PENGUIN BOOKS

RENAISSANCE DRAMATISTS

GENERAL ED

GEOR

PLAYS

The Renaissance Dramatists serie. _____ *_____ ____* text, with a mimimum of interference, *__ __ _____ __ _____ ___ _____ __* *the original editions. Therefore the texts of these plays follow the original spellings,* *reproduce the punctuation of the early editions and manuscripts and are accompanied* *by extensive explicatory Notes. Where appropriate, the volumes will also include* *a Glossary and List of Historical, Mythological and Geographical Names.*

GEORGE CHAPMAN was born in around 1559 in Hitchin, Hertfordshire. Little is known of his early life but he may have been university educated. He emerged as a poet in 1594 with the publication of *The Shadow Of Night* and then as a dramatist in 1596 with the first staging of his comedy *The Blinde begger of Alexandria*. Chapman was associated with a group of 'freethinkers' that included Sir Walter Ralegh, Christopher Marlowe, the poet Matthew Roydon and the scientist Thomas Harriot. He was friends with Ben Jonson, with whom he collaborated (along with John Marston) on the satire *Eastward Hoe* (1605), though the relationship eventually ended in acrimony. From 1604 Chapman received patronage from Prince Henry, holding the post of 'sewer-in-ordinary' until the Prince's death in 1612. His other attempts to acquire courtly patronage were less successful and he seems to have been troubled by debt for a substantial period of his life.

Chapman is usually best remembered for his massive *The Whole Works Of Homer; Prince Of Poetts* (1616), referred to as it was by Keats in 'On First Looking into Chapman's Homer'. There are, however, many extant works from his other areas of literary endeavour. These include the eight comedies, *The Blinde begger of Alexandria* (1596), *An Humerous dayes Myrth* (1597), *All Fooles* (1599), *May-Day* (1601–2), *Sir Gyles Goosecappe Knight* (1602), *The Gentleman Usher* (1602–3), *The Widdowes Teares* (1604–5), and *Monsieur D'Olive* (1605), and the collaborative satire *Eastward Hoe* (1605). Four tragedies survive: *Bussy D'Ambois* (1604), *The Revenge Of Bussy D'Ambois* (1610–11), the double play *The Conspiracie, And Tragedie Of Charles Duke of Byron, Marshall of France* (1607–8) and *Caesar And Pompey*

(1604–5); as does *The Tragedie Of Chabot Admirall Of France* (1611–13; revised by Shirley *c.*1635), which seems to be a reworking of one of Chapman's plays by James Shirley. There is also his only surviving masque, *The Memorable Masque of the two Honourable Houses or Innes of Court; the Middle Temple, and Lyncolnes Inne* (1613). Among his extant poetic works are *Ovids Banquet of Sence* (1595), his continuation of Marlowe's *Hero And Leander* (1598) and *The Teares of Peace* (1609). After the publication of his complete Homer, Chapman ceased to produce major works and appears just to have written minor translations and occasional verse. He died, seemingly in poverty, in 1634.

JONATHAN HUDSTON was educated at Nottingham High School and St John's College, Oxford. He works as a journalist for BBC South West and lives in West Dorset.

JOHN PITCHER is Vice President of St John's College, Oxford, and Visiting Research Professor at the University of Ulster at Coleraine.

GEORGE CHAPMAN
Plays and Poems

Edited with an Introduction and Notes by
JONATHAN HUDSTON

Texts prepared by
RICHARD ROWLAND

PENGUIN BOOKS

PENGUIN BOOKS

Published by the Penguin Group
Penguin Books Ltd, 27 Wrights Lane, London w8 5tz, England
Penguin Putnam Inc., 375 Hudson Street, New York, New York 10014, USA
Penguin Books Australia Ltd, Ringwood, Victoria, Australia
Penguin Books Canada Ltd, 10 Alcorn Avenue, Toronto, Ontario, Canada m4v 3b2
Penguin Books (NZ) Ltd, 182–190 Wairau Road, Auckland 10, New Zealand

Penguin Books Ltd, Registered Offices: Harmondsworth, Middlesex, England

This edition first published 1998
1 3 5 7 9 10 8 6 4 2

Set in 9.5/12 pt PostScript Monotype Garamond
Typeset by Rowland Phototypesetting Ltd, Bury St Edmunds, Suffolk
Printed in England by Clays Ltd, St Ives plc

CONTENTS

SERIES STATEMENT   vi

ACKNOWLEDGEMENTS   viii

CHRONOLOGY   x

INTRODUCTION   xv

FURTHER READING   xxxvi

TEXTUAL PROCEDURE   xxxviii

PLAYS

All Fooles   3

Bussy D'Ambois   73

The Widdowes Teares   145

POEMS

'Hymnus in Noctem'   223

Ovids Banquet of Sence   239

'De Guiana, Carmen Epicum'   277

'To *M. Harriots*'   283

Euthymiae Raptus; or The Teares of Peace   289

'A good woman'   325

NOTES   329

GLOSSARY   433

LIST OF HISTORICAL, MYTHOLOGICAL AND GEOGRAPHICAL NAMES   441

SERIES STATEMENT

All editions are compromises, especially perhaps editions of drama. Dramatic speeches in verse or prose, entrances and exits of characters, stage directions, scene divisions, are communicated to us in manuscripts, typescripts and printed books. From these we receive a whole range of impressions: what the dramatist hoped to achieve, how his or her play was performed, last year or four centuries ago, and how a director and actors might present it to us again. The text of a play is a record, a memory, sometimes even a monument to what has been written and played, and adapted by actors, but it is also the ground from which that play may return to the special life of the theatre, where written or typeset words become speech, and where the book, with its conventions of silent reading, gives way to the space and sounds of the auditorium, and the spectacle of performance.

Editors of drama in English have to choose the best way of passing on play texts to modern readers, who may also be actors and audiences. One choice is to modernize or normalize the texts. With older plays (written before 1700), this involves changing the format as well as the spellings of the original texts, and the punctuation, capitals and italics, so that the words and sentences and phrases look modern. The intention is to reduce what is taken to be too difficult in these older texts for modern readers. This compromise is largely rejected in this series, as for the most part unnecessary, but also because it may impair what the past has to tell us. The punctuation and spelling we encounter in older play texts may of course come from compositors or scribes, rather than from the dramatist, but still their additions and idiosyncrasies bear the imprint of the past. Even where we judge them to be wrong in the way they printed or copied a text, a Renaissance compositor or a scribe is likely to be more interestingly and informatively wrong than a twentieth-century editor who changes the texts to make them easier for us.

For these reasons, the texts of the plays in this series reproduce, wherever possible, the spelling and punctuation of the first printed editions and manuscripts. Original readings are modified only where this is essential (type damaged during printing, turned letters, patently impossible punctuation), and there is a record of significant modifications of spelling and punctuation included in the Textual Notes at the back of each volume. Until the late seventeenth century, the modern distinctions between the letters *i* and *j*, and *u* and *v* were not observed in the printing house, and printers still used *vv* for *w*, a long *s*-letter shape for our *s*, and so forth. All these forms are modernized in this series. Speech prefixes are expanded, regularized and set in small capitals, and abbreviations are silently expanded, except those still in modern use, such as ampersands and *etc.* Where necessary, the act and scene divisions of the original texts are regularized and expanded, as are stage directions, entrances and exits, which are printed in italic, with the names of speaking parts in small capitals. Any words added to the original texts are enclosed within square brackets. Other changes, for example to the lineation of prose and verse, and to the divisions of the verse, are left to the discretion (and arguments) of the volume editors. Details of how specific plays have been edited are given in Textual Procedure. In all of this, the aim of the series is to produce a standard textual frame, within which there is a scrupulously prepared version of the text, minimally interfered with, but accompanied by adequate explicatory Notes, a Glossary and a List of Historical, Mythological and Geographical Names.

John Pitcher

ACKNOWLEDGEMENTS

Franco Basso prepared the Commentary on Chapman's extended Gloss to 'Hymnus in Noctem' in *The Shadow Of Night* (1594). In particular he corrected the Latin misprints. He also gave invaluable assistance with other Latin materials.

The Introduction and Notes feature many quotations from works by Chapman which aren't included in this volume. These excerpts come from four standard modern collections, and I hope those inspired to read more of Chapman's plays, poems and translations will seek them out. They are: *The Plays of George Chapman: The Comedies*, ed. Allan Holaday (Urbana, USA: University of Illinois Press, 1970); *The Plays of George Chapman: The Tragedies with Sir Gyles Goosecappe*, ed. Allan Holaday (Cambridge: D. S. Brewer, 1987); *The Poems of George Chapman*, ed. Phyllis Brooks Bartlett (New York: MLA, 1941), and the two-volume edition of *Chapman's Homer* (*The Iliad* and *The Odyssey and Lesser Homerica*), ed. Allardyce Nicoll (London: Routledge & Kegan Paul, 1957). The text of the plays and poems in this Penguin volume have been checked against the Holaday and Bartlett editions. I'm grateful also to the other copyright holders acknowledged in more detail where their works are quoted.

Every effort has been made to trace or contact all copyright holders. The publishers will be glad to make good any omissions brought to their attention.

Thanks are due to the following copyright holders for permission to reproduce from the following:

Renaissance Self-Fashioning by Stephen Jay Greenblatt (London: University of Chicago Press, 1980). Copyright © 1980 by The University of Chicago.
Forms of Nationhood: The Elizabethan Writing of England by Richard Helgerson (London: University of Chicago Press, 1992). Copyright © 1992 by The University of Chicago.
'Furious Insolence: The Social Meaning of Poetic Inspiration in the 1590s'

by John Huntington in *Modern Philology*, 94 (1997). Copyright © 1997 by The University of Chicago.

Raymond B. Waddington, *The Mind's Empire: Myth and Form in George Chapman's Narrative Poems* (1974). Copyright © 1974 The Johns Hopkins University Press.

John Huntington, 'Philosophical Seduction in Chapman, Davies, and Donne', *English Literary History*, 44, (1977) pp. 43–5. Copyright © 1977 The Johns Hopkins University Press.

By permission of Oxford University Press:

Robert S. Miola, *Shakespeare and Classical Comedy*, 1994, p. 174; Susan Snyder (editor), translated by Josuah Sylvester, *The Divine Weeks and Works of Guillaume de Saluste Sieur du Bartas*, 1979, p. 118.

John W. Shirley, *Thomas Harriot: A Biography*, 1983, p. 65.

John W. Shirley (editor), 'Harriot, Hill, Warner And The New Philosophy' in *Thomas Harriot: Renaissance Scientist*, 1974, p. 107.

Reprinted by permission of the publishers and the Loeb Classical Library from *Seneca: Moral Essays*, Volume III, translated by John W. Basore, Cambridge, Mass.: Harvard University Press, 1935.

Reprinted by permission of the Peters Fraser & Dunlap Group Ltd:

Frank Kermode, 'The Banquet of Sense', *Shakespeare, Spenser, Donne* (London: Routledge & Kegan Paul, 1971), pp. 84–115.

CHRONOLOGY

1559? George Chapman born near Hitchin, Hertfordshire, second son of small landowner. Mother was daughter of royal huntsman, granddaughter of John Grimestone of Uxborough – a Protestant family involved throughout the century in Government service in France. Later pupil at Hitchin Grammar School.

1574? 'Sent to the University [Oxford?] where he was observed to be most excellent in the Latin and Greek tongues' but 'took no degree there' according solely to Anthony Wood, *Athenae Oxonienses* (1691–2). No other evidence.

1578–87? Servingman for some of this time to rich diplomat and soldier Sir Ralph Sadler (1507–87), who administered the royal manor of Hitchin for the Crown and was ordered in 1580 and 1584 to keep Mary Queen of Scots a prisoner.

1582–92? Soldier for some of this time in wars of the Low Countries. Dedicatory letter to the *Crowne of all Homers Workes* refers to an episode at Ghent in 1582; 'Hymnus in Cynthiam' in *The Shadow Of Night* recounts ambush of Spanish troops at Nymeghen in 1591, under Sir Francis Vere.

1592? Links established with free-thinking group around Sir Walter Ralegh, including Christopher Marlowe (d. 1593) and the scientist Thomas Harriot.

1594 *The Shadow Of Night.*

1595 *Ovids Banquet of Sence*, 'A Coronet for his Mistresse *Philosophie*', 'The amorous Zodiack' (translation).

1596 *The Blinde begger of Alexandria* (comedy printed 1598), first surviving play for the Admiral's Men. 'De Guiana, Carmen Epicum' in praise of Ralegh's voyage to Guiana.

1597   *An Humerous dayes Myrth* (printed 1599), first English 'humours' comedy.

1598   Adds four sestyads to Christopher Marlowe's *Hero And Leander*; publishes translation of *Seaven Bookes Of The Iliades* by Homer, with dedication to the Earl of Essex as '*The Most Honored now living Instance of the Achilleian vertues*'; *Achilles Shield* (translation of Homer) also dedicated to Essex. Listed by Francis Meres in *Palladis Tamia* as one of the best writers of comedy and tragedy.

1599   *All Fooles* (comedy possibly revised 1600–1601, printed 1605). Imprisoned for debt.

1600   Starts writing for the Chapel Children, newly revived company of boy actors.

1601   Earl of Essex executed after abortive revolt against Elizabeth I.

1601–2   *May-Day* (printed 1609) adapted from Italian comedy *L'Allesandro* (*c.*1545) by Alessandro Piccolomini.

1602   *Sir Gyles Goosecappe Knight* (comedy printed 1606).

1602–3   *The Gentleman Usher* (tragi-comedy printed 1606), *The Old Joiner of Aldgate* (lost comedy) for the Children at Paul's based on real-life rivalry for rich heiress. Chapman was unsuccessfully sued for libel.

1604   Appointed 'sewer-in-ordinary' (head-waiter/food-taster) to Prince Henry. *Bussy D'Ambois* (tragedy printed 1607).

1604–5   *Caesar And Pompey* (tragedy possibly revised 1612–13, printed 1631), *The Widdowes Teares* (tragi-comedy printed 1612).

1605   City comedy *Eastward Hoe* with Ben Jonson and John Marston, *Monsieur D'Olive* (comedy printed 1606). In September Chapman and Jonson were imprisoned for anti-Scottish satire in *Eastward Hoe*; freed in October.

1607–8   *The Conspiracie, And Tragedie Of Charles Duke of Byron, Marshall of France* (printed 1608). Main written source by Chapman's cousin Sir Edward Grimestone. After protests by French ambassador, theatres shut down, plays published in censored form. Chapman bemoans his 'poore dismembered poemes'.

1609 *Homer Prince of Poets . . . twelve Bookes of his Iliads* (translation) dedicated to Prince Henry and Queen Anne. *Euthymiae Raptus; Or The Teares of Peace.*

1610–11 *The Revenge Of Bussy D'Ambois* (tragedy printed 1613). Possible revision of *Bussy D'Ambois* (printed 1641).

1611 The complete *Iliads.*

1611–13 *The Tragedie Of Chabot Admirall Of France* (printed 1639, revised by James Shirley, probably *c.*1635).

1612 *Petrarchs Seven Penitentiall Psalms, Paraphrastically Translated: With other Philosophicall Poems, and a Hymne to Christ upon the Crosse. An Epicede Or Funerall Song* (about the 'most disastrous' death of Prince Henry on November 6).

1613 *The Memorable Masque of the two Honourable Houses or Innes of Court; the Middle Temple, and Lyncolnes Inne* performed on February 15 to celebrate the marriage of Princess Elizabeth. Imprisoned – possibly for debt.

1614 *Eugenia: Or True Nobilities Trance* mourns the death of Lord Russell. *Andromeda Liberata. Or The Nuptials Of Perseus and Andromeda* written to celebrate the controversial marriage of the Earl of Somerset and Lady Francis Howard, after her divorce from the Earl of Essex. *A Free And Offenceles Justification Of Andromeda liberata* to protest that an allegorical reference to a 'barraine Rocke' was not meant to offend the Earl of Essex or others. Translation of the first twelve books of *Homer's Odysses.*

1614–19 Probably living with elder brother in Hitchin to escape imprisonment for debt, and so forced to give up plays and concentrate on translations. Described in court in 1617 as one 'of meane or poore estate' who 'doth now live in remote places and is hard to be founde'.

1615 The complete *Odysses* dedicated to Earl of Somerset.

1616 *The Whole Works Of Homer* (translation), *The Divine Poem Of Musaeus* (translation of the original Greek epic *Hero and Leander*) dedicated to Inigo Jones.

1618 *The Georgicks Of Hesiod* (translation) dedicated to Francis Bacon.

1622 'Pro Vere, Autumni Lachrymae': A plea to the King to help out Sir Horace Vere (brother of Sir Francis) at the siege of Mannheim. Lawsuit victory quashes debt.

1623–4? 'An Invective . . . against Mr. Ben: Johnson': An attack on his former 'deare friend' probably written soon after Jonson's 'sacred deske' was burned in 1623.

1624 The *Crowne of all Homers Workes* (translation). One copy dedicated to Sir Ralph Sadler's grandson.

1629 Translation of the *fifth Satyre of Juvenall*.

1634 Chapman dies May 12. Buried at St Giles-in-the-Field in London, with monument erected by Inigo Jones to '*Georgius Chapmanius, poeta Homericus, Philosophus verus (etsi Christianus poeta)*'.

INTRODUCTION

Chapman believed that no artist was '*so strictly and inextricably confined to all the lawes of learning, wisedome and truth as a Poet*'.[1] So it's surprising to find a mistake in the second sentence of his first published work. The dedicatory letter to *The Shadow Of Night* (1594) declares that men must, among other attributes, 'have the eyes of *Graea* (as *Hesiodus armes Perseus* against *Medusa*) before they can cut of the viperous head of benumming ignorance'. In fact, the Graeae are three sisters born already ancient who only have one eye between them. Pointing out this error is not merely pedantic or scoffing, like Ben Jonson laughing at Shakespeare for giving Bohemia a coastline in *The Winters Tale* (1610–11), 'wher [there] is no Sea neer by some 100 Miles'.[2] Chapman took unusual care with *The Shadow Of Night*, but this error – one of several – shows that from the very start of his career he found it difficult to fulfil his ambition for greatness. His mind does unexpected things – peculiar even to Chapman himself. The word 'strange' is often used by him as a term of self-description. In 'To the Understander', a preface composed in 1598 for *Achilles Shield*, a translation from Homer's *Iliad*, he says: '. . . *the truth is, my desire and strange disposition in all thinges I write is to set downe uncommon and most profitable coherents for the time*'.[3] Chapman's choice of words immediately shows off his 'desire'. The use of 'coherents' as a noun meaning 'Things which cohere or are connected' is very 'uncommon' indeed; the OED's first citation is not until 1617. Chapman's sense of his own 'strangeness' is here a matter of preening self-satisfaction. Elsewhere his self-estrangement is a cause of perturbations.

Another surprising mistake hints at the importance to Chapman of self-control. Look at this sentence in *The Widdowes Teares* (1604–5): 'But by your leave *Lycus*, *Penelope* is not so wise as her husband *Ulysses*, for he fearing the jawes of the *Syren*, stopt his eares with waxe against her voice' (I.2.13–15). The allusions are to Homer's *Odyssey*. Chapman was obsessed with the works of Homer – possibly more than anyone else who's ever lived – and although this line was written about nine years before he published his initial translation of *Homer's Odysses* (1614), it's impossible to believe that he wasn't already familiar with the famous events of Book XII. Homer shows Ulysses getting his ship's crew to stop their ears with wax while he's bound to the mast so that he can hear the Sirens' voices. Ulysses does not block his own ears with wax. The same mistake is made in *The Tragedie Of Charles Duke of Byron* (1607–8). Henry IV is talking about Byron's past loyalty when tempted by Spaniards:

> . . . they found him still,
> As an unmatcht *Achilles* in the warres,
> So a most wise *Ulisses* to their words,
> Stopping his eares at their enchanted sounds; . . .   (I.i.77–80)

In neither case does the fact of being mistaken seem to contribute anything to an understanding of the characters speaking or the plays' dramatic situations. So it must be assumed that Chapman deliberately changed Homer in these two instances – he didn't when he came to translate Book XII – or he altered the story unconsciously. In either case the error suggests that Chapman didn't believe it was possible to hear the Sirens' voices without being devoured by the sexually threatening 'jawes' referred to in *The Widdowes Teares*. Even an epic figure like Ulysses has literally to harden his outside so as not to lose control within.

The correct interpretation of Chapman's work is for him a matter of perspective. He expects 'ignorants' to miss the point, but hopes that those with more 'judiciall' minds will see.[4] Throughout his career, he uses an analogy from the visual arts to illustrate this phenomenon, namely, what he calls 'optike' pictures. These were popular in the sixteenth and seventeenth centuries; they show different images when seen from different angles. The most famous example of such perspective art is Hans Holbein's painting 'The Ambassadors' (1533) in the National Gallery in London. At the centre of the picture is a death's head which can only be properly discerned from the side. In *Renaissance Self-Fashioning* Stephen Greenblatt comments: 'To see the large death's-head requires a still more radical abandonment of what we take to be "normal" vision; we must throw the entire painting out of perspective in order to bring into perspective what our usual mode of perception cannot comprehend.'[5] The first 'optike' installation in Chapman's work is the fountain in which Corynna bathes in *Ovids Banquet of Sence* (1595), 3.6–9. When it's looked at from a distance, it shows a woman's face, weeping heavily, but closer up this can't be seen. In *All Fooles* (1599) Rynaldo compares Beauty to a cozening picture, like a crow one way, and a swan the other

(I.1.47–8). Women are said by Rynaldo to be like temples, 'wondrous heavenly' on the outside, inside containing painted fowls, furies, and serpents (I.1.87–90). Religion is personified as a woman in the poem *Eugenia* (1614):

> Her lookes were like the pictures that are made,
> To th'optike reason; one way like a shade,
> Another monster like, and every way
> To passers by, and such as made no stay,
> To view her in a right line, face to face,
> She seem'd a serious trifle; all her grace,
> Show'd in her fixt inspection; and then
> She was the onely grace of dames and men: . . .   (ll. 173–80)

The 'fixt inspection' of Religion is a two-way 'face to face' process, with viewing 'in a right line' resulting from inspection *of* her and *by* her.[6] Chapman aims similarly to fix his audience's vision. The poems in this volume all seek to break out of the 'usual mode of perception' and they are included as 'uncommon and most profitable coherents' for the plays. Because so few of Chapman's non-dramatic verses are in print, it has been decided to omit pieces which can be easily obtained elsewhere. Chapman's continuation of Christopher Marlowe's *Hero And Leander* (1598) can be read in Stephen Orgel's edition of *Christopher Marlowe: The Complete Poems and Translations* (London: Penguin Books, 1971), and a selection of Chapman's translations from Homer can be found in *Homer in English*, edited by George Steiner with the assistance of Aminadav Dykman (London: Penguin Books, 1996).

   Interpretations of myth shape Chapman's convictions about the artist's civic and didactic role. In the dedicatory epistle to his translation of *twelve Bookes* of Homer's *Iliads*, ll. 136–8, addressed in 1609 to his patron Prince Henry, man is compared to a tree

> In which, doth Poesie, like the kernell lie
> Obscur'd; though her Promethean facultie
> Can create men, and make even death to live; . . .[7]

This spectacular power is alluded to and glossed in a note to l. 131 of 'Hymnus in Noctem' in *The Shadow Of Night*, where Chapman suggests that just as Prometheus made men with fire fetched from heaven, '*so Poets with the fire of their soules are sayd to create those Harpies, and Centaures, and thereof he calls their soules Geniale*'. Genial doesn't have its modern sense of cheery and good-natured. It means generative, and the root is the same as that of genius. Poets' souls are said to be 'most genial, more-then-humane' ('Hymnus in Noctem', l. 132). Their duty is to fashion monstrous figures to show ordinary men how degenerate they have become, so that, when they view their reflections in 'fixt inspection', they will be shamed into mending their ways.

The ups-and-downs of the Orpheus myth also inspire Chapman's imagination. 'Hymnus in Noctem' casts the story of Orpheus rescuing Eurydice from the underworld as one of 'calming the infernall kinde,/ To wit, the perturbations of his minde' (ll. 149–50). How to conquer perturbations is explained in *The Teares of Peace* (1609), a long poem in which Homer visits the narrator (presented as Chapman himself) in a vision. The narrator breaks into a trance (a state wished for at the start of 'Hymnus in Noctem') and 'so obtainde/ Such bouldnesse, by the sense hee did controule;/ That I set looke, to looke; and soule to soule' (ll. 66–8). The sense of Homer's 'controule' has an empowering effect on the narrator and the pair set themselves in 'fixt inspection'. Homer grants the narrator an audience with the personified female figure of Peace: the narrator and Peace discuss how to put the world right. Their solution is Learning, by which is meant far more than scholarship. Learning can 'Turne blood to soule' (l. 560). Learning is knowing how to control the ignorant body so the soul can curb perturbations and strive to conform to God's Image. Peace castigates the errors of men who do not put their learning to proper uses. The best of such men may be able to write well enough 'to charme/ A wilde of Savadges' (ll. 743–4), but if he can't master perturbations the very point of his being alive is called into question:

> To what end serves he? is his learning tryed
> That comforting, and that creating Fire
> That fashions men? or that which doth inspire
> Citties with civile conflagrations,
> Countries, and kingdomes? That Art that attones
> All opposition to good life, is all;
> Live well ye Learned; and all men ye enthrall.   (ll. 752–8)

The reference to charming a wild of savages again invokes Orpheus, who tamed wild beasts with the music from his lyre, while the creating fire is obviously Promethean. 'Attones' means reconcile, bring into harmony, and the last sentence is an explicit statement of Chapman's belief in the power of setting a good example. His plays make the theatre a space for learning about the good life and countermanding the bad: 'materiall instruction, elegant and sententious excitation to Vertue, and deflection from her contrary; being the soule, lims, and limits of an authenticall Tragedie' asserts the dedicatory epistle to *The Revenge Of Bussy D'Ambois* (1610–11). The last sonnet in the sequence 'A Coronet for his Mistresse *Philosophie*' (1595) also dismisses the notion that the theatres of Athens and Rome were impediments to virtue: 'the seede of memorie/ Have most inspirde, and showne theyr glories there/ To noblest wits, and men of highest doome' (10.3–5).

But Chapman doubted the strength and adequacy of his own creations. One register of this is his use of the word 'trifle' to describe his works, normally in conjunction with two adjectives, either 'strange' or 'serious', or both. The passers-by who look askance at Religion in *Eugenia* see her only as 'a serious trifle'. *The Shadow Of Night* is described in its dedicatory letter as a 'poore and strange trifle'. And in the dedicatory letter to his continuation of Marlowe's translation of *Hero And Leander* (1598), ll. 3–5, Chapman talks of '*being drawne by strange instigation to employ some of my serious time in so trifeling a subject, which yet made the first Author, divine* Musaeus*, eternall*'. Chapman goes on to add that whoever shuns trifles, must also shun the world. And he urges Lady Walsingham to accept the dedication, '*though as a trifle, yet as a serious argument of my affection*'. The tone of this is very difficult to discern. It seems most likely – to begin with – that Chapman is maladroitly expressing a sort of false modesty, he's hedging his bets, he wants to have his trifle and eat it. This impression of false modesty is reinforced elsewhere, for example in the dedicatory letter to *Ovids Banquet of Sence*, where he writes parenthetically of '(not affecting glory for mine owne sleight labors, but desirous others should be more worthely glorious, nor professing sacred Poesie in any degree,) . . .' In a poem commending Ben Jonson's tragedy *Sejanus* (1603) he speaks of only warming himself at the Muses' fire ('In Sejanum Ben. Jonsoni', 1605, l. 119). But then look at these lines addressed in 1598 to the scientist Thomas Harriot ('To *M. Harriots*'):

> Rich mine of knowledge, ô that my strange muse
> Without this bodies nourishment could use,
> Her zealous faculties, onely t'aspire,
> Instructive light from your whole Sphere of fire:

> But woe is me, what zeale or power soever
> My free soule hath, my body will be never
> Able t'attend: never shal I enjoy,
> Th'end of my happles birth: never employ
> That smotherd fervour that in lothed embers,
> Lyes swept from light, and no cleare howre remembers.   (ll. 31–40)

The force of these lines doesn't suggest a writer happy to sit in the cold. Chapman wants and needs to be heated up. Press on that drab word 'instructive', for example, and a lot more comes to light. It's not a word which cries out to be glossed, it can stand by itself, but it's characteristic of Chapman that it sets off cryptic reverberations (the semi-private aspects of his language are often a cause of awkwardness elsewhere). There's an echoing moment towards the end of *Bussy D'Ambois* (1604), when Bussy says that his brain has never been in such need 'of spirit,/ T'instruct and cheere it' (V.2.26–7), and he calls on Apollo to help him:

> . . . O thou King of flames,
> That with thy Musique-footed horse dost strike
> The cleere light out of chrystall, on darke earth;
> And hurlst instructive fire about the world: . . .   (V.2.39–42)

Apollo is the god of sun and music, and the horse is probably Pegasus. It was the stamping of Pegasus' hooves that caused the Muses' sacred fountain at Hippocrene (Hippo = horse) to start flowing. Bussy also summons the devil Behemoth, Apollo's opposite number in Hell, and Maurice Evans, in his edition of the play, suggests that Chapman uses this double invocation to represent 'the common Renaissance distinction between Natural and Demonic Magic as defined, for example, in Pico della Mirandola's *Oration on the Dignity of Man*' [1492].[8] Evans argues persuasively that 'instructive fire' relates to Pico's definition of Natural Magic as 'the utter perfection of natural philosophy' by which the magician 'brings forth into the open the miracles concealed in the recesses of the world, in the depths of nature, and in the storehouses and mysteries of God'. This is the sort of revelatory power attributed to the sun-like Harriot, 'Mayster of all essentiall and true know-ledge', able to make Nature 'all transparent' ('To *M. Harriots*', l. 93). Chapman's complaints to Harriot about the limits on his own zeal and power are matched by an emotionally similar section of *The Teares of Peace*, also presented in confessional mode: 'But woe is me': 'And here, ay me!' In the course of questioning Peace, the Chapmanesque narrator talks about his poor and abject life and his search for grace from God and his Son, and about how God, 'like a carefull guide, hath hal'd [him] on' to the calm shore:

> And here, ay me! (as trembling, I looke back)
> I fall againe, and, in my haven, wracke;
> Still being perswaded (by the shamelesse light)
> That these are dreames, of my retired Night;
> That, all my Reading; Writing; all my paines
> Are serious trifles; and the idle vaines
> Of an unthriftie Angell, that deludes
> My simple fancie; and, by Fate, extendes
> My Birth-accurst life, from the blisse of men: . . .   (ll. 943–51)

Chapman's imagination is so centrifugal, so possessed by certain words, images and situations, that this passage sets off numerous echoes. The opposition between night and light stretches right back to *The Shadow Of Night*. 'Wracke' is an image which may derive from Quintilian's *De Institutione Oratoria* via Erasmus' *Adagia* (1500) and calls to mind Bussy's opening speech in *Bussy D'Ambois* (I.i.32–3) and another by Vandome in *Monsieur D'Olive* (1605): 'O what a second Ruthles Sea of woes/ Wracks mee within my Haven, and on the Shore?' (I.i.174–5). But it's that phrase 'serious trifles' which catches the eye and suggests that Chapman wasn't being falsely modest, but nervous about his fear and misery. *The Teares of Peace* goes on to describe the anguish that is caused by this sudden shipwreck of confidence, as he looks back on his writings. Everything that he most believes in – that he is convinced the Spirit of Heaven has graven in his soul for all eternity – is placed in jeopardy. The reaction to this prospect of spiritual annihilation and isolation is hysterical, the narrator beats his bosom, rages, despairs, and wishes he were dead. But then he goes on to reaffirm what he does believe in – chiefly the supreme importance of self-knowledge – and ends 'All this, I holde' (l. 995). This fluctuation, this movement between Chapman's absolute determination to stay in control, and uncertainty about his own powers and worth, is central to an understanding of his work.[9] The look back which sets off this fluctuation is significant because it links up with the story of Orpheus rescuing Eurydice from the underworld. These lines from 'Hymnus in Noctem' follow those quoted earlier about calming the perturbations of the mind:

> But if in rights observance any man
> Looke backe, with boldnesse less than Orphean,
> Soone falls he to the hell from whence he rose:
> The fiction then would temprature dispose,
> In all the tender motives of the minde,
> To make man worthie his hel-danting kinde.   (ll. 153–8)

Chapman trembles at the thought his own boldness may be less than Orphean, that he might not effectively be a poet. But the fiction – the act and substance of making – acts as a comforting and toughening restorative, and one remembers that the vital Promethean fire is described as a *comforting* and creating fire. Chapman's imagination needs to operate, he feels, in a structure of philosophical certainty and classical, mythological confidence. He creates the goddess of Ceremonie in his continuation of Marlowe's *Hero And Leander* as a totem of order and another 'optike' picture to be 'viewed' in 'fixt inspection':

> Her face was changeable to everie eie;
> One way lookt ill, another graciouslie;
> Which while men viewd, they cheerfull were & holy:
> But looking off, vicious and melancholy: (III.125–8)

Ceremonie carries a 'Mathematique Christall' which refracts the rays from her bright eyes and burns Confusion to death, 'And all estates of men distinguisheth'.[10] The totalizing, anatomizing side of Chapman's imagination likes everything to be in its place and everyone to know his or her place, a predilection which shapes his later expressions of Stoicism.[11]

But Chapman too is 'changeable'. His plays set themselves questions of strangeness and power, freedom and control, they dream of liberation and are fascinated by constriction, partly because he wasn't sure about the accuracy of his own self-diagnosis, and partly because he wanted relief from it. His first surviving plays are comedies.[12] He seems to have been able to write these quite easily and to have enjoyed doing so. They released in him a sort of merry chipmunkish quality, like D. H. Lawrence in his short stories as opposed to some of his novels. The prologue to *All Fooles* toys with the very unChapman-like view that the customer is always right. Chapman normally professed to despise the 'base, ignoble, barbarous, giddie' multitude – but the mischievous thrust of the prologue is that everyone is a fool, old poets included.[13] The awkwardness of some of Chapman's other work tends to evaporate in the lighter-hearted atmosphere of the comedies, which can feel cruder, but also more spontaneous, more direct, more fluent. Particularly in the early plays of the 1600s, Chapman tries to make fun out of facets of his own persona. The plays attempt optic settings together of the serious and the trifling, the wisdom and romance of verse and the wit and friendship of prose. *Sir Gyles Goosecappe Knight* (1602) sets out to make the strange entertaining, and the entertaining strange. Both the main characters in this play are presented as 'strange'. Sir Gyles himself is a foolish knight, while Clarence is modelled partly on Chaucer's Troilus (with his friend Earl Momford as Pandarus and his beloved Eugenia as Criseyde), but is more obviously a version of Chapman himself.[14] Clarence is poor, deep, studious and austere, a scholarly poet and philosopher, who scorns the world, speaks in paradoxes and riddles, writes 'Strange stuffe' (III.ii.90) and is generally to be found in search of 'the blacke Springes/ And unreveald Originall of Things' (II.i.11–12). He believes 'there is no disease of the mind but one, and that is *Ignorance*' (V.ii.31–2); he's Chapman to a T. So it's meant to be all the more amusing that he's structurally twinned with the idiotic figure of Goosecappe, who is a ridiculously bad poet, and has a series of bizarre interests and talents, from being able to dance on egg-shells without breaking them, to guessing the price of gloves, sewing lifelike pictures of whales, and carving leopards' heads. There's never any doubt that Clarence will win Eugenia, although he is forced to lie in bed and pretend to be extremely sick to get her attention, and to expound upon his most cherished notions from this compromising position. Clarence is finally successful, partly because Eugenia herself is prepared to act a 'strange part' (V.ii.134) to make her choice of him, but mostly because the economy of Chapman's plays demands that cleverness is irresistible. Sir Gyles is also promised the bride he wants, and the play ends with the prospect of multiple nuptials. It should be remembered that in Renaissance England fathers and guardians had the power to arrange marriages for sons as well as daughters. The fun of plays such as *All Fooles* and *Sir Gyles Goosecappe Knight*, for young people in the fictions and the audience, lies in fantasies of freedom, in being able to choose a spouse. Marriage in such circumstances is given a terrific erotic charge; in *Sir Gyles Goosecappe Knight* one bridegroom is said to have got so excited as the moment of betrothal came that he fainted and died. At least he saved himself from the discovery that actually being married is no guarantee of contentment in Chapman's plays. Husbands often stray, or their wives suspect they do, while wives themselves are so tormented by husbands' 'sowre and combersome' jealousy, that some even think it might be better not to be married.[15]

Chapman's first play to have survived is *The Blinde begger of Alexandria*. This was first performed on 12 February 1596 by the Admiral's Men at The Rose Theatre in London, and was very successful. By April 1597 the play had been performed more than 22 times, or just under twice a month. That might not sound much in modern-day terms, but the Admiral's Men ran a repertory system with a large number of plays. The company's most popular play of the mid-1590s was the lost and anonymous *Wise Men of Westchester*, performed 37 times between 1594 and 1597, or about once a month. The traditional view of *The Blinde begger* is that it's a knockabout farce of little importance, written for money. But think for a moment of Chapman as a sort of Elizabethan Woody Allen, and it's obvious that early successes should not be left out of the picture, any more than *Bananas* (1971) or *Take the Money and Run* (1969) should be excluded to concentrate on *Interiors* (1978). An awareness of Chapman's early plays fends off the temptation offered by hindsight of viewing everything through the prism of *Bussy D'Ambois*.

A clue about what made *The Blinde begger* so popular can be found in the edition printed in 1598. The title page speaks of the eponymous beggar 'most pleasantly discoursing his variable humours in disguised shapes full of conceite and pleasure', and the text of the play has been cut accordingly. Scenes focus on the antics of the main character, who plays four roles in all: that of a blind beggar and holy man, a Jewish money-lender with a big nose, a mad count in a velvet cloak (named Count Hermes, after the trickster god of mythology), and the warlike Duke Cleanthes. This character is originally the son of a shepherd, as was the hero of Marlowe's *Tamburlaine the Great* (1587–8), and throughout the play he tricks and confounds his enemies, who are trapped in a world of singular identities. He even enjoys cuckolding himself, and he ends up as King of Egypt. This one-man compendium of possibilities was probably played by Edward Alleyn, a leading member of the Admiral's Men and one of the most distinguished actors of the 1590s, who was very well known for his portrayals of Tamburlaine and also Barabas in Marlowe's *The Jew of Malta* (1592). The fantasy of a rise from obscure origins to magnificent power is what seems to have appealed to the audience. Some of the other characters who are important in the early parts of the play simply disappear later, taking Chapman's more expansive generic ideas with them.

His next surviving play was *An Humerous dayes Myrth*, also written for the Admiral's Men and first acted in February 1597. The first of Chapman's six plays to be set in France, *An Humerous dayes Myrth* was another success, being performed more than twenty times by 1598. The animating figure is Lemot, who typically aspires to a sort of royal status, and aims to preside over another display of variable humours. This is made clear almost as soon as he appears in the play's second scene:

> I [will] sit like an old King in an old fashion play, having his wife,
> his counsel, his children, and his foole about him, to whome he
> will sit and point very learnedly as foloweth;
> My counsell grave, and you my noble peeres,
> My tender wife, and you my children deare,
> And thou my foole – . . .   (I.ii.11 – 16)

Lemot's imaginary family and entourage are plainly described in prose, but in the verse which follows their qualities and roles are assigned to them. His children are 'deare' and his wife is 'tender' because he says they are. It's no accident that Lemot's name is French for 'the word' because his creations mimic the original acts of God. 'In the beginning was the Word, and the Word was with God, and the Word was God' (John 1.1). Lemot soon goes on to demonstrate his power by correctly forecasting exactly how one of the next characters to appear will speak and behave. He functions as a playwright within a play, able to manipulate the other characters, because he is flexible and witty, and they are settled inside their given traits. Characters are made predictable by their humours, and the comedy of the resulting situations is best explained by French philosopher Henri Bergson's theory of laughter.[16] According to Bergson, audiences laugh at people whose minds and bodies are so stiff that they can't react flexibly enough to situations; and laughter then acts as a warning to such people to perk themselves up, to save themselves from the mortification of matter. The handing out of humours among characters in *An Humerous dayes Myrth* might seem a small advance from *The Blinde begger* but it introduced a new form to the English stage – the comedy of humours, taken up by Jonson the year after, with *Every Man in His Humour*, and continued in 1599 with *Every Man Out of His*

Humour. Jonson and Chapman went on to produce the finest example of another new generic strain in 1605, when they collaborated with John Marston on the city comedy *Eastward hoe.*

At the turn of the century Chapman started to write for the Chapel Children, a new boys' company based at the indoor Blackfriars Theatre, which was over the River Thames from The Rose, and closer to the city. All of his plays for the next decade were to be written for children's companies. Jonson and Marston also linked up with boys' companies in 1599–1600. Chapman's job was to create dramas which would enable the children's companies successfully to compete for audiences with their adult rivals, such as Shakespeare's company the King's Men. The children's companies sought to stand out in a busy marketplace by encouraging theatrical innovations and experiments. All the companies of the time, like television stations today, also kept a close eye on each other's output, pinching ideas and parodying each other. It's partly for such commercial reasons that Chapman's plays become more heterogenous, but there are still clear lines of continuity. The plays in this volume are his best comedy (*All Fooles*), best tragedy (*Bussy D'Ambois*) and best tragi-comedy (*The Widdowes Teares*). *The Conspiracie, And Tragedie Of Charles Duke of Byron* is the main omission. It's weightier than *All Fooles*, but a selection of work in three genres spans Chapman's move from public to private theatres and gives a fuller sense of his career in the reigns of both Elizabeth I and James I.

Chapman's characters have hard outsides. Their insides – even in the heroes' soliloquies – are not open to the kind of introspective gaze found in Shakespeare's *Hamlet* (1600). To be or not to be is scarcely a question for Rynaldo in *All Fooles* or Tharsalio in *The Widdowes Teares*, nor Bussy until he's about to die. These characters know what they want to be and do, and their moments alone are less opportunities to talk to themselves than chances to address their chosen tutelary spirits, or let the audience know what they think is going to happen next. *The Widdowes Teares* starts with this stage direction: 'THARSALIO *Solus* [Alone], *with a Glasse in his hand making readie*'. Tharsalio is looking in the mirror (the 'glasse') to help him consolidate the new self that he intends to show to the outside world. His opening words display the bent of his character to the audience, and offer a commentary on the unsatisfactory state of the world as he sees it. The key to Tharsalio's success is going to be the impression that others take of him, and so it is with Chapman's characters in general. Even Clarence in *Sir Gyles Goosecappe*

Knight is said to behave when he's by himself as 'in a *Criticke Synods* curious eyes' (V.ii.64). The expectation of being looked at and judged helps to explain why characters put so much energy into fixing the image they want others to see. They seek control by shutting themselves off to everything but their own imperatives (like Ulysses 'stopping his eares'). The effort devoted to externalization leaves much potentially obscured ('you may see the preparation; but the designe lies hidden in the brests of the wise' – *The Widdowes Teares*, I.l.47–8) and the odd, distinctive rhythms of Chapman's plots derive from the subsequent interplay of the outer and the inner. His plays become dramas of altered states, of the secret and the unexpected, to expose and test the limitations of what their characters (and their spectators) want to be and do. Up until *The Conspiracie, And Tragedie Of Charles Duke of Byron* things nearly always happen suddenly. Characters take each other, and often themselves, by surprise. They find things strange. The word 'sudden' is used a dozen times in *Bussy D'Ambois*, from Fortune's gifts coming suddenly to Bussy in Act I to the 'sudden outcrie' of his murder in Act V, while the word 'strange' recurs in the plays again and again.

Chapman associates changes with penetrations, particularly into bodies and female enclaves. A recurring image in the early plays is that of women having their protective barriers broken down. Men think of women as forts to be attacked; advances towards marriage are military manoeuvres. 'I can come/ To lay no battry to the Fort I seeke' moans Fortunio in the first scene of *All Fooles* (I.1.21–2), prompting Rynaldo to get all the ins-and-outs of the action going. In the first scene of *The Widdowes Teares*, Tharsalio tells his brother about his plans to woo a wealthy widow: 'Your way is, not to winne *Penelope* by suite, but by surprise. The Castle's carried by a sodaine assault, that would perhaps sit out a twelve-moneths siege' (I.1.139–42). This is the rationale of Tharsalio's bold intrusions across the stage in Acts I and II. In *Monsieur D'Olive* there's a joke about the sexualization of these rude entries; as Vandome batters on the doors at the back of the stage, a servant pops his head out to defend the women within, saying 'I [am] the Giant set to guard the same:/ My name is *Dildo*' (V.i.32–3). It's because his characters like to appear so hard that Chapman's favourite word for the effectiveness of language and spectacle is 'piercing'. So Marcellina in *Monsieur D'Olive* tells Vandome, 'Speake man, my heart is armed with a mourning habit of such proofe, that there is none greater without, to pierce it' (V.i.66–7). Few people in Chapman are ever persuaded of anything by rational argument

('So, through mens refuse eares, will nothing pearse/ Thats good, or elegant; but the sword; the herse;' – *The Teares of Peace*, ll. 601–602), which is strange in a writer ostensibly so committed to the civilizing functions of rhetoric. In his poem commending Jonson's *Sejanus* he says 'the sense/ That thy Spectators have of good or ill,/ Thou inject'st joyntly to thy Readers soules' ('In Sejanum Ben. Jonsoni', ll. 99–101). Jonson is thus figured as a moral doctor whose art works intravenously on the human spirit. A similar scientific capability is wished for Thomas Harriot: 'O had your perfect eye Organs to pierce/ Into that Chaos whence this stiffled verse/ By violence breakes' ('To *M. Harriots*', ll. 41–3). The process of piercing is multifarious. Strozza in *The Gentleman Usher* (1602–3) gains the gift of prophecy after being shot in the side with an arrow. The widow Eudora starts to fancy Tharsalio in *The Widdowes Teares* after bawdy insinuations about his sexual prowess open 'wounds in her lookes' (II.3.8–9). Things happen in Chapman's works after the body is breached or cut up or tortured or pierced. At the end of *The Gentleman Usher*, old Duke Alphonso only relents in his pursuit of a young woman after she has destroyed her face with a poisonous ointment, his people are nearly in a state of insurrection and his son Vincentio has almost been killed. He seeks forgiveness from Vincentio with these words: 'Beleeve then sonne,/ And know me pierst as deeply with thy wounds' ... (V.iv.79–80). No wonder Bussy asserts that a politician, to be successful, must leave no marks on the skin of his enemies but 'like lightening melt/ The very marrow' (IV.2.165–6). Bussy is unsuccessful, and is shot from offstage by unseen assailants – prompting him to ask himself one of the great questions of western philosophy:

> ... is my bodie then
> But penetrable flesh? And must my minde
> Follow my blood? Can my divine part adde
> No aide to th'earthly in extremitie?
> Then these divines are but for forme, not fact: ...   (V.3.125–9)

The faculties of the body affect what the soul can do – remember Chapman's complaints to Harriot about the limits imposed on his 'zeale and power' by treacherous and unruly flesh. Hence Chapman's frequently expressed hatred of the body, and hence the desirability of hard unpierceable fixity. Near his death Bussy tries to recover and says: 'I am up/ Heere like a Roman Statue;/ I will stand/ Till death hath made me marble' (V.3.139–41). Bussy wants to be his own statue-maker: *The Teares of Peace* describes the job of cutting away perturbations as analogous to the work of the 'Statuarie' hewing redundant matter out of stone (ll. 366–84). The task can't be done 'without Art' (l. 382): the struggles of Bussy and Byron are akin to those of the artist.[17]

Chapman put his heroes into degenerate worlds in part because they are liberations of his own fantasies of greatness and power, of moving from the shades into the centre, of what that might entail, and what might ensue. This projection was something picked up by his friends. The character of Bellamont in Thomas Dekker and John Webster's play *Northward Hoe* (1605) is an affectionate if teasing portrait of Chapman. At the start of Act IV he enters in his nightcap, '*with leaves in his hand, his man after him with lights, Standish and Paper*', and when his man goes out he says, 'Why should not I bee an excellent statesman? I can in the wryting of a tragedy, make *Caesar* speake better than ever his ambition could: when I write of *Pompey* I have *Pompeies* soule within me, and when I personate a worthy Poet, I am then truly my selfe, a poore unpreferd scholler.'[18] Bellamont goes on to imagine himself standing on a stage behind the Duke of Byron, or some such figure, who will step up to the French king and point him out, saying '*Sire, voyla, il et votre treshumble serviteur, le plu sage, è divine espirit, monsieur Bellamont*' or recommend him as a very worthy man 'to bee one of your privy Chamber, or Poet Lawreat'.[19] Of course the portrait of Bellamont proves nothing, but it does suggest that at least two of Chapman's contemporaries, who were well disposed towards him, believed that he put himself into his works. This impression is reinforced by verbal resonances. For instance, Monsieur tells Bussy that when he goes to court: 'Thou shalt have Glosse enough, and all things fit/ T'enchase in all shew, thy long smother'd spirit: . . .'. (I.1.111–12) It's notable that Bussy is promised a hard outside – an encasement – but the key word here is 'smother'd'. It's the word Chapman uses when he describes the state of his inner life to Harriot and laments that he will never be able to employ 'that smotherd fervour that in lothed embers,/ Lyes swept from light, and no cleare howre remembers' (ll. 39–40). Bussy is a dream of what would happen if that 'smotherd fervour' were to be employed.

Bussy is seen as a weird survivor of the Golden Age and a harbinger of its possible return. The Golden Age is Chapman's image of the ideal society, to be longed for in the Iron Age of Elizabethan and Jacobean England. Hesiod first wrote of the Iron Age in *Works and Days* and when Chapman translated this poem in 1618, he commented in the margin: 'This fift age he only prophecied of; almost three thousand years since; which falling out in this age especially true, shows how divine a Truth inspired him.'[20] The Iron Age 'eates it selfe', wastes away through rust and envy and idleness.[21] The myth of the world's decline was expanded out of Hesiod by Ovid, and its terms reverberate through the works of Chapman and many other writers of the time. Thus Byron exclaims, in a speech in *The Tragedie Of Charles Duke of Byron* which T. M. Parrott takes to represent 'Chapman's view of the degeneration of England under the peaceful reign of James I':[22]

> But men them-selves, in steed of bearing fruites,
> Growe rude, and foggie, over-growne with weedes,
> Their spirits, and freedomes smootherd in their ease; . . . . (IV.i.8 – 10)

In the same play, Byron takes the state of this world to justify his conspiracy against Henry IV:

> Wee must reforme and have a new creation
> Of State and government; and on our *Chaos*
> Will I sit brooding up another world. (I.ii.29 – 31)

He later wishes for a life without subjection ('the Lion,/ Serves not the Lion; nor the horse the horse,/ As man serves man' – IV.1.141 – 3), and the Republican tinge of this (which trickled down into the English Revolution) is specifically associated with the Golden Age. In *The Gentleman Usher*, Strozza harks back to the Golden days when no man was Prince:

> . . . Had all beene vertuous men,
> There never had beene Prince upon the earth,
> And so no subject; all men had been Princes:
> A vertuous man is subject to no Prince,
> But to his soule and honour; . . . (V.iv.56 – 60)

This theme is taken up by the King in *Bussy D'Ambois*, eulogizing Bussy:

> . . . Kings had never borne
> Such boundlesse eminence over other men,
> Had all maintain'd the spirit and state of *D'Ambois*; . . . (III.2.95 – 7)

The prospect of recreating a Golden Age is held out in 'De Guiana', which Chapman may have been commissioned to write by Sir Walter Ralegh, who felt that his first expedition to Guiana in 1595 needed promoting. The poem subsequently served as the preface to Lawrence Keymis's account of a second voyage there in 1596. Queen Elizabeth is urged to let her breath go forth upon the waters 'and create/ A golden worlde in this our yron age' (ll. 31–2). Elizabeth is also referred to as 'our most sacred Maide':

> . . . whose barrennesse
> Is the true fruite of vertue, that may get,
> Beare and bring foorth anew in all perfection,
> What heretofore savage corruption held
> In barbarous *Chaos*; . . .   (ll. 25–8)

Chapman's only surviving masque returned in 1613 to the subject of the new world and the Golden Age, and the scenery featured a huge artificial rock, which suddenly split open to reveal 'a rich and refulgent Mine of golde'.[23]

The opposite of the Golden Age is Chaos. The myth of Chaos again stems from Hesiod, and was developed in Ovid's *Metamorphoses*. A world in chaos is the premise of *The Shadow Of Night*.

> And we (without the harmonie was usd,
> When Saturnes golden scepter stroke the strings
> Of Civill governement) make all our doings
> Savour of rudenesse, and obscuritie,
> And in our formes shew more deformitie,
> Then if we still were wrapt, and smoothered
> In that confusion, out of which we fled.
>
> ('Hymnus in Noctem', ll. 194–200)

The artist's role is to create 'Civill' forms but these lines suggest that the state of the world makes 'obscuritie' inevitable. The reappearance of that word 'smoothered' only reinforces the impression that the artist can never achieve the epiphanic moment wished for in *Ovids Banquet of Sence* where Chapman is outlining philosophers' theories about the apprehension of knowledge, and Ovid is listening to Corynna singing: 'My life that in my flesh a Chaos is/ Should to a Golden worlde be thus dygested' (25.3–4).

The strength and weakness of Chapman's work is interdependent in a way consistent with his own 'changeable' personality the nature of his dramatic characters, and his belief that poems too should have hard 'rinds' to repel the vulgar multitude.[24] Hard outsides may lend protection, but what's inside may be softer and all the more penetrable because of that. Chapman's constant urge to totalize – which can be registered through his obsessive use of the word 'all' ('all our doings', 'all perfection', 'All this, I holde', 'That Art that attones/ All opposition to good life, is all') – also suggests more uncertainty than control.[25] But Chapman's need to create does produce some astonishing syntheses, and unexpected moments of extraordinary complexity and power. He thought himself strange – and it is strange that his works have rarely been regarded as more than 'serious trifles'.

Notes

1 George Chapman, 'The Preface to the Reader', *Chapman's Homer: The Iliad*, ed. Allardyce Nicoll (London: RKP, 1957), p. 14, ll. 25–27.

2 Quoted in slightly emended form from ll. 209–10 of 'Informations be Ben Johnston to W. D. when he came to Scotland upon foot 1619'. 'W. D.' is William Drummond of Hawthornden: the 'Informations' a report by Drummond of his conversations with Jonson.

3 See *Chapman's Homer: The Iliad*, p. 548, ll. 17–19.

4 See the dedicatory letter to *Ovids Banquet of Sence*: '. . . which though ignorants will esteeme spic'd, and too curious, yet such as have the judiciall perspective, will see it hath, motion, spirit and life.' Chapman's consistent emphasis on the importance of judgement is part of a wider development traced during the last Elizabethan and early Jacobean years by Leo Salingar, 'Jacobean Playwrights and "Judicious" Spectators', *Proceedings of the British Academy*, LXXV (1989), pp. 1–23. Salingar relates the use of words such as judging, judgement, judicial and judicious, to a Gentlemanly requirement for knowledge and understanding, i.e. classical learning.

5 Stephen Greenblatt, *Renaissance Self-Fashioning* (Chicago and London: University of Chicago Press, 1980), p. 19. The frontispiece of Greenblatt's book is 'The Ambassadors'. Chapman's interest in 'optike' pictures was far from unique: see Inga Stina-Ewbank, 'Webster's Realism or, "A Cunning Piece Wrought Perspective"' in *John Webster*, ed. Brian Morris (London: Ernest Benn, 1970), pp. 157–78, and John Creaser, 'Enigmatic Ben Jonson', in *English Comedy*, eds. Michael Cordner, Peter Holland, and John Kerrigan (Cambridge: Cambridge University Press, 1994), pp. 100–118.

6 The importance of viewing 'in a right line' is stressed again in the final 'optike'

example in Chapman's work, in *The Tragedie Of Chabot Admirall Of France* (1611 – 13), I.1.68 – 80:

> As of a Picture wrought to opticke reason,
> That to all passers by, seemes as they move
> Now woman, now a Monster, now a Divell,
> And till you stand, and in a right line view it,
> You cannot well judge what the maine forme is,
> So men that view him but in vulgar passes,
> Casting but laterall, or partiall glances
> At what he is, suppose him weake, unjust,
> Bloody, and monstrous, but stand free and fast,
> And judge him by no more than what you know
> Ingenuously, and by the right laid line
> Of truth, he truely, will all stiles deserve
> Of wise, just, good, a man both soule and nerve.

7 The image of the 'kernell' possibly derives from Ovid's *Fasti* via Marsilio Ficino's *Omnia Opera* (1561): 'There is a god in us, we are inflamed at his rousing./ That impulse holds the kernels of the sacred mind.' Translated and quoted by Joel F. Wilcox, 'Ficino's Commentary on Plato's *Ion* and Chapman's Inspired Poet in the *Odyssey*', *Philological Quarterly*, 64 (1985), p. 196.

8 George Chapman, *Bussy D'Ambois*, ed. by Maurice Evans (London: Ernest Benn, 1965), pp. 104 – 5. Pico is quoted from Pico della Mirandola, *Oration on the Dignity of Man*, ed. by Paul O. Kristeller (Chicago: 1948), Sec. 33, p. 249.

9 Millar Maclure detects 'a kind of manic-depressive alternation' in Chapman, or melancholy to use the time's own term. Maclure quotes from Thomas Walkington's *The Opticke Glasse of Humours* (1607), f. 64v: 'The melancholic man is said of the wise to be *aut Deus aut Daemon*, either angel of heaven or friend of hell, for in whomsoever this humour hath dominion, the soule is either wrapt up into an *Elysium* and paradise of blisse by a heavenly contemplation, or into a direfull hellish purgatory by a cynicall meditation.' See *George Chapman: A Critical Study* (Toronto: 1966), p. 35. The novelist Alan Garner, himself a manic-depressive, writes suggestively of links between the condition, 'the ancient, mystical experience of "black sight",' and the 'madness' of poetic inspiration. See 'Fierce Fires & Shramming Cold' in *The Voice That Thunders* (London: The Harvill Press, 1997), pp. 208 – 22. Chapman's idea of 'black sight' animates *The Shadow Of Night* and the vision of Homer in *The Teares of Peace*.

10 For a study of 'Ceremonie' see D. J. Gordon, 'The Renaissance Poet as Classicist', in *The Renaissance Imagination*, ed. Stephen Orgel (Berkeley and Los Angeles: University of California Press, 1975), pp. 102 – 33.

11 See, for example, the poem 'Pleasd with thy place' in the 1612 volume *Petrarchs Seven Penitentiall Psalms, Paraphrastically Translated: With other Philosophicall Poems, and a*

Hymne to Christ upon the Cross. The first half of the poem elaborates on a passage in the *Discourses* of the Stoic Epictetus. It starts:

> God hath the whole world perfect made, & free;
> His parts to th'use of all. Men then, that be
> Parts of that all, must as the generall sway
> Of that importeth, willingly obay
> In everie thing, without their powres to change.

These lines – and those immediately following – are also used in *The Revenge Of Bussy D'Ambois* by the hero Clermont (III.iv.58–75). Clermont speaks the second half of the poem at IV.i.137–57. It's often been remarked that the Stoic attitude does not make for exciting drama.

12 Chapman was listed by Francis Meres in *Palladis Tamia* (1598) as one of the best writers of tragedy and comedy, so it is possible that early tragedies may not have survived.

13 The description of the multitude comes from Chapman's prose introduction to *A Free And Offenceles Justification, Of A Lately Publisht and most maliciously misinterpreted Poeme; Entituled Andromeda liberata* (1614), ll. 64–5, which can be read in *The Poems of George Chapman*, ed. Phyllis Brooks Bartlett (New York: MLA, 1941).

14 See Geoffrey Chaucer's *Troilus and Criseyde* (*c.*1385).

15 See *All Fooles*, I.2.61.

16 See Henri Bergson, *Le Rire: essai sur la signification du comique* (1900).

17 See Commentary on ll. 27–30 of 'To *M. Harriots*' for a view of the way in which Bussy is partly a dramatization of Chapman's social and poetic stance.

18 Thomas Dekker and John Webster, *Northward Hoe* (printed 1607), IV.i.6–10, quoted (with u's regularized to v's) from *The Dramatic Works of Thomas Dekker*, Vol. II, ed. Fredson Bowers (Cambridge: Cambridge University Press, 1955). Chapman probably started work on his tragedy *Caesar And Pompey* in 1604–5: the play was printed in 1631.

19 *Northward Hoe*, IV.1.56–60.

20 Quoted from Maclure's *George Chapman*, p. 215.

21 George Chapman, 'To his loving friend M. *J. Fletcher* concerning his Pastorall, being both a Poeme and a play', *Poems*, p. 364. John Fletcher's 'Pastorall' was *The Faithfull Shepheardesse* (printed 1609).

22 See *The Plays of George Chapman: The Tragedies, Volume 2*, ed. T. M. Parrott (New York and London, 1910), p. 614.

23 George Chapman, *The Memorable Masque of the two Honourable Houses or Innes of Court; the Middle Temple and Lyncolnes Inne*, ll. 158–9 of the prose description prefacing the Masque. The performance was spectacularly lavish, costing the two Inns of Court more than £1,500.

24 See *A Free And Offenceles Justification Of Andromeda liberata*, ll. 22–32: 'ever (I say) enclosing within the Rinde, some fruit of knowledge howsoever darkened; and (by reason of the obscurity) of ambiguous and different construction . . . This Ambiguity in the sence, hath given scope to the varietie of expositions; while Poets in al ages (challenging, as their Birth-rights, the use and application of these fictions) have ever beene allowed to fashion both, *pro & contra*, to their owne offencelesse, and judicious occasions.'

25 Chapman's addiction to the word 'all' is further discussed in the last section of the main 'Notes To *Poems*'.

FURTHER READING

Bliss, Lee, *The World's Perspective* (Brighton: Harvester Press, 1983). Mostly about John Webster, but Chapters I and II feature *The Widdowes Teares* and *Bussy D'Ambois*.

Bradbrook, M. C., *George Chapman* (Harlow: Longman, 1977). Pamphlet in the British Council series *Writers and their Work*.

Braunmuller, A. R., *Natural Fictions: George Chapman's Major Tragedies* (Delaware, USA: University of Delaware Press, 1992).

Burrow, Colin, *Epic Romance: Homer to Milton* (Oxford: Clarendon Press, 1993). Two sections of Chapter 7 cover Chapman's translations of Homer.

Eliot, T. S., *The Varieties of Metaphysical Poetry*, ed. Ronald Schuchard (London: Faber, 1993). Late in his life Eliot regretted that he'd never had occasion to write an essay about Chapman, whom he regarded as a great poet and dramatist. Best to look in the index of this volume for signposts to a few stimulating thoughts by Eliot and thorough footnotes.

Hunter, G. K., *English Drama 1586–1642: The Age of Shakespeare* (Oxford: Clarendon Press, 1997).

Ide, Richard S., *Possessed with Greatness: The Heroic Tragedies of Chapman and Shakespeare* (London: Scolar Press, 1980).

Maclure, Millar, *George Chapman: A Critical Study* (Toronto: Toronto University Press, 1966).

Muir, Edwin, ' "Royal Man": Notes on the tragedies of George Chapman', *Essays on Literature and Society* (London: Hogarth Press, 1965 enlarged and revised edition).

Snare, Gerald, *The Mystification Of George Chapman* (Durham, USA, and London: Duke University Press, 1989).

Waddington, Raymond B., *The Mind's Empire: Myth and Form in George Chapman's Narrative Poems* (Baltimore and London: Johns Hopkins University Press, 1974). Includes a chapter on *Bussy D'Ambois*.

Waith, Eugene M., *The Herculean Hero in Marlowe, Chapman, Shakespeare and Dryden* (London: Chatto & Windus, 1962). Chapter 4 concentrates on *Bussy D'Ambois*.

— *Ideas of Greatness: Heroic Drama in England* (London: RKP, 1971). Part of Chapter 3 looks at the tragedies and *The Widdowes Teares*.

TEXTUAL PROCEDURE

This edition of Chapman's Plays and Poems follows the principles set out in the Series Statement. Act and scene divisions are regularized in the light of modern editorial convention, and rendered in English, but Chapman's idiosyncratic Latin designations are recorded in the Textual Notes. Also in the Textual Notes is a record of all differences between the base texts and the ones printed here, including the modification of unintelligible or seriously misleading punctuation.

The texts of all three plays in this volume appear to have been printed from Chapman's own manuscripts, since they all contain spelling forms and Latin stage directions which were unusual to him. *All Fooles* is a sufficiently well-printed text to suggest that it was set from Chapman's fair copy, or perhaps a transcript of it, while *Bussy D'Ambois*, with its lack of attention to crucial entrances and exits and its inaccurate assignment of speech prefixes, may well have been printed from the writer's rather less polished working papers. Neither text shows any sign that the manuscript used by the printer had been annotated for use in the theatre. *The Widdowes Teares* differs in this respect. There are many confusions in lineation, and verse and prose are often set wrongly, which may point to hasty composition and a heavily, perhaps incompletely revised manuscript, but stage directions such as '*shee strikes*' and '*Shut the tomb*' also suggest that the author's papers had been worked on in the theatre by a prompter. The printing of the early editions of the poems was probably supervised by Chapman himself.

Stage directions – so often, as here, a distinctive and revealing feature of the way a dramatist conceives his stage business – are only expanded or interpolated where absolutely necessary, although the names of speaking parts in the stage directions are regularized and set in small capitals. Where Chapman wanted to indicate an unusual piece of staging – throughout Act IV of *The Widdowes Teares*, for instance – or where he wished a line to be spoken as an aside, he ensured that his intentions were reflected in the printed text. In the places where it is not absolutely clear what he wanted, modern editors have been keen to close down interpretative possibilities by too freely adding stage directions; this edition, by contrast, preserves the open-endedness of the earliest texts wherever possible. All additions and expansions are enclosed in square brackets.

Early printers were sometimes careless about the lineation of verse in the text of plays, and occasionally, especially if working from a manuscript which was hard to read or heavily revised, they would set verse as prose (or even the other way round, as they do, for example, in *Bussy D'Ambois*, I.2.99–102 and 173–5). Some relineation has been undertaken in this edition, particularly in *The Widdowes Teares*; once again, the alterations are recorded in the Textual Notes.

PLAYS

All Fooles

Actors.

GOSTANZO. ⎱
MAR. ANTONIO. ⎰ Knights.

VALERIO, sonne to GOSTANZO.

FORTUNIO, elder sonne to MARC. ANTONIO.

RYNALDO, the younger.

DARIOTTO. ⎱
CLAUDIO. ⎰ Courtiers.

CORNELIO, A start-up Gentleman.

CURIO, a Page.

KYTE, a Scrivener.

FRAUNCES POCK, a Surgeon.

GAZETTA, wife to COR[NELIO]

BELLANORA, daughter to GOSTANZO.

GRATIANA, Stolne wife to VALERIO.

[DRAWER.]

Prologus.

The fortune of a Stage (like Fortunes selfe)
Amazeth greatest judgements: And none knowes
The hidden causes of those strange effects,
That rise from this Hell, or fall from this Heaven:
   Who can shew cause, why your wits, that in-ayme
At higher Objects, scorne to compose Playes;
(Though we are sure they could, would they vouchsafe it?)
Should (without meanes to make) judge better farre,
Then those that make, and yet yee see they can;
For without your applause, wretched is he   10
That undertakes the Stage, and he's more blest,
That with your glorious favours can contest.
    Who can shew cause, why th'ancient Comick vaine
Of Eupolis and Cratinus (now reviv'd,
Subject to personall application)
Should be exploded by some bitter splenes?
Yet merely Comicall, and harmelesse jestes
(Though nere so witty) be esteem'd but toyes,
If voide of th'other satyrismes sauce?
    Who can shew cause why quick Venerian jestes,   20
Should sometimes ravish? sometimes fall farre short,
Of the just length and pleasure of your eares?
When our pure Dames, thinke them much less obscene,
Then those that winne your Panegyrick splene?
But our poore doomes (alas) you know are nothing;
To your inspired censure, ever we
Must needs submit, and there's the mistery.
   Great are the giftes given to united heades,
To gifts, attyre, to faire attyre, the stage
Helps much, for if our other audience see   30
You on the stage depart before we end,
Our wits goe with you all, and we are fooles;
So Fortune governes in these stage events,
That merit beares least sway in most contents.

Auriculas Asini quis non habet?
How we shall then appeare, we must referre
To Magicke of your doomes, that never erre.

All Fooles

Act I. Scene 1

Enter RYNALDO, FORTUNIO, VALERIO.

RYNALDO Can one selfe cause, in subjects so alike
    As you two are, produce effects so unlike?
    One like the Turtle, all in mournefull straines,
    Wailing his fortunes? Th'other like the Larke
    Mounting the sky in shrill and cheerefull notes,
    Chaunting his joyes aspir'd, and both for love:
    In one, love rayseth by his violent heate,
    Moyst vapours from the heart into the eyes,
    From whence they drowne his brest in dayly showers;
    In th'other, his divided power infuseth   10
    Onely a temperate and most kindly warmth,
    That gives life to those fruites of wit and vertue,
    Which the unkinde hand of an uncivile father,
    Had almost nipt in the delightsome blossome.

FORTUNIO O brother love rewards our services
    With a most partiall and injurious hand,
    If you consider well our different fortunes:
    Valerio loves, and joyes the dame he loves:
    I love, and never can enjoy the sight
    Of her I love, so farre from conquering   20
    In my desires assault, that I can come
    To lay no battry to the Fort I seeke;
    All passages to it, so strongly kept,
    By straite guard of her Father.

RYNALDO   I dare sweare,
    If just desert in love measur'd reward,
    Your fortune should exceede *Valerios* farre:
    For I am witnes (being your Bedfellow)
    Both to the dayly and the nightly service,

You doe unto the deity of love,
30   In vowes, sighes, teares, and solitary watches,
He never serves him with such sacrifice,
Yet hath his Bowe and shaftes at his commaund:
Loves service is much like our humorous Lords;
Where Minions carry more then Servitors,
The bolde and carelesse servant still obtaines:
The modest and respective, nothing gaines;
You never see your love, unlesse in dreames,
He, *Hymen* puts in whole possession:
What different starres raign'd when your loves were borne,
40   He forc't to weare the Willow, you the horne?
But brother, are you not asham'd to make
Your selfe a slave to the base Lord of love,
Begot of Fancy, and of Beauty borne?
And what is Beauty? a meere Quintessence,
Whose life is not in being, but in seeming;
And therefore is not to all eyes the same,
But like a cousoning picture, which one way
Shewes like a Crowe, another like a Swanne:
And upon what ground in this Beauty drawne?
50   Upon a Woman, a most brittle creature,
And would to God (for my part) that were all.
FORTUNIO But tell me brother, did you never love?
RYNALDO You know I did, and was belov'd againe,
And that of such a Dame, as all men deem'd
Honour'd, and made me happy in her favours;
Exceeding faire she was not; and yet faire
In that she never studied to be fayrer
Then Nature made her; Beauty cost her nothing,
Her vertues were so rare, they would have made
60   An *Aethyop* beautifull: At least, so thought
By such as stood aloofe, and did observe her
With credulous eyes: But what they were indeed
Ile spare to blaze, because I lov'd her once,
Onely I found her such, as for her sake
I vow eternall warres against their whole sexe,
Inconstant shuttle-cocks, loving fooles, and jesters,

Men rich in durt and tytles, sooner woone
With the most vile, then the most vertuous:
Found true to none: if one amongst whole hundreds
Chance to be chaste, she is so proude withall,   70
Wayward and rude, that one of unchaste life,
Is oftentimes approv'd, a worthier wife:
Undressed, sluttish, nasty, to their husbands,
Spung'd up, adorn'd, and painted to their lovers:
All day in cesselesse uprore with their housholdes,
If all the night their husbands have not pleas'd them:
Like hounds, most kinde, being beaten and abus'd,
Like wolves, most cruell, being kindelyest us'd.
FORTUNIO Fye, thou prophan'st the deity of their sexe.
RYNALDO Brother I read, that *Aegipt* heretofore,   80
Had Temples of the richest frame on earth;
Much like this goodly edifice of women,
With Alablaster pillers were those Temples,
Uphelde and beautified, and so are women:
Most curiously glaz'd, and so are women;
Cunningly painted too, and so are women;
In out-side wondrous heavenly, so are women:
But when a stranger view'd those phanes within,
In stead of Gods and Goddesses, he should finde
A painted fowle, a fury, or a serpent,   90
And such celestiall inner parts have women.
VALERIO *Rynaldo*, the poore Foxe that lost his tayle,
Perswaded others also to loose theirs:
Thy selfe, for one perhaps that for desert
Or some defect in thy attempts refus'd thee,
Revil'st the whole sexe, beauty, love and all:
I tell thee, Love, is Natures second sunne,
Causing a spring of vertues where he shines,
And as without the Sunne, the Worlds great eye,
All colours, beauties, both of Arte and Nature,   100
Are given in vaine to men, so without love
All beauties bred in women are in vaine;
All vertues borne in men lye buried,
For love informes them as the Sunne doth colours,

And as the Sunne reflecting his warme beames
Against the earth, begets all fruites and flowers:
So love, fayre shining in the inward man,
Brings foorth in him the honourable fruites
Of valour, wit, vertue, and haughty thoughts,
110 Brave resolution, and divine discourse:
O tis the Paradice, the heaven of earth,
And didst thou know the comfort of two hearts,
In one delicious harmony united?
As to joy one joy, and thinke both one thought,
Live both one life, and therein double life:
To see their soules met at an enter-view
In their bright eyes, at parle in their lippes,
Their language kisses: And t'observe the rest,
Touches, embraces, and each circumstance
120 Of all loves most unmatched ceremonies:
Thou wouldst abhorre thy tongue for blasphemy,
O who can comprehend how sweet love tastes,
But he that hath been present at his feastes?
RYNALDO Are you in that vaine too *Valerio*?
Twere fitter you should be about your charge,
How Plow and Cart goes forward: I have knowne
Your joyes were all imployde in husbandry,
Your study was how many loades of hay
A meadow of so many acres yeelded;
130 How many Oxen such a close would fat?
And is your rurall service now converted
From *Pan* to *Cupid*? and from beastes to women?
O if your father knew this, what a lecture
Of bitter castigation he would read you?
VALERIO My father? why my father? does he thinke
To rob me of my selfe? I hope I know
I am a Gentleman, though his covetous humour
And education hath transform'd me Bayly,
And made me overseer of his pastures,
140 Ile be my selfe, in spight of husbandry.
  Enter GRATIANA.

And see bright heaven here comes my husbandry,

> *Amplectitur eam.*

Here shall my cattle graze, here *Nectar* drinke,
Here will I hedge and ditch, here hide my treasure,
O poore *Fortunio*, how wouldst thou tryumph,
If thou enjoy'dst this happines with my Sister?

FORTUNIO I were in heaven if once twere come to that.

RYNALDO And me thinkes tis my heaven that I am past it,
And should the wretched Machevilian,
The covetous knight your father see this sight
Lusty *Valerio?*

VALERIO   Sfoote Sir if he should,   150
He shall perceive ere long my skill extends
To something more, then sweaty husbandry.

RYNALDO Ile beare thee witnes, thou canst skill of dice,
Cards, tennis, wenching, dauncing, and what not?
And this is something more then husbandry:
Th'art knowne in Ordinaries, and *Tabacco* shops,
Trusted in Tavernes and in vaulting houses,
And this is something more then husbandry:
Yet all this while, thy father apprehends thee
For the most tame and thriftie Groome in *Europe*.   160

FORTUNIO Well, he hath venter'd on a mariage
Would quite undoe him, did his father know it.

RYNALDO Know it? alas Sir where can he bestow
This poore Gentlewoman he hath made his wife,
But his inquisitive father will heare of it?
Who, like the dragon to th'esperean fruite,
Is to his haunts? slight hence, the olde knight comes.

> *Intrat* GOSTANZO.

GOSTANZO *Rynaldo.*

RYNALDO   Whose that calles? what Sir *Gostanzo?*

> *Omnes aufugiunt.*

How fares your Knighthood Sir?

GOSTANZO   Say who was that
Shrunke at my entry here? was't not your brother?   170

RYNALDO He shrunke not sir, his busines call'd him hence.

GOSTANZO And was it not my sonne that went out with him?

RYNALDO I saw not him, I was in serious speech
    About a secret busines with my brother.

GOSTANZO Sure twas my sonne, what made he here? I sent him
    About affaires to be dispacht in hast.

RYNALDO Well sir, lest silence breed unjust suspect,
    Ile tell a secret I am sworne to keep,
    And crave your honoured assistance in it.

GOSTANZO What ist *Rynaldo*?

180 RYNALDO   This sir, twas your sonne.

GOSTANZO And what yong gentlewoman grac'st their company?

RYNALDO Thereon depends the secret I must utter:
    That gentlewoman hath my brother maryed.

GOSTANZO Maryed? what is she?

RYNALDO   Faith sir, a gentlewoman:
    But her unusering dowry must be tolde
    Out of her beauty.

GOSTANZO   Is it true *Rynaldo*?
    And does your father understand so much?

RYNALDO That was the motion sir, I was entreating
    Your sonne to make to him, because I know
190   He is well spoken, and may much prevaile
    In satisfying my father, who much loves him,
    Both for his wisedome and his husbandry.

GOSTANZO Indeede he's one can tell his tale I tell you,
    And for his husbandry —

RYNALDO   O sir, had you heard,
    What thrifty discipline he gave my brother,
    For making choyce without my fathers knowledge,
    And without riches, you would have admyr'd him.

GOSTANZO Nay, nay, I know him well, but what was it?

RYNALDO That in the choyce of wives men must respect
200   The chiefe wife, riches, that in every course
    A mans chiefe Load-starre should shine out of riches,
    Love nothing hartely in this world but riches;
    Cast off all friends, all studies, all delights,
    All honesty, and religion for riches:
    And many such, which wisedome sure he learn'd
    Of his experient father; yet my brother,

So soothes his rash affection, and presumes
So highly on my fathers gentle nature,
That he's resolv'd to bring her home to him,
And like enough he will.

GOSTANZO   And like enough,   210
Your silly father too, will put it up,
An honest knight, but much too much indulgent
To his presuming children.

RYNALDO   What a difference
Doth interpose it selfe, twixt him and you?
Had your sonne us'd you thus?

GOSTANZO   My sonne? alas
I hope to bring him up in other fashion,
Followes my husbandry, sets early foote
Into the world; he comes not at the citty,
Nor knowes the citty Artes.

RYNALDO   But dice and wenching.   *Aversus.*

GOSTANZO Acquaints himselfe with no delight but getting,   220
A perfect patterne of sobriety,
Temperance and husbandry to all my housholde,
And what's his company I pray? not wenches.

RYNALDO Wenches? I durst be sworne he never smelt
A wenches breath yet, but me thinkes twere fit
You sought him out a wife.

GOSTANZO   A wife *Rynaldo*?
He dares not looke a woman in the face.

RYNALDO Sfoote holde him to one, your sonne such a sheep?

GOSTANZO Tis strange in earnest.

RYNALDO Well sir, though for my thriftlesse brothers sake,   230
I little care how my wrong'd father takes it,
Yet for my fathers quiet, if your selfe
Would joyne hands with your wise and toward Sonne,
I should deserve it some way.

GOSTANZO   Good *Rynaldo*,
I love you and your father, but this matter
Is not for me to deale in: And tis needlesse,
You say your brother is resolv'd, presuming
Your father will allow it.

Enter MARC ANTONIO.

RYNALDO　　　　　　　　See my father:
Since you are resolute not to move him Sir,
240　　　In any case conceale the secret　　　　　　*Abscondit se.*
By way of an attonement, let me pray
You will.

GOSTANZO Upon mine honour.

RYNALDO　　　　　　　　Thankes Sir.

MARC ANTONIO God save thee honourable Knight *Gostanzo.*

GOSTANZO Friend *Marc Antonio*? welcome, and I thinke
I have good newes to welcome you withall.

RYNALDO He cannot holde.

MARC ANTONIO　　　　　　What newes I pray you Sir?

GOSTANZO You have a forward, valiant eldest Sonne,
But wherein is his forwardnes, and valour?

MARC ANTONIO I know not wherein you intend him so.

250　　GOSTANZO Forward before, valiant behinde, his duety,
That he hath dar'd before your due consent
To take a wife.

MARC ANTONIO A wife sir? what is she?

GOSTANZO One that is rich enough, her hayre pure Amber,
Her forehead mother of pearle, her faire eyes
Two wealthy diamants: her lips, mines of Rubies:
Her teeth, are orient pearle; her necke, pure Ivory.

MARC ANTONIO Jest not good Sir, in an affayre so serious,
I love my sonne, and if his youth reward me
With his contempt of my consent in mariage:
260　　Tis to be fear'd that his presumption buildes not
Of his good choyce, that will beare out it selfe,
And being bad, the newes is worse then bad.

GOSTANZO What call you bad? is it bad to be poore?

MARC ANTONIO The world accounts it so; but if my sonne
Have in her birth and vertues helde his choice,
Without disparagement, the fault is lesse.

GOSTANZO Sits the winde there? blowes there so calme a gale
From a contemned and deserved anger?
Are you so easie to be disobay'd?

270　　MARC ANTONIO What should I doe? if my enamour'd sonne

Have been so forward; I assure my selfe
He did it more to satisfie his love,
Then to incense my hate, or to neglect me.

GOSTANZO A passing kinde construction; suffer this,
You ope him doores to any villany,
He'le dare to sell, to pawne, runne ever ryot,
Despise your love in all, and laugh at you:
And that knights competency you have gotten
With care and labour, he with lust and idlenesse
Will bring into the stypend of a begger;   280
All to maintaine a wanton whirly-gig,
Worth nothing more then she brings on her back,
Yet all your wealth too little for that back:
By heaven I pitty your declining state,
For be assur'd your sonne hath set his foote,
In the right path-way to consumption:
Up to the heart in love; and for that love,
Nothing can be too deare his love desires:
And how insatiate and unlymited,
Is the ambition and the beggerly pride   290
Of a dame hoysed from a beggers state,
To a state competent and plentifull,
You cannot be so simple not to know.

MARC ANTONIO I must confesse the mischiefe: But alas
Where is in me the power of remedy?

GOSTANZO Where? in your just displeasure: cast him off,
Receive him not, let him endure the use
Of their enforced kindnesse that must trust him
For meate and money, for apparrell, house,
And every thing belongs to that estate,   300
Which he must learne with want of misery,
Since pleasure and a full estate hath blinded
His dissolute desires.

MARC ANTONIO   What should I doe?
If I should banish him my house and sight,
What desperate resolution might it breed?
To runne into the warres, and there to live
In want of competencie: and perhaps

Taste th'unrecoverable losse of his chiefe limbes,
Which while he hath in peace, at home with me,
310   May with his spirit, ransome his estate
From any losse his mariage can procure.

GOSTANZO Ist true? No let him runne into the warre,
And lose what limbes he can: better one branch
Be lopt away, then all the whole tree should perish:
And for his wants, better young want then olde;
You have a younger sonne at *Padoa*,
I like his learning well, make him your heire,
And let your other walke: let him buy wit
Att's owne charge, not at's fathers, if you loose him,
320   You loose no more then that was lost before,
If you recover him, you finde a sonne.

MARC ANTONIO I cannot part with him.

GOSTANZO   If it be so,
And that your love to him be so extreame,
In needfull daungers, ever chuse the least:
If he should be in minde to passe the Seas,
Your sonne *Rynaldo* (who tolde me all this)
Will tell me that, and so we shall prevent it:
If by no sterne course you will venture that,
Let him come home to me with his faire wife:
330   And if you chaunce to see him, shake him up,
As if your wrath were hard to be reflected,
That he may feare hereafter to offend
In other dissolute courses: At my house
With my advice and my sonnes good example,
Who shall serve as a glasse for him to see
His faults, and mend them to his president:
I make no doubt but of a dissolut Sonne
And disobedient, to send him home
Both dutifull and thriftie.

MARC ANTONIO   O *Gostanzo*!
340   Could you do this, you should preserve your selfe,
A perfect friend of mee, and mee a Sonne.

GOSTANZO Remember you your part, and feare not mine:
Rate him, revile him, and renounce him too:

Speake, can you doo't man?

MARC ANTONIO   Ile do all I can.

                                   Exit MARC ANTONIO.

GOSTANZO Ahlas good man, how Nature over-wayes him.

    RYNALDO *comes foorth.*

RYNALDO God save you Sir.

GOSTANZO   *Rynaldo,* All the Newes
    You told mee as a secret, I perceive
    Is passing common; for your Father knowes it,
    The first thing he related, was the Marriage.

RYNALDO And was extreamly moov'd?

GOSTANZO   Beyond all measure: 350
    But I did all I could to quench his furie:
    Told him how easie t'was for a young man
    To runne that Amorous course: and though his choyce
    Were nothing rich, yet shee was gentlie borne,
    Well quallified and beautifull: But hee still
    Was quite relentles, and would needes renounce him.

RYNALDO My Brother knowes it well, and is resolv'd
    To trayle a Pyke in Field, rather then bide
    The more feard push of my vext Fathers furie.

GOSTANZO Indeed that's one way: but are no more meanes   360
    Left to his fine wits, then t'incence his Father
    With a more violent rage, and to redeeme
    A great offence with greater?

RYNALDO   So I told him:
    But to a desperat minde all breath is lost.

GOSTANZO Go to, let him be wise, and use his friendes,
    Amongst whom, Ile be formost to his Father:
    Without this desperate errour he intends
    Joynd to the other, Ile not doubt to make him
    Easie returne into his Fathers favour:
    So he submit himselfe, as duetie bindes him: 370
    For Fathers will be knowne to be them selves,
    And often when their angers are not deepe,
    Will paint an outward Rage upon their lookes.

RYNALDO All this I told him Sir; but what sayes hee?
    I know my Father will not be reclaymde,

Heele thinke that if he wincke at this offence,
T'will open doores to any villanie:
Ile dare to sell, to pawne, and run all ryot,
To laugh at all his patience, and consume
380   All he hath purchast to an honord purpose,
In maintenance of a wanton Whirligigg,
Worth nothing more then she weares on her backe.

GOSTANZO The very words I usd t'incense his Father,
But good *Rinaldo* let him be advisde:
How would his Father grieve, should he be maynd,
Or quite miscarie in the ruthles warre?

RYNALDO I told him so; but better farr (sayd hee)
One branch should utterly be lopt away,
Then the whole Tree of all his race should perish:
390   And for his wants, better yong want, then eld.

GOSTANZO By heaven the same words still I usde t'his Father.
Why comes this about?—Well, good *Rinaldo*,
If hee dare not indure his Fathers lookes,
Let him and his faire wife come home to me,
Till I have quallified his Fathers passion,
He shall be kindly welcome, and be sure
Of all the intercession I can use.

RYNALDO I thanke you sir, Ile try what I can doe,
Although I feare me I shall strive in vaine.

GOSTANZO Well, try him, try him.   *Exit.*
400   RYNALDO   Thanks sir, so I will.
See, this olde politique dissembling Knight,
Now he perceives my Father so affectionate,
And that my brother may hereafter live
By him and his, with equall use of either,
He will put on a face of hollowe friendship.
But this will prove an excellent ground to sowe
The seede of mirth amongst us; Ile go seeke
Valerio and my brother, and tell them
Such newes of their affaires, as they'le admire.   *Exit.*

[*Act I. Scene 2*]

Enter GAZETTA, BELLANORA, GRATIANA.

GAZETTA How happie are your fortunes above mine?
 Both still being woode and courted: still so feeding
 On the delightes of love, that still you finde
 An appetite to more; where I am cloyde,
 And being bound to love sportes, care not for them.

BELLANORA That is your fault *Gazetta*, we have Loves
 And wish continuall company with them
 In honour'd marriage rites, which you enjoy.
 But seld or never can we get a looke
 Of those we love, *Fortunio* my deare choyce   10
 Dare not be knowne to love me, nor come neere
 My Fathers house, where I as in a prison
 Consume my lost dayes, and the tedious nights,
 My Father guarding me for one I hate;
 And *Gratiana* here my brothers love,
 Joyes him by so much stelth, that vehement feare
 Drinkes up the sweetnesse of their stolne delightes:
 Where you enjoye a husband, and may freely
 Performe all obsequies you desire to love.

GAZETTA Indeede I have a husband, and his love   20
 Is more then I desire, being vainely jelouse:
 Extreames, though contrarie, have the like effects,
 Extreame heate mortifies like extreame colde:
 Extreame love breedes sacietie as well
 As extreame Hatred: and too violent rigour,
 Tempts Chastetie as much, as too much Licence:
 There's no mans eye fixt on mee but doth pierce
 My Husbandes soule: If any aske my wel-fare?
 Hee straight doubts Treason practis'd to his bed:
 Fancies but to himselfe all likelihoods   30
 Of my wrong to him, and layes all on mee
 For certaine trueths; yet seekes he with his best,
 To put Disguise on all his Jelosie,
 Fearing perhaps, least it may teach me that,

Which otherwise I should not dreame upon:
Yet lives he still abrode, at great expence,
Turns merely Gallant from his Farmers state,
Uses all Games and recreations:
Runnes Races with the Gallants of the Court,
40   Feastes them at home, and entertaines them costly,
And then upbraydes mee with their companie:
    Enter CORNELIO.
See see, wee shalbe troubl'd with him now.

CORNELIO Now Ladyes, what plots have we now in hand?
They say, when onely one Dame is alone,
Shee plots some mischiefe; but if three together,
They plot three hundred: Wife, the Ayre is sharpe,
Y'ad best to take the house least you take cold.

GAZETTA Ahlas this time of yeere yeeldes no such danger.

CORNELIO Goe, in I say; a friend of yours attends you.

50 GAZETTA Hee is of your bringing, and may stay.

CORNELIO Nay stand not chopping Logicke; in I pray.

GAZETTA Yee see, Gentlewomen, what my happines is,
These humors raigne in mariage; humors, humors.
                              Exit, he followeth.

GRATIANA Now by my Sooth I am no fortune teller,
And would be loth to proove so; yet pronounce
This at adventure, that t'were indecorum
This Heffer should want hornes.

BELLANORA   Fie on this Love,
I rather wish to want, then purchase so.

GRATIANA In deede such Love is like a Smokie fire
60   In a cold morning; though the Fire be cheerefull,
Yet is the Smoke so sowre and combersome,
T'were better lose the Fire, then finde the Smoke:
Such an attendant then as Smoke to Fire,
Is Jelosie to Love: Better want both,
Then have both.
    Enter VALERIO *and* FORTUNIO.

VALERIO   Come *Fortunio*, now take hold
On this occasion, as my selfe on this:
One couple more would make a Barly-breake.

FORTUNIO I feare *Valerio*, wee shall breake too soone,
    Your Fathers Jelosie, Spy-all, will displease us.

VALERIO Well Wench, the daye will come his Argus eyes   70
    Will shut, and thou shalt open: Sfoote, I thinke
    Dame *Natures* memorie begins to fayle her:
    If I write but my Name in Mercers Bookes,
    I am as sure to have at sixe months end
    A Rascole at my elbow with his Mace,
    As I am sure my Father's not farre hence:
    My Father yet hath ought *Dame Nature* debt
    These threescore yeeres and ten, yet cals not on him:
    But if shee turne her Debt-booke over once,
    And finding him her debtor, do but send   80
    Her Sergeant *John Death* to arrest his body,
    Our Soules shall rest Wench then, and the free Light
    Shall triumph in our faces; where now Night,
    In imitation of my Fathers frownes,
    Lowres at our meeting:
      Enter RYNALDO.
                      See where the Scholler comes.

RYNALDO Downe on your knees; poore lovers reverence learning.

FORTUNIO I pray thee why *Rinaldo*?

RYNALDO   Marke what cause
    Flowes from my depth of knowledge to your loves,
    To make you kneele and blesse me while you live.

VALERIO I pray thee good Scholard give us cause.   90

RYNALDO Marke then, erect your eares: you know what horror
    Would flye on your love from your fathers frownes,
    If he should knowe it. And your sister here,
    (My brothers sweete hart) knowes aswell what rage
    Would sease his powers for her, if he should knowe
    My brother woo'd her, or that she lov'd him:
    Is not this true? speake all.

OMNES   All this is true.

RYNALDO It is as true that now you meete by stelth
    In depth of midnight, kissing out at grates,
    Clime over walles. And all this Ile reforme.   100

VALERIO By Logicke?

RYNALDO   Well sir, you shall have all meanes
    To live in one house, eate and drinke together,
    Meete and kisse your fils.

VALERIO   All this by learning?

RYNALDO I, and your frowning father know all this.

VALERIO I marry, small learning may prove that.

RYNALDO Nay he shall know it, and desire it too,
    Welcome my Brother to him, and your wife,
    Entreating both to come and dwell with him.
    Is not this strange?

FORTUNIO   I, too strange to be true.

110 RYNALDO Tis in this head shall worke it: Therefore heare;
    Brother this Lady you must call your wife,
    For I have tolde her sweet harts Father here
    That she is your wife; and because my Father
    (Who now beleeves it) must be quieted
    Before you see him, you must live a while
    As husband to her, in his Fathers house.
    Valerio here's a simple meane for you
    To lye at racke and manger with your wedlocke,
    And brother, for your selfe to meete as freely
120   With this your long desir'd and barred love.

FORTUNIO You make us wonder.

RYNALDO   Peace, be ruld by mee,
    And you shall see to what a perfect shape
    Ile bring this rude Plott, which blind Chaunce (the Ape
    Of Counsaile and advice) hath brought foorth blind.
    Valerio, can your heat of love forbeare
    Before your Father, and allow my Brother
    To use some kindnes to your wife before him?

VALERIO I, before him, I do not greatlie care,
    Nor anie where in deed; my Sister heere
130   Shall be my spie: if shee will wrong her selfe,
    And give her right to my wife, I am pleasd.

FORTUNIO My dearest life I know, will never feare
    Anie such will or thought in all my powers:
    When I court her then, thinke I thinke tis thee:
    When I embrace her, hold thee in mine Armes:

Come, let us practise gainst wee see your Father.

VALERIO Soft Sir, I hope you need not do it yet,
  Let mee take this time.

RYNALDO   Come, you must not touch her.

VALERIO No not before my Father?

RYNALDO   No nor now,
  Because you are so soone to practise it;   140
  For I must bring them to him presentlie.
  Take her *Fortunio*, goe, hence man and wife,
  Wee will attend you rarely with fixt faces.
  Valerio keepe your countenaunce, and conseave
  Your Father in your forged sheepishnes,
  Who thinks thou dar'st not looke upon a Wench,
  Nor knowest at which end to begin to kisse her.   *Exeunt.*

Finis Actus Primi.

Act II. Scene 1

GOSTANZO, MARC. ANTONIO.

GOSTANZO It is your owne too simple lenitie,
  And doting indulgence showne to him still
  That thus hath taught your Sonne to be no Sonne,
  As you have us'd him, therefore so you have him:
  Durst my Sonne thus turne rebell to his dutie,
  Steale up a match unshuting his estate
  Without all knowledge of or friend or father;
  And to make that good with a worse offence
  Resolve to runne beyond Sea to the warres?
  Durst my Sonne serve me thus? well, I have stayd him,   10
  Though much against my disposition,
  And this howre I have set for his repayre,
  With his young mistresse and concealed wife,
  And in my house here they shall sojourne both
  Till your blacke angers storme be over-blowne.

MARC ANTONIO My angers storme? Ah poore *Fortunio*,

One gentle word from thee would soone resolve
The storme of my rage to a showre of teares.

GOSTANZO In that vaine still? well *Marc Antonio*,
Our olde acquaintance and long neighbourhood
Ties my affection to you, and the good
Of your whole house; in kinde regard whereof
I have advisde you for your credite sake,
And for the tender welfare of your sonne,
To frowne on him a little; if you do not
But at first parle take him to your favour,
I protest utterly to renownce all care
Of you and yours, and all your amities.
They say hee's wretched that out of himselfe
Cannot draw counsell to his propper weale,
But hee's thrice wretched that has neither counsell
Within himselfe, nor apprehension
Of counsaile for his owne good, from another.

MARC ANTONIO Well, I will arme my selfe against this weaknes
The best I can; I long to see this *Hellene*
That hath enchaunted my young *Paris* thus,
And's like to set all our poore *Troye* on fire.

    Enter VALERIO *with a* PAGE.
    MARC. *retyres himselfe.*

GOSTANZO Here comes my Sonne; withdraw, take up your stand,
You shall heare odds betwixt your Sonne and mine.

VALERIO Tell him I can not doo't: Shall I be made
A foolish Novice, my Purse set a broch
By everie cheating come you seaven? to lend
My Money and be laught at? tell him plaine
I professe Husbandrie, and will not play
The Prodigall like him, gainst my profession.

GOSTANZO Here's a Sonne.

MARC ANTONIO   An admirable sparke.

PAGE Well sir, Ile tell him so.   *Exit* PAGE.

VALERIO   Sfoote, let him lead
A better Husbands life, and live not idlely,
Spending his time, his coyne, and selfe on Wenches.

GOSTANZO Why what's the matter Sonne?

VALERIO Cry mercie Sir; why there comes messengers
　　From this and that brave Gallant: and such Gallants,
　　As I protest I saw but through a Grate.

GOSTANZO And what's this Message?

VALERIO 　　　　　　　　　　Faith Sir, hee's disappoynted
　　Of payments; and disfurnisht of meanes present:
　　If I would do him the kind office therefore
　　To trust him but some seven-night with the keeping
　　Of fourtie Crownes for mee, hee deeply sweares
　　As hee's a Gentleman, to discharge his trust,
　　And that I shall eternally endeare him   60
　　To my wisht service, he protestes and contestes.

GOSTANZO Good words *Valerio*; but thou art too wise
　　To be deceiv'd by breath: Ile turne thee loose
　　To the most cunning Cheater of them all.

VALERIO Sfoote, Hee's not ashamde besides to charge mee
　　With a late Promise: I must yeeld in deed,
　　I did (to shift him with some contentment)
　　Make such a frivall promise.

GOSTANZO 　　　　　　　　　I, well done,
　　Promises are no Fetters: with that tongue
　　Thy promise past, unpromise it againe.   70
　　Wherefore has Man a Tongue, of powre to speake,
　　But to speake still to his owne private purpose?
　　Beastes utter but one sound; but Men have change
　　Of speach and Reason, even by Nature given them:
　　Now to say one thing, and an other now,
　　As best may serve their profitable endes.

MARC ANTONIO Ber-Ladie sound instructions to a Sonne.

VALERIO Nay Sir, he makes his claime by debt of friendship.

GOSTANZO Tush, Friendship's but a Terme boy: the fond world
　　Like to a doting Mother glases over   80
　　Her Childrens imperfections with fine tearmes:
　　What she calls Frindship and true humane kindnes,
　　Is onely want of true Experience:
　　Honestie is but a defect of Witt,
　　Respect but meere Rusticitie and Clownerie.

MARC ANTONIO Better and better. Soft, here comes my Sonne.

Enter FORTUNIO, RYNALDO, *and* GRATIANA.

RYNALDO *Fortunio*, keepe your countenance: See sir here
 The poore young married couple, which you pleasd
 To send for to your house.

GOSTANZO   *Fortunio* welcome,
90 And in that welcome I imploy your wives,
 Who I am sure you count your second selfe.   *He kisses her.*

FORTUNIO Sir, your right noble favours do exceede
 All powre of worthy gratitude by words,
 That in your care supplie my Fathers place.

GOSTANZO *Fortunio*, I can not chuse but love you,
 Being Sonne to him who long time I have lov'd:
 From whose just anger, my house shall protect you,
 Till I have made a calme way to your meetings.

FORTUNIO I little thought Sir, that my Fathers love
100 Would take so ill, so sleight a fault as this.

GOSTANZO Call you it sleight? Nay though his spirit take it
 In higher manner then for your lov'd sake,
 I would have wisht him; yet I make a doubt,
 Had my Sonne done the like, if my affection
 Would not have turnd to more spleene, then your Fathers:
 And yet I quallifie him, all I can,
 And doubt not but that time and my perswasion,
 Will worke out your excuse: since youth and love
 Were th'unresisted orgaines to seduce you:
110 But you must give him leave, for Fathers must
 Be wonne by penitence and submission,
 And not by force or opposition.

FORTUNIO Ahlas Sir, what advise you mee to doe?
 I know my Father to be highly moov'd,
 And am not able to endure the breath
 Of his exprest displeasure, whose hote flames
 I thinke my absence soonest would have quencht.

GOSTANZO True Sir, as fire with oyle, or else like them
 That quench the fire with pulling downe the house:
120 You shall remaine here in my house conceal'd
 Till I have wonne your Father to conceive
 Kinder opinion of your oversight.

Valerio entertaine *Fortunio*
And his faire wife, and give them conduct in.
VALERIO Y'are welcome sir.
GOSTANZO   What sirha is that all?
No entertainment to the Gentlewoman?
VALERIO Forsooth y'are welcome by my Fathers leave.
GOSTANZO What no more complement? kisse her you
        sheepes-head,
Why when? Go go Sir, call your Sister hither.   *Exit* VAL[ERIO].
Ladie, youle pardon our grosse bringing up?   130
Wee dwell farre off from Court you may perceive:
The sight of such a blazing Starre as you,
Dazles my rude Sonnes witts.
GRATIANA   Not so good Sir,
The better husband, the more courtlie ever.
RYNALDO In deed a Courtier makes his lipps go farre,
As he doth all things else.
        Enter VALERIO, BELLANORA.
GOSTANZO   Daughter recive
This Gentlewoman home, and use her kindly.   *She kisses her.*
BELLANORA My Father bids you kindly welcome Lady,
And therefore you must needes come well to mee.
GRATIANA Thanke you for-soth.
GOSTANZO   Goe Dame, conduct am in.   140
        Exeunt RYNALDO, FORTUNIO, BELLANORA, GRATIANA.
Ah errant Sheepes-head, hast thou liv'd thus long,
And dar'st not looke a Woman in the face?
Though I desire especially to see
My Sonne a Husband, Shall I therefore have him
Turne absolute Cullion? Lets see, kisse thy hand.
Thou kisse thy hand? thou wip'st thy mouth by th'masse.
Fie on thee Clowne; They say the world's growne finer,
But I for my part, never saw Young men
Worse fashin'd and brought up then now adayes.
Sfoote, when my selfe was young, was not I kept   150
As farre from Court as you? I thinke I was:
And yet my Father on a time invited
The Dutchesse of his house; I beeing then

About some five and twentie yeares of age,
Was thought the onelie man to entertaine her:
I had my Conge; plant my selfe of one legg,
Draw backe the tother with a deepe fetcht honor:
Then with a Bell regard advant mine eye
With boldnes on her verie visnomie.

160 Your Dauncers all were counterfets to mee:
And for discourse in my faire Mistresse presence,
I did not as you barraine Gallants doe,
Fill my discourses up drinking *Tobacco*;
But on the present furnisht ever more
With tales and practisde speeches; as some times,
What ist a clocke? What stuff's this Petticoate?
What cost the making? What the Frindge and all?
And what she had under her Petticoate?
And such like wittie complements: and for need,

170 I could have written as good Prose and Verse,
As the most beggerlie Poet of am all,
Either *Accrostique*, *Exordion*,
Epithalamions, *Satyres*, *Epigrams*,
Sonnets in Doozens, or your *Quatorzanies*,
In any Rime *Masculine*, *Feminine*,
Or *Sdruciolla*, or *cooplets*, *Blancke Verse*:
Y'are but bench-whistlers now a dayes to them
That were in our times: well, about your Husbandrie,
Go, for I'fayth th'art fit for nothing else.

      Exit VAL[ERIO] *prodit* MAR[C ANTONIO].

180 MARC ANTONIO Ber-Ladie you have plaide the Courtier rarelie.

GOSTANZO But did you ever see so blanck a Foole,
 When he should kisse a Wench, as my Sonne is?

MARC ANTONIO Ahlas tis but a little bashfulnes,
 You let him keepe no companie, nor allow him
 Monie to spend at Fence and Dauncing-scholes,
 Y'are too seveere y'faith.

GOSTANZO   And you too supple.
 Well Sir, for your sake I have staide your Sonne
 From flying to the warres: now see you rate him,
 To staie him yet from more expencefull courses,

Wherein your lenitie will encourage him.   190

MARC ANTONIO   Let me alone, I thank you for this kindnes. *Exeunt.*

> *Enter* VALERIO *and* RYNALDO.

RYNALDO   So, are they gone? Now tell me brave *Valerio*
  Have I not wonne the wreath from all your wits,
  Brought thee t'enjoy the most desired presence
  Of thy deare love at home? and with one labour
  My brother t'enjoy thy sister, where
  It had beene her undooing t'have him seene,
  And make thy father crave what he aborres:
  T'entreate my brother home t'enjoy his daughter,
  Commaund thee kisse thy wench, chide for not kissing,   200
  And worke all this out of a Machevil,
  A miserable Politician?
  I thinke the like was never plaid before!

VALERIO   Indeede I must commend thy wit of force,
  And yet I know not whose deserves most praise
  Of thine, or my wit: thine for plotting well,
  Mine, that durst undertake and carrie it
  With such true forme.

RYNALDO   Well, th'evening crownes the daie,
  Persever to the end, my wit hath put
  Blinde Fortunne in a string into your hand,   210
  Use it discreetlie, keepe it from your Father,
  Or you may bid all your good daies good night.

VALERIO   Let me alone boy.

RYNALDO   Well sir, now to varie
  The pleasures of our wits, thou knowst *Valerio*
  Here is the new turnd Gentlemans faire wife,
  That keepes thy wife and sister companie;
  With whome the amorous Courtier *Dariotto*
  Is farre in love, and of whome her sowre husband
  Is passing jelous, puts on Eagles eies
  To prie into her carriage. Shall wee see   220
  If he be now from home, and visite her?

> *Enter* GAZETTA *sowing,* CORNELIO *following.*

  See, see, the prisoner comes.

VALERIO   But soft Sir, see

Her jelous Jaylor followes at her heeles:
Come, we will watch some fitter time to boord her,
And in the meane time seeke out our mad crue.
My spirit longs to swagger.
RYNALDO   Goe too youth,
Walke not too boldly; if the Sergeants meete you,
You may have swaggering worke your bellie full.
VALERIO No better Copesmates,   GAZETTA *sits and singes sowing.*
230   Ile go seeke am out with this light in my hand,
The slaves grow proud with seeking out of us.

Exeunt.

CORNELIO A prettie worke, I pray what flowers are these?
GAZETTA The Pancie this.
CORNELIO   O thats for lovers thoughtes.
Whats that, a Columbine?
GAZETTA No, that thankles Flower fitts not my Garden.
CORNELIO Hmm? yet it may mine:
This were a prettie present for some friend,
Some gallant Courtier, as for *Dariotto*,
One that adores you in his soule I know.
240 GAZETTA Mee? why mee more then your selfe I pray?
CORNELIO O yes, hee adores you, and adhornes mee:
Yfaith deale plainelie; Doe not his kisses relish
Much better then such Pessants as I am?
GAZETTA Whose kisses?
CORNELIO   *Dariottoes,* does he not
The thing you wot on?
GAZETTA   What thing good Lord?
CORNELIO Why Lady, lie with you?
GAZETTA   Lie with mee?
CORNELIO I with you.
GAZETTA   You with mee indeed.
CORNELIO Nay I am told that he lies with you too,
And that he is the onely Whore-maister
About the Cittie.
250 GAZETTA   Yf he be so onely,
Tis a good hearing that there are no more.

CORNELIO Well Mistresse well, I will not be abusde,
    Thinke not you daunce in Netts; for though you do not
    Make brode profession of your love to him,
    Yet do I understand your darkest language,
    Your treads ath'toe, your secret jogges and wringes:
    Your entercourse of glaunces: every tittle
    Of your close Amorous rites I understand,
    They speake as loud to mee, as if you said,
    My dearest *Dariotto*, I am thine.   260

GAZETTA Jesus what moodes are these? did ever Husband
    Follow his Wife with Jelosie so unjust?
    That once I lov'd you, you your selfe will sweare.
    And if I did, where did you lose my Love?
    In deed this strange and undeserved usage,
    Hath powre to shake a heart were nere so setled:
    But I protest all your unkindnes, never
    Had strength to make me wrong you, but in thought.

CORNELIO No, not with *Dariotto*?
GAZETTA   No by heaven.
CORNELIO No Letters past, nor no designes for meeting?   270
GAZETTA No by my hope of heaven.
CORNELIO   Well, no time past,
    Goe goe; goe in and sow.
GAZETTA   Well, bee it so.   *Exit* GAZETTA.
CORNELIO Suspition is (they say) the first degree
    Of deepest wisedome: and how ever others
    Inveygh against this mood of Jelousy,
    For my part I suppose it the best curb,
    To check the ranging appetites that raigne
    In this weake sexe: my neighbours poynt at me
    For this my jelousy; but should I doe
    As most of them doe; let my wife fly out   280
    To feasts and revels, and invite home Gallants,
    Play *Menelaus*, give them time and place,
    While I sit like a well-taught wayting-woman,
    Turning her eyes upon some worke or picture,
    Read in a Booke, or take a fayned nap,
    While her kind Lady takes one to her lap?

No, let me still be poynted at, and thought
A jelouse Asse, and not a wittally Knave.
I have a shew of Courtyers haunt my house,
In shew my friends, and for my profit too:
But I perceive um, and will mock their aymes,
With looking to their marke, I warrant um:
I am content to ride abroad with them,
To revell, dice, and fit their other sports;
But by their leaves ile have a vigilant eye
To the mayne chaunce still. See my brave Comrades.

> *Enter* DARIOTTO [*and* PAGE,] CLAUDIO *and* VALERIO:
> VALERIO *putting up his Sword.*

DARIOTTO Well, wag, well, wilt thou still deceive thy father,
And being so simple a poore soule before him,
Turne swaggerer in all companies besides?

CLAUDIO Hadst thou bin rested, all would have come forth.

VALERIO Soft, sir, there lyes the poynt; I do not doubt,
But t'have my pennyworths of these Rascals one day:
Ile smoke the buzzing Hornets from their nests,
Or else ile make their lether Jerkins stay.
The whorson hungry Horse-flyes; Foot, a man
Cannot so soone, for want of Almanacks,
Forget his day but three or foure bare moneths,
But strait he sees a sort of Corporals,
To lye in Ambuscado to surprize him.

DARIOTTO Well, thou hadst happy fortune to escape um.

VALERIO But they thought theirs was happier to scape me.
I walking in the place, where mens law suites
Are heard and pleaded, not so much as dreaming
Of any such encounter, steps me forth
Their valiant fore-man, with the word, I rest you.
I made no more adoe, but layd these pawes
Close on his shoulders, tumbling him to earth;
And there sate he on his *posteriors*,
Like a Baboone; and turning me about,
I strayt espyed the whole troope issuing on me.
I stept me backe, and drawing my olde friend heere,
Made to the midst of them, and all unable

T'endure the shock, all rudely fell in rout,
And downe the stayres they ranne with such a fury,
As meeting with a troope of Lawyers there,
Man'd by their Clyents: some with ten, some with twenty,
Some five, some three; he that had least, had one:
Upon the stayres they bore them downe afore them:
But such a rattling then was there amongst them
Of ravisht Declarations, Replications,   330
Rejoynders and Petitions; all their bookes
And writings torne and trod on, and some lost,
That the poore Lawyers comming to the Barre,
Could say nought to the matter, but instead,
Were fayne to rayle and talke besides their bookes
Without all order.
CLAUDIO   Fayth, that same vayne of rayling
Became now most applausive; your best Poet,
Is he that rayles grossest.
DARIOTTO   True, and your best foole
Is your broad rayling foole.
VALERIO   And why not, sir?
For by the gods, to tell the naked trueth,   340
What objects see men in this world, but such
As would yeeld matter to a rayling humour?
When he that last yere carryed after one
An empty Buckram bag, now fills a Coach,
And crowds the Senate with such troops of Clyents,
And servile followers, as would put a mad spleene
Into a Pigeon.
DARIOTTO   Come, pray leave these crosse capers,
Let's make some better use of precious time.
See, here's *Cornelio*: come, Lad, shall we to dice?
CORNELIO Any thing I.
CLAUDIO   Well sayd, how does thy wife?   350
CORNELIO In health, God save her.
VALERIO   But where is she, man?
CORNELIO Abroad about her businesse.
VALERIO   Why, not at home?
Foot, my masters, take her to the Court,

And this rare Lad her husband: and doest heare?
Play me no more the miserable Farmer,
But be advisde by friends, sell all ith countrey,
Be a flat Courtier, follow some great man,
Or bring thy wife there, and sheele make thee great.

CORNELIO What, to the Court? then take me for a Gull.

360 VALERIO Nay, never shun it to be cald a Gull:
For I see all the world is but a Gull:
One man Gull to another in all kinds:
A Marchant to a Courtyer is a Gull:
A Clyent to a Lawyer is a Gull:
A marryed man to a Bacheler, a Gull:
A Bacheler to a Cuckold is a Gull:
All to a Poet, or a Poet to himselfe.

CORNELIO Hark *Dariotto*, shall we gull this Guller?

DARIOTTO He gulls his father, man, we cannot gull him.

370 CORNELIO Let me alone. – Of all mans wits alive,
I most admyre *Valerioes*, that hath stolne,
By his meere industry, and that by spurts,
Such qualities, as no wit else can match,
With plodding at perfection every houre;
Which, if his father knew eche gift he has,
Were like enough to make him give all from him:
I meane besides his dycing and his wenching,
He has stolne languages, th'Italian, Spanish,
And some spice of the French, besides his dauncing,
380 Singing, playing on choyce Instruments:
These has he got, almost against the hayre.

CLAUDIO But hast thou stolne all these, *Valerio*?

VALERIO Toyes, toyes, a pox; and yet they be such toyes,
As every Gentleman would not be without.

CORNELIO Vayne glory makes yee judge um lyte yfayth.

DARIOTTO Afore heaven I was much deceyv'd in him:
But hee's the man indeed that hides his gifts,
And sets them not to sale in every presence.
I would have sworne, his soule were far from musike;
390 And that all his choyce musike was to heare
His fat beastes bellow.

CORNELIO   Sir, your ignorance
  Shall eftsoone be confuted. Prythee *Val*,
  Take thy *Theorbo* for my sake a little.
VALERIO By heaven, this moneth I toucht not a *Theorbo*.
CORNELIO Toucht a *Theorbo*? marke the very word.
  Sirra, goe fetch.   *Exit* PAGE.
VALERIO If you will have it, I must needs confesse,
  I am no husband of my qualityes.
    He untrusses and capers.
CORNELIO See what a Caper there was!
CLAUDIO   See agayne.
CORNELIO The best that ever; and how it becomes him!   400
DARIOTTO O that his father saw these qualityes!
    Enter a PAGE *with an Instrument.*
CORNELIO Nay, that's the very wonder of his wit,
  To carry all without his fathers knowledge.
DARIOTTO Why, we might tell him now.
CORNELIO   No but we could not,
  Although we think we could: his wit doth charme us.
  Come sweet *Val*, touch and sing.
DARIOTTO   Foote, will you heare
  The worst voyce in Italy?
    Enter RINALDO.
CORNELIO   O God, sir.   *He sings.*
  Courtiers, how like you this?
DARIOTTO   Beleeve it excellent.
CORNELIO Is it not naturall?
VALERIO   If my father heard me,
  Foot, hee'd renounce me for his naturall sonne.   410
DARIOTTO By heaven, *Valerio*, and I were thy father,
  And lov'd good qualities as I doe my life,
  Ide disinherit thee: for I never heard
  Dog howle with worse grace.
CORNELIO   Go to, Signeur Courtier,
  You deale not courtly now to be so playne,
  Nor nobly, to discourage a young Gentleman,
  In vertuous qualityes, that has but stolne um.
CLAUDIO Call you this touching a *Theorbo*?

OMNES   Ha, ha, ha.

Exeunt all but VALERIO *and* RYNALDO.

VALERIO How now, what's heere?

RYNALDO   Zoones, a plot layd to gull thee.
420   Could thy wit thinke the voyce was worth the hearing?
      This was the Courtiers and the Cuckolds project.

VALERIO And ist eene so? tis very well, Maister Courtier,
      And Dan Cornuto, ile cry quit with both:
      And first, ile cast a jarre betwixt them both,
      With firing the poore cuckolds jelousy.
      I have a tale will make him madde,
      And turne his wife divorced loose amongst us.
      But first let's home, and entertayne my wife.
      O father, pardon, I was borne to gull thee.   *Exeunt.*

Finis Actus secundi.

Act III. Scene 1

Enter FORTUNIO, BELLANORA, GRATIANA,
GOSTANZO *following closely.*

FORTUNIO How happy am I, that by this sweet meanes
      I gayne accesse to your most loved sight,
      And therewithall to utter my full love,
      Which but for vent would burne my entrayles up!

GOSTANZO Byth masse they talke too softly.

BELLANDRA   Little thinks
      The austere mind my thrifty father beares,
      That I am vowd to you, and so am bound
      From him: who for more riches he would force
      On my disliking fancy.

FORTUNIO   Tis no fault,
10   With just deeds to defraud an injury.

GOSTANZO My daughter is perswading him to yeeld
      In dutifull submission to his father.

Enter VALERIO.

VALERIO Do I not dreame? do I behold this sight

With waking eyes? or from the Ivory gate
Hath *Morpheus* sent a vision to delude me?
Ist possible that I a mortall man,
Should shrine within mine armes so bright a Goddesse,
The fayre *Gratiana*, beautyes little world!

GOSTANZO What have we heere?

VALERIO My dearest Myne of Gold,   20
    All this that thy white armes enfold,
    Account it as thine owne free-hold.

GOSTANZO Gods my deare soule, what sudden change is here!
    I smell how this geare will fall out yfayth.

VALERIO *Fortunio*, sister; come, let's to the garden.   *Exeunt.*

GOSTANZO Sits the wind there yfayth? see what example
    Will worke upon the dullest appetite.
    My sonne last day so bashfull, that he durst not
    Looke on a wench, now courts her; and byrlady,
    Will make his friend *Fortunio* weare his head   30
    Of the right moderne fashion. What *Rinaldo*.

      Enter RYNALDO.

RYNALDO I feare I interrupt your privacy.

GOSTANZO Welcome, *Rinaldo*, would't had bin your hap
    To come a little sooner, that you might
    Have seene a handsome sight: but let that passe,
    The short is, that your sister *Gratiana*
    Shall stay no longer here.

RYNALDO   No longer, sir?
    Repent you then so soone your favour to her,
    And to my brother?

GOSTANZO   Not so, good *Rinaldo*;
    But to prevent a mischiefe that I see   40
    Hangs over your abused brothers head.
    In briefe, my sonne has learn'd but too much courtship.
    It was my chaunce even now to cast mine eye
    Into a place whereto your sister entred:
    My metamorphosde sonne: I must conceale
    What I saw there: but to be playne, I saw
    More then I would see: I had thought to make
    My house a kind receypt for your kind brother;

But ide be loth his wife should find more kindnesse,
Then she had cause to like of.

50 RYNALDO   What's the matter?

Perhaps a little complement or so.

GOSTANZO Wel, sir, such complement perhaps may cost
Marryed *Fortunio* the setting on:
Nor can I keepe my knowledge; He that lately
Before my face I could not get to looke
Upon your sister; by this light, now kist her,
Embrac't and courted with as good a grace,
As any Courtyer could: and I can tell you
(Not to disgrace her) I perceyv'd the Dame
60 Was as far forward as himselfe, byth masse.

RYNALDO You should have schoold him for't.

GOSTANZO   No, Ile not see't:
For shame once found, is lost; Ile have him thinke
That my opinion of him is the same
That it was ever; it will be a meane,
To bridle this fresh humour bred in him.

RYNALDO Let me then schoole him; foot, ile rattle him up.

GOSTANZO No, no, *Rinaldo*, th'onely remedy,
Is to remove the cause; carry the object
From his late tempted eyes.

RYNALDO   Alas, sir, whither?
70 You know, my father is incent so much,
Heele not receyve her.

GOSTANZO   Place her with some friend
But for a time, till I reclayme your father:
Meane time your brother shall remaine with me.

To himself. RYNALDO The care's the lesse then, he has still his
      longing,
To be with this Gulls daughter.

GOSTANZO   What resolve you?
I am resolv'd she lodges here no more:
My friends sonne shall not be abusde by mine.

RYNALDO Troth, sir, ile tell you what a sudden toy
Comes in my head; what think you if I brought her
Home to my fathers house?

GOSTANZO   I mary, sir;   80
Would he receyve her?

RYNALDO   Nay, you heare not all:
I meane, with use of some device or other.

GOSTANZO As how, *Rinaldo*?

RYNALDO   Mary sir, to say,
She is your sonnes wife, maryed past your knowledge.

GOSTANZO I doubt, last day he saw her, and will know her
To be *Fortunioes* wife.

RYNALDO   Nay, as for that
I wil pretend she was even then your sonnes wife,
But faynde by me to be *Fortunioes*,
Onely to try how he would take the matter.

GOSTANZO 'Fore heaven 'twere pretty.

RYNALDO   Would it not doe well?   90

GOSTANZO Exceeding well in sadnesse.

RYNALDO   Nay, good sir,
Tell me unfaynedly, do ye lik't indeed.

GOSTANZO The best that ere I heard.

RYNALDO   And do you thinke
Heele swallow downe the Gudgion?

GOSTANZO   A my life
It were a grosse gob would not downe with him,
An honest knight, but simple, not acquainted
With the fine slights and policies of the world,
As I my selfe am.

RYNALDO   Ile go fetch her strait:
And this jest thrive, 'twill make us princely sport:
But you must keepe our counsell, second all,   100
Which to make likely, you must needs sometimes
Give your sonne leave (as if you knew it not)
To steale and see her at my fathers house.

GOSTANZO I, but see you then that you keepe good gard
Over his forward new begun affections:
For by the Lord, heele teach your brother else,
To sing the Cuckooes note: spirit will breake out,
Though never so supprest and pinioned.

RYNALDO Especially your sonnes: what would he be,

110   If you should not restrayne him by good counsell?
       GOSTANZO Ile have an eye on him, I warrant thee.
       Ile in and warne the Gentlewoman to make ready.
       RYNALDO Wel, sir, and ile not be long after you. *Exit* GOSTANZO.
       Heaven, heaven, I see these Politicians
       (Out of blind Fortunes hands) are our most fooles.
       Tis she that gives the lustre to their wits,
       Still plodding at traditionall devices:
       But take um out of them to present actions,
       A man may grope and tickle um like a Trowt,
120   And take um from their close deere holes, as fat
       As a Phisician; and as giddy-headed,
       As if by myracle heaven had taken from them,
       Even that which commonly belongs to fooles.
       Well, now let's note what black ball of debate,
       Valerioes wit hath cast betwixt *Cornelio*,
       And the inamoured Courtyer; I beleeve
       His wife and he will part: his jelousy
       Hath ever watcht occasion of divorce,
       And now *Valerioes* villany will present it.
130   See, here comes the twyn-Courtier his companion.
            Enter CLAUDIO.
       CLAUDIO *Rinaldo*, well encountred.
       RYNALDO   Why? what newes?
       CLAUDIO Most sudden and infortunate, *Rinaldo*:
       Cornelio is incenst so 'gainst his wife,
       That no man can procure her quiet with him.
       I have assayd him, and made *Marc Antonio*,
       With all his gentle Rethorike second me,
       Yet all I feare me will be cast away.
       See, see, they come: joyne thy wit, good *Rinaldo*,
       And helpe to pacify his yellow fury.
140   RYNALDO With all my heart, I consecrate my wit
       To the wisht comfort of distressed Ladies.
            Enter CORNELIO, MARC ANTONIO, VALERIO, PAGE.
       CORNELIO Will any man assure me of her good behaviour?
       VALERIO Who can assure a jelous spirit? you may be afrayd of the
       shaddow of your eares, and imagine them to be hornes: if you will

assure your selfe, appoynt keepers to watch her.

CORNELIO And who shall watch the keepers?

MARC ANTONIO To be sure of that, be you her keeper.

VALERIO Well sayd, and share the hornes your selfe:
For that's the keepers fee.

CORNELIO But say I am gone out of town, and must trust others;   150
how shall I know if those I trust be trusty to me?

RYNALDO Mary, sir, by a singular instinct, given naturally to all you
maryed men, that if your wives play legerdeheele, though you bee
a hundred miles off, yet you shall be sure instantly to find it in
your forheads.

CORNELIO Sound doctrine I warrant you: I am resolv'd ifaith.

PAGE Then give me leave to speak, sir, that hath all this while bene
silent: I have heard you with extreme patience, now therefore
pricke up your eares, and vouchsafe me audience.

CLAUDIO Good boy, a mine honour.   160

CORNELIO Pray what are you, sir?

PAGE I am here, for default of better, of counsel with the fayre
Gazetta, and though her selfe had bene best able to defend her
selfe, if she had bin here, and would have pleasd to put forth the
Buckler, which Nature hath given all women, I meane her tongue.

VALERIO Excellent good boy.

PAGE Yet since she either vouchsafes it not, or thinks her innocence
a sufficient shield against your jelous accusations, I wil presume
to undertake the defence of that absent and honorable Lady, whose
sworne Knight I am; and in her of all that name (for Lady is   170
growne a common name to their whole sex) which sex I have ever
loved from my youth, and shall never cease to love, till I want wit
to admire.

MARC ANTONIO An excellent spoken boy.

VALERIO Give eare, *Cornelio*, heere is a yong *Mercurio* sent to perswade
thee.

CORNELIO Well, sir, let him say on.

PAGE It is a heavy case, to see how this light sex is tumbled and tost
from post to piller, under the unsavory breath of every humourous
Peasant: *Gazetta*, you sayd, is unchaste, disloyall, and I wot not   180
what; Alas, is it her fault? is shee not a woman? did she not suck
it (as others of her sex doe) from her mothers brest? and will you

condemne that, as her fault, which is her Nature? Alas, sir, you
must consider, a woman is an unfinisht Creature, delivered hastyly
to the world, before Nature had set to that Seale which should
have made them perfect. Faultes they have (no doubt) but are wee
free? Turne your eye into your selfe (good Signeur *Cornelio*) and
weygh your owne imperfections with hers: If shee be wanton
abroad, are not you wanting at home? if she be amorous, are not

190   you jelous? If she be high set, are not you taken downe? If she be
a Courtizan, are not you a Cuckold?

CORNELIO Out you rogue.

RYNALDO On with thy speech, boy.

MARC ANTONIO You doe not well, *Cornelio*, to discourage the bashfull
youth.

CLAUDIO Forth, boy, I warrant thee.

PAGE But if our owne imperfections will not teach us to beare with
theirs; yet let their vertues perswade us: let us indure their bad
qualities for their good; allow the prickle for the Rose; the bracke

200   for the Velvet; the paring for the cheese, and so forth: if you say
they range abroad, consider it is nothing but to avoyd idlenesse at
home: their nature is still to be doing: keepe um a doing at home;
let them practise one good quality or other, either sowing, singing,
playing, chiding, dauncing or so, and these will put such idle toyes
out of their heads into yours: but if you cannot find them variety
of businesse within dores, yet at least imitate the ancient wise
Citizens of this City, who used carefully to provide their wives
gardens neere the towne, to plant, to graft in, as occasion served,
onely to keepe um from idlenesse.

210 VALERIO Everlasting good boy.

CORNELIO I perceyve your knavery, sir, and will.yet have patience.

RYNALDO Forth, my brave *Curio*.

PAGE As to her unquietnesse (which some have rudely tearm'd
shrewishnesse) though the fault be in her, yet the cause is in you.
What so calme as the sea of it own nature? Arte was never able
to equall it: your dycing tables, nor your bowling alleys are not
comparable to it; yet if a blast of wind do but crosse it, not so
turbulent and violent an element in the world: So (nature in lieu
of womens scarcity of wit, having indued them with a large portion

220   of will) if they may (without impeach) injoy their willes, no quieter

creatures under heaven: but if the breath of their husbands mouthes once crosse their wils, nothing more tempestuous. Why then, sir, should you husbands crosse your wives wils thus, considering the law allowes them no wils at all at their deaths, because it intended they should have their willes while they lived?

VALERIO Answere him but that, *Cornelio*.

CORNELIO All shall not serve her turne, I am thinking of other matters.

MARC ANTONIO Thou hast halfe wonne him, Wag; ply him yet a little further.   230

PAGE Now (sir) for these Cuckooish songs of yours, of Cuckolds, hornes, grafting, and such like; what are they, but meere imaginary toyes, bred out of your owne heads, as your owne, and so by tradition delivered from man to man, like Scar-crowes, to terrify fooles from this earthly paradice of wedlock, coyn'd at first by some spent Poets, superannated Bachelers, or some that were scarce men of their hands; who, like the Foxe, having lost his taile, would perswade others to lose theirs for company? Agayne, for your Cuckold, what is it but a meere fiction? shew me any such creature in nature; if there be, I could never see it, neyther could   240 I ever find any sensible difference betwixt a Cuckold and a Christen creature. To conclude, let Poets coyne, or fooles credit what they list; for mine owne part, I am cleere of this opinion, that your Cuckold is a meere *Chymæra*, and that there are no Cuckoldes in the world, but those that have wives: and so I will leave them.

CORNELIO Tis excellent good, sir; I do take you, sir, d'ye see? to be, as it were bastard to the sawcy Courtier, that would have me father more of your fraternity, d'ye see? and so are instructed (as we heare) to second that villayne with your toung, which he has acted   250 with his Tenure piece, d'ye see?

PAGE No such matter, a my credit, sir.

CORNELIO Wel, sir, be as be may, I scorn to set my head against yours, d'ye see? when in the meane time I will fircke your father, whether you see or no.   *Exit drawing his rapier.*

RYNALDO Gods my life, *Cornelio*.   *Exit.*

VALERIO Have at your father ifaith, boy, if he can find him.

MARC ANTONIO See, he comes here, he has mist him.

Enter DARIOTTO.

DARIOTTO How now, my hearts, what, not a wench amongst you?
260 　　　Tis a signe y'are not in the grace of wenches,
　　　That they will let you be thus long alone.

VALERIO Well, *Dariotto*, glory not too much,
　　　That for thy briske attyre and lips perfumde,
　　　Thou playest the Stallyon ever where thou com'st;
　　　And like the husband of the flocke, runn'st through
　　　The whole towne heard, and no mans bed secure:
　　　No womans honour unattempted by thee.
　　　Thinke not to be thus fortunate for ever:
　　　But in thy amorous conquests at the last
270 　　　Some wound will slice your mazer: *Mars* himselfe
　　　Fell into *Vulcans* snare, and so may you.

DARIOTTO Alas, alas, fayth I have but the name:
　　　I love to court and wynne; and the consent,
　　　Without the act obtayn'd, is all I seeke.
　　　I love the victory that drawes no bloud.

CLAUDIO O, tis a high desert in any man
　　　To be a secret Lecher; I know some,
　　　That (like thy selfe) are true in nothing else.

MARC ANTONIO And, me thinks, it is nothing, if not told;
280 　　　At least the joy is never full before.

VALERIO Well, *Dariotto*, th'hadst as good confesse,
　　　The Sunne shines broad upon your practises:
　　　Vulcan will wake and intercept you one day.

DARIOTTO Why, the more jelous knave and coxcombe he.
　　　What, shall the shaking of his bed a little
　　　Put him in motion? It becomes him not;
　　　Let him be duld and stald, and then be quiet.
　　　The way to draw my costome to his house,
　　　Is to be mad and jelous; tis the sauce
　　　That whets my appetite.

290 VALERIO　　　　　　　　Or any mans:
　　　Sine periculo friget lusus.
　　　They that are jelous, use it still of purpose
　　　To draw you to their houses.

DARIOTTO　　　　　　　I, by heaven,

I am of that opinion. Who would steale
Out of a common Orchard? Let me gayne
My love with labour, and injoy't with feare,
Or I am gone.

 Enter RYNALDO.

RYNALDO   What, *Dariotto* here?
 Foot, dar'st thou come neere *Cornelioes* house?

DARIOTTO Why? is the Bull run mad? what ayles he, trow?

RYNALDO I know not what he ayles; but I would wish you   300
 To keepe out of the reach of his sharpe hornes:
 For by this hand heele gore you.

DARIOTTO   And why me,
 More then thy selfe, or these two other whelps?
 You all have basted him as well as I.
 I wonder what's the cause.

RYNALDO   Nay, that he knowes,
 And sweares withall, that wheresoere he meets you,
 Heele marke you for a marker of mens wives.

VALERIO Pray heaven he be not jelous by some tales
 That have bin told him lately: did you never
 Attempt his wife? hath no Loves Harbenger,   310
 No looks, no letters past twixt you and her?

DARIOTTO For lookes I cannot answere; I bestow them
 At large, and carelesly, much like the Sunne:
 If any be so foolish to apply them
 To any private fancy of their owne,
 (As many doe) it's not my fault, thou knowest.

VALERIO Well, *Dariotto*, this set face of thine
 (If thou be guilty of offence to him)
 Comes out of very want of wit and feeling
 What danger haunts thee: for *Cornelio*   320
 Is a tall man, I tell you; and 'twere best
 You shund his sight awhile, till we might get
 His patience, or his pardon: for past doubt
 Thou dyest if he but see thee.

 Enter CORNELIO.

RYNALDO   Foot, he comes.

DARIOTTO Is this the Cockatrice that kils with sight?

How doest thou boy? ha?

CORNELIO   Well.

DARIOTTO   What, lingring still
About this paltry towne? hadst thou bin rulde
By my advice, thou hadst by this time bene
A gallant Courtyer, and at least a Knight:

330   I would have got thee dubd by this time certayne.

CORNELIO And why then did you not your selfe that honour?

DARIOTTO Tush, tis more honour still to make a Knight,
Then tis to be a Knight: to make a Cuckold,
Then tis to be a Cuckold.

CORNELIO   Y'are a villayne.

DARIOTTO God shield man: villayne?

CORNELIO   I, ile prove thee one.

DARIOTTO What, wilt thou prove a villayne? By this light
Thou deceyv'st me then.

CORNELIO   Well, sir, thus I prove it.   *Drawes.*

OMNES Hold, hold, rayse the streets.

CLAUDIO   *Cornelio.*

RYNALDO Hold, *Dariotto*, hold.

VALERIO   What, art thou hurt?

DARIOTTO A scratch, a scratch.

340   VALERIO   Goe sirra, fetch a Surgeon.

                                              [*Exit* PAGE.]

CORNELIO Youle set a badge on the jelous fooles head, sir;
Now set a Coxcombe on your owne.

VALERIO What's the cause of these warres, *Dariotto*?

DARIOTTO Foot, I know not.

CORNELIO   Well, sir, know and spare not;
I will presently bee divorst, and then take her amongst ye.

RYNALDO Divorst? nay good *Cornelio*.

CORNELIO   By this sword
I will, the world shall not disswade me.   *Exit.*

VALERIO Why this has bin your fault now *Dariotto*,
You youths have fashions when you have obtein'd

350   A Ladies favour, straight your hat must weare it,
Like a Jacke-daw that when he lights upon
A dainty morsell, kaas and makes his brags,

And then some kite doth scoope it from him straight,
Where if he fed without his dawish noise,
He might fare better, and have lesse disturbance:
Forbeare it in this case; and when you prove,
Victorious over faire *Gazettas* Forte,
Doe not for pittie sound your trumpe for joy,
But keepe your valour close, and 'tis your honour.

    Enter PAGE *and* POCK.

POCK God save you Signior *Dariotto*.   360

DARIOTTO I know you not Sir, your name I pray?

POCK My name is *Pock* Sir; a practitioner in Surgery.

DARIOTTO *Pock* the Surgeon, y'are welcome Sir, I know a Doctor of
    your name maister *Pocke*.

POCK My name has made many Doctors Sir.

RYNALDO Indeede tis a worshipfull name.

VALERIO Mary is it, and of an auncient discent.

POCK Faith Sir I could fetch my pedigree far, if I were so dispos'd.

RYNALDO Out of France at least.

POCK And if I stood on my armes as others doe –   370

DARIOTTO No doe not *Pock*, let others stand a their armes, and thou
    a thy legs as long as thou canst.

POCK Though I live by my bare practise, yet I could shew good
    cardes for my Gentilitie.

VALERIO Tush thou canst not shake off thy gentry *Pock*, tis bred i'th
    bone; but to the maine *Pock*, what thinkest thou of this gentlemans
    wound, *Pock*, canst thou cure it *Pock*?

POCK The incision is not deepe, nor the Orifice exorbitant, the
    Pericranion is not dislocated, I warrant his life for forty crownes,
    without perishing of any joynt.   380

DARIOTTO Faith *Pock*, tis a joynt I would be loath to loose, for the
    best joynt of Mutton in Italy.

RYNALDO Would such a scratch as this hazard a mans head?

POCK I Byr-lady Sir, I have knowen some have lost there heads for
    a lesse matter I can tell you, therefore sir you must keepe good
    dyet: if you please to come home to my house till you be perfectly
    cur'd, I shall have the more care on you.

VALERIO Thats your onely course to have it well quickly.

POCK By what time would he have it well sir?

390 DARIOTTO A very necessary question, canst thou limit the time?

POCK O sir, cures are like causes in law, which may be lengthned or
shortned at the discretion of the Lawyer, he can either keepe it
greene with replications or rejoinders, or sometimes skinne it faire
a'th outside for fashion sake, but so he may be sure 'twill breake
out againe by a writt of error, and then has he his suite new to
begin, but I will covenant with you, that by such a time Ile make
your head as sound as a Bell, I will bring it to suppuration, and
after I will make it coagulate and growe to a perfect *Cycatrice*, and
all within these ten dayes, so you keepe a good dyet.

400 DARIOTTO Well come *Pock*, weele talke farther on't within, it drawes
neere dinner time; what's a clock boye?

PAGE By your clock sir it should be almost one, for your head rung
noone some halfe houre agoe.

DARIOTTO Ist true sir?

VALERIO Away let him alone, though he came in at the window he
sets the gates of your honor open I can tell you.

DARIOTTO Come in *Pock*, come, apply; and for this deede
Ile give the Knave a wound shall never bleed:
So sir I thinke this knock rings lowd acquittance,
410 For my ridiculouse –   *Exeunt all but* RYNALDO *and* VALERIO.

RYNALDO Well sir to turne our heads to salve your licence:
Since you have usd the matter so unwisely,
That now your father has discern'd your humor,
In your too carelesse usage in his house,
Your wife must come from his house to *Antonios*,
And he, to entertaine her must be tould
She is not wife to his sonne, but to you:
Which newes will make his simple wit triumphe
Over your father; and your father thinking
420 He still is guld, will still account him simple:
Come sir, prepare your villanous witt to faine
A kinde submission to your fathers fury,
And we shall see what harty policie,
He will discover, in his fained Anger,
To blinde *Antonios* eyes, and make him thinke,
He thinkes her hartely to be your wife.

VALERIO O I will gull him rarely with my wench,
    Lowe kneeling at my heeles before his furie,
    And injury shalbe salv'd with injurie.   *[Exeunt.]*

Finis Actus 3.

Act IV. Scene 1

MARC ANTONIO: GOSTANZO.

MARC ANTONIO You see how too much wisdome evermore,
    Out-shootes the truth: you were so forwards still,
    To taxe my ignorance, my greene experience
    In these gray haires, for giving such advantage,
    To my sonnes spirit, that he durst undertake
    A secret match, so farre short of his woorth:
    Your sonne so seasoned with obedience,
    Even from his youth, that all his actions relish
    Nothing but dutie, and your angers feare:
    What shall I say to you, if it fall out   10
    That this most precious sonne of yours, has plaide
    A part as bad as this, and as rebellious:
    Nay more has grosely guld your witt withall?
    What if my sonne has undergone the blame
    That appertain'd to yours? and that this wench
    With which my sonne is charg'd, may call you father:
    Shall I then say you want experience?
    Y'are greene, y'are credulous; easie to be blinded.
GOSTANZO Ha, ha, ha, good *Marc Antonio*, when't comes to that;
    Laugh at me, call me foole, proclaime me so,   20
    Let all the world take knowledge I am an Asse.
MARC ANTONIO O the good God of Gods,
    How blinde is Pride? what Eagles we are still,
    In matters that belong to other men?
    What Beetles in our owne? I tell you Knight,
    It is confest to be as I have tould you;
    And *Gratiana*, is by young *Rinaldo*,

And your white sonne, brought to me as his wife:
How thinke you now Sir?

GOSTANZO   Even just as before,

30   And have more cause to thinke honest *Credulity*,
Is a true Loadstone to draw on *Decrepity*:
You have a hart to open to imbrace,
All that your eare receives: alas good man,
All this is but a plot for entertainment
Within your house, for your poore sonnes yong wife
My house without huge danger cannot holde.

MARC ANTONIO Iſt possible, what danger Sir I pray?

GOSTANZO Ile tell you Sir, twas time to take her thence:
My sonne that last day you saw could not frame,

40   His lookes to entertaine her, now bir-lady
Is grone a Courtier: for my selfe unseene,
Saw when he courted her, imbrac't and kist her,
And I can tell you left not much undone,
That was the proper office of your sonne.

MARC ANTONIO What world is this?

GOSTANZO   I tolde this to *Rinaldo*,
Advising him to fetch her from my house,
And his yong wit not knowing where to lodge her
Unlesse with you: and saw that could not be,
Without some wyle: I presently suggested

50   This queint devise, to say she was my sonnes:
And all this plot, good *Marc Antonio*,
Flow'd from this fount, onely to blinde your eyes.

MARC ANTONIO Out of how sweete a dreame have you awak't
            me?
By heaven, I durst have laid my part in heaven
All had bin true; it was so lively handled,
And drawne with such a seeming face of trueth:
Your sonne had cast a perfect vaile of griefe
Over his face, for his so rash offence,
To seale his love with act of marriage,

60   Before his father had subscrib'd his choyce:
My sonne (my circumstance lessening the fact)
Intreating me to breake the matter to you,

And joyning my effectuall perswasions,
With your sonnes penitent submission,
Appease your fury; I at first assented,
And now expect their comming to that purpose.

GOSTANZO T'was well, t'was well, seeme to beleeve it still,
Let Art end what Credulitie began,
When they come, suite your words and lookes to theirs,
Second my sad Sonnes fain'd submission,   70
And see in all points how my braine will answere,
His disguisde griefe, with a set countenance
Of rage and choller; now observe and learne
To schoole your sonne by me.

Intrant RYNALDO, VALERIO, GRATIANA.

MARC ANTONIO   On with your maske;
Here come the other maskers sir.

RYNALDO   Come on I say,
Your Father with submission wilbe calm'd;
Come on; downe a your knees.

GOSTANZO   Villaine durst thou
Presume to gull thy Father? doost thou not
Tremble to see my bent and cloudy browes
Ready to thunder on thy gracelesse head,   80
And with the bolt of my displeasure cut
The thred of all my living from thy life,
For taking thus a beggar to thy wife?

VALERIO Father, if that part I have in your blood,
If teares, which so aboundantly distill
Out of my inward eyes: and for a neede,
Can drowne these outward ([*aside to* RYNALDO] lend me thy hand-
        kercher)
And being indeed as many drops of blood,
Issuing from the Creator of my hart,
Be able to beget so much compassion,   90
Not on my life, but on this lovely Dame,
Whom I hold dearer —

GOSTANZO   Out upon thee villaine.

MARC ANTONIO Nay good *Gostanzo*, thinke you are a Father.

GOSTANZO I will not heare a word; out, out upon thee:

       Wed without my advise, my love, my knowledge,

       I, and a begger too, a trull, a blowse?

RYNALDO You thought not so last day, when you offerd her

       A twelve months boord for one nights lodging with her.

GOSTANZO Goe too, no more of that, peace good *Rinaldo*,

100   It is a fault that onely she and you know.

RYNALDO Well sir, go on I pray.

GOSTANZO   Have I fond wretch,

       With utmost care and labour brought thee up,

       Ever instructing thee, omitting never

       The office of a kinde and carefull Father,

       To make thee wise and vertuous like thy father:

       And hast thou in one acte everted all?

       Proclaim'd thy selfe to all the world a foole?

       To wedde a begger?

VALERIO   Father, say not so.

GOSTANZO Nay shees thy owne, here, rise foole, take her to thee,

110   Live with her still, I know thou countst thy selfe

       Happy in soule, onely in winning her:

       Be happy still, heere, take her hand, enjoy her,

       Would not a sonne hazard his Fathers wrath,

       His reputation in the world? his birth-right,

       To have but such a messe of broth as this?

MARC ANTONIO Be not so violent, I pray you good *Gostanzo*,

       Take truce with passion, licence your sad sonne,

       To speake in his excuse.

GOSTANZO   What? what excuse?

       Can any orator in this case excuse him?

120   What can he say? what can be said of any?

VALERIO Ahlas sir, heare me, all that I can say

       In my excuse, is but to shew loves warrant.

GOSTANZO Notable wagge.

VALERIO   I know I have committed

       A great impiety, not to moove you first

       Before the dame, I meant to make my wife.

       Consider what I am, yet young, and greene,

       Beholde what she is, is there not in her,

       I, in her very eye, a power to conquer,

Even age it selfe and wisdome? Call to minde
Sweete Father, what your selfe being young have bin,   130
Thinke what you may be, for I doe not thinke
The world so farre spent with you, but you may
Looke back on such a beauty, and I hope
To see you young againe, and to live long
With young affections, wisdome makes a man
Live young for ever: and where is this wisdome
If not in you? ahlas I know not what
Rests in your wisedome to subdue affections,
But I protest it wrought with me so strongly,
That I had quite bin drownd in seas of teares   140
Had I not taken hold in happy time
Of this sweete hand; my hart had beene consum'de
T'a heape of Ashes with the flames of love,
Had it not sweetly bin asswag'd and cool'd,
With the moist kisses of these sugred lippes.

GOSTANZO   O puisant wag, what huge large thongs he cuts
     Out of his friend *Fortunios* stretching leather.

MARC ANTONIO   He knows he does it but to blinde my eyes.

GOSTANZO   O excellent, these men will put up any thing.

VALERIO   Had I not had her, I had lost my life,   150
     Which life indeed I would have lost before
     I had displeasd you, had I not receav'd it
     From such a kinde, a wise, and honour'd Father.

GOSTANZO   Notable Boy.

VALERIO   Yet doe I here renounce
     Love, life and all, rather then one houre longer
     Indure to have your love eclipsed from me.

GRATIANA   O I can hold no longer, if thy words
     Be us'd in earnest my *Valerio*,
     Thou woundst my hart, but I know tist in jest.

GOSTANZO   No ile be sworne she has her lyripoope too.   160

GRATIANA   Didst thou not sweare to love me, spight of Father,
     And all the world? That nought should sever us
     But death it selfe?

VALERIO   I did, but if my father
     Will have his sonne foresworne, upon his soule,

      The blood of my black perjurie shall lye,

      For I will seeke his favour though I dye.

GOSTANZO No, no, live still my sonne, thou well shalt know,

      I have a fathers hart, come joyne your hands,

      Still keepe thy vowes, and live together still,

170   Till cruell death set foote betwixt you both.

VALERIO O speake you this in earnest?

GOSTANZO   I by heaven.

VALERIO And never to recall it?

GOSTANZO   Not till death.

RYNALDO Excellent sir, you have done like your selfe:

      What would you more *Valerio*?

VALERIO   Worshipfull Father.

RYNALDO Come sir, come you in, and celebrate your joyes.

Exeunt all save the old men.

GOSTANZO O *Marc Antonio*,

      Had I not armd you with an expectation,

      Would not this make you pawne your very soule,

      The wench had bin my sonnes wife?

MARC ANTONIO   Yes by heaven:

180   A knaverie thus effected might deceive

      A wiser man then I, for I ahlas,

      Am noe good polititian, plaine beleeving

      Simple honesty, is my policy still.

GOSTANZO The visible markes of folly, honesty,

      And quick Credulitie his yonger brother.

      I tell you *Marc Antonio* there is mutch

      In that young boy my Sonne.

MARC ANTONIO   Not much honesty,

      If I may speake without offence to his father.

GOSTANZO O God you cannot please me better sir,

190   H'as honesty enough to serve his turne,

      The lesse honesty ever the more wit,

      But goe you home, and use your daughter kindly,

      Meane time Ile schoole your sonne: and do you still

      Dissemble what you know, keepe off your sonne,

      The wench at home must still be my sonnes wife,

      Remember that, and be you blinded still.

MARC ANTONIO You must remember too, to let your sonne
    Use his accustom'd visitations,
    Onely to blinde my eyes.

GOSTANZO   He shall not faile:
    But still take you heede, have a vigilant eye,   200
    On that slie childe of mine, for by this light,
    Heele be too bould with your sonnes forhead els.

MARC ANTONIO Well sir let me alone, Ile beare a braine.   *Exeunt*.
     Enter VALERIO, RYNALDO.

VALERIO Come they are gone.

RYNALDO   Gone, they were farre gone heere.

VALERIO Guld I my father, or guld he himselfe?
    Thou toldst him *Gratiana* was my wife,
    I have confest it, he has pardoned it.

RYNALDO Nothing more true, enow can witnesse it.
    And therefore when he comes to learne the truth,
    (As certainly for all these slie disguises,   210
    Time will strip Truth into her nakednesse)
    Thou hast good plea against him to confesse,
    The honor'd Action, and to claime his pardon.

VALERIO Tis true, for all was done he deeply swore
    Out of his hart.

RYNALDO   He has much faith the whiles,
    That swore a thing, so quite against his hart.

VALERIO Why this is pollicie.

RYNALDO   Well see you repaire,
    To *Gratiana* daily, and enjoy her
    In her true kinde; and now we must expect
    The resolute, and ridiculous divorce,   220
    Cornelio hath sued against his wedlock.

VALERIO I thinke it be not so; the Asse dotes on her.

RYNALDO It is too true, and thou shalt answere it,
    For setting such debate twixt man and wife:
    See, we shall see the solemne maner of it.

     Enter CORNELIO, DARIOTTO, CLAUDIO, NOTARIE, PAGE,
     GAZETTA, BELLANORA, GRATIANA.

BELLANORA Good Signior *Cornelio* let us poore Gentlewomen
    intreate you to forbeare.

CORNELIO Talke no more to me, Ile not be made Cuckold in my owne house: Notarie read me the divorce.

230 GAZETTA My deare *Cornelio*, examine the cause better before you condemne me.

CORNELIO Sing to me no more Syren, for I will heare thee no more, I will take no compassion on thee.

PAGE Good Signior *Cornelio* be not too mankinde against your wife, say y'are a cuckold (as the best that is may be so at a time) will you make a trumpet of your owne hornes?

CORNELIO Goe too sir, are a rascall, ile give you a fee for pleading for her one day, *Notary* doe you your office.

VALERIO Goe too Signior, looke better to your wife, and be better
240 advised, before you grow to this extremitie.

CORNELIO Extremity? go too, I deale but too mercifully with her: If I should use extremitie with her I might hang her, and her copes-mate my drudge here. How say you Maister *Notary*, might I not doe it by law?

NOTARY Not hang am, but you may bring them both to a white sheete.

CORNELIO Nay by the masse they have had too much of the sheete already.

NOTARY And besides you may set capitall letters on their fore-
250 heads.

CORNELIO What's that to the capitall letter thats written in mine? I say for all your law, maister *Notary* that I may hang am. May I not hang him that robs me of mine honour, as well as he that robs me of my horse?

NOTARY No sir your horse is a chattell.

CORNELIO Soe is honour, a man may buy it with his peny, and if I may hang a man for stealing my horse (as I say) much more for robbing mee of my honour; for why? if my horse be stolne, it may bee my owne fault; for why? eyther the stable is not strong enough,
260 or the pasture not well fenc't, or watcht, or so foorth: But for your wife that keepes the stable of your honour: Let her be lockt in a brazen towre, let *Argus* himselfe keepe her, yet can you never bee secure of your honour, for why? she can runne through all with her serpent nodle: besides you may hang a locke upon your horse, and so can you not upon your wife.

RYNALDO But I pray you Sir what are the presumptions on which you would build this divorce?

CORNELIO Presumption enough Sir, for besides their entercourse, or commerce of glances that past betwixt this cockrill-drone, and her, at my table the last Sunday night at supper, their winckes, their beckes (due gard) their treads a'the toe (as by heaven I sweare she trode once upon my toe instead of his) this is chiefly to be noted, the same night she would needs lie alone; and the same night her dog barkt, did not you heare him *Valerio*?

VALERIO And understand him too, Ile be sworne of a booke.

CORNELIO Why very good, if these be not manifest presumptions now, let the world be judge: Therefore without more ceremony, Maister *Notarie* plucke out your Instrument.

NOTARY I will sir, if there be no remedie.

CORNELIO Have you made it strong in law Maister *Notary*? have you put in words enough?

NOTARY I hope so sir, it has taken me a whole skinne of Parchment you see.

CORNELIO Very good, and is Egresse and Regresse in?

NOTARY Ile warrant you sir, it is *forma Juris*.

CORNELIO Is there no hoale to be found in the Ortography?

NOTARY None in the world sir.

CORNELIO You have written *Sunt* with an *S* have you not?

NOTARY Yes that I have.

CORNELIO You have done the better for quietnesse sake: and are none of the Autenticall dashes over the head left out? if there be Maister *Notary* an error will lye out.

NOTARY Not for a dashe over head sir I warrant you, if I should oversee; I have seene that tryed in *Butiro et Caseo*, in *Butler* and *Casons* case, *Decimo sexto* of Duke *Anonimo*.

RYNALDO Y'ave gotten a learned Notarie *Signior Cornelio*.

CORNELIO Hees a shroad fellow indeed, I had as leeve have his head in a matter of fellony, or Treason, as any Notary in *Florence*. Read out Maister *Notary*, harken you mistresse, Gentlemen marke I beseech you.

OMNES We will all marke you sir, I warrant you.

NOTARY I thinke it would be something tedious to read all, and therfore Gentlemen the summe is this: That you *Signior Cornelio*

Gentleman, for divers and sundry waighty and mature consider-
ations, you especially moving, specifying all the particulars of your
wives enormities in a scedule hereunto annexed, the transcript
whereof is in your owne tenure, custodie, occupation, and keeping:
That for these the afore said premises, I say, you renounce, disclaime
310 and discharge *Gazetta* from being your leeful, or your lawfull wife:
And that you eftsoones devide, disjoyne, seperate, remove, and
finally eloigne, sequester, and divorce her, from your bed and your
boord; That you forbid her all accesse, repaire, egresse or regresse
to your person, or persons, mansion or mansions, dwellings,
habitations, remainenances or abodes, or to any shop, sellar, Sollar,
easements chamber, dormer, and so forth, now in the tenure,
custody, occupation or keeping of the said *Cornelio*; notwithstanding
all former contracts, covenants, bargaines, conditions, agreements,
compacts, Promises, vowes, affiances, assurances, bonds, billes,
320 indentures, pole-deedes, deeds of guift, defesances, feoffments,
endowments, vowchers, double vowchers, privie entries, actions,
declarations, explications, rejoinders, surrejoinders, rights, inter-
ests, demands, claymes, or titles whatsoever, heretofore betwixt
the one and the other party, or parties, being had, made, past,
covenanted and agreed, from the beginning of the world, till the
day of the date hereof, given the 17. of November 1500. and so
forth, here Sir you must set to your hand.

CORNELIO What els maister *Notary*? I am resolute ifaith.

GAZETTA Sweete husband forbeare.

330 CORNELIO Avoyde, I charge thee in name of this divorce: Thou
mightst have lookt to it in time, yet this I will doe for thee; if thou
canst spie out any other man that thou wouldest cuckolde, thou
shalt have my letter to him: I can do no more: more Inke maister
Notary, I wright my name at large.

NOTARY Here is more Sir.

CORNELIO Ah asse that thou could not know thy happinesse till thou
hadst lost it. How now? my nose bleed? shall I write in blood?
what onely three drops? Sfoote thi's Ominous: I will not set my
hand toot now certaine, Maister *Notary* I like not this abodement:
340 I will deferre the setting too of my hand till the next court day:
keepe the divorce I pray you, and the woman in your house
together.

OMNES Burne the divorce, burne the divorce.

CORNELIO Not so Sir, it shall not serve her turne. Maister *Notary*, keep it at your perill, and gentlemen you may be gone a Gods name, what have you to doe to flocke about me thus? I am neither *Howlet*, nor *Cuckooe*: gentlewomen for gods sake medle with your owne cases, it is not fit you should haunt these publike assemblies.

OMNES Well, farewell *Cornelio*.

VALERIO Use the gentlewoman kindely maister *Notary*.   350

[NOTARY] As mine owne wife, I assure you Sir.

                    Exeunt [*all but* CLAUDIO *and* CORNELIO].

CLAUDIO Signior *Cornelio* I cannot but in kindenes tell you that *Valerio* by counsaile of *Rinaldo* hath whispered all this jealosie into your eares, not that he knew any just cause in your wife, but only to be revengd on you, for the gull, you put upon him, when you drew him with his glory to touch the *Theorbo*.

CORNELIO May I beleeve this?

CLAUDIO As I am a gentleman: and if this accident of your nose had not falne out, I would have told you this before you set too your hand.   360

CORNELIO It may well be, yet have I cause enough
To perfect my divorce, but it shall rest,
Till I conclude it with a Counterbuffe,
Given to these noble rascals: *Claudio* thankes:
What comes of this, watch but my braine a little,
And yee shall see, if like two partes in me,
I leave not both these gullers wits Imbrierd,
Now I perceive well where the wilde winde sits,
Heres Gull for Gull and wits at warre with wits.   *Exeunt.*

Act V. Scene 1

RYNALDO *solus.*

Fortune the great commandresse of the world,
Hath divers wayes to advance her followers:
To some she gives honour without deserving,
To other some deserving without honour,
Some wit, some wealth: and some wit without wealth:

Some wealth without wit, some, nor wit nor wealth
But good smocke-faces: or some qualities,
By nature without judgement, with the which
They live in sensuall acceptation,
10 And make show onely, without touche of substance;
My fortune is to winne renowne by Gulling,
Gostanzo, Dariotto, and *Cornelio*:
All which suppose in all their different kindes,
Their witts entyre, and in themselves no piece,
All at one blow, my helmet yet unbruisde,
I have unhorst, laid flat on earth for Guls;
Now in what taking poore *Cornelio* is,
Betwixt his large divorce, and no divorce,
I long to see, and what he will resolve:
20 I lay my life he cannot chew his meate,
And lookes much like an Ape had swallowed pilles,
And all this comes of bootelesse jealousie:
And see where bootlesse jealousie appeares.

    Enter CORNELIO.

Ile bourd him straight; how now *Cornelio*?
Are you resolv'd on the divorce or no?

CORNELIO What's that to you? looke to your owne affaires,
The time requires it; are not you engag'd
In some bonds forfeit for *Valerio*?

RYNALDO Yes, what of that?

CORNELIO   Why so am I my selfe,
30 And both our dangers great, he is arrested
On a recognizance, by a usuring slave.

RYNALDO Arrested? I am sorry with my hart,
It is a matter may import me much,
May not our bayle suffize to free him thinke you?

CORNELIO I thinke it may, but I must not be seene in't,
Nor would I wish you, for we both are parties,
And liker farre to bring our selves in trouble,
Then beare him out: I have already made
Meanes to the officers to sequester him
40 In private for a time, till some in secret
Might make his Father understand his state,

Who would perhaps take present order for him,
Rather then suffer him t'endure the shame
Of his imprisonment; Now, would you but goe
And breake the matter closely to his Father,
(As you can wisely doo't) and bring him to him,
This were the onely way to save his credit,
And to keepe off a shrowd blow from our selves.

RYNALDO I know his Father will be moov'd past measure.

CORNELIO Nay if you stand on such nice ceremonies,   50
Farewell our substance: Extreame diseases
Aske extreame remedies, better he should storme
Some little time, then we be beate for ever
Under the horred shelter of a prison.

RYNALDO Where is the place?

CORNELIO   Tis at the Halfe Moone Taverne,
Hast, for the matter will abide no staye.

RYNALDO Heaven send my speed be equall with my hast.   *Exit.*

CORNELIO Goe shallow scholler, you that make all Guls,
You that can out-see cleere-ey'd jeolousie,
Yet make this slight a Milstone, where your braine   60
Sticks in the midst amazd: This Gull to him
And to his fellow Guller, shall become
More bitter then their baiting of my humour:
Heere at this Taverne shall *Gostanzo* finde,
Fortunio, Dariotto, Claudio,
And amongst them, the ringleader his sonne,
His husband, and his Saint *Valerio,*
That knowes not of what fashion Dice are made,
Nor ever yet lookt towards a red Lettice,   70
(Thinkes his blinde Sire) at drinking and at Dice,
With all their wenches, and at full discover
His owne grose folly, and his sonnes distempers,
And both shall know (although I be no scholler)
Yet I have thus much Latin, as to say
Iam sumus ergo pares.   *Exit.*

[*Act V. Scene 2*]

Enter VALERIO, FORTUNIO, CLAUDIO, PAGE, GRATIANA,
GAZETTA, BELLANORA. *A* DRAWER *or two, setting a Table.*

VALERIO Set me the Table heere, we will shift roomes,
　　To see if Fortune will shift chances with us:
　　Sit Ladies, sit, *Fortunio* place thy wench,
　　And *Claudio* place you *Dariottos* mistresse,
　　I wonder where that neate spruce slave becomes:
　　I thinke he was some Barbers sonne by th'masse,
　　Tis such a picked fellow, not a haire
　　About his whole Bulke, but it stands in print,
　　Each Pinne hath his due place, not any point,
10　　But hath his perfect tie, fashion, and grace,
　　A thing whose soule is specially imployde
　　In knowing where best Gloves, best Stockings, Wasecotes,
　　Curiously wrought are solde; sacks Milleners shops
　　For all new tyres and fashions, and can tell yee
　　What new devices of all sorts there are:
　　And that there is not in the whole *Rialto*,
　　But one new-fashion'd Wast-cote, or one Night-cap,
　　One paire of Gloves, pretty or well perfum'd,
　　And from a paire of Gloves of halfe a crowne,
20　　To twenty crownes, will to a very scute
　　Smell out the price: and for these womanly parts
　　He is esteem'd a witty Gentleman.
FORTUNIO See where he comes.
　　　　Enter DARIOTTO.
DARIOTTO　　　　　　　　God save you lovely Ladies.
VALERIO I, well said lovely *Paris*, your wall eye,
　　Must ever first be gloting on mens wives,
　　You thinke to come upon us, being halfe drunke,
　　And so to part the freshest man amongst us,
　　But you shall over-take us, Ile be sworne.
DARIOTTO Tush man where are your dice? lets fall to them.
30　CLAUDIO We have bin at am. Drawer, call for more.
VALERIO First lets have Wine, Dice have no perfect edge,

Without the liquid whetstone of the Sirrope.

FORTUNIO True, and to welcome *Dariotto*'s latenes,
He shall (unpledg'd) carouze one crowned cup
To all these Ladies health.

DARIOTTO   I am well pleasd.

VALERIO Come on, let us varie our sweete time
With sundry excercises. Boy? Tabacco.
And Drawer, you must get us musique too,
Call's in a cleanly noyse, the slaves grow lowzy.

DRAWER You shall have such as we can get you sir.   *Exit.*

DARIOTTO Let's have some Dice: I pray thee, they are clenly.   40

VALERIO Page, Let mee see that Leafe?

PAGE   It is not Leafe Sir,
Tis pudding cane *Tabacco.*

VALERIO   But I meane,
Your Linstock sir, what leafe is that I pray?

PAGE I pray you see sir, for I cannot read.

VALERIO Sfoote a rancke stincking Satyre: this had been
Enough to have poysned everie man of us.

DARIOTTO And now you speake of that, my Boy once lighted
A pipe of Cane *Tabacco* with a peece
Of a vild Ballad, and Ile sweare I had   50
A singing in my head a whole weeke after.

VALERIO Well, th'old verse is, *A potibus incipe io-c-um.*

Enter DRAWER *with Wine and a Cupp.*

Drawer, fill out this Gentlemans Carowse,
And harden him for our societie.

DARIOTTO Well Ladies heere is to your honourd healths.

FORTUNIO What *Dariotto*, without hat or knee?

VALERIO Well said *Fortunio*, O y'are a rare Courtier,
Your knee good Signior, I beseech your knee.

DARIOTTO Nay pray you, lets take it by degrees *Valerio*;
On our feete first, for this will bring's too soone   60
Upon our knees.

VALERIO   Sir, there are no degrees
Of order in a Taverne, heere you must,
I chargd yee, runne all a head: Slight, Courtier, downe;
I hope you are no Elephant, you have Joynts?

DARIOTTO Well Sir, heere's to the Ladies on my knees.

VALERIO Ile be their pledge.

    Enter GOSTANZO *and* RINALDO.

FORTUNIO   Not yet *Valerio*,

    This hee must drinke unpledgd.

VALERIO Hee shall not, I will give him this advantage.

GOSTANZO How now? whats heere? are these the Officers?

RYNALDO Slight, I would all were well.

    Enter CORNELIO.

70   VALERIO   Heere is his pledge:

    Heere's to our common friend, *Cornelioes* health.

DARIOTTO Health to *Gazetta*, Poyson to her husband.   *He kneeles.*

CORNELIO Excellent Guestes: these are my dayly Guestes.

VALERIO Drawer make even th'impartiall skales of Justice,

    Give it to *Claudio*, and from him fill round.

    Come *Dariotto*, sett mee, let the rest

    Come in when they have done the Ladyes right.

GOSTANZO Sett mee, doe you know what belongs to setting?

RYNALDO What a dull slave was I to be thus gull'd.

80   CORNELIO Why *Rinald*, what meant you to intrap your friend,

    And bring his Father to this spectacle?

    You are a friend in deed.

RYNALDO   Tis verie good Sir,

    Perhaps my friend, or I, before wee part,

    May make even with you.

FORTUNIO   Come, lets sett him round.

VALERIO Doe so: at all. A plague upon these Dice.

    Another health, sfoote I shall have no lucke,

    Till I be druncke: come on, heere's to the comfort,

    The Cavalier my Father should take in mee,

    If he now saw mee, and would do me right.

90   FORTUNIO Ile pledge it, and his health *Valerio*.

GOSTANZO Heere's a good Husband.

RYNALDO   I pray you have patience Sir.

VALERIO Now have at all, an't were a thousand pound.

GOSTANZO Hold Sir, I barr the Dice.

VALERIO   What Sir, are you there?

    Fill's a fresh pottle, by this light, Sir Knight,

You shall do right.

    Enter MARC ANTONIO.

GOSTANZO   O thou ungratious villaine.

[VALERIO] Come, come, wee shall have you now thunder foorth
    Some of your thriftie sentences, as gravely:
    For as much *Valerius* as every thing has time, and a Pudding has
    two: yet ought not satisfaction to swerve so much from defalcation
    of well dispos'd people, as that indemnitie should prejudice what   100
    securitie doth insinuate: a tryall yet once againe.

MARC ANTONIO Heere's a good sight, y'are well encountred sir,
    Did not I tell you you'd oreshoote your selfe
    With too much wisedome?

VALERIO   Sir, your wisest do so.
    Fill the old man some wine.

GOSTANZO   Heere's a good Infant.

MARC ANTONIO Why Sir: Ahlas Ile wager with your wisedome,
    His consorts drew him to it, for of him selfe
    He is both vertuous, bashfull, innocent:
    Comes not at Cittie: knowes no Cittie Art,
    But plies your Husbandrie; dares not view a Wench.   110

VALERIO Father, hee comes upon you.

GOSTANZO   Heere's a Sonne.

MARC ANTONIO Whose wife is *Gratiana* now I pray?

GOSTANZO Sing your old song no more, your braine's too short
    To reach into these pollicies.

MARC ANTONIO   Tis true,
    Mine eye's soone blinded: and your selfe would say so,
    If you knew all: Where lodg'd your Sonne last night?
    Doe you know that with all your pollicie?

GOSTANZO Youle say he lodg'd with you, and did not I
    Foretell you: all this must for cullour sake
    Be brought about, onely to blinde your eyes?   120

MARC ANTONIO By heaven I chaunc't this morne, I know not why,
    To passe by *Gratianas* bed-chamber,
    And whom saw I fast by her naked side,
    But your *Valerio*?

GOSTANZO   Had you not warning given?
    Did not I bidd you watch my Courtier well,

Or hee would set a Crest a your Sonnes head?

MARC ANTONIO That was not all, for by them on a stoole,

My Sonne sate laughing, to see you so gull'd.

GOSTANZO Tis too too plaine.

MARC ANTONIO Why Sir, do you suspect it

The more for that?

130 GOSTANZO Suspect it? is there any

So grosse a wittoll, as if t'were his wife,

Would sit by her so tamelie?

MARC ANTONIO Why not Sir,

To blind my eyes?

GOSTANZO Well Sir, I was deceiv'd,

But I shall make it proove a deare deceipt

To the deceiver.

RYNALDO Nay Sir, lets not have

A new infliction, set on an old fault:

Hee did confesse his fault upon his knees,

You pardned it, and swore twas from your hart.

GOSTANZO Swore; a great peece of worke, the wretch shall know

140 I have a Daughter heere to give my land too,

Ile give my Daughter all: the prodigall

Shall not have one poore House to hide his head in.

FORTUNIO I humblie thanke you Sir, and vow all duetie

My life can yeelde you.

GOSTANZO Why are you so thankfull?

FORTUNIO For giving to your Daughter all your Lands,

Who is my Wife, and so you gave them mee.

GOSTANZO Better, and better.

FORTUNIO Pray Sir be not moov'd,

You drew mee kindlie to your house, and gave mee

Accesse to woe your Daughter, whom I lov'd:

150 And since (by honord mariage) made my wife.

GOSTANZO Now all my Choller flie out in your witts:

Good trickes of Youth y'faith, no *Indecorum*,

Knights sonne, Knights daughter; *Marc Antonio*

Give mee your hand: There is no remedie,

Mariage is ever made by Destenie.

RYNALDO Scilence my Maisters, now heere all are pleas'd,

Onelie but *Cornelio*: who lackes but perswasion
To reconcile himselfe to his faire wife:
Good Sir will you (of all men our best speaker)
Perswade him to receive her into grace?   160

GOSTANZO That I will gladlie, and he shalbe rul'd. Good *Cornelio*: I
have heard of your wayward Jelosie, and I must tell you plaine
as a friend, y'are an Asse: you must pardon me, I knew your
Father.

RYNALDO Then you must pardon him, indeed Sir.

GOSTANZO Understand mee: put case *Dariotto* lov'd your wife,
whereby you would seeme to refuse her; would you desire to have
such a Wife as no man could love but your selfe?

MARC ANTONIO Answere but that *Cornelio*.

GOSTANZO Understand mee: Say *Dariotto* hath kist your wife, or   170
perform'de other offices of that nature, whereby they did converse
togeather at bedd and at boord, as friendes may seeme to doe:

MARC ANTONIO Marke but the now understand mee.

GOSTANZO Yet if there come no proofes, but that her actions were
cleanlie, or indiscreete private, why t'was a signe of modestie: and
will you blow the Horne your selfe, when you may keepe it to
your selfe? Goe to, you are a Foole, understand mee?

VALERIO Doe understand him *Cornelio*.

GOSTANZO Nay *Cornelio* I tell you againe, I knew your Father; Hee
was a wise Gentleman, and so was your Mother: mee thinkes I   180
see her yet, a lustie stoute Woman, bore great Children, you were
the verie skundrell of am all; but let that passe: As for your Mother,
shee was wise, a most flippant tongue she had, and could set out
her Taile with as good grace as any shee in *Florence*, come cut and
long-tayle; and she was honest enough too: But yet by your leave
she would tickle *Dob* now and then, as well as the best on am; By
Jove it's true *Cornelio*, I speake it not to flatter you: your Father
knew it well enough, and would he do as you do, thinke you? set
Rascalles to undermine her, or looke to her water, (as they say)?
No, when he saw twas but her humour (for his owne quietnesse   190
sake) hee made a Backe-doore to his house for convenience, gott
a Bell to his fore doore, and had an odd fashion in ringing, by
which shee and her Mayde knew him; and would stand talking to
his next neighbour to prolong time, that all thinges might be ridde

clenly out a the way before he came, for the credite of his Wife:
This was wisedome now, for a mans owne quiet.

MARC ANTONIO Heere was a man *Cornelio*.

GOSTANZO What I say? Young men thinke old men are fooles; but
old men know young men are fooles.

200 CORNELIO Why harke you, you two Knights; Doe you thinke I will
forsake *Gazetta?*

GOSTANZO And will you not?

CORNELIO Why theer's your wisedome; why did I make shew of
Divorce thinke you?

MARC ANTONIO Pray you why Sir?

CORNELIO Onelie to bridle her stout stomack: and how did I draw
on the cullour for my divorce? I did traine the Woodcocke *Dariotto*
into the net, drew him to my house, gave him opportunitie with
my wife (as you say my Father dealt with his wives friendes) onely
210 to traine him in: let him alone with my wife in her bed-chamber;
and sometimes founde him a bedd with her, and went my way
backe againe softlie, onelie to draw him into the Pitte.

GOSTANZO This was well handled in deed *Cornelio*.

MARC ANTONIO I marrie Sir, now I commend your wisedome.

CORNELIO Why, if I had been so minded as you thinke, I could have
flung his Pantable downe the staires, or doone him some other
disgrace: but I winckt at it, and drew on the good foole more and
more, onelie to bring him within my compasse.

GOSTANZO Why, this was pollicie in graine.

220 CORNELIO And now shal the world see I am as wise as my father.

VALERIO Is't come to this? then will I make a speech in praise of
this reconcilement, including therein the praise and honor of the
most fashionable and autenticall *HORNE*: stande close Gentles,
and be silent.   *He gets into a chaire.*

GOSTANZO Come on, lets heare his wit in this potable humour.

VALERIO The course of the world (like the life of man) is said to be
devided into severall ages: As wee into Infancie, Childhood, Youth,
and so forward to Old-age: So the World into the Golden age, the
Silver, the Brasse, the Iron, the Leaden, the Wooden; and now
230 into this present age, which wee tearme the *Horned age*: not that
but former ages have injoyde this benefite as well as our times;
but that in ours it is more common, and neverthelesse pretious.

It is said, that in the Golden age of the world, the use of Gold was not then knowne: an argument of the simplicitie of that age; least therefore succeeding ages should hereafter impute the same fault to us, which wee lay upon the first age; that wee living in the Horned age of the world, should not understand the use, the vertue, the honour, and the very royaltie of the Horne; I will in briefe sound the prayses thereof, that they who are alreadie in possession of it, may beare their heades aloft, as beeing proud of   240 such loftie acowtrementes: And they that are but in possibilitie, may be ravisht with a desire to be in possession.

A Trophey so honorable, and unmatchably powerfull, that it is able to raise any man from a Beggar to an Emperours fellow, a Dukes fellow, a Noble-mans fellow, Aldermans fellow; so glorious, that it deserves to be worne (by most opinions) in the most conspicuous place about a man: For what worthier Crest can you beare then the Horne? which if it might be seene with our mortall eyes, what a wonderfull spectacle would there be? and how highly they would ravish the beholders? But their substaunce is incor-   250 porall, not falling under sence, nor mixt of the grosse concretion of Elementes, but a quintessence beyond them; a spirituall essence invisible, and everlasting.

And this hath been the cause that many men have called their beeing in question, whether there be such a thing in *rerum natura*, or not; because they are not to be seene: as though nothing were that were not to be seene? Who ever saw the Winde? yet what wonderfull effectes are seene of it? It drives the cloudes, yet no man sees it: It rockes the House, beares downe Trees, Castles, Steeples, yet who sees it? In like sort does your Horne, it swelles   260 the Forehead, yet none sees it: it rockes the Cradle, yet none sees it: so that you plainely perceive Sence, is no Judge of Essence. The Moone to any mans sence, seemes to be Horned; yet who knowes not the Moone to be ever perfectly round: So likewise your Heades seeme ever to be round, when in deed they are oftentimes Horned: for their originall, it is unsearchable: Naturall they are not; for there is [no] Beast borne with Hornes, more then with Teeth: Created they were not, for *Ex nihilo nihil fit*; Then will you aske mee, How came they into the world? I know not; but I am sure Women brought them into this part of the world, howsoever some   270

Doctors are of opinion that they came in with the Divell: and not unlike; for, as the Divell brought Sinne into the worlde; but the Woman brought it to the Man: so it may very well be that the Divell brought Hornes into the world; but the Woman brought them to the man.

For their power it is generall over the world, no Nation so barbarous, no Countrey so proude, but doth equall homage to the Horne. *Europa* when shee was carried through the Sea by the *Saturnian* Bull, was said (for feare of falling) to have held by the Horne: and what is this but a plaine shewing to us, that all *Europe*, which tooke name from that *Europa*, should likewise hold by the Horne: So that I say, it is universall over the face of the world, general over the face of *Europe*, and common over the face of this Countrey. What Cittie, what Towne, what Village, what Streete? nay what House can quit it selfe of this prerogative? I have read that the Lion once made a Proclamation through all the Forrest, that all Horned Beastes should depart foorthwith upon paine of death: If this Proclamation should be made through our Forrest, Lord what pressing, what running, what flying, would there be even from all the parts of it? he that had but a bunch of Flesh in his head would away: and some foolishly fearefull, would imagine the shadow of his Eares to be Hornes: Ahlas how desart would this Forrest be left?

To conclude: for there force it is irrevitable, for were they not irrevitable, then might eyther propernesse of person secure a man, or wisedome prevent am; or greatnesse exempt, or riches redeeme them, but present experience hath taught us, that in this case, all these stand in no steade: for we see the properst men take part of them, the best wits cannot avoide them (for then should Poets be no cuckolds) nor can money redeeme them, for then would rich-men fine for their hornes, as they do for offices: But this is held for a maxime, that there are more rich cuckolds then poore; lastly for continuance of the horne it is undeterminable till death: Neither doe they determine with the wives death, (howsoever ignorant writers holde opinion they doe); For as when a knight dies, his Ladie still retaines the title of Ladie; when a company is cast yet the Captaine still retaines the title of Captaine; So though the wife die by whom this title came to her husband, yet by the

curtesie of the City, he shalbe a cuckold during life, let all ignorant
asses prate what they list.   310

GOSTANZO Notable wag, come sir shake hands with him,
In whose high honour you have made this speech.

MARC ANTONIO And you sir come, joyne hands, y'are one
amongst them.

GOSTANZO Very well done, now take your severall wives,
And spred like wilde-geese, though you now grow tame:
Live merily together and agree,
Hornes cannot be kept off with jealousie.

FINIS.

Epilogue.

Since all our labours are as you can like,
We all submit to you; nor dare presume,
To thinke ther's any reall worth in them:
Sometimes feastes please the Cookes, and not the guestes,
Sometimes the guestes, and curious Cookes contemne them:
Our dishes we intirely dedicate
To our kinde guestes, but since yee differ so,
Some to like onely mirth without taxations,
Some to count such workes trifles, and such like,
We can but bring you meate, and set you stooles,   10
And to our best cheere say, you all are (   ) welcome.

Bussy D'Ambois

[Dramatis Personae

BUSSY D'AMBOIS
KING HENRY (III of France)
MONSIEUR, the king's brother
THE DUKE OF GUISE
THE COUNT OF MONTSURRY
BEAUMOND, a courtier
BARRISOR
L'ANOU ⎫ courtiers, and
PYRHOT ⎬ enemies of BUSSY
  (sometimes ⎭ D'AMBOIS
  PYRRHOT)
BRISAC ⎫ courtiers, and friends
MELYNELL ⎭ of BUSSY D'AMBOIS
COMOLET, a friar (later UMBRA, his
  ghost)
MAFFE, steward of MONSIEUR
BEHEMOTH, master of the
  underworld spirits
CARTOPHYLAX, a devil

DUCHESS (Elenor), wife of GUISE
TAMYRA, Countess of MONTSURRY
BEAUPRE, niece to the DUCHESS
PYRA (sometimes PYRHA), a
  woman of the court
ANNABLE (sometimes ANNABELL),
  maid to the DUCHESS
PERO, maid to TAMYRA
CHARLOTTE, maid to BEAUPRE

NUNCIUS (a messenger)
Attendants, pages, servants, devils,
  murderers]

Bussy D'Ambois: A Tragedie.

Act I. Scene 1

BUSSY *solus.*

Fortune, not Reason, rules the state of things,
Reward goes backwards, Honor on his head;
Who is not poore, is monstrous; only Need
Gives forme & worth to every humane seed.
As Cedars beaten with incessant stormes,
So great men flourish; and doe imitate
Unskilfull statuaries, who suppose
(In forging a Colossus) if they make him
Stroddle enough, stroote, and looke big, and gape,
Their worke is goodly: so our Tympanouse statists   10
(In their affected gravitie of voice,
Sowernesse of countenance, maners crueltie,
Authoritie, wealth, and all the spawne of Fortune)
Thinke they beare all the kingdomes worth before them;
Yet differ not from those Colossicke Statues,
Which with Heroique formes, without o'respread,
Within are nought but morter, flint and lead.
Man is a Torch borne in the winde; a Dreame
But of a shadow, summ'd with all his substance;
And as great Seamen using all their powers   20
And skils in *Neptunes* deepe invisible pathes,
In tall ships richly built and ribd with brasse,
To put a Girdle round about the world,
When they have done it (comming neere their Haven)
Are glad to give a warning peece, and call
A poore staid fisher-man, that never past
His Contries sight, to waft and guide them in:
So when we wander furthest through the waves
Of Glassie Glorie and the Gulfes of State,

30 Topt with all Titles, spreading all our reaches,
    As if each private Arme would sphere the world;
    Wee must to vertue for her guide resort,
    Or wee shall shipwracke in our safest Port.   *Procumbit.*

      [*Enter*] MONSIEUR *with two Pages.*

MONSIEUR There is no second place in Numerous State
    That holds more than a Cypher: In a King
    All places are contain'd. His words and lookes
    Are like the flashes and the bolts of *Jove*,
    His deedes inimitable, like the Sea
    That shuts still as it opes, and leaves no tracts,
40 Nor prints of President for poore mens facts:
    There's but a Thred betwixt me and a Croune;
    I would not wish it cut, unlesse by nature;
    Yet to prepare mee for that likely Fortune,
    Tis fit I get resolved spirits about mee.
    I followd *D'Ambois* to this greene Retreat;
    A man of spirit beyond the reach of feare,
    Who (discontent with his neglected worth)
    Neglects the light, and loves obscure Abodes;
    But he is yoong and haughtie, apt to take
50 Fire at advancement, to beare state and flourish;
    In his Rise therefore shall my bounties shine:
    None lothes the world so much, nor loves to scoffe it,
    But gold and grace will make him surfet of it.
    What, *D'Ambois?*

BUSSY   He sir.

MONSIEUR   Turn'd to Earth, alive?
    Up man, the Sunne shines on thee.

BUSSY   Let it shine.
    I am no mote to play in't, as great men are.

MONSIEUR Think'st thou men great in state, motes in the sunne?
    They say so that would have thee freeze in shades,
    That (like the grosse Sicilian Gurmundist)
60 Emptie their Noses in the Cates they love,
    That none may eat but they. Do thou but bring
    Light to the Banquet Fortune sets before thee,
    And thou wilt loth leane Darkenesse like thy Death.

Who would beleeve thy Mettall could let sloth
Rust and consume it? If *Themistocles*
Had liv'd obscur'd thus in th'Athenian state,
Xerxes had made both him and it his slaves.
If brave *Camillus* had lurckt so in Rome,
He had not five times beene dictator there,
Nor foure times triumpht. If *Epaminondas*   70
(Who liv'd twice twentie yeeres obscur'd in *Thebs*)
Had liv'd so still, he had beene still unnam'd,
And paid his Countrie nor himselfe their right:
But putting foorth his strength, he rescude both
From imminent ruine; and like Burnisht Steele,
After long use he shin'd; for as the light
Not only serves to shew, but render us
Mutually profitable; so our lives
In acts exemplarie, not only winne
Our selves good Names, but doth to others give   80
Matter for vertuous Deedes, by which wee live.
BUSSY What would you wish me doe?
MONSIEUR   Leave the troubled streames,
    And live as Thrivers doe, at the Well head.
BUSSY At the Well head? Alas what should I doe
    With that enchanted Glasse? See divels there?
    Or (like a strumpet) learne to set my lookes
    In an eternall Brake, or practise juggling,
    To keepe my face still fast, my hart still loose;
    Or beare (like Dames Schoolemistresses their Riddles)
    Two Tongues, and be good only for a shift;   90
    Flatter great Lords, to put them still in minde
    Why they were made Lords: or please portly Ladies
    With a good carriage, tell them idle Tales,
    To make their Physicke worke; spend a mans life
    In sights and visitations, that will make
    His eies as hollow as his Mistresse heart:
    To doe none good, but those that have no neede;
    To gaine being forward, though you breake for haste
    All the Commandements ere you breake your fast,

100   But Beleeve backewards, make your Period
    And Creedes last Article, I beleeve in God:
    And (hearing villanies preacht) t'unfold their Art
    Learne to commit them? Tis a great mans Part.
    Shall I learne this there?

MONSIEUR   No, thou needst not learne,
    Thou hast the Theorie, now goe there and practise.

BUSSY I, in a thridbare suit; when men come there,
    They must have high Naps, and goe from thence bare:
    A man may drowne the parts of ten rich men
    In one poore suit; Brave Barks, and outward Glosse
110   Attract Court eies, be in-parts ne're so grosse.

MONSIEUR Thou shalt have Glosse enough, and all things fit
    T'enchase in all shew, thy long smother'd spirit:
    Be rul'd by me then. The rude Scythians
    Painted blinde Fortunes powerfull hands with wings,
    To shew her gifts come swift and suddenly,
    Which if her Favorite be not swift to take,
    He loses them forever. Then be rul'd:
    Stay but a while heere, and I'le send to thee.

                  Exit MONSIEUR [*and Pages.*] *Manet* BUSSY.

BUSSY What will he send? some Crounes? Is it to sow them
120   Upon my spirit, and make them spring a Croune
    Worth Millions of the seede Crounes he will send:
    But hee's no husband heere; A smooth plaine ground
    Will never nourish any politicke seede;
    I am for honest Actions, not for great:
    If I may bring up a new fashion,
    And rise in Court with vertue; speede his plow:
    The King hath knowne me long as well as hee,
    Yet could my Fortune never fit the length
    Of both their understandings till this houre.
130   There is a deepe nicke in times restlesse wheele
    For each mans good, when which nicke comes it strikes;
    As Rhetoricke, yet workes not perswasion,
    But only is a meane to make it worke:
    So no man riseth by his reall merit,
    But when it cries Clincke in his Raisers spirit:

Many will say, that cannot rise at all,
Mans first houres rise, is first steppe to his fall.
I'le venture that; men that fall low must die,
As well as men cast headlong from the skie.
    Enter MAFFE.

MAFFE Humor of Princes! Is this man indu'd   140
    With any merit worth a thousand Crounes?
    Will my Lord have me be so ill a Steward
    Of his Revenue, to dispose a summe
    So great with so small cause as shewes in him?
    I must examine this: Is your name *D'Ambois*?

BUSSY Sir?

MAFFE   Is your name *D'Ambois*?

BUSSY   Who have wee heere?
    Serve you the *Monsieur*?

MAFFE   How?

BUSSY   Serve you the *Monsieur*?

MAFFE Sir, y'are very hot. I serve the *Monsieur*,
    But in such place as gives me the Command
    Of all his other servants: And because   150
    His Graces pleasure is, to give your good
    A Passe through my Command, Me thinks you might
    Use me with more good fashion.

BUSSY   Crie you mercie.
    Now you have open'd my dull eies, I see you;
    And would be glad to see the good you speake of:
    What might I call your name?

MAFFE   Monsieur *Maffe*.

BUSSY Monsieur *Maffe*? Then good Monsieur *Maffe*,
    Pray let me know you better.

MAFFE   Pray doe so,
    That you may use me better. For your selfe,
    By your no better outside, I would judge you   160
    To be a Poet; Have you given my Lord
    Some Pamphlet?

BUSSY ·   Pamphlet?

MAFFE   Pamphlet sir, I say.

BUSSY Did his wise excellencie leave the good

That is to passe your charge, to my poore use,
To your discretion?

MAFFE   Though he did not sir,
I hope tis no bad office to aske reason,
How that his grace gives mee in charge, goes from me?

BUSSY   That's very perfect, sir.

MAFFE   Why very good, sir;
I pray then give me leave: If for no Pamphlet,
170   May I not know what other merit in you,
Makes his compunction willing to relieve you?

BUSSY   No merit in the world sir.

MAFFE   That is strange.
Y'are a poore souldier, are you?

BUSSY   That I am sir.

MAFFE   And have Commanded?

BUSSY   I, and gone without sir.

MAFFE   I see the man: A hundred Crounes will make him
Swagger, and drinke healths to his highnes bountie;
And sweare he could not be more bountifull.
So ther's nine hundred Crounes, saft; heere tall souldier,
His grace hath sent you a whole hundred Crounes.

180   BUSSY   A hundred sir? naie doe his Highnes right;
I know his hand is larger, and perhaps
I may deserve more than my outside shewes:
I am a scholar, as I am a souldier,
And I can Poetise; and (being well encourag'd)
May sing his Fame for giving; yours for delivering
(Like a most faithfull Steward) what he gives.

MAFFE   What shall your subject be?

BUSSY   I care not much,
If to his excellence I sing the praise
Of faire great Noses, And to your Deserts
190   The reverend vertues of a faithfull Steward;
What Qualities have you sir (beside your chaine
And velvet Jacket)? Can your worship dance?

MAFFE   A merrie Fellow faith: It seemes my Lord
Will have him for his Jester; And beleeve it,
Such men are now no fooles, Tis a Knights place:

If I (to save my Lord some Crounes) should urge him
T'abate his Bountie, I should not be heard;
I would to heaven I were an errant Asse,
For then I should be sure to have the Eares
Of these great men, where now their Jesters have them: 200
Tis good to please him, yet Ile take no notice
Of his preferment, but in policie
Will still be grave and serious, lest he thinke
I feare his wodden dagger: Heere sir *Ambo*,
A thousand Crounes I bring you from my Lord;
Serve God, play the good husband, you may make
This a good standing living, Tis a Bountie,
His Highnes might perhaps have bestow'd better.
BUSSY Goe, y'are a Rascall; hence, Away you Rogue.
MAFFE What meane you sir?
BUSSY   Hence; prate no more;   210
Or by thy villans blood thou prat'st thy last:
A Barbarous Groome, grudge at his masters Bountie:
But since I know he would as much abhorre
His hinde should argue what he gives his friend,
Take that Sir, for your aptnesse to dispute.   *Exit.*
MAFFE These Crounes are sown in blood, blood be their fruit. *Exit.*

[*Act I. Scene 2*]

HENRY, GUISE, MONTSURRY, DUCHESS, TAMYRA,
BEAUPRE, PERO, CHARLOTTE, PYRA, ANNABLE.

HENRY Dutchesse of *Guise*, your Grace is much enricht,
In the attendance of this English virgin,
That will initiate her Prime of youth,
(Dispos'd to Court conditions) under hand
Of your preferd instructions and Command,
Rather than anie in the English Court,
Whose Ladies are not matcht in Christendome,
For gracefull and confirm'd behaviours;
More than the Court, where they are bred is equall'd.

10   GUISE I like not their Court forme, it is too crestfalne,
          In all observance; making Semi-gods
          Of their great Nobles; and of their old Queene
          An ever-yoong, and most immortall Goddesse.
     HENRY Assure you Cosen *Guise*, so great a Courtier,
          So full of majestie and Roiall parts,
          No Queene in Christendome may boast her selfe,
          Her Court approoves it, Thats a Court indeede;
          Not mixt with Rudenesse us'd in common houses;
          But, as Courts should be th'abstracts of their kingdomes,
20   In all the Beautie, State, and Worth they hold;
          So is hers, amplie, and by her inform'd.
          The world is not contracted in a man,
          With more proportion and expression
          Than in her Court, her Kingdome: Our French Court
          Is a meere mirror of confusion to it:
          The King and subject, Lord and everie slave
          Dance a continuall Haie; Our Roomes of State,
          Kept like our stables; No place more observ'd
          Than a rude Market place: And though our Custome
30   Keepe this assur'd deformitie from our sight,
          Tis nere the lesse essentiallie unsightlie,
          Which they would soone see, would they change their forme
          To this of ours, and then compare them both;
          Which we must not affect, because in Kingdomes,
          Where the Kings change doth breede the Subjects terror,
          Pure Innovation is more grosse than error.
     MONTSURRY No Question we shall see them imitate
          (Though a farre off) the fashions of our Courts,
          As they have ever Ap't us in attire;
40   Never were men so wearie of their Skins,
          And apt to leape out of themselves as they;
          Who when they travell to bring foorth rare men,
          Come home deliver'd of a fine French suit:
          Their Braines lie with their Tailors, and get babies
          For their most compleat issue; Hee's first borne
          To all the morall vertues, that first greetes
          The light with a new fashion, which becomes them

Like Apes, disfigur'd with the attires of men.

HENRY No Question they much wrong their reall worth,
   In affectation of outlandish Scumme;   50
   But they have faults, and wee; They foolish-proud,
   To be the Pictures of our vanitie;
   We proud, that they are proud of foolerie.
      Enter MONSIEUR, D'AMBOIS.

MONSIEUR Come mine owne sweet heart I will enter thee.
   Sir, I have brought this Gentleman t'attend you;
   And pray, you would vouchsafe to doe him grace.

HENRY *D'Ambois*, I thinke.

BUSSY   Thats still my name, my Lord,
   Though I be something alter'd in attire.

HENRY I like your alteration, and must tell you,
   I have expected th'offer of your service;   60
   For we (in feare to make milde vertue proud)
   Use not to seeke her out in any man.

BUSSY Nor doth she use to seeke out any man:
   He that will winne, must wooe her; shee's not shamelesse.

MONSIEUR I urg'd her modestie in him, my Lord,
   And gave her those Rites, that he saies shee merits.

HENRY If you have woo'd and won, then Brother weare him.

MONSIEUR Th'art mine, my love; See here's the Guises *Duches*; The
   Countesse of *Mountsurreaue*; *Beaupres*, come I'le enseame thee;
   Ladies, y'are too many to be in Counsell: I have heere a friend,   70
   that I would gladlie enter in your Graces.

DUCHESS If you enter him in our Graces, me thinks by his blunt
   behaviour, he should come out of himselfe.

TAMYRA Has he never beene Courtier, my Lord?

MONSIEUR Never, my Ladie.

BEAUPRE And why did the Toy take him inth'head now?

BUSSY Tis leape yeere, Ladie, and therefore verie good to enter a
   Courtier.

TAMYRA The man's a Courtier at first sight.

BUSSY I can sing prickesong, Ladie, at first sight; and why not be a   80
   Courtier as suddenly?

BEAUPRE Heere's a Courtier rotten before he be ripe.

BUSSY Thinke mee not impudent, Ladie, I am yet no Courtier, I desire to be one, and would gladly take entrance (Madam) under your Princely Colours.

GUISE Sir, know you me?

BUSSY My Lord?

GUISE I know not you: Whom doe you serve?

BUSSY Serve, my Lord?

90 GUISE Go to Companion; Your Courtship's too saucie.

BUSSY Saucie? Companion? Tis the *Guise*, but yet those termes might have beene spar'd of the Guiserd. Companion? Hee's jealous by this light: are you blinde of that side Sir? Ile to her againe for that. Forth Madam, for the honour of Courtship.

GUISE Cease your Courtshippe, or by heaven Ile cut your throat.

BUSSY Cut my throat? cut a whetstone; good *Accius Nævius*, doe as much with your tongue as he did with a Rasor; cut my throat?

GUISE Ile doe't, by this hand.

BUSSY That hand dares not doe't; y'ave cut too many throates alreadie
100 *Guise*; and Robb'd the Realme of many thousand Soules, more precious than thine owne. Come Madam, talke on; Sfoote, can you not talke? Talke on I say, more Courtship, as you love it.

Enter BARRISOR, L'ANOU, PYRHOT.

BARRISOR What new-come Gallant have wee heere, that dares mate the *Guise* thus?

L'ANOU Sfoote tis *D'Ambois*; The Duke mistakes him (on my life) for some Knight of the new edition.

BUSSY Cut my throat? I would the King fear'd thy cutting of his throat no more than I feare thy cutting of mine.

GUISE So sir, so.

110 PYRHOT Heere's some strange distemper.

BARRISOR Heere's a sudden transmigration with *D'Ambois*, out of the Knights ward, into the Duches bed.

L'ANOU See what a Metamorphosis a brave suit can worke.

PYRHOT Slight, step to the *Guise* and discover him.

BARRISOR By no meanes, let the new suit worke, wee'll see the issue.

GUISE Leave your Courtship.

BUSSY I will not. I say, mistresse, and I will stand unto it, that if a woman may have three servants, a man may have threescore
120 mistresses.

GUISE Sirha, Ile have you whipt out of the Court for this insolence.

BUSSY Whipt? Such another syllable out a th'presence, if thou dar'st
for thy Dukedome.

GUISE Remember, Poultron.

MONSIEUR Pray thee forbeare.

BUSSY Passion of death! Were not the King heere, he should strow
the Chamber like a rush.

MONSIEUR But leave Courting his wife then.

BUSSY I will not: Ile Court her in despight of him. Not Court her!
Come Madam, talke on; Feare me nothing: Well maist thou drive   130
thy master from the Court; but never *D'Ambois.*

MONSIEUR His great heart will not downe, tis like the Sea
That partly by his owne internall heat,
Partly the starr's dailie and nightly motion,
Ardor and light, and partly of the place
The divers frames; And chiefly by the Moone,
Bristled with surges, never will be wonne,
(No, not when th'hearts of all those powers are burst)
To make retreat into his setled home,
Till he be croun'd with his owne quiet fome.   140

HENRY You have the mate. Another.

GUISE No more.

                    Exit GUISE, *after him the* KING, MONSIEUR *whispering.*

BARRISOR Why heer's the Lion, skard with the throat of a dunghill
Cocke; a fellow that has newlie shak'd off his shackles; Now does
he crow for that victorie.

L'ANOU Tis one of the best Jigges that ever was acted.

PYRHOT Whom does the *Guise* suppose him to be, troe?

L'ANOU Out of doubt, some new denizond Lord; and thinks that
suit come new out a th'Mercers bookes.

BARRISOR I have heard of a fellow, that by a fixt imagination looking   150
upon a Bulbaiting, had a visible paire of hornes grew out of his
forhead: and I beleeve this Gallant, overjoied with the conceit of
Monsieurs cast suit, imagines himselfe to be the *Monsieur.*

L'ANOU And why not? as well as the Asse, stalking in the Lions case,
beare himselfe like a Lion, roaring all the huger beasts out of the
Forrest?

PYRHOT Peace, he lookes this way.

BARRISOR Marrie let him looke sir, what will you say now if the
　　Guise be gone to fetch a blanquet for him?

160　L'ANOU Faith I beleeve it for his honour.

PYRHOT But, if *D'Ambois* carrie it cleane?　　　*Exeunt* LADIES.

BARRISOR True, when he curvets in the blanquet.

PYRHOT I marie sir.

L'ANOU Sfoote, see how he stares on's.

BARRISOR Lord blesse us, let's away.

BUSSY Now sir, take your full view: how does the Object please ye?

BARRISOR If you aske my opinion sir, I thinke your suit sits as well
　　as if't had beene made for you.

BUSSY So sir, and was that the subject of your ridiculous joilitie?

170　L'ANOU What's that to you sir?

BUSSY Sir, I have observ'd all your fleerings; and resolve your selves
　　yee shall give a strickt account for't.

　　　Enter BRISAC, MELYNELL.

PYRHOT O strange credulitie! Doe you thinke your selfe such a
　　singular subject for laughter, that none can fall into our meriment
　　but you?

BARRISOR This jealousie of yours sir, confesses some close defect in
　　your selfe, that wee never dream'd of.

L'ANOU We held discourse of a perfum'd Asse, that being disguis'd
　　with a Lions case, imagin'd himselfe a Lion: I hope that toucht
180　not you.

BUSSY So sir: Your descants doe marvellous well fit this ground, wee
　　shall meete where your Buffonly laughters will cost ye the best
　　blood in your bodies.

BARRISOR For lifes sake let's be gone; hee'll kill's outright.

BUSSY Goe at your pleasures, Ile be your Ghost to haunt you, and
　　yee sleepe an't, hang mee.

L'ANOU Goe, goe sir, Court your mistresse.

PYRHOT And be advis'd: we shall have odds against you.

BUSSY Tush, valour stands not in number: Ile maintaine it, that one
190　man may beat three boies.

BRISAC Nay you shall have no ods of him in number sir: hee's a
　　gentleman as good as the proudest of you, and yee shall not wrong
　　him.

BARRISOR Not sir?

MELYNELL Not sir: Though he be not so rich, hee's a better man
than the best of you; And I will not endure it.

L'ANOU Not you sir?

BRISAC No sir, nor I.

BUSSY I should thanke you for this kindnesse, if I thought these
perfum'd muske-Cats (being out of this priviledge) durst but once   200
mew at us.

BARRISOR Does your confident spirit doubt that sir? Come follow
us and trie.

L'ANOU Come sir, wee'll lead you a dance.   *Exeunt.*

Finis Actus primi.

Act II. Scene 1

HENRY, GUISE, BEAUMOND, *and Attendants.*

HENRY This desperate quarrell sprung out of their envies
To *D'Ambois* sudden braverie, and great spirit.

GUISE Neither is worth their envie.

HENRY   Lesse then either
Will make the Gall of Envie overflow;
She feedes on outcast entrailes like a Kite:
In which foule heape, if any ill lies hid,
She sticks her beake into it, shakes it up,
And hurl's it all abroad, that all may view it.
Corruption is her Nutriment; but touch her
With any precious ointment, and you kill her: 10
When she findes any filth in men, she feasts,
And with her blacke throat bruits it through the world
(Being sound and healthfull) But if she but taste
The slenderest pittance of commended vertue,
She surfets of it, and is like a flie,
That passes all the bodies soundest parts,
And dwels upon the sores; or if her squint eie
Have power to finde none there, she forges some:
She makes that crooked ever which is strait;

20   Call's valour giddinesse, Justice Tyrannie:
   A wise man may shun her, she not her selfe;
   Whither soever she flies from her Harmes,
   She beares her Foe still claspt in her owne Armes:
   And therefore cousen *Guise* let us avoid her.
    Enter NUNCIUS.

NUNCIUS What *Atlas*, or *Olympus* lifts his head
   So farre past Covert, that with aire enough
   My words may be inform'd? And from his height
   I may be seene, and heard through all the world?
   A tale so worthie, and so fraught with wonder,
30   Sticks in my jawes, and labours with event.

HENRY Com'st thou from *D'Ambois?*

NUNCIUS   From him, and the rest
   His friends and enemies; whose sterne fight I saw,
   And heard their words before, and in the fray.

HENRY Relate at large what thou hast seene and heard.

NUNCIUS I saw fierce *D'Ambois*, and his two brave friends
   Enter the Field, and at their heeles their foes;
   Which were the famous souldiers; *Barrisor*,
   L'Anou, and *Pyrrhot*, great in deedes of Armes:
   All which arriv'd at the evenest peece of earth
40   The field affoorded; The three Challengers
   Turn'd head, drew all their rapiers, and stoode ranckt:
   When face to face the three Defendants met them,
   Alike prepar'd, and resolute alike,
   Like bonfires of Contributorie wood:
   Everie mans looke shew'd, Fed with eithers spirit,
   As one had beene a mirror to another,
   Like formes of life and death each tooke from other;
   And so were life and death mixt at their heights,
   That you could see no feare of death, for life;
50   Nor love of life, for death: But in their browes
   Pyrrho's Opinion in great letters shone;
   That life and death in all respects are one.

HENRY Past there no sort of words at their encounter?

NUNCIUS As *Hector*, twixt the Hosts of *Greece* and *Troy*,
   (When *Paris* and the Spartane King should end

The nine yeeres warre) held up his brasen launce
For signall, that both Hosts should cease from Armes,
And heare him speake: So *Barrisor* (advis'd)
Advanc'd his Naked Rapier twixt both sides,
Ript up the Quarrell, and compar'd six lives,   60
Then laid in ballance with six idle words,
Offer'd remission and contrition too;
Or else that he and *D'Ambois* might conclude
The others dangers. *D'Ambois* lik'd the last;
But *Barrisors* friends (being equally engag'd
In the maine Quarrell) never would expose
His life alone, to that they all deserv'd.
And (for the other offer of remission)
D'Ambois (that like a Lawrell put in fire,
Sparkl'd and spit) did much much more than scorne,   70
That his wrong should incense him so like chaffe,
To goe so soone out; and like lighted paper,
Approove his spirit at once both fire and ashes:
So drew they lots, and in them Fates appointed,
That *Barrisor* should fight with firie *D'Ambois*;
Pyrhot with *Melynell*; with *Brisac L'Anou*:
And then like flame and Powder they commixt,
So spritely, that I wisht they had beene spirits,
That the ne're shutting wounds, they needes must open,
Might as they open'd, shut, and never kill: 80
But *D'Ambois* sword (that lightned as it flew)
Shot like a pointed Comet at the face
Of manly *Barrisor*; and there it stucke:
Thrice pluckt he at it, and thrice drew on thrusts,
From him, that of himselfe was free as fire;
Who thrust still as he pluckt, yet (past beliefe!)
He with his subtle eie, hand, bodie, scap't;
At last the deadly bitten point tugg'd off,
On fell his yet undaunted Foe so fiercely,
That (only made more horrid with his wound)   90
Great *D'Ambois* shrunke, and gave a little ground;
But soone return'd, redoubled in his danger,
And at the heart of *Barrisor* seal'd his anger:

Then, as in *Arden* I have seene an Oke
Long shooke with tempests, and his loftie toppe
Bent to his roote, which being at length made loose
(Even groaning with his weight) he gan to Nodde
This way and that: as loth his curled Browes
(Which he had oft wrapt in the skie with stormes)
100   Should stoope: and yet, his radicall fivers burst,
Storme-like he fell, and hid the feare-cold Earth.
So fell stout *Barrisor*, that had stoode the shockes
Of ten set Battles in your Highnesse warre,
Gainst the sole souldier of the world, *Navarre*.

GUISE   O pitious and horrid murther!

BEAUMOND   Such a life
Me thinkes had mettall in it to survive
An age of men.

HENRY   Such, often soonest end.
Thy felt report cals on, wee long to know
On what events the other have arriv'd.

110   NUNCIUS   Sorrow and furie, like two opposite fumes,
Met in the upper Region of a Cloud,
At the report made by this worthies fall,
Brake from the earth, and with them rose Revenge,
Entring with fresh powers his two noble friends;
And under that ods fell surcharg'd *Brisac*,
The friend of *D'Ambois*, before fierce *L'Anou*;
Which *D'Ambois* seeing, as I once did see
In my yoong travels through *Armenia*,
An angrie Unicorne in his full carier
120   Charge with too quicke an eie a Jeweller,
That watcht him for the Treasure of his browe;
And ere he could get shelter of a tree,
Naile him with his rich Antler to the Earth:
So *D'Ambois* ranne upon reveng'd *L'Anou*,
Who eying th'eager point borne in his face,
And giving backe, fell backe, and in his fall
His foes uncurbed sword stopt in his heart:
By which time all the life strings of the tw'other

Were cut, and both fell as their spirits flew
Upwards: and still hunt Honour at the view.   130
And now (of all the six) sole *D'Ambois* stood
Untoucht, save only with the others blood.

HENRY All slaine outright?

NUNCIUS   All slaine outright but he,
Who kneeling in the warme life of his friends
(All feebled with the blood, his Rapier raind)
He kist their pale cheekes, and bade both farewell;
And see the bravest man the French earth beares.
    Enter MONSIEUR, D'AMBOIS *bare.*

BUSSY Now is the time, y'are Princely vow'd my friend,
Performe it Princely, and obtaine my pardon.

MONSIEUR Else Heaven, forgive not me: Come on brave friend.   140
If ever Nature held herselfe her owne,
When the great Triall of a King and subject
Met in one blood, both from one bellie springing:
Now proove her vertue and her greatnesse One,
Or make the t'one the greater with the t'other,
(As true Kings should) and for your brothers love,
(Which is a speciall species of true vertue)
Doe that you could not doe, not being a King.

HENRY Brother I know your suit; these wilfull murthers
Are ever past our pardon.

MONSIEUR   Manly slaughter   150
Should never beare th'account of wilfull murther;
It being a spice of justice, where with life
Offending past law, equall life is laid
In equall ballance, to scourge that offence
By law of reputation, which to men
Exceedes all positive law, and what that leaves
To true mens valours (not prefixing rights
Of satisfaction, suited to their wrongs)
A free mans eminence may supplie and take.

HENRY This would make everie man that thinks him wrongd,   160
Or is offended, or in wrong or right,
Lay on this violence, and all vaunt themselves
Law-menders and suppliers though meere Butchers;

Should this fact (though of justice) be forgiven?

MONSIEUR O no, my Lord; it would make Cowards feare
To touch the reputations of full men;
When only they are left to impe the law,
Justice will soone distinguish murtherous mindes
From just revengers: Had my friend beene slaine
(His enemie surviving) he should die,
Since he had added to a murther'd fame
(Which was in his intent) a murther'd man;
And this had worthily beene wilfull murther:
But my friend only sav'd his fames deare life,
Which is above life, taking th'under value,
Which in the wrong it did, was forfeit to him;
And in this fact only preserves a man
In his uprightnesse; worthie to survive
Millions of such as murther men, alive.

HENRY Well brother, rise, and raise your friend withall
From death to life: and *D'Ambois*, let your life
(Refin'd by passing through this merited death)
Be purg'd from more such foule pollution;
Nor on your scape, nor valour more presuming,
To be againe so violent.

BUSSY   My Lord,
I loth as much a deede of unjust death,
As law it selfe doth; and to Tyrannise,
Because I have a little spirit to dare,
And power to doe, as to be Tyranniz'd;
This is a grace that (on my knees redoubled)
I crave to double this my short lifes gift;
And shall your royall bountie Centuple,
That I may so make good what God and nature
Have given mee for my good: since I am free,
(Offending no just law) let no law make
By any wrong it does, my life her slave:
When I am wrong'd and that law failes to right me,
Let me be King my selfe (as man was made)
And doe a justice that exceedes the law:
If my wrong passe the power of single valour

To right and expiate; then be you my King,
And doe a Right, exceeding Law and Nature:
Who to himselfe is law, no law doth neede,
Offends no King, and is a King indeede.

HENRY   Enjoy what thou intreat'st, we give but ours.

BUSSY   What you have given, my Lord, is ever yours.

     Exit Rex cum BEAUMOND, [NUNCIUS *and Attendants*].

GUISE   Mort dieu, who would have pardon'd such a murther? *Exit.*

MONSIEUR   Now vanish horrors into Court attractions,
 For which let this balme make thee fresh and faire.

BUSSY   How shall I quite your love?

MONSIEUR   Be true to the end: 210
 I have obtain'd a Kingdome with my friend.   *Exeunt.*

[*Act II. Scene 2*]

MONTSURRY, TAMYRA, BEAUPRE, PERO *with a Booke,*
CHARLOTTE, PYRHA.

MONTSURRY   He will have pardon sure.

TAMYRA   Twere pittie else:
 For though his great spirit something overflow,
 All faults are still borne, that from greatnesse grow:
 But such a sudden Courtier saw I never.

BEAUPRE   He was too sudden, which indeede was rudenesse.

TAMYRA   True, for it argued his no due conceit
 Both of the place, and greatnesse of the persons:
 Nor of our sex: all which (we all being strangers
 To his encounter) should have made more maners
 Deserve more welcome.

MONTSURRY   All this fault is found   10
 Because he lov'd the Dutchesse and left you.

TAMYRA   Ahlas, love give her joy; I am so farre
 From Envie of her honour, that I sweare,
 Had he encounterd me with such proud sleight,
 I would have put that project face of his
 To a more test, than did her Dutchesship.

BEAUPRE Why (by your leave my Lord) Ile speake it heere,
  (Although she be my ante) she scarce was modest,
  When she perceiv'd the Duke her husband take
20 Those late exceptions to her servants Courtship
  To entertaine him.

TAMYRA   I, and stand him still,
  Letting her husband give her servant place:
  Though he did manly, she should be a woman.
      Enter GUISE.

GUISE *D'Ambois* is pardond: wher's a king? where law?
  See how it runnes, much like a turbulent sea;
  Heere high, and glorious, as it did contend
  To wash the heavens, and make the stars more pure:
  And heere so low, it leaves the mud of hell
  To every common view: come count *Montsurry*
  We must consult of this.

30 TAMYRA   Stay not, sweet Lord.

MONTSURRY Be pleas'd, Ile strait returne.   *Exit cum* GUISE.

TAMYRA   Would that would please me.

BEAUPRE Ile leave you Madam to your passions.
  I see, ther's change of weather in your lookes.
                Exit cum suis [CHARLOTTE *and* PYRHA].

TAMYRA I cannot cloake it: but, as when a fume,
  Hot, drie and grosse, within the wombe of earth
  Or in her superficies begot:
  When extreame cold hath stroke it to her heart,
  The more it is comprest, the more it rageth;
  Exceeds his prisons strength that should containe it,
40 And then it tosseth Temples in the aire;
  Alle barres made engines, to his insolent fury:
  So, of a sudden, my licentious fancy
  Riots within me: not my name and house
  Nor my religion to this houre observ'd
  Can stand above it: I must utter that
  That will in parting breake more strings in me,
  Than death when life parts: and that holy man
  That, from my cradle, counseld for my soule,
  I now must make an agent for my bloud.

Enter MONSIEUR.

MONSIEUR Yet, is my Mistresse gratious?

TAMYRA   Yet unanswer'd?   50

MONSIEUR Pray thee regard thine owne good, if not mine,
   And cheere my Love for that; you do not know
   What you may be by me, nor what without me;
   I may have power t'advance and pull downe any.

TAMYRA Thats not my study: one way I am sure
   You shall not pull downe me: my husbands height
   Is crowne to all my hopes: and his retiring
   To any meane state, shalbe my aspiring:
   Mine honour's in mine owne hands, spite of kings.

MONSIEUR Honour, whats that? your second maidenhead: 60
   And what is that? a word: the word is gone,
   The thing remaines: the rose is pluckt, the stalke
   Abides: an easie losse where no lack's found:
   Beleeve it ther's as small lacke in the losse,
   As there is paine i'th'losing: archers ever
   Have two strings to a bow: and shall great *Cupid*
   (Archer of archers both in men and women)
   Be worse provided than a common archer?
   A husband and a friend all wise wives have.

TAMYRA Wise wives they are that on such strings depend,   70
   With a firme husband, weighing a dissolute friend.

MONSIEUR Still you stand on your husband, so doe all
   The common sex of you, when y'are encounterd
   With one ye cannot fancie: all men know
   You live in court heere by your owne election,
   Frequenting all our solemne sports and triumphs,
   All the most youthfull companie of men:
   And wherefore doe you this? To please your husband?
   Tis grosse and fulsome: if your husbands pleasure
   Be all your Object, and you aime at Honour,   80
   In living close to him, get you from Court,
   You may have him at home; these common Put-ofs
   For common women serve: my honor? husband?
   Dames maritorious, ne're were meritorious:
   Speake plaine and say I do not like you Sir,

Y'are an illfavor'd fellow in my eie,
And I am answer'd.

TAMYRA   Then I pray be answer'd:
For in good faith my Lord I do not like you
In that sort you like.

MONSIEUR   Then have at you heere:

90   Take (with a politique hand) this rope of Pearle;
And though you be not amorous: yet be wise:
Take me for wisdome; he that you can love
Is neere the further from you.

TAMYRA   Now it comes
So ill prepar'd, that I may take a poison,
Under a medicine as good cheape as it:
I will not have it were it worth the world.

MONSIEUR Horror of death: could I but please your eie,
You would give me the like, ere you would loose me:
Honor and husband?

TAMYRA   By this light my Lord

100   Y'are a vile fellow: and Ile tell the King
Your occupation of dishonouring Ladies
And of his Court: a Lady cannot live
As she was borne; and with that sort of pleasure
That fits her state: but she must be defam'd
With an infamous Lords detraction:
Who would endure the Court if these attempts,
Of open and profest lust must be borne?
Whose there? [*To* PERO] come on Dame, you are at your booke
When men are at your mistresse; have I taught you

110   Any such waiting womans qualitie?

MONSIEUR Farewell good husband.   *Exit* MONSIEUR.
TAMYRA   Farewell wicked Lord.
        Enter MONTSURRY.
MONTSURRY Was not the *Monsieur* heere?
TAMYRA   Yes, to good purpose.
And your cause is as good to seeke him too
And haunt his company.
MONTSURRY   Why what's the matter?
TAMYRA Matter of death, were I some husbands wife:

    I cannot live at quiet in my chamber
    For opportunities almost to rapes
    Offerd me by him.

MONTSURRY   Pray thee beare with him:
    Thou know'st he is a Bachelor, and a Courtier,
    I, and a Prince: and their prerogatives   120
    Are, to their lawes, as to their pardons are
    Their reservations, after Parliaments
    One quits another: forme gives al their essence:
    That Prince doth high in vertues reckoning stand
    That will entreat a vice, and not command:
    So far beare with him: should another man
    Trust to his priviledge, he should trust to death:
    Take comfort then (my comfort) nay triumph,
    And crown thy selfe, thou part'st with victory:
    My presence is so only deare to thee,   130
    That other mens appeare worse than they be.
    For this night yet, beare with my forced absence:
    Thou know'st my businesse; and with how much weight,
    My vow hath charg'd it.

TAMYRA   True my Lord, and never
    My fruitlesse love shall let your serious profit,
    Yet, sweet Lord, do not stay, you know my soule
    Is so long time without me, and I dead
    As you are absent.

MONTSURRY   By this kisse, receive
    My soule for hostage, till I see my love.

TAMYRA The morne shall let me see you.

MONTSURRY   With the sunne   140
    Ile visit thy more comfortable beauties.

TAMYRA This is my comfort, that the sunne hath left
    The whole worlds beauty ere my sunne leaves me.

MONTSURRY Tis late night now indeed: farewell my light.   *Exit.*

TAMYRA Farewell my light and life: But not in him.
    Alas, that in the wane of our affections
    We should supplie it with a full dissembling,
    In which each yoongest maid is growne a mother;
    Frailtie is fruitfull, one sinne gets another:

150   Our loves like sparkles are that brightest shine,
      When they goe out; most vice shewes most divine:
      Goe maid, to bed, lend me your booke I pray:
      Not like your selfe, for forme; Ile this night trouble
      None of your services: Make sure the doores,
      And call your other fellowes to their rest.

PERO I will, yet I will watch to know why you watch.   *Exit.*

TAMYRA Now all the peacefull regents of the night,
      Silently-gliding exhalations,
      Languishing windes, and murmuring fals of waters,
160   Sadnesse of heart, and ominous securenesse,
      Enchantments, dead sleepes, all the friends of rest,
      That ever wrought upon the life of man,
      Extend your utmost strengths; and this charm'd houre
      Fix like the Center; make the violent wheeles
      Of Time and Fortune stand; and Great Existens
      (The Makers treasurie) now not seeme to bee,
      To all but my approaching friends and mee:
      They come, alas they come, feare, feare and hope
      Of one thing, at one instant fight in mee:
170   I love what most I loath, and cannot live
      Unlesse I compasse that that holds my death:
      For love is hatefull without love againe,
      And he I love, will loth me, when he sees
      I flie my sex, my vertue, my Renowne,
      To runne so madly on a man unknowne.   *The Vault opens.*
      See, see the gulfe is opening, that will swallow
      Me and my fame for ever; I will in,
      And cast my selfe off, as I ne're had beene.   *Exit.*
        Ascendit Frier [COMOLET] *and* D'AMBOIS.

COMOLET Come worthiest sonne, I am past measure glad,
180   That you (whose worth I have approov'd so long)
      Should be the Object of her fearefull love;
      Since both your wit and spirit can adapt
      Their full force to supplie her utmost weakenesse:
      You know her worths and vertues, for Report
      Of all that know, is to a man a knowledge:
      You know besides, that our affections storme,

Rais'd in our blood, no Reason can reforme.
Though she seeke then their satisfaction,
(Which she must needes, or rest unsatisfied)
Your judgement will esteeme her peace thus wrought,   190
Nothing lesse deare, than if your selfe had sought:
And (with another colour, which my Art
Shall teach you to lay on) your selfe must seeme
The only agent, and the first Orbe Move,
In this our set, and cunning world of Love.

BUSSY   Give me the colour (my most honour'd Father)
And trust my cunning then to lay it on.

COMOLET   Tis this, good sonne; Lord *Barrisor* (whom you slew)
Did love her dearely, and with all fit meanes
Hath urg'd his acceptation, of all which   200
She keepes one letter written in his blood:
You must say thus then, That you heard from mee
How much her selfe was toucht in conscience
With a Report (which is in truth disperst)
That your maine quarrell grew about her love,
Lord *Barrisor* imagining your Courtship
Of the great *Guises* Duchesse in the Presence,
Was by you made to his elected mistresse:
And so made me your meane now to resolve her,
Chosing (by my direction) this nights depth,   210
For the more cleere avoiding of all note
Of your presumed presence, and with this
(To cleere her hands of such a lovers blood)
She will so kindely thanke and entertaine you,
(Me thinkes I see how) I, and ten to one,
Shew you the confirmation in his blood,
Lest you should thinke report and she did faine,
That you shall so have circumstantiall meanes,
To come to the direct, which must be used:
For the direct is crooked; Love comes flying;   220
The height of love is still wonne with denying.

BUSSY   Thankes honour'd Father.

COMOLET   She must never know
That you know any thing of any love

    Sustain'd on her part: For learne this of mee;
    In any thing a woman does alone,
    If she dissemble, she thinkes tis not done;
    If not dissemble, nor a little chide,
    Give her her wish, she is not satisfi'd;
    To have a man thinke that she never seekes,
230   Does her more good than to have all she likes:
    This frailtie sticks in them beyond their sex;
    Which to reforme, reason is too perplex:
    Urge reason to them, it will doe no good;
    Humour (that is the charriot of our foode
    In everie bodie) must in them be fed,
    To carrie their affections by it bred.
    Stand close.

      Enter TAMYRA.

TAMYRA Alas, I feare my strangenesse will retire him:
    If he goe backe, I die; I must prevent it,
240   And cheare his onset with my sight at least,
    And thats the most; though everie step he takes
    Goes to my heart, Ile rather die than seeme
    Not to be strange to that I most esteeme.

COMOLET Madam.

TAMYRA   Ah.

COMOLET   You will pardon me, I hope,
    That, so beyond your expectation,
    (And at a time for visitants so unfit)
    I (with my noble friend heere) visit you:
    You know that my accesse at any time
    Hath ever beene admitted; and that friend
250   That my care will presume to bring with mee,
    Shall have all circumstance of worth in him,
    To merit as free welcome as my selfe.

TAMYRA O father, but at this suspicious houre
    You know how apt best men are to suspect us,
    In any cause, that makes suspicious shadow
    No greater than the shadow of a haire:
    And y'are to blame: what though my Lord and husband
    Lie foorth to night? and since I cannot sleepe

When he is absent, I sit up to night,
Though all the doores are sure, & all our servants   260
As sure bound with their sleepes; yet there is one
That sits above, whose eie no sleepe can binde:
He sees through doores, and darkenesse, and our thoughts;
And therefore as we should avoid with feare,
To thinke amisse our selves before his search;
So should we be as curious to shunne
All cause that other thinke not ill of us.

BUSSY Madam, tis farre from that: I only heard
By this my honour'd father, that your conscience
Was something troubled with a false report;   270
That *Barrisors* blood should something touch your hand,
Since he imagin'd I was courting you,
When I was bold to change words with the Duchesse,
And therefore made his quarrell; which my presence
(Presum'd on with my father at this season,
For the more care of your so curious honour)
Can well resolve your Conscience, is most false.

TAMYRA And is it therefore that you come good sir?
Then crave I now your pardon and my fathers,
And sweare your presence does me so much comfort,   280
That all I have, it bindes to your requitall:
Indeede sir, tis most true that a report
Is spread, alleaging that his love to mee
Was reason of your quarrell, and because
You shall not thinke I faine it for my glorie,
That he importun'd me for his Court service,
Ile shew you his owne hand, set downe in blood
To that vaine purpose: Good Sir, then come in.
Father I thanke you now a thousand fold.

                    Exeunt TAMYRA *and* D'AMBOIS.

COMOLET May it be worth it to you honour'd daughter.   290

                              Descendit Fryar.

                    Finis Actus secundi.

Act III. Scene 1

BUSSY, TAMYRA

TAMYRA O my deare servant, in thy close embraces,
    I have set open all the dores of danger
    To my encompast honor, and my life:
    Before I was secure against death and hell;
    But now am subject to the hartlesse feare
    Of every shadow, and of every breath,
    And would change firmnesse with an aspen leafe:
    So confident a spotlesse conscience is;
    So weake a guilty: O the dangerous siege
10   Sin laies about us! and the tyranny
    He exercises when he hath expugn'd:
    Like to the horror of a winters thunder,
    Mixt with a gushing storme, that suffer nothing
    To stirre abroad on earth, but their own rages,
    Is sin, when it hath gather'd head above us:
    No roofe, no shelter can secure us so,
    But he will drowne our cheeks in feare or woe.

BUSSY Sin is a coward Madam, and insults
    But on our weaknesse, in his truest valour:
20   And so our ignorance tames us, that we let
    His shadowes fright us: and like empty clouds
    In which our faulty apprehensions fordge
    The formes of Dragons, Lions, Elephants,
    When they hold no proportion: the slie charmes
    Of the witch policy makes him, like a monster
    Kept onely to shew men for Goddesse money:
    That false hagge often paints him in her cloth
    Ten times more monstrous than he is in troth:
    In three of us, the secret of our meeting,
30   Is onely guarded, and three friends as one
    Have ever beene esteem'd: as our three powers
    That in our one soule, are, as one united:
    Why should we feare then? for my truth I sweare

Sooner shall torture, be the Sire to pleasure,
And health be grievous to men long time sicke,
Than the deare jewell of your fame in me,
Be made an outcast to your infamy;
Nor shall my value (sacred to your vertues)
Onely give free course to it, from my selfe:
But make it flie out of the mouths of kings 40
In golden vapours, and with awfull wings.

TAMYRA It rests as all kings seales were set in thee. *Exit* D'AMBOIS.
    It is not I, but urgent destiny, *Manet* TAMYRA.
    That (as great states men for their generall end
    In politique justice, make poore men offend)
    Enforceth my offence to make it just:
    What shall weake Dames doe, when th'whole worke of Nature
    Hath a strong finger in each one of us?
    Needs must that sweep away the silly cobweb
    Of our still-undone labours; that laies still 50
    Our powers to it: as to the line, the stone,
    Not to the stone, the line should be oppos'd;
    We cannot keepe our constant course in vertue:
    What is alike at all parts? every day
    Differs from other: every houre and minute:
    I, every thought in our false clock of life,
    Oft times inverts the whole circumference:
    We must be sometimes one, sometimes another:
    Our bodies are but thicke clouds to our soules;
    Through which they cannot shine when they desire: 60
    When all the starres, and even the sunne himselfe,
    Must stay the vapors times that he exhales
    Before he can make good his beames to us:
    O how can we, that are but motes to him,
    Wandring at randon in his orderd rayes,
    Disperse our passions fumes, with our weake labors,
    That are more thick & black than all earths vapors?
      Enter MONTSURRY.

MONTSURRY Good day, my love: what up and ready too!
TAMYRA Both, (my deare Lord) not all this night made I
    My selfe unready, or could sleepe a winke. 70

MONTSURRY Ahlasse, what troubled my true love, my peace,
From being at peace within her better selfe?
Or how could sleepe forbeare to sease thy beauties
When he might challenge them as his just prise?

TAMYRA I am in no powre earthly, but in yours;
To what end should I goe to bed my Lord,
That wholly mist the comfort of my bed?
Or how should sleepe possesse my faculties,
Wanting the proper closer of mine eies?

80 MONTSURRY Then will I never more sleepe night from thee:
All mine owne Businesse, all the Kings affaires
Shall take the day to serve them: Everie night
Ile ever dedicate to thy delight.

TAMYRA Nay, good my Lord esteeme not my desires
Such doters on their humours, that my judgement
Cannot subdue them to your worthier pleasure:
A wives pleas'd husband must her object be
In all her acts, not her sooth'd fantasie.

MONTSURRY Then come my love, Now pay those Rites to sleepe
90 Thy faire eies owe him: shall we now to bed?

TAMYRA O no my Lord, your holy Frier saies,
All couplings in the day that touch the bed,
Adulterous are, even in the married;
Whose grave and worthie doctrine, well I know,
Your faith in him will liberally allow.

MONTSURRY Hee's a most learned and Religious man;
Come to the Presence then, and see great *D'Ambois*
(Fortunes proud mushrome shot up in a night)
Stand like an *Atlas* underneath the King;

100 Which greatnesse with him *Monsieur* now envies
As bitterly and deadly as the *Guise*.

TAMYRA What, he that was but yesterday his maker?
His raiser and preserver?

MONTSURRY   Even the same.
Each naturall agent workes but to this end,
To render that it works on, like it selfe;
Which since the *Monsieur* in his act on *D'Ambois*,
Cannot to his ambitious end effect,

But that (quite opposite) the King hath power
(In his love borne to *D'Ambois*) to convert
The point of *Monsieurs* aime on his owne breast,   110
He turnes his outward love to inward hate:
A Princes love is like the lightnings fume,
Which no man can embrace, but must consume.   *Exeunt.*

[*Act III. Scene 2*]

HENRY, D'AMBOIS, MONSIEUR, GUISE, DUTCHES, ANNABELL, CHARLOT, *Attendants.*

HENRY Speake home my *Bussy*, thy impartiall wordes
Are like brave Faulcons that dare trusse a Fowle
Much greater than themselves; Flatterers are Kites
That checke at nothing; thou shalt be my Eagle,
And beare my thunder underneath thy wings:
Truths words like jewels hang in th'eares of Kings.
BUSSY Would I might live to see no Jewes hang there
In steede of jewels; sycophants I meane,
Who use truth like the Divell, his true Foe,
Cast by the Angell to the pit of feares,   10
And bound in chaines; truth seldome decks Kings eares:
Slave flatterie (like a Rippiers legs rowl'd up
In bootes of haie-ropes) with Kings soothed guts
Swadled and strappl'd, now lives only free.
O tis a subtle knave; how like the plague
Unfelt, he strikes into the braine of truth,
And rageth in his entrailes when he can,
Worse than the poison of a red hair'd man.
HENRY Flie at him and his broode, I cast thee off,
And once more give thee surname of mine Eagle.   20
BUSSY Ile make you sport enough then, let me have
My lucerns too (or dogges inur'd to hunt
Beasts of most rapine) but to put them up,
And if I trusse not, let me not be trusted:
Shew me a great man (by the peoples voice,

Which is the voice of God) that by his greatnesse
Bumbasts his private roofes, with publique riches;
That affects royaltie, rising from a clapdish;
That rules so much more than his suffering King,
30 That he makes kings of his subordinate slaves:
Himselfe and them graduate like woodmongers
(Piling a stacke of billets) from the earth,
Raising each other into steeples heights;
Let him convey this on the turning proppes
Of Protean Law, and (his owne counsell keeping)
Keepe all upright; let me but Hawlke at him,
Ile play the Vulture, and so thumpe his liver,
That (like a huge unlading Argosea)
He shall confesse all, and you then may hang him.
40 Shew me a Clergie man, that is in voice
A Larke of Heaven; in heart a Mowle of earth;
That hath good living, and a wicked life;
A temperate looke, and a luxurious gut;
Turning the rents of his superfluous Cures
Into your Phesants and your Partriches;
Venting their Quintessence as men read Hebrew:
Let me but hawlke at him, and, like the other,
He shall confesse all, and you then may hang him.
Shew me a Lawyer that turnes sacred law
50 (The equall rendrer of each man his owne,
The scourge of Rapine and Extortion,
The Sanctuarie and impregnable defence
Of retir'd learning, and oppressed vertue)
Into a Harpye, that eates all but's owne,
Into the damned sins it punisheth;
Into the Synagogue of theeves and Atheists;
Blood into gold, and justice into lust:
Let me but hawlke at him, as at the tother,
He shall confesse all, and you then may hang him.
   Enter MONTSURRY, TAMYRA, *and* PERO.
60 GUISE Where will you finde such game as you would hawlke at?
BUSSY Ile hawlke about your house for one of them.
GUISE Come, y'are a glorious Ruffin, and runne proud

Of the Kings headlong graces; hold your breath,
Or by that poison'd vapour not the King
Shall backe your murtherous valour against me.

BUSSY I would the King would make his presence free
But for one charge betwixt us: By the reverence
Due to the sacred space twixt kings and subjects,
Heere would I make thee cast that popular purple,
In which thy proud soule sits and braves thy soveraigne.   70

MONSIEUR Peace, peace, I pray thee peace.

BUSSY   Let him peace first
That made the first warre.

MONSIEUR   Hee's the better man.

BUSSY And therefore may doe worst?

MONSIEUR   He has more titles.

BUSSY So *Hydra* had more heads.

MONSIEUR   Hee's greater knowne.

BUSSY His greatnesse is the peoples, mine's mine owne.

MONSIEUR Hee's noblie borne.

BUSSY   He is not, I am noble.
And noblesse in his blood hath no gradation,
But in his merit.

GUISE   Th'art not nobly borne,
But bastard to the Cardinall of *Ambois*.

BUSSY Thou liest proud Guiserd; let me flie (my Lord).   80

HENRY Not in my face (my Eagle); violence flies
The Sanctuaries of a Princes eies.

BUSSY Still shall we chide? and fome upon this bit?
Is the *Guise* only great in faction?
Stands he not by himselfe? Prooves he th'Opinion
That mens soules are without them? Be a Duke,
And lead me to the field.

GUISE   Come, follow me.

HENRY Stay them, stay, *D'Ambois*; Cosen *Guise*, I wonder
Your equall disposition brookes so ill
A man so good, that only would uphold   90
Man in his native noblesse, from whose fall
All our dissentions rise; that in himselfe
(Without the outward patches of our frailtie,

Riches and honour) knowes he comprehends
Worth with the greatest: Kings had never borne
Such boundlesse eminence over other men,
Had all maintain'd the spirit and state of *D'Ambois*,
Nor had the full impartiall hand of nature
That all things gave in her originall,
100   Without these definite terms of Mine and Thine,
Beene turn'd unjustly to the hand of Fortune:
Had all preserv'd her in her prime, like *D'Ambois*,
No envie, no disjunction had dissolv'd,
Or pluck'd out one sticke of the golden fagot,
In which the world of *Saturne* was compris'd,
Had all beene held together with the nerves,
The genius and th'ingenuous soule of *D'Ambois*.
Let my hand therefore be the Hermean rodde
To part and reconcile, and so conserve you,
110   As my combin'd embracers and supporters.

BUSSY Tis our Kings motion, and wee shall not seeme
(To worst eies) womanish, though wee change thus soone
Never so great grudge for his greater pleasure.

GUISE I seale to that, and so the manly freedome
That you so much professe, heereafter proove not
A bold and glorious licence to deprave:
To mee his hand shall proove the Hermean rodde
His grace affects, in which submissive signe
On this his sacred right hand, I lay mine.

120 BUSSY Tis well my Lord, and so your worthie greatnesse
Engender not the greater insolence,
Nor make you thinke it a Prerogative,
To racke mens freedomes with the ruder wrongs;
My hand (stucke full of lawrell, in true signe
Tis wholly dedicate to righteous peace)
In all submission kisseth th'other side.

HENRY Thankes to ye both: and kindly I invite ye
Both to a banquet where weele sacrifice
Full cups to confirmation of your loves;
130   At which (faire Ladies) I entreat your presence.

     Exeunt HENRY, D'AMBOIS, *Ladies* [*and Attendants*].

MONSIEUR What had my bounty drunke when it rais'd him?

GUISE Y'ave stucke us up a very proper flag

    That takes more winde than we with all our sailes.

MONSIEUR O so he spreds and flourishes.

GUISE   He must downe,

    Upstarts should never perch too neere a crowne.

MONSIEUR Tis true my Lord; and as this doting hand,

    Even out of earth, (like *Juno*) strooke this giant,

    So *Joves* great ordinance shalbe heere implide

    To strike him under th'*AEtna* of his pride:

    To which worke lend your hands and let us cast   140

    Where we may set snares for his gadding greatnes:

    I thinke it best, amongst our greatest women:

    For there is no such trap to catch an upstart

    As a loose downfall; and indeed their fals

    Are th'ends of all mens rising: if great men

    And wise make scapes to please advantage

    Tis with a woman: women that woorst may

    Still hold mens candles: they direct and know

    All things amisse in all men; and their women

    All things amisse in them: through whose charmd mouthes   150

    We may see all the close scapes of the Court:

    When the most royall beast of chace (being old,

    And cunning in his choice of layres and haunts)

    Can never be discover'd to the bow,

    The peece or hound: yet where his custome is

    To beat his vault, and he ruts with his hinde,

    The place is markt, and by his Venery

    He still is taken. Shall we then attempt

    The chiefest meane to that discovery heere,

    And court our greatest Ladies greatest women,   160

    With shews of love, and liberall promises?

    Tis but our breath. If something given in hand,

    Sharpen their hopes of more, twilbe well venterd.

GUISE No doubt of that: and tis an excellent point

    Of our devis'd investigation.

MONSIEUR I have already broke the ice, my Lord,

    With the most-trusted woman of your Countesse,

And hope I shall wade through to our discovery.

MONTSURRY Take say of her my Lord, she comes most fitly
And we will to the other.

Enter CHARLOTTE, ANNABLE, PERO.

170 GUISE   Y'are engag'd.

ANNABLE Nay pray my Lord forbeare.

MONTSURRY   What skittish, servant?

ANNABLE No my Lord I am not so fit for your service.

CHARLOTTE Pray pardon me now my Lord? my Lady expects me.

GUISE Ile satisfie her expectation, as far as an unkle may.

MONSIEUR Well said: a spirit of Courtship of all hands: Now mine
owne *Pero*: hast thou remembred mee for the discovery I entreated
thee to make concerning thy Mistresse? speak boldly, and be sure
of all things I have promised.

PERO Building on that you have sworne (my Lord) I may speake:
180 and much the rather, because my Lady hath not trusted me with
that I can tell you; for now I cannot be said to betray her.

MONSIEUR That's all one: so it bee not to one that will betray thee:
foorth I beseech thee.

PERO To tell you truth, my Lord, I have made a strange discovery.

MONSIEUR Excellent *Pero* thou reviv'st me: may I sincke quicke into
earth heere, if my tongue discover it.

PERO Tis thus then: This last night my Lord lay foorth: and I wondring
my Ladies sitting up, stole at midnight from my pallat: and (having
before made a hole both through the wall and arras to her inmost
190 chamber) I saw *D'Ambois* and she set close at a banquet.

MONSIEUR *D'Ambois*?

PERO Even he my Lord.

MONSIEUR Dost thou not dreame wench?

PERO No my Lord, he is the man.

MONSIEUR The divell he is, and thy Lady his dam: infinite regions
betwixt a womans tongue and her heart: is this our Goddesse of
chastity? I thought I could not be so sleighted, if shee had not her
freight besides: and therefore plotted this with her woman: deare
Pero I will advance thee for ever: but tell mee now: Gods pretious
200 it transformes me with admiration: sweet *Pero*, whom should she
trust with his conveiance? Or, all the doores being made sure, how
could his conveiance bee performed?

PERO Nay my Lord, that amazes me: I cannot by any study so much
as guesse at it.

MONSIEUR Well, lets favour our apprehensions with forbearing that
a little: for if my heart were not hoopt with adamant, the conceipt
of this would have burst it: but hearke thee.   *Whispers.*

CHARLOTTE I sweare to your Grace, all that I can conjecture touching
my Lady your Neece, is a strong affection she beares to the English
Mylor.   210

GUISE All quod you? tis enough I assure you, but tell me –

[*Whispers with* CHARLOTTE.]

MONTSURRY I pray thee resolve me: the Duke will never imagine
that I am busie about's wife: hath *D'Ambois* any privy accesse to
her?

ANNABLE No my Lord, *D'Ambois* neglects her (as she takes it) and
is therefore suspicious that either your Countesse, or the Lady
Beaupre hath closely entertaind him.

MONTSURRY Ber lady a likely suspition, and very neere the life, if
she marks it; especially of my wife.

MONSIEUR Come we'l put off all, with seeming onely to have courted;   220
away drie palme: sh'as a liver as hard as a bisket: a man may goe
a whole voyage with her, and get nothing but tempests at her
windpipe.

GUISE Heer's one (I thinke) has swallowd a porcupine, she casts
pricks from her tongue so.

MONTSURRY And heer's a peacock seemes to have devour'd one of
the Alpes, she has so swelling a spirit, and is so cold of her
kindnesse.

CHARLOTTE We be no windfals my Lord; ye must gather us with
the ladder of matrimony, or we'l hang till we be rotten.   230

MONSIEUR Indeed that's the way to make ye right openarses. But
ahlas ye have no portions fit for such husbands as we wish you.

PERO Portions my Lord, yes and such portions as your principality
cannot purchase.

MONSIEUR What, woman? what are those portions?

PERO Riddle my riddle my Lord.

MONSIEUR I, marry, wench, I thinke thy portion is a right riddle, a
man shall never finde it out: but lets heare it.

PERO You shall my Lord.

240   What's that, that being most rar's most cheape?

                   That if you sow, you never reape?

                   That when it growes most, most you in it?

                   And still you lose it when you win it:

                   That when tis commonest, tis dearest,

                   And when tis farthest off 'tis neerest?

MONSIEUR Is this your portion?

PERO Even this my Lord.

MONSIEUR Beleeve me I cannot riddle it.

PERO No my Lord, tis my chastity, which you shall neither riddle
250   nor fiddle.

MONSIEUR Your chastity? let me begin with the end of you; how is
     a womans chastitie neerest a man, when tis furthest off?

PERO Why my Lord, when you cannot get it, it goes toth' heart on
     you; and that I thinke comes most neere you: and I am sure it
     shall bee farre enough off; and so I leave you to my mercy.

                                        Exeunt women.

MONSIEUR Farewell riddle.

GUISE Farewell Medlar.

MONTSURRY Farewell winter plum.

MONSIEUR Now my Lords, what fruit of our inquisition? feele you
260   nothing budding yet? Speake good my Lord *Mountsurry.*

MONTSURRY Nothing but this: *D'Ambois* is negligent in observing
     the Duchesse, and therefore she is suspicious that your Neece or
     my wife closely entertaines him.

MONSIEUR Your wife, my Lord? Thinke you that possible?

MONTSURRY Alas, I know she flies him like her last houre.

MONSIEUR Her last houre? why that comes upon her the more she
     flies it: Does *D'Ambois* so, thinke you?

MONTSURRY Thats not worth the answering: Tis horrible to think
     with what monsters womens imaginations engrosse them when
270   they are once enamour'd, and what wonders they will worke for
     their satisfaction. They will make a sheepe valiant, a Lion fearefull.

MONSIEUR And an Asse confident, my Lord, tis true, and more will
     come forth shortly, get you to the banquet.

                         Exit GUISE *cum* MONTSURRY.

O the unsounded Sea of womens bloods,

That when tis calmest, is most dangerous;
Not any wrincle creaming in their faces,
When in their hearts are *Scylla* and *Charibdis*,
Which still are hid in monster-formed cloudes,
Where never day shines, nothing ever growes,
But weeds and poisons, that no states-man knowes;   280
Not *Cerberus* ever saw the damned nookes
Hid with the vailes of womens vertuous lookes:
I will conceale all yet, and give more time
To *D'Ambois* triall, now upon my hooke;
He awes my throat; else like *Sybillas* Cave
It should breath oracles; I feare him strangely,
And may resemble his advanced valour
Unto a spirit rais'd without a circle,
Endangering him that ignorantly rais'd him,
And for whose furie he hath learn'd no limit.   290

    Enter D'AMBOIS.

How now, what leap'st thou at?
BUSSY   O royall object.
MONSIEUR Thou dream'st awake: Object in th'emptie aire?
BUSSY Worthie the head of *Titan*, worth his chaire.
MONSIEUR Pray thee what mean'st thou?
BUSSY   See you not a Croune
  Empale the forehead of the great King *Monsieur*?
MONSIEUR O fie upon thee.
BUSSY   Sir, that is the Subject
  Of all these your retir'd and sole discourses.
MONSIEUR Wilt thou not leave that wrongfull supposition?
  This still hath made me doubt thou dost not love me.
  Wilt thou doe one thing for me then syncerelie?   300
BUSSY I, any thing, but killing of the King.
MONSIEUR Still in that discord, and ill taken note?
BUSSY Come, doe not doubt me, and command mee all things.
MONSIEUR I will not then, and now by all my love
  Shewne to thy vertues, and by all fruits else
  Alreadie sprung from that affection,
  I charge thee utter (even with all the freedome
  Both of thy noble nature and thy friendship)

The full and plaine state of me in thy thoughts.

310 BUSSY What, utter plainly what I thinke of you?
Why this swims quite against the streame of greatnesse:
Great men would rather heare their flatteries,
And if they be not made fooles, are not wise.

MONSIEUR I am no such great foole, and therefore charge thee
Even from the roote of thy free heart, display mee.

BUSSY Since you affect it in such serious termes,
If your selfe first will tell me what you thinke
As freely and as heartily of mee,
Ile be as open in my thoughts of you.

320 MONSIEUR A bargaine, of mine honour; and make this,
That proove wee in our full dissection
Never so foule, live still the sounder friends.

BUSSY What else Sir? come begin, and speake me simply.

MONSIEUR I will sweare. I thinke thee then a man,
That dares as much as a wilde horse or Tyger;
As headstrong and as bloodie; and to feede
The ravenous wolfe of thy most Caniball valour,
(Rather than not employ it) thou would'st turne
Hackster to any whore, slave to a Jew,

330 Or English usurer, to force possessions,
And cut mens throates of morgaged estates;
Or thou would'st tire thee like a Tinkers wife,
And murther market folkes, quarrell with sheepe,
And runne as mad as *Ajax*; serve a Butcher,
Doe any thing but killing of the King:
That in thy valour th'art like other naturals,
That have strange gifts in nature, but no soule
Diffus'd quite through, to make them of a peece,
But stoppe at humours, that are more absurd,

340 Childish and villanous than that hackster, whore,
Slave, cut-throat, Tinkers bitch, compar'd before:
And in those humours would'st envie, betray,
Slander, blaspheme, change each houre a religion;
Doe any thing, but killing of the King;
That in that valour (which is still my dunghill,
To which I carrie all filth in thy house)

Th'art more ridiculous and vaine-glorious
Than any Mountibancke; and impudent
Than any painted bawde; which, not to sooth
And glorifie thee like a *Jupiter Hammon,*   350
Thou eat'st thy heart in vineger; and thy gall
Turns all thy blood to poison, which is cause
Of that Tode-poole that stands in thy complexion;
And makes thee (with a cold and earthie moisture,
Which is the damme of putrifaction,
As plague to thy damn'd pride) rot as thou liv'st;
To study calumnies and treacheries;
To thy friends slaughters, like a Scrich-owle sing,
And to all mischiefs, but to kill the King.

BUSSY So: Have you said?

MONSIEUR   How thinkest thou? Doe I flatter?   360
Speake I not like a trustie friend to thee?

BUSSY That ever any man was blest withall;
So heere's for mee. I thinke you are (at worst)
No divell, since y'are like to be no king;
Of which, with any friend of yours Ile lay
This poore Stilladoe heere, gainst all the starres,
I, and gainst all your treacheries, which are more;
That you did never good, but to doe ill;
But ill of all sorts, free and for it selfe:
That (like a murthering peece, making lanes in armies,   370
The first man of a ranke, the whole ranke falling)
If you have once wrong'd one man, y'are so farre
From making him amends, that all his race,
Friends and associates fall into your chace:
That y'are for perjuries the verie prince
Of all intelligencers; and your voice
Is like an Easterne winde, that where it flies,
Knits nets of Catterpillars, with which you catch
The prime of all the fruits the kingdome yeeldes.
That your politicall head is the curst fount   380
Of all the violence, rapine, crueltie,
Tyrannie & Atheisme flowing through the realme.
That y'ave a tongue so scandalous, twill cut

> A perfect Crystall; and a breath that will
> Kill to that wall a spider; you will jest
> With God, and your soule to the divell tender
> For lust; kisse horror, and with death engender.
> That your foule bodie is a Lernean fenne
> Of all the maladies breeding in all men.
> 390   That you are utterlie without a soule:
> And (for your life) the thred of that was spunne,
> When *Clotho* slept, and let her breathing rocke
> Fall in the durt; and *Lachesis* still drawes it,
> Dipping her twisting fingers in a boule
> Defil'd, and croun'd with vertues forced soule.
> And lastly (which I must for Gratitude
> Ever remember) That of all my height
> And dearest life, you are the onlie spring,
> Only in royall hope to kill the king.
> 400   MONSIEUR   Why now I see thou lov'st mee, come to the banquet.
>
> *Exeunt.*

Finis Actus tertii.

Act IV. Scene 1

HENRY, MONSIEUR, GUISE, MONTSURRY, BUSSY,
DUCHESS, TAMYRA, BEAUPRE, PERO, CHARLOTTE,
ANNABLE, PYRHA, *with foure Pages.*

> HENRY   Ladies, ye have not done our banquet right,
> Nor lookt upon it with those cheerefull raies
> That lately turnd your breaths to flouds of gold;
> Your looks, me thinks, are not drawne out with thoughts,
> So cleere and free as heeretofore, but fare
> As if the thicke complexions of men
> Governd within them.
> BUSSY   Tis not like, my Lord,
> That men in women rule; but contrary,
> For as the Moone (of all things God created)

Not only is the most appropriate image   10
Or glasse to shew them how they wax and wane,
But in her light and motion, likewise beares
Imperiall influences that command
In all their powers, and make them wax & wane;
So women, that (of all things made of nothing)
Are the most perfect images of the Moone
(Or still-unweand sweet Moon-calves with white faces)
Not only are paternes of change to men:
But as the tender Moon-shine of their beauties
Cleeres, or is cloudy, make men glad or sad.   20

MONSIEUR But heere the Moones are chang'd (as the King notes)
And either men rule in them, or some power
Beyond their voluntary motions:
For nothing can recover their lost faces.

BUSSY None can be alwaies one: our griefes and joies
Hold severall scepters in us, and have times
For their predominance: which griefe now, in them
Doth claime, as proper to his diademe:
And grief's a naturall sicknesse of the bloud,
That time to part, asks as his comming had;   30
Onely sleight fooles griev'd, suddenly are glad;
A man may say t'a dead man, be reviv'd,
As well as to one sorrowfull, be not griev'd.
And therefore (Princely mistresse) in all warres
Against these base foes that insult on weaknesse,
And still fight hous'd, behinde the shield of Nature,
Of tyrannous law, treachery, or beastly need,
Your servant cannot helpe; authority heere
Goes with corruption; something like some States,
That back woorst men: valure to them must creepe   40
That (to themselves left) would feare him asleepe.

DUCHESS Ye all take that for granted, that doth rest
Yet to be prov'd; we all are as we were,
As merry, and as free in thought as ever.

GUISE And why then can ye not disclose your thoughts?

TAMYRA Me thinks the man hath answerd for us well.

MONSIEUR The man? why Madam d'ee not know his name?

TAMYRA Man is a name of honour for a King:
    Additions take away from each chiefe thing:
50   The Schoole of Modesty, not to learne, learnes Dames:
    They sit in high formes there, that know mens names.
MONSIEUR Harke sweet heart, heer's a bound set to your valure:
    It cannot enter heere; no, not to notice
    Of what your name is; your great Eagles beake
    (Should you flie at her) had as good encounter
    An Albion cliffe, as her more craggy liver.
BUSSY Ile not attempt her Sir; her sight and name
    (By which I only know her) doth deter me.
HENRY So do they all men else.
MONSIEUR   You would say so
    If you knew all.
60   TAMYRA   Knew all my Lord? what meane you?
MONSIEUR All that I know Madam.
TAMYRA   That you know? speake it.
MONSIEUR No tis enough I feele it.
HENRY   But me thinkes
    Her Courtship is more pure than heeretofore:
    True Courtiers should be modest, but not nice:
    Bold, but not impudent: pleasure love, not vice.
MONSIEUR Sweet heart: come hither, what if one should make
    Horns at *Mountsurry?* would it strike him jealous
    Through all the proofes of his chaste Ladies vertues?
BUSSY No I thinke not.
MONSIEUR   Not if I nam'd the man
70   With whom I would make him suspicious
    His wife hath armd his forehead?
BUSSY   So, you might
    Have your great nose made lesse indeed: and slit:
    Your eies thrust out.
MONSIEUR   Peace, peace, I pray thee peace.
    Who dares doe that? the brother of his King?
BUSSY Were your King brother in you: all your powers
    (Stretcht in the armes of great men and their bawds)
    Set close downe by you; all your stormie lawes
    Spouted with Lawyers mouths; and gushing bloud,

Like to so many Torrents: all your glories
(Making you terrible, like enchaunted flames,   80
Fed with bare cockescombes: and with crooked hammes):
All your prerogatives, your shames and tortures:
All daring heaven, and opening hell about you:
Were I the man, ye wrong'd so and provok'd:
(Though ne're so much beneath you) like a box tree
I would (out of the toughnesse of my root)
Ramme hardnesse, in my lownesse, and like death
Mounted on earthquakes, I would trot through all
Honors and horrors: through fowle and faire,
And from your whole strength tosse you into aire.   90

MONSIEUR Goe, th'art a divell; such another spirit
Could not be stild, from all Th'Armenian dragons.
O my Loves glory: heire to all I have:
(That's all I can say, and that all I sweare):
If thou outlive me, as I know thou must,
Or else hath nature no proportiond end
To her great labors: she hath breath'd a spirit
Into thy entrailes, of effect to swell
Into another great *Augustus Cæsar.*
Organes, and faculties fitted to her greatnesse: 100
And should that perish like a common spirit,
Nature's a Courtier and regards no merit.

HENRY Heer's nought but whispering with us: like a calme
Before a tempest, when the silent aire
Laies her soft eare close to the earth to hearken
For that she feares is comming to afflict her;
Some fate doth joine our eares to heare it comming.
Come, my brave eagle, let's to Covert flie:
I see Almighty *Æther* in the smoake
Of all his clowds descending: and the skie   110
Hid in the dimme ostents of Tragedy.

Exit HENRY *with* D'AMBOIS *and Ladies.*

GUISE Now stirre the humour, and begin the brawle.
MONTSURRY The King and *D'Ambois* now are growen all one.
MONSIEUR Nay, they are two my Lord.
MONTSURRY   How's that?

MONSIEUR   No more.

MONTSURRY I must have more my Lord.

MONSIEUR   What, more than two?

MONTSURRY How monstrous is this?

MONSIEUR   Why?

MONTSURRY   You make me Horns.

MONSIEUR Not I, it is a worke, without my power,
    Married mens ensignes are not made with fingers:
    Of divine Fabrique they are, Not mens hands;
120   Your wife, you know, is a Meere *Cynthia,*
    And she must fashion hornes out of her Nature.

MONTSURRY But doth she? dare you charge her? speak false
              Prince.

MONSIEUR I must not speake my Lord: but if yow'le use
    The learning of a noble man, and read,
    Heer's something to those points: soft you must pawne
    Your honour having read it to returne it.

MONTSURRY Not I, I pawne mine Honour, for a paper?

MONSIEUR You must not buie it under.

                            Exeunt GUISE *and* MONSIEUR.

    Enter TAMYRA, PERO.

MONTSURRY   Keepe it then!
    And keepe fire in your bosome.

TAMYRA   What saies he?

MONTSURRY You must make good the rest.

130 TAMYRA   How fares my Lord?
    Takes my Love any thing to heart he saies?

MONTSURRY Come y'are a –

TAMYRA   What my Lord?

MONTSURRY   The plague of *Herod*
    Feast in his rotten entrailes.

TAMYRA   Will you wreake
    Your angers just cause given by him, on mee?

MONTSURRY By him?

TAMYRA   By him my Lord, I have admir'd
    You could all this time be at concord with him,
    That still hath plaid such discords on your honour.

MONTSURRY Perhaps tis with some proud string of my wives.

TAMYRA How's that, my Lord?

MONTSURRY   Your tongue will still admire,
  Till my head be the miracle of the world.   140

TAMYRA O woe is mee.   *She seemes to sound.*

PERO   What does your Lordship meane?
  Madam, be comforted; my Lord but tries you.
  Madam? Helpe good my Lord, are you not mov'd?
  Doe your set lookes print in your words, your thoughts?
  Sweete Lord, cleere up those eies, for shame of Noblesse:
  Mercilesse creature; but it is enough,
  You have shot home, your words are in her heart;
  She has not liv'd to beare a triall now.

MONTSURRY Looke up my love, and by this kisse receive
  My soule amongst thy spirits for supplie   150
  To thine, chac'd with my furie.

TAMYRA   O my Lord,
  I have too long liv'd to heare this from you.

MONTSURRY Twas from my troubled blood, and not from mee:
  I know not how I fare; a sudden night
  Flowes through my entrailes, and a headlong Chaos
  Murmurs within mee, which I must digest;
  And not drowne her in my confusions,
  That was my lives joy, being best inform'd:
  Sweet, you must needes forgive me, that my love
  (Like to a fire disdaining his suppression)   160
  Rag'd being discourag'd; my whole heart is wounded
  When any least thought in you is but touch't,
  And shall be till I know your former merits:
  Your name and memorie altogether crave
  In loth'd oblivion their eternall grave;
  And then you must heare from me, ther's no meane
  In any passion I shall feele for you:
  Love is a rasor cleansing being well us'd,
  But fetcheth blood still being the least abus'd:
  To tell you briefly all; The man that left mee   170
  When you appear'd, did turne me worse than woman,
  And stab'd me to the heart thus, [*Making horns.*] with his hand.

TAMYRA O happie woman! Comes my staine from him?

It is my beautie, and that innocence prooves,
That slew *Chyaeæra*, rescu'd *Peleus*
From all the savage beasts in *Peleon*;
And rais'd the chaste Athenian prince from Hell:
All suffering with me; they for womens lusts,
I for a mans; that the Augean stable
Of his foule sinne would emptie in my lappe:
How his guilt shunn'd me! sacred innocence
That where thou fear'st, art dreadfull; and his face
Turn'd in flight from thee, that had thee in chace:
Come, bring me to him: I will tell the serpent
Even to his teeth (whence, in mine honors soile,
A pitcht field starts up twixt my Lord and mee)
That his throat lies, and he shall curse his fingers,
For being so govern'd by his filthie soule.

MONTSURRY   I know not, if himselfe will vaunt t'have beene
The princely author of the slavish sinne,
Or any other; he would have resolv'd mee,
Had you not come; not by his word, but writing,
Would I have sworne to give it him againe,
And pawn'd mine honour to him for a paper.

TAMYRA   See how he flies me still: Tis a foule heart
That feares his owne hand: Good my Lord make haste
To see the dangerous paper: Be not nice
For any trifle, jeweld with your honour,
To pawne your honor; and with it conferre
My neerest woman heere, in all she knowes;
Who (if the sunne or *Cerberus* could have seene
Anie staine in mee) might as much as they:
And *Pero*, heere I charge thee by my love,
And all proofes of it, (which I might call bounties)
By all that thou hast seene seeme good in mee,
And all the ill which thou shouldst spit from thee,
By pity of the wound, my Lord hath given mee,
Not as thy Mistresse now, but a poore woman
(To death given over): rid me of my paines,
Powre on thy powder: cleere thy breast of me:
My Lord is only heere: heere speake thy worst,

180

190

200

210

Thy best will doe me mischiefe; If thou spar'st mee,
Never shine good thought on thy memorie:
Resolve my Lord, and leave me desperate.

PERO My Lord? My Lord hath plaid a prodigals part,
To breake his Stocke for nothing; and an insolent,
To cut a Gordian when he could not loose it:
What violence is this, to put true fire
To a false traine? To blow up long crown'd peace
With sudden outrage? and beleeve a man   220
Sworne to the shame of women, gainst a woman
Borne to their honours: Ile attend your Lordship.

TAMYRA No, I will write (for I shall never more
Speake with the fugitive) where I will defie him,
Were he ten times the brother of my king.   *Exeunt.*

[*Act IV. Scene 2*]

Musicke: and TAMYRA *enters with her maid, bearing a letter.*

TAMYRA Away, deliver it: O may my lines   *Exit* PERO.
(Fild with the poison of a womans hate
When he shall open them) shrinke up his eies
With torturous darkenesse, such as stands in hell,
Stucke full of inward horrors, never lighted;
With which are all things to be fear'd, affrighted;
Father?

           Ascendit BUSSY *with* COMOLET.

BUSSY How is it with my honour'd mistresse?

TAMYRA O servant helpe, and save me from the gripes
Of shame and infamie.

BUSSY   What insensate stocke,
Or rude inanimate vapour without fashion,   10
Durst take into his Epimethean breast
A box of such plagues as the danger yeeldes,
Incurd in this discoverie? He had better
Ventur'd his breast in the consuming reach
Of the hot surfets cast out of the cloudes,
Or stoode the bullets that (to wreake the skie)

The *Cyclops* ramme in *Joves* artillerie.

COMOLET Wee soone will take the darkenesse from his face

That did that deede of darkenesse; wee will know

20 What now the *Monsieur* and your husband doe;

What is contain'd within the secret paper

Offerd by *Monsieur*, and your loves events:

To which ends (honour'd daughter) at your motion,

I have put on these exorcising Rites,

And, by my power of learned holinesse

Vouchsaft me from above, I will command

Our resolution of a raised spirit.

TAMYRA Good father raise him in some beauteous forme,

That with least terror I may brooke his sight.

30 COMOLET Stand sure together then, what ere ye see,

And stirre not, as ye tender all our lives.

Occidentalium legionum spiritalium imperator (*magnus ille* Behemoth) *veni,*
veni, comitatus cum Astaroth *locotenente invicto. Adjuro te per stygis inscrutabi-*
lia arcana, per ipsos irremeabiles anfractus averni: adesto ô Behemoth, *tu cui*
pervia sunt Magnatum scrinia; veni, per Noctis et tenebrarum abdita profundis-
sima; (*Thunder.*) *per labentia sydera; per ipsos motus horarum furtivos, Heca-*
tesque altum silentium: Appare in forma spiritali, lucente splendida et amabili.

Thunder. Ascendit [BEHEMOTH, CARTOPHYLAX, *and other devils*].

BEHEMOTH What would the holy Frier?

COMOLET   I would see

What now the *Monsieur* and *Mountsurrie* doe;

40 And see the secret paper that the *Monsieur*

Offer'd to Count *Montsurry*, longing much

To know on what events the secret loves

Of these two honor'd persons shall arrive.

BEHEMOTH Why call'dst thou me to this accursed light?

To these light purposes? I am Emperor

Of that inscrutable darkenesse, where are hid

All deepest truths, and secrets never seene,

All which I know, and command Legions

Of knowing spirits that can doe more than these.

50 Any of this my guard that circle mee

In these blew fires, and out of whose dim fumes

Vast murmurs use to breake, and from their soundes

Articulat voices, can doe ten parts more
Than open such sleight truths, as you require.

COMOLET From the last nights black depth, I cald up one
Of the inferior ablest ministers,
And he could not resolve mee; send one then
Out of thine owne command, to fetch the paper
That *Monsieur* hath to shew to Count *Montsurry.*

BEHEMOTH I will: *Cartophylax*: thou that properly   60
Hast in thy power all papers so inscribde:
Glide through all barres to it and fetch that paper.

CARTOPHYLAX I will.   *a torch removes.*

COMOLET   Till he returnes (great prince of darknesse)
Tell me, if *Monsieur* and the Count *Montsurry*
Are yet encounterd.

BEHEMOTH   Both them and the *Guise*
Are now together.

COMOLET   Shew us all their persons,
And represent the place, with all their actions.

BEHEMOTH The spirit will strait returne: and then Ile shew thee:

                                          [*The torch returns.*]

See he is come; why broughtst thou not the paper?

CARTOPHYLAX He hath prevented me, and got a spirit   70
Rais'd by another, great in our command,
To take the guard of it before I came.

BEHEMOTH This is your slacknesse, not t'invoke our powers
When first your acts, set foorth to their effects;
Yet shall you see it, and themselves: behold
They come heere & the Earle now holds the paper.

        Ent[*er*] MONSIEUR, GUISE, MONTSURRY *with a paper.*

BUSSY May we not heare them?

COMOLET   No, be still and see.

BUSSY I will go fetch the paper.

COMOLET   Do not stir:
Ther's too much distance and too many lockes
Twixt you & them (how neere so e're they seeme)   80
For any man to interrupt their secrets.

TAMYRA O honord spirit: flie into the fancie

Of my offended Lord: and do not let him
Beleeve what there the wicked man hath written.

BEHEMOTH Perswasion hath already enterd him
Beyond reflection; peace till their departure.

MONSIEUR There is a glasse of inke wherein you see
How to make ready black fac't Tragedy:
You now discerne, I hope through all her paintings
90   Her gasping wrinkles, and fames sepulchres.

GUISE Thinke you he faines my Lord? what hold you now?
Doe we maligne your wife: or honour you?

MONSIEUR What stricken dumbe? nay fie, Lord be not danted:
Your case is common: were it ne're so rare
Beare it as rarely: now to laugh were manly:
A woorthy man should imitate the weather
That sings in tempests: and being cleere is silent.

GUISE Goe home my Lord, and force your wife to write
Such loving stuffe to *D'Ambois* as she usde
100   When she desir'd his presence.

MONSIEUR   Doe my Lord,
And make her name her conceald messenger:
That close and most inennerable Pander
That passeth all our studies to exquire:
By whom convay the letter to her love:
And so you shall be sure to have him come
Within the thirsty reach of your revenge;
Before which, lodge an ambush in her chamber
Behind the arras of your stoutest men
All close and soundly armd: and let them share
110   A spirit amongst them, that would serve a thousand.
            Enter PERO *with a Letter.*

GUISE Yet stay a little: see she sends for you.

MONSIEUR Poore, loving lady, she'le make all good yet,
Thinke you not so my Lord?   MONTSURRY *stabs* PERO *and exit.*

GUISE   Ahlas poore soule.

MONSIEUR This was ill done y'faith.

PERO   T'was nobly done.
And I forgive his Lordship from my soule.

MONSIEUR Then much good doo't thee *Pero*: hast a letter?

PERO I hope it be, at least, if not a volume
    Of worthy curses for your perjury.
MONSIEUR Now out upon her.
GUISE   Let me see, my Lord.
MONSIEUR You shall presently: how fares my *Pero*?   120
    Whose there?
        Enter servant.
                    Take in this maid, sh'as caught a clap:
    And fetch my surgeon to her; come my Lord,
    We'l now peruse our letter.   *Exeunt* MONSIEUR, GUISE.
PERO   Furies rise
    Out of the blacke lines, and torment his soule.   *Lead her out.*
TAMYRA Hath my Lord slaine my woman?
BEHEMOTH   No, she lives.
COMOLET What shall become of us?
BEHEMOTH   All I can say
    Being cald thus late, is briefe, and darkly this:
    If *D'Ambois* mistresse, stayne not her white hand
    With his forst bloud he shall remaine untoucht:
    So father, shall your selfe, but by your selfe: 130
    To make this Augurie plainer: when the voice
    Of *D'Ambois* shall invoke me I will rise,
    Shining in greater light: and shew him all
    That will betide ye all; meane time be wise,
    And let him curb his rage, with policy.   *Descendit cum suis.*
BUSSY Will he appeare to me, when I invoke him?
COMOLET He will: be sure.
BUSSY   It must be shortly then:
    For his darke words have tied my thoughts on knots
    Till he dissolve, and free them.
TAMYRA   In meane time
    Deare servant, till your powerfull voice revoke him,   140
    Be sure to use the policy he advis'd:
    Lest fury in your too quicke knowledge taken
    Of our abuse, and your defence of me
    Accuse me more than any enemy:
    And Father, you must on my Lord impose
    Your holiest charges, and the churches power

To temper his hot spirit: and disperse
The cruelty and the bloud, I know his hand
Will showre upon our heads, if you put not
150 Your finger to the storme, and hold it up,
As my deare servant heere must do with *Monsieur*.

BUSSY Ile sooth his plots: and strow my hate with smiles
Till all at once the close mines of my heart
Rise at full date, and rush into his bloud:
Ile bind his arme in silke, and rub his flesh,
To make the vaine swell, that his soule may gush
Into some kennell, where it longs to lie,
And policy shalbe flanckt with policy.
Yet shall the feeling center where wee meet
160 Grone with the wait of my approaching feet:
Ile make th'inspired threshals of his Court
Sweat with the weather of my horrid steps
Before I enter: yet will I appeare
Like calme security, before a ruine;
A politician, must like lightening melt
The very marrow, and not Print the skin:
His waies must not be seene: the superficies
Of the greene center must not taste his feet,
When hell is plowd up with his wounding tracts:
170 And all his harvest reap't, from hellish facts.   *Exeunt.*

Finis Actus Quarti.

Act V. Scene 1

MONTSURRY *bare, unbrac't, pulling* TAMYRA *in,* COMOLET*, One
bearing light, a standish and paper, which sets a Table.*

COMOLET My Lord remember that your soule must seeke
Her peace, as well as your revengefull bloud:
You ever, to this houre have prov'd your selfe
A noble, zealous, and obedient sonne,
T'our holy mother: be not an apostate:
Your wives offence serves not, (were it the woorst

You can imagine, without greater proofes)
To sever your eternall bonds, and harts;
Much lesse to touch her with a bloudy hand:
Nor is it manly (much lesse husbandly)   10
To expiate any frailty in your wife,
With churlish strokes, or beastly ods of strength:
The stony birth of clowds, will touch no lawrell:
Nor any sleeper; your wife is your lawrell:
And sweetest sleeper; do not touch her then:
Be not more rude than the wild seed of vapor,
To her that is more gentle than it rude;
In whom kind nature sufferd one offence
But to set of, her other excellence.

MONTSURRY Good father leave us: interrupt no more   20
  The course I must run for mine honour sake.
  Relie on my love to her, which her fault
  Cannot extinguish; will she but disclose
  Who was the hatefull minister of her love,
  And through what maze he serv'd it, we are friends.

COMOLET It is a damn'd worke to pursue those secrets,
  That would ope more sinne, and proove springs of slaughter;
  Nor is't a path for Christian feete to touch;
  But out of all way to the health of soules,
  A sinne impossible to be forgiven: 30
  Which he that dares commit –

MONTSURRY   Good father cease:
  Tempt not a man distracted; I am apt
  To outrages that I shall ever rue:
  I will not passe the verge that boundes a Christian,
  Nor breake the limits of a man nor husband.

COMOLET Then God inspire ye both with thoughts and deedes
  Worthie his high respect, and your owne soules. *Exit* COMOLET.

MONTSURRY Who shall remoove the mountaine from my heart,
  Ope the seventimes-heat furnace of my thoughts,
  And set fit outcries for a soule in hell?   40

                MONTSURRY *turnes a key.*

  O now it nothing fits my cares to speake,
  But thunder, or to take into my throat

The trumpe of Heaven; with whose determinate blasts
The windes shall burst, and the enraged seas
Be drunke up in his soundes; that my hot woes
(Vented enough) I might convert to vapour,
Ascending from my infamie unseene;
Shorten the world, preventing the last breath
That kils the living, and regenerates death.

50   TAMYRA My Lord, my fault (as you may censure it
With too strong arguments) is past your pardon:
But how the circumstances may excuse mee
God knowes, and your more temperate minde heereafter
May let my penitent miseries make you know.

  MONTSURRY Heereafter? Tis a suppos'd infinite,
That from this point will rise eternally:
Fame growes in going; in the scapes of vertue
Excuses damne her: They be fires in Cities
Enrag'd with those windes that lesse lights extinguish.

60   Come Syren, sing, and dash against my rockes
Thy ruffin Gallie, laden for thy lust:
Sing, and put all the nets into thy voice,
With which thou drew'st into thy strumpets lappe
The spawne of *Venus*; and in which ye danc'd;
That, in thy laps steede, I may digge his toombe,
And quit his manhoode with a womans sleight,
Who never is deceiv'd in her deceit.
Sing, (that is, write) and then take from mine eies
The mists that hide the most inscrutable Pandar

70   That ever lapt up an adulterous vomit:
That I may see the divell, and survive
To be a divell, and then learne to wive:
That I may hang him, and then cut him downe,
Then cut him up, and with my soules beams search
The crankes and cavernes of his braine, and studie
The errant wildernesse of a womans face;
Where men cannot get out, for all the Comets
That have beene lighted at it; though they know
That Adders lie a sunning in their smiles,

80   That Basilisks drinke their poison from their eies,

And no way there to coast out to their hearts;
Yet still they wander there, and are not stai'd
Till they be fetter'd, nor secure before
All cares distract them; nor in humane state
Till they embrace within their wives two breasts
All *Pelion* and *Cythæron* with their beasts.
Why write you not?

TAMYRA   O good my Lord forbeare
In wreake of great sins, to engender greater,
And make my loves corruption generate murther.

MONTSURRY It followes needefully as childe and parent;   90
The chaine-shot of thy lust is yet aloft,
And it must murther; tis thine owne deare twinne:
No man can adde height to a womans sinne.
Vice never doth her just hate so provoke,
As when she rageth under vertues cloake.
Write: For it must be; by this ruthlesse steele,
By this impartiall torture, and the death
Thy tyrannies have invented in my entrailes,
To quicken life in dying, and hold up
The spirits in fainting, teaching to preserve   100
Torments in ashes, that will ever last.
Speake: Will you write?

TAMYRA   Sweete Lord enjoine my sinne
Some other penance than what makes it worse:
Hide in some gloomie dungeon my loth'd face,
And let condemned murtherers let me downe
(Stopping their noses) my abhorred foode.
Hang me in chaines, and let me eat these armes
That have offended: Binde me face to face
To some dead woman, taken from the Cart
Of Execution, till death and time   110
In graines of dust dissolve me; Ile endure:
Or any torture that your wraths invention
Can fright all pittie from the world withall:
But to betray a friend with shew of friendship,
That is too common, for the rare revenge
Your rage affecteth; heere then are my breasts,

Last night your pillowes; heere my wretched armes,
As late the wished confines of your life:
Now breake them as you please, and all the boundes
120 Of manhoode, noblesse, and religion.

MONTSURRY Where all these have beene broken, they are kept,
In doing their justice there: Thine armes have lost
Their priviledge in lust, and in their torture
Thus they must pay it.   *Stabs her.*

TAMYRA   O Lord.

MONTSURRY   Till thou writ'st
Ile write in wounds (my wrongs fit characters)
Thy right of sufferance. Write.

TAMYRA   O kill me, kill me:
Deare husband be not crueller than death;
You have beheld some *Gorgon*: Feele, ô feele
How you are turn'd to stone; with my heart blood
130 Dissolve your selfe againe, or you will grow
Into the image of all Tyrannie.

MONTSURRY As thou art of adulterie, I will still
Proove thee my like in ill, being most a monster:
Thus I expresse thee yet.   *Stabs her againe.*

TAMYRA   And yet I live.

MONTSURRY I, for thy monstrous idoll is not done yet:
This toole hath wrought enough: now Torture use
  Ent[er] servants [and place TAMYRA *on rack].*
This other engine on th'habituate powers
Of her thrice damn'd and whorish fortitude.
Use the most madding paines in her that ever
140 Thy venoms sok'd through, making most of death;
That she may weigh her wrongs with them, and then
Stand vengeance on thy steepest rocke, a victor.

TAMYRA O who is turn'd into my Lord and husband?
Husband? My Lord? None but my Lord and husband.
Heaven, I aske thee remission of my sinnes,
Not of my paines: husband, ô helpe me husband.
  Ascendit COMOLET.

COMOLET What rape of honour and religion?
O wracke of nature.   *Falls and dies.*

TAMYRA   Poore man: ô my father,
   Father? looke up; ô let me downe my Lord,
   And I will write.

MONTSURRY   Author of prodigies!   150
   What new flame breakes out of the firmament,
   That turnes up counsels never knowne before?
   Now is it true, earth mooves, and heaven stands still;
   Even Heaven it selfe must see and suffer ill:
   The too huge bias of the world hath swai'd
   Her backe-part upwards, and with that she braves
   This Hemisphere, that long her mouth hath mockt:
   The gravitie of her religious face
   (Now growne too waighty with her sacriledge
   And here discernd sophisticate enough)   160
   Turnes to th'*Antipodes*: and all the formes
   That her illusions have imprest in her,
   Have eaten through her backe: and now all see,
   How she is riveted with hypocrisie:
   Was this the way? was he the meane betwixt you?

TAMYRA He was, he was, kind innocent man he was.

MONTSURRY Write, write a word or two.

TAMYRA   I will, I will.
   Ile write, but in my bloud that he may see,
   These lines come from my wounds and not from me.   *Writes.*

MONTSURRY Well might he die for thought: me thinkes the frame   170
   And shaken joints of the whole world should crack
   To see her parts so disproportionate;
   And that his generall beauty cannot stand
   Without these staines in the particular man.
   Why wander I so farre? heere, heere was she
   That was a whole world without spot to me:
   Though now a world of spots; oh what a lightning
   Is mans delight in women? what a bubble,
   He builds his state, fame, life on, when he marries?
   Since all earths pleasures are so short and small,   180
   The way t'njoy it, is t'abjure it all:
   Enough: I must be messenger my selfe,
   Disguis'd like this strange creature: in, Ile after,

To see what guilty light gives this cave eies,
And to the world sing new impieties.

Exeunt [Servants], He puts the Frier in the vault and follows, She
wraps her self in the Arras.

[*Act V. Scene 2*]

D'AMBOIS *with two Pages.*

BUSSY Sit up to night, and watch, Ile speake with none
But the old frier, who bring to me.

PAGES   We will Sir.   *Exeunt.*

BUSSY What violent heat is this? me thinks the fire
Of twenty lives doth on a sudden flash
Through all my faculties: the aire goes high
In this close chamber, and the frighted earth   *Thunder.*
Trembles, and shrinkes beneath me: the whole house
Crackes with his shaken burthen; blesse me, heaven.

Enter Umbra COMOLET.

UMBRA Note what I want, my sonne, and be forewarnd:
10   O there are bloudy deeds past and to come,
I cannot stay: a fate doth ravish me:
Ile meet thee in the chamber of thy love.   *Exit.*

BUSSY What dismall change is heere? the good old Frier
Is murtherd; being made knowne to serve my love;
Note what he wants? he wants his utmost weed,
He wants his life, and body: which of these
Should be the want he meanes, and may supplie me
With any fit forewarning? this strange vision,
(Together with the darke prediction
20   Us'd by the Prince of darknesse that was raisd
By this embodied shadowe) stir my thoughts
With reminiscion of the Spirits promise;
Who told me, that by any invocation
I should have power to raise him; though it wanted
The powerfull words, and decent rites of art;
Never had my set braine such need of spirit,
T'instruct and cheere it; now then, I will claime

Performance of his free and gentle vow,
T'appeare in greater light; and make more plaine
His rugged oracle: I long to know   30
How my deare mistresse fares; and be informd
What hand she now holds on the troubled bloud
Of her incensed Lord: me thought the Spirit,
(When he had utterd his perplext presage)
Threw his chang'd countenance headlong into clowdes;
His forehead bent, as it would hide his face;
He knockt his chin against his darkned breast,
And strooke a churlish silence through his powrs;
Terror of darknesse: O thou King of flames,
That with thy Musique-footed horse dost strike   40
The cleere light out of chrystall, on darke earth;
And hurlst instructive fire about the world:
Wake, wake the drowsie and enchanted night,
That sleepes with dead eies in this heavy riddle:
Or thou great Prince of shades where never sunne
Stickes his far-darted beames: whose eies are made,
To see in darknesse: and see ever best
Where sense is blindest: open now the heart
Of thy abashed oracle: that for feare,
Of some ill it includes, would faine lie hid,   50
And rise thou with it in thy greater light.

    Thunders. Surgit Spiritus [BEHEMOTH] *cum suis.*

BEHEMOTH Thus to observe my vow of apparition,
   In greater light: and explicate thy fate:
   I come; and tell thee that if thou obay
   The summons that thy mistresse next wil send thee,
   Her hand shalbe thy death.
BUSSY   When will she send?
BEHEMOTH Soone as I set againe, where late I rose.
BUSSY Is the old Frier slaine?
BEHEMOTH   No, and yet lives not.
BUSSY Died he a naturall death?
BEHEMOTH   He did.
BUSSY   Who then,
   Will my deare mistresse send?

60   BEHEMOTH   I must not tell thee.

BUSSY Who lets thee?

BEHEMOTH   Fate.

BUSSY   Who are Fates ministers?

BEHEMOTH The *Guise* and *Monsieur.*

BUSSY   A fit paire of sheeres
 To cut the threds of kings, and kingly spirits,
 And consorts fit to sound forth harmony,
 Set to the fals of kingdomes: shall the hand
 Of my kinde Mistresse kill me?

BEHEMOTH   If thou yeeld,
 To her next summons; y'are faire warnd: farewell.

             Exit [*with Devils*].

BUSSY I must fare well, how ever: though I die,
 My death consenting with his augurie;
70   Should not my powers obay when she commands,
 My motion must be rebell to my will:
 My will, to life: If when I have obaid,
 Her hand should so reward me, they must arme it,
 Binde me and force it: or I lay my soule
 She rather would convert it, many times
 On her owne bosome: even to many deaths:
 But were there danger of such violence,
 I know tis far from her intent to send:
 And who she should send, is as far from thought
80   Since he is dead, whose only meane she usde.   *Knocks.*
 Whose there? looke to the dore: and let him in,
 Though politicke *Monsieur,* or the violent *Guise.*

   Enter MONTSURRY *like the Frier.*

MONTSURRY Haile to my worthy sonne.

BUSSY O lying Spirit: welcome loved father.
 How fares my dearest mistresse?

MONTSURRY   Well, as ever,
 Being well as ever thought on by her Lord:
 Whereof she sends this witnesse in her hand
 And praies, for urgent cause, your speediest presence,

BUSSY What? writ in bloud?

MONTSURRY   I, tis the inke of lovers.

BUSSY O tis a sacred witnesse of her love.   90
 So much elixer of her bloud as this
 Dropt in the lightest dame, would make her firme
 As heat to fire: and like to all the signes,
 Commands the life confinde in all my vaines;
 O how it multiplies my bloud with spirit,
 And makes me apt t'encounter death and hell:
 But, come kinde Father; you fetch me to heaven,
 And to that end your holy weed was given.   *Exeunt.*

[*Act V. Scene 3*]

 Enter MONSIEUR, GUISE *above.*

MONSIEUR Now shall we see, that Nature hath no end,
 In her great workes, responsive to their worths,
 That she who makes so many eies, and soules,
 To see and foresee, is starke blinde herselfe:
 And as illiterate men say Latine praiers
 By roote of heart, and daily iteration;
 In whose hot zeale, a man would thinke they knew
 What they ranne so away with, and were sure
 To have rewards proportion'd to their labours;
 Yet may implore their owne confusions   10
 For any thing they know, which oftentimes
 It fals out they incurre: So Nature laies
 A masse of stuffe together, and by use,
 Or by the meere necessitie of matter,
 Ends such a worke, fils it, or leaves it emptie,
 Of strength, or vertue, error or cleere truth;
 Not knowing what she does; but usually
 Gives that which wee call merit to a man,
 And beleeve should arrive him on huge riches,
 Honour, and happinesse, that effects his ruine;   20
 Right as in ships of warre, whole lasts of powder
 Are laid (men thinke) to make them last, and gard them;
 When a disorder'd sparke that powder taking,
 Blowes up with sudden violence and horror

       Ships that kept emptie, had sail'd long with terror.

GUISE He that observes, but like a worldly man,
       That which doth oft succeede, and by th'events
       Values the worth of things; will thinke it true,
       That Nature workes at randome, just with you:
30   But with as much decorum she may make
       A thing that from the feete up to the throat
       Hath all the wondrous fabrike man should have,
       And leave it headlesse for an absolute man,
       As give a whole man valour, vertue, learning,
       Without an end more excellent than those,
       On whom she no such worthie part bestowes.

MONSIEUR Why you shall see it here, here will be one
       Yoong, learned, valiant, vertuous, and full mand;
       One on whom Nature spent so rich a hand,
40   That, with an ominous eie, she wept to see
       So much consum'd her vertuous treasurie;
       Yet, as the windes sing through a hollow tree,
       And (since it lets them passe through) let it stand;
       But a tree solid, since it gives no way
       To their wilde rages, they rend up by th'roote:
       So this full creature now shall reele and fall,
       Before the franticke pufs of purblinde chance
       That pipes thorow emptie men, and makes them dance:
       Not so the Sea raves on the Lybian sandes,
50   Tumbling her billowes in each others necke:
       Not so the surges of the *Euxine* Sea
       (Neere to the frostie Pole, where free *Bootes*
       From those darke-deepe waves turns his radiant Teame)
       Swell being enrag'd, even from their inmost drop,
       As Fortune swings about the restlesse state
       Of vertue, now throwne into all mens hate.

     Intrat Umbra COMOLET *to the* COUNTESSE, *wrapt in a Canapie.*

UMBRA Revive those stupid thoughts, and sit not thus,
       Gathering the horrors of your servants slaughter,
       (So urg'd by your hand, and so imminent)
60   Into an idle fancie; but devise
       How to prevent it; watch when he shall rise,

And with a sudden outcrie of his murther,
Blow his retreat before he be engag'd.

TAMYRA   O father, have my dumbe woes wak'd your death?
When will our humane griefes be at their height?
Man is a tree, that hath no toppe in cares;
No roote in comforts; all his power to live
Is given to no end, but t'have power to grieve.

UMBRA   Tis the just curse of our abus'd creation,
Which wee must suffer heere, and scape heereafter: 70
He hath the great mind that submits to all,
He sees inevitable; he the small
That carps at earth, and her foundation shaker,
And rather than himselfe, will mend his maker.   *Exit.*

D'AMBOIS *at the gulfe.*

TAMYRA   Away, (my love) away, thou wilt be murther'd.

BUSSY   Murther'd? I know not what that Hebrew meanes:
That word had ne're beene nam'd had all beene *D'Ambois.*
Murther'd? By heaven he is my murtherer
That shewes me not a murtherer; what such bugge
Abhorreth not the very sleepe of *D'Ambois?*   80
Murther'd? Who dares give all the roome I see
To *D'Ambois* reach? or looke with any oddes
His fight i'th' face, upon whose hand sits death;
Whose sword hath wings, and everie feather pierceth?
Let in my politique visitants, let them in,
Though entring like so many moving armours,
Fate is more strong than arms, and slie than treason,
And I at all parts buckl'd in my fate:
Dare they not come?

Enter murtherers with Frier at the other dore.

TAMYRA   They come.

I MURDERER   Come all at once.

UMBRA   Backe coward murtherers, backe.

OMNES   Defend us heaven.   90

Exeunt all but the first.

I MURDERER   Come ye not on?

BUSSY   No, slave, nor goest thou off.
Stand you so firme? Will it not enter heere?

You have a face yet: so in thy lifes flame   [*Kills him.*]
I burne the first rites to my mistresse fame.

UMBRA Breath thee brave sonne against the other charge.

BUSSY O is it true then that my sense first told mee?
Is my kinde father dead?

TAMYRA   He is, my love.
Twas the Earle my husband in his weede that brought thee.

BUSSY That was a speeding sleight, and well resembled.
100 Where is that angrie Earle my Lord? Come forth
And shew your owne face in your owne affaire;
Take not into your noble veines the blood
Of these base villans, nor the light reports
Of blister'd tongues, for cleere and weightie truth:
But me against the world, in pure defence
Of your rare Ladie, to whose spotlesse name
I stand heere as a bulwarke, and project
A life to her renowne, that ever yet
Hath beene untainted even in envies eie,
110 And where it would protect, a sanctuarie.
Brave Earle come forth, and keepe your scandall in:
Tis not our fault if you enforce the spot,
Nor the wreake yours if you performe it not.

      Enter MONTSURRY *with all the murtherers.*

MONTSURRY Cowards, a fiend or spirit beat ye off?
They are your owne faint spirits that have forg'd
The fearefull shadowes that your eies deluded:
The fiend was in you; cast him out then thus.

      D'AMBOIS *hath* MONTSURRY *downe.*

TAMYRA Favour my Lord, my love, ô favour him.

BUSSY I will not touch him: Take your life, my Lord,
And be appeas'd: *Pistolls shot within.* [BUSSY *falls.*]
120   O then the coward Fates
Have maim'd themselves, and ever lost their honour.

UMBRA What have ye done slaves? irreligious Lord?

BUSSY Forbeare them, father; tis enough for me
That *Guise* and *Monsieur*, Death and Destinie,
Come behinde *D'Ambois*: is my bodie then
But penetrable flesh? And must my minde

Follow my blood? Can my divine part adde
No aide to th'earthly in extremitie?
Then these divines are but for forme, not fact:
Man is of two sweet Courtly friends compact;   130
A mistresse and a servant: let my death
Define life nothing but a Courtiers breath.
Nothing is made of nought, of all things made,
Their abstract being a dreame but of a shade.
Ile not complaine to earth yet, but to heaven,
And (like a man) looke upwards even in death.
Proppe me, true sword, as thou hast ever done:
The equall thought I beare of life and death,
Shall make me faint on no side; I am up
Heere like a Roman Statue; I will stand   140
Till death hath made me marble: ô my fame
Live in despight of murther; take thy wings
And haste thee where the gray-eyd morne perfumes
Her Rosie chariot with Sabæan spices;
Flie, where the evening from th'Iberean vales,
Takes on her swarthy shoulders *Heccate*
Cround with a grove of oakes: flie where men feele
The burning axeltree: and those that suffer
Beneath the chariot of the Snowy Beare:
And tell them all that *D'Ambois* now is hasting   150
To the eternall dwellers; that a thunder
Of all their sighes together (for their frailties
Beheld in me) may quit my worthlesse fall
With a fit volley for my funerall.

UMBRA Forgive thy murtherers.

BUSSY   I forgive them all;
And you my Lord, their fautor; for true signe
Of which unfain'd remission, take my sword;
Take it, and only give it motion,
And it shall finde the way to victorie
By his owne brightnesse, and th'inherent valour   160
My fight hath still'd into't, with charmes of spirit.
And let me pray you, that my weighty bloud
Laid in one skale of your impertiall splene

May sway the forfeit of my worthy love
Waid in the other: and be reconcilde
With all forgivenesse to your matchlesse wife.

TAMYRA   Forgive thou me deare servant, and this hand
That lead thy life to this unworthy end,
Forgive it, for the bloud with which tis staind
170   In which I writ the summons of thy death:
The forced summons, by this bleeding wound,
By this heere in my bosome: and by this
That makes me hold up both my hands embrewd
For thy deare pardon.

BUSSY   O, my heart is broken.
Fate, nor these murtherers, *Monsieur*, nor the *Guise*,
Have any glorie in my death, but this:
This killing spectacle: this prodigie:
My sunne is turnd to blood gainst whose red beams
Pindus and *Ossa* (hid in endlesse snow),
180   Laid on my heart and liver, from their vains
Melt like two hungrie torrents eating rockes
Into the Ocean of all humane life,
And make it bitter, only with my bloud:
O fraile condition of strength, valure; vertue,
In me (like warning fire upon the top
Of some steepe Beakon, on a steeper hill)
Made to expresse it: like a falling starre
Silently glanc't, that like a thunderbolt,
Lookt to have stucke and shooke the firmament.   *Moritur.*

190   UMBRA   Son of the earth, whom my unrested soule
Rues t'have begotten in the faith of heaven
(Since thy revengefull Spirit hath rejected
The charitie it commands, and the remission
To serve and worship, the blind rage of bloud);
Assay to gratulate and pacifie,
The soule fled from this worthy by performing
The Christian reconcilement he besought
Betwixt thee and thy Lady, let her wounds
Manlesly digd in her, be easd and cur'd
200   With balme of thine owne teares: or be assur'd

Never to rest free from my haunt and horror.

MONTSURRY See how she merits this: still sitting by
    And mourning his fall, more than her owne fault.

UMBRA Remove, deare daughter, and content thy husband:
    So piety wils thee, and thy servants peace.

TAMYRA O wretched piety, that art so distract
    In thine owne constancy; and in thy right
    Must be unrighteous: if I right my friend
    I wrong my husband: if his wrong I shunne,
    The duty of my friend I leave undone;   210
    Ill plays on both sides; heere and there, it riseth;
    No place, no good so good, but ill compriseth;
    My soule more scruple breeds, than my bloud, sinne,
    Vertue imposeth more than any stepdame:
    O had I never married but for forme,
    Never vowd faith but purposd to deceive:
    Never made conscience of any sinne,
    But clok't it privately and made it common:
    Nor never honord beene, in blood, or mind,
    Happy had I beene then, as others are   220
    Of the like licence; I had then beene honord:
    Liv'd without envy: custome had benumbd
    All sense of scruple, and all note of frailty:
    My fame had beene untoucht, my heart unbroken:
    But (shunning all) I strike on all offence.
    O husband? deare friend? O my conscience?

MONTSURRY I must not yeeld to pity nor to love
    So servile and so traiterous: cease my bloud
    To wrastle with my honour, fame and judgement:
    Away, forsake my house, forbeare complaints   230
    Where thou hast bred them: heere all things full
    Of their owne shame and sorrow, leave my house.

TAMYRA Sweet Lord forgive me, and I will be gone,
    And till these wounds, that never balme shall close
    Till death hath enterd at them (so I love them
    Being open'd by your hands) by death be cur'd
    I never more will grieve you with my sight:
    Never endure that any roofe shall part

          Mine eies and heaven: but to the open deserts

240   (Like to hunted Tygres) I will flie:

          Eating my heart, shunning the steps of men,

          And looke on no side till I be arriv'd.

MONTSURRY I do forgive thee, and upon my knees

          (With hands held up to heaven) wish that mine honor

          Would suffer reconcilement to my love:

          But since it will not, honor, never serve

          My Love with flourishing object till it sterve:

          And as this Taper, though it upwards looke,

          Downwards must needs consume, so let our love;

250   As having lost his hony, the sweet taste

          Runs into savor, and will needs retaine

          A spice of his first parents, till (like life)

          It sees and dies; so let our love: and lastly,

          And when the flame is sufferd to looke up

          It keepes his luster: but, being thus turnd downe

          (His naturall course of usefull light inverted)

          His owne stuffe puts it out: so let our love

          Now turne from me, as heere I turne from thee,

          And may both points of heavens strait axeltree

260   Conjoine in one, before thy selfe and me.

                        Exeunt [MONTSURRY *and* TAMYRA] *severally.*

UMBRA My terrors are strook inward, and no more

          My pennance will allow they shall enforce

          Earthly afflictions but upon my selfe:

          Farewell brave relicts of a compleat man:

          Looke up and see thy spirit made a star,

          Joine flames with *Hercules*: and when thou setst

          Thy radiant forhead in the firmament,

          Make the vast continent, cracke with thy receit,

269   Spred to a world of fire: and th'aged skie,

          Chere with new sparkes of old humanity.   [*Exit.*]

                Finis Actus Quinti & ultimi.

The Widdowes Teares

The Actors

THARSALIO *the wooer.*

LYSANDER *his brother.*

GOVERNOUR *of Cyprus.*

LYCUS *ser[vant] to the widdow Countesse.*

[CLINIAS, *another servant to the widow Countess*]

ARGUS, *Gent[leman] Usher.*

[REBUS, *suitor to the widow Countess*

HIARBUS
PSORABEUS } *friends of Rebus*]

HY[LUS], *Nephew to Tharsalio, and Sonne to Lysander.*

CAPTAINE *of the watch.*

2. SOULDIERS.

EUDORA *the widdow Countesse.*

CYNTHIA, *wife to Lysander.*

STHENIO
IANTHE } *Gent[lewomen] attending on Eudora*

ERO, *waiting woman to Cynthia.*

[LAODICE, *daughter to Eudora.*

ARSACE, *a panderess.*

TOMASIN, *a courtesan.*

Guard, Six Sylvans, Grooms.]

To the right Vertuous and truly *noble Gentleman*,
Mʀ Jo. REED of Mitton,
in the countie of Glocester Esquire.

Sir, if any worke of this nature be worth the presenting to Friends Worthie, and
Noble; I presume this, will not want much of that value. Other Countrie men
have thought the like worthie of Dukes and Princes acceptations; Injusti sdegnii;
Il Pentamento Amorose: Calisthe, Pastor fido, &c. *(all being but plaies)*
were all dedicate to Princes of Italie. And therefore [*I*] *only discourse to shew my*
love to your right vertuous and noble disposition. This poor Comedie (of many
desired to see printed) I thought not utterly unworthie that affectionate designe in
me: Well knowing that your free judgement weighs nothing by the Name, or
Forme; or any vaine estimation of the vulgar; but will accept acceptable matter,
as well in Plaies; as in many lesse materialls, masking in more serious Titles.   10
And so, till some worke more worthie I can select, and perfect, out of my other
Studies, that may better expresse me; and more fit the gravitie of your ripe
inclination, I rest,

Yours at all parts most truly affected,
Geo. Chapman.

The Widdowes Teares. A Comedie

Act I. Scene 1

THARSALIO *Solus, with a Glasse in his hand making readie.*
Thow blinde imperfect Goddesse, that delights
(Like a deepe-reaching Statesman) to converse
Only with Fooles: Jealous of knowing spirits;
For feare their piersing Judgements might discover
Thy inward weaknesse, and despise thy power;
Contemne thee for a Goddesse; Thou that lad'st
Th'unworthy Asse with gold; while worth and merit
Serve thee for nought; (weake Fortune) I renounce
Thy vaine dependance, and convert my dutie
And sacrifices of my sweetest thoughts,   10
To a more Noble Deitie. Sole friend to worth,
And Patronesse of all good Spirits, *Confidence.*
Shee be my Guide, and hers the praise of these
My worthie undertakings.

> *Enter* LYSANDER *with a Glasse in his hand,* CYNTHIA, HYLUS,
> ERO.

LYSANDER Morrow Brother; Not readie yet?

THARSALIO No; I have somewhat of the Brother in me; I dare say,
your Wife is many times readie, and you not up. Save you sister;
how, are you enamoured of my presence? how like you my aspect?

CYNTHIA Faith no worse then I did last weeke, the weather has
nothing chang'd the graine of your complexion.   20

THARSALIO A firme proofe, 'tis in graine, and so are not all com-
plexions. A good Souldiers face Sister.

CYNTHIA Made to be worne under a Bever.

THARSALIO I, and 'twould shew well enough under a maske too.

LYSANDER So much for the face.

THARSALIO But is there no object in this suite to whet your tongue
upon?

LYSANDER None, but Fortune send you well to weare it: for shee
best knowes how you got it.

30   THARSALIO Faith, 'tis the portion shee bestowes upon yonger
Brothers, valour, and good clothes: Marry, if you aske how we
come by this new suite, I must take time to answere it: for as the
Ballad saies, in written Bookes I find it. Brother these are the
blossomes of spirit: and I will have it said for my Fathers honour,
that some of his children were truly begotten.

LYSANDER Not all?

THARSALIO Shall I tell you brother that I know will rejoyce you? my
former suites have been all spenders, this shall be a speeder.

LYSANDER A thing to bee heartily wisht; but brother, take heede you
40   be not gull'd, be not too forward.

THARSALIO 'T had beene well for me, if you had follow'd that
counsaile: You were too forward when you stept into the world
before me, and gull'd me of the Land, that my spirits and parts
were indeed borne too.

CYNTHIA May we not have the blessing to know the aime of your
fortunes, what coast, for heavens love?

THARSALIO Nay, tis a project of State: you may see the preparation;
but the designe lies hidden in the brests of the wise.

LYSANDER May we not know't?

50   THARSALIO Not unlesse you'le promise mee to laugh at it, for without
your applause, Ile none.

LYSANDER The qualitie of it may bee such as a laugh will not be ill
bestow'd upon't; pray heaven I call not *Arsace* sister.

CYNTHIA What? the Pandresse?

THARSALIO Know you (as who knowes not) the exquisite Ladie of
the Palace? The late Governours admired Widdow? The rich and
haughtie Countesse *Eudora*? Were not shee a Jewell worth the
wearing, if a man knew how to win her?

LYSANDER How's that? how's that?

60   THARSALIO Brother, there is a certaine Goddesse called *Confidence*,
that carries a maine stroke in honourable preferments. Fortune
waits upon her; *Cupid* is at her becke; shee sends them both of
errands. This Deitie doth promise me much assistance in this
businesse.

LYSANDER But if this Deitie should draw you up in a basket to your

Countesses window, and there let you hang for all the wits in the
Towne to shoot at: how then?

THARSALIO If shee doe, let them shoote their bolts and spare not:
I have a little Bird in a Cage here that sings me better comfort.
What should be the barre? you'le say, I was Page to the Count her   70
husband. What of that? I have thereby one foote in her favour
alreadie; Shee has taken note of my spirit, and survaid my good
parts, and the picture of them lives in her eie: which sleepe, I
know, can not close, till shee have embrac't the substance.

LYSANDER All this savors of the blind Goddesse you speake of.

THARSALIO Why should I despaire, but that *Cupid* hath one dart in
store for her great Ladiship, as well as for any other huge Ladie,
whom she hath made stoope Gallant, to kisse their worthie fol-
lowers. In a word, I am assured of my speede. Such faire attempts
led by a brave resolve, are evermore seconded by Fortune.   80

CYNTHIA But brother, have I not heard you say, your own eares
have been witnesse to her vowes, made solemnly to your late Lord;
in memorie of him, to preserve till death, the unstain'd honour of
a Widdowes bed? If nothing else, yet that might coole your
confidence.

THARSALIO Tush sister, suppose you should protest with solemne
oath (as perhaps you have done) if ever Heaven heares your praiers,
that you may live to see my Brother nobly interred, to feede only
upon fish, and not endure the touch of flesh, during the wretched
Lent of your miserable life; would you beleeve it Brother?   90

LYSANDER I am therein most confident.

THARSALIO Indeed, you had better beleeve it then trie it: but pray
Sister tell me, you are a woman: doe not you wives nod your heads,
and smile one upon an other when yee meete abroade?

CYNTHIA Smile? why so?

THARSALIO As who should say, are not we mad Wenches, that can
lead our blind husbands thus by the noses? do you not brag
amongst your selves how grosly you abuse their honest credulities?
how they adore you for Saints: and you beleeve it? while you
adhorne their temples, and they beleeve it not? how you vow   100
Widdow-hood in their life time, and they beleeve you, when even
in the sight of their breathlesse corse, ere they be fully cold, you
joine embraces with his Groome, or his Phisition, and perhaps his

poisoner; or at least by the next Moone (if you can expect so long) solemnely plight new Hymineall bonds, with a wild, confident, untamed Ruffine?

LYSANDER As for example?

THARSALIO And make him the top of his house, and soveraign Lord of the Palace, as for example. Looke you Brother, this glasse is mine.

LYSANDER What of that?

THARSALIO While I am with it, it takes impression from my face; but can I make it so mine, that it shall be of no use to any other? will it not doe his office to you or you: and as well to my Groome as to my selfe? Brother, Monopolies are cryed downe. Is it not madnes for me to beleeve, when I have conquer'd that Fort of chastitie the great Countesse; that if another man of my making, and mettall, shall assault her: her eies and eares should lose their function, her other parts their use, as if Nature had made her all in vaine, unlesse I only had stumbl'd into her quarters?

CYNTHIA Brother: I feare me in your travaile, you have drunck too much of that Italian aire, that hath infected the whole masse of your ingenuous Nature; dried up in you all sap of generous disposition, poisond the very Essence of your soule, and so polluted your senses, that whatsoever enters there, takes from them contagion, and is to your fancie represented as foule and tainted, which in it selfe perhaps is spotlesse.

THARSALIO No sister, it hath refin'd my senses, and made mee see with cleare eies, and to judge of objects, as they truly are, not as they seeme, and through their maske to discerne the true face of thinges. It tells me how short liv'd Widdowes teares are, that their weeping is in truth but laughing under a Maske, that they mourne in their Gownes, and laugh in their Sleeves, all which I beleeve as a Delphian Oracle: and am resolv'd to burne in that faith. And in that resolution doe I march to the great Ladie.

LYSANDER You lose time Brother in discourse, by this had you bore up with the Ladie and clapt her aboord, for I knowe your confidence will not dwell long in the service.

THARSALIO No, I will performe it in the Conquerours stile. Your way is, not to winne *Penelope* by suite, but by surprise. The Castle's carried by a sodaine assault, that would perhaps sit out a twelve-

moneths siege. It would bee a good breeding to my yong Nephew
here, if hee could procure a stand at the Palace, to see with what
alacritie Ile a-coast her Countesship, in what garbe I will woo her,
with what facilitie I will winne her.

LYSANDER It shall goe hard but weele heare your entertainement for
your confidence sake.

THARSALIO And having wonne her, Nephew, this sweet face
Which all the Citie saies, is so like me,
Like me shall be preferr'd, for I will wed thee   150
To my great widdowes Daughter and sole Heire,
The lovely sparke, the bright *Laodice.*

LYSANDER A good pleasant dreame.

THARSALIO   In this eie I see
That fire that shall in me inflame the Mother,
And that in this shall set on fire the Daughter.
It goes Sir in a bloud; beleeve me brother,
These destinies goe ever in a bloud.

LYSANDER These diseases doe, brother, take heede of them:
Fare you well; take heede you be not baffeld.

                              Exeunt LYSANDER, CYNTHIA,
                              HYLUS, ERO. *Manet* THARSALIO.

THARSALIO Now thou that art the third blind Deitie   160
That governes earth in all her happinesse,
The life of all endowments, *Confidence;*
Direct and prosper my intention.
Command thy servant Deities, Love and Fortune
To second my attempts for this great Ladie,
Whose Page I lately was; That shee, whose bord
I might not sit at, I may boord a bed
And under bring, who bore so high her head.   *Exit.*

[*Act I. Scene 2*]

[*Enter*] LYSANDER, LYCUS.

LYCUS 'Tis miraculous that you tell me Sir: he come to woo our
Ladie Mistris for his wife?

LYSANDER 'Tis a phrensie he is possest with, and wil not be cur'd

but by some violent remedie. And you shall favour me so much
to make me a spectator of the Scene. But is shee (say you) alreadie
accessible for Suiters? I thought shee would have stood so stifly
on her Widdow vow, that shee would not endure the sight of a
Suiter.

LYCUS Faith Sir, *Penelope* could not barre her gates against her woers,
but shee will still be Mistris of her selfe. It is as you know, a
certaine Itch in femall bloud, they love to be su'd to: but sheele
hearken to no Suiters.

LYSANDER But by your leave *Lycus, Penelope* is not so wise as her
husband *Ulysses,* for he fearing the jawes of the *Syren,* stopt his
eares with waxe against her voice. They that fear the Adders sting,
will not come neare her hissing. Is any Suiter with her now?

LYCUS A Spartan Lord, dating himselfe our great Viceroies Kinsman,
and two or three other of his Countrie Lords, as spots in his train.
He comes armed with his Altitudes letters in grace of his person,
with promise to make her a Duchesse if shee embrace the match.
This is no meane attraction to her high thoughts; but yet shee
disdaines him.

LYSANDER And how then shall my brother presume of acceptance?
yet I hold it much more under her contentment, to marrie such a
Nastie braggart, then under her honour to wed my brother: A
Gentleman (though I sai't) more honourably descended than that
Lord: who perhaps, for all his Ancestrie would bee much troubled
to name you the place where his Father was borne.

LYCUS Nay I hold no comparison betwixt your brother and him.
And the Venerean disease, to which they say, he has beene long
wedded, shall I hope first rot him, ere shee endure the savour of
his Sulphurous breath. Well, her Ladiship is at hand; y'are best
take you to your stand.

LYSANDER Thankes good friend *Lycus.*   *Exit.*

> *Enter* ARGUS *barehead, with whome another Usher* LYCUS *joynes,*
> *going over the Stage.* HIARBAS, *and* PSORABEUS *next,* REBUS *single*
> *before* EUDORA, LAODICE, STHENIO *bearing her traine,* IANTHE
> *following.*

REBUS I admire Madame, you can not love whome the Viceroy loves.

HIARBAS And one whose veines swell so with his bloud, Madam, as
they doe in his Lordship.

PSORABEUS A neare and deare Kinsman his Lordship is to his Alti-
tude, the Viceroy; In care of whose good speede here, I know his
Altitude hath not slept a sound sleepe since his departure.   40

EUDORA I thanke *Venus* I have, ever since he came.

REBUS You sleepe away your Honour, Madam, if you neglect me.

HIARBAS Neglect your Lordship? that were a negligence no lesse
than disloialtie.

EUDORA I much doubt that Sir; It were rather a presumption to take
him, being of the bloud Viceroiall.

REBUS Not at all, being offered Madame.

EUDORA But offered ware is not so sweet you know. They are the
graces of the Viceroy that woo me, not your Lordships, and I
conceive it should be neither Honor nor Pleasure to you, to be   50
taken in for an other mans favours.

REBUS Taken in Madam? you speake as I had no house to hide my
head in.

EUDORA I have heard so indeed, my Lord, unlesse it be another
mans.

REBUS You have heard untruth then; These Lords can well witnesse
I can want no houses.

HIARBAS Nor Palaces neither my Lord.

PSORABEUS Nor Courts neither.

EUDORA Nor Temples I thinke neither; I beleeve wee shall have a   60
God of him.

Enter THARSALIO.

ARGUS See the bold fellow; whether will you Sir?

THARSALIO Away, all honour to you Madam?

EUDORA How now base companion?

THARSALIO Base Madame? hees not base that fights as high as your
lips.

EUDORA And does that beseeme my servant?

THARSALIO Your Court-servant Madam.

EUDORA One that waited on my boord?

THARSALIO That was only a preparation to my weight on your bed   70
Madam.

EUDORA How dar'st thou come to me with such a thought?

THARSALIO Come to you Madam? I dare come to you at midnight,
and bid defiance to the proudest spirit that haunts these your loved

shadowes; and would any way make terrible the accesse of my
love to you.

EUDORA Love me? love my dogge.

THARSALIO I am bound to that by the proverb Madam.

EUDORA Kennell without with him, intrude not here. What is it thou
80   presum'st on?

THARSALIO On your judgement Madam, to choose a Man, and not
a Giant, as these are that come with Titles, and Authoritie, as they
would conquer, or ravish you. But I come to you with the liberall
and ingenuous Graces, Love, Youth, and Gentrie; which (in no
more deform'd a person then my selfe) deserve any Princesse.

EUDORA In your sawcie opinion Sir, and sirha too; get gone; and let
this malipert humour returne thee no more, for afore heaven Ile
have thee tost in blanquets.

THARSALIO In blanquets Madam? you must adde your sheetes, and
90   you must be the Tosser.

REBUS Nay then Sir y'are as grosse as you are sawcie.

THARSALIO And all one Sir, for I am neither.

REBUS Thou art both.

THARSALIO Thou liest; keepe up your smiter Lord *Rebus*.

HIARBAS Usest thou thus his Altitudes Cosen?

REBUS The place thou know'st protects thee.

THARSALIO Tie up your valour then till an other place turne me
loose to you, you are the Lord (I take it) that wooed my great
Mistris here with letters from his Altitude; which while she was
100   reading, your Lordship (to entertaine time) strodl'd and skal'd your
fingers; as you would shew what an itching desire you had to get
betwixt her sheetes.

HIARBAS Slight, why does your Lordship endure him?

REBUS The place, the place my Lord.

THARSALIO Be you his Attorney Sir.

HIARBAS What would you doe Sir?

THARSALIO Make thee leape out at window, at which thou cam'st
in: Whores-sonne bag-pipe Lords.

EUDORA What rudenesse is this?

110   THARSALIO What tamenesse is it in you Madam, to sticke at the
discarding of such a suiter? A leane Lord, dub'd with the lard of
others? A diseased Lord too, that opening certaine Magick

Characters in an unlawfull booke, up-start as many aches in's
bones, as there are ouches in's skinne. Send him (Mistris) to the
Widdow your Tennant; the vertuous Pandresse *Arsace*. I perceive
he has crownes in's Purse, that make him proud of a string; let
her pluck the Goose therefore, and her maides dresse him.

PSORABEUS Still my Lord suffer him?

REBUS The place Sir, beleeve it the place.

THARSALIO O good Lord *Rebus*; The place is never like to be yours   120
and you neede respect it so much.

EUDORA Thou wrong'st the noble Gentleman.

THARSALIO Noble Gentleman? A tumor, an impostume hee is
Madam; a very hault-boy, a bag-pipe; in whom there is nothing
but winde, and that none of the sweetest neither.

EUDORA Quitt the House of him by 'thead and Shoulders.

THARSALIO Thankes to your Honour Madame, and my Lord Cosen
the Viceroy shall thanke you.

REBUS So shall he indeede sir.

LYCUS, ARGUS Will you be gone sir?   130

THARSALIO Away poore Fellowes.

EUDORA What is he made of? or what Devill sees
Your childish, and effeminate spirits in him,
That thus yee shun him? Free us of thy sight;
Be gone, or I protest thy life shall goe.

THARSALIO Yet shall my Ghost stay still; and haunt those beauties,
And glories, that have rendered it immortall.
But since I see your bloud runnes (for the time)
High, in that contradiction that fore-runs
Truest agreements (like the Elements   140
Fighting before they generate;) and that Time
Must be attended most, in thinges most worth;
I leave your Honour freely; and commend
That life you threaten, when you please, to be
Adventur'd in your service; so your Honour
Require it likewise.

EUDORA   Doe not come againe.

THARSALIO Ile come again, beleeve it, and againe.   *Exit.*

EUDORA If he shall dare to come againe, I charge you
Shut dores upon him.

ARGUS   You must shut them (Madam)
150   To all men else then, if it please your Honour,
         For if that any enter, hele be one.

EUDORA I hope, wise Sir, a Guard will keepe him out.

ARGUS Afore Heaven, not a Guard (ant please your Honour.)

EUDORA Thou liest base Asse; One man enforce a Guard?
         Ile turne yee all away (by our Iles Goddesse)
         If he but set a foote within my Gates.

PSORABEUS [*to Rebus*] Your Honour shall doe well to have him
         poison'd.

HIARBAS Or begg'd of your Cosen the Viceroy.   *Exeunt.*

[*Act I. Scene 3*]

         LYSANDER *from his stand.*

LYSANDER This braving wooer, hath the successe expected; The
         favour I obtain'd, made me witnesse to the sport; And let his
         Confidence bee sure, Ile give it him home. The newes by this,
         is blowne through the foure quarters of the Cittie. Alas good
         Confidence: but the happinesse is he has a forehead of proofe;
         the staine shall never stick there whatsoever his reproch be.

         Enter THARSALIO.

LYSANDER What? in discourse?

THARSALIO Hell and the Furies take this vile encounter.
         Who would imagine this Saturnian Peacock
10   Could be so barbarous to use a spirit
         Of my erection, with such lowe respect?
         Fore heaven it cuts my gall; but Ile dissemble it.

LYSANDER What? my noble Lord?

THARSALIO Well Sir, that may be yet, and meanes to be.

LYSANDER What meanes your Lordship then to hang that head that
         hath beene so erected? it knocks Sir at your bosome to come in
         and hide it selfe.

THARSALIO Not a jot.

LYSANDER I hope by this time it needes feare no hornes.

20 THARSALIO Well Sir, but yet that blessing runs not alwaies in a bloud.

LYSANDER What blanqueted? O the Gods! spurn'd out by Groomes like a base Bisogno? thrust out by'th head and shoulders?

THARSALIO You doe well Sir to take your pleasure of me, (I may
turne tables with you ere long.)

LYSANDER What has thy wits fine engine taken cold? art stuff't inth
head? canst answere nothing?

THARSALIO Truth is, I like my entertainment the better that 'twas
no better.

LYSANDER Now the Gods forbid that this opinion should run in a
bloud.   30

THARSALIO Have not you heard this principle, All thinges by strife
engender?

LYSANDER Dogges and Cats doe.

THARSALIO And men and women too.

LYSANDER Well Brother, in earnest, you have now set your confi-
dence to schoole, from whence I hope't has brought home such
a lesson as will instruct his master never after to begin such
attempts as end in laughter.

THARSALIO Well Sir, you lesson my Confidence still; I pray heavens
your confidence have not more shallow ground (for that I know)   40
then mine you reprehend so.

LYSANDER My confidence? in what?

THARSALIO May be you trust too much.

LYSANDER Wherein?

THARSALIO In human frailtie.

LYSANDER Why brother know you ought that may impeach my
confidence, as this successe may yours? hath your observation
discovered any such frailtie in my wife (for that is your aime I
know) then let me know it.

THARSALIO Good, good. Nay, Brother, I write no bookes of Obser-   50
vations, let your confidence beare out it selfe, as mine shall me.

LYSANDER That's scarce a Brothers speech. If there be ought wherein
your Brothers good might any way be question'd can you
conceale it from his bosome?

THARSALIO So, so. Nay my saying was but generall. I glanc't at no
particular.

LYSANDER Then must I presse you further. You spake (as to your
selfe, but yet I over-heard) as if you knew some disposition of

weaknesse where I most had fixt my trust. I challenge you to let
60   me know what 'twas.

THARSALIO Brother? are you wise?

LYSANDER Why?

THARSALIO Be ignorant. Did you never heare of *Actæon*?

LYSANDER What then?

THARSALIO Curiositie was his death. He could not be content to
     adore *Diana* in her Temple, but he must needes dogge her to her
     retir'd pleasures, and see her in her nakednesse. Doe you enjoy
     the sole priviledge of your wives bed? have you no pretie *Paris* for
     your Page? No yong *Adonis* to front you there?

70 LYSANDER I thinke none: I know not.

THARSALIO Know not still Brother. Ignorance and credulitie are
     your sole meanes to obtaine that blessing. You see your greatest
     Clerkes, your wisest Politicians, are not that way fortunate, your
     learned Lawyers would lose a dozen poore mens causes to gaine
     a lease ant, but for a Terme. Your Phisition is jelous of his. Your
     Sages in generall, by seeing too much oversee that happinesse.
     Only your block-heardly Tradesman; your honest meaning Cittizen;
     your not-headed Countrie Gentleman; your unapprehending
     Stinckerd is blest with the sole prerogative of his Wives chamber.
80   For which he is yet beholding, not to his starres, but to his
     ignorance. For if he be wise, Brother, I must tell you the case
     alters. How doe you relish these thinges Brother?

LYSANDER Passing ill.

THARSALIO So do sick men solid meates: hearke you brother, are
     you not jelous?

LYSANDER No: doe you know cause to make me?

THARSALIO Hold you there; did your wife never spice your broth
     with a dramme of sublimate? hath shee not yeelded up the Fort
     of her Honour to a staring Soldado? and (taking courage from her
90   guilt) plaid open banckrout of all shame, and runne the Countrie
     with him? Then blesse your Starres, bow your knees to *Juno*. Looke
     where shee appeares.

Enter CYNTHIA, HYLUS, [*and* ERO.]

CYNTHIA We have sought you long Sir, there's a Messenger within,
     hath brought you letters from the Court, and desires your speech.

LYSANDER I can discover nothing in her lookes. Goe, Ile not be
   long.

CYNTHIA Sir, it is of weight the bearer saies: and besides, much
   hastens his departure. Honourable Brother! crie mercie! what, in
   a Conquerours stile? but come and overcome?   100

THARSALIO A fresh course.

CYNTHIA Alas you see of how sleight mettall Widdowes vowes are
   made.

THARSALIO And that shall you prove too ere long.

CYNTHIA Yet for the honour of our sexe, boast not abroade this
   your easie conquest; another might perhaps have staid longer
   below staires, it but was your confidence, that surpris'd her love.

HYLUS My uncle hath instructed me how to accoast an honorable
   Ladie; to win her, not by suite, but by surprise.

THARSALIO The Whelp and all.

HYLUS Good Uncle let not your neare Honours change your manners,   110
   bee not forgetfull of your promise to mee, touching your Ladies
   daughter *Laodice*. My fancie runns so upon't, that I dreame every
   night of her.

THARSALIO A good chicken, goe thy waies, thou hast done well; eate
   breade with thy meate.

CYNTHIA Come Sir, will you in?

LYSANDER Ile follow you.

CYNTHIA Ile not stirre a foot without you. I can not satisfie the
   messengers impatience.

LYSANDER *He takes* THAR. *aside.* Wil you not resolve me brother?   120

THARSALIO Of what?

> LYSANDER *stamps and goes out vext with* CYNTHIA, HYLUS,
>   ERO.

So, there's venie for venie, I have given't him 'ith speeding place
for all his confidence. Well out of this perhaps there may bee
moulded matter of more mirth, then my baffling. It shall goe
hard but Ile make my constant sister act as famous a Scene as
Virgil did his Mistris; who caus'd all the Fire in Rome to faile so
that none could light a torch but at her nose. Now forth: At this
house dwells a vertuous Dame, sometimes of worthy Fame, now
like a decai'd Merchant turn'd Broker, and retailes refuse com-
modities for unthriftie Gallants. Her wit I must imploy upon this   130

businesse to prepare my next encounter, but in such a fashion as shall make all split. Ho? Madam *Arsace*? pray heaven the Oister-wives have not brought the newes of my woing hether amongst their stale Pilcherds.

Enter ARSACE, TOMASIN.

ARSACE What? my Lord of the Palace?

THARSALIO Looke you.

ARSACE Why, this was done like a beaten Souldier.

THARSALIO Hearke, I must speake with you. I have a share for you in this rich adventure. You must bee the Asse chardg'd with Crownes to make way to the Fort, and I the Conquerour to follow, and seise it. Seest thou this jewell?

ARSACE Is't come to that? why *Tomasin.*

TOMASIN Madam.

ARSACE Did not one of the Countesses Serving-men tell us that this Gentleman was sped?

TOMASIN That he did, and how her honour grac't and entertained him in very familiar manner.

ARSACE And brought him downe staires her selfe.

TOMASIN I forsooth, and commanded her men to beare him out of dores.

THARSALIO Slight, pelted with rotten egges?

ARSACE Nay more, that he had alreadie possest her sheetes.

TOMASIN No indeede Mistris, twas her blanquets.

THARSALIO Out you yong hedge-sparrow, learne to tread afore you be fledge.   *He kicks her out.*
Well have you done now Ladie?

ARSACE O my sweet kilbuck.

THARSALIO You now, in your shallow pate, thinke this a disgrace to mee, such a disgrace as is a battered helmet on a souldiers head, it doubles his resolution. Say, shall I use thee?

ARSACE Use me?

THARSALIO O holy reformation! how art thou fallen downe from the upper-bodies of the Church to the skirts of the Citie! honestie is stript out of his true substance into verball nicetie. Common sinners startle at common termes, and they that by whole moun-taines swallow downe the deedes of darknesse; A poore mote of

a familiar word, makes them turne up the white o'th eie. Thou art
the Ladies Tennant.

ARSACE For terme Sir.

THARSALIO A good induction, be successefull for me, make me Lord   170
of the Palace, and thou shalt hold thy Tenement to thee and thine
heirs for ever, in free smockage, as of the manner of Panderage,
provided alwaies –

ARSACE Nay if you take me unprovided –

THARSALIO Provided I say, that thou mak'st thy repaire to her
presently with a plot I will instruct thee in; and for thy surer accesse
to her greatnesse, thou shalt present her, as from thy selfe with
this jewell.

ARSACE So her old grudge, stand not betwixt her and me.

THARSALIO Feare not that.   180

Presents are present cures for femall grudges,
Make bad, seeme good; alter the case with Judges.   *Exeunt.*

Finis Actus Primi

Act II. Scene 1

LYSANDER, THARSALIO.

LYSANDER So now we are our selves. Brother, that ill relisht speech
you let slip from your tongue, hath taken so deepe hold of my
thoughts, that they will never give me rest, till I be resolv'd what
'twas you said, you know, touching my wife.

THARSALIO Tush: I am wearie of this subject, I said not so.

LYSANDER By truth it selfe you did: I over-heard you. Come, it shall
nothing move me, whatsoever it be; pray thee unfold briefly what
you know.

THARSALIO Why briefly Brother, I know my sister to be the wonder
of the Earth; and the Envie of the Heavens; Vertuous, Loiall, and   10
what not. Briefly, I know shee hath vow'd, that till death and after
death, sheele hold inviolate her bonds to you, and that her black
shal take no other hew; all which I firmely beleeve. In briefe

Brother, I know her to be a woman. But you know brother, I have
other yrons on th' anvile.   *Exiturus.*

LYSANDER You shall not leave mee so unsatisfied; tell mee what tis
you know.

THARSALIO Why Brother; if you be sure of your wives loialtie for
terme of life: why should you be curious to search the Almanacks
for aftertimes: whether some wandring *Aeneas* should enjoy your
reversion; or whether your true Turtle would sit mourning on a
wither'd branch, till *Atropos* cut her throat: Beware of curiositie,
for who can resolve you? youle say perhaps her vow.

LYSANDER Perhaps I shall.

THARSALIO Tush, her selfe knowes not what shee shall doe, when
shee is transform'd into a Widdow. You are now a sober and staid
Gentleman. But if *Diana* for your curiositie should translate you
into a monckey; doe you know what gambolds you should play?
your only way to bee resolv'd is to die and make triall of her.

LYSANDER A deare experiment, then I must rise againe to bee resolv'd.

THARSALIO You shall not neede. I can send you speedier advertise-
ment of her constancie, by the next Ripier that rides that way with
Mackerell. And so I leave you.   *Exit* THARSALIO.

LYSANDER All the Furies in hell attend thee; h'as given me
A bone to tire on with a pestilence; slight know?
What can he know? what can his eie observe
More then mine owne, or the most piersing sight
That ever viewed her? by this light I thinke
Her privat'st thought may dare the eie of heaven,
And challenge th'envious world to witnesse it.
I know him for a wild corrupted youth,
Whom prophane Ruffins, Squires to Bawds, and Strumpets,
Drunckards, speud out of Taverns, into'th sinkes
Of Tap-houses, and Stewes, Revolts from manhood,
Debaucht perdu's, have by their companies
Turn'd Devill like themselves, and stuft his soule
With damn'd opinions, and unhallowed thoughts
Of womanhood, of all humanitie,
Nay Deitie it selfe.
        Enter LYCUS.

LYCUS   Welcome friend *Lycus.*

LYCUS Have you met with your capricious brother?   50

LYSANDER He parted hence but now.

LYCUS And has he yet resolv'd you of that point you brake with me about?

LYSANDER Yes, he bids me die for further triall of her constancie.

LYCUS That were a strange Phisicke for a jealous patient; to cure his thirst with a draught of poison. Faith Sir, discharge your thoughts an't; thinke 'twas but a Buzz devis'd by him to set your braines a work, and divert your eie from his disgrace. The world hath written your wife in highest lines of honour'd Fame: her vertues so admir'd in this Ile, as the report thereof sounds in forraigne eares; and   60 strangers oft arriving here, (as some rare sight) desire to view her presence, thereby to compare the Picture with the originall. Nor thinke he can turne so farre rebell to his bloud,
Or to the Truth it selfe to misconceive
Her spotlesse love and loialtie; perhaps
Oft having heard you hold her faith so sacred
As you being dead, no man might stirre a sparke
Of vertuous love, in way of second bonds;
As if you at your death should carrie with you
Both branch and roote of all affection.   70
T'may be, in that point hee's an Infidell,
And thinkes your confidence may over-weene.

LYSANDER So thinke not I.

LYCUS Nor I: if ever any made it good.
I am resolv'd of all, sheele prove no changling.

LYSANDER Well, I must yet be further satisfied;
And vent this humour by some straine of wit,
Somewhat Ile doe; but what, I know not yet.   *Exeunt.*

[*Act II. Scene 2*]

Enter STHENIO, IANTHE.

STHENIO Passion of Virginitie, *Ianthe*, how shall we quit our selves of this Pandresse, that is so importunate to speake with us? Is shee knowne to be a Pandresse?

IANTHE I, as well as we are knowne to be waiting women.

STHENIO A shrew take your comparison. Lets cal out *Argus* that bold
Asse that never weighs what he does or saies; but walkes and
talkes like one in a sleepe; to relate her attendance to my Ladie,
and present her.

IANTHE Who? ant please your Honour? None so fit to set on any
dangerous exploit. Ho? *Argus*?

    Enter ARGUS *bare.*

ARGUS Whats the matter Wenches?

STHENIO You must tell my Ladie here's a Gentle-woman call'd *Arsace*,
her Honours Tennant, attends her, to impart important businesse
to her.

ARGUS I will presently.   *Exit* ARGUS.

IANTHE Well, shee has a welcome present, to beare out her unwel-
come presence: and I never knew but a good gift would welcome
a bad person to the purest. *Arsace*?

    Enter ARSACE.

ARSACE I, Mistris.

STHENIO Give me your Present, Ile doe all I can, to make way both
for it and your selfe.

ARSACE You shall binde me to your service Ladie.

STHENIO Stand unseene.

    Enter LYCUS, EUDORA, LAODICE, ARGUS *comming to* EUDORA.

ARGUS Here's a Gentle-woman (ant please your Honour) one of
your Tennants, desires accesse to you.

EUDORA What Tennant? what's her name?

ARGUS *Arsace*, she saies Madam.

EUDORA *Arsace*? what the Bawde?

ARGUS The Bawd Madam? *shee strikes*, that's without my privitie.

EUDORA Out Asse, know'st not thou the Pandresse *Arsace*?

STHENIO Shee presents your Honour with this Jewell?

EUDORA This jewell? how came shee by such a jewell? Shee has had
great Customers.

ARGUS Shee had neede Madam, shee sits at a great Rent.

EUDORA Alas for your great Rent: Ile keepe her jewell, and keepe
you her out, yee were best: speake to me for a Pandresse?

ARGUS What shall we doe?

STHENIO Goe to; Let us alone. *Arsace*?

ARSACE I Ladie.

STHENIO You must pardon us, we can not obtaine your accesse. 40

ARSACE Mistris *Sthenio*, tell- her Honour, if I get not accesse to her, and that instantly shee's undone.

STHENIO This is some thing of importance. Madam, shee sweares your Honour is undone if she speake not with you instantly.

EUDORA Undone?

ARSACE Pray her for her Honours sake to give mee instant accesse to her.

STHENIO Shee makes her businesse your Honour Madame, and entreates for the good of that, her instant speech with you.

EUDORA How comes my Honour in question? Bring her to mee. 50

　　　ARSACE *comes forward.*

ARSACE Our *Cypriane* Goddesse save your good Honor.

EUDORA Stand you off I pray: How dare you Mistris importune accesse to me thus, considering the last warning I gave for your absence?

ARSACE Because, Madam, I have been mov'd by your Honours last most chast admonition, to leave the offensive life I led before.

EUDORA I? have you left it then?

ARSACE I, I assure your Honour, unlesse it be for the pleasure of two or three poore Ladies, that have prodigall Knights to their husbands.

EUDORA Out on thee Impudent. 60

ARSACE Alas Madam, wee would all bee glad to live in our callings.

EUDORA Is this the reform'd life thou talk'st on?

ARSACE I beseech your good Honour mistake me not, I boast of nothing but my charitie, that's the worst.

EUDORA You get these jewels with charitie, no doubt. But whats the point in which my Honour stands endanger'd I pray?

ARSACE In care of that Madam, I have presum'd to offend your chast eies with my presence. Hearing it reported for truth and generally, that your Honor will take to husband a yong Gentleman of this Citie called *Tharsalio*. 70

EUDORA I take him to husband?

ARSACE If your Honour does, you are utterly undone, for hees the most incontinent, and insatiate Man of Women that ever *Venus* blest with abilitie to please them.

EUDORA Let him be the Devill; I abhorre his thought, and could I be inform'd particularly of any of these slanderers of mine Honour, he should as dearely dare it, as any thing wherein his life were endanger'd.

ARSACE Madam, the report of it is so strongly confident, that I feare
80 the strong destinie of marriage is at worke in it. But if it bee
Madam: Let your Honours known vertue resist and defie it for
him: for not a hundred will serve his one turne. I protest to your
Honour, when (*Venus* pardon mee) I winckt at my unmaidenly
exercise, I have knowne nine in a Night made mad with his love.

EUDORA What tell'st thou mee of his love? I tell thee I abhorre him;
and destinie must have an other mould for my thoughts, then
Nature or mine Honour, and a Witchcraft above both, to trans-
forme mee to another shape, as soone as to an other conceipt of
him.

90 ARSACE Then is your good Honour just as I pray for you, and good
Madam, even for your vertues sake, and comfort of all your
Dignities, and Possessions; fixe your whole Woman-hood against
him. Hee will so inchant you, as never man did woman: Nay a
Goddesse (say his light huswives) is not worthie of his sweetnesse.

EUDORA Goe to, be gone.

ARSACE Deare Madam, your Honours most perfect admonitions
have brought mee to such a hate of these imperfections, that I
could not but attend you with my dutie, and urge his unreasonable
manhood to the fill.

100 EUDORA Man-hood, quoth you?

ARSACE Nay Beastly-hood, I might say, indeede Madam, but for
saving your Honour; Nine in a night said I?

EUDORA Goe to, no more.

ARSACE No more Madame? that's enough one would thinke.

EUDORA Well be gone I bid thee.

ARSACE Alas Madam, your Honour is the chiefe of our Citie, and to
whom shall I complaine of these inchastities, (being your Ladiships
reform'd Tennant) but to you that are chastest?

EUDORA I pray thee goe thy waies, and let me see this reformation
110 you pretend continued.

ARSACE I humbly thanke your good Honour, that was first cause of
it.

EUDORA Here's a complaint as strange as my Suiter.

ARSACE I beseech your good Honour thinke upon him, make him
an example.

EUDORA Yet againe?

ARSACE All my dutie to your Excellence.   *Exit.* ARSACE.

EUDORA These sorts of licentious persons, when they are once
reclaim'd, are most vehement against licence. But it is the course
of the world to dispraise faults and use them; that so we may use   120
them the safer. What might a wise Widdow resolve upon this point
now? Contentment is the end of all worldly beings: Beshrow her;
would shee had spared her newes.

> [EUDORA, STHENIO, *and* IANTHE *exit as* REBUS, HIARBAS,
> PSORABEUS *enter.*]

REBUS See if shee take not a contrarie way to free her selfe of us.

HIARBAS You must complaine to his Altitude.

PSORABEUS All this for triall is; you must indure
That will have wives, nought else, with them is sure.   *Exeunt.*

[*Act II. Scene 3*]

THARSALIO, ARSACE.

THARSALIO Hast thou beene admitted then?

ARSACE Admitted? I, into her heart, Ile able it; never was man so
prais'd with a dispraise; nor so spoken for in being rail'd on. Ile
give you my word; I have set her hart upon as tickle a pin as the
needle of a Diall; that will never let it rest, till it be in the right
position.

THARSALIO Why dost thou imagine this?

ARSACE Because I saw *Cupid* shoot in my words, and open his wounds
in her lookes. Her bloud went and came of errands betwixt her
face and her heart; and these changes I can tell you are shrewd   10
tell-tales.

THARSALIO Thou speak'st like a Doctrisse in thy facultie; but howso-
ever, for all this foile, Ile retrive the game once againe, hee's a
shallow gamster that for one displeasing cast gives up so faire a
game for lost.

ARSACE Well, 'twas a villanous invention of thine, and had a swift
operation, it tooke like sulphure. And yet this vertuous Countesse

hath to my eare spun out many a tedious lecture of pure sisters
thred against concupiscence. But ever with such an affected zeale,
as my minde gave me, shee had a kinde of secret titillation to grace
my poore house sometimes; but that shee fear'd a spice of the
Sciatica, which as you know ever runs in the bloud.

THARSALIO And as you know, sokes into the bones. But to say truth,
these angrie heates that breake out at the lips of these streight lac't
Ladies, are but as symptoms of a lustfull fever that boiles within
them. For wherefore rage wives at their husbands so, when they
flie out, for zeale against the sinne?

ARSACE No, but because they did not purge that sinne.

THARSALIO Th'art a notable Syren, and I sweare to thee, if I prosper,
not only to give thee thy mannor-house gratis, but to marrie thee
to some one Knight or other, and burie thy trade in thy Ladiship:
Goe be gone.   *Exit.* ARSACE.

　　Enter LYCUS.

THARSALIO What newes *Lycus*? where's the Ladie?

LYCUS Retir'd into her Orchard.

THARSALIO A pregnant badge of love, shee's melancholy.

LYCUS 'Tis with the sight of her Spartane wooer. But howsoever tis
with her, you have practis'd strangely upon your Brother.

THARSALIO Why so?

LYCUS You had almost lifted his wit off the hinges. That sparke
jelousie falling into his drie melancholy braine, had well neare set
the whole house on fire.

THARSALIO No matter, let it worke; I did but pay him in's owne
coine; Sfoot hee plied me with such a volley of unseason'd
scoffs, as would have made Patience it selfe turne Ruffine, attiring
it selfe in wounds and bloud: but is his humour better qualified
then?

LYCUS Yes, but with a medicine ten parts more dangerous then the
sicknesse: you know how strange his dotage ever was on his wife;
taking speciall glorie to have her love and loialtie to him so
renown'd abroad. To whom shee oftentimes hath vow'd constancie
after life, till her owne death had brought forsooth, her widdow-
troth to bed. This he joi'd in strangely, and was therein of infallible
beliefe, till your surmise began to shake it; which hath loos'd it so,

as now there's nought can settle it, but a trial, which hee's resolv'd upon.

THARSALIO As how man? as how?

LYCUS Hee is resolv'd to follow your advise, to die, and make triall of her stablenesse, and you must lend your hand to it.

THARSALIO What to cut's throat?

LYCUS To forge a rumour of his death, to uphold it by circumstance, 60 maintaine a publicke face of mourning, and all thinges appertaining.

THARSALIO I, but the meanes man: what time? what probabilitie?

LYCUS Nay, I thinke he has not lickt his Whelpe into full shape yet, but you shall shortly heare ant.

THARSALIO And when shall this strange conception see light?

LYCUS Forthwith: there's nothing staies him, but some odde businesse of import, which hee must winde up; least perhaps his absence by occasion of his intended triall bee prolonged above his aimes.

THARSALIO Thankes for this newes i'faith. This may perhaps prove happie to my Nephew. Truth is I love my sister well and must 70 acknowledge her more then ordinarie vertues. But shee hath so possest my brothers heart with vowes, and disavowings, seal'd with oathes of second nuptialls; as in that confidence, hee hath invested her in all his state, the ancient inheritance of our Familie: and left my Nephew and the rest to hang upon her pure devotion; so as he dead, and shee matching (as I am resolv'd shee will) with some yong Prodigall; what must ensue, but her post-issue beggerd, and our house alreadie sinking, buried quick in ruin. But this triall may remove it, and since tis come to this; marke but the issue *Lycus*, for all these solemne vowes, if I doe not make her prove in 80 the handling as weake as a wafer; say I lost my time in travaile. This resolution then has set his wits in joynt againe, hee's quiet.

LYCUS Yes, and talkes of you againe in the fairest manner, listens after your speede.

THARSALIO Nay hee's passing kinde, but I am glad of this triall for all that.

LYCUS Which he thinkes to be a flight beyond your wing.

THARSALIO But hee will change that thought ere long. My Bird you saw even now, sings me good newes, and makes hopefull signes to me. 90

LYCUS Somewhat can I say too, since your messengers departure, her Ladiship hath beene something alter'd, more pensive then before, and tooke occasion to question of you, what your addictions were? of what tast your humor was? of what cut you wore your wit? and all this in a kind of disdainefull scorne.

THARSALIO Good Callenders *Lycus*. Well Ile pawne this jewell with thee, my next encounter shall quite alter my brothers judgement. Come lets in, he shall commend it for a discreet and honourable attempt.

100 Mens judgments sway on that side fortune leanes,
Thy wishes shall assist me.

LYCUS   And my meanes.   *Exeunt*.

[*Act II. Scene 4*]

ARGUS, CLINIAS, STHENIO, IANTHE.

ARGUS I must confesse I was ignorant, what 'twas to court a Ladie till now.

STHENIO And I pray you what is it now?

ARGUS To court her I perceive, is to woo her with letters from Court, for so this Spartane Lords Court discipline teacheth.

STHENIO His Lordship hath procur'd a new Pacquet from his Altitude.

CLINIAS If he bring no better ware then letters in's pacquet, I shall greatly doubt of his good speede.

10 IANTHE If his Lordship did but know how gracious his Aspect is to my Ladie in this solitarie humour.

CLINIAS Well these retir'd walkes of hers are not usuall; and bode some alteration in her thoughts. What may bee the cause *Sthenio*?

STHENIO Nay twould trouble *Argus* with his hundred eies to descrie the cause.

IANTHE *Venus* keepe her upright, that shee fall not from the state of her honour; my feare is that some of these Serpentine suiters will tempt her from her constant vow of widdow-hood. If they doe, good night to our good daies.

20 STHENIO 'Twere a sinne to suspect her; I have been witnesse to so many of her fearfull protestations to our late Lord against that course; to her infinite oathes imprinted on his lips, and seal'd in

his heart with such imprecations to her bed, if ever it should
receive a second impression; to her open and often detestations
of that incestuous life (as shee term'd it) of widdowes marriages;
as being but a kinde of lawfull adulterie; like usurie, permitted by
the law, not approv'd. That to wed a second, was no better then
to cuckold the first: That women should entertaine wedlocke as
one bodie, as one life, beyond which there were no desire, no
thought, no repentance from it, no restitution to it. So as if the   30
conscience of her vowes should not restraine her, yet the worlds
shame to breake such a constant resolution, should represse any
such motion in her.

ARGUS   Well, for her vowes, they are gone to heaven with her husband,
they binde not upon earth: And as for Womens resolutions, I must
tell you, The Planets, and (as *Ptolomie* saies) the windes have a great
stroke in them. Trust not my learning if her late strangenesse, and
exorbitant solitude, be not hatching some new Monster.

IANTHE   Well applied *Argus*; Make you husbands Monsters?

ARGUS   I spoke of no husbands: but you Wenches have the pregnant   40
wits, to turne Monsters into husbands, as you turne husbands into
monsters.

STHENIO   Well *Ianthe*, 'twere high time we made in, to part our Ladie
and her Spartane wooer.

IANTHE   We shall appeare to her like the two fortunate Stars in a
tempest, to save the shipwrack of her patience.

STHENIO   I, and to him to, I beleeve; For by this time he hath spent
the last dramme of his newes.

ARGUS   That is, of his wit.

STHENIO   Just good wittals.   50

IANTHE   If not, and that my Ladie be not too deep in her new dumps,
we shall heare from his Lordship; what such a Lord said of his
wife the first night hee embrac't her: To what Gentleman such a
Count was beholding for his fine children. What yong Ladie, such
an old Count should marrie; what Revells: what presentments are
towards; and who penn'd the Pegmas; and so forth: and yet for
all this, I know her harsh Suiter hath tir'd her to the uttermost
scruple of her forbearance, and will doe more, unlesse we two,
like a paire of Sheres, cut a-sunder the thred of his discourse.

STHENIO   Well then, lets in; But my masters, waite you on your charge   60 at your perils, see that you guard her approch from any more intruders.

IANTHE Excepting yong *Tharsalio*.

STHENIO True, excepting him indeede, for a guard of men is not able to keepe him out ant please your Honour.

ARGUS O Wenches, that's the propertie of true valour, to promise like a Pigmey, and performe like a Giant. If he come, Ile bee sworne Ile doe my Ladies commandement upon him.

IANTHE What? beate him out?

70 STHENIO If hee should, *Tharsalio* would not take it ill at his handes, for he does but his Ladies commandement.

> *Enter* THARSALIO.

ARGUS Well, by *Hercules* he comes not here.

STHENIO By *Venus* but hee does: or else shee hath heard my Ladies praiers, and sent some gracious spirit in his likenesse to fright away that Spartane wooer, that hants her.

THARSALIO There stand her Sentinells.

ARGUS Slight the Ghost appeares againe.

THARSALIO Save yee my qondam fellowes in Armes; save yee; my women.

80 STHENIO Your Women Sir?

THARSALIO 'Twill be so. What no courtesies? No preparation of grace? Observe me I advise you for your owne sakes.

IANTHE For your owne sake, I advise you to pack hence, lest your impudent valour cost you dearer then you thinke.

CLINIAS What senselesse boldnesse is this *Tharsalio*?

ARGUS Well said *Clinias*, talke to him.

CLINIAS I wonder that notwithstanding the shame of your last entertainment, and threatnings of worse; you would yet presume to trouble this place againe.

90 THARSALIO Come, y'are a widgine; Off with your hat Sir, acknowledge: forecast is better then labour. Are you squint ey'd? can you not see afore you? A little foresight I can tell you might sted you much as the Starres shine now.

CLINIAS 'Tis well sir, tis not for nothing your brother is asham'd on you. But Sir, you must know, wee are chardg'd to barre your entrance.

THARSALIO But Wifler, know you, that who so shall dare to execute
that charge, Ile be his Executioner.

ARGUS By *Jove, Clinias,* me thinks, the Gentleman speakes very
honourably.   100

THARSALIO Well I see this house needes reformation, here's a fellow
stands behind now, of a forwarder insight then yee all. What place
hast thou?

ARGUS What place you please Sir.

THARSALIO Law you Sir. Here's a fellow to make a Gentleman Usher
Sir, I discharge you of the place, and doe here invest thee into his
roome, make much of thy haire, thy wit will suit it rarely. And for
the full possession of thine office; Come, Usher me to thy Ladie:
and to keep thy hand supple, take this from me.

ARGUS No bribes Sir, ant please your Worship.   110

THARSALIO Goe to, thou dost well; but pocket it for all that; it's no
impaire to thee: the greatest doo't.

ARGUS Sir, tis your love onely that I respect, but since out of your
love you please to bestow it upon me, it were want of Courtship
in mee to refuse it; Ile acquaint my Ladie with your comming.

Exit. ARGUS.

THARSALIO How say by this? have not I made a fit choise, that hath
so soone attain'd the deepest mysterie of his profession: Good
sooth Wenches, a few courtsies had not beene cast away upon
your new Lord.

STHENIO Weele beleeve that, when our Ladie has a new Sonne of   120
your getting.

Enter ARGUS, EUDORA, REBUS, HIARBUS, PSORABEUS.

EUDORA Whats the matter? whose that, you say, is come?

ARGUS The bold Gentleman, ant please your Honour.

EUDORA Why thou flering Asse thou.

ARGUS Ant please your Honour.

EUDORA Did not I forbid his approch by all the charge and dutie of
thy service?

THARSALIO Madam, this fellow only is intelligent; for he truly under-
stood your command according to the stile of the Court of *Venus;*
that is, by contraries: when you forbid you bid.   130

EUDORA By heaven Ile discharge my house of yee all.

THARSALIO You shall not neede Madame, for I have alreadie

casheer'd your officious Usher here, and chos'd this for his Suc-
cessor.

EUDORA O incredible boldnesse!

THARSALIO Madam, I come not to command your love with enforst
letters, not to woo you with tedious stories of my Pedigree, as hee
who drawes the thred of his descent from *Ledas* Distaffe; when
'tis well knowne his Grandshire cried Coniskins in Sparta.

140 REBUS Whom meane you Sir?

THARSALIO Sir, I name none, but him who first shall name himselfe.

REBUS The place Sir, I tell you still; and this Goddesses faire presence,
or else my reply should take a farre other forme upon't.

THARSALIO If it should Sir, I would make your Lordship an anser.

ARGUS Anser's Latine for a Goose, ant please your honor.

EUDORA Well noted Gander; and what of that?

ARGUS Nothing, ant please your Honor, but that he said he would
make his Lordship an answere.

EUDORA Thus every foole mocks my poore Suiter. Tell mee thou
150 most frontlesse of all men, did'st thou (when thou had'st meanes
to note me best) ever observe so base a temper in mee, as to give
any glance at stooping to my Vassall?

THARSALIO Your drudge Madam, to doe your drudgerie.

EUDORA Or am I now so skant of worthie Suiters,
That may advance mine honour; advance my estate;
Strengthen my alliance (if I list to wed)
That I must stoop to make my foot my head?

THARSALIO No but your side, to keepe you warme a bed.
But Madame vouchsafe me your patience to that points serious
160 answere. Though I confesse to get higher place in your graces, I
could wish my fortunes more honourable; my person more gra-
tious, my minde more adorn'd with Noble and Heroicall vertues;
yet Madame (that you thinke not your bloud disparadg'd by mixture
with mine) daine to know this: howsoever I once, only for your
love, disguis'd my selfe in the service of your late Lord and mine;
yet my descent is as honourable as the proudest of your Spartane
attempters; who by unknown quills or conduits under ground,
drawes his Pedigree from *Lycurgus* his great Toe, to the Viceroies
little finger, and from thence to his owne elbow, where it will
170 never leave itching.

REBUS Tis well Sir, presume still of the place.

THARSALIO Sfoot Madame, am I the first great personage that hath
stoopt to disguises for love? what thinke you of our Countrie-man
Hercules; that for love put on *Omphales* Apron, and sate spinning
amongst her Wenches, while his Mistris wore his Lyons skin and
Lamb-skin'd him, if he did not his businesse?

EUDORA Most fitly thou resembl'st thy selfe to that violent outlaw,
that claim'd all other mens possessions as his owne by his meere
valour. For what lesse hast thou done? Come into my house, beate
away these Honourable persons?   180

THARSALIO That I will Madam. Hence ye Sparta-Velvets.

PSORABEUS Hold, shee did not meane so.

THARSALIO Away I say, or leave your lives I protest here.

HIARBAS Well Sir, his Altitude shall know you.

REBUS Ile doe your errand Sir.

                    Exeunt [REBUS, HIARBUS, PSORABEUS].

THARSALIO Doe good Cosen Altitude; and beg the reversion of the
next Ladie: for *Dido* has betrotht her love to me. By this faire hand
Madam, a faire riddance of this Calidonian Bore.

EUDORA O most prodigious audaciousnesse!

THARSALIO True Madam; O fie upon am, they are intollerable. And   190
I can not but admire your singular vertue of patience, not common
in your sexe; and must therefore carrie with it some rare indowment
of other Masculine and Heroicall vertues. To heare a rude Spartane
court so ingenuous a Ladie, with dull newes from Athens, or the
Vicerois court; how many dogs were spoil'd at the last Bull-baiting;
what Ladies dub'd their husbands Knights, and so forth.

EUDORA But hast thou no shame? No sense of what disdain I shew'd
thee in my last entertainment? chacing thee from my presence,
and charging thy dutie, not to attempt the like intrusion for thy
life; and dar'st thou yet approch mee in this unmannerly manner?   200
No question this desperate boldnesse can not choose but goe
accompanied with other infinite rudenesses.

THARSALIO Good Madam, give not the Child an unfit name, terme
it not boldnes, which the Sages call true confidence, founded on
the most infallible Rocke of a womans constancie.

EUDORA If shame can not restraine thee, tell mee yet if any brainlesse
foole would have tempted the danger attending thy approch.

THARSALIO No Madam, that proves I am no Foole: Then had I been
here a Foole, and a base low-sprited Spartan, if for a Ladies froune,
210   or a Lords threates, or for a Guard of Groomes, I should have
shrunke in the wetting, and suffer'd such a delicious flower to
perish in the stalke, or to be savadgely pluckt by a prophane finger.
No Madam: First let me be made a Subject for disgrace; let your
remorselesse Guard seaze on my despised bodie, bind me hand
and foot, and hurle me into your Ladiships bed.

EUDORA O Gods: I protest thou dost more and more make me
admire thee.

THARSALIO Madam, ignorance is the mother of admiration: know
me better, and youle admire me lesse.

220 EUDORA What would'st thou have mee know? what seekes thy com-
ming? why dost thou hant me thus?

THARSALIO Only Madam, that the *AEtna* of my sighes, and *Nilus*
of my teares, pour'd forth in your presence, might witnesse to
your Honor the hot and moist affection of my hart, and worke
me some measure of favour, from your sweete tongue, or your
sweeter lips, or what else your good Ladiship shall esteeme more
conducible, to your divine contentment.

EUDORA Pen and Inck-horne I thanke thee. This you learn'd when
you were a Serving-man.

230 THARSALIO Madam, I am still the same creature; and I will so tie my
whole fortunes to that stile, as were it my happinesse (as I know
it will be) to mount into my Lords succession, yet vow I never to
assume other Title, or State, then your servants: Not approching
your boord, but bidden: Not pressing to your bed, but your pleasure
shall be first known if you will command me any service.

EUDORA Thy vowes are as vaine as a Ruffins othes; as common as
the aire; and as cheape as the dust. How many of the light huswives,
thy Muses, hath thy love promist this service besides, I pray thee?

THARSALIO Compare shadowes to bodies, Madam; Pictures to the
240   life; and such are they to you, in my valuation.

EUDORA I see wordes will never free me of thy boldnesse, and will
therefore now use blowes; and those of the mortallest enforcement.
Let it suffice Sir, that all this time, and to this place, you enjoy
your safetie; keepe backe: No one foote follow mee further; for I

protest to thee, the next threshold past, lets passe a prepar'd
Ambush to thy latest breath.   *Exit.* EUDORA.

THARSALIO This for your Ambush! *He drawes.* Dare my love with
death?   [*Exit.*]

CLINIAS Slight; follow ant please your Honour.

ARGUS Not I by this light.   250

CLINIAS I hope Gentle-women you will.

STHENIO Not we Sir, we are no parters of fraies.

CLINIAS Faith nor Ile be any breaker of customes.   *Exeunt.*

Finis Actus Secundi.

Act III. Scene 1

Enter LYSANDER *and* LYCUS *booted.*

LYCUS Would any heart of Adamant, for satisfaction of an
ungrounded humour, racke a poore Ladies innocencie as you
intend to doe? It was a strange curiositie in that Emperour, that
ript his Mothers wombe to see the place he lay in.

LYSANDER Come do not lode me with volumes of perswasion; I am
resolv'd, if shee be gold shee may abide the tast; lets away. I wonder
where this wild brother is.

Enter CYNTHIA, HYLUS, *and* ERO.

CYNTHIA Sir.

LYSANDER I pray thee wife shew but thy selfe a woman;
And be silent: question no more the reason   10
Of my journey, which our great Viceroies charge
Urg'd in this letter doth enforce me to.

CYNTHIA Let me but see that letter, there is somthing
In this presaging bloud of mine, tells me
This sodaine journey can portend no good;
Resolve me sweet, have not I given you cause
Of discontent, by some misprision,
Or want of fit observance? let mee know
That I may wreake my selfe upon my selfe.

LYSANDER Come wife, our love is now growne old and staid,   20
And must not wanton it in tricks of Court,

> Nor enterchang'd delights of melting lovers;
> Hanging on sleeves, sighing, loth to depart;
> These toies are past with us; our true loves substance
> Hath worne out all the shew; let it suffice,
> I hold thee deare: and thinke some cause of weight
> With no excuse to be dispenst with all,
> Compells me from thy most desir'd embraces;
> I stay but for my Brother, came he not in last night?

30 HYLUS For certaine no sir, which gave us cause of wonder, what accident kept him abrode.

CYNTHIA Pray heaven it prove not some wild resolution, bred in him by his second repulse from the Countesse.

LYSANDER Trust me I something feare it, this insatiate spirit of aspiring, being so dangerous and fatall; desire mounted on the wings of it, descends not but headlong.

HYLUS Sir, sir, heres my Uncle.

> *Enter* THARSALIO.

LYSANDER What wrapt in carelesse cloake, face hid in hat unbanded! these are the ditches brother, in which outraging colts plunge both
40 themselves and their riders.

THARSALIO Well, wee must get out as well as wee may, if not, there's the making of a grave sav'd.

CYNTHIA That's desperately spoken brother, had it not been happier the colt had beene better broken, and his rider not fallen in?

THARSALIO True sister, but wee must ride colts before wee can breake them, you know.

LYSANDER This is your blind Goddesse *Confidence*.

THARSALIO Alas brother, our house is decaid, and my honest ambition to restore it, I hope be pardonable. My comfort is: the
50 Poet that pens the storie wil write ore my head *magnis tamen excidit ausis*;
> Which in our native Idiome, lets you know,
> His mind was high, though Fortune was his Foe.

LYSANDER A good resolve brother, to out-jest disgrace: come, I had been on my journey but for some private speech with you: lets in.

THARSALIO Good brother stay a little, helpe out this ragged colt out of the ditch.

> [*Uncloaks and reveals a splendid suit.*]

LYSANDER How now.

THARSALIO Now I confesse my oversight, this have I purchas'd by
my confidence.   60

LYSANDER I like you brother, 'tis the true Garb you know,
What wants in reall worth supply in show.

THARSALIO In show? alas 'twas even the thing it selfe,
I op't my counting house, and tooke away
These simple fragments of my treasurie,
Husband my Countesse cri'd take more, more yet,
Yet, I in hast, to pay in part my debt,
And prove my selfe a husband of her store,
Kist and came of; and this time tooke no more.

CYNTHIA But good brother –   70

THARSALIO Then were our honor'd spousall rites perform'd,
Wee made all short, and sweet, and close, and sure.

LYSANDER Hee's wrap't.

THARSALIO Then did my Ushers, and chiefe Servants stoope,
Then made my women curtsies, and envied
Their Ladies fortune: I was magnified.

LYSANDER Let him alone, this spirit will soone vanish.

THARSALIO Brother and sister as I love you, and am true servant
To *Venus*, all the premises are serious and true,
And the conclusion is: the great Countesse is mine,   80
The Palace is at your service, to which I invite
You all to solemnize my honour'd nuptialls.

LYSANDER Can this be credited!

THARSALIO Good brother doe not you envie my fortunate
atchievement?

LYSANDER Nay I ever said, the attempt was commendable.

THARSALIO Good.

LYSANDER If the issue were successefull.

THARSALIO A good state-conclusion, happie events make good the
worst attempts. Here are your widdow-vowes sister; thus are yee   90
all in your pure naturalls; certaine morall disguises of coinesse,
which the ignorant cal modestie, ye borrow of art to cover your
buske points; which a blunt and resolute encounter, taken under
a fortunate aspect, easily disarms you off; and then alas what are
you? poore naked sinners, God wot: weake paper walls thrust

downe with a finger; this is the way on't, boile their appetites to
a full height of lust; and then take them downe in the nicke.

CYNTHIA Is there probabilitie in this; that a Ladie so great, so
vertuous, standing on so high termes of honour, should so soone
stoope?

THARSALIO You would not wonder sister, if you knew the lure shee
stoop't at: greatnesse? thinke you that can curb affection? no, it
whets it more; they have the full streame of bloud, to beare them:
the sweet gale of their sublim'd spirits to drive them: the calme of
ease to prepare them: the sun-shine of fortune to allure them:
Greatnesse to waft them safe through all Rocks of infamie: when
youth, wit, and person come aboord once, tell me sister, can you
chuse but hoise saile, and put forward to the maine?

LYSANDER But let me wonder at this frailtie yet;
Would shee in so short time weare out his memorie,
So soone wipe from her eies, nay, from her heart,
Whom I my selfe, and this whole Ile besides,
Still remember with griefe, th'impression of
His losse taking worthily such roote in us;
Howe thinke you wife?

CYNTHIA I am asham'd ant, and abhorre to thinke,
So great and vow'd a patterne of our sexe,
Should take into her thoughts, nay to her bed,
(O staine to woman-hood) a second love.

LYCUS In so short time.

CYNTHIA   In any time.

LYSANDER   No, wife?

CYNTHIA By *Juno* no; sooner a lothsom Tode.

THARSALIO High words beleeve me, and I thinke sheele keep them;
next turne is yours Nephew; you shall now marrie my noblest
Ladie-Daughter; the first marriage in *Paphos* next my nuptialls shall
be yours; these are strange occurents brother, but pretie and
patheticall: if you see mee in my chaire of Honour; and my
Countesse in mine armes; you will then beleeve, I hope, I am Lord
of the Palace, then shall you trie my great Ladies entertainment;
see your handes free'd of mee, and mine taking you to advancement.

LYSANDER Well, all this rids not my businesse; wife you shall bee
there to partake the unexpected honour of our House. *Lycus*, and

I will make it our recreation by the way, to thinke of your Revells
and Nuptiall sports; Brother my stay hath beene for you; Wife
pray thee bee gone, and soone prepare for the solemnitie, a Moneth
returnes mee.

CYNTHIA   Heavens guide your journey.

LYSANDER   Fare-well.

THARSALIO   Fare-well Nephew; prosper in virilitie, but doe you heare;
keepe your hand from your voice, I have a part for you in our
Hymeneall shew.   140

HYLUS   You speake too late for my voice, but Ile discharge the part.
                                    Exeunt CYNTHIA, HYLUS [*and* ERO].

LYSANDER   Occurrents call yee them; foule shame confound them
all; that impregnable Fort of chastitie and loyaltie, that amazement
of the world, O yee Deities could nothing restraine her? I tooke
her spirit to bee too haughtie for such a depression.

THARSALIO   But who commonly more short heeld, then they that
are high 'ith in-step?

LYSANDER   Mee thinkes yet shame should have controul'd so sodaine
an appetite.

THARSALIO   Tush, shame doth extinguish lust as oile doth fire,   150
The bloud once het, shame doth enflame the more,
What they before by art dissembled most,
They act more freely; shame once found is lost;
And to say truth Brother; what shame is due to't? or what congru-
ence doth it carrie, that a yong Ladie, Gallant, Vigorous, full of
Spirit, and Complexion; her appetite newe whetted with Nuptiall
delights; to be confind to the speculation of a deaths head, or for
the losse of a husband, the world affording flesh enough, make
the noone-tide of her yeares, the sunne-set of her pleasures?

LYCUS   And yet there have been such women.   160

THARSALIO   Of the first stamp perhaps, when the mettal was purer
then in these degenerate daies; of later yeares, much of that coine
hath beene counterfait, and besides so crackt and worne with use,
that they are growne light, and indeede fit for nothing, but to be
turn'd over in play.

LYSANDER   Not all brother.

THARSALIO   My matchlesse sister only excepted: for shee, you know
is made of an other mettall, then that shee borrow'd of her mother.

But doe you brother sadly intend the pursuite of this triall?

170 LYSANDER Irrevocably.

THARSALIO Its a high project: if it be once rais'd, the earth is too
weake to beare so waightie an accident, it cannot bee conjur'd
downe againe, without an earth-quake, therefore beleeve shee will
be constant.

LYSANDER No, I will not.

THARSALIO Then beleeve shee will not be constant.

LYSANDER Neither, I will beleeve nothing but what triall enforces;
will you hold your promise for the governing of this project with
skill, and secrecie?

180 THARSALIO If it must needes bee so. But hearke you brother; have
you no other Capricions in your head to intrap my sister in her
frailtie, but to prove the firmenesse of her widdow vowes after
your suppos'd death?

LYSANDER None in the world.

THARSALIO Then here's my hand, Ile be as close, as my Ladies shoe
to her foote that pinches and pleases her, and will beare on with
the plot, till the vessell split againe.

LYSANDER Forge any death, so you can force beliefe. Say I was
poison'd, drown'd.

190 THARSALIO Hang'd.

LYSANDER Any thing, so you assist it with likely circumstance, I
neede not instruct you: that must bee your imploiment *Lycus*.

LYCUS Well Sir.

THARSALIO But brother you must set in to; to countenance truth
out, a herse there must be too; Its strange to thinke how much
the eie prevailes in such impressions; I have marckt a Widdow,
that just before was seene pleasant enough, follow an emptie herse,
and weepe devoutly.

LYCUS All those thinges leave to me.

200 LYSANDER But brother for the bestowing of this herse in the monu-
ment of our Familie, and the marshalling of a Funerall.

THARSALIO Leave that to my care, and if I doe not doe the mourner,
as lively as your Heire, and weepe as lustily as your Widdow, say
there's no vertue in Onions; that being done, Ile come to visit the
distrest widdow; apply old ends of comfort to her griefe, but the
burden of my song shall be to tell her wordes are but dead comforts;

and therefore counsaile her to take a living comfort, that might
Ferrit out the thought of her dead husband, and will come prepar'd
with choise of suiters; either my Spartane Lord for grace at the
Viceroies Court, or some great Lawyer that may soder up her   210
crackt estate, and so forth. But what would you say brother, if you
should finde her married at your arrivall?

LYSANDER By this hand, split her Wezand.

THARSALIO Well, forget not your wager, a stately chariot with foure
brave Horses of the Thracian breede, with all appurtenances. Ile
prepare the like for you, if you prove Victor; but well remembred,
where will you lurke the whiles?

LYSANDER Mewd up close, some short daies journey hence, *Lycus*
shall know the place; write still how all things passe. Brother adiew;
all joy attend you.   220

THARSALIO Will you not stay our nuptiall now so neare?

LYSANDER I should be like a man that heares a tale
And heedes it not; one absent from himselfe.
My wife shall attend the Countesse, and my Sonne.

THARSALIO Whom you shal hear at your returne call me
Father; adiew: *Jove* be your speede.
My Nuptialls done, your Funeralls succeed.   *Exeunt.*

[*Act III. Scene 2*]

Enter ARGUS *barehead.*

ARGUS A Hall, a hall: who's without there?

Enter two or three with cushions.

Come on, y'are proper Groomes, are yee not? Slight I thinke y'are
all Bridegroomes, yee take your pleasures so. A companie of
dormice. Their Honours are upon comming, and the roome not
readie. Rushes and seates instantly.

Enter THARSALIO.

THARSALIO Now, alas fellow *Argus*, how thou art comberd with an
office?

ARGUS Perfume sirrha, the roome's dampish.

THARSALIO Nay you may leave that office to the Ladies, theyle
perfume it sufficiently.   10

ARGUS Cry mercie Sir, here's a whole *Chorus* of *Sylvans* at hand,
cornetting, and tripping ath' toe, as the ground they troad on were
too hot for their feete. The device is rare; and there's your yong
Nephew too, he hangs in the clouds Deified with *Hymens* shape.

THARSALIO Is he perfect in's part? has not his tongue learn'd of the
Sylvans to trip ath' Toe?

ARGUS Sir, beleeve it, he does it pretiously for accent and action, as
if hee felt the part he plaid: hee ravishes all the yong Wenches in
the Palace: Pray *Venus* my yong Ladie *Laodice* have not some little
20 prick of *Cupid* in her, shee's so diligent at's rehearsall.

THARSALIO No force, so my next vowes be heard, that if *Cupid* have
prickt her, *Hymen* may cure her.

ARGUS You meane your Nephew Sir that presents *Hymen*.

THARSALIO Why so, I can speake nothing but thou art within me:
fie of this wit of thine, 'twill be thy destruction. But howsoever
you please to understand, *Hymen* send the boy no worse fortune:
And where's my Ladies honour?

ARGUS At hand Sir, with your unparagond sister, please you take
your chaire of Honour Sir?

30 THARSALIO Most serviceable *Argus*, the Gods reward thy service;
for I will not.

> *Enter* EUDORA, *leading* CYNTHIA, LAODICE, STHENIO,
> IANTHE, ERO, *with others following.*

EUDORA Come sister, now we must exchange that name
For stranger Titles, let's dispose our selves
To entertaine these *Sylvane* Revellers,
That come to grace our loved Nuptialls.
I feare me we must all turne Nymphs to night,
To side those sprightly wood-Gods in their dances;
Can you doo't nimbly sister? slight what aile you,
Are you not well?

CYNTHIA Yes Madam.

EUDORA But your lookes,
40 Mee thinkes, are cloudie; suiting ill the Sunne-shine
Of this cleare honour to your husbands house.
Is there ought here that sorts not with your liking?

THARSALIO Blame her not Mistris, if her lookes shew care.
Excuse the Merchants sadnesse that hath made

A doubtfull venture of his whole estate;
His livelyhood, his hopes, in one poore bottome,
To all encounters of the Sea and stormes.
Had you a husband that you lov'd as well,
Would you not take his absent plight as ill?
Cavill at every fancie? not an object   50
That could present it selfe, but it would forge
Some vaine objection, that did doubt his safetie;
True love is ever full of jealousie.

EUDORA Jealous? of what? of every little journey?
Meere fancie then is wanton; and doth cast
At those sleight dangers there, too doting glances;
Misgiving mindes ever provoke mischances:
Shines not the Sunne in his way bright as here?
Is not the aire as good? what hazard doubt you?

ARGUS His horse may stumble if it please your Honour;   60
The raine may wet, the winde may blow on him;
Many shrewd hazards watch poore travailers.

EUDORA True, and the shrewdest thou hast reckend us.
Good sister, these cares fit yong married wives.

CYNTHIA Wives should be stil yong in their husbands loves.
Time beares no Sythe should bear down them before him.
Our lives he may cut short, but not our loves.

THARSALIO Sister be wise, and ship not in one Barke,
All your abilitie: if he miscarrie,
Your well tried wisedome should look out for new.   70

CYNTHIA I wish them happie windes that runne that course,
From me tis farre; One Temple seal'd our troth
One Tomb, one houre shall end, and shroud us both.

THARSALIO Well, y'are a *Phoenix*; there, be that your cheere:
Love, with your husband be, your wisedome here.
Hearke, our sports challenge it; Sit dearest Mistris.

EUDORA Take your place worthiest servant.

THARSALIO Serve me heaven,   *Musique.*
As I my heavenly Mistris; Sit rare sister.
      Musique: [HYLUS *as*] HYMEN *descends; and sixe* SYLVANES *enter
      beneath, with Torches.*

ARGUS A hall, a hall: let no more Citizens in there.   80

LAODICE O, not my Cosen see; but *Hymens* selfe.

STHENIO He does become it most enflamingly.

HYMEN Haile honor'd Bridegroom, and his Princely bride,
    With the most fam'd for vertue, *Cynthia*;
    And this yong Ladie, bright *Laodice*,
    One rich hope of this noblest Familie.

STHENIO Hearke how he courts: he is enamour'd too.

LAODICE O grant it *Venus*, and be ever honour'd.

HYMEN In grace and love of you, I *Hymen* searcht
90   The groves and thickets that embrace this Palace
    With this clear-flam'd, and good aboding Torch
    For summons of these fresh and flowrie *Sylvans*,
    To this faire presence; with their winding Haies,
    Active and Antique dances to delight
    Your frolick eies, and helpe to celebrate
    These noblest nuptialls; which great Destinie,
    Ordain'd past custome and all vulgar object
    To be the readvancement of a house,
    Noble and Princely, and restore this Palace
100   To that name, that six hunderd Summers since
    Was in possession of this Bridegroomes Ancetors,
    The ancient and most vertue-fam'd *Lysandri*.
    Sylvans! the Courtships you make to your Dryads,
    Use to this great Bride, and these other Dames,
    And heighten with your sports, my nuptiall flames.

LAODICE O would himselfe descend, and me command.

STHENIO Dance; and his heart catch in an others hand.

    SYLVANS, *take out the Bride and the rest: They dance, after which,*
    and all set in their places, HYMEN.

HYMEN Now, what the Power and my Torches influence
    Hath in the blessings of your Nuptiall joyes
110   (Great Bride and Bridegroome) you shall amply part
    Betwixt your free loves, and forgoe it never.

OMNES Thankes to great *Hymen*, and faire *Sylvanes* ever.   *Exeunt.*

Finis Actus Tertii.

Act IV. Scene 1

THARSALIO, LYCUS, *with his Arme in a skarfe, a nightcap on's head.*

LYCUS I hope Sir by this time.

THARSALIO Put on man, by our selves.

LYCUS The edge of your confidence is well taken off; would you not
bee content to with-draw your wager?

THARSALIO Faith fellow *Lycus*, if my wager were weakely built, this
unexpected accident might stagger it. For the truth is, this strain
is extraordinarie, to follow her husbands bodie into the Tombe,
and there for his companie to burie her selfe quick: it's new and
stirring, but for all this, Ile not despaire of my wager.

LYCUS Why Sir, can you thinke such a passion dissembl'd?   10

THARSALIO All's one for that, What I thinke I thinke; In the meane
time forget not to write to my Brother, how the plot hath succeeded,
that the newes of his death hath taken; a funerall solemnitie
perform'd, his suppos'd Corse bestow'd in the monument of our
Familie, thou and I horrible mourners: But above all that his
intollerable vertuous Widow, for his love; and (for her love) *Ero*
her hand-maid, are discended with his Corse into the vault; there
wipe their eies time out of minde, drinke nothing but their own
teares, and by this time are almost dead with famine. There's a
point will sting it (for you say tis true); where left you him?   20

LYCUS At *Dipolis* Sir, some twentie miles hence.

THARSALIO He keepes close.

LYCUS I sir, by all meanes; skulks unknowne under the name of a
strange Knight.

THARSALIO That may carrie him without discrying, for there's a
number of strange Knights abroad. You left him well?

LYCUS Well Sir, but for this jealous humour that hants him.

THARSALIO Well, this newes will absolutely purge that humor. Write
all, forget not to describe her passion at thy discoverie of his
slaughter: did shee performe it well for her husbands wager?   30

LYCUS Performe it, call you it? you may jest; men hunt Hares to
death for their sports, but the poore beasts die in earnest: you
wager of her passions for your pleasure, but shee takes little

pleasure in those earnest passions. I never saw such an extasie of
sorrow, since I knew the name of sorrow. Her hands flew up to
her head like Furies, hid all her beauties in her dischevel'd haire,
and wept as she would turne fountaine. I would you and her
husband had beene behind the Arras but to have heard her. I
assure you Sir, I was so transported with the spectacle, that in
40   despight of my discretion, I was forc't to turne woman, and beare
a part with her. Humanitie broke loose from my heart, and stream'd
through mine eies.

THARSALIO In prose, thou weptst. So have I seen many a moist
Auditor doe at a play; when the storie was but a meere fiction:
And didst act the Nuntius well? would I had heard it: could'st
thou dresse thy lookes in a mournefull habite?

LYCUS Not without preparation Sir; no more then my speech, twas
a plaine acting of an enterlude to me, to pronounce the part.

THARSALIO As how for heavens sake?

50   LYCUS *Phœbus* addrest his chariot towards the West
To change his wearied Coursers, and so forth.

THARSALIO Nay on, and thou lov'st me.

LYCUS *Lysander* and my selfe beguild the way
With enterchang'd discourse, but our chiefe Theame,
Was of your dearest selfe, his honour'd wife;
Your love, your vertue, wondrous constancie.

THARSALIO Then was her Cu to whimper; on.

LYCUS When sodainly appear'd as far as sight
A troope of horse, arm'd as we might descerne,
60   With Javelines, Speares, and such accoutrements.
He doubted nought (As Innocencie ever
Is free from doubting ill.)

THARSALIO There dropt a teare.

LYCUS   My minde misgave me.
They might be mountaners. At their approch
They us'd no other language but their weapons,
To tell us what they were; *Lysander* drew,
And bore him selfe *Achilles* like in fight,
And as a Mower sweepes off t'heads of Bents,
So did *Lysanders* sword shave off the points
70   Of their assaulting lances.

His horse at last, sore hurt, fell under him;
I, seeing I could not rescue, us'd my spurres
To flie away.

THARSALIO What from thy friend?

LYCUS I in a good quarrell, why not?

THARSALIO Good; I am answer'd.

LYCUS A lance pursued me, brought me back againe;
And with these wounds left me t'accompanie
Dying *Lysander*. Then they rifl'd us,
And left us.   80
They gone; my breath not yet gone, gan to strive
And revive sense: I with my feeble joynts
Crawl'd to *Lysander*, stirr'd him, and withall
He gaspst; cried *Cynthia*! and breath'd no more.

THARSALIO O then shee howl'd out right.

LYCUS Passengers came and in a Chariot brought us
Streight to a Neighbour Towne; where I forthwith
Coffind my friend in leade; and so convaid him
To this sad place.

THARSALIO 'Twas well; and could not show but strangely.   90

LYCUS Well Sir, this tale pronounc't with terrour, suited with action,
clothed with such likely circumstance; My wounds in shew, her
husbands herse in sight, thinke what effect it wrought: And if you
doubt, let the sad consequence of her retreat to his Tombe, bee
your wofull instructer.

THARSALIO For all this, Ile not despaire of my wager:
These Grieves that sound so lowd, prove alwaies light,
True sorrow evermore keepes out of sight.
This straine of mourning wi'th' Sepulcher, like an over-doing
Actor, affects grosly, and is indeede so farre forc't from the life,   100
that it bewraies it selfe to be altogether artificiall. To set open a
shop of mourning! Tis palpable. Truth, the substance, hunts not
after the shadow of popular Fame. Her officious ostentation of
sorrow condemnes her sinceritie. When did ever woman mourne
so unmeasurably, but shee did dissemble?

LYCUS O Gods! a passion thus borne; thus apparell'd with teares,
sighes, swownings, and all the badges of true sorrow, to be dis-
sembl'd! by *Venus* I am sorrie I ever set foot in't. Could shee, if

shee dissembl'd, thus dally with hunger, be deafe to the barking
of her appetite, not having these foure daies reliev'd nature with
one dramme of sustenance?

THARSALIO For this does shee looke to bee Deified, to have Hymnes
made of her, nay to her: The Tomb where she is to be no more
reputed the ancient monument of our Familie the *Lysandri*; but
the new erected Altar of *Cynthia*: To which all the Paphian widdowes
shall after their husbands Funeralls, offer their wet muckinders,
for monuments of the danger they have past, as Sea-men doe their
wet garments at *Neptunes* Temple after a shipwracke.

LYCUS Well, Ile apprehend you, at your pleasure: I for my part will
say; that if her faith bee as constant as her love is heartie, and
unaffected, her vertues may justly challenge a Deitie to enshrine
them.

THARSALIO I, there's an other point too. But one of those vertues
is enough at once. All natures are not capable of all gifts. If the
braine of the West were in the heads of the learned; then might
Parish-Clerkes be common counsaile men, and Poets Aldermens
deputies. My sister may turne *Niobe* for love; but till *Niobe* bee
turn'd to a Marble, Ile not despaire but shee may prove a woman.
Let the triall runne on, if shee doe not out-runne it, Ile say Poets
are not Prophets, Prognosticators are but Mountibankes, and none
tell true but woodmongers.   *Exit.*

LYCUS A sweet Gentleman you are. I mervaile what man? what
woman? what name? what action doth his tongue glide over, but
it leaves a slime upon't? Well, Ile presently to *Dipolis*, where *Lysander*
staies; and will not say but shee may prove fraile:
But this Ile say, if she should chance to breake,
Her teares are true, though womens truths are weake.   *Exit.*

[*Act IV. Scene 2*]

Enter LYSANDER *like a Souldier disguisde at all parts, a halfe Pike,*
gorget, &c, he discovers the Tombe, lookes in and wonders, &c.
O Miracle of nature! womens glorie;
Mens shame; and envie of the Deities!
Yet must these matchlesse creatures be suspected;

Accus'd; condemn'd! Now by th'immortall Gods,
They rather merit Altars, Sacrifice,
Then love and courtship.
Yet see the Queene of these lies here interred;
Tearing her haire, and drowned in her teares.
Which *Jove* should turne to Christall; and a Mirrour
Make of them; wherein men may see and wonder   10
At womens vertues. Shall shee famish then?
Will men (without disswasions) suffer thus
So bright an Ornament to earth, tomb'd quick,
In Earths darke bosome? Ho! who's in the Tombe there?
  [*He opens the tomb:* ERO *discovered.*]
ERO [*within*] Who calls? whence are you?
LYSANDER I am a Souldier of the watch and must enter.
ERO Amongst the dead?
LYSANDER Doe the dead speake? ope or Ile force it open.
ERO What violence is this? what seeke you here
  Where nought but death and her attendants dwell?   20
LYSANDER What wretched soules are you that thus by night
  Lurke here amongst the dead?
ERO   Good Souldier doe not stirre her,
  Shee's weake, and quickly seiz'd with swowning and passions,
  And with much trouble shall we both recall
  Her fainting spirits.
  Five daies thus hath shee wasted; and not once
  Season'd her Pallate with the tast of meate;
  Her powers of life are spent; and what remaines
  Of her famisht spirit, serves not to breath but sigh.
  Shee hath exil'd her eies from sleepe, or sight,   30
  And given them wholly up to ceaselesse teares
  Over that ruthfull herse of her deare Spouse,
  Slaine by Bandittos, Nobly borne *Lysander.*
LYSANDER And hopes shee with these heavie notes and cries
  To call him from the dead? In these five daies
  Hath shee but made him stirre a finger or fetch
  One gasp of that forsaken life shee mournes?
  Come, honour'd Mistris; I admire your vertues;
  But must reprove this vaine excesse of mone;

40 Rowse your selfe Ladie, and looke up from death,
   [CYNTHIA *is discovered.*]
 Well said, tis well; stay by my hand and rise.
 This Face hath beene maintain'd with better huswiferie.

CYNTHIA What are you?

LYSANDER   Ladie, I am Sentinell,
 Set in this hallowed place, to watch and guard
 On forfait of my life, these monuments
 From Rape, and spoile of sacrilegious handes,
 And save the bodies, that without you see
 Of crucified offenders; that no friends
 May beare them hence, to honour'd buriall.

50 CYNTHIA Thou seem'st an honest Souldier; pray thee then
 Be as thou seem'st; betake thee to thy charge
 And leave this place; adde not affliction
 To the afflicted.

LYSANDER   You misname the children.
 For what you terme affliction now, in you
 Is but selfe-humour; voluntarie Penance
 Impos'd upon your selfe: and you lament
 As did the *Satyre* once, that ran affrighted
 From that hornes sound that he himselfe had winded.
 Which humour to abate, my counsaile tending your term'd
   affliction,

60 What I for Phisicke give, you take for poison.
 I tell you honour'd Mistris, these ingredients
 Are wholesome, though perhaps they seeme untoothsome.

ERO This Souldier sure, is some decai'd pothecarie.

LYSANDER Deere Ghost be wise, and pittie your faire selfe
 Thus, by your selfe unnaturally afflicted:
 Chide back, heart-breaking grones, clear up those lamps,
 Restore them to their first creation:
 Windowes for light; not sluces made for teares.
 Beate not the senselesse aire with needlesse cries,
70 Banefull to life, and bootlesse to the dead.
 This is the Inne, where all *Deucalions* race
 Sooner or later, must take up their lodging;
 No priviledge can free us from this prison;

    No teares, no praiers, can redeeme from hence
    A captiv'd soule; Make use of what you see:
    Let this affrighting spectacle of death
    Teach you to nourish life.

ERO Good [Mistris] heare him: this is a rare Souldier.

LYSANDER Say that with abstinence you should unlose
    The knot of life: Suppose that in this Tombe   80
    For your deare Spouse, you should entomb your selfe
    A living Corse; Say that before your houre
    Without due Summons from the Fates, you send
    Your hastie soule to hell: can your deare Spouse
    Take notice of your faith and constancie?
    Shall your deare Spouse revive to give you thankes?

CYNTHIA Idle discourser.

LYSANDER   No, your moanes are idle.
    Goe to I say, be counsail'd; raise your selfe:
    Enjoy the fruits of life, there's viands for you,
    Now, live for a better husband. No? will you none?   90

ERO For love of courtesie, good Mistris, eate,
    Doe not reject so kinde and sweet an offer,
    Who knowes but this may be some *Mercurie*
    Disguis'de, and sent from *Juno* to relieve us?
    Did ever any lend unwilling eares
    To those that came with messages of life?

CYNTHIA I pray thee leave thy Rhetorique.

ERO By my soule; to speake plaine truth, I could rather wish t'employ
    my teeth then my tongue, so your example would be my warrant.

CYNTHIA Thou hast my warrant.

LYSANDER   Well then, eate my wench,   100
    Let obstinacie starve. Fall to.

ERO Perswade My Mistris first.

LYSANDER   Slight tell me Ladie,
    Are you resolv'd to die? If that be so,
    Choose not (for shame) a base, and beggars death:
    Die not for hunger, like a Spartane Ladie;
    Fall valiantly upon a sword, or drinke
    A noble death, expell your griefe with poison,
    There 'tis, seize it. [*offering his sword.*] Tush you dare not die.

110   Come, Wench, thou hast not lost a husband;
        Thou shalt eate, th'art now within the place
        Where I command.

ERO I protest sir.

LYSANDER Well said; eate, and protest, or Ile protest
        And doe thou eate; thou eat'st against thy will,
        That's it thou would'st say.

ERO It is.

LYSANDER And under such a protestation
        Thou lost thy Maiden-head.

120   For your owne sake good Ladie forget this husband,
        Come you are now become a happy Widdow,
        A blessednesse that many would be glad of.
        That and your husbands Inventorie together,
        Will raise you up husbands enow. What thinke you of me?

CYNTHIA Trifler, pursue this wanton Theame no further;
        Lest (which I would be loth) your speech provoke
        Uncivill language from me; I must tell you,
        One joynt of him I lost, was much more worth
        Then the rackt valew of thy entire bodie.

130 ERO O know what joynt shee meanes.

LYSANDER   Well, I have done.
        And well done frailtie; proface, how lik'st thou it?

ERO Very toothsome Ingrediens surely sir,
        Want but some lycor to incorporate them.

LYSANDER There tis, carouse.

ERO   I humbly thanke you Sir.

LYSANDER Hold pledge me now.

ERO   Tis the poison Sir,
        That preserves life, I take it.   *bibit Ancill.*

LYSANDER   Doe so, take it.

ERO Sighing has made me somthing short-winded.
        Ile pledge y'at twice.

LYSANDER   Tis well done; doe me right.

ERO I pray sir, have you beene a Pothecarie?

140 LYSANDER Marrie have I wench; A womans Pothecarie.

ERO Have you good Ingredients?
        I like your Bottle well. Good Mistris tast it.

Trie but the operation, twill fetch up
The roses in your cheekes againe.
Doctor *Verolles* bottles are not like it;
There's no *Guaicum* here, I can assure you.

LYSANDER This will doe well anone.

ERO   Now fie upon't.
O I have lost my tongue in this same lymbo.
The spring an't's spoil'd me thinkes; it goes not off
With the old twange.   150

LYSANDER Well said wench, oile it well; twill make it slide well.

ERO *Aristotle* saies sir, in his Posterionds –

LYSANDER This wench is learned; And what saies he?

ERO That when a man dies, the last thing that moves is his heart, in
a woman her tongue.

LYSANDER Right; and addes further, that you women are
A kind of spinners; if their legs be pluckt off,
Yet still they'le wag them; so will you your tongues.
With what an easie change does this same weaknesse
Of women, slip from one extreame t'another?   160
All these attractions take no hold of her;
No not to take refection; 'T must not be thus.
Well said wench; Tickle that Helicon.
But shall we quit the field with this disgrace
Given to our Oratorie? Both not gaine
So much ground of her as to make her eate?

ERO Faith the truth is sir; you are no fit Organe
For this businesse;
Tis quite out of your Element:
Let us alone, sheele eate I have no feare;   170
A womans tongue best fits a womans eare.
Jove never did employ *Mercurie*,
But *Iris* for his Messenger to *Juno*.

LYSANDER Come, let me kisse thee wench; wilt undertake
To make thy Mistris eate?

ERO   It shall goe harde Sir
But I will make her turne flesh and bloud,
And learne to live as other mortalls doe.

LYSANDER Well said: the morning hasts; next night expect me.

ERO With more provision good Sir.

LYSANDER   Very good.   *Exiturus.*

180 ERO And bring more wine.   *Shee shuts up the Tomb.*

LYSANDER   What else; shalt have enough:

O *Cynthia*, heire of her bright puritie,

Whose name thou dost inherit; Thow disdainst

(Sever'd from all concretion) to feede

Upon the base foode of grosse Elements.

Thou all art soule; All immortalitie.

Thou fasts for *Nectar* and *Ambrosia*,

Which till thou find'st, and eat'st above the starres,

To all foode here thou bidd'st celestiall warrs.   *Exit.*

[*Act IV. Scene 3*]

CYNTHIA, ERO, *the Tombe opening.*

ERO So; lets aire our dampish spirits, almost stifl'd in this grose muddie Element.

CYNTHIA How sweet a breath the calmnesse of the night inspires the aire withall?

ERO Well said; Now y'are your selfe: did not I tell you how sweet an operation the Souldiers bottle had? And if there be such vertue in the bottle; what is there in the Souldier? know, and acknowledge his worth when hee comes in any case Mistris.

CYNTHIA So Maide.

10 ERO Gods my patience? did you looke forsooth that *Juno* should have sent you meate from her owne Trencher, in reward of your widdowes teares? you might sit and sigh first till your heart-strings broke, Ile able't.

CYNTHIA I feare me thy lips have gone so oft to the bottle, that thy tongue-strings are come broken home.

ERO Faith the truth is, my tongue hath beene so long tied up, that tis cover'd with rust, and I rub it against my pallat as wee doe suspected coines, to trie whether it bee currant or no. But now Mistris for an upshot of this bottle; let's have one carouse to the

20 good speede of my old Master, and the good speede of my new.

CYNTHIA So Damzell.

ERO You must pledge it, here's to it. Doe me right I pray.

CYNTHIA You say I must.

ERO Must? what else?

CYNTHIA How excellent ill this humour suites our habite?

ERO Goe to Mistris, do not thinke but you and I shall have good
sport with this jest, when we are in private at home. I would to
Venus we had some honest shift or other to get off withall; for Ile
no more ant; Ile not turne Salt-peeter in this vault for never a
mans companie living; much lesse for a womans. Sure I am the   30
wonder's over, and 'twas only for that, that I endur'd this; and so
a my conscience did you. Never denie it.

CYNTHIA Nay pray thee take it to thee.

    Enter LYSANDER.

CYNTHIA Hearke I heare some footing neare us.

ERO Gods me 'tis the Souldier Mistris, by *Venus* if you fall to your
late black *Santus* againe, Ile discover you.

LYSANDER What's here? The maid hath certainly prevail'd with her;
mee thinkes those cloudes that last night cover'd her lookes are
now disperst: Ile trie this further. Save you Lady.

ERO Honourable Souldier? y'are welcome; please you step in sir?   40

LYSANDER With all my heart sweet heart; by your patience Ladie;
why this beares some shape of life yet. Damzell, th'ast performd
a service of high reckoning, which cannot perish unrewarded.

ERO Faith Sir, you are in the way to doe it once, if you have the heart
to hold on.

CYNTHIA Your bottle has poisond this wench sir.

LYSANDER A wholsome poison it is Ladie, if I may judge; of which
sort here is one better bottle more.
Wine is ordaind to raise such hearts as sinke,
Whom wofull starres distemper; let him drinke.   50
I am most glad I have beene some meane to this part of your
recoverie, and will drinke to the rest of it.

ERO Goe to Mistris, pray simper no more; pledge the man of Warre
here.

CYNTHIA Come y'are too rude.

ERO Good.

LYSANDER Good sooth Ladie y'are honour'd in her service; I would
have you live, and shee would have you live freely; without which

life is but death. To live freely is to feast our appetites freely;
60   without which humanes are stones; to the satisfaction whereof I
drinke Ladie.

CYNTHIA Ile pledge you Sir.

ERO Said like a Mistris; and the Mistris of your selfe; pledge him in
love too: I see hee loves you; Shee's silent, shee consents sir.

LYSANDER O happy starres. And now pardon Ladie; [*kisses her.*] me
thinks these are all of a peece.

ERO Nay if you kisse all of a peece wee shall n'ere have done: Well
twas well offer'd, and as well taken.

CYNTHIA If the world should see this.

70   LYSANDER The world! should one so rare as your selfe, respect the
vulgar world?

CYNTHIA The praise I have had, I would continue.

LYSANDER What, of the vulgar? Who hates not the vulgar, deserves
not love of the vertuous. And to affect praise of that we despise,
how rediculous it is?

ERO Comfortable doctrine, Mistris, edifie, edifie. Me thinkes even
thus it was when *Dido* and *Aeneas* met in the Cave; And hearke
me thinks I heare some of the hunters.   *She shuts the tomb.*

Finis Actus Quarti

Act V. Scene I

Enter THARSALIO, LYCUS.

LYCUS Tis such an obstinacie in you Sir,
As never was conceipted, to runne on
With an opinion against all the world,
And what your eies may witnes; to adventure
The famishment for griefe of such a woman
As all mens merits met in any one,
Could not deserve.

THARSALIO   I must confesse it *Lycus*,
Weele therefore now prevent it if we may,
And that our curious triall hath not dwelt
10   Too long on this unnecessarie hant:

Griefe, and all want of foode, not having wrought
Too mortally on her divine disposure.

LYCUS I feare they have, and shee is past our cure.

THARSALIO I must confesse with feare and shame as much.

LYCUS And that shee will not trust in any thing
What you perswade her to.

THARSALIO   Then thou shalt hast
And call my brother from his secret shroude,
Where he appointed thee to come and tell him
How all thinges have succeeded.

LYCUS   This is well.
If (as I say) the ill be not so growne,   20
That all help is denied her. But I feare
The matchlesse Deme is famisht.

        THARSALIO *looks into the tomb.*

THARSALIO   Slight, whose here?
A Souldier with my sister? wipe, wipe, see!
Kissing by *Jove*; shee, as I lay tis shee.

LYCUS What? is shee well Sir?

THARSALIO   O no, shee is famisht;
Shee's past our comfort, shee lies drawing on.

LYCUS The Gods forbid.

THARSALIO   Looke thou, shee's drawing on.
How saist thou?

LYCUS   Drawing on? Illustrious witchcrafts.

THARSALIO Lies shee not drawing on?

LYCUS   Shee drawes on fairely.
Your sister Sir? This shee? can this be shee?   30

THARSALIO She, she, she, and none but she.   *He dances and sings.*
Shee only Queene of love, and chastitie,
O chastitie; This women be.

LYCUS Slight tis prodigious.

THARSALIO   Horse, horse, horse,
Foure Chariot Horses of the Thracian breede,
Come, bring me, brother. O the happiest evening,
That ever drew her vaile before the Sunne.
Who is't canst tell?

LYCUS   The Souldier Sir that watches

     The bodies crucified in this hallow'd place.

40   Of which to lose one, it is death to him,

     And yet the lustfull knave is at his Venerie,

     While one might steale one.

THARSALIO   What a slave was I

     That held not out my mindes strength constantly,

     That shee would prove thus? O incredible?

     A poore eight-pennie Souldier? Shee that lately

     Was at such height of interjection,

     Stoope now to such a base conjunction?

     By heaven I wonder now I see't in act,

     My braine could ever dreame of such a thought.

50   And yet, tis true: Rare, pereles, is't not *Lycus*?

LYCUS I know not what it is; Nor what to say.

THARSALIO O had I held out (villaine that I was,)

     My blessed confidence but one minute longer,

     I should have beene eternis'd. Gods my fortune,

     What an unspeakable sweet sight it is?

     O eies Ile sacrifice to your deare sense.

     And consecrate a Phane to Confidence.

LYCUS But this you must at no hand tell your brother.

     Twill make him mad: For he that was before

60   So scurg'd but only with bare jealousie,

     What would he be, if he should come to know it?

THARSALIO He would be lesse mad: for your only way

     To cleare his jealousie, is to let him know it.

     When knowledge comes suspicion vanishes.

     The Sunne-beames breaking forth swallow the mists.

     But as for you Sir Gallant; howsoever

     Your banquet seemes sweet in your lycorous pallat,

     It shall be sure to turne gall in your maw.

     Thy hand a little *Lycus* here without.

LYCUS To what?

70 THARSALIO   No bootie serve you sir Soldado

     But my poore sister? Come, lend me thy shoulder,

     Ile climb the crosse; it will be such a cooler

     To my Venerean Gentlemans hot liver,

     When he shall finde one of his crucified

Bodies stolne downe, and he to be forthwith
Made fast in place thereof, for the signe
Of the lost Sentinell. Come glorifie
Firme Confidence in great Inconstancie.
And this beleeve (for all prov'd knowledge sweares)
He that beleeves in errour, never errs.   *Exeunt.*   80

[Act V. Scene 2]

The Tomb opens, LYSANDER, CYNTHIA, ERO.

LYSANDER Tis late; I must away.

CYNTHIA   Not yet sweet love.

LYSANDER Tempt not my stay, tis dangerous. The law is strict, and
not to bee dispenst with. If any Sentinell be too late in's watch,
or that by his neglect one of the crucified bodies should be stollen
from the crosse, his life buyes it.

CYNTHIA A little stay will not endanger them.
The daies proclaimer has not yet given warning.
The Cock yet has not beate his third alarme.

LYSANDER What? shall we ever dwell here amongst
Th'Antipodes? Shall I not enjoy   10
The honour of my fortune in publique?
Sit in *Lysanders* chaire? Raigne in his wealth?

CYNTHIA Thou shalt, thou shalt; though my love to thee
Hath prov'd thus sodaine and for hast lept over
The complement of wooing,
Yet only for the worlds opinion –

LYSANDER Marke that againe.

CYNTHIA I must maintaine a forme in parting hence.

LYSANDER Out upon't, Opinion the blind Goddesse of Fooles, Foe
to the vertuous; and only friend to undeserving persons, contemne   20
it. Thou know'st thou hast done vertuously; thou hast strangly
sorrow'd for thy husband, follow'd him to death; further thou
could'st not, thou hast buried thy selfe quick (O that 'twere true)
spent more teares over his carcase, then would serve a whole
Citie of saddest widdowes in a plague time; besides sighings, and
swownings, not to be credited.

CYNTHIA True; but those complements might have their time for
fashion sake.

LYSANDER Right, Opinion and Fashion. Sfoot what call you time?
30 t'hast wept these foure whole daies.

ERO Nay berladie almost five.

LYSANDER Looke you there; nere upon five whole daies.

CYNTHIA Well goe and see; Returne, weele goe home.

[*Exeunt* CYNTHIA *and* ERO *into the tomb.*]

LYSANDER Hell be thy home, Huge Monsters damne yee, and your
whole creation! O yee Gods; in the height of her mourning in a
Tomb, within sight of so many deaths! her husbands beleev'd
bodie in her eie. He dead, a few daies before; this mirrour of
Nuptiall chastitie; this Votresse of widdow-constancie: to change
her faith; exchange kisses, embraces, with a stranger; and but my
40 shame with-stood, to give the utmost earnest of her love, to an
eight-pennie Sentinell: in effect, to prostitute her selfe upon her
husbands Coffin! Lust, impietie, hell, womanhood it selfe, adde if
you can one step to this.

Enter CAPTAINE *with two or three Souldiers.*

CAPTAINE One of the crucified bodies taken downe!

LYSANDER Enough.   [*Exit into the tomb.*]

CAPTAINE And the Sentinell not to be heard off?

1 SOLDIER No sir.

CAPTAINE Make out; hast, search about for him; does none of you
know him? nor his name?

50 2 SOLDIER Hee's but a stranger here of some foure daies standing;
and we never set eie on him, but at setting the watch.

CAPTAINE For whom *serves* he? you looke well to your watch masters.

1 SOLDIER For *Seigneur Stratio*, and whence he is, tis ignorant to us;
we are not correspondent for any, but our owne places.

CAPTAINE Y'are eloquent. Abroad I say, let me have him.

                                                              Exeunt [*soldiers*].

This negligence will by the Governour be wholly cast on me, he
hereby will suggest to the Viceroy, that the Citie guards are very
carelessly attended.

He loves mee not I know; because of late
60 I knew him but of meane condition;
But now by fortunes injudicious hand,

Guided by bribing Courtiers, hee is rais'd
To this high seate of honour. Nor blushes he,
To see him selfe advanc't over the heads
Of ten times higher worths; but takes it all
Forsooth, to his merits; and lookes (as all
Upstarts doe) for most huge observance.
Well, my minde must stoope to his high place,
And learne within it selfe to sever him
From that, and to adore Authoritie   70
The Goddesse, how ever borne by an unworthie beast;
And let the Beasts dull apprehension take
The honour done to *Isis*, done to himselfe.
I must sit fast, and bee sure to give
No hold to these fault-hunting enemies.   *Exit.*

[*Act V. Scene 3*]

Tomb opens, and LYSANDER *within lies along,* CYNTHIA *and* ERO.

LYSANDER   Pray thee disturbe me not; put out the lights.

ERO   Faith Ile take a nap againe.

CYNTHIA   Thou shalt not rest before I be resolv'd
   What happy winde hath driven thee back to harbour?
   Was it my love?

LYSANDER   No.

CYNTHIA   Yet say so (sweet) that with the thought thereof
   I may enjoy all that I wish in earth.

LYSANDER   I am sought for. A crucified body is stolne while I loiter'd
   here; and I must die for't.   10

CYNTHIA   Die? All the Gods forbid; O this affright
   Torments me ten parts more then the sad losse
   Of my deare husband.

LYSANDER   (Damnation) I believe thee.

CYNTHIA   Yet heare a womans wit,
   Take counsaile of Necessitie and it.
   I have a bodie here which once I lov'd
   And honour'd above all; but that time's past.

LYSANDER   It is, revenge it heaven.

20 CYNTHIA That shall supply at so extrem a need
   The vacant Gibbet.

  LYSANDER Cancro! What? thy husbands bodie?

  CYNTHIA What hurt is't, being dead it save the living?

  LYSANDER O heart hold in, check thy rebellious motion.

  CYNTHIA Vexe not thy selfe deare love, nor use delay.
   Tempt not this danger, set thy handes to worke.

  LYSANDER I can not doo't; my heart will not permit
   My handes to execute a second murther.
   The truth is I am he that slew thy husband.

30 CYNTHIA The Gods forbid.

  LYSANDER It was this hand that bath'd my reeking sword
   In his life bloud, while he cried out for mercie,
   But I remorselesse, panch't him, cut his throat,
   He with his last breath crying, *Cynthia*.

  CYNTHIA O thou hast told me newes that cleaves my heart,
   Would I had never seene thee, or heard sooner
   This bloudie storie; yet see, note my truth;
   Yet I must love thee.

  LYSANDER   Out upon thee Monster.
   Goe, tell the Governour; Let me be brought
40   To die for that most famous villanie;
   Not for this miching base transgression
   Of truant negligence.

  CYNTHIA   I can not doo't.
   Love must salve any murther: Ile be judge
   Of thee deare love, and these shall be thy paines
   In steede of yron, to suffer these soft chaines.

  LYSANDER O I am infinitely oblig'd.

  CYNTHIA Arise I say, thou saver of my life.
   Doe not with vaine-affrighting conscience
   Betray a life, that is not thine but mine:
   Rise and preserve it.

50 LYSANDER   Ha? thy husbands bodie?
   Hang't up you say, in steede of that that's stolne;
   Yet I his murtherer, is that your meaning?

  CYNTHIA It is my Love.

  LYSANDER   Thy love amazes me,

The point is yet how we shall get it thither,
Ha? Tie a halter about's necke, and dragge him to the Gallowes:
Shall I my love?

CYNTHIA   So you may doe indeede,
Or if your owne strength will not serve, wee'le aide
Our handes to yours, and beare him to the place.
For heavens love come, the night goes off apace.

LYSANDER All the infernall plagues dwell in thy soule;   60
Ile fetch a crow of yron to breake the coffin.

CYNTHIA Doe love, be speedie.

LYSANDER   As I wish thy damnation.

                                                Shut the Tomb.

O I could teare my selfe into Atomes; off with this Antick, the
shirt that *Hercules* wore for his wife, was not more banefull. Is't
possible there should be such a latitude in the Sphere of this sexe,
to entertaine such an extention of mischiefe, and not turne Devill?
What is a woman? what are the worst when the best are so past
naming? As men like this, let them trie their wives againe. Put
women to the test; discover them; paint them, paint them ten
parts more then they doe themselves, rather then looke on them   70
as they are; Their wits are but painted that dislike their painting.
Thou foolish thirster after idle secrets, and ills abrode; looke home,
and store and choke thee; there sticks an *Achelous* horne of ill,
copie enough.
As much as *Alizon* of streames receives,
Or loftie *Ida* showes of shadie leaves.
      Enter THARSALIO.
Who's that?

THARSALIO I wonder *Lycus* failes me. Nor can I heare whats become
of him. Hee would not certaine ride to Dipolis to call my brother
back, without my knowledge.   80

LYSANDER My brothers voice; what makes he here abouts so
untimely? Ile slip him.   *Exiturus.*

THARSALIO Who goes there?

LYSANDER A friend.

THARSALIO Deare friend, lets know you. A friend least look't for
but most welcome, and with many a long looke expected here.
What sir unbooted? have you beene long arriv'd?

LYSANDER Not long, some two houres before night.

THARSALIO Well brother, y'have the most rare, admirable, unmatch-
able wife, that ever suffer'd for the sinne of a husband. I cannot
blame your confidence indeede now; 'tis built on such infallible
ground; *Lycus* I thinke be gone to call you to the rescue of her life;
why shee! O incomprehensible!

LYSANDER I have heard all related since my arrivall, weele meet to
morrow.

THARSALIO What hast brother? But was it related with what untoller-
able paines, I and my Mistris, her other friends, Matrones and
Magistrates, labour'd her diversion from that course?

LYSANDER Yes, yes.

THARSALIO What streame of teares she powr'd out; what tresses of
her haire she tore! and offer'd on your suppos'd herse!

LYSANDER I have heard all.

THARSALIO But above all; how since that time, her eies never har-
bour'd winck of slumber, these six daies; no nor tasted the least
dramme of any sustenance.

LYSANDER How is that assurd?

THARSALIO Not a scruple.

LYSANDER Are you sure there came no Souldier to her nor brought
her victualls?

THARSALIO Souldier? what Souldier?

LYSANDER Why some Souldier of the watch, that attends the executed
bodies: well brother I am in hast; to morrow shall supply this
nights defect of conference; Adieu.   *Exit.*

THARSALIO A Souldier? of the watch? bring her victualls? Goe to
brother I have you in the winde; hee's unharnest of all his travailing
accoutrements. I came directly from's house, no word of him
there; he knowes the whole relation; hee's passionate: All collec-
tions speake he was the Souldier. What should be the riddle of this?
that he is stolne hether into a Souldiers disguise? he should have
staid at *Dipolis* to receive news from us. Whether he suspected our
relation; or had not patience to expect it, or whether that furious,
frantique capricious Devill jealousie hath tost him hether on his
hornes, I can not conjecture. But the case is cleare, hee's the
Souldier. Sister, looke to your fame, your chastetie's uncover'd.

Are they here still? here beleeve it both most wofully weeping
over the bottle.   *He knocks.*

ERO Who's there?

THARSALIO *Tharsalio,* open.

ERO Alas Sir, tis no boote to vexe your sister, and your selfe, she is
desperate, and will not heare perswasion, she's very weak.   130

THARSALIO Here's a true-bred chamber-maid. Alas, I am sorrie for't;
I have brought her meat and Candian wine to strengthen her.

ERO O the very naming an't, will drive her into a swowne; good Sir
forbeare.

THARSALIO Yet open sweet, that I may blesse mine eies with sight
of her faire shrine; and of thy sweetest selfe (her famous Pandresse)
open I say. Sister? you heare me well, paint not your Tomb without;
wee know too well what rotten carcases are lodg'd within; open I
say.

> ERO *opens, and hee sees her head layd on the coffin, &c.*

Sister I have brought you tidings to wake you out of this sleeping   140
mummerie.

ERO Alas shee's faint, and speech is painefull to her.

THARSALIO Well said frubber, was there no Souldier here lately?

ERO A Souldier? when?

THARSALIO This night, last night, tother night; and I know not how
many nights and daies.

CYNTHIA Whose there?

ERO Your brother Mistris, that asks if there were not a souldier here.

CYNTHIA Here was no souldier.

ERO Yes Mistris I thinke here was such a one though you tooke no   150
heede of him.

THARSALIO Goe to sister; did not you joyne kisses, embraces, and
plight indeede with him the utmost pledge of Nuptiall love with
him? Deni't, deni't; but first heare me a short storie. The Souldier
was your disguis'd husband, dispute it not. That you see yonder,
is but a shadow, an emptie chest containing nothing but aire. Stand
not to gaze at it, tis true. This was a project of his owne contriving
to put your loialtie and constant vowes to the test; y'are warned,
be arm'd.   *Exit.*

ERO O fie a these perils.   160

CYNTHIA O *Ero*! we are undone.

ERO Nay, you'd nere be warn'd; I ever wisht you to withstand the
push of that Souldiers pike, and not enter him too deep into your
bosom, but to keep sacred your widowes vowes made to *Lysander*.

CYNTHIA Thou did'st, thou did'st.

ERO Now you may see th'event. Well our safetie lies in our speed:
heele doe us mischiefe, if we prevent not his comming. Lets to
your Mothers: and there cal out your mightiest friends to guard
you from his furie. Let them begin the quarrell with him for
170   practising this villanie on your sexe to intrappe your frailties.

CYNTHIA Nay I resolve to sit out one brunt more;
To trie to what aime heele enforce his project:
Were he some other man, unknowne to me,
His violence might awe me; but knowing him
As I doe, I feare him not. Do thou
But second me, thy strength and mine shall master
His best force, if he should prove outragious.
Despaire they say makes cowardes turne couragious.
Shut up the Tomb.   *Shut the Tomb.*

[*Act V. Scene 4*]

Enter one of the Souldiers sent out before to seeke the Sentinell.

1 SOLDIER All paines are lost in hunting out this Souldier; his fear
(adding wings to his heeles) out-goes us as farre as the fresh Hare
the tir'd hounds. Who goes there?

Enter 2. Souldier another way.

2 SOLDIER A friend.

1 SOLDIER O, your successe and mine touching this Sentinell, tells,
I suppose, one tale; hee's farre enough I undertake by this time.

2 SOLDIER I blame him not: the law's severe (though just and can
not be dispenc'd.)

1 SOLDIER Why should the lawes of *Paphos*, with more rigour, then
10   other Citie lawes, pursue offenders? that not appeas'd with their
lives forfait, exact a justice of them after death? And if a Souldier
in his watch forsooth lose one of the dead bodies, he must die
for't: It seems the State needed no souldiers when that was made
a law.

2 SOLDIER So we may chide the fire for burning us; or say the Bee's
not good because she stings; Tis not the body the law respects,
but the souldiers neglect; when the watch (the guard and safetie
of the Citie) is left abandon'd to all hazards. But let him goe; and
tell me if your newes sort with mine, for *Lycus*, apprehended they
say, about *Lysanders* murther.   20

1 SOLDIER Tis true; hee's at the Captaines lodge under guard, and
tis my charge in the morning to unclose the leaden coffin, and
discover the bodie; The Captaine will assay an old conclusion
often approv'd; that at the murtherers sight the bloud revives
againe, and boiles a fresh; and every wound has a condemning
voice to crie out guiltie gainst the murtherer.

2 SOLDIER O world, if this be true; his dearest friend, his bed
companion, whom of all his friends he cull'd out for his bosome!

1 SOLDIER Tush man, in this topsie turvy world, friendship and
bosom kindnes, are but made covers for mischief, meanes to   30
compasse il. Near-allied trust, is but a bridge for treson. The
presumptions crie loud against him; his answeres found disjonted;
cross-legd tripping up one another. He names a Town whether
he brought *Lysander* murther'd by Mountainers; thats false, some
of the dwellers have been here, and all disclaim it. Besides, the
wounds he bears in show, are such as shrews closely give their
husbands, that never bleede, and finde to be counterfait.

2 SOLDIER O that jade falshood is never sound of all; but halts of
one legge still.
    Truth's pace is all upright; sound every where,   40
    And like a die, sets ever on a square.
    And how is *Lycus* his bearing in this condition?

1 SOLDIER Faith (as the manner of such desperate offenders is till it
come to the point) carelesse, and confident, laughing at all that
seeme to pittie him. But leave it to th'event. Night, fellow Souldier,
youle not meet me in the morning at the Tomb, and lend me your
hand to the unrigging of *Lysanders* herse?

2 SOLDIER I care not if I do, to view heavens power in this unbottomd
seller.
    Bloud, though it sleep a time, yet never dies.   50
    The Gods on murtherers fixe revengefull eies.   *Exeunt.*

[*Act V. Scene 5*]

LYSANDER *solus with a crow of yron, and a halter which he laies*
        downe, and puts on his disguise againe.

Come my borrow'd disguise, let me once more
Be reconcild to thee, my trustiest friend;
Thou that in truest shape hast let me see
That which my truer selfe hath hid from me,
Helpe me to take revenge on a disguise,
Ten times more false and counterfait then thou.
Thou, false in show, hast been most true to me;
The seeming true hath prov'd most false then thee.
Assist me to behold this act of lust,

10   Note, with a Scene of strange impietie,
Her husbands murtherd corse! O more then horror!
Ile not beleeve't untri'd; If shee but lift
A hand to act it; by the fates her braines flie out,
Since shee has madded me; let her beware my hornes,
For though by goring her, no hope be showne
To cure my selfe, yet Ile not bleede alone.   *He knocks.*

ERO Who knocks?

LYSANDER The souldier; open.   *She opens and he enters.*
See sweet, here arte the engines that must doo't,

20   Which with much feare of my discoverie
I have at last procur'd.
Shall we about this worke? I feare the morne
Will over-take's; my stay hath been prolong'd
With hunting obscure nookes for these emploiments,
The night prepares a way; come, art resolv'd?

CYNTHIA I, you shall finde me constant.

LYSANDER I, so I have, most prodigiously constant,
Here's a rare halter to hugge him with.

ERO Better you and I joyne our handes and beare him thether, you
30   take his head.

CYNTHIA I, for that was alwaies heavier then's whole bodie besides.

LYSANDER You can tell best that loded it.

ERO Ile be at the feet; I am able to beare against you I warrant you.

LYSANDER Hast thou prepar'd weake nature to digest
 A sight so much distastfull; hast ser'd thy heart
 It bleede not at the bloudie spectacle?
 Hast arm'd thy fearefull eies against th'affront
 Of such a direfull object?
 Thy murther'd husband ghastly staring on thee;
 His wounds gaping to affright thee; his bodie   40
 Soild with gore? fore heaven my heart shruggs at it.
CYNTHIA So does not mine,
 Love's resolute; and stands not to consult
 With pettie terrour; but in full carrier
 Runnes blind-fold through an Armie of misdoubts,
 And interposing feares; perhaps Ile weepe
 Or so, make a forc't face and laugh againe.
LYSANDER O most valiant love!
 I was thinking with my selfe as I came;
 How if this brake to light; his bodie knowne;   50
 (As many notes might make it) would it not fixe
 Upon thy fame an unremoved Brand
 Of shame and hate? They that in former times
 Ador'd thy vertue, would they not abhorre
 Thy lothest memorie?
CYNTHIA   All this I know.
 But yet my love to thee swallowes all this;
 Or whatsoever doubts can come against it.
 Shame's but a feather ballanc't with thy love.
LYSANDER Neither feare nor shame? you are steele toth'proofe
 (But I shall yron you): Come then lets to worke. 60
 Alas poore Corps how many martyrdomes
 Must thou endure? mangl'd by me a villaine,
 And now expos'd to foule shame of the Gibbet?
 Fore pietie, there is somewhat in me strives
 Against the deede, my very arme relents
 To strike a stroke so inhumane,
 To wound a hallow'd herse? suppose twere mine,
 Would not my Ghost start up and flie upon thee?
CYNTHIA No, Ide mall it down againe with this.
 She snatches up the crow.

70   LYSANDER How now?   *He catches at her throat.*

CYNTHIA Nay, then Ile assay my strength; a Souldier and afraid of
a dead man? A soft-roed milk-sop? come Ile doot my selfe.

LYSANDER And I looke on? give me the yron.

CYNTHIA No, Ile not lose the glorie ant. This hand, *&c.*

LYSANDER Pray thee sweet, let it not bee said the savage act was
thine; deliver me the engine.

CYNTHIA Content your selfe, tis in a fitter hand.

LYSANDER Wilt thou first? are not thou the most —

CYNTHIA Ill-destin'd wife of a transform'd monster;

80   Who to assure him selfe of what he knew,
Hath lost the shape of man.

LYSANDER   Ha? crosse-capers?

CYNTHIA Poore Souldiers case; doe not we know you Sir?
But I have given thee what thou cam'st to seeke.
Goe *Satyre,* runne affrighted with the noise
Of that harsh sounding horne thy selfe hast blowne,
Farewell; I leave thee there my Husbands Corps,
Make much of that.   *Exit cum* ERO.

LYSANDER   What have I done?
O let me lie and grieve, and speake no more.

    [Enter] CAPTAINE, LYCUS *with a guard of three or foure Souldiers.*

CAPTAINE Bring him away; you must have patience Sir: If you can
90   say ought to quit you of those presumptions that lie heavie on
you, you shall be heard. If not, tis not your braves, nor your
affecting lookes can carrie it. We must acquite our duties.

LYCUS Y'are Captaine ath' watch Sir.

CAPTAINE You take me right.

LYCUS So were you best doe mee; see your presumptions bee strong;
or be assured that shall prove a deare presumption, to brand me
with the murther of my friend. But you have beene suborn'd by
some close villaine to defame me.

CAPTAINE Twill not be so put off friend *Lycus,* I could wish your
100   soule as free from taint of this foule fact; as mine from any such
unworthy practise.

LYCUS Conduct mee to the Governour him selfe; to confront before
him your shallow accusations.

CAPTAINE First Sir, Ile beare you to *Lysanders* Tombe, to confront

the murther'd body; and see what evidence the wounds will yeeld
against you.

LYCUS Y'are wise Captaine. But if the bodie should chance not to
speake; If the wounds should bee tongue-tied Captaine; where's
then your evidence Captaine? will you not be laught at for an
officious Captaine?

CAPTAINE Y'are gallant Sir.

LYCUS Your Captainship commands my service no further.

CAPTAINE Well Sir, perhaps I may, if this conclusion take not; weele
trie what operation lies in torture, to pull confession from you.

LYCUS Say you so Captaine? but hearke you Captaine, Might it not
concurre with the qualitie of your office, ere this matter grow to
the height of a more threatning danger; to winck a little at a by
slip, or so?

CAPTAINE How's that?

LYCUS To send a man abroad under guard of one of your silliest
shack-rags; that he may beate the knave, and run's way. I meane
this on good termes Captaine; Ile be thankfull.

CAPTAINE Ile thinke ont hereafter. Meane time I have other emploi-
ment for you.

LYCUS Your place is worthily replenisht Captaine. My dutie Sir;
Hearke Captaine, there's a Mutinie in your Armie; Ile go raise the
Governour.   *Exiturus.*

CAPTAINE No hast Sir; heele soone be here without your summons.
    Souldiers thrust up LYSANDER *from the Tomb.*

1 SOLDIER Bring forth the Knight ath' Tomb; have we met with you
Sir?

LYSANDER Pray thee souldier use thine office with better temper.

2 SOLDIER Come convay him to the Lord Governour.

LYSANDER First afore the Captaine Sir. Have the heavens nought
else to doe, but to stand still, and turne all their malignant aspects
upon one man?

2 SOLDIER Captaine here's the Sentinell wee sought for; hee's some
new prest Souldier, for none of us know him.

CAPTAINE Where found you him?

1 SOLDIER My truant was mich't Sir into a blind corner of the Tomb.

CAPTAINE Well said, guard him safe, but for the Corps?

1 SOLDIER For the Corps Sir? bare misprision, there's no bodie,

nothing. A meere blandation; a *deceptio visus*. Unlesse this souldier for hunger have eate up *Lysanders* bodie.

LYCUS Why, I could have told you this before Captaine; the body was borne away peece-meale by devout Ladies of *Venus* order, for the man died one of *Venus* Martyrs. And yet I heard since 'twas seene whole ath' other side the downes upon a Colestafe betwixt two huntsmen, to feede their dogges withall. Which was a miracle Captaine.

150 CAPTAINE Mischiefe in this act hath a deepe bottom; and requires more time to sound it. But you Sir, it seemes, are a Souldier of the newest stamp. Know you what tis to forsake your stand? There's one of the bodies in your charge stolne away; how answere you that? See here comes the Governour.

> *Enter a Guard bare after the* GOVERNOUR: THARSALIO, ARGUS,
> CLINIAS, *before* EUDORA, CYNTHIA, LAODICE, STHENIO,
> [HYLUS], IANTHE, ERO, *&c.*

GUARD Stand aside there.

CAPTAINE Roome for a strange Governour. The perfect draught of a most brainelesse, imperious upstart. O desert! where wert thou, when this woodden dagger was guilded over with the Title of Governour?

160 GUARD Peace Masters; heare my Lord.

THARSALIO All wisedome be silent; Now speakes Authoritie.

GOVERNOUR I am come in person to discharge Justice.

THARSALIO Of his office.

GOVERNOUR The cause you shall know hereafter; and it is this. A villaine, whose very sight I abhorre; where is he? Let mee see him.

CAPTAINE Is't *Lycus* you meane my Lord?

GOVERNOUR Goe to sirrha y'are too malipert; I have heard of your Sentinells escape; looke too't.

CAPTAINE My Lord, this is the Sentinell you speake of.

170 GOVERNOUR How now Sir? what time a day ist?

ARGUS I can not shew you precisely, ant please your Honour.

GOVERNOUR What? shall we have replications? Rejoinders?

THARSALIO Such a creature, a Foole is, when hee bestrides the back of Authoritie.

GOVERNOUR Sirrha, stand you forth. It is supposed thou hast committed a most inconvenient murther upon the body of *Lysander*.

LYCUS My good Lord, I have not.

GOVERNOUR Peace varlet; dost chop with me? I say it is imagined
thou hast murther'd *Lysander*. How it will be prov'd I know not.
Thou shalt therefore presently bee had to execution, as justice in   180
such cases requireth. Souldiers take him away: bring forth the
Sentinell.

LYCUS Your Lordship will first let my defence be heard.

GOVERNOUR Sirrha; Ile no fending nor proving. For my part I am
satisfied, it is so: thats enough for thee. I had ever a Sympathy in
my minde against him. Let him be had away.

THARSALIO A most excellent apprehension. Hee's able yee see to
judge of a cause at first sight, and heare but two parties. Here's a
second *Solon*.

EUDORA Heare him my Lord; presumptions oftentimes,   190
(Though likely grounded) reach not to the truth.
And truth is oft abus'd by likelyhood.
Let him be heard my Lord.

GOVERNOUR Madam, content your selfe. I will doe justice; I will not
heare him. Your late Lord was my Honourable Predecessour: But
your Ladiship must pardon me. In matters of justice I am blinde.

THARSALIO Thats true.

GOVERNOUR I know no persons. If a Court favorite write to mee in
a case of justice; I will pocket his letter, and proceede. If a Suiter
in a case of justice thrusts a bribe into my hand, I will pocket his   200
bribe, and proceede. Therefore Madam, set your heart at rest: I
am seated in the Throne of justice; and I will doe justice; I will
not heare him.

EUDORA Not heare him my Lord?

GOVERNOUR No my Ladie: and moreover put you in mind, in whose
presence you stand; if you Parrat to me long; goe to.

THARSALIO Nay the Vice must snap his Authoritie at all he meetes,
how shalt else be knowne what part he plaies?

GOVERNOUR Your husband was a Noble Gentleman, but Alas hee
came short, hee was no Statesman. Hee has left a foule Citie   210
behinde him.

THARSALIO I, and I can tell you twill trouble his Lordship and all
his Honorable assistants of Scavingers to sweepe it cleane.

GOVERNOUR It's full of vices, and great ones too.

THARSALIO And thou none of the meanest.

GOVERNOUR But Ile turne all topsie turvie; and set up a new discipline amongst you. Ile cut of all perisht members.

THARSALIO Thats the Surgeons office.

GOVERNOUR Cast out these rotten stinking carcases for infecting the
220 whole Citie.

ARGUS Rotten they may be, but their wenches use to pepper them; and their Surgeons to perboile them; and that preserves them from stinking, ant please your Honour.

GOVERNOUR Peace Sirrha, peace; and yet tis well said too. A good pregnant fellow yfaith. But to proceede. I will spew drunkennesse out ath' Citie.

THARSALIO In to th' Countrie.

GOVERNOUR Shifters shall cheate and sterve; And no man shall doe good but where there is no neede. Braggarts shall live at the head
230 and the tumult that hant Tavernes. Asses shall beare good qualities, and wise men shall use them. I will whip lecherie out ath' Citie, there shall be no more Cuckolds. They that heretofore were errand Cornutos, shall now bee honest shop-keepers, and justice shall take place. I will hunt jelousie out of my Dominion.

THARSALIO Doe heare Brother?

GOVERNOUR It shall be the only note of love to the husband, to love the wife: And none shall be more kindly welcome to him then he that cuckolds him.

THARSALIO Beleeve it a wholsome reformation.

240 GOVERNOUR Ile have no more Beggers. Fooles shall have wealth, and the learned shall live by their wits. Ile have no more Banckrouts. They that owe money shall pay it at their best leisure: And the rest shall make a vertue of imprisonment; and their wives shall helpe to pay their debts. Ile have all yong widdowes spaded for marrying againe. For the old and wither'd, they shall be confiscate to unthriftie Gallants, and decai'd Knights. If they bee poore they shall bee burnt to make Sope ashes, or given to Surgeons Hall, to bee stampt to salve for the French mesells. To conclude, I will Cart pride out ath' Towne.

250 ARGUS Ant please your Honour Pride ant be nere so beggarly will looke for a Coch.

GOVERNOUR Well said a mine Honour. A good significant fellow yfaith: What is he? he talkes much; does he follow your Ladiship?

ARGUS No ant please your Honour, I goe before her.

GOVERNOUR A good undertaking presence; A well-promising fore-
head, your Gentleman Usher Madam?

EUDORA Yours if you please my Lord.

GOVERNOUR Borne ith' Citie?

ARGUS I ant please your Honour, but begot ith' Court.

GOVERNOUR Tressellegg'd?   260

ARGUS I, ant please your Honour.

GOVERNOUR The better, it beares a bredth; makes roome a both
sides. Might I not see his pace?

ARGUS Yes ant please your Honour.   ARGUS *stalkes.*

GOVERNOUR Tis well, tis very well. Give me thy hand: Madame I
will accept this propertie at your hand, and wil weare it thred-bare
for your sake. Fall in there, sirrha. And for the matter of *Lycus*
Madam, I must tell you, you are shallow: there's a State point in't!
hearke you: The Viceroy has given him, and wee must uphold
correspondence. Hee must walke; say one man goes wrongfully   270
out ath' world, there are hundreds to one come wrongfully into
th' world.

EUDORA Your Lordship will give me but a word in private.

THARSALIO Come brother; we know you well: what meanes this
habite? why staid you not at *Dipolis* as you resolv'd, to take
advertisement from us of your wives bearing?

LYSANDER O brother, this jealous phrensie has borne mee headlong
to ruine.

THARSALIO Go to, be comforted; uncase your selfe; and discharge
your friend.   280

GOVERNOUR Is that *Lysander* say you? And is all his storie true?
Berladie Madam this jealousie will cost him deare: he undertooke
the person of a Souldier; and as a Souldier must have justice.
Madam, his Altitude in this case can not dispence. *Lycus*, this
Souldier hath acquited you.

THARSALIO And that acquitall Ile for him requite; the body lost is
by this time restor'd to his place.

1 SOLDIER It is my Lord.

THARSALIO These are State points, in which your Lordships time
Has not yet train'd your Lordship; please your Lordship   290

To grace a Nuptiall we have now in hand,
> HYLUS *and* LAODICE *stand together.*

Twixt this yong Ladie and this Gentleman.
Your Lordship there shall heare the ample storie.
And how the Asse wrapt in a Lyons skin
Fearefully rord; but his large eares appeard
And made him laught at, that before was feard.

GOVERNOUR Ile goe with you. For my part, I am at a non plus.
> EUDORA *whispers with* CYNTHIA.

THARSALIO Come brother; thanke the Countesse: she hath swet
To make your peace. Sister give me your hand.

300 So; brother let your lips compound the strife,
And thinke you have the only constant Wife.   *Exeunt.*

FINIS

POEMS

'Hymnus in Noctem'
(From *THE SHADOW OF NIGHT*, 1594)

[Dedication]

TO MY DEARE AND
MOST WORTHY FRIEND
MASTER MATHEW ROYDON.

It is an exceeding rapture of delight in the deepe search of knowledge,
(none knoweth better then thy selfe sweet *Mathew*) that maketh men
manfully indure th'extremes incident to that *Herculean* labour: from
flints must the *Gorgonean* fount be smitten. Men must be shod by
Mercurie, girt with *Saturnes* Adamantine sword, take the shield from
Pallas, the helme from *Pluto*, and have the eyes of *Graea* (as *Hesiodus
armes Perseus* against *Medusa*) before they can cut of the viperous head
of benumming ignorance, or subdue their monstrous affections to
most beautifull judgement.

    How then may a man stay his marvailing to see passion-driven   10
men, reading but to curtoll a tedious houre, and altogether hidebownd
with affection to great mens fancies, take upon them as killing censures
as if they were judgements Butchers, or as if the life of truth lay
tottering in their verdits.

    Now what a supererogation in wit this is, to thinke skil so mightilie
pierst with their loves, that she should prostitutely shew them her
secrets, when she will scarcely be lookt upon by others but with
invocation, fasting, watching; yea not without having drops of their
soules like an heavenly familiar. Why then should our *Intonsi Catones*
with their profit-ravisht gravitie esteeme her true favours such ques-   20
tionlesse vanities, as with what part soever thereof they seeme to be
something delighted, they queimishlie commende it for a pretie toy.
Good Lord how serious and eternall are their Idolatrous platts for
riches! no marvaile sure they here do so much good with them. And
heaven no doubt will grovill on the earth (as they do) to imbrace
them. But I stay this spleene when I remember my good *Mat.* how
joyfully oftentimes you reported unto me, that most ingenious *Darbie*,
deepe searching *Northumberland*, and skill-imbracing *heire of Hunsdon*

had most profitably entertained learning in themselves, to the vitall
30   warmth of freezing science, & to the admirable luster of their true
Nobilitie, whose high deserving vertues may cause me hereafter strike
that fire out of darknesse, which the brightest Day shall envie for
beautie. I should write more, but my hasting out of towne taketh me
from the paper, so preferring thy allowance in this poore and strange
trifle, to the passport of a whole Cittie of others, I rest as resolute as
Seneca, satisfying my selfe if but a few, if one, or if none like it.

> *By the true admirour of thy vertues*
> *and perfectly vowed friend.*
> G. CHAPMAN

Hymnus in Noctem.

Great Goddesse to whose throne in[1] Cynthian fires,
This earthlie Alter endlesse fumes exspires,
Therefore, in fumes of sighes and fires of griefe,
To fearefull chances thou sendst bold reliefe,
Happie, thrise happie, Type, and[2] nurse of death,
Who breathlesse, feedes on nothing but our breath,
In whom must vertue and her issue live,
Or dye for ever; now let humor give
Seas to mine eyes, that I may quicklie weepe
The shipwracke of the world: or let soft sleepe   10
(Binding my sences) lose my working soule,
That in her highest pitch, she may controule
The court of skill, compact of misterie,
Wanting but franchisement[3] and memorie
To reach all secrets: then in blissfull trance,
Raise her (deare Night) to that perseverance,
That in my torture, she all earths may sing,
And force to tremble in her trumpeting
Heavens christall[4] temples: in her powrs implant
Skill of my griefs, and she can nothing want.   20

   Then like fierce bolts, well rammd with heate & cold
In Joves Artillerie; my words unfold,
To breake the labyrinth of everie eare,
And make ech frighted soule come forth and heare,
Let them breake harts, as well as yeelding ayre,
That all mens bosoms (pierst with no affaires,
But gaine of riches) may be lanced wide,
And with the threates of vertue terrified.

   Sorrowes deare soveraigne, and the queene of rest,
That when unlightsome, vast, and indigest   30
The formelesse matter of this world did lye,
Fildst every place with thy Divinitie,

Why did thy absolute and endlesse sway,
Licence heavens torch, the scepter of the Day,
Distinguisht intercession to thy throne,
That long before, all matchlesse rulde alone?
Why letst thou order, orderlesse disperse,
The fighting parents of this universe?
When earth, the ayre, and sea, in fire remaind,
40 When fire, the sea, and earth, the ayre containd,
When ayre, the earth, and fire, the sea enclosde
When sea, fire, ayre, in earth were indisposde,
Nothing, as now, remainde so out of kinde,
All things in grosse, were finer than refinde,
Substance was sound within, and had no being,
Now forme gives being; all our essence seeming,
Chaos had soule without a bodie then,
Now bodies live without the soules of men,
Lumps being digested; monsters, in our pride.
50 And as a wealthie fount, that hils did hide,
Let forth by labor of industrious hands,
Powres out her treasure through the fruitefull strands,
Seemely divided to a hunderd streames,
Whose bewties shed such profitable beames,
And make such Orphean Musicke in their courses,
That Citties follow their enchanting forces,
Who running farre, at length ech powres her hart
Into the bosome of the gulfie desart,
As much confounded there, and indigest,
60 As in the chaos of the hills comprest:
So all things now (extract out of the prime)
Are turnd to chaos, and confound the time.
A stepdame Night of minde about us clings,
Who broodes beneath her hell obscuring wings,
Worlds of confusion, where the soule defamde,
The bodie had bene better never framde,
Beneath thy soft, and peace-full covert then,
(Most sacred mother both of Gods and men)
Treasures unknowne, and more unprisde did dwell;
70 But in the blind borne shadow of this hell,

This horrid stepdame, blindnesse of the minde,
Nought worth the sight, no sight, but worse then blind,
A Gorgon that with brasse, and snakie brows,
(Most harlot-like) her naked secrets shows:
For in th'expansure, and distinct attire,
Of light, and darcknesse, of the sea, and fire,
Of ayre, and earth, and all, all these create,
First set and rulde, in most harmonious state,
Disjunction showes, in all things now amisse,
By that first order, what confusion is: 80
Religious curb, that manadgd men in bounds,
Of publique wellfare; lothing private grounds,
(Now cast away, by selfe-lov's paramores)
All are transformd to Calydonian bores,
That kill our bleeding vines, displow our fields,
Rend groves in peeces; all things nature yeelds
Supplanting: tumbling up in hills of dearth,
The fruitefull disposition of the earth,
Ruine creates men: all to slaughter bent,
Like envie, fed with others famishment.   90
　　And what makes men without the parts of men,
Or in their manhoods, lesse then childeren,
But manlesse natures? all this world was namde
A world of him, for whom it first was framde,
(Who (like a tender Chevrill,) shruncke with fire
Of base ambition, and of selfe-desire,
His armes into his shoulders crept for feare
Bountie should use them; and fierce rape forbeare,
His legges into his greedie belly runne,
The charge of hospitalitie to shunne)   100
In him the world is to a lump reverst,
That shruncke from forme, that was by forme disperst,
And in nought more then thanklesse avarice,
Not rendring vertue her deserved price.
Kinde Amalthaea was transferd by Jove,
Into his sparckling pavement, for her love,
Though but a Goate, and giving him her milke,
Basenesse is flintie; gentrie softe as silke,

In heavens she lives, and rules a living signe
110   In humane bodies: yet not so divine,
That she can worke her kindnesse in our harts.

    The sencelesse Argive ship, for her deserts,
Bearing to Colchos, and for bringing backe,
The hardie Argonauts, secure of wracke,
The fautor and the God of gratitude,
Would not from number of the starres exclude.
A thousand such examples could I cite,
To damne stone-pesants, that like Typhons fight
Against their Maker, and contend to be
120   Of kings, the abject slaves of drudgerie:
Proud of that thraldome: love the kindest lest,
And hate, not to be hated of the best.

    If then we frame mans figure by his mind,
And that at first, his fashion was assignd,
Erection in such God-like excellence
For his soules sake, and her intelligence:
She so degenerate, and growne deprest,
Content to share affections with a beast,
The shape wherewith he should be now indude,
130   Must beare no signe of mans similitude.

He cals them Promethean   Therefore* Promethean Poets with the coles
Poets in this high conceipt,   Of their most geniale, more-then-humane soules
by a figurative comparison   In living verse, created men like these,
betwixt them, that as Pro.   With shapes of Centaurs, Harpies, Lapithes,
with fire fetcht from heaven,   That they in prime of erudition,
made men: so Poets with   When almost savage vulgar men were growne,
the fire of their soules are   Seeing them selves in those Pierean founts,
sayd to create those   Might mend their mindes, asham'd of such accounts.
Harpies, and Centaures,   So when ye heare, the† sweetest Muses sonne,
and thereof he calls their   With heavenly rapture of his Musicke, wonne
soules Geniale.   Rockes, forrests, floods, and winds to leave their course

†*Calliope is cald the*   In his attendance: it bewrayes the force
sweetest Muse, her name   His wisedome had, to draw men growne so rude
being by signification,   To civill love of Art, and Fortitude.
Cantus suavitas, vel   And not for teaching others⁵ insolence,
modulatio.   Had he his date-exceeding excellence

With soveraigne Poets, but for use applyed,
And in his proper actes exemplified;
And that in calming the infernall kinde,
To wit, the perturbations of his minde,   150
And bringing his Eurydice from hell,
(Which Justice signifies) is proved well.
But if in rights observance any man
Looke backe, with boldnesse lesse then Orphean,
Soone falls he to the hell from whence he rose:
The fiction then would temprature dispose,
In all the tender motives of the minde,
To make man worthie his hel-danting kinde.
The golden chaine of Homers high device
Ambition is, or cursed avarice,   160
Which all Gods haling being tyed to Jove,
Him from his setled height could never move:
Intending this, that though that powrefull chaine
Of most Herculean vigor to constraine
Men from true vertue, or their pristine states
Attempt a man that manlesse changes hates,
And is enobled with a deathlesse love
Of things eternall, dignified above:
Nothing shall stirre him from adorning still
This shape with vertue, and his powre with will.   170
   But as rude painters that contend to show
Beasts, foules or fish, all artlesse to bestow
On every side his native counterfet,
Above his head, his name had neede to set:
So men that will be men, in more then face,
(As in their foreheads) should in actions place
More perfect characters, to prove they be
No mockers of their first nobilitie:
Else may they easly passe for beasts or foules:
Soules praise our shapes, and not our shapes our soules.   180
      And as when Chloris paints th'ennamild meads,
A flocke of shepherds to the bagpipe treads
Rude rurall dances with their countrey loves:
Some a farre off observing their removes,

Turnes, and returnes, quicke footing, sodaine stands,
Reelings aside, od actions with their hands;
Now backe, now forwards, now lockt arme in arme,
Now hearing musicke, thinke it is a charme,
That like loose froes at Bacchanalean feasts,
190   Makes them seeme franticke in their barraine jestes;
And being clusterd in a shapelesse croude,
With much lesse admiration are allowd.
So our first excellence, so much abusd,
And we (without the harmonie was usd,
When Saturnes golden scepter stroke the strings
Of Civill governement) make all our doings
Savour of rudenesse, and obscuritie,
And in our formes shew more deformitie,
Then if we still were wrapt, and smoothered
200   In that confusion, out of which we fled.

    And as when hosts of starres attend thy flight,
(Day of deepe students, most contentfull night)
The morning (mounted on the Muses[6] stead)
Ushers the sonne from[7] Vulcans golden bed,
And then from forth their sundrie roofes of rest,
All sorts of men, to sorted taskes addrest,
Spreade this inferiour element: and yeeld
Labour his due: the souldier to the field,
States-men to counsell, Judges to their pleas,
210   Merchants to commerce, mariners to seas:
All beasts, and birds, the groves and forrests range,
To fill all corners of this round Exchange,
Till thou (deare Night, ô goddesse of most worth)
Letst thy sweet seas of golden humor forth
And Eagle-like dost with thy starrie wings,
[8]Beate in the foules, and beasts to Somnus lodgings,
And haughtie Day to the infernall deepe,
Proclaiming scilence, studie, ease, and sleepe.
All things before thy forces put in rout,
220   Retiring where the morning fir'd them out.

    So to the chaos of our first descent,
(All dayes of honor, and of vertue spent)

We basely make retrait, and are no lesse
Then huge impolisht heapes of filthinesse.
Mens faces glitter, and their hearts are blacke,
But thou (great Mistresse of heavens gloomie racke)
Art blacke in face, and glitterst in thy heart.
There is thy glorie, riches, force, and Art;
Opposed earth, beates blacke and blewe thy face,
And often doth thy heart it selfe deface,   230
For spite that to thy vertue-famed traine,
All the choise worthies that did ever raigne
In eldest age, were still preferd by Jove,
Esteeming that due honor to his love.
There shine they: not to sea-men guides alone,
But sacred presidents to everie one.
There fixt for ever, where the Day is driven,
Almost foure hundred times a yeare from heaven.
In hell then let her sit, and never rise,
Till Morns leave blushing at her cruelties.   240
    Meane while, accept, as followers of thy traine,
(Our better parts aspiring to thy raigne)
Vertues obscur'd, and banished the day,
With all the glories of this spongie sway,
Prisond in flesh, and that poore flesh in bands
Of stone, and steele, chiefe flowrs of vertues Garlands.
    O then most tender fortresse of our woes,
That bleeding lye in vertues overthroes,
Hating the whoredome of this painted light:
Raise thy chast daughters, ministers of right,   250
The dreadfull and the just Eumenides,
And let them wreake the wrongs of our disease,
Drowning the world in bloud, and staine the skies
With their spilt soules, made drunke with tyrannies.
    Fall Hercules from heaven in tempestes hurld,
And cleanse this beastly stable of the world:
⁹Or bend thy brasen bow against the Sunne,
As in Tartessus, when thou hadst begunne

Thy taske of oxen: heat in more extreames
260   Then thou wouldst suffer, with his envious beames:
Now make him leave the world to Night and dreames.
Never were vertues labours so envy'd
As in this light: shoote, shoote, and stoope his pride:
Suffer no more his lustfull rayes to get
The Earth with issue: let him still be set
In Somnus thickets: bound about the browes,
With pitchie vapours, and with Ebone bowes.
    [10]Rich-tapird sanctuarie of the blest,
Pallace of Ruth, made all of teares, and rest,
270   To thy blacke shades and desolation,
I consecrate my life; and living mone,
Where furies shall for ever fighting be,
And adders hisse the world for hating me,
Foxes shall barke, and Night-ravens belch in grones,
And owles shall hollow my confusions:
There will I furnish up my funerall bed,
Strewd with the bones and relickes of the dead.
Atlas shall let th'Olimpick burthen fall,
To cover my untombed face withall.
280   And when as well, the matter of our kind,
As the materiall substance of the mind,
Shall cease their revolutions, in abode
Of such impure and ugly period,
As the old essence, and insensive prime:
Then shall the ruines of the fourefold time,
Turnd to that lumpe (as rapting Torrents rise)
For ever murmure forth my miseries.
    Ye living spirits then, if any live,
Whom like extreames, do like affections give,
290   Shun, shun this cruell light, and end your thrall,
In these soft shades of sable funerall:
From whence with ghosts, whom vengeance holds from rest,
Dog-fiends and monsters hanting the distrest,
As men whose parents tyrannie hath slaine,
Whose sisters rape, and bondage do sustaine.

But you that ne'er had birth, nor ever prov'd,
How deare a blessing tis to be belov'd,
Whose friends idolatrous desire of gold,
Do scorne, and ruine have your freedome sold:
Whose vertues feele all this, and shew your eyes,   300
Men made of Tartar, and of villanies:
Aspire th'extraction, and the quintessence
Of all the joyes in earths circumference:
With ghosts, fiends, monsters: as men robd and rackt,
Murtherd in life: from shades with shadowes blackt:
Thunder your wrongs, your miseries and hells,
And with the dismall accents of your knells,
Revive the dead, and make the living dye
In ruth and terror of your torturie:
Still all the powre of Art into your grones,   310
Scorning your triviall and remissive mones,
Compact of fiction, and hyperboles,
(Like wanton mourners, cloyd with too much ease)
Should leave the glasses of the hearers eyes
Unbroken, counting all but vanities.
But paint, or else create in serious truth,
A bodie figur'd to your vertues ruth,
That to the sence may shew what damned sinne,
For your extreames this Chaos tumbles in.
But wo is wretched me, without a name: 320
Vertue feeds scorne, and noblest honor, shame:
Pride bathes in teares of poore submission,
And makes his soule, the purple he puts on.
    Kneele then with me, fall worme-like on the ground,
And from th'infectious dunghill of this Round,
From mens brasse wits, and golden foolerie,
Weepe, weepe your soules, into felicitie:
Come to this house of mourning, serve the night,
To whom pale day (with whoredome soked quite)
Is but a drudge, selling her beauties use   330
To rapes, adultries, and to all abuse.
Her labors feast imperiall Night with sports,
Where Loves are Christmast, with all pleasures sorts:

And whom her fugitive, and far-shot rayes
Disjoyne, and drive into ten thousand wayes,
Nights glorious mantle wraps in safe abodes,
And frees their neckes from servile labors lodes:
Her trustie shadowes, succour men dismayd,
Whom Dayes deceiptfull malice hath betrayd:
340   From the silke vapors of her Iveryport,
Sweet Protean dreames she sends of every sort:
Some taking formes of Princes, to perswade
Of men deject, we are their equals made,
Some clad in habit of deceased friends,
For whom we mournd, and now have wisht amends,
And some (deare favour) Lady-like attyrd,
With pride of Beauties full Meridian fir'd:
Who pitie our contempts, revive our harts:
For wisest Ladies love the inward parts.

350   If these be dreames, even so are all things else,
That walke this round by heavenly sentinels:
But from Nights port of horne she greets our eyes
With graver dreames inspir'd with prophesies,
Which oft presage to us succeeding chances,
We prooving that awake, they shew in trances.
If these seeme likewise vaine, or nothing are
Vaine things, or nothing come to vertues share:
For nothing more then dreames, with us shee findes:
Then since all pleasures vanish like the windes,
360   And that most serious actions not respecting
The second light, are worth but the neglecting,
Since day, or light, in anie qualitie,
For earthly uses do but serve the eye.
And since the eyes most quicke and dangerous use,
Enflames the heart, and learnes the soule abuse,
Since mournings are preferd to banquettings,
And they reach heaven, bred under sorrowes wings.
Since Night brings terror to our frailties still,
And shamelesse Day, doth marble us in ill.

370   All you possest with indepressed spirits,
Indu'd with nimble, and aspiring wits,

Come consecrate with me, to sacred Night
Your whole endevours, and detest the light.
Sweete Peaces richest crowne is made of starres,
Most certaine guides of honord Marinars,
No pen can any thing eternall wright,
That is not steept in humor of the Night.

   Hence beasts, and birds to caves and bushes then,
And welcome Night, ye noblest heires of men,
Hence Phebus to thy glassie strumpets bed,   380
And never more let[11] Themis daughters spred,
Thy golden harnesse on thy rosie horse,
But in close thickets run thy oblique course.

   See now ascends, the glorious Bride of Brides,
Nuptials, and triumphs, glittring by her sides,
Juno and Hymen do her traine adorne,
Ten thousand torches round about them borne:
Dumbe Silence mounted on the Cyprian starre,
With becks, rebukes the winds before his carre,
Where she advanst; beates downe with cloudie mace,   390
The feeble light to blacke Saturnius pallace:
Behind her, with a brase[12] of silver Hynds,
In Ivorie chariot, swifter then the winds,
Is great[13] Hyperions horned daughter drawne
Enchantresse-like, deckt in disparent lawne,
Circkled with charmes, and incantations,
That ride huge spirits, and outragious passions:
Musicke, and moode, she loves, but love she hates,
(As curious Ladies do, their publique cates)
This traine, with meteors, comets, lightenings,   400
The dreadfull presence of our Empresse sings:
Which grant for ever (ô eternall Night)
Till vertue flourish in the light of light.

                     Explicit Hymnus.

GLOSS

1 He cals these Cynthian fiers of *Cynthius* or the Sunne. In whose beames the fumes and vapors of the earth are exhald. The earth being as an aulter, and those fumes as sacrificing smokes, because they seeme pleasing to her in resembling her. That the earth is cald an aulter, *Aratus* in *Astronomicis* testifies in these verses:

> 'Αλλ' ἄρα καὶ περὶ κεῖνο θυτήριον ἀρχαίη νὺξ &c.
> *Nox antiqua suo curru convolvitur Aram*
> *Hanc circum, quae signa dedit certissima nautis*
> *Commiserata virûm metuendos undique casus.*

In which verses the substance of the first foure verses is exprest.

2 Night is cald the nurse or mother of death by *Hesiodus* in *Theogonia*, in these verses repeating her other issue:

> *Nox peperit fatumque malum, Parcamque nigrantem*
> *Et mortem & somnum, diversâque somnia: natos*
> *Hos peperit, nulli dea nox conjuncta marito.*

3 *Plato* saith *discere* is nothing else but *reminisci*.

4 The heavenly abodes are often called, celestiall temples by *Homer & aliis*.

5 Insolence is here taken for rarenesse or unwontednesse.

6 *Lycophron* in *Alexandra*, affirmes the morning useth to ride upon *Pegasus* in his verses:

> *Aurora montem Phagium advolaverat*
> *Velocis altum nuper alis Pegasi.*

7 Vulcan is said by *Natalis Comes* in his *Mythologie*, to have made a golden bed for the Sunne, wherein he swum sleeping till the morning.

8 *Quae lucem pellis sub terras: Orpheus.*

9 Here he alludes to the fiction of *Hercules*, that in his labor at *Tartessus* fetching away the oxen, being (more then he liked) heat with the beames of the Sunne, he bent his bow against him, &c. *Ut ait Pherecides in 3.lib. Historiarum.*

10 This *Periphrasis* of the Night he useth, because in her the blest, (by whom he intends the vertuous) living obscurelie are relieved and quieted, according to those verses before of *Aratus, Commiserata virûm metuendos undique casus.*

11 *Themis* daughters are the three houres, *viz. Dice, Irene,* and *Eunomia,* begotten by Jupiter. They are said to make ready the horse & chariot of the Sun every morning. *ut Orph.*

> *Et Jovis & Themidis Horae de semine natae, &c.*

12 Cynthia or the Moone, is said to be drawne by two white hindes, *ut ait Calimachus.*

> *Aurea nam domitrix Tityi sunt arma Diana*
> *Cuncta tibi & zona, & iuga quae cervicibus aurea*
> *Cervarum imponis currum cum ducis ad aureum.*

13 *Hesiodus* in *Theogonia* cals her the daughter of *Hyperion*, and *Thya, in his versibus.*

> *Thia parit Solem magnum, Lunamqúe nitentem*
> *Auroram quae fert lucem mortalibus almam*
> *Coelicolisqúe Deis cunctis, Hyperionis almi*
> *Semine concepit, namque illos Thia decora.*

So is she said to weare partie-coloured garments: the rest intimates her Magick authoritie.

FINIS.

For the rest of his owne invention, figures and similes, touching their aptnesse and noveltie he hath not laboured to justifie them, because he hopes they wil be proud enough to justifie themselves, and prove sufficiently authenticall to such as understand them; for the rest, God helpe them, I can not (do as others), make day seeme a lighter woman then she is, by painting her.

Ovids Banquet of Sence

[Dedication]

TO THE TRULIE
Learned, and my worthy Friende,
Ma. *Mathew Royden.*

Such is the wilfull povertie of judgements (sweet *Ma:*) wandring like
pasportles men, in contempt of the divine discipline of Poesie, that
a man may well feare to frequent their walks: The prophane multitude
I hate, & onelie consecrate my strange Poems to these serching spirits,
whom learning hath made noble, and nobilitie sacred; endevoring
that materiall Oration, which you call *Schema*; varying in some rare
fiction, from popular custome, even for the pure sakes of ornament
and utilitie; This of *Euripides* exceeding sweetly relishing with mee;
Lentem coquens ne quicquam olentis addito.

But that Poesie should be as perviall as Oratorie, and plainnes her   10
speciall ornament, were the plaine way to barbarisme: and to make
the Asse runne proude of his eares; to take away strength from Lyons,
and give Cammels hornes.

That, *Enargia*, or cleerenes of representation, requird in absolute
Poems is not the perspicuous delivery of a lowe invention; but high,
and harty invention exprest in most significant, and unaffected phrase;
it serves not a skilfull Painters turne, to draw the figure of a face onely
to make knowne who it represents; but hee must lymn, give luster,
shaddow, and heightening; which though ignorants will esteeme spic'd,
and too curious, yet such as have the judiciall perspective, will see it   20
hath, motion, spirit and life.

There is no confection made to last, but it is admitted more cost
and skill then presently to be used simples; and in my opinion, that
which being with a little endevour serched, ads a kinde of majestie to
Poesie; is better then that which every Cobler may sing to his patch.

Obscuritie in affection of words, & indigested concets, is pedanticall
and childish; but where it shroudeth it selfe in the hart of his subject,
utterd with fitnes of figure, and expressive Epethites; with that darknes

wil I still labour to be shaddowed: rich Minerals are digd out of the
30   bowels of the earth, not found in the superficies and dust of it; charms
made of unlerned characters are not consecrate by the Muses which
are divine artists, but by *Evippes* daughters, that challengd them with
meere nature, whose brests I doubt not had beene well worthy
commendation, if their comparison had not turnd them into Pyes.

Thus (not affecting glory for mine owne sleight labors, but desirous
others should be more worthely glorious, nor professing sacred Poesie
in any degree,) I thought good to submit to your apt judgment:
acquainted long since with the true habit of Poesie, and now since
your labouring wits endevour heaven-high thoughts of Nature, you
40   have actual meanes to sound the philosophical conceits, that my new
pen so seriously courteth. I know, that empty, and dark spirits, wil
complaine of palpable night: but those that before-hand, have a
radiant, and light-bearing intellect, will say they can passe through
Corynnas Garden without the helpe of a Lanterne.

Your owne most worthily
and sincerely affected,
George Chapman.

Ovids Banquet of Sence.

The Argument.

Ovid, newly enamoured of Julia, *(daughter to* Octavius Augustus Caesar, *after by him called* Corynna,) *secretly convaid himselfe into a Garden of the Emperors Court: in an Arbor whereof,* Corynna *was bathing; playing upon her Lute, and singing: which* Ovid *over-hearing, was exceedingly pleasde with the sweetnes of her voyce, & to himselfe uttered the comfort he conceived in his sence of Hearing.*   *Auditus.*

   Then the odors shee usde in her bath, breathing a rich savor, hee expresseth the joy he felt in his sence of Smelling.   *Olfactus.*

   Thus growing more deeplie enamoured, in great contentation with himselfe, he venters to see her in the pride of her nakednesse: which dooing by stealth, he   10 *discovered the comfort hee conceived in Seeing, and the glorie of her beautie.*   *Visus.*

   Not yet satisfied, hee useth all his Art to make knowne his being there, without her offence: or (being necessarily offended) to appease her: which done, he entreats a kisse to serve for satisfaction of his Tast, which he obtaines.   *Gustus.*

   Then proceedes he to entreaty for the fift sence and there is interrupted.   *Tactus.*

NARRATIO.

The Earth, from heavenly light conceived heat,
Which mixed all her moyst parts with her dry,
When with right beames the Sun her bosome beat,
And with fit foode her Plants did nutrifie;
   They (which to Earth, as to theyr Mother cling
In forked rootes) now sprinckled plenteously
   With her warme breath; did hasten to the spring,
Gather their proper forces, and extrude
All powre but that, with which they stood indude.

2

*Cyrrhus is a surname
of the Sun, from a towne
called* Cyrrha, *where he
was honored.*

Then did *Cyrrhus fill his eyes with fire,
Whose ardor curld the foreheads of the trees,
And made his greene-love burne in his desire,
When youth, and ease, (Collectors of loves fees)
    Entic'd *Corynna* to a silver spring,
Enchasing a round Bowre; which with it sees,*
    (As with a Diamant dooth an ameld Ring.)
Into which eye, most pittifully stood
Niobe, shedding teares, that were her blood.

*By Prosopopaeia, he
makes ye fountaine ye eye
of the round Arbor, as a
Diamant seemes to be the
eye of a Ring: and therefore
sayes, the Arbor sees with
the Fountaine.*

3

Stone *Niobe*, whose statue to this Fountaine,
In great *Augustus Caesars* grace was brought
From *Sypilus*, the steepe *Mygdonian* Mountaine:
That statue tis, still weepes for former thought,
    Into thys spring *Corynnas* bathing place;
So cunningly to optick reason wrought,
    That a farre of, it shewd a womans face,
Heavie, and weeping; but more neerely viewed,
Nor weeping, heavy, nor a woman shewed.

20

4

In Sommer onely wrought her exstasie;
And that her story might be still observed,
Octavius caus'd in curious imagrie,
Her fourteene children should at large be carved,
    Theyr fourteene brests, with fourteene arrowes gored
And set by her, that for her seede so starved
    To a stone Sepulcher herselfe deplored,
In Ivory were they cut; and on each brest,
In golden Elements theyr names imprest.

30

5

Her sonnes were *Sypilus*, *Agenor*, *Phaedimus*,
Ismenus, *Argus*, and *Damasicthen*,
The seaventh calde like his Grandsire, *Tantalus.*
Her Daughters, were the fayre *Astiochen*,

40

Chloris, *Naeera*, and *Pelopie*,
Phaeta, proud *Phthia*, and *Eugigen*,
 All these apposde to violent *Niobe*
Had lookes so deadly sad, so lively doone,
As if Death liv'd in theyr confusion.

6

Behind theyr Mother two Pyramides
Of freckled Marble, through the Arbor viewed,
On whose sharp brows, *Sol*, and *Tytanides*
In purple and transparent glasse were hewed,
 Through which the Sun-beames on the statues staying,   50
Made theyr pale bosoms seeme with blood imbrewed,
 Those two sterne Plannets rigors still bewraying
To these dead forms, came living beauties essence
Able to make them startle with her presence.

7

In a loose robe of Tynsell foorth she came,
Nothing but it betwixt her nakednes
And envious light. The downward-burning flame,
Of her rich hayre did threaten new accesse,
 Of ventrous *Phaeton* to scorch the fields:
And thus to bathing came our Poets Goddesse,   60
 Her handmaides bearing all things pleasure yeelds
To such a service; Odors most delighted,
And purest linnen which her lookes had whited.

8

Then cast she off her robe, and stood upright,
As lightning breakes out of a laboring cloude;
Or as the Morning heaven casts off the Night,
Or as that heaven cast off it selfe, and showde
 Heavens upper light, to which the brightest day
Is but a black and melancholy shroude:
 Or as when *Venus* striv'd for soveraine sway   70
Of charmfull beautie, in yong Troyes desire,
So stood *Corynna* vanishing her tire.

9

A soft enflowered banck embrac'd the founte;
Of *Chloris* ensignes, an abstracted field;
Where grew Melanthy, great in Bees account,
Amareus, that precious Balme dooth yeeld,
   Enameld Pansies, us'd at Nuptials still,
Dianas arrow, *Cupids* crimson shielde,
    Ope-morne, night-shade, and *Venus* navill,
80   Solemne Violets, hanging head as shamed,
And verdant Calaminth, for odor famed.

10

Sacred Nepenthe, purgative of care,
And soveraine Rumex that doth rancor kill,
Sya, and Hyacinth, that Furies weare,
White and red Jessamines, Merry, Melliphill:
   Fayre Crowne-imperiall, Emperor of Flowers,
Immortall Amaranth, white Aphrodill,
    And cup-like Twillpants, stroude in *Bacchus* Bowres,
These cling about this Natures naked Jem,
90   To taste her sweetes, as Bees doe swarme on them.

11

And now shee usde the Founte, where *Niobe*,
Toomb'd in her selfe, pourde her lost soule in teares,
Upon the bosome of this Romaine *Phoebe*;
Who; bathd and Odord; her bright lyms she rears,
   And drying her on that disparent grounde;
Her Lute she takes t'enamoure hevenly eares,
    And try if with her voyces vitall sounde,
She could warme life through those cold statues spread,
And cheere the Dame that wept when she was dead.

12

100   And thus she sung, all naked as she sat,
Laying the happy Lute upon her thigh,
Not thinking any neere to wonder at
The blisse of her sweet brests divinitie.

The Song of CORYNNA.

T'is better to contemne then love,
And to be fayre then wise;
For soules are rulde by eyes:
And Joves *Bird, ceaz'd by* Cypris *Dove,*
It is our grace and sport to see,
Our beauties sorcerie,
That makes (like destinie) 110
Men followe us the more wee flee;
That sets wise Glosses on the foole,
And turns her cheekes to bookes,
Where wisdome sees in lookes
Derision, laughing at his schoole,
   Who (loving) proves, prophanenes, holy;
   Nature, our fate, our wisdome, folly.

13

While this was singing, *Ovid* yong in love
With her perfections, never proving yet
How mercifull a Mistres she would prove, 120
Boldly embrac'd the power he could not let
   And like a fiery exhalation
Followd the sun, he wisht might never set;
   Trusting heerein his constellation
Rul'd by loves beames, which *Julias* eyes erected,
Whose beauty was the star his life directed.

14

And having drencht his anckles in those seas,
He needes would swimme, and car'd not if he drounde:
Loves feete are in his eyes; for if he please
The depth of beauties gulfye floodd to sounde, 130
   He goes upon his eyes, and up to them,
At the first steap he is; no shader grounde
   Coulde *Ovid* finde; but in loves holy streame
Was past his eyes, and now did wett his eares,
For his high Soveraignes silver voice he heares.

15

Whereat his wit, assumed fierye wings,
Soring above the temper of his soule,
And he the purifying rapture sings
Of his eares sence, takes full the Thespian boule
    And it carrouseth to his Mistres health,
Whose sprightfull verdure did dull flesh controle,
    And his conceipt he crowneth with the wealth
Of all the Muses in his pleased sences,
When with the eares delight he thus commences:

16

Now Muses come, repayre your broken wings,
(Pluckt, and prophan'd by rusticke Ignorance,)
With feathers of these notes my Mistres sings;
And let quick verse hir drooping head advance
    From dungeons of contempt to smite the starrs;
In *Julias* tunes, led forth by furious trance
    A thousand Muses come to bid you warrs,
Dive to your Spring, and hide you from the stroke,
All Poets furies will her tunes invoke.

17

Never was any sence so sette on fire
With an immortall ardor, as myne eares;
Her fingers to the strings doth speeche inspire
And numberd laughter; that the deskant beares
    To hir sweete voice; whose species through my sence
My spirits to theyr highest function reares;
    To which imprest with ceaseles confluence
It useth them, as propper to her powre
Marries my soule, and makes it selfe her dowre;

18

Me thinks her tunes flye guilt, like *Attick* Bees
To my eares hives, with hony tryed to ayre;
My braine is but the combe, the wax, the lees,
My soule the Drone, that lives by their affayre.

140

150

160

O so it sweets, refines, and ravisheth,
And with what sport they sting in theyr repayre:
   Rise then in swarms, and sting me thus to death
Or turne me into swounde; possesse me whole,   170
Soule to my life, and essence to my soule.

19

Say gentle Ayre, ô does it not thee good
Thus to be smit with her correcting voyce?
Why daunce ye not, ye daughters of the wood?
Wither for ever, if not now rejoyce.
   Rise stones, and build a Cittie with her notes,
And notes infuse with your most Cynthian noyse,
   To all the Trees, sweete flowers, and christall Flotes,
That crowne, and make this cheerefull Garden quick,
Vertue, that every tuch may make such Musick.   180

20

O that as man is cald a little world
The world might shrink into a little man,
To heare the notes about this Garden hurld,
That skill disperst in tunes so Orphean
   Might not be lost in smiting stocks and trees
That have no eares; but growne as it began
   Spred theyr renownes, as far as *Phoebus* sees
Through earths dull vaines; that shee like heaven might move,
In ceaseles Musick, and be fill'd with love.

21

In precious incense of her holy breath,   190
My love doth offer Hecatombs of notes
To all the Gods; who now despise the death
Of Oxen, Heifers, Wethers, Swine, and Goates.
   A Sonnet in her breathing sacrifiz'd,
Delights them more then all beasts bellowing throates,
   As much with heaven, as with my hearing priz'd.
And as guilt Atoms in the sunne appeare,
So greete these sounds the grissells of myne eare,

22

Whose pores doe open wide to theyr regreete,
200   And my implanted ayre, that ayre embraceth
Which they impresse; I feele theyr nimble feete
Tread my eares Labyrinth; theyr sport amazeth
     They keepe such measure; play themselves and dance.
And now my soule in *Cupids* Furnace blazeth,
     Wrought into furie with theyr daliance:
And as the fire the parched stuble burns,
So fades my flesh, and into spyrit turns.

23

Sweete tunes, brave issue, that from *Julia* come;
Shooke from her braine, armd like the Queene of Ire;
For first* conceived in her mentall wombe,
And nourisht with her soules discursive fire,
     They grew into the power of her thought;
She gave them dounye plumes from her attire,
     And them to strong imagination brought:
That, to her voice; wherein most movinglye
Shee (blessing them with kysses) letts them flye.

In this allusion to the birth of Pallas; *he shewes the conceipt of her Sonnet; both for matter and note, and by Metaphor hee expresseth how shee delivered her words, & tunes, which was by commission of the order, Philosophers set downe in apprehension of our knowledge, and by effection of our sences, for first they affirme, the species of every object propagates it selfe by our spirites to our common sence, that, delivers it to the imaginative part, that to the Cogitative: the Cogitative to the Passive Intelect; the Passive Intelect, to that which is called* Dianoia, *or* Discursus; *and that delivers it up to the minde, which order hee observes in her utterance.*

24

Who flye rejoysing; but (like noblest mindes)
In giving others life themselves do dye,
Not able to endure earthes rude unkindes
Bred in my soveraigns parts too tenderly;
220   O that as* Intellects themselves transite
To eache intellegible quallitie,
     My life might passe into my loves conceit,
Thus to be form'd in words, her tunes, and breath,
And with her kysses, sing it selfe to death.

The Philosopher saith, Intellectus in ipsa intellegibilia transit, *upon which is grounded thys invention, that in the same manner his life might passe into hys* Mistres conceite, *intending his intellectuall life, or soule: which by this Analogie, should bee* Intellectus, & *her conceit,* Intelligibilis.

25

This life were wholy sweete, this onely blisse,
Thus would I live to dye; Thus sence were feasted,
My life that in my flesh a Chaos is
Should to a Golden worlde be thus dygested;
   Thus should I rule her faces Monarchy,   230
Whose lookes in severall Empires are invested
   Crown'd now with smiles, and then with modesty,
Thus in her tunes division I should raigne,
For her conceipt does all, in every vaine.

26

My life then turn'd to that, t'each note, and word
Should I consorte her looke; which sweeter sings,
Where songs of solid harmony accord,
Rulde with Loves rule; and prickt with all his stings;
   Thus should I be her notes, before* they be;   *This hath reference to the order
While in her blood they sitte with fierye wings   of her utterance, exprest before.
   Not vapord in her voyces stillerie,
Nought are these notes her breast so sweetely frames,
But motions, fled out of her spirits flames.

27

For as when steele and flint together smit,
With violent action spitt forth sparkes of fire,
And make the tender tynder burne with it;
So my loves soule doth lighten her desire
   Upon her spyrits in her notes* pretence;   *So is thys lykewise referd to the
And they convaye them (for distinckt attire)   order abovesaid, for the more
   To use the Wardrobe of the common sence: perspicuitie.
From whence in vailes of her rich breath they flye,
And feast the eare with this felicitye.

28

Me thinks they rayse me from the heavy ground
And move me swimming in the yeelding ayre:
As Zephirs flowry blasts doe tosse a sounde;
Upon their wings will I to Heaven repayre,

And sing them so, Gods shall descend and heare
Ladies must bee ador'd that are but fayre,
But apt besides with art to tempt the eare
In notes of Nature, is a Goddesse part,
Though oft, mens natures notes, please more then Art.

29

But heere are Art and Nature both confinde,
Art casting Nature in so deepe a trance
That both seeme deade, because they be divinde,
Buried is Heaven in earthly ignorance,
Why breake not men then strumpet Follies bounds,
To learne at this pure virgine utterance?
No; none but *Ovids* eares can sound these sounds,
Where sing the harts of Love and Poesie,
Which make my Muse so strong she works too hye.

30

Now in his glowing eares her tunes did sleepe,
And as a silver Bell, with violent blowe
Of Steele or Iron, when his soundes most deepe,
Doe from his sides and ayres soft bosome flowe,
A great while after murmures at the stroke,
Letting the hearers eares his hardnes knowe,
So chid the Ayre to be no longer broke:
And left the accents panting in his eare
Which in this Banquet his first service were.

31

Olfactus.

Heerewith, as *Ovid* something neerer drew,
Her Odors, odord with her breath and brest,
Into the sensor of his savor flew,
As if the Phenix hasting to her rest
Had gatherd all th'Arabian Spicerie
T'enbalme her body in her Tombe, her nest,
And there lay burning gainst *Apollos* eye,
Whose fiery ayre straight piercing *Ovids* braine
Enflamde his Muse with a more odorouse vaine.

32

And thus he sung, come soveraigne Odors, come
Restore my spirits now in love consuming,   290
Wax hotter ayre, make them more savorsome,
My fainting life with fresh-breath'd soule perfuming,
    The flames of my disease are violent,
And many perish on late helps presuming,
    With which hard fate must I yet stand content,
As Odors put in fire most richly smell,
So men must burne in love that will excell.

33

And as the ayre is rarefied with heate
But thick and grosse with Summer-killing colde,
So men in love aspire perfections seate,   300
When others, slaves to base desire are sold,
    And if that men neere *Ganges* liv'd by sent
Of Flowres, and Trees, more I a thousand fold
    May live by these pure fumes that doe present
My Mistres quickning, and consuming breath
Where her wish flyes with power of life and death.

34

Me thinks, as in these liberall fumes I burne
My Mistres lips be neere with kisse-entices,
And that which way soever I can turne,
She turns withall, and breaths on me her spices,   310
    As if too pure for search of humaine eye
She flewe in ayre disburthening Indian prizes,
    And made each earthly fume to sacrifice.
With her choyse breath fell *Cupid* blowes his fire,
And after, burns himselfe in her desire.

35

Gentle, and noble are theyr tempers framde,
That can be quickned with perfumes and sounds,
And they are cripple-minded, Gowt-wit lamde,
That lye like fire-fit blocks, dead without wounds,

320   Stird up with nought, but hell-descending gaine,
    The soule of fooles that all theyr soules confounds,
     The art of Pessants and our Nobles staine,
    The bane of vertue and the blisse of sinne.
    Which none but fooles and Pessants glorie in.

36

    Sweete sounds and Odors, are the heavens, on earth
    Where vertues live, of vertuous men deceast,
    Which in such like, receive theyr second birth
    By smell and* hearing endlesly encreast;
     They were meere flesh were not with them delighted,
    And every such is perisht like a beast
     As all they shall that are so foggye sprighted,
    Odors feede love, and love cleare heaven discovers,
    Lovers weare sweets then; sweetest mindes, be lovers.

*By this allusion drawne from the effects of sounds and Odors, he imitates the eternitie of Vertue: saying, the vertues of good men live in them, because they stir up pure enclinations to the like, as if infusde in perfumes & sounds: Besides, he infers, that such as are neyther delighted with sounds (intending by sounds all utterance of knowledge, as well as musicall affections,) nor with Odors, (which properly drye the braine & delight the instruments of the soule, making them more capable of her faculties) such saith hee, perrish without memorie.

37

    Odor in heate and drynes is consite
    Love then a fire is much thereto affected;
    And as ill smells do kill his appetite
    With thankfull savors it is still protected;
     Love lives in spyrits, and our spyrits be
    Nourisht with Odors, therefore love refected;
340   And ayre lesse corpulent in quallitie
    Then Odors are, doth nourish vitall spyrits
    Therefore may they be prov'd of equall merits.

38

    O soveraigne Odors; not of force to give
    Foode to a thing that lives nor let it dye,
    But to ad life to that did never live;
    Nor to ad life, but immortallitie.

Since they pertake her heate that like the fire
Stolne from the wheeles of *Phoebus* waggonrie
   To lumps of earth, can manly lyfe inspire;
Else be these fumes the lives of sweetest dames   350
That (dead) attend on her for novell frames.

39

Rejoyce blest Clime, thy ayre is so refinde
That while shee lives no hungry pestilence
Can feede her poysoned stomack with thy kynde;
But as the Unicorns pregredience
   To venomd Pooles, doth purdge them with his horne,
And after him the desarts Residence
   May safely drinke, so in the holesome morne
After her walke, who there attends her eye,
Is sure that day to tast no maladye.   360

40

Thus was his course of Odors sweet and sleight,
Because he long'd to give his sight assaye,
And as in fervor of the summers height,
The sunne is so ambitious in his sway
   He will not let the Night an howre be plast,
So in this *Cupids* Night (oft seene in day
   Now spred with tender clouds these Odors cast,)
Her sight, his sunne so wrought in his desires,
His savor vanisht in his visuale fires.

41

So vulture love on his encreasing liver,   370
And fruitfull entrails egerly did feede,
And with the goldnest Arrow in his Quiver,
Wounds him with longings, that like Torrents bleeds,
   To see the Myne of knowledge that enricht
His minde with povertie, and desperate neede:
   A sight that with the thought of sight bewitcht,
A sight taught Magick his deepe misterie,
         Quicker in danger then* *Dianas* eye.

*Allusion to the
transformation of Acteon
with the sight of Diana.

42

Stay therefore *Ovid*, venter not, a sight
380 May prove thy rudenes, more then shew thee loving,
And make thy Mistres thinke thou think'st her light:
Which thought with lightest Dames is nothing moving.
 The slender hope of favor thou hast yet
Should make thee feare, such grosse conclusions proving:
 Besides, the Thicket *Floras* hands hath set
To hide thy theft, is thinne and hollow harted,
Not meete to have so high a charge imparted.

43

And should it keepe thy secrets, thine owne eye
Would fill thy thoughts so full of lightenings,
390 That thou must passe through more extremitie.
Or stand content to burne beneath theyr wings,
 Her honor gainst thy love, in wager layde,
Thou would'st be prickt with other sences stings,
 To tast, and feele, and yet not there be staide:
These casts, he cast, and more, his wits more quick
Then can be cast, by wits Arithmetick.

44

A simile, Forward, and back, and forward went he thus,
expressing the Like wanton *Thamysis*, that hastes to greete
manner of his The brackish Court of old *Oceanus*;
minds contention
in the desire of her And as by Londons bosome she doth fleet
sight, and feare of Casts herselfe proudly through the Bridges twists,
her displeasure. Where (as she takes againe her Christall feete:)
  She curls her silver hayre like Amorists,
Smoothes her bright cheekes, adorns her browes with ships
And Empresse-like along the Coast she trips.

45

Till comming neere the Sea, she heares him rore,
Tumbling her churlish billowes in her face,
Then, more dismaid, then insolent before
Charg'd to rough battaile, for his smooth embrace,

She crowcheth close within her winding bancks,   410
And creepes retreate into her peacefull Pallace;
   Yet straite high-flowing in her female prancks
Againe shee will bee wanton, and againe,
By no meanes stayde, nor able to containe.

46

So *Ovid* with his strong affections striving,
Maskt in a friendly Thicket neere her Bowre,
Rubbing his temples, fainting, and reviving,
Fitting his garments, praying to the howre,
   Backwards, and forwards went, and durst not venter,
To tempt the tempest of his Mistres lowre,   420
   Or let his eyes her beauties ocean enter;
At last, with prayer he pierceth *Junos* eare,
Great Goddesse of audacitie and feare,

47

Great Goddesse of audacitie, and feare,
Queene of Olympus, *Saturns* eldest seede,
That doost the scepter over *Samos* beare,
And rul'st all Nuptiale rites with power, and meede,
   Since thou in nature art the meane to mix
Still sulphure humors, and canst therefore speede
   Such as in Cyprian sports theyr pleasures fix,   430
Venus herselfe, and *Mars* by thee embracing,
Assist my hopes, me and my purpose gracing.

48

Make love within me not too kinde but pleasing,
Exiling Aspen feare out of his forces,
My inward sight, with outward seeing, easing,
And if he please further to stretch his courses,
   Arme me with courage to make good his charges,
Too much desire to please, pleasure divorces,
   Attemps, and not entreats get Ladies larges,
Wit is with boldnes prompt, with terror danted,   440
And grace is sooner got of Dames then graunted.

49

Visus.

This sayde, he charg'd the Arbor with his eye,
Which pierst it through, and at her brests reflected,
Striking him to the hart with exstasie:
As doe the sun-beames gainst the earth prorected,
  With their reverberate vigor mount in flames,
And burne much more then where they were directed,
  He saw th'extraction of all fayrest Dames:
The fayre of Beauty, as whole Countries come
And shew theyr riches in a little Roome.

450

50

Heere *Ovid* sold his freedome for a looke,
And with that looke was ten tymes more enthralde,
He blusht, lookt pale, and like a fevour shooke,
And as a* burning vapor being exhalde
  Promist by *Phoebus* eye to be a star,
Heavens walles denying to be further scalde
  The force dissolves that drewe it up so far:
And then it lightens gainst his death and fals,
So *Ovids* powre, this powrefull sight appals.

**This simile expresseth
the cause and substance of
those exhalations which
vulgarly are called falling
starres: so* Homer *and*
Virgill *calls them,*
Stellas cadentes,
Homer *comparing the
descent of* Pallas *among
the Troyans to a falling
Starre.*

51

This beauties fayre is an enchantment made
By natures witchcraft, tempting men to buy
With endles showes, what endlessly will fade,
Yet promise chapmen all eternitie:
  But like to goods ill got a fate it hath,
Brings men enricht therewith to beggerie
  Unlesse th'enricher be as rich in fayth,
Enamourd (like good selfe-love) with her owne,
Seene in another, then tis heaven alone.

52

For sacred beautie, is the fruite of sight,
The curtesie that speakes before the tongue,
The feast of soules, the glory of the light,
Envy of age, and everlasting young,

470

Pitties Commander, *Cupids* richest throne,
Musick intransed, never duely sung,
    The summe and court of all proportion:
And that I may dull speeches best afforde,
All Rethoricks flowers in lesse then in a worde.

53

Then is the truest wisdome can be thought,
Spight of the publique *Axiom* worldings hold,
That nothing wisdome is, that getteth nought,   480
This all-things-nothing, since it is no gold.
    Beautie enchasing love, love gracing beautie,
To such as constant simpathies enfold,
    To perfect riches dooth a sounder duetie
Then all endevors, for by all consent
All wealth and wisdome rests in true Content.

54

Contentment is our heaven, and all our deedes
Bend in that circle, seld or never closde,
More then the letter in the word preceedes,
And to conduce that compasse is reposde.   490
    More force and art in beautie joynd with love,
Then thrones with wisdome, joyes of them composde
    Are armes more proofe gainst any griefe we prove,
Then all their vertue-scorning miserie
Or judgments graven in Stoick gravitie,

55

But as weake colour alwayes is allowde
The proper object of a humaine eye,
Though light be with a farre more force endowde
In stirring up the visuale facultie,
    This colour being but of vertuous light   500
A feeble Image; and the cause dooth lye
    In th'imperfection of a humaine sight,
So this for love, and beautie, loves cold fire
May serve for my praise, though it merit higher.

56

With this digression, wee will now returne
To *Ovids* prospect in his fancies storme:
Hee thought hee sawe the Arbors bosome burne,
Blaz'd with a fire wrought in a Ladyes forme:
    Where silver past the least: and Natures vant
510   Did such a precious miracle performe,
      Shee lay, and seemd a flood of Diamant
Bounded in flesh: as still as *Vespers* hayre,
When not an Aspen leafe is styrrd with ayre.

57

*The amplification of this
simile, is taken from the
blisfull state of soules in
Elisium, as Virgill
faines: and expresseth a
regenerate beauty in all
life & perfection, not
intimating any rest of
death. But in peace of
that eternall spring, he
poynteth to that life of life
thys beauty-clad naked
Lady.

Shee lay* at length, like an immortall soule
At endlesse rest in blest *Elisium*:
And then did true felicitie enroule
So fayre a Lady, figure of her kingdome.
    Now *Ovids* Muse as in her tropicke shinde,
And hee (strooke dead) was meere heaven-borne become,
      So his quick verse in equall height was shrinde:
Or els blame mee as his submitted debter,
That never Mistresse had to make mee better.

58

[*]*He calls her body (as
it were divided with her
breasts,) ye fields of
Paradise, and her armes
& legs the famous Rivers
in it.*

Now as shee lay, attirde in nakednes,
His eye did carve him on that feast of feasts:
Sweet* fields of life which Deaths foote dare not presse,
Flowrd with th'unbroken waves of my Loves brests,
    Unbroke by depth of those her beauties floods:
See where with bent of Gold curld into Nests
      In her heads Grove, the Spring-bird Lameate broods:
530   Her body doth present those fields of peace
Where soules are feasted with the soule of ease.

59

To prove which Parradise that nurseth these,
See see the golden Rivers that renowne it:
Rich *Gehon, Tigris, Phison, Euphrates*,
Two from her bright Pelopian shoulders crowne it,

And two out of her snowye Hills doe glide,
That with a Deluge of delights doe drowne it:
   The highest two, theyr precious streames divide
To tenne pure floods, that doe the body dutie
Bounding themselves in length, but not in beautie.   540

60

These* winde theyr courses through the painted bowres,
And raise such sounds in theyr inflection,
As ceaseles start from Earth fresh sorts of flowers,
And bound that booke of life with every section.
   In these the Muses dare not swim for drowning,
Theyr sweetnes poisons with such blest infection,
     And leaves the onely lookers on them swouning,
These forms so decks, and colour makes so shine,
That Gods for them would cease to be divine.

*Hee intends the office of her fingers in attyring her, touching thys of theyr courses, in theyr inflection following, theyr playing upon an Instrument.

61

Thus though my love be no *Elisium*   550
That cannot move, from her prefixed place;
Yet have her feete no powre from thence to come,
For where she is, is all *Elisian* grace:
   And as those happy men are sure of blisse
That can performe so excellent a race
     As that Olympiad where her favor is,
So shee can meete them; blessing them the rather
And give her sweetes, as well as let men gather.

62

Ah how should I be so most happy then
T'aspire that place, or make it come to mee?   540
To gather, or be given, the flowre of women?
Elisium must with vertue gotten bee,
   With labors of the soule and continence,
And these can yeeld no joy with such as she,
     Shee is a sweet *Elisium* for the sence
And Nature dooth not sensuall gifts infuse
But that with sence, shee still intends their use.

63

The sence is given us to excite the minde,
And that can never be by sence exited
But first the sence must her contentment finde,
We therefore must procure the sence delighted,
    That so the soule may use her facultie;
Mine Eye then to this feast hath her invited;
    That she might serve the soveraigne of mine Eye,
Shee shall bide Time, and Time so feasted never
Shall grow in strength of her renowne for ever.

64

Betwixt mine Eye and object, certayne lynes,
Move in the figure of a Pyramis,
Whose chapter in mine eyes gray apple shines,
The base within my sacred object is:
    On this will I inscribe in golden verse
The mervailes raigning in my soveraigns blisse,
    The arcks of sight, and how her arrowes pierse:
This in the Region of the ayre shall stand
In Fames brasse Court, and all her Trumps commaund.

65

Rich Beautie, that ech Lover labors for,
Tempting as heapes of new-coynd-glowing Gold,
(Rackt of some miserable Treasurer)
Draw his desires, and them in chaynes enfold
    Urging him still to tell it, and conceale it,
But Beauties treasure never can be told:
    None can peculier joy, yet all must steale it.
O Beautie, this same bloody siedge of thine
Starves me that yeeld, and feedes mee till I pine.

66

And as a Taper burning in the darke
(As if it threatned every watchfull eye
That viewing burns it,) makes that eye his marke,
And hurls guilt Darts at it continually,

    Or as it envied, any eye but it
Should see in darknes, so my Mistres beautie   600
    From foorth her secret stand my hart doth hit:
And like the Dart of *Cephalus* dooth kill
Her perfect Lover, though shee meane no ill.

67

Thus, as the innocence of one betraide
Carries an *Argus* with it, though unknowne,
And Fate, to wreake the trecherie bewraide;
Such vengeance hath my Mistres Beautie showne
    On me the Traitor to her modestie,
So unassailde, I quite am overthrowne,
    And in my tryumph bound in slaverie.   610
O Beauty, still thy Empire swims in blood,
And in thy peace, Warre stores himselfe with foode.

68

O Beautie, how attractive is thy powre?
For as the lives heate clings about the hart,
So all Mens hungrie eyes do haunt thy Bowre,
Raigning in Greece, Troy swum to thee in Art;
    Remov'd to Troy, Greece followd thee in feares;
Thy drewst each Syreles sworde, each childles Dart
    And pulld'st the towres of Troy about thine eares:
Shall I then muse that thus thou drawest me?   620
No, but admire, I stand thus farre from thee.

69

Heerewith shee rose like the Autumnale Starre
Fresh burnisht in the loftie Ocean floode,
That darts his glorious influence more farre
Then any Lampe of bright *Olympus* broode;
    Shee lifts her lightning arms above her head,
And stretcheth a Meridian from her blood,
    That slept awake in her *Elisian* bed:
Then knit shee up, lest loose, her glowing hayre
Should scorch the Center and incense the ayre.   630

70

Thus when her fayre hart-binding hands had tied
Those liberall Tresses, her high frontier part,
Shee shrunk in curls, and curiously plied
Into the figure of a swelling hart:
    And then with Jewels of devise, it graced:
One was a Sunne graven at his Eevens depart,
    And under that a Mans huge shaddow* placed,
Wherein was writ, in sable Charectry,
Decrescente nobilitate, crescunt obscuri.

*At the Sun going downe, shadowes grow longest, whereupon this Embleme is devised.

71

640

An other was an Eye in Saphire set,
And close upon it a fresh Lawrell spray,
The skilfull Posie was, *Medio* caret,
To showe not eyes, but meanes must truth display.
    The third was an *Apollo** with his Teme
About a Diall and a worlde in way,
    The Motto was, *Teipsum et orbem,*
Graven in the Diall; these exceeding rare
And other like accomplements she ware.

*Sight is one of the three sences that hath his medium extrinsecally, which now (supposed wanting,) lets the sight by the close apposition of the Lawrell: the application wherof hath many constructions.

*The Sun hath as much time to compasse a Diall as the world, & therefore ye world is placed in the Dyall, expressing the conceite of the Emprese morally which hath a far higher intention.

72

650

Not *Tygris*, *Nilus*, nor swift *Euphrates*,
Quoth *Ovid* now, can more subdue my flame,
I must through hell adventure to displease,
To tast and touch, one kisse may worke the same:
    If more will come, more then much more I will;
Each naturall agent doth his action frame,
    To render that he works on like him styll:
The fire on water working doth induce
Like qualitie unto his owne in use.

73

But Heaven in her a sparckling temper blewe
(As love in mee) and so will soone be wrought,
Good wits will bite at baits most strang and new,   660
And words well plac'd, move things were never thought;
    What Goddesse is it *Ovids* wits shall dare
And he disgrace them with attempting nought?
    My words shall carry spirits to ensnare,
The subtlest harts affecting sutes importune,
"Best loves are lost for wit when men blame Fortune.

74

With this, as she was looking in her Glasse,   NARRATIO.
She saw therein* a mans face looking on her: [*]*Ovid* standing
Whereat she started from the frighted Grasse,   behind her, his
As if some monstrous Serpent had been shown her: face was seene in
    Rising as when (the sunne in *Leos* signe)   the Glasse.
Auriga with the heavenly Goate upon her,
    Shows her horn'd forehead with her Kids divine,
Whose rise, kils Vines, Heavens face with storms disguising;
No man is safe at sea, the Haedy rising.

75

So straight wrapt shee her body in a Clowde,
And threatned tempests for her high disgrace,
Shame from a Bowre of Roses did unshrowde
And spread her crimson wings upon her face;
    When running out, poore *Ovid* humbly kneeling   680
Full in the Arbors mouth, did stay her race
    And saide; faire Nimph, great Goddesse have some feeling
Of *Ovids* paines; but heare: and your dishonor
Vainely surmisde, shall vanish with my horror.

76

Traytor to Ladies modesties (said shee)
What savage boldnes hardned thee to this?
Or what base reckoning of my modestie?
What should I thinke thy facts proude reason is?

Love (sacred Madam) love exhaling mee
690   (Wrapt in his Sulphure,) to this clowde of his
Made my affections his artillerie,
Shot me at you his proper Cytadell,
And loosing all my forces, heere I fell.

77

This Glosse is common, as thy rudenes strange
Nor to forbeare these private times, (quoth she)
Whose fixed Rites, none shoulde presume to change
Not where there is adjudg'd inchastitie;
Our nakednes should be as much conceald
As our accomplishments desire the eye:
700   It is a secrete not to be revealde,
But as Virginitie, and Nuptialls clothed,
And to our honour all to be betrothed.

78

It is a want, where our aboundance lyes,
Given a sole dowre t'enrich chast *Hymens* Bed,
A perfect Image of our purities,
And glasse by which our actions should be dressed.
That tells us honor is as soone defild
And should be kept as pure, and incompressed,
But sight attainteth it: for Thought Sights childe
710   Begetteth sinne; and Nature bides defame,
When light and lawles eyes bewray our shame.

79

Deere Mistresse (answerd *Ovid*,) to direct
Our actions, by the straitest rule that is,
We must in matters Morrall, quite reject
Vulgar Opinion, ever led amisse
And let autentique Reason be our guide,
The wife of Truth, and Wisdoms Governisse:
The nature of all actions must be waide,
And as they then appeare, breede love or loathing,
720   Use makes things nothing huge, and huge things nothing.

80

As in your sight, how can sight simply beeing
A Sence receiving essence to his flame
Sent from his object, give it harme by seeing
Whose action* in the Seer hath his frame?

   All excellence of shape is made for sight,
Else, to be like a Beast were no defame;

   Hid Beauties lose theyr ends, and wrong theyr right:
And can kinde love, (where no harms kinde can be)
Disgrace with seeing that is given to see?

*Actio cernendi in
homine vel animali,
vidente collocanda est.
Aristot.

81

Tis I (alas) and my hart-burning Eye
Doe all the harme, and feele the harme wee doo:
I am no Basiliske, yet harmles I
Poyson with sight, and mine owne bosome too;

   So am I to my selfe a Sorceresse
Bewitcht with my conceites in her I woo:

   But you unwrongd, and all dishonorlesse
No ill dares touch, affliction, sorcerie,
One kisse of yours can quickly remedie.

730

82

I could not times observe, as others might
Of cold affects, and watry tempers framde,
Yet well assurde the wounder of your sight
Was so farre of from seeing you defamde,

   That ever in the Phane of Memorie
Your love shall shine by it, in mee enflamde.

   Then let your powre be clad in lenitie,
Doe not (as others would) of custome storme,
But prove your wit as pregnant as your forme.

740

83

Nor is my love so suddaine, since my hart
Was long loves *Vulcan*, with his pants unrest,
Ham'ring the shafts bred this delightsome smart:
And as when *Jove* at once from East and West

750

Cast off two Eagles, to discerne the sight
Of this world Center, both his Byrds joyned brest
  In Cynthian *Delphos*, since *Earths navill* hight:
So casting off my ceaseles thoughts to see
My harts true Center, all doe meete in thee.

84

Cupid that acts in you, suffers in mee
To make himselfe one tryumph-place of twaine,
Into your tunes and odors turned hee,
And through my sences flew into my braine
  *Where rules the Prince of sence, whose Throne hee takes,
And of my Motions engines framd a chaine
  To leade mee where hee list; and heere hee makes
Nature (my* fate) enforce mee: and resignes
The raines of all, to you, in whom hee shines.

*In Cerebro est
principium sentiendi, et
inde nervi, qui
instrumenta sunt motus
voluntarii oriuntur.
*Natura est
unjuscuiusque Fatum,
ut* Theophr.

85

For yeelding love then, doe not hate impart,
Nor let mine Eye, your carefull Harbengere
That hath purvaide your Chamber in my hart,
Be blamde for seeing who it lodged there;
  The freer service merrits greater meede,
Princes are serv'd with unexpected chere,
  And must have things in store before they neede:
Thus should faire Dames be wise and confident,
Not blushing to be noted excellent.

770

86

Now, as when Heaven is muffled with the vapors
His long since just divorced wife the Earth,
In envie breathes, to maske his spurrie Tapers
From the unrich aboundance of her birth,
  When straight the westerne issue of the Ayre
Beates with his flowrie wings those Brats of dearth,
  And gives *Olympus* league to shew his fayre,
So fled th'offended shaddowes of her cheere,
And showd her pleased count'nance full as cleere.

780

Which for his fourth course made our Poet court her. &c.

87

This motion of my soule, my fantasie   *Gustus.*
   Created by three sences put in act,
   Let justice nourish with thy simpathie,
   Putting my other sences into fact,
    If now thou grant not, now changde that offence;   *Alterationem pati est*
To suffer change, doth perfect sence compact: *sentire.*
   Change then, and suffer for the use of sence,
Wee live not for our selves, the Eare, and Eye,
And every sence, must serve societie.

88

To furnish then, this Banquet where the tast
Is never usde, and yet the cheere divine,
The neerest meane deare Mistres that thou hast
To blesse me with it, is a kysse of thine,
   Which grace shall borrow organs of my touch
T'advance it to that inward* taste of mine   **He intends the common sence*
   Which makes all sence, and shall delight as much   *which is* centrum sensibus
Then with a kisse (deare life) adorne thy feast   et speciebus, *& cals it last*
And let (as Banquets should) the last be best.   *because it dooth,* sapere in
                                       effectione sensuum.

89

I see unbidden Guests are boldest still,   *Corynna.*
   And well you showe how weake in soule you are
That let rude sence subdue your reasons skill
And feede so spoilefully on sacred fare;
   In temper of such needles feasts as this
We show more bounty still the more we spare,
   Chiefly where birth and state so different is:
Ayre too much rarefied breakes forth in fire,   810
And favors too farre urg'd do end in ire.

90

Ovid. The difference of our births (imperiall Dame)
Is heerein noted with too triviall eyes
For your rare wits; that should your choices frame
To state of parts, that most doth royalize,
  Not to commend mine owne; but that in yours
Beyond your birth, are perrils soveraignties
  Which (urgd) your words had strook with sharper powers;
Tis for mere looke-like Ladies, and for men
820 To boast of birth that still be childeren,

91

Running to Father straight to helpe theyr needs;
True dignities and rites of reverence,
Are sowne in mindes, and reapt in lively deedes,
And onely pollicie makes difference
  Twixt States, since vertue wants due imperance,
Vertue makes honor, as the soule doth sence,
  And merit farre exceedes inheritance,
The Graces fill loves cup, his feasts adorning,
Who seekes your service now, the Graces scorning.

92

830 Pure love (said she) the purest grace pursues,
And there is contact, not by application
Of lips or bodies, but of bodies vertues,
As in our elementale Nation
  Stars by theyr powers, which are theyr heat and light
Do heavenly works, and that which hath probation
  By vertuall contact hath the noblest plight,
Both for the lasting and affinitie
It hath with naturall divinitie.

93

Ovid replied; in thys thy vertuall presence
840 (Most fayre *Corynna*) thou canst not effuse
The true and solid parts of thy pure essence
But doost the superficiall beames produce

Of thy rich substance; which because they flow
Rather from forme then from the matters use
    Resemblance onely of thy body showe
Whereof they are thy wondrous species,
And t'is thy substance must my longings ease.

94

Speake then sweet ayre, that giv'st our speech event
And teach my Mistres tractabilitie,
That art to motion most obedient,   850
And though thy nature, swelling be and high
    And occupiest so infinite a space,
Yet yeeldst to words, and art condenst thereby
    Past nature prest into a little place
Deare soveraigne then, make ayre thy rule in this,
And me thy worthy servant with a kisse.

95

Ovid (sayd shee) I am well pleasd to yeeld:
Bountie by vertue cannot be abusde:
Nor will I coylie lyft *Minervas* shielde
Against *Minerva*, honor is not brusde   860
    With such a tender pressure as a kisse,
Nor yeelding soone to words, though seldome usde,
    Nicenes in civill favours, folly is:
Long sutes make never good a bad detection,
Nor yeelding soone, makes bad, a good affection.

96

To some I know, (and know it for a fault)
Order and reverence, are repulst in skaling,
When pryde and rudenes, enter with assault,
Consents to fall, are worse to get then falling:
    Willing resistance, takes away the will,   870
And too much weakenes tis to come with calling:
    Force in these frayes, is better man then skyll
Yet I like skill, and *Ovid* if a kis
May doe thee so much pleasure, heere it is.

97

Her mooving towards him, made *Ovids* eye
Beleeve the Firmament was comming downe
To take him quick to immortalitie,
And that th'Ambrosian kisse set on the Crowne:
　　Shee spake in kissing, and her breath infusde
880　　Restoring syrrop to his tast, in swoune:
　　　　And hee imaginde *Hebes* hands had brusde
A banquet of the Gods into his sence,
Which fild him with this furious influence.

98

The motion of the Heavens that did beget
The golden age, and by whose harmonie
Heaven is preservd, in mee on worke is set,
All instruments of deepest melodie
　　Set sweet in my desires to my loves liking
With this sweet kisse in mee theyr tunes apply,
890　　　　As if the best Musitians hands were striking:
This kisse in mee hath endlesse Musicke closed,
Like *Phoebus* Lute, on *Nisus* Towrs imposed.

99

And as a Pible cast into a Spring,
Wee see a sort of trembling cirkles rise,
One forming other in theyr issuing
Till over all the Fount they circulize,
　　So this perpetuall-motion-making kisse,
Is propagate through all my faculties,
　　　　And makes my breast an endlesse Fount of blisse,
900　　Of which, if Gods could drink, theyr matchlesse fare
Would make them much more blessed then they are.

100

Qua ratione fiat Eccho.　But* as when sounds doe hollow bodies beate,
Ayre gatherd there, comprest, and thickned,
The selfe same way shee came doth make retreate,
And so effects the sounde reechoed

Onely in part, because shee weaker is
In that redition, then when first shee fled:
 So I alas, faint eccho of this kisse,
Onely reiterate a slender part
Of that high joy it worketh in my hart.   910

101

And thus with feasting, love is famisht more,
Without my touch are all things turnd to gold,
And till I touch, I cannot joy my store:
To purchase others, I my selfe have sold,
 Love is a wanton famine, rich in foode,
But with a richer appetite controld,
  An argument in figure and in Moode,
Yet hates all arguments: disputing still
For Sence, gainst Reason, with a sencelesse will.

102

Then sacred Madam, since my other sences   *Tactus*
Have in your graces tasted such content,
Let wealth not to be spent, feare no expences,
But give thy bountie true eternizement:
 Making my sences ground-worke, which is, Feeling,
Effect the other, endlesse excellent,
  Their substance with flint-softning softnes steeling:
Then let mee feele, for know sweet beauties Queene,
Dames may be felt, as well as heard or seene.

103

For if wee be allowd to serve the Eare
With pleasing tunes, and to delight the Eye   930
With gracious showes, the Taste with daintie cheere,
The Smell with Odors, ist immodestie
 To serve the sences Emperor, sweet Feeling
With those delights that fit his Emperie?
  Shall Subjects free themselves, and bind theyr King?
Mindes taint no more with bodies touch or tyre,
Then bodies nourish with the mindes desire.

104

The minde then cleere, the body may be usde,
Which perfectly your touch can spritualize;
940 As by the great elixer is trans-fusde
Copper to Golde, then grant that deede of prise:
  Such as trans-forme into corrupt effects
What they receave from Natures purities,
  Should not wrong them that hold her due respects:
To touch your quickning side then give mee leave,
Th'abuse of things, must not the use bereave.

105

Heere-with, even glad his arguments to heare,
Worthily willing to have lawfull grounds
To make the wondrous power of Heaven appeare,
950 In nothing more then her perfections found,
  Close to her navill shee her Mantle wrests,
Slacking it upwards, and the foulds unwound,
  Showing *Latonas* Twinns, her plenteous brests
The Sunne and *Cynthia* in theyr tryumph-robes
Of Lady-skin; more rich then both theyr Globes.

106

Whereto shee bad, blest *Ovid* put his hand:
Hee, well acknowledging it much too base
For such an action, did a little stand,
Enobling it with tytles full of grace,
960 And conjures it with charge of reverend verse,
To use with pietie that sacred place,
  And through his Feelings organ to disperse
Worth to his spirits, amply to supply
The porenes of his fleshes facultie.

107

And thus hee sayd: King of the King of Sences,
Engines of all the engines under heaven,
To health, and life, defence of all defences,
Bountie by which our nourishment is given,

Beauties bewtifier, kinde acquaintance maker,
Proportions odnes that makes all things even,   970
   Wealth of the laborer, wrongs revengement taker,
Patterne of concord, Lord of exercise,
And figure of that power the world did guise:

                              108
Deere Hand, most dulie honord in this
And therefore worthy to be well employde:
Yet know, that all that honor nothing is,
Compard with that which now must be enjoyd:
   So thinke in all the pleasures these have showne
(Liken'd to this) thou wert but meere anoyde,
   That all hands merits in thy selfe alone   980
With this one touch, have more then recompence,
And therefore feele, with feare and reverence.

                              109
See *Cupids* Alps which now thou must goe over,
Where snowe that thawes the Sunne doth ever lye:
Where thou maist plaine and feelingly discover
The worlds fore-past, that flow'd with Milke and Honny:
   Where, (like an Empresse seeing nothing wanting
That may her glorious child-bed bewtifile)
   Pleasure her selfe lyes big with issue panting:
Ever deliverd, yet with childe still growing,   990
Full of all blessings, yet all blisse bestowing.

                              110
This sayd, hee layde his hand upon her side,
Which made her start like sparckles from a fire,
Or like *Saturnia* from th'Ambrosian pride
Of her morns slumber, frighted with admire
   When *Jove* layd young *Alcydes* to her brest,
So startled shee, not with a coy retire,
   But with the tender temper shee was blest,
Proving her sharpe, unduld with handling yet,
Which keener edge on *Ovids* longings set.   1000

111

And feeling still, he sigh'd out this effect;
Alas why lent not heaven the soule a tongue?
Nor language, nor peculier dialect,
To make her high conceits as highly sung,
   But that a fleshlie engine must unfold
A spirituall notion; birth from Princes sprung
   Pessants must nurse, free vertue waite on gold
And a profest though flattering enemie,
Must pleade my honor, and my libertie.

112

1010
O nature how doost thou defame in this
Our humane honors? yoking men with beasts
And noblest mindes with slaves? thus beauties blisse,
Love and all vertues that quick spirit feasts
   Surfet on flesh; and thou that banquests mindes,
Most bounteous Mistresse, of thy dull-tongu'd guests
   Reapst not due thanks; thus rude frailetie bindes
What thou giv'st wings; thus joyes I feele in thee
Hang on my lips and will not utterd be.

113

Sweete touch the engine that loves bow doth bend,
1020
The sence wherewith he feeles him deified,
The object whereto all his actions tend,
In all his blindenes his most pleasing guide,
   For thy sake will I write the Art of love,
Since thou doost blow his fire and feede his pride
   Since in thy sphere his health and life doth move,
For thee I hate who hate societie
And such as self-love makes his slaverie.

114

In these dog-dayes how this contagion smoothers
The purest bloods with vertues diet fined
1030
Nothing theyr owne, unlesse they be some others
Spite of themselves, are in themselves confined

And live so poore they are of all despised,
Theyr gifts, held down with scorne should be divined,
    And they like Mummers mask, unknowne, unprised:
A thousand mervailes mourne in some such brest
Would make a kinde and worthy Patrone blest.

115

To mee (deere Soveraigne) thou art Patronesse,
And I, with that thy graces have infused,
Will make all fat and foggy braines confesse,
Riches may from a poore verse be deduced: 1040
    And that Golds love shall leave them groveling heere,
When thy perfections shall to heaven be Mused,
    Deckt in bright verse, where Angels shall appeare
The praise of vertue, love, and beauty singing,
Honor to Noblesse, shame to Avarice bringing.

116

Heere *Ovid* interupted with the view
Of other Dames, who then the Garden painted,
Shrowded himselfe, and did as death eschew
All note by which his loves fame might be tainted:
    And as when mighty *Macedon* had wun   1050
The Monarchie of Earth, yet when hee fainted,
    Griev'd that no greater action could be doone,
And that there were no more worlds to subdue,
So loves defects, loves Conqueror did rue.

117

But as when expert Painters have displaid,
To quickest life a Monarchs royall hand
Holding a Scepter, there is yet bewraide
But halfe his fingers; when we understand
    The rest not to be seene; and never blame
The Painters Art, in nicest censures skand: 1060
    So in the compasse of this curious frame,
Ovid well knew there was much more intended,
With whose omition none must be offended.

Intentio, animi actio.
Explicit convivium.

De Guiana, Carmen Epicum

(1596)

What worke of honour and eternall name,
For all the worlde t'envie and us t'atchieve,
Filles me with furie, and gives armed handes
To my heartes peace, that els would gladlie turne
My limmes and every sence into my thoughtes
Rapt with the thirsted action of my mind?
O *Clio, Honors Muse*, sing in my voyce,
Tell the attempt, and prophecie th'exploit
Of his *Eliza*-consecrated sworde,
That in this peacefull charme of *Englands* sleepe,   10
Opens most tenderlie her aged throte,
Offring to poure fresh youth through all her vaines,
That flesh of brasse, and ribs of steele retaines.

Riches, and *Conquest*, and *Renowme* I sing,
Riches with honour, *Conquest* without bloud,
Enough to seat the Monarchie of earth,
Like to *Joves* Eagle, on *Elizas* hand.
Guiana, whose rich feet are mines of golde,
Whose forehead knockes against the roofe of Starres,
Stands on her tip-toes at faire *England* looking,   20
Kissing her hand, bowing her mightie breast,
And every signe of all submission making,
To be her sister, and the daughter both
Of our most sacred Maide: whose barrennesse
Is the true fruite of vertue, that may get,
Beare and bring foorth anew in all perfection,
What heretofore savage corruption held
In barbarous *Chaos*; and in this affaire
Become her father, mother, and her heire.

30 Then most admired Soveraigne, let your breath
 Goe foorth upon the waters, and create
 A golden worlde in this our yron age,
 And be the prosperous forewind to a Fleet,
 That seconding your last, may goe before it
 In all successe of profite and renowme:
 Doubt not but your election was divine,
 (As well by *Fate* as your high judgement ordred)
 To raise him with choise Bounties, that could adde
 Height to his height; and like a liberall vine,
40 Not onelie beare his vertuous fruit aloft,
 Free from the Presse of squint-eyd *Envies* feet,
 But decke his gracious Proppe with golden bunches,
 And shroude it with broad leaves of *Rule* oregrowne
 From all blacke tempestes of invasion.

 Those Conquests that like generall earthquakes shooke
 The solid world, and made it fall before them,
 Built all their brave attemptes on weaker groundes,
 And lesse persuasive likelihoods then this;
 Nor was there ever princelie Fount so long
50 Powr'd foorth a sea of Rule with so free course,
 And such ascending Majestie as you:
 Then be not like a rough and violent wind,
 That in the morning rends the Forrestes downe,
 Shoves up the seas to heaven, makes earth to tremble,
 And toombes his wastfull braverie in the Even:
 But as a river from a mountaine running,
 The further he extends, the greater growes,
 And by his thriftie race strengthens his streame,
 Even to joyne battale with th'imperious sea
60 Disdaining his repulse, and in despight
 Of his proud furie, mixeth with his maine,
 Taking on him his titles and commandes:
 So let thy soveraigne Empire be encreast,
 And with *Iberian Neptune* part the stake,
 Whose *Trident* he the triple worlde would make.
 You then that would be wise in Wisdomes spight,

Directing with discredite of direction,
And hunt for honour, hunting him to death,
With whome before you will inherite gold,
You will loose golde, for which you loose your soules;   70
You that choose nought for right, but certaintie,
And feare that value will get onlie blowes,
Placing your faith in *Incredulitie*.
Sit till you see a woonder, *Vertue* rich:
Till *Honour* having golde, rob golde of honour,
Till as men hate desert that getteth nought,
They loath all getting that deserves not ought,
And use you gold-made men, as dregges of men;
And till your poysoned soules, like Spiders lurking
In sluttish chinckes, in mystes of Cobwebs hide   80
Your foggie bodies, and your dunghill pride.

O *Incredulitie*, the wit of Fooles,
That slovenlie will spit on all thinges faire,
The *Cowards castle*, and the *Sluggards cradle*,
How easie t'is to be an Infidell?

But you *Patrician* Spirites that refine
Your flesh to fire, and issue like a flame
On brave endevours, knowing that in them
The tract of heaven in morne-like glorie opens,
That know you cannot be the Kinges of earth,   90
(Claiming the Rightes of your creation)
And let the Mynes of earth be Kinges of you;
That are so farre from doubting likelie driftes,
That in things hardest y'are most confident;
You that know death lives, where power lives unusde,
Joying to shine in waves that burie you,
And so make way for life even through your graves;
That will not be content like horse to hold
A thread-bare beaten waie to home affaires:
But where the sea in envie of your raigne,   100
Closeth her wombe, as fast as tis disclosde,
That she like *Avarice* might swallowe all,

And let none find right passage through her rage:
There your wise soules as swift as *Eurus* lead
Your Bodies through, to profit and renowne,
And skorne to let your bodies chooke your soules,
In the rude breath and prisoned life of beastes:
You that heerein renounce the course of earth,
And lift your eies for guidance to the starres,
That live not for your selves, but to possesse
Your honour'd countrey of a generall store;
In pitie of the spoyle rude self-love makes,
Of them whose lives and yours one aire doth feede,
One soile doeth nourish, and one strength combine;
You that are blest with sence of all things noble
In this attempt your compleat woorthes redouble.

But how is *Nature* at her heart corrupted,
(I meane even in her most ennobled birth?)
How in excesse of Sence is Sence bereft her?
That her most lightening-like effectes of lust
Wound through her flesh, her soule, her flesh unwounded;
And she must neede incitements to her good,
Even from that part she hurtes. O how most like
Art thou (heroike Author of this Act)
To this wrong'd soule of *Nature*: that sustainst
Paine, charge, and perill for thy countreys good,
And she much like a bodie numb'd with surfets,
Feeles not thy gentle applications
For the health, use, & honor of her powers.
Yet shall my verse through all her ease-lockt eares
Trumpet the Noblesse of thy high intent,
And if it cannot into act proceed,
The fault and bitter pennance of the fault
Make red some others eyes with penitence,
For thine are cleare; and what more nimble spirites
Apter to byte at such unhooked baytes,
Gaine by our losse; that must we needs confesse
Thy princelie valure would have purchast us.
Which shall be fame eternall to thy name,

Though thy contentment in thy grave desires,   140
Of our advancement, faile deserv'd effect,
O how I feare thy glorie which I love,
Least it should dearelie growe by our decrease.
Natures that stick in golden-graveld springs,
In mucke-pits cannot scape their swallowings.

But we shall foorth I know; Golde is our Fate,
Which all our actes doeth fashion and create.

Then in the *Thespiads* bright Propheticke Fount,
Me thinkes I see our Liege rise from her throne,
Her eares and thoughtes in steepe amaze erected,   150
At the most rare endevour of her power.
And now she blesseth with her woonted Graces
Th'industrious Knight, the soule of this exploit,
Dismissing him to convoy of his starres.
And now for love and honour of his woorth,
Our twise-borne Nobles bring him Bridegroome-like,
That is espousde for vertue to his love
With feastes and musicke, ravishing the aire,
To his *Argolian* Fleet, where round about
His bating Colours English valure swarmes   160
In haste, as if *Guianian Orenoque*
With his Fell waters fell upon our shore.
And now a wind as forward as their spirits,
Sets their glad feet on smooth *Guianas* breast,
Where (as if ech man were an *Orpheus*)
A world of Savadges fall tame before them,
Storing their theft-free treasuries with golde,
And there doth plentie crowne their wealthie fieldes,
There *Learning* eates no more his thriftlesse books,
Nor *Valure* Estridge-like his yron armes.   170
There *Beautie* is no strumpet for her wantes,
Nor *Gallique* humours putrifie her bloud:
But all our Youth take *Hymens* lightes in hand,
And fill each roofe with honor'd progenie.
There makes *Societie* Adamantine chaines,

And joins their harts with wealth, whom wealth disjoyn'd.
There healthfull Recreations strowe their meades,
And make their mansions daunce with neighborhood,
That here were drown'd in churlish *Avarice*.
180   And there do Pallaces and temples rise
Out of the earth, and kisse th'enamored skies,
Where new *Britania*, humblie kneeles to heaven,
The world to her, and both at her blest feete,
In whom the Circles of all Empire meet.

G C.

'To *M. Harriots*'
(from *Achilles Shield*, 1598)

TO MY ADMIRED AND SOULE-
LOVED FRIEND
Mayster of all essentiall and true knowledge,
M. Harriots.

To you whose depth of soule measures the height,
And all dimensions of all workes of weight,
Reason being ground, structure and ornament,
To all inventions, grave and permanent,
And your cleare eyes the Spheres where *Reason* moves;
This Artizan, this God of rationall loves
Blind *Homer*; in this shield, and in the rest
Of his seven bookes, which my hard hand hath drest,
In rough integuments I send for censure,
That my long time and labours deepe extensure   10
Spent to conduct him to our envious light,
In your allowance may receive some right
To their endevours; and take vertuous heart
From your applause, crownd with their owne desert.
Such crownes suffice the free and royall mind,
But these subjected hangbyes of our kind,
These children that will never stand alone,
But must be nourisht with corruption,
Which are our bodies; that are traitors borne,
To their owne crownes their soules: betraid to scorne,   20
To gaudie insolence and ignorance:
By their base fleshes frailties, that must daunce,
Prophane attendance at their states and birth,
That are meere servants to this servile earth,
These must have other crownes for meedes then merits,
Or sterve themselves, and quench their fierie spirits.

Thus as the soule upon the flesh depends,
Vertue must wait on wealth; we must make friends,
Of the unrighteous *Mammon*, and our sleights,
30 Must beare the formes of fooles or Parasites.
Rich mine of knowledge, ô that my strange muse
Without this bodies nourishment could use,
Her zealous faculties, onely t'aspire,
Instructive light from your whole Sphere of fire:
But woe is me, what zeale or power soever
My free soule hath, my body will be never
Able t'attend: never shal I enjoy,
Th'end of my happles birth: never employ
That smotherd fervour that in lothed embers,
40 Lyes swept from light, and no cleare howre remembers.
O had your perfect eye Organs to pierce
Into that Chaos whence this stiffled verse
By violence breakes: where Gloweworme like doth shine
In nights of sorrow, this hid soule of mine:
And how her genuine formes struggle for birth,
Under the clawes of this fowle Panther earth;
Then under all those formes you should discerne
My love to you, in my desire to learne.
Skill and the love of skill do ever kisse:
50 No band of love so stronge as knowledge is;
Which who is he that may not learne of you,
Whom learning doth with his lights throne endow?
What learned fields pay not their flowers t'adorne
Your odorous wreathe? compact, put on and worne,
By apt and Adamantine industrie,
Proposing still demonstrate veritie,
For your great object, farre from plodding gaine,
Or thirst of glorie; when absurd and vayne,
Most students in their whole instruction are,
60 But in traditions meere particular:
Leaning like rotten howses, on out beames,
And with true light fade in themselves like dreames.
True learning hath a body absolute,
That in apparant sence it selfe can suite,

Not hid in ayrie termes as if it were
Like spirits fantastike that put men in feare,
And are but bugs form'd in their fowle conceites,
Nor made for sale glas'd with sophistique sleights;
But wrought for all times proofe, strong to bide prease,
And shiver ignorants like *Hercules*,   70
On their owne dunghils; but our formall Clearkes
Blowne for profession, spend their soules in sparkes,
Fram'de of dismembred parts that make most show,
And like to broken limmes of knowledge goe.
When thy true wisedome by thy learning wonne
Shall honour learning while there shines a Sunne;
And thine owne name in merite; farre above,
Their Timpanies of state that armes of love,
Fortune or blood shall lift to dignitie;
Whome though you reverence, and your emperie   80
Of spirit and soule, be servitude they thinke
And but a beame of light broke through a chink
To all their watrish splendor: and much more
To the great Sunne, and all thinges they adore,
In staring ignorance: yet your selfe shall shine
Above all this in knowledge most divine,
And all shall homage to your true-worth owe,
You comprehending all, that all, not you.
    And when thy writings that now errors Night
Chokes earth with mistes, breake forth like easterne light,   90
Showing to every comprehensive eye,
High fectious brawles becalmde by unitie,
Nature made all transparent, and her hart
Gripte in thy hand, crushing digested Art
In flames unmeasurde, measurde out of it,
On whose head for her crowne thy soule shall sitte,
Crownd with Heavens inward brightnes shewing cleare
What true man is, and how like gnats appeare:
O fortune-glossed Pompists, and proud Misers,
That are of Arts such impudent despisers;   100
Then past anticipating doomes and skornes,
Which for selfe grace ech ignorant subornes,

Their glowing and amazed eyes shall see
How short of thy soules strength my weake words be,
And that I do not like our Poets preferre
For profit, praise, and keepe a squeaking stirre
With cald on muses to unchilde their braines
Of winde and vapor: lying still in paynes,
Of worthy issue; but as one profest
110 In nought but truthes deare love the soules true rest.
      Continue then your sweet judiciall kindnesse,
To your true friend, that though this lumpe of blindnes,
This skornefull, this despisde, inverted world,
Whose head is furie-like with Adders curlde,
And all her bulke a poysoned Porcupine,
Her stings and quilles darting at worthes devine,
Keepe under my estate with all contempt,
And make me live even from my selfe exempt,
Yet if you see some gleames of wrastling fire,
120 Breake from my spirits oppression, shewing desire
To become worthy to pertake your skill,
(Since vertues first and chiefe steppe is to will)
Comfort me with it and prove you affect me,
Though all the rotten spawne of earth reject me.
For though I now consume in poesie,
Yet *Homer* being my roote I can not die.
But lest to use all Poesie in the sight,
Of grave philosophie shew braines too light
To comprehend her depth of misterie,
130 I vow t'is onely strong necessitie
Governes my paines herein, which yet may use
A mans whole life without the least abuse.
And though to rime and give a verse smooth feet,
Uttering to vulgar pallattes passions sweet
Chaunce often in such weake capriccious spirits,
As in nought else have tollerable merits,
Yet where high *Poesies* native habite shines,
From whose reflections flow eternall lines:
Philosophy retirde to darkest caves
140 She can discover: and the proud worldes braves

Answere in any thing but impudence,
With circle of her general excellence.
For ample instance *Homer* more then serveth,
And what his grave and learned Muse deserveth,
Since it is made a Courtly question now,
His competent and partles judge be you;
If these vaine lines and his deserts arise
To the high serches of your serious eyes
As he is English: and I could not chuse
But to your Name this short inscription use,   150
As well assurde you would approve my payne
In my traduction; and besides this vayne
Excuse my thoughts as bent to others ames:
Might my will rule me, and when any flames
Of my prest soule break forth to their own show,
Thinke they must hold engraven regard of you.
Of you in whom the worth of all the Graces,
Due to the mindes giftes, might embrew the faces
Of such as skorne them, and with tiranous eye
Contemne the sweat of vertuous industrie.   160
But as ill lines new fild with incke undryed,
An empty Pen with their owne stuffe applied
Can blot them out: so shall their wealth-burst wombes
Be made with emptie Penne their honours tombes.

FINIS.

Euthymiae Raptus;
Or The Teares of Peace
(1609)

TO THE HIGH
BORN PRINCE OF MEN,
HENRIE,
THRICE-ROYALL
INHERITOUR TO THE
UNITED KINGDOMS
OF GREAT
Britanne.

The Teares of Peace.

Inductio.

Now that our Soveraign, the great King of Peace,
Hath (in her grace) outlabour'd *Hercules*;
And, past his Pillars, stretcht her victories;
Since (as he were sole Soule, t'all Royalties)
He moves all Kings, in this vast Universe,
To cast chaste Nettes, on th'impious lust of *Mars*;
See, All; and imitate his goodnesse still;
That (having cleard so well, warres outward ill)
Hee, God-like, still employes his firme desires,
To cast learn'd ynke upon those inwarde fires,   10
That kindle worse Warre, in the mindes of men,
Like to incense the outward Warre againe:
Selfe-love, inflaming so, mens sensuall bloud,
That all good, publique, drownes in private good;
And that, sinks under, his owne over-freight;
Mens Reasons, and their Learnings, shipwrackt quite;
And their Religion, that should still be One,
Takes shapes so many, that most know't in none.
Which, I admiring (since, in each man shinde
A light so cleere, that by it, all might finde   20
(Being well informd) their object perfect Peace,
Which keepes the narrow path to Happinesse)
In that discourse; I shund, (as is my use)
The jarring preace, and all their times abuse;
T'enjoy least trodden fieldes, and fre'est shades;
Wherein (of all the pleasure that invades
The life of man, and flies all vulgar feet,
Since silent meditation is most sweet)
I sat to it; discoursing what maine want
So ransackt man; that it did quite supplant   30
The inward Peace I spake of; letting in
(At his loose veines) sad warre, and all his sinne.

When, sodainely, a comfortable light
Brake through the shade; and, after it, the sight
Of a most grave, and goodly person shinde;
With eys turnd upwards, & was outward, blind;
But, inward; past, and future things, he sawe;
And was to both, and present times, their lawe.
His sacred bosome was so full of fire,
That t'was transparent; and made him expire
His breath in flames, that did instruct (me thought)
And (as my soule were then at full) they wrought.
At which, I casting downe my humble eyes,
Not daring to attempt their fervencies;
He thus bespake me; Deare minde, do not feare
My strange apparance; Now t'is time t'outweare
Thy bashfull disposition, and put on
As confident a countnance, as the Sunne.
For what hast thou to looke on, more divine,
And horrid, then man is; as hee should shine,
And as he doth? what, free'd from this worlds strife;
What he is entring; and what, ending life?
All which, thou onely studiest, and dost knowe;
And, more then which, is onely sought for showe.
Thou must not undervalue what thou hast,
In weighing it with that, which more is grac't;
The worth that weigheth inward, should not long
For outward prices. This should make thee strong
In thy close value; Nought so good can be
As that which lasts good, betwixt God, and thee.
Remember thine owne verse – Should Heaven turn Hell,
For deedes well done, I would do ever well.

    This heard, with joy enough, to breake the twine
Of life and soule, so apt to breake as mine;
I brake into a trance, and then remainde
(Like him) an onely soule; and so obtainde
Such bouldnesse, by the sense hee did controule;
That I set looke, to looke; and soule to soule.
I view'd him at his brightest; though, alas,
With all acknowledgement, of what hee was

40

50

60

70

Beyond what I found habited in me;
And thus I spake; O thou that (blinde) dost see
My hart, and soule; what may I reckon thee?
Whose heavenly look showes not; nor voice sounds man?
I am (sayd hee) that spirit *Elysian*,
That (in thy native ayre; and on the hill
Next *Hitchins* left hand) did thy bosome fill,
With such a flood of soule; that thou wert faine
(With acclamations of her Rapture then)
To vent it, to the Echoes of the vale;   80
When (meditating of me) a sweet gale
Brought me upon thee; and thou didst inherit
My true sense (for the time then) in my spirit;
And I, invisiblie, went prompting thee,
To those fayre Greenes, where thou didst english me.

   Scarce he had uttered this, when well I knewe
It was my Princes *Homer*; whose deare viewe
Renew'd my gratefull memorie of the grace
His Highnesse did me for him: which, in face,
Me thought the Spirit show'd, was his delight;   90
And added glory to his heavenly plight:
Who tould me, he brought stay to all my state;
That hee was Angell to me; Starre, and Fate;
Advancing Colours of good hope to me;
And tould me, my retired age should see
Heavens blessing, in a free, and harmelesse life,
Conduct me, through Earths peace-pretending strife,
To that true Peace, whose search I still intend,
And to the calme Shore of a loved ende.

   But now, as I cast round my ravisht eye,   100
To see, if this free Soule had companie;
Or that, alone, hee lovingly pursude
The hidden places of my Solitude;
He rent a Cloude downe, with his burning hand
That at his backe hung, twixt me, and a Land
Never inhabited; and sayd; Now, behould
What maine defect it is that doth enfould

The World, in ominous flatteries of a Peace
So full of worse then warre; whose sterne encrease
110   Devours her issue. With which words, I view'd
A Lady, like a Deitie indew'd;
(But weeping, like a woman) and made way
Out of one Thicket, that sawe never day,
Towards another; bearing underneath
Her arme, a Coffine, for some prize of death;
And after her (in funerall forme) did goe
The woddes foure-footed Beasts, by two, and two;
A Male, and Female, matcht, of everie kinde;
And after them; with like instinct enclinde,
120   The ayrie Nation felt her sorrowes stings;
Fell on the earth, kept rancke, and hung their wings.
Which sight I much did pittie, and admire;
And longd to knowe the dame that could inspire
Those Bestials, with such humane Forme, and ruthe;
And how I now should knowe, the hidden Truthe
(As *Homer* promist) of that maine defect
That makes men, all their inward Peace reject
For name of outward: Then hee took my hand;
Led to her; and would make my selfe demand,
130   (Though he could have resolv'd me) what shee was?
And from what cause, those strange effects had pass?
For whom, She bore that Coffine? and so mournd?
To all which; with all mildnesse, she returnd
Aunswere; that she was Peace; sent down from heaven
With charge, from the Almightie Deitie given,
T'attend on men; who now had banisht her
From their societies, and made her erre
In that wilde desert; onely Humane love
(Banisht in like sort) did a long time prove
140   That life with her; but now, alas, was dead,
And lay in that wood to bee buried;
For whom she bore that Coffine, and did mourne;
And that those Beasts were so much humane, borne,
That they, in nature, felt a love to Peace;
For which, they followd her, when men did cease.

This went so neere her heart, it left her tongue;
And (silent) she gave time, to note whence sprung
Mens want of Peace, which was from want of love:
And I observ'd now, what that peace did prove
That men made shift with, & did so much please.   150
For now, the Sunne declining to the Seas,
Made long misshapen shadowes; and true Peace
(Here walking in his Beames) cast such encrease
Of shaddowe from her; that I saw it glide
Through Citties, Courts, and Countryes; and descride,
How, in her shadowe only, men there liv'd,
While shee walkt here ith Sunne: and all that thriv'd
Hid in that shade their thrift; nought but her shade
Was Bullwarke gainst all warre that might invade
Their Countries, or their Consciences; since Love   160
(That should give Peace, her substance) now they drove
Into the Deserts; where hee sufferd Fate,
And whose sad Funerals Beasts must celebrate.
With whom, I freely wisht, I had beene nurst;
Because they follow Nature, at their wurst;
And at their best, did teach her. As wee went
I felt a scruple, which I durst not vent,
No not to Peace her selfe, whom it concernd,
For feare to wrong her; So well I have learnd,
To shun injustice, even to doves, or flies;   170
But, to the Divell, or the Destinies,
Where I am just, and knowe I honour Truth,
Ile speake my thoughts, in scorne of what ensu'th.
Yet (not resolv'd in th'other) there did shine
A Beame of *Homers* fre'er soule, in mine,
That made me see, I might propose my doubt;
Which was; If this were true Peace I found out,
That felt such passion? I prov'd her sad part;
And prayd her call, her voice out of her hart
(There, kept a wrongfull prisoner to her woe)   180
To answere, why shee was afflicted so.
Or how, in her, such contraries could fall;
That taught all joy, and was the life of all?

Shee aunswered; Homer tould me that there are
Passions, in which corruption hath no share;
There is a joy of soule; and why not then
A griefe of soule, that is no skathe to men?
For both are Passions, though not such as raigne
In blood, and humor, that engender paine.
190 Free sufferance for the truth, makes sorrow sing,
And mourning farre more sweet, then banqueting.
Good, that deserveth joy (receiving ill)
Doth merit justly, as much sorrow still:
And is it a corruption to do right?
Griefe, that dischargeth Conscience, is delight:
One sets the other off. To stand at gaze
In one position, is a stupide maze,
Fit for a Statue. This resolv'd me well,
That Griefe, in Peace, and Peace in Griefe might dwell.

200 And now fell all things from their naturall Birth:
Passion in Heaven; Stupiditie, in Earth,
Inverted all; the Muses, Vertues, Graces,
Now sufferd rude, and miserable chaces
From mens societies, to that desert heath;
And after them, Religion (chac't by death)
Came weeping, bleeding to the Funerall:
Sought her deare Mother Peace; and downe did fall,
Before her, fainting, on her horned knees;
Turnd horne, with praying for the miseries
210 She left the world in; desperate in their sinne;
Marble, her knees pearc't; but heaven could not winne
To stay the weightie ruine of his Glorie
In her sad Exile; all the memorie
Of heaven, and heavenly things, rac't of all hands;
Heaven moves so farre off, that men say it stands;
And Earth is turnd the true, and moving Heaven;
And so tis left; and so is all Truth driven
From her false bosome; all is left alone,
Till all bee orderd with confusion.

Thus the poore broode of Peace; driven, & distrest, 220
Lay brooded all beneath their mothers breast;

Who fell upon them weeping, as they fell:
All were so pinde, that she containde them well.
And in this Chaos, the digestion
And beautie of the world, lay thrust and throwne.
In this dejection, Peace pourd out her Teares,
Worded (with some pause) in my wounded Eares.

Invocatio.

O ye three-times-thrice sacred Quiristers,
Of Gods great Temple; the small Universe
Of ruinous man: (thus prostrate as ye lye   230
Brooded, and Loded with Calamitie,
Contempt, and shame, in your true mother, Peace)
As you make sad my soule, with your misease:
So make her able fitly to disperse
Your sadnesse, and her owne, in sadder verse.
Now (olde, and freely banisht with your selves
From mens societies; as from rockes, and shelves)
Helpe me to sing, and die, on our Thames shore;
And let her lend me, her waves to deplore
(In yours, and your most holy Sisters falls)   240
Heavens fall, and humane Loves, last funeralls.
    And thou, great Prince of men; let thy sweete graces
Shine on these teares; and drie, at length, the faces
Of Peace, and all her heaven-allyed brood;
From whose Doves eyes, is shed the precious blood
Of Heavens deare Lamb, that freshly bleeds in them.
Make these no toyes then; gird the Diadem
Of thrice great Britaine, with their Palm and Bayes:
And with thy Eagles feathers, daigne to raise
The heavie body of my humble Muse;   250
That thy great *Homers* spirit in her may use
Her topless flight, and beare thy Fame above
The reach of Mortalls, and their earthly love;
To that high honour, his *Achilles* wonne,
And make thy glory farre out-shine the Sunne.

While this small time gave Peace (in her kinde Throes)
Vent for the violence of her sodaine woes;
She turnd on her right side, and (leaning on
Her tragique daughters bosome) lookt upon
260 My heavy lookes, drownd in imploring teares
For her, and that so wrongd deare Race of hers.
At which, even Peace, exprest a kinde of Spleene;
And, as a carefull Mother, I have seene
Chide her lov'd Childe, snatcht with som feare from danger:
So Peace chid me; and first shed teares of anger.

The Teares of Peace.

Peace. Thou wretched man, whome I discover, borne
To want, and sorrowe, and the Vulgars scorne:
Why haunt'st thou freely, these unhaunted places,
Emptie of pleasures? empty of all Graces,
270 Fashions, and Riches; by the best pursude
With broken Sleepe, Toyle, Love, Zeale, Servitude;
With feare and trembling, with whole lives, and Soules?
While thou break'st sleepes, digst under Earth, like moules,
To live, to seeke me out, whome all men fly:
And think'st to finde, light in obscuritie,
Eternitie, in this deepe vale of death:
Look'st ever upwards, and liv'st still beneath;
Fill'st all thy actions, with strife, what to thinke,
Thy Braine with Ayre, and skatterst it in inke:
280 Of which thou mak'st weeds for thy soule to weare,
As out of fashion, as the bodies are.
Interlo I grant their strangenesse, and their too ill grace,
And too much wretchednesse, to beare the face
Or any likenesse of my soule in them:
Whose Instruments, I rue with many a Streame
Of secret Teares for their extream defects,
In uttering her true forms: but their respects
Need not be less'ned, for their being strange,
Or not so vulgar, as the rest that range

With headlong Raptures, through the multitude: 290
Of whom they get grace, for their being rude.
Nought is so shund by Virtue, throwne from Truth,
As that which drawes the vulgar Dames, and Youth.
Truth must confesse it: for where lives there one,   *Pea*
That *Truth* or *Vertue*, for themselves alone,
Or seekes, or not contemns? All, all pursue
Wealth, Glory, Greatnesse, Pleasure, Fashions new.
Who studies, studies these: who studies not
And sees that studie, layes the vulgar Plot;
That all the Learning he gets living by,   300
Men but for forme, or humour dignifie
(As himselfe studies, but for forme, and showe,
And never makes his speciall end, to knowe)
And that an idle, ayrie man of Newes,
A standing Face; a propertie to use
In all things vile, makes Booke-wormes, creepe to him:
How scorns he bookes, and booke-worms! O how dim
Burnes a true Soules light, in his Bastard eyes!
And, as a Forrest over-grow'n breedes Flyes,
Todes, Adders, Savadges, that all men shunne;   310
When, on the South-side, in a fresh May Sunne,
In varied Heards, the Beasts lie out, and sleepe,
The busie Gnatts, in swarms a buzzing keepe,
And guild their empty bodies (lift aloft)
In beames, that though they see all, difference nought:
So, in mens meerly outward, and false Peace,
Insteade of polisht men, and true encrease,
She brings forth men, with vices over-growne:
Women, so light, and like, fewe knowe their owne:
For milde and humane tongues, tongues forkt that sting: 320
And all these (while they may) take Sunne, and spring,

*   *   *   *   *

To help them sleep, and florish: on whose beames,
And branches, up they clime, in such extreams
Of proude confusion, from just Lawes so farre,
That in their Peace, the long Robe sweeps like warre.

Int.	That Robe serves great men: why are great so rude?
Peac.	Since great, and meane, are all but multitude.
	For regular Learning, that should difference set
	Twixt all mens worths, and make the meane, or great,
330	As that is meane or great (or chiefe stroke strike)
	Serves the Plebeian and the Lord alike.
	Their objects, showe their learnings are all one;
	Their lives, their objects; Learning lov'd by none.
Int.	You meane, for most part: nor would it displease
	That most part, if they heard; since they professe,
	Contempt of learning: Nor esteeme it fit,
	Noblesse should study, see, or count'nance it.
Pea.	Can men in blood be Noble, not in soule?
	Reason abhorres it; since what doth controule
340	The rudenesse of the blood, and makes it Noble
	(Or hath chiefe meanes, high birth-right to redouble,
	In making manners soft, and man-like milde,
	Not suffering humanes to runne proude, or wilde)
	Is Soule, and learning; (or in love, or act)
	In blood where both faile then, lyes Nobless wrackt.
Interlo.	It cannot be denyde: but could you prove,
	As well, that th'act of learning, or the love,
	(Love being the act in will) should difference set,
	Twixt all mens worths, and make the meane or great,
350	As learning is, or great, or meane in them;
	Then cleare, her Right, stood to mans Diadem.
Pea.	To prove that Learning (the soules actuall frame;
	Without which, tis a blanke; a smoke-hid flame)
	Should sit great Arbitresse, of all things donne,
	And in your soules, (like Gnomons in the Sunne)
	Give Rules to all the circles of your lives;
	I prove it, by the Regiment God gives
	To man, of all things; to the soule, of man;
	To Learning, of the Soule. If then it can
360	Rule, live; of all things best, is it not best?
	O who, what god makes greatest, dares make least?
	But, to use their tearms; Life is Roote and Crest

To all mans Cote of Nobless; his soule is
Field to that Cote; and learning differences
All his degrees in honour, being the Cote.
And as a Statuarie, having got   *Simi.*
An Alabaster, bigge enough to cut
A humane image in it: till he hath put
His tooles, and art to it; hew'n, formd, left none
Of the redundant matter in the Stone;   370
It beares the image of a man, no more,
Then of a Woolf, a Cammell, or a Boare:
So when the Soule is to the body given;
(Being substance of Gods Image, sent from heaven)
It is not his true Image, till it take
Into the Substance, those fit forms that make
His perfect Image; which are then imprest
By Learning and impulsion; that invest
Man with Gods forme in living Holinesse,
By cutting from his Body the excesse   380
Of Humors, perturbations and Affects;
Which Nature (without Art) no more ejects,
Then without tooles, a naked Artizan
Can, in rude stone, cut th' Image of a man.
How then do Ignorants? who, oft, we trie,   *Int.*
Rule perturbations, live more humanely
Then men held learnd?
Who are not learn'd indeed;   *Pea.*
More then a house fram'd loose, (that still doth neede
The haling up, and joyning) is a house: 390
Nor can you call, men meere Religious,
(That have good wills, to knowledge) Ignorant;
For, virtuous knowledge hath two waies to plant;
By Powre infus'd, and Acquisition;
The first of which, those good men, graft upon;
For good life is th'effect, of learnings Act;
Which th'action of the minde, did first compact
By infusde love to Learning gainst all ill,
Conquests first step, is to all good, the will.

Int.   If *Learning* then, in love or act must be,
          Meane to good life, and true humanitie;
          Where are our Scarre-crowes now, or men of ragges,
          Of Titles meerely, Places, Fortunes, Bragges,
          That want and scorne both? Those inverted men?
          Those dungeons; whose soules no more containe
          The actuall light of Reason, then darke beasts?
          Those Cloudes, driven still, twixt Gods beame and their brests?
          Those Giants, throwing goulden hils gainst heaven?
          To no one spice of true humanitie given?

Peace.   Of men, there are three sorts, that most foes be
          To Learning and her love; themselves and me:
          Active, Passive, and *Intellective* men:
          Whose selfe-loves; Learning, and her love disdaine.
          Your Active men, consume their whole lifes fire,
          In thirst of State-height, higher still and higher,
          (Like seeled Pigeons) mounting, to make sport,
          To lower lookers on; in seeing how short
          They come of that they seeke, and with what trouble;
          Lamely, and farre from Nature, they redouble

420   Their paines in flying, more then humbler witts,
          To reach death, more direct. For Death that sits,
          Upon the fist of Fate, past highest Ayre,
          (Since she commands all lives, within that Sphere)
          The higher men advance; the neerer findes
          Her seeled Quarries; when, in bitterest windes,
          Lightnings, and thunders, and in sharpest hayles
          Fate casts her off at States; when lower Sayles
          Slide calmely to their ends. Your *Passive* men
          (So call'd of onely passing time in vaine)

430   Passe it, in no good exercise; but are
          In meates, and cuppes laborious; and take care
          To lose without all care their Soule-spent Time;
          And since they have no meanes, nor Spirits to clime,
          Like Fowles of Prey, in any high affaire;
          See how like Kites they bangle in the Ayre,
          To stoope at scraps, and garbidge; in respect,
          Of that which men of true peace should select;

And how they trot out, in their lives, the Ring;
With idlely iterating oft one thing,
A new-fought Combat, an affaire at Sea; 440
A Marriage, or a Progresse, or a Plea.
No Newes, but fits them, as if made for them,
Though it be forg'd, but of a womans dreame;
And stuffe with, such stolne ends, their manlesse breasts,
(Sticks, rags, and mud) they seem meer Puttock nests:
Curious in all mens actions, but their owne;
All men, and all things censure, though know none.
Your Intellective men, they study hard
Not to get knowledge, but for meere rewarde.
And therefore that true knowledge that should be 450
Their studies end, and is in Nature free,
Will not be made their Broker; having powre
(With her sole selfe) to bring both Bride, and dowre.
They have some shadowes of her (as of me,
Adulterate outward peace) but never see
Her true and heavenly face. Yet those shades serve
(Like errant Knights, that by enchantments swerve,
From their true Ladyes being; and embrace
An ougly Witch, with her phantastique face)
To make them thinke, *Truths* substance in their arms: 460
Which that they have not, but her shadowes charmes,
See if my proofes, be like their Arguments
That leave *Opinion* still, her free dissents.
They have not me with them; that all men knowe
The highest fruite that doth of knowledge grow;
The Bound of all true formes, and onely Act;
If they be true, they rest; nor can be rackt
Out of their posture, by *Times* utmost strength;
But last the more of force, the more of length;
For they become one substance with the Soule; 470
Which Time with all his adjuncts shall controule.
But since, men wilfull may beleeve perchance
(In part of Errors two-folde Ignorance,
Ill disposition) their skills looke as hie
And rest in that divine Securitie;

See if their lives make proofe of such a Peace,
For Learnings Truth makes all lifes vain war cease;
It making peace with God, and joines to God;
Whose information drives her Period
480   Through all the Bodies passive Instruments;
And by reflection gives them Soule-contents,
Besides, from perfect Learning you can never
Wisedome (with her faire Reigne of Passions) sever;
For Wisedome is nought else, then Learning fin'd,
And with the understanding Powre combin'd;
That is, a habite of both habits standing;
The Bloods vaine humours, ever countermaunding.
But, if these showe, more humour then th'unlearn'd;
If in them more vaine passion be discern'd;
490   More mad Ambition, more lust; more deceipt;
More showe of golde, then gold; then drosse, less weight;
If Flattery, Avarice have their soules so given,
Headlong, and with such divelish furies driven;
That fooles may laugh at their imprudencie,
And Villanes blush at their dishonestie;
Where is true Learning, proov'd to separate these
And seate all forms in her Soules height, in peace?
Raging *Euripus*, that (in all their Pride)
Drives Shippes gainst roughest windes, with his fierce Tide,
500   And ebbes and flowes, seven times in everie daie;
Toyles not on Earth with more irregulare swaye,
Nor is more turbulent, and mad then they.
And shine; like gould-worms, whom you hardly finde,
By their owne, light; not seene; but heard like winde.
But this is Learning; To have skill to throwe
Reignes on your bodies powres, that nothing knowe;
And fill the soules powers, so with act, and art,
That she can curbe the bodies angrie part;
All perturbations; all affects that stray
510   From their one object; which is to obay
Her Soveraigne Empire; as her selfe should force
Their functions onely, to serve her discourse;

And, that; to beat the streight path of one ende
Which is, to make her substance still contend,
To be Gods Image; in informing it,
With knowledge; holy thoughts, and all formes fit
For that eternitie, ye seeke in way
Of his sole imitation; and to sway,
Your lifes love so, that hee may still be Center
To all your pleasures; and you, (here) may enter   520
The next lifes peace; in governing so well
Your sensuall parts, that you, as free may dwell
Of vulgare Raptures, here; as when calme death
Dissolves that learned Empire, with your Breath.
To teach, and live thus, is the onely use,
And end of Learning, Skill that doth produce
But tearmes, and tongues, and Parrating of Arte,
Without that powre to rule the errant part;
Is that which some call, learned ignorance;
A serious trifle; error in a trance.   530
And let a Scholler, all earths volumes carrie,
He will be but a walking dictionarie:
A meere articulate Clocke, that doth but speake
By others arts; when wheeles weare, or springs breake,
Or any fault is in him; hee can mend
No more then clockes; but at set howres must spend
His mouth, as clocks do; If too fast, speech goe
Hee cannot stay it; nor haste if too slowe.
So that, as Travaylers, seeke their peace through storms,
In passing many Seas, for many forms,   540
Of forreigne government; indure the paine
Of many faces seeing; and the gaine
That Strangers make, of their strange-loving humors;
Learn tongues; keep note books, all to feed the tumors
Of vaine discourse at home; or serve the course
Of State employment, never having force
T'employ themselves; but idle complements
Must pay their paines, costs, slaveries, all their Rents;
And, though they many men knowe, get few friends:
So covetous Readers; setting many endes   550

To their much skill to talke; studiers of Phrase;
Shifters in Art; to flutter in the Blaze
Of ignorant count'nance; to obtaine degrees
And lye in Learnings bottome, like the Lees,
To be accounted deepe, by shallow men;
And carve all Language, in one glorious Pen;
May have much fame for learning: but th'effect
Proper to perfect Learning; to direct
Reason in such an Art, as that it can

560   Turne blood to soule, and make both, one calme man;
So making peace with God; doth differ farre
From Clearkes that goe with God & man to warre.

Int.   But may this Peace, and mans true Empire then,
By learning be obtainde? and taught to men?

Pea.   Let all men judge; who is it can denie,
That the rich crowne of ould Humanitie,
Is still your birth-right? and was ne're let downe
From heaven, for rule of Beasts lives, but your owne?
You learne the depth of Arts; and (curious) dare

570   By them (in Natures counterfaits) compare
Almost with God; to make perpetually
Motion like heavens; to hang sad Rivers by
The ayre, in ayre; and earth, twixt earth and heaven
By his owne paise. And are these vertues given
To powrefull Art, and Vertue's selfe denied?
This proves the other, vaine, and falsified,
Wealth, Honour, and the Rule of Realmes doth fall
In lesse then Reasons compasse; yet, what all
Those things are given for (which is living well)

580   Wants discipline, and reason to compell.
O foolish men! how many waies ye vex
Your lives with pleasing them? and still perplex
Your liberties, with licence? every way
Casting your eyes, and faculties astray
From their sole object? If some few bring forth
(In Nature, freely) something of some worth;
Much rude and worthlesse humour runs betwixt;
(Like fruit in deserts) with vile matter mixt.

Nor (since they flatter flesh so) they are bould
(As a most noble spectacle) to behould   590
Their owne lives; and (like sacred light) to beare
There Reason inward: for the Soule (in feare
Of everie sort of vice, shee there containes)
Flies out; and wanders about other mens;
Feeding, and fatting, her infirmities.
    And as in auntient Citties, t'was the guise
To have some Ports of sad, and haplesse vent,
Through which, all executed men they sent;
All filth; all offall, cast from what purg'd sinne;
Nought, chaste, or sacred, there going out, or in: 600
So, through mens refuse eares, will nothing pearse
Thats good, or elegant; but the sword; the herse;
And all that doth abhorre, from mans pure use,
Is each mans onely Siren; only Muse.
And thus, for one God; one fit good; they prise
These idle, foolish, vile varieties.
Wretched estate of men, by fortune blest;   *Int.*
That being ever idle, never rest;
That have goods, ere they earne them; and for that,
Want art to use them. To bee wonderd at   610
Is Justice; for Proportion, Ornament;
None of the Graces, is so excellent.
Vile things, adorne her: me thought, once I sawe
How, by the Seas shore, she sat giving lawe
Even to the streames, and fish (most loose, and wilde)
And was (to my thoughts) wondrous sweet and milde;
Yet fire flew from her that dissolved Rocks;
Her lookes, to Pearle turnd pebble; and her locks,
The rough, and sandy bankes, to burnisht gould;
Her white left hand, did goulden bridles holde;   620
And, with her right, she wealthy gifts did give;
Which with their left hands, men did still receive;
Upon a world in her chaste lappe, did lye,
A little Ivory Book, that show'd mine eye,
But one Page onely; that one verse containde,
Where all Arts, were contracted, and explainde;

All policies of Princes, all their forces;
Rules for their feares, cares, dangers, pleasures, purses,
All the fayre progresse of their happinesse here,
630   Justice converted, and composed there.
All which I thought on, when I had exprest
Why great men, of the great states they possest,
Enjoyd so little; and I now must note
The large straine of a verse, I long since wrote.
Which (me thought) much joy, to men poore presented;
God hath made none (that all might be) contented.

Peace.   It might (for the capacitie it beares)
Be that concealed and expressive verse,
That Justice, in her Ivorie Manuell writ;
640   Since all Lines to mans Peace, are drawne in it.
For great men; though such ample stuffe they have
To shape contentment; yet, since (like a wave)
It flittes, and takes all formes, retayning none;
(Not fitted to their patterne, which is one)
They may content themselves; God hath not given,
To men meere earthly, the true Joyes of heaven;
And so their wilde ambitions either stay;
Or turne their headstrong course, the better way.
For poore men; their cares may be richly easde;
650   Since rich (with all they have) live as displeasde.

Int.   You teach me to be plaine. But whats the cause,
That great, and rich, whose stares winne such applause;
With such enforc't, and vile varieties,
Spend time; nor give their lives glad sacrifice;
But when they eate, and drinke, with tales, jests, sounds;
As if (like frantique men, that feele no wounds)
They would expire in laughters? and so erre
From their right way; that like a Travayler,
(Weariest when neerest to his journeys ende)
660   Time best spent ever, with most paine they spend?

Pea.   The cause, is want of Learning; which (being right)
Makes idlenesse a paine; and paine delight.
It makes men knowe, that they (of all things borne
Beneath the silver Moone, and goulden Morne)

Being onely formes of God; should onely fix
One forme of life to those formes; and not mix
With Beastes in formes of their lives. It doth teach,
To give the soule her Empire; and so reach
To rule of all the bodies mutinous Realme;
In which (once seated) She then takes the Helme,   670
And governes freely; stering to one Port.
Then, (like a man in health) the whole consort
Of his tun'd body, sings; which otherwise,
Is like one full of weiward maladies,
Still out of tune; and (like to Spirits raisde
Without a Circle) never is appaisde.
And then, they have no strength, but weakens them;
No greatnes, but doth crush them into streame;
No libertie, but turnes into their snare;
Their learnings then, do light them but to erre;   680
Their ornaments, are burthens; their delights,
Are mercinarie, servile Parasites,
Betraying, laughing; Feends, that raisde in feares,
At parting, shake their Roofes about their eares;
Th'imprison'd thirst, the fortunes of the Free;
The Free, of Rich; Rich, of Nobilitie;
Nobilitie, of Kings; and Kings, Gods thrones;
Even to their lightning flames; and thunder-stones.
O liberall Learning, that well usde, gives use
To all things good; how bad is thy abuse!   690
When, onely thy divine reflection can
(That lights but to thy love) make good a man;
How can the regular Body of thy light,
Informe, and decke him? the Ills infinite,
That (like beheaded *Hydra's* in that Fen
Of bloud, and flesh, in lewd illiterate men)
Aunswere their amputations, with supplyes
That twist their heads, and ever double rise;
Herculean Learning conquers; And O see
How many, and of what fowle formes they be?   700
Unquiet, wicked thoughts; unnumbred passions;
Poorenesse of Counsailes; howrely fluctuations;

(In entercourse) of woes, and false delights;
Impotent wils to goodnesse; Appetites
That never will bee bridl'd; satisfied;
Nor knowe how, or with what to be supplyed;
Feares, and distractions, mixt with greedinesse;
Stupidities of those things ye possesse;
Furies for what ye lose; wrongs done for nonce;
For present, past, and future things, at once   710
Cares vast, and endlesse; miseries, swolne with pride;
Vertues despisde, and vices glorified.
All these, true Learning calmes, and can subdue:
But who turnes learning this way? All pursue
Warre with each other, that exasperates these;
For things without; whose ends are inward peace;
And yet those inward Rebels they maintaine.
And as your curious sort of Passive men,
Thrust their heads through the Roofs of Rich & Poore;
Through all their lives, and fortunes, and explore   720
Forraigne, and home-affayres; their Princes Courts,
Their Counsaile, and Bedchambers for reports;
And (like free-booters) wander out, to win
Matter to feede their mutinous Route within;
(Which are the greedier still) and overshoote
Their true-sought inward Peace, for outward boote;
So Learned men, in controversies spend
(Of tongues, and tearmes, readings, and labours pend)
Their whole lives studies; Glorie, Riches, Place,
In full crie, with the vulgare giving Chace;   730
And never, with their learnings true use strive
To bridle strifes within them; and to live
Like men of Peace, whome Art of Peace begat:
But, as their deedes, are most adulterate,
And showe them false Sons, to their Peacefull Mother,
In those warres; so their Arts, are prov'd no other.
And let the best of them, a search impose
Upon his Art: for all the things shee knowes
(All being referd, to all, to her unknowne)
They will obtaine the same proportion   740

That doth a little brooke that never ran
Through Summers Sunne; compar'd with th'Ocean.
But, could he Oracles speake; and wright to charme
A wilde of Savadges; take Natures Arme,
And plucke into his search, the Circuit
Of Earth, and Heaven; the Seas space, and the spirit
Of everie Starre: the Powers of Herbs, and Stones;
Yet touch not, at his perturbations;
Nor give them Rule, and temper to obay
Imperiall Reason; in whose Soveraigne sway,   750
Learning is wholly us'd, and dignified;
To what end serves he? is his learning tryed
That comforting, and that creating Fire
That fashions men? or that which doth inspire
Citties with civile conflagrations,
Countries, and kingdomes? That Art that attones
All opposition to good life, is all;
Live well ye Learned; and all men ye enthrall.
Alas they are discourag'd in their courses;   *Interlo.*
And (like surpris'd Forts) beaten from their forces.   ·   760
Bodies, on Rights of Soules did never growe
With ruder Rage, then barbarous Torrents flowe
Over their sacred Pastures; bringing in
Weedes, and all rapine; Temples now begin
To suffer second deluge; Sinne-drownde Beasts,
Making their Altars crack; and the filde Nests
Of vulturous Fowles, filling their holy places;
For wonted Ornaments, and Religious graces.
The chiefe cause is, since they themselves betraie;   *Pea.*
Take their Foes baites, for some particular swaie   770
T'invert their universall; and this still,
Is cause of all ills else; their living ill.
Alas! that men should strive for others swaie;   *Int.*
But first to rule themselves: And that being waie
To all mens Bliss; why is it trod by none?
And why are rules so dully lookt upon
That teach that lively Rule?
O horrid thing!   *Pea.*

Tis Custome powres into your common spring
780 Such poyson of Example, in things vaine;
That Reason nor Religion can constraine
Mens sights of serious things; and th'onely cause
That neither humane nor celestiall lawes
Drawe man more compasse; is his owne slacke bent
T'intend no more his proper Regiment,
Where; if your Active men (or men of action)
Their Policie, Avarice, Ambition, Faction,
Would turne to making strong, their rule of Passion,
To search, and settle them, in Approbation
790 Of what they are, and shalbe (which may be
By Reason, in despight of Policie)
And in one true course, couch their whole Affaires
To one true blisse, worth all the spawne of theirs;
If halfe the idle speech, men Passive spend,
At sensuall meetings, when they recommend
Their sanguine Soules, in laughters, to their Peace,
Were spent in Counsailes how they might decrease
That frantique humour of ridiculous blood
(Which addes, they vainely thinke, to their lives flood)
800 And so converted, in true humane mirth,
To speech, what they shall be (dissolv'd from Earth)
In bridling it in flesh; with all the scope
Of their owne knowledge here; and future hope:
If (last of all) your Intellective men
Would mixe the streames of every jarring Penne
In one calme Current; that like land flouds, now
Make all Zeales bounded Rivers over-flowe;
Firme Truth, with question, every howre pursue;
And yet will have no question, all is true:
810 Search in that troubled Ocean, for a Ford
That by it selfe runnes; and must beare accord
In each mans self; by banishing falshood there,
Wrath, lust, pride, earthy thoughts; before elsewhere.
(For, as in one man, is the world inclosde,
So to forme one, it should be all disposde:)

If all these would concurre to this one end,
It would aske all their powres; and all would spend
Life with that reall sweetnesse, which they dreame
Comes in with objects that are meere extreame:
And make them outward pleasures still apply   820
Which never can come in, but by that key;
Others advancements, others Fames desiring;
Thirsting, exploring, praysing, and admiring;
Like lewd adulterers, that their owne wives scorne,
And other mens, with all their wealth, adorne.

Why, in all outraying, varied joyes, and courses,
That in these errant times, tire all mens forces,
Is this so common wonder of our dayes?
That in poore foretimes, such a fewe could raise
So many wealthy Temples, and these none?   830
All were devout then; all devotions one;
And to one end converted; and when men
Give up themselves to God; all theirs goes then:
A few well-given, are worth a world of ill;
And worlds of Powre, not worth one poore good-will.

And what's the cause, that (being but one *Truth*) spreds
About the world so manie thousand heads,
Of false Opinions, all self-lov'd as true?
Onely affection, to things more then due:
One Error kist, begetteth infinite.   840
How can men finde truth, in waies opposite?
And with what force, they must take opposite wayes
When all have opposite objects? *Truth* displaies
One coloured ensigne; and the world pursues
Ten thousand colours: see (to judge, who use
Truth in their Arts;) what light their lives doe give:
For wherefore doe they study, but to live?
See I Eternities streight milke-white waie,
And One, in this lifes crooked vanities straie;
And, shall I thinke he knowes Truth, following Error?   850
This; onely this; is the infallible myrror,
To showe, why Ignorants, with learn'd men vaunt,
And why your learn'd men, are so ignorant,

Why every Youth, in one howre will be old
In every knowledge; and why Age doth mould.
Then; As in Rules of true Philosophie
There must be ever due Analogie
Betwixt the Powre that knowes, and that is knowne,
So surely joynde that they are ever one;
860   The understanding part transcending still
To that it understands, that, to his skill;
All, offering to the Soule, the Soule to God;
(By which do all things make their Period
In his high Powre; and make him, All in All;
So, to ascend, the high-heaven-reaching Skale
Of mans true Peace; and make his Art entire,
By calming all his Errors in desire;
(Which must preceede, that higher happinesse)
Proportion still, must traverse her accesse
870   Betwixt his powre, and will; his Sense and Soule;
And evermore th'exorbitance controule
Of all forms, passing through the bodies Powre,
Till in the soule they rest, as in their Towre.

Int.   But; as Earths grosse and elementall fire,
Cannot maintaine it selfe; but doth require
Fresh matter still, to give it heate, and light;
And, when it is enflam'd; mounts not upright;
But struggles in his lame impure ascent;
Now this waie works, and then is that waie bent,
880   Not able, straight, t'aspire to his true Sphere
Where burns the fire, eternall, and sincere;
So, best soules here; with heartiest zeales enflam'd
In their high flight for heaven; earth-broos'd and lam'd)
Make many faint approches; and are faine,
With much unworthy matter, to sustaine
Their holiest fire; and with sick feathers, driven,
And broken Pinions, flutter towards heaven.

Peace.   The cause is, that you never will bestowe
Your best, t'enclose your lives, twixt God, and you;
890   To count the worlds Love, Fame, Joy, Honour, nothing;
But life, (with all your love to it) betrothing

To his love; his recomfort; his rewarde;
Since no good thought calls to him, but is heard.
Nor neede you, thinke this strange; since he is there,
Present: within you; ever, everywhere
Where good thoughts are; for Good hath no estate
Without him; nor himselfe is, without That:
If then, this Commerce stand twixt you entire;
Trie, if he either, grant not each desire;
Or so conforme it, to his will, in staie;   900
That you shall finde him, there, in the delaie,
As well as th'instant grant; And so proove, right
How easie, his deare yoke is; and how light
His equall burthen: whether this Commerce
Twixt God and man, be so hard, so perverse
(In composition); as, the Raritie,
Or no-where-patterne of it, doth implie?
Or if, in worthy contemplation
It do not tempt, beyond comparison
Of all things worldly? Sensualitie,   910
Nothing so easie; all Earths Companie,
(Like Rubarb, or the drugges of *Thessalie*)
Compar'd, in taste with that sweet? O trie then
If, that contradiction (by the God of men)
Of all the lawe, and Prophets, layd upon
The tempting Lawyer; were a lode, that None
Had powre to stand beneath? If Gods deare love,
Thy Conscience do not, at first sight approve
Deare, above all things? And, so passe this shelfe;
To love (withall) thy Neighbour as thy selfe?   920
Not, love as much; but as thy selfe; in this,
To let it be as free, as thine owne is;
Without respect of profit, or reward,
Deceipt, or flatterie; politique regard,
Or anie thing, but naked Charitie.
I call, even God, himselfe; to testifie   *Interlo.*
(For men, I know but fewe) that farre above
All to be here desir'd; I rate his love.

Thanks to his still-kist-hand, that hath so fram'd
930   My poore, and abject life; and so, inflam'd
My soule with his sweete, all-want-seasoning love;
In studying to supply, though not remove,
My desert fortunes, and unworthinesse,
With some wisht grace from him; that might expresse
His presence with me; and so dignifie,
My life, to creepe on earth; behold the skie,
And give it meanes enough, for this lowe plight;
Though, hitherto, with no one houres delight,
Heartie or worthie; but in him alone;
940   Who, like a carefull guide, hath hal'd me on;
And (every minute, sinking) made me swimme,
To this calme Shore; hid, with his Sonne, in him:
And here, ay me! (as trembling, I looke back)
I fall againe, and, in my haven, wracke;
Still being perswaded (by the shamelesse light)
That these are dreames, of my retired Night;
That, all my Reading; Writing; all my paines
Are serious trifles; and the idle vaines
Of an unthriftie Angell, that deludes
950   My simple fancie; and, by Fate, extendes
My Birth-accurst life, from the blisse of men:
And then; my hands I wring; my bosome, then
Beate, and could breake ope; fill th'inraged Ayre;
And knock at heaven, with sighs; invoke Despaire,
At once, to free the tyr'd Earth of my lode;
That these recoiles, (that, Reason doth explode;
Religion damns; and my arm'd Soule defies;
Wrastles with Angels; telling Heaven it lies,
If it denie the truth, his Spirit hath writ,
960   Graven, in my soule, and there eternisde it)
Should beat me from that rest; and that is this;
That these prodigious Securities
That all men snore-in (drowning in vile lives
The Soules of men, because the bodie thrives)
Are Witch-crafts damnable; That all learnings are
Foolish, and false, that with those vile lives square;

That these sowre wizzards, that so gravely scorne
Learning with good life; kinde gainst kinde suborne;
And are no more wise, then their shades, are men;
Which (as my finger, can goe to my Penne)   970
I can demonstrate; that our knowledges,*   *Knowledge of our selves.
(Which we must learne, if ever we professe
Knowledge of God; or have one Notion true)
Are those, which first, and most we should pursue;
That, in their searches, all mens active lives,
Are so farre short of their contemplatives;
As Bodies are of Soules; This life, of Next:
And, so much doth the Forme, and whole Context
Of matter, serving one; exceede the other;
That Heaven, our Father is; as Earth our Mother.   980
And therefore; in resemblance to approve,
Who are the true bredde; fatherd by his love;
As Heaven it selfe, doth only, virtually
Mix with the Earth; his Course still keeping hie,
And Substance, undisparag'd; (though his Beames
Are dround in many dung-hils; and their Steames,
(To us) obscure him; yet he ever shines:)
So though our soules beames, digge in bodies Mines,
To finde them rich discourses, through their Senses;
And meet with many myddins of offences,   990
Whose Vapours choke their Organes; yet should they
Disperse them by degrees; because their swaie
(In Powre) is absolute; And (in that Powre) shine
As firme as heaven; heaven, nothing so divine.
All this, I holde; and since, that all truth else,
That all else knowe, or can holde; staies and dwelles
On these grounds uses; and should all contend
(Knowing our birth here, serves but for this end
To make true meanes, and waies, t'our second life)
To plie those studies; and holde every strife   1000
To other ends (more then to amplifie,
Adorne, and sweeten these, deservedly)
As balls cast in our Race; and but grasse knitt
From both sides of our Path; t'ensnare our wit:

And thus, because, the gaudie vulgar light
Burns up my good thoughts, form'd in temperate Night,
Rising to see, the good Moone oftentimes
(Like the poore virtues of these vicious times)
Labour as much to lose her light; as when
She fills her waning horns; And how (like men
Raisd to high Places) Exhalations fall
That would be thought Starres; Ile retire from all
The hot glades of Ambition; Companie,
That (with their vainenesse) make this vanitie;
And coole to death, in shaddowes of this vale:
To which end, I will cast this Serpents skale;
This loade of life, in life; this fleshie stone;
This bond, and bundle of corruption;
This breathing Sepulcher; this spundge of griefe;
This smiling Enemie; this household-thiefe;
This glasse of ayre; broken with lesse then breath;
This Slave, bound face to face, to death, till death;
And consecrate my life, to you, and yours:
In which objection; if that Powre of Powers
That hath reliev'd me thus farre; with a hand
Direct, and most immediate; still will stand
Betwixt me, and the Rapines of the Earth;
And give my poore paines, but such gratious birth,
As may sustaine me, in my desert Age,
With some powre, to my will; I still will wage
Warre with that false Peace, that exileth you;
And (in my prayd for freedome) ever vow,
Teares in these shades, for your teares; till mine eyes
Poure out my soule in better sacrifise.

Peace. Nor doubt (good friend) but God, to whom I see
Your friendlesse life converted; still will be
A rich supply for friends; And still be you
Sure Convertite to him. This, this way rowe
All to their Countrie. Thinke how hee hath shew'd
You wayes, and by wayes; what to bee pursew'd,
And what avoyded. Still, in his hands be,
If you desire to live, or safe, or free.

1010

1020

1030

1040

No longer dayes take; Nature doth exact
This resolution of thee, and this fact:
The Foe hayles on thy head; and in thy Face
Insults, and trenches; leaves thee, no worlds grace;
The walles; in which thou art besieged, shake.
Have done; Resist no more: but if you take
Firme notice of our speech, and, what you see;
And will adde paines to write all; let it be   1050
Divulged too. Perhappes, of all, some one
May finde some good: But might it touch upon
Your gratious Princes liking; hee might doe
Good to himselfe, and all his kingdomes too:
So virtuous, a great Example is;
And that, hath thankt, as small a thing as this;
Here being stuffe, and forme, for all true Peace;
And so, of all mens perfect Happinesse.
To which, if hee shall lend his Princely eare,
And give commandement (from your selfe) to heare   1060
My state; tell him you know me; and that I,
That am the Crowne of Principalitie,
(Though thus cast off by Princes) ever vow
Attendance at his foote; till I may growe
Up to his bosome; which (being deaw'd in time
With these my Teares) may to my comforts clyme:
Which (when all Pleasures, into Palseys turne,
And Sunne-like Pomp; in his own clowds shal mourne)
Will be acceptive. Meane space I will pray,
That hee may turne, some toward thought this way;   1070
While the round whirlewindes, of the earths delights
Dust betwixt him and me; and blinde the sights
Of all men ravisht with them; whose encrease
(You well may tell him) fashions not true Peace.
The Peace that they informe; learns but to squat,
While the slye legall foe (that levels at
Warre, through those false lights) soudainly runs by
Betwixt you, and your strength; and while you lye,

Couching your eares; and flatting everie lymme
1080   So close to earth, that you would seeme to him
The Earth it selfe: yet hee knowes who you are;
And, in that vantage, poures on, ready warre.

Conclusio.

Thus, by the way, to humane Loves interring,
These marginall, and secret teares referring
To my disposure (having all this howre
Of our unworldly conference, given powre
To her late-fainting issue, to arise)
She raisde her selfe, and them; The Progenies
Of that so civile Desert, rising all;
1090   Who fell with her; and to the Funerall
(She bearing still the Coffine) all went on.
And, now gives Time, her states description.
Before her flew Affliction, girt in storms,
Gasht all with gushing wounds; and all the formes
Of bane, and miserie, frowning in her face;
Whom Tyrannie, and Injustice, had in Chace;
Grimme Persecution, Povertie, and Shame;
Detraction, Envie, foule Mishap and lame;
Scruple of Conscience; Feare, Deceipt, Despaire;
1100   Slaunder, and Clamor, that rent all the Ayre;
Hate, Warre, and Massacre; uncrowned Toyle;
And Sickenes (t'all the rest, the Base, and Foile)
Crept after; and his deadly weight, trode downe
Wealth, Beautie, and the glorie of a Crowne.
These usherd her farre of; as figures given,
To showe, these Crosses borne, make peace with heaven:
But now (made free from them) next her, before;
Peacefull, and young, Herculean silence bore
His craggie Club; which up, aloft, hee hild;
1110   With which, and his forefingers charme hee stild
All sounds in ayre; and left so free, mine eares,
That I might heare, the musique of the Spheres,

And all the Angels, singing, out of heaven;
Whose tunes were solemne (as to Passion given)
For now, that Justice was the Happinesse there
For all the wrongs to Right, inflicted here.
Such was the Passion that Peace now put on;
And on, all went; when soudainely was gone
All light of heaven before us; from a wood
Whose sight, fore-seene (now lost) amaz'd wee stood,   1120
The Sunne still gracing us; when now (the Ayre
Inflam'd with Meteors) we discoverd, fayre,
The skipping Gote; the Horses flaming Mane;
Bearded, and trained Comets; Starres in wane;
The burning sword; the Firebrand, flying Snake;
The Lance; the Torch; the Licking fire; the Drake:
And all else Metors, that did ill abode;
The thunder chid; the lightning leapt abrode;
And yet, when Peace came in, all heaven was cleare;
And then, did all the horrid wood appeare;   1130
Where mortall dangers, more then leaves did growe;
In which wee could not, one free steppe bestowe;
For treading on some murtherd Passenger,
Who thither, was by witchcraft, forc't to erre,
Whose face, the bird hid, that loves Humans best;
That hath the bugle eyes, and Rosie Breast;
And is the yellow Autumns Nightingall.
Peace made us enter here secure of all;
Where, in a Cave, that through a Rocke did eate
The monster, Murther, held his impious Seat: 1140
A heape of panting Harts, supported him;
On which, he sate, gnawing a reeking lymme,
Of some man newly murtherd. As he eate
His grave-digg'd Browes, like stormy Eaves did sweat;
Which, like incensed Fennes, with mists did smoke;
His hyde was rugged, as an aged Oke
With heathie Leprosies; that still hee fed
With hote, raw lyms, of men late murthered.
His Face was like a Meteor, flashing blood;
His head all bristl'd, like a thornie wood;   1150

His necke cast wrinkles, like a Sea enrag'd;
And, in his vast Armes, was the world engag'd,
Bathing his hands in everie cruell deed;
Whose Palmes were hell-deepe lakes of boyling lead;
His thighes were mines of poyson, torment, griefe;
In which digg'd Fraude, and Trecherie, for reliefe;
Religions Botcher, Policie; and Pride;
Oppression, Slaverie, Flatterie glorified;
Atheisme, and Tyranny, and gaine unjust;
Franticke Ambition, Envie, shagge-heard Lust;   1160
Both sorts of Ignorance; and Knowledge swell'd;
And over these, the ould wolfe Avarice held
A goulden Scourge, that dropt, with blood and vapor;
With which, he whipt them to their endlesse labor.
From under heapes, cast from his fruitfull thyes,
(As ground, to all their damn'd Impieties)
The mourneful Goddesse, drew dead Humane Love;
Nor could they let her entrie, though they strove;
And furnac't on her, all their venemous breath;
(For; though all outrage breakes the Peace of death)   1170
She Coffind him; and forth to Funerall
All helpt to beare him: But to sound it all,
My Trumpet fayles; and all my forces shrinke.
Who can enact to life, what kils to thinke?
Nor can the Soules beames bear, through blood & flesh,
Formes of such woe, and height, as now, afresh,
Flow'd from these Objects: to see Poesie
Prepar'd to doe the speciall obsequie,
And sing the Funerall Oration;
How it did showe, to see her tread upon   1180
The breast of Death; and on a Furie leane;
How, to her Fist, (as rites of service then)
A Cast of Ravens flew; On her shoulders, how
The Foules, that to the Muses Queene we vow,
(The Owle, and Heronshawe) sate, how, for her hayre,
A haplesse Comet, hurld about the Ayre
Her curled Beames: whence sparkes, like falling starres,
Vanisht about her; and with windes adverse,

Were still blowne back; To which the Phoenix flew;
And (burning on her head) would not renew: 1190
How her divine Oration did move,
For th'unredeemed losse of humane Love;
Object mans future state to reasons eye;
The soules infusion; Immortalitie;
And prove her formes firme, that are here imprest;
How her admirde straines, wrought on every Beast;
And made the woods cast their Immanitie,
Up to the Ayre; that did to Citties flye
In Fewell for them: and, in Clowds of smoke,
Ever hang over them; cannot be spoke;   1200
Nor how to Humane love (to Earth now given)
A lightening stoop't, and ravisht him to heaven,
And with him Peace, with all her heavenly seede:
Whose outward Rapture, made me inward bleed;
Nor can I therefore, my Intention keepe;
Since Teares want words, & words want teares to weepe.

Corollarium ad *Principem*.

Thus shooke I this abortive from my Braine;
Which, with it, laie in this unworthy paine:
Yet since, your HOMER had his worthy hand
In vent'ring this delaie of your Command,   1210
To end his *Iliades*; deigne (Great Prince of men)
To holde before it your great Shielde; and then
It may, doe service, worthy this delaie,
To your more worthy Pleasure; and I maie
Regather the sperst fragments of my spirits,
And march with HOMER through his deathless merits,
To your undying graces. Nor did he
Vanish with this slight vision; but brought me
Home to my Cabine; and did all the waie
Assure me of your Graces constant staie   1220
To his soules Being, wholly naturalliz'd
And made your Highenesse subject; which he priz'd,

Past all his honours helde in other Lands;
And that (because a Princes maine state stands
In his owne knowledge, and his powre within)
These works that had chiefe virtue to beginne
Those informations; you would holde most deare;
Since false Joyes, have their seasons to appeare
Just as they are; but these delights were ever
1230   Perfect and needefull, and would irke you never.
   I praying for this happie worke of heaven
In your sweete disposition; the calme Even
Tooke me to rest; and he with wings of Fire,
To soft Ayres supreame Region did aspire.

*By the ever most humbly and truly dedicated
to your most Princely graces,*

Geo. Chapman.

A Good Woman

A woman good, and faire (which no dame can
Esteeme much easier found then a good man)
Sets not her selfe to shew, nor found would be:
Rather her vertues flie abroad then she.
Dreames not on fashions, loves no gossips feasts,
Affects no newes, no tales, no guests, no jeasts:
Her worke, and reading writs of worthiest men:
Her husbands pleasure, well taught childeren:
Her housholds fit provision to see spent,
As fits her husbands will, and his consent: 10
Spends pleasingly her time, delighting still,
To her just dutie, to adapt her will.
Vertue she loves, rewards and honors it,
And hates all scoffing, bold and idle wit:
Pious and wise she is, and treads upon
This foolish and this false opinion,
That learning fits not women; since it may
Her naturall cunning helpe, and make more way
To light, and close affects: for so it can
Courbe and compose them too, as in a man: 20
And, being noble, is the noblest meane,
To spend her time: thoughts idle and uncleane,
Preventing and suppressing: to which end
She entertaines it: and doth more commend
Time spent in that, then houswiferies low kindes,
As short of that, as bodies are of minds.
If it may hurt, is powre of good lesse great,
Since food may lust excite, shall she not eate?
    She is not Moon-like, that the Sunne, her spouse
Being furthest off, is cleare and glorious: 30
And being neare, growes pallid and obscure:
But in her husbands presence, is most pure,

In all chast ornaments, bright still with him,
And in his absence, all retir'd and dim:
With him still kind and pleasing, still the same;
Yet with her weeds, not putting off her shame:
But when for bed-rites her attire is gone,
In place thereof her modest shame goes on.
Not with her husband lies, but he with her:

40 And in their love-joyes doth so much prefer
Modest example, that she will not kisse
Her husband, when her daughter present is.
When a just husbands right he would enjoy,
She neither flies him, nor with moods is coy.
One, of the light dame savours, th'other showes
Pride, nor from loves ingenuous humor flowes.

Geometrae dicunt, lineas And as *Geometricians approve,
& superficies, non seipsis That lines, nor superficies, do move
moveri, sed motus Themselves, but by their bodies motions go:
corporum comitari. So your good woman never strives to grow
Strong in her owne affections and delights,
But to her husbands equall appetites,
Earnests and jeasts, and lookes austerities,
Her selfe in all her subject powres applies.

A good wife in most Since lifes chiefe cares on him are ever laid,
cares, should ever *In cares she ever comforts, undismaid,
undismaid comfort her Though her heart grieves, her lookes yet makes it sleight,
husband. Dissembling evermore, without deceit.

*Simile. *And as the twins of learn'd *Hippocrates*,
60 If one were sicke, the other felt disease:
A good wife watcheth If one rejoyc't; joy th'others spirits fed:
her husbands serious If one were griev'd, the other sorrowed:
thoughts in his lookes, *So fares she with her husband; every thought
and applies her owne to (Weightie in him) still watcht in her, and wrought.
them.
*Simile. *And as those that in Elephants delight,
Never come neare them in weeds rich and bright;
Nor Buls approch in scarlet; since those hewes,
Through both those beasts, enrag'd affects diffuse:
And as from Tygres, men the Timbrels sound
70 And Cimbals keepe away; since they abound

Thereby in furie, and their owne flesh teare:
So when t'a good wife, it is made appeare,
That rich attire, and curiositie
In wires, tires, shadowes, do displease the eye
Of her lov'd husband; musicke, dancing, breeds
Offence in him; she layes by all those weeds,
Leaves dancing, musicke; and at every part
Studies to please; and does it from her heart.
As greatnesse in a Steede; so dignitie
Needs in a woman, courbe, and bit, and eie,   80
If once she weds, shee's two for one before:
Single againe, she never doubles more.

NOTES

All Fooles

All Fooles was first known as *the world Rones a whelles* (*The World Runs On Wheels*) and was written for the Admiral's Men at the Rose Theatre on the Bankside in London. The Rose's owner and financier Philip Henslowe kept a diary, which first refers to the play on 22 January 1598. Notes about it continue until 2 July 1599, when Henslowe records: 'Lent unto thomas dowton the 2 of July 1599 to paye mr chapman in full payment for his Boocke called the world Rones a whelles & now all foolles but the foolle some of xxx.' There's no record of any performance at the Rose although it's likely that the Admiral's Men would have wanted to stage what Henslowe had paid for. Chapman moved on shortly afterwards to write for the newly formed Chapel Children. This company of boy actors played at an indoor theatre set up in an old Dominican monastery in Blackfriars, between Ludgate Hill in London and the River Thames. *All Fooles* was acted at Blackfriars, and it may have been revised in 1600–1601 for performance there. For example, the parody in Act III of a well-known passage from John Lyly's *Euphues* (1578) may have been inserted as a cheeky assertion of one-upmanship over the old style of plays produced by Lyly with an earlier incarnation of the Chapel Children, who performed at a different venue in Blackfriars between 1576 and 1584. But other details, such as a date still given in the 1500s at IV.1.326, suggest that if there was any revision, it was not thorough. The *Prologus* and Epilogue were almost certainly added for the play's first performance at Blackfriars. References in the *Prologus* to '*bitter splenes*' and '*satyrisme*' set the play above the so-called War of the Theatres (1599–1602). But here, too, certain details, such as references to features usually found in outdoor theatres, like the '*Hell*' and the '*Heaven*', make it impossible to be certain about the play's history between 2 July 1599 and 31 December 1604. On 1 January 1605 it was acted at court for King James I, an event which shows it must have attained some repute. The play was printed in 1605. Since then it's rarely been staged.

All Fooles shows Chapman turning to Roman literary sources to find forms for the new experiences of London city life. London became a metropolis during Chapman's lifetime. Between 1550 and 1600 the population increased by about half to around 250,000, dwarfing other English cities. London was felt to be a new Rome; as Barbara Everett points out ('Donne: A London Poet', *English Poets: British Academy Chatterton Lectures*, Oxford, Clarendon Press, 1988), its growth enabled English writers for the first time to make full imaginative use of metropolitan Roman satirists such as Horace,

Juvenal and Persius. Donne's 'Satire I' is among the works about modern urban life indebted to Persius' 'Satire I', and so too is *All Fooles*. Chapman's pronouncement in the *Prologus* that '*merit beares least sway in most contents*' is consistent with the thrust of Persius' 'Satire I', as summarized in a note prefixed to the Penguin translation of *The Satires of Horace and Persius* by Niall Rudd: '. . . Persius says that he expects to have few readers because the Romans do not want poetry to have any bearing on real life. Fashionable verse is false and affected, written without a proper apprenticeship to the craft and designed solely to win applause. This decadence in literary taste is directly related to the general decadence in morals. Romans have lost their traditional virility' (London: Penguin, 1987), p. 208. A line from Persius' 'Satire I' is quoted in Chapman's *Prologus*: 'Auriculas Asini quis non habet?' Who doesn't have asses' ears? *All Fooles* swaps asses' ears for those traditional insults to virility, the cuckold's horns. The penultimate speech of the play is a long encomium to the present age – 'the *Horned age*' (V.2.230) – the decadent end of a world run down from the Golden Age through the Silver, the Brass, the Iron, the Leaden and the Wooden. The joke shared by Chapman and Persius is the idea of universal foolery. Persius' 'Satire I' goes on in ll. 123–6 of Rudd's translation:

> . . . If you've caught the spirit of brave Cratinus
> or are pale from devotion to angry Eupolis and the Grand Old Man,
> if you've an ear for a concentrated brew, then look at this.
> I want a reader with his ears well steamed by that comic vinegar,
> . . .

Aristophanes (the 'Grand Old Man'), Cratinus and Eupolis were the most distinguished practitioners of Greek Old Comedy, which through Greek Middle and Greek New Comedy provided the basis hundreds of years later for Roman New Comedy. The quotation from Persius and the references in the *Prologus* to Cratinus and Eupolis suggest that *All Fooles* was presented as a play intended to make its audience think about the proper nature of comedy, wit, judgement and satire – the last in particular being one of the subjects of the War of the Theatres.

All Fooles is a suave refashioning of two plays by the Roman dramatist Terence, a 'concentrated brew' of *Heautontimorumenos* (*The Self-Tormentor*) and *Adelphi* (*The Brothers*). Terence was much studied in sixteenth-century English grammar schools and it's likely that Chapman first read his works as a pupil at Hitchin Grammar School, which was famous for its productions of plays. The plots of Terence's works are difficult to summarize, but in essence the plot of *All Fooles* is largely adapted from *The Self-Tormentor*, while *The Brothers* accounts more for the characterization of Gostanzo and Marc Antonio. Chapman's adaptation of previous plays means that *All Fooles* should technically be known as a 'contaminatio', like *The Brothers*, which itself draws on two lost plays by the Greek New Comedy writer Menander. Other contemporary 'contaminatios' include Shakespeare's *The Comedie of Errors* (1594) and Ben Jonson's first surviving play *The Case is Altered* (1597–8). Both Jonson and Shakespeare combine different works by the Roman dramatist Plautus. Roman New Comedy was one of the most important sources for Renaissance drama as a whole, and the plays of Terence and Plautus helped to form the repertory of characters adapted by Chapman for *All Fooles*. The intriguer Rynaldo is based on the crafty slave of Roman comedies, although he's elevated to the rather superior status of a graduate of the University of Padua. The brothers Fortunio and Valerio ascend from being lusty adolescents to gallants about town. Gratiana – a prostitute in *The Self-Tormentor* – becomes Valerio's secret wife. Gostanzo is a type of the *senex* – the old man – a bit like the old gentleman Kno'well in the revised version of Jonson's comedy *Every Man in His Humour* (printed 1616) or Polonius in Shakespeare's tragedy *Hamlet* (1600), as he's described by the critic Robert S. Miola: 'Like a Terentian father, he gives self-consciously sage advice and speaks in *sententiae*; he recalls his heyday gone by; he acts an uncomprehending target for jokes and repartee' (*Shakespeare and Classical Comedy*, Oxford: Clarendon Press, 1994), p. 174. Gostanzo is 'an uncomprehending target,' all the more comically because he wants to be as knowing and adroit as Rynaldo; this is why Rynaldo teases him in Act III. Scene 1 by repeating his own words back to him in seeming innocence. Rynaldo takes Gostanzo's frequent errors to prove that would-be politicians are the biggest fools around when they're not being helped by the goddess Fortune:

> Tis she that gives the lustre to their wits,
> Still plodding at traditionall devices:
> But take um out of them to present actions,
> A man may grope and tickle um like a Trowt, . . .   (III.1.116–19)

Chapman's aim in all his plays is to give his audience something new. *Bussy D'Ambois* (1604) follows Bussy's complicated course as he seeks to 'bring up a new fashion,/ And rise in Court with vertue' (I.1.125–6). 'It's new and stirring,' comments Tharsalio on the action of *The Widdowes Teares* (1604–5), IV.1.8–9. In *All Fooles* the agent of Chapman's experimentalism is Rynaldo, pitting 'present actions' against 'traditionall devices'.

All Fooles checks its characters' passion for tricks and intrigue. Gostanzo comically fancies himself as a Machiavellian figure, partitioning the common lands of language. He urges his son Valerio to espouse the competitive individualism which animates most of the play – everyone gulling everybody else:

> Wherefore has Man a Tongue, of powre to speake,
> But to speake still to his owne private purpose?
> Beastes utter but one sound; but Men have change
> Of speech and Reason, even by Nature given them:
> Now to say one thing, and an other now,
> As best may serve their profitable endes.   (II.1.71–6)

The fifth line quoted here is an example of the rhetorical figure known as epanalepsis, in which the same word is repeated at the beginning and end of a line. It's used because Gostanzo's outlook is based on an atomised view of society, in which everyone must start and finish by looking after themselves. Other people are as much tools to be used as words. But in schooling his son in 'politique' behaviour and encouraging Valerio to exploit the gaps between the senses of words, Gostanzo sets up his own hoodwinking. Take the different uses of the word 'husbandry'. For Gostanzo this means digging ditches and looking after cattle, for Valerio it means the much more exciting stewardship of women. Such deceptions are played for their comic value, they are never really felt as threatening. There's no true discord in the world of light New Comedy – something will always emerge to make things all right, a concealed fact about birth for example. As Gostanzo says when capitulating near the end: 'Now all my Choller flie out in your witts:/ Good trickes of Youth y'faith, no *Indecorum*, . . .' (V.2.151–2). The passion for tricks and intrigue is safely contained in *All Fooles*, but it will reappear more dangerously in *Bussy D'Ambois* and *The Widdowes Teares*. In *Bussy D'Ambois*, for example, Gostanzo's attitude to language is shared by the much more accomplished Machiavellian Monsieur (see the scene where he tries to seduce Tamyra by saying that Honour is just a word – II.2.59ff.). In *The Widdowes Teares*, 'crosse capers' prove almost tragic.

FURTHER READING

Altman, Joel B., *The Tudor Play of Mind: Rhetorical Inquiry and the Development of Elizabethan Drama* (Berkeley and Los Angeles: University of California Press, 1978)
Chapman, George, *All Fools*, ed. Frank Manley (Lincoln, USA: University of Nebraska Press, 1968)

NOTE ON THE TEXT

The text is based on the first edition of *All Fooles* in the library of Worcester College, Oxford. The title page of the first quarto calls it AL FOOLE⸀; the S is crazily reversed and the typeface looks like it's been chosen by a harlequin. Inside, at the head of the play, it's called *All Fooles* and this less eccentric appellation has been taken as the title of the text in this volume. It's been checked against the standard modern text in *The Plays of George Chapman: The Comedies*, ed. Allan Holaday (Urbana, USA: University of Illinois Press, 1970), where the introduction to *All Fooles* is concerned more with textual than critical matters. The Illinois edition prints *All Fooles* with the following dedicatory sonnet, addressed 'To my long lovd and Honourable *friend Sir Thomas Walsingham Knight*':

Should I expose to every common eye,
    The least allow'd birth of my shaken braine;
And not entitle it perticulerly
    To your acceptance, I were wurse then vaine.
And though I am most loth to passe your sight
    with any suche light marke of vanitie,
Being markt with Age for Aimes of greater weight,
    and drownd in dark Death-ushering melancholy,
Yet least by others stealth it be imprest,
    without my pasport, patcht with others wit,
Of two enforst ills I elect the least;
    and so desire your love will censure it;
        Though my old fortune keepe me still obscure,
        The light shall still bewray my ould love sure.

The authenticity of this sonnet has been questioned. It appears in only one copy of the first edition of *All Fooles*, owned by the University of Texas Library. It's inserted into the volume on a different-sized leaf of paper. The lines were first reprinted by a nineteenth-century editor called J. P. Collier, who worked from the edition that's now in Texas when he prepared a copy of the play for inclusion in Robert Dodsley's *Select Collection of Old Plays* (1825). T. M. Parrott, in his edition of *The Plays of George Chapman: The Comedies* (New York and London: Russell & Russell, 1914), pp. 725–7, argued the sonnet was a forgery by Collier. But Professor Parrott later changed his mind. Phyllis Brooks Bartlett, in her edition of *The Poems of George Chapman* (New York: MLA, 1941), p. 470, reports Parrott telling her that he now thought the sonnet was by Chapman, but possibly written instead for the printing of *May-Day* in 1611 or *The Widdowes Teares* in 1612. Bartlett also believed the sonnet was genuine. There are notes which do sound like Chapman ('Aimes of greater weight', 'Death-ushering melancholy', 'obscure') and there are similarities between the second line of the sonnet and l. 1207 of *The Teares of Peace* (1609): 'Thus shooke I this abortive from my Braine', and 23.2 of *Ovids Banquet of Sence* (1595): 'Shooke from her braine'. Chapman also dedicated other works to the Walsingham family: the continuation of Marlowe's *Hero And Leander* (1598) to Lady Walsingham, *The Conspiracie, And Tragedie Of Charles Duke of Byron* (1607–8) to Sir Thomas Walsingham, Knight, and his son Thomas Walsingham, Esquire. The Byron dedication starts: 'SIR, though I know, you ever stood little affected to these unprofitable rites of Dedication; (which disposition in you, hath made me hetherto dispence with your right in my other impressions) . . .' Parrott first pointed out that Chapman would hardly have written this if *All Fooles* had been dedicated to Walsingham three years earlier. However, there may have been a distinction in Chapman's mind between public and private dedications, and Bartlett notes that three extra dedicatory sonnets are included in a few copies of his translation of *The Iliads Of Homer* (1611). Overall it seems likely that the sonnet is genuine, but not so likely that it was written to accompany *All Fooles*.

TEXTUAL NOTES

This edition is based on the copy of the first quarto in the Library of Worcester College, Oxford. In the notes that follow, the first readings are from this edition and the second readings record those of the base text.

Actors

13 Bellanora] Bellonora
15 Gratiana,] ~ ∧

Prologus

27 mistery] *misery in corrected* Q; mistery *in uncorrected*

Act I. Scene 1

1 alike] a like
55 favours;] ~,
66 jesters,] ~;
67 durt and tytles,] ~, ~~ ∧
76 them:] ~,
81 richest] riches
97 sunne] sonne
162 it.] *uncorrected* Q; ~? *in corrected*
194 husbandry-] ~.
224–6 Wenches . . . wife] Q *lines*: Wenches . . . breath/ Yet . . . wife
224 be sworne] besworne
227 looke] lookee
233 wise] wife
238–42 See . . . will] Q *lines*: See . . . Sir,/ In . . . secret/ By . . . will
238 father:] ~,
240 SD] *Set as part of l. 240 in* Q
241 attonement,] ~ ∧
264 sonne] soone
279 labour,] ~;
315 olde;] ~,
322–3 If . . . esteame] Q *prints as one line*

339 thriftie.] ~,
364 lost.] ~,
368 other,] ~;

Act I. Scene 2

0.1 BELLANORA] *Bellonora*
14 hate;] ~ ∧
23 Extreame] Extreames
48 danger.] ~,
52 Gentlewomen] Gentle women
69 Jelosie,] ~ ∧
76 Father's] Fathers
82 and] And
86 learning.] ~ ∧
90 Scholard] Scholards
96 him:] ~,
101 Logicke?] ~.
109 I,] ~ ∧
118 wedlocke,] ~ ∧
128 I,] ~ ∧
147.01 SD *Primi*] *Prima*

Act II. Scene 1

0.1 SD MARC ANTONIO] *Marcantonio (and at l. 19)*
9 warres?] ~.
37 Troye] *Trope*
37.02 SD *himselfe.*] ~,
86 Better . . . Sonne] Q *lines*: Better . . . better/ Soft . . . Sonne
86 FORTUNIO] *Fortunion*
109 orgaines] organies
119 house:] ~,
128 What . . . sheepes-head] Q *lines*:

What . . . compliment/ Kisse
. . . sheepes-head
136 SD VALERIO] *Volerio*
137 *her.*] ~ ∧
140 conduct am] conduct-am
148 Young men] Youngmen
165 times,] ~ ∧
172 *Accrostique*] accrostique
172–6 *Exordion . . . cooplets*] *italics
throughout in* Q
176 *Blanke Verse*] *roman in* Q
217, 238,
244, 269 *Dariotto*] *Doriotto*
226–7 Goe . . . you] Q *prints as one line*
227 boldly; . . . you,] ~,. . . ~;
229 SD GAZETTA] *Gazetto*
236 Hmm] Him
242 plainelie;] ~,
244 not ∧] ~?
308 sees] fees
336–8 Fayth . . . grossest] Q *lines:*
Fayth . . . became/ Now . . . is/
He . . . grossest
385 um] on
407–8 O God . . . this?] Q *prints as one
line*
418 Ha] ha
422–5 And . . . jelousy] Q *prints as prose*
422 Maister] mast ∧

Act III. Scene 1

78–80 Troth . . . house?] Q *prints as
prose*
86 To] to
122 by] be
312 lookes] looke
336–7 What . . . then] Q *lines:* What
. . . villayne?/ By . . . then
339, 343,
348, 360 *Dariotto*] *Darioto*
344–7 Foot . . . me] Q *prints as prose*
349 obtein'd] obtei'nd

359 'tis] ti's
362 Surgery.] ~,
370 doe-] ~,
371 others] other
377 *Pock?*] ~.
383 hazard] hazards
389 sir?] ~.
390 time?] ~.
410 ridiculouse-] ~.
411 licence:] ~,

Act IV. Scene 1

9 feare:] ~,
13 withall?] ~.
19–20 when't . . . so] Q *prints as one line*
36 holde.] ~:
52 your] our
74.01 SD RYNALDO,] ~ ∧
74–5 on . . . sir] Q *prints as one line*
75 sir.] ~,
76–7 Your . . . knees] Q *prints as one
line*
77 knees.] ~:
92 dearer-] ~?
108 so.] ~,
112 hand,] ~ ∧
125 wife.] ~ ∧
127 her,] ~ ∧
129 wisdome? Call] ~, call
142 hand;] ~,
151 before ∧] ~,
161–3 Didst . . . selfe?] Q *lines:* Didst
. . . world/ That . . . selfe
181 ahlas] ah las
184–5 The . . . brother] Q *prints as one
line*
187–8 Not . . . father] Q *prints as one
line*
216 hart.] ~:
239 Signior,] ~ ∧
241 her:] ~,
243 here. How] ~, how

251 mine?] minde,
252 am. May] ~, may
271 beckes (due gard)] ~, due gard,
272 this] This
286 Ortography?] ~.
294 *et*] *&*
298 *Florence*. Read] ~, read
337 it. How] ~, how
344 turne.] ~ ∧
349 Well] well
350 *Notary*.] ~,
364 Given] given
369 *Exeunt*] roman in Q

Act V. Scene 1

8 By] by
12, 65 *Dariotto*] *Darioto*
15 blow,] ~;
54 prison.] ~,
55 Halfe] halfe
66 sonne,] ~ ∧
71 With all] Withall

Act V. Scene 2

4 *Dariottos*] *Dariotos*
20 crownes,] ~:
24 I,] ~ ∧
30 am.] ~,
33 *Dariotto's*] *Darioto's*
37 excercises.] ~,
39 Call's] Calls
42–3 It . . . *Tabacco*] Q *prints as one line*
43 *Tabacco*.] ~:
43–4 But . . . pray] Q *prints as one line*

44 pray?] ~ ∧
59–61 Nay . . . knees] Q *prints as prose*
61–3 Sir . . . downe;] Q *lines*: Sir . . .
Taverne/ Heere . . . head/
Slight . . . downe
63 yee,] ~ ∧
72 DARIOTTO] *Clau*
76 the rest] mee rest
95 villaine.] ~,
96 VALERIO] *no speech-prefix in* Q
104 wisedome?] ~.
115 eye's] eyes
121 why,] ~ ∧
128 gull'd.] ~,
129–30 Why . . . that?] Q *prints as one
line*
132–3 Why . . . eyes?] Q *prints as one
line*
135 To] to
154 hand:] ~,
161 rul'd. Good] ~ ∧ good
188 do, thinke] ~ ∧ ~
234 age;] ~,
267 is [no] Beast] is Beast
275 man.] ~,
280 *Europe*] *Europa*
294 conclude:] ~ ∧ ('To conclude' *is
not indented in* Q)
302 poore;] ~,
305 doe);] ~) ∧
312 speech.] ~:

Epilogue

5 *them*:] ~,

COMMENTARY

As explained in the Headnote, *All Fooles* adapts two comedies by the Roman dramatist
Terence. *Heautontimorumenos* (*The Self-Tormentor*) is abbreviated below as *ST*; *Adelphi*
(*The Brothers*) as *BR*.

The Actors

Gostanzo: Also the name of the foolish old lover (the *vecchio innamorato*) in the Italian comedy *L'Allesandro* (*c.*1545) by Alessandro Piccolomini. Chapman's comedy *May-Day* (1601-2) is an adaptation of the Italian play.

Fortunio: Another name taken from *L'Allesandro* where Fortunio is a woman disguised as a boy.

Cornelio ... Gentleman: In *L'Allesandro*, Cornelio is in love with Gostanzo's daughter. In *All Fooles* the derivation of his name from the Latin *cornus*, or horn, fits the theme of cuckoldry. Cornelio is a 'start-up Gentleman' because he is an upstart. A 'startup' is also kind of large-soled high-sided boot originally worn by rustics – compare ll. 92-4 of 'Hymnus in Cynthiam' in *The Shadow Of Night* (1594): 'Accounting it no meede but mockerie,/When her steepe browes alreadie prop the skie,/To put on startups ...'

Prologus

4 *this Hell ... Heaven*: Both the '*Hell*' and the '*Heaven*' were features more usually found in an outdoor theatre such as the Rose, not an indoor one such as Blackfriars, a sign perhaps that if the *Prologus* was written for a Blackfriars premiere in 1600-1601 that Chapman was still adjusting to his new surroundings. The '*Hell*' is the area under the stage. The '*Heaven*' – more usually known as 'the heavens' – is the cover above the stage, designed to protect the actors from the weather and also as a place to let things down from. The 'heavens' were painted with pictures of the sun, the moon and the stars, and possibly the signs of the zodiac.

13-19 *Who can ... sauce*: The references to '*personall application*', '*bitter splenes*' and '*satyrisme*' all suggest the War of the Theatres (1599-1602), in its origins a clash between Ben Jonson and John Marston.

27 *mistery*: The corrected Quarto reads '*misery*' but the uncorrected '*mistery*' has been preferred as seeming in fact more likely to be accurate. All modern editors of *All Fooles* have adopted '*mistery*' and taken it to refer back to the questions posed in ll. 20-22.

28-32 *Great ... fooles*: Young gallants paid extra to sit '*on the stage*' at Blackfriars where their '*faire attyre*' could be admired. They sometimes used to walk off before the end, one of several embarrassing practices satirized by Thomas Dekker in Chapter VI of *The guls Horne-booke* (1609). As it wasn't possible to sit on the stage of an outdoor theatre like the Rose, Chapman's reference to this practice is another pointer to the possible date of the *Prologus*.

35 *Auriculas ... habet?*: 'Who doesn't have asses' ears?' From Persius' 'Satire I', l. 121. See Headnote.

Act I. Scene 1

47 *cousoning picture*: See Introduction for a discussion of Chapman's interest in such pictures.

69–76 *Found true . . . pleas'd them*: Compare Juvenal's 'Satire VI', ll. 166–99, 461–6, 474–80. See Headnote for discussion of Roman literary sources.

92 *the poore Foxe*: One of Aesop's fables tells how the fox lost his tail in a trap and tried to persuade the others to lose theirs, but, according to Aesop, they wouldn't. Rynaldo's name is meant to be foxy – like Reynard.

97–123 *I tell . . . feastes*: Valerio's assertions suggest that one of the 'feastes' at which he's been present is *Ovids Banquet of Sence* (1595). Compare, for example, I.1.105–6 and 1.3–4: 'When with right beames the Sun her bosome beat/ And with fit foode her Plants did nutrifie.' In the poem's next stanza the sun makes 'greene-love burne in his desire' (2.3). Both the play and the poem are calling on Neoplatonic ideas expressed by Marsilio Ficino (1433–99) in *Ficino's Commentary on Plato's Symposium*, edited and translated by Sears Jayne, *University of Missouri Studies*, 19 (1944). Compare Commentary on stanzas 1 and 2 of *Ovids Banquet of Sence*, in particular Ficino's comparison of love to the sun: 'the sun turns many flowers and leaves towards itself' ('*Commentary*', p. 200).

141 SD *Amplectitur eam*: 'Embraces her'.

166 *dragon . . . fruite*: The golden apples of the Hesperides were guarded by the dragon Ladon, which had many heads and never slept.

167 SD *Intrat Gostanzo*: 'Enter Gostanzo'.

168 SD *Omnes aufugiunt*: 'Everyone runs away'.

219 SD *Aversus*: 'Aside'.

240 SD *Abscondit se*: 'Hides himself'.

253–6 *One that . . . Ivory*: Gostanzo's attitude towards Gratiana's poverty, also expressed at I.1.263 and I.1.289–93, is more facetious than Demea's opposition to Pamphilia's suitability as a wife for his son Aeschinus in *BR*, 728–9.

260–61 *Tis . . . selfe*: 'It's to be feared that his presumptuous behaviour doesn't stem from having made a good choice, because that by itself would justify what he's done.'

270–73 *What . . . neglect me*: Marc Antonio's relaxed attitude is similar to that of Menedemus when told about his son Clinia's lovelife in *ST*, 463–6.

275 *You . . . villany*: Translated from *ST*, 481.

284 *By heaven . . . state*: Compare *ST*, 463.

294–5 *mischiefe . . . remedy*: 'Mischiefe' and 'remedy' are both legal terms. In the law of the time a mischiefe was 'a condition in which a person suffers a wrong or is under some disability, esp. one for which equity affords a remedy' (*OED*).

306 *runne into the warres*: In *ST*, 117ff, Menedemus' son Clinia has run away to serve in the army in Asia.

316 *Padoa*: The university at Padua in Italy was founded in the thirteenth century and was famous in England for its learning.

Act I. Scene 2

101–3 *you shall . . . your fils*: Compare Terence's comedy *Eunuchus* (*The Eunuch*), 372–3.

111 *Brother . . . wife*: Compare *ST*, 332.

117–8 *Valerio . . . wedlocke*: Compare *ST*, 328. The phrase 'at racke and manger' (derived from feeding animals) means 'in the midst of abundance and plenty, wanting for nothing' (*OED*).

138–9 *Come . . . nor now*: Compare *ST*, 376–7.

Act II. Scene 1

20 *Our olde . . . neighbourhood*: Gostanzo and Marc Antonio are more like the brothers in *BR* than Chremes and Menedemus in *ST*, who have only known each other for about three months.

179 SD *prodit*: 'Comes forward'.

205–8 *And yet . . . forme*: Compare *The Eunuch*, 1044–6.

226 *swagger*: Compare ll. 36–8 of Chapman's address 'To the Understander' prefixed to *Achilles Shield* (1598): '*Swaggering is a new worde amongst them and rounde-headed custome gives it priviledge with much imitation, being created, as it were, by a naturall Prosopopeia without etimologie or derivation*'.

232–6 *what flowers . . . may mine*: The upturned tips of the columbine resemble horns; hence, they were associated with cuckoldry. There is also a possible allusion to Ophelia's speech about flowers including the pansy and columbine in Shakespeare's tragedy *Hamlet* (1600), IV.v.176–80. Albert H. Tricomi believes this points towards 'a turn-of-the-century rather than a Jacobean revision' of *All Fooles*. See 'The Dates of the Plays of George Chapman', *English Literary Renaissance*, XII (1982), pp. 242–66.

286 *takes . . . lap*: A euphemism for copulation. Compare Hamlet to Ophelia in *Hamlet*, III.ii.108–14.

291–2 *mock . . . marke*: Make them misfire by keeping close watch on their target.

336–8 *that same . . . grossest*: An allusion to the War of the Theatres.

347 *crosse capers*: Compare *The Widdowes Teares* (1604–5), V.5.61.

Act III. Scene 1

14–15 *or from . . . delude me*: The 'Ivory gate' is the gate of false deluding dreams according to Homer's *Odyssey*, XIX.562 and Virgil's *Aeneid*, VI.893–6. Compare ll. 340–49 of 'Hymnus in Noctem' in *The Shadow Of Night* (1594).

28 *last day*: One night has passed between Acts II and III, as in *ST*, 410.

62 *For shame . . . lost*: Possibly a variant of the proverb 'Past shame past amendment'. Difficult to paraphrase, but means something like: 'Once somebody's cause for shame has been found out about, their shame is lost because once it's known about there's no point in them being ashamed any more.' Compare *The Widdowes Teares*, III.1.153.

90–93 *Would it . . . I heard*: Compare Gostanzo's approval of Rynaldo's plans with Chremes' expressions of pleasure to Syrus in *ST*, 760–70.

109–11 *what would . . . warrant thee*: Compare *ST*, 591–3.

123 *Even that . . . fooles*: i.e. some degree of common sense.

146 *watch the keepers*: A proverbial phrase derived from Juvenal's 'Satire VI', ll. 347–8: '*Quis custodiet ipsos custodes*' – the Latin meaning 'Who will guard the guardians?'

199–200 *prickle . . . cheese*: Compare John Lyly's *Euphues* (1578): 'As therefore the sweetest Rose hath his prickel, the finest velvet his brack, the fairest floure his bran.' Brack means flaw. The addition of the cheese points up Chapman's parodic intentions. More generally in this scene the Page's speeches mock Lyly's famously peculiar style, known as Euphuism, marked particularly by heavy use of antitheses. Albert H. Tricomi (see Commentary on II.1.232–4) argues that Chapman's use of Lyly is another sign of *All Fooles* being revised at the turn of the century rather than 1603–4. By that time he says 'Lyly was already passé'. And he writes: 'Imitations and parodies of the Euphuistic style became prominent in the 1590s and at the end of the decade turned toward the biting (or shaggy) style of Juvenal. Under these circumstances practitioners of the Juvenalian style – Marston, for example – parodied Lyly as well' ('Dates', p. 244). See also Commentary on V.2.226–310.

205–9 *but . . . idlenesse*: Such gardens were places for women to meet their lovers. The young Puritan wife Florila in Chapman's comedy *An Humerous dayes Myrth* (1597) is given a garden by her old husband, and she meets courtiers there.

224 *no wils*: Laws passed in the reign of Henry VII and Henry VIII meant that married women were not allowed to make wills without their husbands' consent, a situation that didn't change until the Married Women's Property Act of 1882. This was one reason for widows' attractiveness in the marriage market; young men and impoverished gentlemen hoped to keep widows' fortunes for themselves. See Notes to *The Widdowes Teares*.

237–8 *Foxe . . . company*: Compare I.1.92 and Commentary.

270–71 *Mars . . . snare*: Vulcan used a net to catch Venus and Mars committing adultery. Compare *Bussy D'Ambois* (1604), V.1.62, and *The Teares of Peace* (1609), l. 6.

291 *Sine periculo friget lusus*: 'No fun without danger.'

369 *out of France*: The English thought France was the home of syphilis or pox – punning on the surgeon's name Pock.

395 *writt of error*: A writ which calls for a new trial on the grounds of earlier error.

402–3 *head rung noone*: From the proverb 'To ring one's head at noon', which means to beat somebody about the head.

408 *I'll give . . . bleed*: 'I'll get my own back by secretly cuckolding him'.

409 *rings lowd acquittance*: 'Pays in full'.

Act IV. Scene 1

23–5 *What Eagles . . . our owne*: The image is imaginatively expanded from *ST*, 502–5.

53 *Out . . . awak't me*: Possibly derived from *ST*, 857.

61 *my circumstance . . . fact*: The 'fact' is that Valerio deceived his father by marrying without his permission. Marc Antonio has been asked to approach Gostanzo because when he thought that his son had similarly deceived him he was not angry. This is the 'circumstance' which 'lessens' Marc Antonio's view of the seriousness of what Valerio has done.

114–15 *birth-right . . . broth*: A Biblical allusion. Esau sells his birthright for a mess of pottage in Genesis 25:29–34.

146–7 *What huge . . . leather*: Compare the proverb: 'To cut large thongs of other men's leather.'

173 *like your selfe*: i.e. like a fool.

209–11 *And therefore . . . nakednesse*: Compare the title page of Robert Greene's novel *Pandosto* (1588): 'Pandosto. The Triumph of Time. Wherein is discovered by a pleasant Historie, that although by the meanes of sinister fortune Truth may be concealed, yet by Time in spight of fortune it most manifestly revealed.' Chapman's lines are briefly discussed in relation to *Pandosto*'s title page by D. J. Gordon in his essay '*Veritas Filia Temporis*: Hadrianus Junius and Geoffrey Whitney' in *The Renaissance Imagination*, ed. Stephen Orgel (Berkeley and Los Angeles: University of California Press, 1975), pp. 220–32.

245–6 *white sheete*: Worn by adulterers as a sign of public penance.

249–50 *capitall . . . foreheads*: Bound on offenders' foreheads to indicate their crime.

262 *brazen towre*: A mythological allusion. Danaë was shut in a bronze chamber ('brazen towre') by her father Acrisius, after he was warned by an oracle that Danae's son would kill him. Zeus then visited Danae in a shower of gold, after which she gave birth to Perseus. The expression 'brazen towre' may be derived from Christopher Marlowe's translation of *All Ovids Elegies*, II.xix.27.

271 *due gard*: 'God help us'.

288 *with an S*: Instead of with a rude C.

294–5 *Butiro . . . Anonimo*: *Butiro* is Latin for butter, *caseo* for cheese. *Decimo sexto* is the sixteenth chapter, *Anonimo* means Anonymous.

327–8 *1500 . . . forth*: A pointer to the play's composition in the late 1590s, and also an indication that if it was revised after 1600, it wasn't thought necessary to revise so thoroughly as to change this.

347 *Howlet . . . Cuckooe*: The owl is mobbed by other birds, and Cornelio supposes the cuckoo to be similarly unpopular, probably because it lays eggs in other birds' nests, i.e. behaves like a cuckolder. Compare III.1.107.

366–7 *And yee . . . Imbrierd*: 'You'll see me so entangle these tricksters, they'll be like two parts of me.' Chapman's use of the word 'Imbrierd' – meaning 'to be entangled as in briers' – is the first cited in the *OED*.

Act V. Scene 1

11–16 *My fortune . . . Guls*: *The Eunuch*, 923ff, was probably the source for what happens from here. In *The Eunuch*, Parmeno is boasting like Rynaldo about the success of his tricks, when he's approached by one of his victims with a plausible-sounding story. Parmeno betrays his master's whereabouts to his master's father, to try to avoid landing himself and his master in trouble. Compare Rynaldo and Valerio. In both cases the fathers are reconciled with their sons.

53–4 *then . . . prison*: 'Horred' has the old Latin sense of bristling with rocks. Hence the meaning is: 'Than we be trapped (by that storm) in a harbour so rocky it's like a prison.'

60–61 *a Milstone . . . amazd*: The reference to 'a Milstone' derives from the proverb 'to see far in a millstone', interpreted as 'A claim to acuteness, often used ironically' by Morris Palmer Tilley in *A Dictionary of the Proverbs in England in the Sixteenth and Seventeenth Centuries* (Ann Arbor, Michigan: University of Michigan Press, 1950). Cornelio imagines Rynaldo's head ('braine') stuck in the middle of a millstone, while 'midst' also suggests a pun on sight-baffling mist.

69 *red Lettice*: i.e. a red lattice, once a common mark of an alehouse or inn.

75 *Iam . . . pares*: 'So now we're equal.' In Volume 2 of his edition of *The Plays of George Chapman: The Comedies* (New York and London, 1914), p. 722, T. M. Parrott noted that the same phrase is used three times in Martial II.18.

Act V. Scene 2

5 *I wonder where . . . becomes*: 'I wonder what's become of.'

16 *Rialto*: The market in Venice, although the play is set in Florence (IV.1.298).

46–51 *Sfoote . . . weeke after*: 'Sfoote' is a contraction of the oath 'God's foot'. Gallants' tobacco smoking was a common subject of satire. Chapman was also interested in smoking as a form of physical infusion akin to the spiritual wonderings of art: 'which entring in at the mouth walkes through the Regions of a mans brayne, drives out all ill Vapours but itselfe' – from Monsieur D'Olive's encomium on tobacco in *Monsieur D'Olive* (1605), II.ii.254–6.

52 *A . . . io-c-um*: Latin for 'Let the drinks begin the joking.'

64 *Elephant . . . Joynts*: It was thought that elephants didn't have joints and so couldn't kneel.

76 *Sett mee*: 'Make me a bet, set a stake'.

96–101 *Come . . . againe*: Valerio speaks nonsensically to mock his father, in V.2.98–9 adapting the proverb 'Everything has an end and a pudding has two'.

124–42 *Had you . . . head in*: Compare Gostanzo's reactions to finally being put right with those of the angrily vengeful Chremes in *ST*, 900–918.

184–5 *come . . . long-tayle*: Proverbial, meaning 'Come one and all, long tail or bobtail.'

186 *tickle Dob*: There's no entry for '*Dob*' in the *OED* but it's probably a slang term for the penis. A 'tickle-tail' was a loose or wanton woman.

198–9 *Young . . . fooles*: A common proverb.

206 *Onelie to . . . stomack*: Cornelio says that he sought to curb his wife's sexuality by frightening her with the prospect of divorce. But to get the evidence for his divorce, he had to leave Dariotto and his wife alone in bed. In other words he too reveals himself to be a fool by encouraging the very thing that, in his jealousy, he ostensibly wanted to prevent. He's all the more of a fool because in another ironical twist he proudly thinks he's as 'wise' as his father (V.2.220). Cornelio's words echo those of the page in Act III. Scene 1 who mocked him by talking of the 'ancient wise Citizens' who planted gardens for their wives 'onely to keepe um from idlenesse'. Cornelio's train of thought is elaborated upon in the long speech by Valerio which follows, about how men should be proud to be cuckolds. And Cornelio's relationship with Gazetta also foreshadows that of Lysander and his wife in *The Widdowes Teares*. Lysander wants his wife to be chaste, but by his own actions corrupts her.

225 *potable*: 'Appropriate to drinking, flowing, intoxicated'. The only citation of this word in the *OED*.

226–310 *The course . . . they list*: Parrott suggests another parody of Lyly: 'the comic theme of the oration combined with the affected gravity of the treatment shows that Chapman is ridiculing the formal and elaborate discourses with which Lyly's work abounds' (*The Comedies*, p. 710). Compare Commentary on III.1.199–200.

268 *Ex nihilo nihil fit*: 'Nothing is made from nothing'. A philosophical assertion also found in *Bussy D'Ambois*, V.3.133–4.

286–8 *Lion . . . death*: An allusion to a well-known fable found in Sir Thomas More's *History of Richard III* (1543).

Epilogue

10–11 *stooles . . . welcome*: The 'stooles' are used for sitting on the stage, as in the *Prologus*, ll. 28–32. But they're also mentioned to provoke expectations of the rhyme left jokily unspoken in the next line – 'fooles'.

Bussy D'Ambois

Bussy D'Ambois was popular throughout the seventeenth century. It was probably first performed in 1604 by the Children of the Queen's Revels, as the Chapel Children became known that year. In 1605–6, the company's manager Edward Kirkham moved over to the Children at Paul's, and he must have taken *Bussy D'Ambois* with him, because when it was printed in 1607 and reprinted in 1608, the title page says it was 'often presented' there. Chapman wrote a follow-up in 1610–11, *The Revenge Of Bussy D'Ambois*, in which Bussy is given a fictional brother called Clermont, who avenges Bussy's death then kills himself. *The Revenge* was staged by a new incarnation of the Queen's Revels, who probably revived *Bussy D'Ambois* – in a reworked form

– as a commercially sensible tie-in (see 'Note on the Text' below). The Queen's Revels were managed from 1610 to 1616 by the heroic actor and playwright Nathan Field, who was well known for playing Bussy in *Bussy D'Ambois*. Field took the play with him when he joined the King's Men, Shakespeare's old company, in 1616, and he continued to star as Bussy until he died in 1619. The King's Men kept the play in their repertoire for another two decades, and it was acted at court in 1634 and 1638. *Bussy D'Ambois* was revived in the Restoration, and savagely criticized by John Dryden in his dedication to *The Spanish Fryar* (1681). It was 'improved' by Thomas D'Urfey in 1691 as *Bussy D'Ambois or The Husband's Revenge*. In his dedication, D'Urfey ranked Chapman's play among 'the Topping Tragedies' of the time, but since then it's hardly ever been performed in any of its three versions.

No written source has been found for Chapman's knowledge of the historical Bussy. It's possible that his scandalous life features in a lost play before Chapman's, to judge by the parodic-sounding line 'for trusty *Damboys* now the deed is done' (IV.1.138– 9) in Thomas Dekker's *Satiromastix* (1601); or it may simply be that Bussy was a legendary figure. There's a portrait of '*Monsieur Lambois*' as a 'most queint' French lover in Act III. Scene 1 of Chapman's own *Sir Gyles Goosecappe Knight* (1602), so even though the existence of any earlier drama is uncertain, it does seem likely that enough about Bussy was still commonly known for Chapman to be able to pick up details from English gossip, with extra information perhaps coming from his relative Edward Grimestone, whose family were diplomats in Paris. Louis de Clermont de Bussy d'Amboise was born in 1549 and brought up in the French court. By the age of 18 he was the commander of a military company. He was noted for bravery, and famous for duelling. In 1572 he used the cover of the St Bartholomew's Day massacre of Protestants in Paris to kill his Huguenot cousin Antoine de Clermont; he inherited his victim's estate. Two years later he began to affiliate himself with the Duke of Alençon, the Monsieur of *Bussy D'Ambois* and the brother of the French King Henry III. The pair's alliance made the King uneasy. In 1575 Bussy was forced to leave court after a series of contretemps; a gang tried to assassinate him in the street, probably with the King's connivance. Monsieur made him a colonel, and when Monsieur became Duke of Anjou in 1576 he made Bussy Governor of the province. In Flanders in 1578 Bussy was involved in the long-running and eventually fruitless negotiations over Monsieur's proposed marriage to the English Queen Elizabeth I (the English party was led by Sir Francis Walsingham, cousin of Sir Thomas Walsingham, to whom Chapman dedicated *The Conspiracie, And Tragedie Of Charles Duke of Byron* in 1608). Bussy was also a minor poet and scholar, he had an affair with Marguerite de Valois, wife of Henry IV, and he acted like a law unto himself. Fearsomely irascible and unruly, his behaviour as Governor of Anjou made him unpopular with both his subjects and his superiors. He was killed in 1579, after Monsieur decided to sacrifice him for the sake of reconciliation with the King. Monsieur gave the King evidence suggesting that Bussy was having an affair with the wife of the Comte de Montsoreau, Chapman's Montsurry. The King tipped off Montsoreau, and the Count then forced his wife to write a letter summoning her lover. Bussy died in an ambush at Montsoreau's chateau, after leaping out of a window and impaling himself on an iron railing. Monsieur was in England at the time, courting Elizabeth I.

Chapman turned Bussy's short life into his most theatrical play. He made free with the facts, insofar as he knew them, ideas being more important in shaping his first surviving tragedy. All the action of *Bussy D'Ambois* is condensed into two days, during which eight men die, a woman is tortured, a maid is stabbed, several devils are raised and a ghost appears to a roll of thunder. The result of this unhistorical foreshortening is to make the drama starker and more exciting. Its impact is sensational, partly because Chapman used his boy actors in a new way. R. A. Foakes first suggested that the style of the children's performance helped Chapman venture into extremities of sin, cruelty and sexual violence: 'the artifice of the dialogue, of the boys playing heroes, prevented the horror from taking its full effect, while giving the audience a thrill. It works in its own way, allowing actual tortures, the extremes of cruelty to women, to be carried out on stage, while the audience simultaneously knew the whole thing was fantastic, a charade acted by boys' (see p. 56 of 'Tragedy at the Children's Theatres after 1600: A Challenge to the Adult Stage' in *The Elizabethan Theatre* II, ed. D. Galloway (Toronto: Macmillan in collaboration with the University of Waterloo, 1970). Chapman uses all the resources of the stage to shape a series of physically telling events, such as Tamyra going into an opening vault to meet Bussy. Tamyra herself draws attention to the symbolism of this: 'See, see the gulfe is opening, that will swallow/ Me and my fame for ever . . .' (II.2.176–7). One reason for the fictional sharpening of events is to jab characters and the audience into wondering what lies behind them. Chapman always wanted his style to carry the prospect of further revelations and this dark philosophical shadowing is vital to the play's world of paradox and oscillation.

Arthur Koestler's theorizing about the life of the Second World War fighter pilot Richard Hillary is strangely congruent with *Bussy D'Ambois*. 'Usually we live and move on the plane of the *vie triviale*, but occasionally in moments of elation, danger etc we find ourselves transferred to the plane of the *vie tragique*, with its uncommon-sense cosmic perspective. One of the miseries of the human condition is that we can neither live permanently on the one nor on the other plane, but oscillate between the two' (see 'The Birth of a Myth' in *The Yogi and the Commissar and Other Essays*, London: Jonathan Cape, 1945; also pp. 200–202 of *The Fatal Englishman* by Sebastian Faulks, London: Vintage, 1997). *Bussy D'Ambois* is a difficult play because of the way it tries to dramatize the woeful convictions expressed in Chapman's poems, such as 'To *M. Harriots*' (1598), ll. 27–8: 'Thus as the soule upon the flesh depends,/ Vertue must wait on wealth' (see Commentary on ll. 27–30 of the poem). Chapman's play reaches out towards the *vie tragique* while facing up to its relationship with the *vie triviale*, a relationship which must be gone through if an 'uncommon-sense cosmic perspective' is to be realized. Bussy's perspective is set to be stellar ('Looke up and see thy spirit made a star' – V.3.265). This is why he warns his mistress Tamyra against the 'faulty apprehensions' (III.1.22) of the *vie triviale* to which he is constantly subject. In Act I. Scene 1, Monsieur fancies him as a type of the Malcontent ('discontent with his neglected worth' – I.1.47) who is common in other plays of the period, and he errs in supposing that Bussy will be ruled by him and 'wait on wealth'. Monsieur sends his steward Maffe to pay Bussy 1,000 crowns. 'I see the man,' says Maffe (I.1.175), but his confidence is also misplaced. Maffe runs through several stereotypical suppositions, thinking first that Bussy is a pamphlet-writing poet, then a poor soldier, then a jester armed with the wooden dagger of the Vice in the old Morality plays. The laughing courtiers in the next scene also mistake him, and they pay for their presumptions with their lives. Bussy's brutality – and his genius – is that he doesn't fit into any instrumental role assigned to him by others. He has an epic excessiveness, he is full of himself, he believes that he can do no wrong – 'Who to himselfe is law, no law doth neede' (II.1.203). *Bussy D'Ambois* is a fascinating play partly because it doesn't rig the terms, or evade the consequences, of encountering the world with such a perspective. It matters enormously that Bussy is a failure politically and a scandal morally, but it's also irrelevant, an oscillation which can be freeze-framed in his own reference to his 'worthlesse fall' (V.3.153). The sense of 'worthlesse' is ambiguous: it can mean that Bussy is lacking in any worth, it can also mean that his fall does not correspond to his worth.

Chapman's heroes live by a code of violent reverberation. Monsieur proposes one interpretation of Bussy's fate in a choric speech at the start of Act V. Scene 3. Nature, he proclaims, 'gives that which wee call merit to a man', only for it to cause 'his ruine', like a warship blowing up. Worth or 'merit' is presented as a state of particularly explosive paradox, and Bussy's role as a hero is to body forth a series of contradictions as dramatically as possible. Perhaps the most original of them all is that genius can be its own destroyer, and Bussy sees that when he dies (V.3.184–7), exclaiming:

> O fraile condition of strength, valure: vertue
> In me (like warning fire upon the top
> Of some steepe Beacon, on a steeper hill)
> Made to expresse it: . . .

This statement of the frailty of strength links *Bussy D'Ambois* with *The Conspiracie, And Tragedie Of Charles Duke of Byron* (1607–8), V.iii.189–98, where there's a choric passage including these lines:

> We have not any strength but weakens us,
> No greatnes but doth crush us into ayre.
> Our knowledges, do light us but to erre,
> Our Ornaments are Burthens: Our delights
> Are our tormentors; . . .

This speech is reshaped into an assertion of the importance of Learning in *The Teares of Peace* (1609), ll. 677–84. Before then, Byron too experiences the world as a state of paradox, as he approaches death (V.iv.62–5):

> ... wretched world,
> Consisting most of parts, that flie each other:
> A firmnesse, breeding all inconstancy,
> A bond of all disjunction; ...

Byron's fate is twice compared with that of the Earl of Essex who was executed in 1601 after an abortive revolt against Elizabeth I. Chapman dedicated his two Homeric translations of 1598 to the Earl of Essex, acclaiming him as '*The Most Honored Now living Instance of the Achilleian vertues*'. Chapman's version of Bussy's career is also shaped by memories of Essex. The suggestion of both plays is that the world can't accommodate such heroic figures, an outcome which reflects both on great men and the world. One effect of the condensation of the action of *Bussy D'Ambois* into two days is to reinforce the inextricability of Bussy's rise and fall ('Mans first houres rise, is first steppe to his fall./ I'le venture that' – I.1.137–8). The penultimate speech of the play describes life as a candle which 'though it upwards looke,/ Downwards must needs consume' (V.3.248–9). The wax burns down until 'It sees and dies' (V.3.253).

This drive towards paradox and moments of vision accounts for much of the notorious slipperiness of *Bussy D'Ambois*. In his poetry and his drama, Chapman is fascinated by forms of doubleness, and intrigued by the perceptual demands of inconstancy in a world of universal instability (see III.1.53–67 and IV.1.25). Hence his continued emphasis on the 'judiciall perspective' and the recurring phenomenon of 'the optike picture' (see Introduction) in which something can seem to be something else or really can be something else and, in *Bussy D'Ambois*, the emphasis on 'seeing' and the reaction of opposites. Juxtapositions, conflicts, resolutions, mirrorings, minglings and transpositions inform the structure, characterization, imagery and linguistic texture of the play. The duel described in Act II. Scene 1 is invented by Chapman to serve as one of the set pieces of a world of polarities. Other examples abound, from single letter changes ('Dames maritorious, ne're were meritorious' – II.2.84) to large plot movements ('I love what most I loath,' says Tamyra, preparing for her affair with Bussy at II.2.170).

The clearest successor to *Bussy D'Ambois* is Chapman's tragi-comedy *The Widdowes Teares*, which was probably written shortly afterwards. Both plays start with their heroes alone on the stage, scorning Fortune and discoursing on the unsatisfactory state of the world. Tharsalio dedicates himself to rising with Confidence, Bussy chooses Virtue as his guide. Both characters go in for the outrageous wooing of women of higher social rank, who find themselves irresistibly attracted to breaking vows made to their husbands. Both Tharsalio and Bussy enjoy the same theatrical coup of suddenly appearing in a splendid new suit of clothes. Further comparison would highlight the extent to which both works experiment with generic juxtapositions. Tragic pressures are brought to bear on the comedic situations of *The Widdowes Teares*, while reductive comic forces surround Bussy. Bussy's progress is echoed again in Chapman's comedy *Monsieur D'Olive* (1605). At the start of the play Monsieur D'Olive lives obscurely away from court, and he takes liberties with the ladies when he arrives. *Bussy D'Ambois* opens up possibilities which Chapman goes on to explore, as if he himself wanted to look again at what he'd done.

Bussy D'Ambois reaches into odd territories. Its story doesn't have enough world-altering weight to resonate still like *The Tragedie of Anthonie, and Cleopatra* (1606–7), although the critic Richard S. Ide believes that Chapman's probings of the heroic code provoked Shakespeare's play (see Ide's *Possessed With Greatness: The Heroic Tragedies of Chapman and Shakespeare*, London: Scolar Press, 1980). Chapman also inspired John Webster. Webster's preface to *The White Divel* (1610: printed 1612) put Chapman top of the contemporary dramatists he admired. Webster learned from Chapman the art of juxtaposing genres to produce dramatic effects of weird landscaping: there's nothing quite like them until the David Lynch film *Blue Velvet* (1986) delves into its own extremities of cruelty and sexual violence. *Bussy D'Ambois* is a work with its peers far into the future. Its strange prefigurings of the ideology of genius look forward to the more esoteric ideas of the Romantics and the Modernists, to Goethe's *The Sorrows of Young Werther* (1774), Hegel's idea of the world-historical individual, and Wyndham Lewis's and Samuel Beckett's paradoxical convictions about having to descend into the hell of life to ascend to the transcendental realm of understanding.

FURTHER READING

Altman, Joel B., *The Tudor Play of Mind: Rhetorical Inquiry and the Development of Elizabethan Drama* (Berkeley and Los Angeles: University of California Press, 1978)

Chapman, George, *Bussy D'Ambois*, ed. Nicholas Brooke (London: Methuen, 1964)

— *Bussy D'Ambois*, ed. Maurice Evans (London: Ernest Benn, 1965)

Digangi, Mario, *The Homoerotics of Early Modern Drama* (Cambridge: Cambridge University Press, 1997), pp. 124–30

Dollimore, Jonathan, *Radical Tragedy: Religion, Ideology and Power in the Drama of Shakespeare and his Contemporaries* (Brighton: John Spiers, 1984), pp. 182–8

Goldberg, Jonathan, *James I And The Politics Of Literature* (Baltimore: Johns Hopkins University Press, 1983)

Krasner, James N., 'The Tragedy of *Bussy D'Ambois* and the Creation of Heroism', *Medieval and Renaissance Drama in England*, IV (1989), pp. 107–21

Lever, J. W., *The Tragedy of State* (London: Methuen, 1987, with new introduction by Jonathan Dollimore), pp. 37–58

Melbourne, Jane, 'The Inverted World of *Bussy D'Ambois*', *Studies in English Literature*, 25 (1985), pp. 381–95

Montuori, Deborah, 'The Confusion of Self and Role in Chapman's *Bussy D'Ambois*', *Studies in English Literature*, 28 (1988), pp. 287–99

NOTE ON THE TEXT

The text is based on the first 1607 Quarto (Q1) of *Bussy D'Ambois* in The Bodleian Library, Oxford. It's been checked against the standard modern text of Q1 in *The Plays of George Chapman: The Tragedies* ed. Allan Holaday (Cambridge: D. S. Brewer, 1987). A second Quarto (Q2) was printed in 1641, declaring on its title page: 'As it hath often been Acted with Great Applause. *Being much corrected and amended by the Author before his death*'. Q1 has been preferred in this edition because in a selection, next to *The Widdowes Teares*, it's of more historical value. It's a different kind of play to Q2, and, the publisher's 1641 assertion notwithstanding, it's also widely believed to be more authentically Chapman's.

Bussy D'Ambois was probably reworked in 1610–11, refreshed to tie in with Chapman's sequel *The Revenge Of Bussy D'Ambois*. In Q2 there are dozens of changes, from the alteration of single words to the creation of new scenes. The nature and quality of these changes is so variable that Nicholas Brooke, in his Revels edition of *Bussy D'Ambois* (London: Methuen, 1964), first suggested that Chapman only went over a prompter's copy of the play, before a more thorough revision was undertaken by the heroic actor and playwright Nathan Field. Other scholars have taken issue with Brooke; there's a useful survey of the complicated arguments in the Holaday edition of *The Tragedies*. Brooke's case is none the less the most widely accepted version of the play's history, because it does make sense. Field knew *Bussy D'Ambois* and Chapman knew him. Bussy was Field's first recorded role; he was well-known for acting the part. From 1610–16 he was the manager of the Queen's Revels, who staged *The Revenge Of Bussy D'Ambois*, and probably the revised version of *Bussy D'Ambois* as well. Chapman called Field his 'loved sonne' in a commendatory poem he wrote in 1612 for Field's play *A Woman is a Weathercocke*.

It's impossible to pick out changes in Q2 which are indisputably Chapman's work. But four passages do stand out. The case for Chapman's authorship of the first and fourth instances is also supported by Brooke and Evans in their editions; the second and third by Evans as well.

The first passage comes between I.1.121 ('he will send: . . .') and I.1.122:

> Like to disparking noble Husbandmen,
> Hee'll put his Plow into me, Plow me up:
> But his unsweating thrift is policie,
> And learning-hating policie is ignorant
> To fit his seed-land soyl; . . .

The last half-line replaces 'But hee's no husband heere' (I.1.122) in Q1. The passage fits smoothly into its context, and shares Chapman's obsession with 'learning' and 'policie'.

The second instance comes between II.2.145 ('But not in him. . . .') and II.2.146: 'In mine owne dark love and light bent to another.' This line matches the play's paradoxical mixings and Chapman's gnomic style.

In the third case Evans makes the plausible suggestion that the 1641 text restores words that were simply missing from Q1, instead of adding any. At III.2.195 in Q1 Monsieur says: 'The divell he is, and thy Lady his dam: infinite regions betwixt a womans tongue and her heart: . . .' This makes a compressed kind of sense but Q2 makes more, and Monsieur's glee is entirely in keeping with the amazed rhythms of his speech and his character: 'The devill he is, and thy Lady his dam: Why this was the happiest shot that ever flew, the just plague of hypocrisie level'd it; Oh the infinite regions betwixt a womans tongue and her heart!'

The fourth instance comes between V.3.136 ('. . . even in death.') and V.3.137:

> And if *Vespasian* thought in majestie
> An Emperour might die standing, why not I? –   *She offers to help him*
> Nay without help, in which I will exceed him;
> For he died splinted with his chamber Groomes. –

Chapman's relative Edward Grimestone referred to this action on p. 990 of his *General Inventorie of the Historie of France* (1607), which was the main source for Chapman's Byron plays and used for *The Revenge Of Bussy D'Ambois*. The lines are of a high quality, and it seems very likely they are authentic.

TEXTUAL NOTES

This edition is based on the copy of the first quarto in The Bodleian Library, Oxford (shelfmark: Mal. 240 [8]). In the notes that follow, the first readings are from this edition and the second readings record those of the base text.

Act I. Scene 1

66 liv'd] lived
83 doe,] ~ ∧
99 fast,] ~?
101 Article,] ~;
103 them?] ~,
110 in-parts] ~ ∧ ~
112 smother'd] smothered
118.1 *Exit* MONSIEUR] *after l. 117 in* Q
118.1 *Manet* BUSSY] *after l. 119 in* Q
138 I'le] Il'e
139.1 *Enter*] *Ent.*
140 MAFFE] *omitted in* Q
140 Princes!] ~.
146 Sir?] ~.
152 Command,] ~;

154 open'd] opened
159 better.] ~,
168 perfect, . . . good,] ~ ∧ ~ ∧
192 Jacket)?] ~) ∧
209, 210 BUSSY] *D'Amb.*

Act I. Scene 2

0.1 DUCHESS] *Elenor*
0.1 PYRA] *Pyr.*
43 deliver'd] delivered
57 BUSSY] *D'Amb.* (*thus all speech-prefixes until l. 129*)
57–8 Thats . . . attire] Q *prints as prose*
58 alter'd] altered
65–6 I . . . merits] Q *prints as prose*
68 Duches;] ~.
98 doe't,] ~ ∧

99–102 That . . . it] Q *prints as verse,*
lining: That . . . many/ Throates
. . . of/ Many . . . owne/ Come
. . . talke?/ Talke . . . it

102.1 PYRHOT] *Pyrlot*

114 Slight,] ~ ∧

118 say,] ~ ∧

135 place ∧] ~,

147 be,] ~ ∧

152 Gallant,] ~ ∧

161 SD] Q2; *omitted in* Q1

172.1 BRISAC,] ~ ∧

173–5 O . . . you] Q *prints as verse,*
lining: O . . . selfe/ Such . . .
into/ Our . . . you

194 sir?] ~.

Act II. Scene 1

0.1 *and Attendants*] Q2; *Nuncius*

12 world ∧] ~;

25 NUNCIUS] Q2; *omitted in* Q1

47 death] ~,

60 lives,] ~;

88 tugg'd] tuggd'd

166 men;] ~,

172 murther'd] murthered

Act II. Scene 2

14 sleight,] ~:

19 perceiv'd] perceived

21 still,] ~.

24 GUISE] *omitted in* Q1

31 pleas'd] pleased

34 but,] ~;

35 grosse,] ~:

48 soule,] ~:

50 unanswer'd] unanswered

61 gone,] ~ ∧

65 i'th'] ith

73 y'are] yare

82 Put-ofs] Q2; Puttofs

108 you] Q2; your

111 TAMYRA] Q2; *Mont.*

134 charg'd] charged

136 not] no

140 you.] Q2; ~:

146 wane] waue

148 mother;] ~,

153 forme;] ~,

175 SD] Q2 (*placed after l. 173*);
omitted in Q1

178.1 SD] Q2; *omitted in* Q1

206 *Barrisor* ∧] ~,

211 note ∧] ~,

222, 268 BUSSY] *D'Amb.*

222 honour'd] honoured

274–5 And . . . (Presum'd] (And . . . ∧
Presum'd

289.1 SD] Q2 (*Exit Tamira/ and*
D'Amb,) *in margin opposite*
ll. 288–9; omitted in Q1

290.1 SD] Q2; *omitted in* Q1

Act III. Scene 1

0.1 BUSSY] *Bucy*

5 feare ∧] ~:

10 us!] ~?

14 rages,] ~;

15 gather'd] gathered

18 BUSSY] *Buc.*

27 him ∧] ~:

43 It] *Ta.* It

47 th'whole] t'whole

71 love,] ~?

Act III. Scene 2

0.1–2 DUTCHES . . . *Attendants*] Q2;
Monts./ Elenor, Tam. Pero.

59.1 SD] Q2; *omitted in* Q1

71–2 Let . . . warre] *one line in* Q

80 Lord).] ~.)

81 face (my Eagle);] ~; (~ ~) ∧

129 your] Q2; yours
130.1 SD] Q2; *Exeunt/ Henry,/ D'Amb./ Ely. Ta. (in margin after l. 130)*
146 wise ∧] Q2; ~;
154 discover'd] discovered
154 bow,] ~ ∧
163 more,] ~;
168 discovery.] ~,
172 service.] ~:
175-8 Well . . . promised] Q *prints as verse, lining:* Well . . . hands/ Now . . . mee/ For . . . concerning/ Thy Mistresse *(then prose)*
197 sleighted,] ~:
207 SD] Q2; *omitted in Q1*
211 me-] ~.
216 Countesse . . . Lady] Lady . . . Countesse (Lady . . . Lady *in* Q2)
224 one ∧] ~:
235 What,] ~ ∧
237 I, marry,] ~ ∧ ~ ∧
255 SD *Exeunt women*] Q2; *Exit.*
267 so,] ~ ~ ∧
291 How] *Mons.* How
291 BUSSY] *D'Amb. (and for rest of scene)*
320 bargaine,] ~ ∧
370 armies,] ~ ∧
400 SD] Q2; *omitted in Q1*

Act IV. Scene 1

0.1 DUCHESS] *Elynor*
7 like, my Lord,] ~ ∧ ~ ~ ∧
43 were,] ~ ∧
52 heer's] hee'rs
57, 69,
71, 75 BUSSY] *Buc.*
79-81 glories ∧ . . . hammes):] ~: . . . ~) ∧

80 flames,] Q2; ~ ∧
94 sweare):] ~).
111.1 *and Ladies*] Q2; *omitted in Q1*
115 What,] ~ ∧
124 read,] ~ ∧
128 SD *Exeunt . . . MONSIEUR*] Q2; *omitted in Q1*
132 a-] Q2 (a.-); ~.
141 SD] Q2; *omitted in Q1*
179 Augean] Egean
181 me!] ~?
209 over):] ~:)
221 a woman ∧] ~~,

Act IV. Scene 2

0.1 TAMYRA] *she*
1 SD] Q2; *omitted in Q1*
6.1 SD] *thus uncorrected* Q1; *Comolet in a* [robe?] *in uncorrected*
7, 9 BUSSY] *D'Amb.*
33 Astaroth] Asaroth
35 et] &
36-7 Hecatesque] Hecatesq. et] &
37.1 SD] Q2; Q1 *places 'Thunder' in margin opposite* tenebrarum ab-/ dita profundissima
44 call'dst] Q2; calledst
53 voices,] ~;
71 command,] ~ ∧
73 t'invoke] t'nvoke
76.1 *with a paper*] Q2; *omitted in Q1*
77 COMOLET] *Mons.*
80 them ∧] ~:
85 BEHEMOTH] *Pre (in* Q1 *text*); *Per (*Q1 *catchword*)
110.1 SD] Q2; *omitted in Q1*
113 SD] Q2; *Exit Mont. (after* y'faith *in l. 114)*
119 see,] ~ ∧
121 SD] Q2; *omitted in Q1*
121 maid,] ~ ∧

124 SD] *opposite l. 123 (as if continuing*
    'Exeunt . . . GUISE')
128 stayne] stay
136,   BUSSY] *Buc.*
137
    168 feet,] ~:
    170 SD] Q2; *omitted in* Q1

Act V. Scene 1

15 then:] ~ ∧
31 commit-] ~;
124 *Stabs her*] Q2; *omitted in* Q1
134 SD] Q2; *omitted in* Q1
136.1 SD] Q2; *omitted in* Q1
146.1 SD] *in margin opposite ll. 147–8*
148 SD] Q2; *omitted in* Q1
158 face ∧] ~:
169 SD] Q2; *omitted in* Q1
175 heere,] Q2; ~ ∧
185.1–2] Q2; *omitted in* Q1

Act V. Scene 2

1 BUSSY] *D'Amb. (and for rest of*
    scene)
2 *Exeunt*] Q2; *Exit*
6 SD] Q2; *omitted in* Q1
8.1 *Umbra* COMOLET] *Vmb.*
    Comol.
27 claime ∧] ~,
29 plain ∧] ~,
43 wake ∧ the] ~, ~
43 night,] ~;
51.1 *Thunders*] Q2 (*roman*); *omitted in*
    Q1
51.1 *suis.*] ~:
52 BEHEMOTH] *Sp. (and for rest*
    of scene)
61 Fates] fates
67 summons;] ~,
68 die;] ~ ∧

70 obay ∧ . . . commands,] ~, . . .
    ~ ∧
72 will, to life:] ~: ~~,
73 me,] ~:
80 *Knocks*] Q2; *omitted in* Q1
84 father.] ~ ∧
85 ever,] ~ ∧
98 *Exeunt*] Q2; *Exit*

Act V. Scene 3

1 Nature] nature
12, 29 Nature] Q2; nature
29 randome,] ~ ∧
43 stand;] Q2; ~ ∧
51 *Euxine*] euxine
56 *Umbra* ∧] *vmbra,*
57 UMBRA] *omitted in* Q1; *Frier*
    Q2
64, 75 TAMYRA] Q2; *Count.*
74 *Exit*] Q2; *omitted in* Q1
83 i'th] ith'
88 fate] Fate
89.1 SD] Q2; *omitted in* Q1
89 1 MURDERER] Q2 (*I*
    Murth.); 1.
90.1 SD *all but the first*] Q2; *omitted in*
    Q1
91 1 MURDERER] 1.
97 He is,] ~~ ∧
110 protect,] ~ ∧
113.1 SD] *all the murtherers*] Q2; *others.*
117.1 SD] Q2; *omitted in* Q1
118 Favour my Lord,] ~ (~~)
120 SD] Q2; *omitted in* Q1
120 Fates] Q2; fates
124 Death and Destinie,] death and
    destinie ∧
143 perfumes] Q2; perfines
144 spices;] ~,
146 shoulders ∧] ~,
162 And] *Bus.* And; Q2 *has* Now
174 broken.] ~ ∧

175 *Guise,*] ~.
179–80 snow), ... liver, ... vains] ~ ∧
  ... ~; ~)
189 *Moritur*] Q2; *omitted in* Q1
190 soule ∧] ~,
191–4 heaven ... bloud);] ~; ... ~) ∧
212 place,] ~:

225 offence.] ~,
231 full ∧] ~,
236 open'd] opened
244 (With hands held] ∧ ~~ (~
260.1 *Exeunt ... severally*] Q2; *omitted in* Q1

COMMENTARY

Act I. Scene 1

SD *Bussy solus*: 'Bussy alone'. In the revised version printed in 1641 (see 'Note on the text') this SD becomes '*Enter* BUSSY D'AMBOIS *poore*', thus making more explicit the contrast with the wealthy appearance of '*MONSIEUR with two Pages*' at I.1.33 SD.

1 *Fortune ... things*: Translated from Plutarch's essay 'Of Fortune' in the *Moralia*, possibly via Cicero's *Tuscan Disputations*, V.25.

10 *Tympanouse statists*: Compare l. 78 of 'To *M. Harriots*' (1598): 'Timpanies of state'.

6–17 *So great ... and lead*: Closely translated from 'To an uneducated Ruler' in Plutarch's *Moralia*.

18–19 *a Dreame ... shadow*: Translated from Pindar's 'Pythian Ode 8', probably out of Erasmus's *Adagia* (1500). The phrase is picked up again at V.3.131–4.

33 SD *Procumbit*: 'He lies down.'

39–40 *no tracts ... facts*: 'No tracks or imprints for poor men to follow as precedents for their actions.'

59–81 *That ... wee live*: Translated from the essay 'Whether it was rightly said, one ought to live in obscurity' in Plutarch's *Moralia* and in ll. 69–70 from his *Life of Camillus*.

100–101 *Beleeve backewards ... in God*: A reference to the Black Magic practice of inverting the liturgy to conjure up devils. Compare the 'black *Santus*' in *The Widdowes Teares* (1604–5), IV.3.36.

113–4 *rude Scythians ... wings*: The barbarous ('rude') Scythians lived north of the Black Sea. Fortune is traditionally represented as 'blind' to emphasize her randomness. Chapman may have seen the Scythians' emblem reproduced in Cartari's *Le Imagini dei Dei degli Antichi* (1568).

118 SD *Manet Bussy*: 'Bussy remains.'

132–3 *As Rhetoricke ... it worke*: Adapted from Plutarch's 'Precepts of Statecraft' in the *Moralia*.

134–9 *So ... skie*: Compare the devil Ophioneus in Chapman's tragedy *Caesar And Pompey* (1604–5), II.i.110–14: 'Nor skils it for degrees in a knave, or a fooles preferment; Thou shalt rise by fortune: let desert rise leisurely enough, and by degrees; fortune preferres headlong, and comes like riches to a man; huge riches being got with little paines, and little with huge paines.' Compare also V.3.19 where 'huge riches' recurs, and *The Widdowes Teares*, I.1.60–63.

140 *Humor*: Elizabethan physiology held that a person's temperament was conditioned by the balance of the body's four fluids – blood, phlegm, choler, melancholy. Blood is particularly linked with sexual passion, e.g. at II.2.49.

189 *faire great Noses*: Monsieur was an ugly man, with a large deformed nose, divided at the end by smallpox, a feature taken to symbolize his two-faced nature.

191–2 *What Qualities ... Jacket*: The 'chaine' and 'Jacket' symbolize the steward's role. Bussy is asking Maffe whether he has any merits ('Qualities') beyond these outward accoutrements. Compare the question put by Bussy about the Guise at III.2.85–6: 'Prooves he th'Opinion/ That mens soules are without them?'

195 *Knights place*: The first of several allusions to James I's creation of a large number of new knights after his accession in 1603. The King's enlargement of his Privy Council by new Scottish knights was frequently satirized. The allusion here is a pointer to the date of the play as post-1603.

204 *wodden dagger*: Traditionally carried by the Vice in the old Morality plays and Interludes, and sometimes carried by Elizabethan jesters. Compare the Governor in *The Widdowes Teares* (1604–5), V.5.158.

Act I. Scene 2

12 *old Queene*: Elizabeth I, who died in 1603. Not a remark likely to have been made on the English stage when she was still alive.

22 *The world ... man*: The Medieval and Renaissance idea is that man is a microcosm of the world.

37–48 *No Question ... of men*: Englishmen's aping of foreign fashions is often satirized in this period.

70 *too many ... Counsell*: Another allusion to James I's enlargement of his Privy Council with new Scottish knights.

77 *leape yeeare*: 1604 was a leap year, and possibly therefore the date of this play. Women are allowed to propose in a leap year. Sexual innuendo runs throughout these lines: a ram is said to 'leap' when he mounts a ewe.

99–100 *y'ave ... Guise*: The Guise played a large part in the St Bartholomew's Day massacre of Protestants in Paris in 1572, the subject of Marlowe's play *Massacre at Paris* (*c.*1592).

106 *Knight ... edition*: An allusion to James I's creation of new Scottish knights.

112 *the Knights ward*: The second-best class of accommodation in the Counters, London's two prisons for debtors. Best was the Master's Side, then the Knight's Ward, then the Twopenny Ward, then the Hole.

135–7 *Ardor ... surges*: Monsieur is explaining why the waves of the sea will never 'retreat' before they've broken. 'Ardor' means burning heat and refers to the sun ('the starr's dailie ... motion'). The next clause means 'partly because of the diverse frames of the place', those being the sea-bed and other features of the land which shape the sea's movement. 'Bristled with surges' means the sea is frothing with waves.

143—4 *Lion . . . Cocke*: Popular superstition held that lions were afraid of cocks crowing.

148 *new denizond*: An allusion to the entourage of James I, newly naturalized from Scotland.

154—6 *the Asse . . . the Forrest*: An allusion to one of Aesop's fables. Compare *The Widdowes Teares*, V.5.94—6.

159 *blanquet*: Being tossed in a blanket was a punishment. Compare *The Widdowes Teares*, I.2.86—8.

181 *descants . . . ground*: In music a 'ground' is a tune, a 'descant' is a melodic accompaniment. Here the 'ground' for comment is Bussy's suit and behaviour, the 'descants' are what Bussy regards as the la-di-da comments of Barrisor and his friends. 'Ground' also means 'this ground we're standing on' – the King's presence-chamber where fighting is not allowed (see Bussy wishing it was at III.2.66—7) – and thus a safe place for insults.

Act II. Scene 1

24 SD *NUNCIUS*: Messenger descended from Greek Tragedy via Seneca, parodied in *The Widdowes Teares*, IV.1.45 ff. Chapman was saturated in the works of Seneca, whose plays were almost certainly written to be read aloud rather than performed, so what couldn't be seen had to be conjured rhetorically. The use in this scene of the Nuncius' traditional epic style fits Chapman's conception of *Bussy D'Ambois* as a heroic tragedy. Seneca's nine plays were a massive influence on Elizabethan and Jacobean drama. Just as Chapman adapted classical sources for comedies such as *All Fooles* and *The Widdowes Teares*, so he turned to Seneca for what may have been his first tragedy. The end of the play draws particularly closely on *Hercules Oetaeus*.

35—42 *I saw . . . met them*: There was a three-sided duel between followers of the King and the Guise in France in 1578, although Bussy was not involved. Duels were common in France: J. W. Lever notes that between 1601 and 1609 some 2,000 French noblemen died fighting duels in defence of their honour (*The Tragedy of State*, London: Methuen, 1987), p. 42.

54—6 *Hector . . . warre*: In Chapman's translation of *The Iliads Of Homer* (1611), III.73—85, Paris offers to fight a duel with Menelaus to end the Trojan War. Hector rushes 'betwixt the fighting hoasts and made the Troyans cease/ By holding up in midst his lance.'

84—7 *Thrice . . . scap't*: In these lines 'He' refers to Bussy, 'him' to Barrisor.

94—101 *an Oke . . . Earth*: Based on a simile in Virgil's *Aeneid*, II.626—32.

110 *two opposite fumes*: 'The exhalations which, when trapped in a cloud, cause thunder by their breaking out' (Note by Maurice Evans in his edition of *Bussy D'Ambois*, London: Ernest Benn, 1965).

119—23 *An angrie . . . Earth*: The treasure of a unicorn's brow is his horn, reckoned to be an antidote against all poisons. The horn was supposed to be obtained by standing in front of a tree, then moving when the unicorn charged, so it impaled itself. Compare Spenser's *Faerie Queene* (1590), II.V.10.

130 *hunt . . . at the view*: A hunting term. 'Pursue Honour like hounds which have spotted their quarry at the end of a chase.'

141–8 *If ever . . . a King*: Monsieur's speech can be paraphrased: 'If Nature can ever be truly herself when a King and his subject (who's also his brother) are in conflict, show now either that the ties of greatness between King and subject and the ties of virtue between brother and brother are as powerful as each other, or demonstrate (as a true King should) that both can be made even greater, by acting in accordance with the special love that exists between us brothers, and doing what you couldn't do if you weren't a King (i.e. pardon Bussy for murder).'

150–59 *Manly . . . and take*: Monsieur argues that the 'manly slaughter' of duelling, where 'equall life is laid in equall ballance', is a type of justice which can redress offences outside the scope of the ordinary law. Men value the natural law of reputation more highly than codified 'positive law', and when positive law does not provide for the satisfactory righting of wrongs, free men should be able to seek their own remedies.

190–204 *This is . . . King indeede*: The King has just said that Bussy 'merited death' (II.1.182). Bussy disagrees. He argues that he has not broken any 'just law', and he kneels at II.1.190 because he wants the King to accept that 'man was made' to be free, and should have the right to act when the ordinary law fails. The King later accepts Bussy's claims when he praises his 'native noblesse' (III.2.91).

Act II. Scene 2

31 SD *Exit cum Guise*: 'He leaves with Guise.'

33 SD *Exit cum suis [Charlotte and Pyrha]*: 'He leaves with them [Charlotte and Pyrha].'

34–41 *as when . . . fury*: Tamyra expounds the classical theory of the cause of earthquakes. The fume is male, the Earth female.

60–63 *Honour . . . Abides*: 'Thing' refers both to the female genitals which Monsieur, drawing on philosophical distinctions, says are unaltered by the loss of the 'second maidenhead' of Honour; and to the penis, hence 'the stalke/ Abides'.

120–23 *their prerogatives . . . their essence*: In paraphrase: 'Princes appear to take laws seriously while Parliament is sitting, then use Royal prerogatives to cancel them out, just as they grant pardons, and effectively negate them with reservations. They are only bothered with appearances.'

164 *the Center*: The centre of the ten revolving spheres of the universe as first mooted by Ptolemy.

178 SD *Ascendit Frier [COMOLET] and* D'AMBOIS: 'Frier [Comolet] and D'Ambois ascend.'

194 *the first Orbe Move*: The Primum Mobile or outer sphere in the Ptolemaic universe, which sets the other ones in motion.

227–8 *If not . . . satisfi'd*: 'If she is not given opportunity to dissemble or show petulance, she's not satisfied even if she gains her wish' (Note by F. S. Boas in his edition of *Bussy D'Ambois* and *The Revenge Of Bussy D'Ambois*, The Belles-Lettres Series: 1905).

234–5 *Humour . . . fed*: The liver was supposed to turn the elements in food into the four humours which would then be taken to the necessary parts of the body by the blood, and there form a person's temperament – that's why people must be 'humoured'.

291 SD *Descendit Fryar*: 'Fryar descends.'

Act III. Scene 1

21–4 *empty clouds . . . no proportion*: A common simile derived from *The Clouds* by Aristophanes. Compare Shakespeare's *The Tragedie of Anthonie, and Cleopatra* (1606–7), IV.xii.2–3.

31 *our three powers*: Three powers were thought to be linked with three parts of the body: the rational soul – the brain; the sensitive soul – the heart; the vegetable soul – the liver.

43 SD *Manet Tamyra*: 'Tamyra remains.'

49–50 *silly cobweb . . . labours*: Possibly an allusion by the adulterous Tamyra to the web woven every day and unwoven every night by Odysseus' chaste wife Penelope to deter suitors. See Homer's *Odyssey*, II.93ff, XIX.139ff, XXXIV.128ff. Compare *The Widdowes Teares*, I.1.139–40 and II.3.18–19.

50–52 *that laies . . . oppos'd*: 'Our powers are set by Nature, just as in wall-building stones should be laid according to the plumb-line that's suspended from above, and not vice versa.' The image may derive from the essay 'How a man may become aware of his progress in virtue' in Plutarch's *Moralia*, or from Aristotle's *Ethics*, V.10.

61–3 *Even . . . to us*: 'Even the sun can't shine on us until the mists his heat drew up ('exhales') have cleared.'

92–3 *All couplings . . . married*: An idea possibly taken from Book III of Plutarch's *Symposium*.

104–5 *Each . . . selfe*: Compare *Ovids Banquet of Sence* (1595), 72.6–7.

Act III. Scene 2

4–5 *thou . . . wings*: Jove's eagle bore thunder beneath its wings. See Commentary on l. 17 of 'De Guiana, Carmen Epicum' (1596).

13 *bootes of haie-ropes*: Hay was sometimes coiled around the legs instead of boots.

18 *red hair'd man*: Red wigs were traditionally worn on the English stage by Jews such as Marlowe's *The Jew of Malta* (1592), where Barabas poisons a well. Compare also ll. 89–90 of Chapman's *A Justification Of A Strange Action Of Nero; In burying with a solemne Funerall, One of the cast Hayres of his Mistresse Poppaea* (1629): 'red hayre on a man is a signe of treachery'.

31–6 *Himselfe . . . upright*: The 'great man' and his 'subordinate slaves' rise high up from the earth, like woodmongers carrying billets on the 'turning proppes' of a cart.

By 'Let him' Bussy is saying what the great man must do to keep the show on the road. It's difficult to 'Keepe all upright', when the wheels of the cart are also those of ever-changing (Protean) law, and the great man has to keep his advisers and everything secret. Overall it's an image of shiftiness.

37 *the Vulture*: An allusion to the eagle feeding on Prometheus' liver. Compare *Ovids Banquet of Sence*, 41.1 and Commentary.

43–6 *luxurious . . . Hebrew*: Bussy is thinking of a clergyman with a taste for expensive food ('luxurious gut') and more than one parish ('superfluous Cures'). 'Quintessence' is the 'fifth essence' of ancient and medieval philosophy, the substance of which heavenly bodies were supposed to be composed; and 'their Quintessence' refers both to the best parts of the revenues ('rents') the clergyman takes from his parishioners, and the best parts of the game birds he spends those revenues on. 'Venting' pictures the clergyman excreting food and money through his back passage – Hebrew is read backwards.

69 *popular purple*: The imperial colour (hence 'braves thy soveraigne'). Guise wore it in Paris to impress the people.

78–9 *Th'art . . . Ambois*: The Cardinal was Georges, Archbishop of Rouen, who died in 1510 and was actually Bussy's great-uncle. Bussy, Monsieur and the Guise are quarrelling about the definition of nobility, Bussy arguing it stems from innate merit, Monsieur and the Guise from pedigrees. Compare Commentary on ll. 327–31 of *The Teares of Peace* (1609).

86 *Duke*: A play on words – 'Duke' derives from 'dux', Latin for leader.

104–5 *sticke . . . Saturne*: The 'world of *Saturne*' is the Golden Age, hence 'golden fagot'.

136–9 *and as . . . his pride*: The 'giant' is Typhon who was destroyed with a thunderbolt ('*Jove*'s great ordinance') when he challenged Jove and was buried under Aetna. Typhon's parentage is uncertain. He was either the child of Juno (with whom Monsieur compares himself) or of Tartarus and Ge (Earth).

147–8 *women . . . candles*: From the proverb: 'He that worst may hold the Candle.' Meaning that women are unsuitable to guide men, but because they do they can cast light on affairs. The candles are also phallic.

221 *drie . . . bisket*: Dryness is a sign of chastity, moistness of amorousness. Compare Shakespeare's *Othello* (1602–4), III.iv.36–44. The liver is the seat of love and passion, so 'hard as a bisket' means Pero is supposed to be unyielding.

229–32 *windfals . . . no portions*: Sexual innuendo. 'Windfals' refers to fruit which is literally and morally 'loose' and so 'falls' easily to the ground. 'Rotten' makes Monsieur think of medlars, which must be eaten when they're rotten and split open, hence the name 'openarses'. 'Portions' means both dowries and virginal sexual parts.

240–45 *What's that . . . neerest*: The answer to Pero's riddle is her maidenhead, i.e. her 'chastity' (III.2.249).

274–7 *O . . . Charibdis*: Probably expanded from ll. 233–6 of Seneca's *Hercules Oetaeus*.

278 *monster-formed*: The clouds are monstrous in themselves, and because they've been formed by Scylla and Charybdis, who want to hide in them. Compare III.1.21–8 and III.1.59.

288 *spirit . . . circle*: The magician's magic circle was supposed to protect him from any devil ('spirit') he raised. Compare ll. 675–6 of *The Teares of Peace*.

351–6 *Thou . . . pride*: 'Eat'st thy heart in vineger' is a phrase meant to indicate Bussy's brooding discontent. 'Gall' refers to the gall-bladder's function in Humour theory of controlling the level of choler in the blood. Bussy's blood is 'poison' because the acidity ('vineger') of his disposition and his bitter gall are unbalancing his humours. Hence the ugly and corrupted 'Tode-poole' of his 'complexion' – meaning skin and temperament. Hence also the 'cold and earthie moisture' like that of the 'Tode-poole' where toads breed. The moisture is 'damme' (mother) to Bussy's putrefaction, and a 'plague' to his pride because pride stems from opposing sorts of humours, which are hot and dry. This is why Bussy's pride is also obstructed ('damn'd'); and there's a further play on 'damn'd' as in cursed.

387 *kisse . . . engender*: Compare *The Revenge Of Bussy D'Ambois* (1610–11), I.ii.32: 'Learne to kisse horror, and with death engender.'

Act IV. Scene 1

54–6 *your great . . . liver*: Compare the references to eagles and Prometheus at III.2.4–5 and III.2.37. Tamyra's liver – the seat of love and passion – is said to be 'craggy' because of her apparent disdain for Bussy.

120–21 *Meere Cynthia . . . Nature*: Cynthia is the Goddess of Chastity and the moon, as in 'Hymnus in Cynthiam' in Chapman's *The Shadow Of Night* (1594). 'Meere' is used in its old sense of 'pure' and in its main modern sense ('She's only a Cynthia'). 'Meere' thus points to the paradox used by Monsieur to torment Montsurry: that the pure chaste moon has 'hornes' (e.g. when it's a quarter-full) but that 'hornes' are also the sign of a cuckold. Monsieur is telling Montsurry that it's in his wife's nature to make him a cuckold.

123 *not speake*: Monsieur promised Pero that he would not say what she told him about Bussy and Tamyra, so he's written it down instead.

141 SD *She seemes to sound*: 'She seems to swoon.'

173–4 *Comes . . . prooves*: 'If the blot on my honour comes from Monsieur, it's a thing of beauty in me, and proves my innocence.' The three stories which follow are put together as examples of innocence in Natalis Comes's compendium *Mythologiae* (1551), to which Chapman often resorted for illustrative material, e.g. in *The Shadow Of Night*.

181–3 *How . . . in chace*: Monsieur left as soon as Tamyra entered at IV.1.128, hence 'How his guilt shunn'd me!' Sacred innocence frightens what it's afraid of – Monsieur, who was hunting it, fled.

185–6 *teeth . . . up*: A reference to Jason (the leader of the Argonauts) or Cadmus or both. They both sowed dragon's teeth from which sprang hostile soldiers.

Act IV. Scene 2

32–7 *Occidentalium . . . amabili*: 'Commander of the western legions of spirits, (the great Behemoth himself) come, come, attended by your invincible lieutenant *Asteroth*. I adjure you by the inscrutable mysteries of the Styx, by those very circles of Avernus from which there is no return: appear O Behemoth, you who can open the strong-boxes of the Great Ones; come, through the deepest secret places of the Night and darkness; through the gliding stars; through the stealthy motions of the hours, and the deep silence of Hecate: show yourself in the form of a spirit, luminous, resplendent, and lovely'. The Styx is one of the nine underworld rivers; the gods swore their most solemn oaths by it. Avernus is a deep lake in woods in Italy, 'the poisonous effluvium from which was said to kill birds flying over it' (*OED*). The lake was supposed to lead to the underworld: metaphorically it stood for 'the infernal regions'. The '*Thunder*' that accompanies the devils' ascent is matched in *Caesar And Pompey*, II.i.24 SD: '*Thunder, and the Gulfe opens, flames issuing; and Ophioneus ascending, with the face, wings, and taile of a Dragon; a skin coate all speckled on the throat.*' The greater detail given here suggests why Tamyra requests 'some beautous forme'.

37.1 SD *CARTOPHYLAX*: Means 'guardian of papers', hence Behemoth's speech at IV.2.60–62.

63 SD *a torch removes*: Cartophylax is carrying a lighted torch, probably soaked in spirits to achieve the 'blew fires' of IV.2.51.

110.1 SD *a Letter*: The one Tamyra wrote and gave Pero to deliver at IV.2.1.

135 SD *Descendit cum suis*: Means that Behemoth descends with his devils.

Act V. Scene 1

13–14 *lawrell . . . sleeper*: Superstition held that lightning never struck laurel trees or people sleeping.

38–40 *Who . . . hell*: Montsurry is 'a soule a hell' because he is about to 'passe the verge that boundes a Christian' (V.1.34) and he feels no faith. This is why he cannot move the 'mountaine' from his heart (compare Jove's crushing giants under mountains at V.3.178–83) or open the Biblical furnace from Daniel 3:19. The word 'set' means 'to write a musical composition for certain voices' (*OED*).

57 *Fame . . . going*: Proverbial from Virgil's *Aeneid*, IV.173–5.

57–9 *in the . . . extinguish*: 'Excuses make things worse, just as fires are made worse by winds that would only put out smaller flames'; i.e. they would not matter in the case of an ordinary person.

61 *ruffin Gallie*: i.e. Bussy.

62 *nets*: Mars and Venus were caught in Vulcan's net when they committed adultery. Compare l. 6 of *The Teares of Peace* and *All Fooles* (1599), III.1.270–71.

64 *spawne of Venus*: Venus' child, i.e. Bussy. Spawn also means semen.

65–7 *That . . . deceit*: Brooke (in his edition of *Bussy D'Ambois*, London: Methuen, 1964) first pointed out that 'quit' has three meanings. Bussy has (ac)quitted his manhood in Tamyra's lap, and will now leave (quit) his life in a tomb because Montsurry is going to (re)quit(e) Bussy by luring him to his death with Tamyra's letter. Tamyra's 'deceit' is her previous show of chastity which didn't deceive Bussy because he was having an affair with her, but Montsurry now gloats because Bussy is going to be deceived.

77 *Comets*: Traditional omens of disaster.

132–3 *I will . . . monster*: 'I am behaving like a monster, because you are, and in stabbing you again, I'm proving that.'

153 *earth . . . still*: It was thought that the heavens moved around the earth, Copernicus suggested otherwise. Compare ll. 215–16 of *The Teares of Peace*.

Act V. Scene 2

39–42 *O thou . . . the world*: See the discussion of this passage in the Introduction.

51 SD *Surgit . . . suis*: Translates as 'The Spirit springs up with his', i.e. Behemoth rises with his devils.

83 *O lying Spirit*: Bussy thinks that Behemoth has lied to him and the Friar is still alive.

Act V. Scene 3

SD *Enter . . . above*: i.e. onto the balcony above the stage.

49–56 *Not so . . . hate*: Closely adapted from Seneca's *Agamemnon*, ll. 64–72, possibly via Comes's *Mythologiae*.

81–3 *Who dares . . . death*: 'Who dares come within my range, or fancies his chances in a face-to-face fight, when the weapon in my hand means death.'

130–31 *Man is . . . servant*: Blood and mind, body and soul, passion and reason.

133–4 *Nothing . . . shade*: 'Everything is created out of nothing, everything comes to nothing, so things' being is insubstantial.' Compare *All Fooles*, V.2.268 and Commentary.

138–9 *The equall . . . side*: Compare Seneca's *Hercules Oetaeus*, ll. 1741–2, where Hercules rises upright amidst the flames of his funeral pyre.

143–51 *haste thee . . . dwellers*: Closely adapted from *Hercules Oetaeus*, ll. 1518–27. 'O splendour of the world, radiant Titan [i.e. the sun],/ at whose first warmth Hecate/ eases the weary mouths of her nocturnal horses,/ tell the Sabaeans who are placed under Aurora [i.e. the dawn, the east],/ tell the Hiberians who are placed under the sunset [i.e. the west],/ and those who suffer under the wagon of the bear [i.e. the arctic],/ and those who are stricken by your incandescent axeltree [i.e. the equator, the tropics],/ tell them that Hercules is hasting down to the eternal spirits,/ and towards the kingdom of the unresting dog,/ from where he shall never come back.' The 'wagon of the bear' is linked with the Arctic because the constellation of the Little Bear includes the Pole Star, although the Great Bear is more usually linked with the figure of the wagon (Chapman's 'chariot'). In Bussy's speech, the sorcerous

Hecate may be 'Cround with a grove of oakes' because groves of oaks were sacred to the Druids who performed rituals there.

157 *take my sword*: Compare Hercules' gift of his bow and arrows to Philoctetes in *Hercules Oetaeus*, l. 1648.

178–83 *My sunne . . . bloud*: These lines draw on the Biblical Book of Revelation 6:12 ('and the moon became as blood') and 8:8–11: 'a great mountain burning with fire was cast into the sea; and the third part of the sea became blood; . . . and the third part of the ships were destroyed . . . and there fell a great star from heaven . . . and many men died of the waters, because they were made bitter.' These verses coalesce with passages in *Hercules Oetaeus*, particularly l. 1228, and ll. 1308–10. Jean Jacquot (in his edition of *Bussy D'Amboise*, Paris, 1960) first suggested they fused in Chapman's mind because of the Latin word '*ossa*'. In l. 1228, Hercules describes the pain he feels in the fire which is burning up his bones: '*Nec ossa durant ipsa* (My bones themselves do not keep their hardness).' Lines 1308–10 read: 'send forth from the Sicilian peak, O father/ the burning Titans on me, to seize Pindus in a hand/ and Ossa, to crush me by hurling a mountain.' Hercules' pyre is on Oeta and he looks out over Pindus and Ossa. Bussy first feels like Hercules as Tamyra's blooded white breasts remind him of Pindus and Ossa, but he also feels like the Titans buried under the mountains 'Laid on' him. Monsieur predicted at III.2.139 that Bussy would be struck 'under th'*AEtna* of his pride'.

189 SD *Moritur*: 'He dies.'

206–11 *O wretched . . . sides*: Adapted from Seneca's *Hercules Oetaeus*, ll. 1027–30.

252 *first parents*: The honey-producing bees, and, more generally, Adam and Eve, as the candle ('Taper' at V.3.248) is an emblem of life.

262 *pennance*: The Friar has come from Purgatory and is about to go back there to continue his penance.

265–70 *Looke up . . . humanity*: Hercules became a star in *Hercules Oetaeus* after burning to death.

The Widdowes Teares

The Widdowes Teares was first printed in 1612 after 'many desired' to see it published. It was probably written in 1604 or early 1605, shortly after *Bussy D'Ambois*. The play was first acted at the indoor Blackfriars theatre by the Children of the Queen's Revels, who in 1609 moved to the indoor Whitefriars, part of an old monastery, and also performed it there. The company's leading actor by this time was Nathan Field, who was well known for playing Bussy in Chapman's tragedy *Bussy D'Ambois* (1604) and may also have appeared as Tharsalio in *The Widdowes Teares*. The last known performance of *The Widdowes Teares* was on 27 February 1613, when it was acted at court for Prince Charles. It was among a group of 108 plays allotted for performance in the 1668/69 theatrical season at the Theatre Royal in London, but there's no record of its performance then, nor of any commercial staging since.

All of Chapman's early plays put women to the test. They are often married to jealous husbands, like Gazetta to Cornelio in *All Fooles* (1599), and their situation is a source of unhappiness to them ('humors, humors' complains Gazetta – I.2.53) and entertainment to others. *The Widdowes Teares* puts a spectacular end to the parade of mere humours. Chapman's new twist is to test out two widows, and give vent to the period's conflicting views about how widows should behave. In theory, widows were respected for being chaste and faithful to the memory of their spouses. In practice, they were expected to be lusty, because they'd had sex before and were bound to want it again. 'Younger men and impoverished gentlemen were particularly attracted to rich widows, hoping to restore their fortune and then outlive the widow ...' remarks Rene Juneja in an essay about *The Widdowes Teares* (see Further Reading below). Tharsalio in *The Widdowes Teares* is an impoverished younger son. He fears that when his older brother Lysander dies, Lysander's wife Cynthia will marry 'some yong Prodigall' (II.3.77) who will speed through what remains of the wealth of their ancient family. Part of the reason Tharsalio pursues the wealthy widow Eudora is that he wants to restore his family's fortunes. He's realistic about widows remarrying, asking rhetorically why should 'a yong Ladie, Gallant, Vigorous, full of Spirit, and Complexion; her appetite newe whetted with Nuptiall delights ... be confind to the speculation of a deaths head' (III.1.155–7). Tharsalio shows none of the abhorrence for the breaking of vows that's expressed by Lysander and Cynthia, nor any of the revulsion for 'honying, and making love/ Over the nasty stie' that so marks *Hamlet* (III.iv.83–4). *The Widdowes Teares* glances several times at Shakespeare's play, and adapts one of its central features. In *Hamlet* (1600) the King's widow marries the man who murdered her husband, although she doesn't know he murdered him. In *The Widdowes Teares*, Lysander's widow commits herself to a man who tells her that he has murdered her husband. Chapman's aim was to go beyond his sources and his own previous comedies.

    The Widdowes Teares is more cynically sophisticated than *All Fooles* and Chapman's earlier humour plays. Characters' names still proclaim their natures, but they're expected to do more than stage a display of 'variable humours', like players in *The Blinde begger of Alexandria* (1596). Tharsalio's name derives from the Greek for boldness and confidence, as well the English word 'tarse', a slang term for the penis. He's meant to put himself about, and he does, but – post-*Bussy D'Ambois* – Chapman is fascinated by the overdrive this can lead to. The savage glitter and exhilarating disillusionment of *The Widdowes Teares* is akin to *The Revengers Tragedie* (printed 1607) by Tourneur or Middleton, where the characters relentlessly overdo the destinies set out for them in their Italianate names. *The Revengers Tragedie* takes the old Morality plays as far as they can go, and *The Widdowes Teares* explores what happens when the spirit of intrigue safely contained in a comedy like *All Fooles* is let out. Chapman's Jacobean drama is more piercing and aggressive; more attention is paid to consequences. As Lycus says, rebuking Tharsalio for questioning Cynthia's sincerity at Lysander's funeral: '. . . you may jest; men hunt Hares to death for their sports, but the poore beasts die in earnest: . . .' (IV.1.31–2). New Comedy has gone sour. Rynaldo in *All Fooles* wants to have fun, 'to sowe/ The seede of mirth amongst us' (I.1.406–7), and Tharsalio too hopes for merriment: 'Not unlesse you'le promise mee to laugh at it, for without your applause, Ile none' (I.1.50–51). But whereas Rynaldo is known for his 'learning', Tharsalio has what some other characters – notably Cynthia and Lysander – regard as a reductive debasing view of humanity. Tharsalio's retort is that his experiences have taught him to '. . . see with cleare eies, and to judge of objects, as they truly are, not as they seeme, and through their maske to discerne the true face of thinges' (I.1.128–31). The play examines whether the knowledge of human weakness is indeed liberating or debilitating, and whether ignorance is better than curiosity. It takes its mordant flavour from the strength of its drive towards the unmasking of frailty.

The source of the main plot of *The Widdowes Teares* is the story of the Widow of Ephesus, as told by the Roman poet Petronius in his *Satyricon*. Chapman was the first dramatist to adapt this tale for the theatre. It's a simple story. The Widow is famous for vowing that she'll be chaste after the death of her husband, but she isn't. When he does die, she follows his body into the tomb, and continues to mourn there, with her maid. Then, after five days of sorrowing and hunger, a soldier arrives. He persuades the maid to share his supper, and they both urge the widow to eat and drink with them. She relents, one thing leads to another, and the soldier and the widow end up having sexual intercourse and spending three nights together. The soldier is supposed to be guarding the bodies of some robbers hung up on crosses nearby, and when the parents of one crucified wretch spot he's not on duty, they take their son's body down for proper burial. The punishment for any soldier losing a body is death. The Widow suggests they avoid this penalty by replacing the missing body with her husband's. This is done overnight, and in the morning people wonder how a dead man managed to ascend the cross. The tale is told as an entertainingly cynical anecdote and all the listeners in the *Satyricon* roar with laughter except one man who says the governor of the province should have crucified the Widow.

Chapman follows Petronius' story quite closely in Acts IV and V, but he also makes some significant changes. The most important twist is that Cynthia's husband Lysander is not really dead. He pretends that he's been killed on a business trip so that he can come back and test her chastity, by disguising himself as the cross-guarding soldier. He doesn't do this in a self-delighting way, like Count Hermes cuckolding himself in *The Blinde begger of Alexandria*. He recoils from the prospect of sexual intercourse and racks Cynthia more by telling her that he murdered her husband. Chapman himself invents the plot of the first half of *The Widdowes Tears* – Tharsalio's wooing of Eudora – to give Lysander motives for this strange behaviour. Lysander laughs at Tharsalio's initial lack of success with Eudora, and Tharsalio repays him by sowing doubts in his mind about Cynthia's chastity. He makes Lysander jealous just as Valerio does Cornelio in *All Fooles*, and the logic of jealousy in Chapman's plays is that it leads to what its sufferers want to avoid. Cornelio's wife Gazetta points out that '. . . too violent rigour,/ Tempts Chastetie as much, as too much Licence' (I.2.25 – 6).

Strange things can happen when history repeats itself. The first part of *The Widdowes Teares* is farce, the second (almost) tragedy. The last two acts of the play are a drama created by Lysander, and the tomb is a simulacrum of the inside of his head, as well as a turning-inside-out of the walled gardens built for women in Chapman's earlier plays and *Ovids Banquet of Sence* (1595). Just as Ovid's eye is at Corynna's 'brests reflected' and compared to the 'reverberate vigor' of sun-beams (see stanza 49), so Lysander's dangerous self-centredness is described by Lycus: '. . . you know how strange his dotage ever was on his wife; taking speciall glorie to have her love and loialtie to him so renown'd abrode' (II.3.48 – 50). It's this reflexive habit of mind that's responsible for the outrageous black comedy of Acts IV and V, the most distinctive feature of *The Widdowes Teares*. Lysander produces Cynthia's actions in the tomb, and he's determined to prove that his wife will not keep her vows: 'Thou shalt eate, th'art now within the place/ Where I command' (IV.2.111 – 12). The warning he's given about the 'Curiositie' of Actaeon – killed by his own hounds after seeing Diana 'in her nakednesse' (I.3.63 – 7) – suggests that he too is to be dogged with the worst scenario he can imagine. So, as soon as Lysander screams 'Lust, impietie, hell, womanhood it selfe, adde if you can one step to this' (V.2.42 – 3), it's clear that things will carry on getting worse. As they do. It takes just seconds for Cynthia to get over the shock of hearing the supposed murderer's own melodramatic account of her husband's death (V.3.35 – 8).

CYNTHIA   O thou hast told me newes that cleaves my heart,

> Would I had never seene thee, or heard sooner
>
> This bloudie storie; yet see, note my truth;
>
> Yet I must love thee.

LYSANDER   Out upon thee Monster.

Lysander's story is Tharsalio's reversed and negated, like the candle in the penultimate speech of *Bussy D'Ambois* (V.3.255 – 7): '. . . being thus turnd downe . . . His owne stuffe puts it out'. *The Widdowes Teares* is another study of reverberation: 'Goe *Satyre*, runne affrighted with the noise/ Of that harsh sounding horne thy selfe hast blowne' (V.5.84 – 5). Chapman then continues to add to Petronius by exploring what could be the wider social consequences of Lysander's destructive inversion, through the soldiers on the watch and the Governor, as Lee Bliss points out in Chapter I of *The World's Perspective* (Brighton: Harvester Press, 1983). The first soldier shows how the play is partly about the making and breaking of bonds: 'Tush man, in this topsie turvy world, friendship and bosom kindnes are but made covers for mischief, meanes to compasse il. Near-allied trust, is but a bridge for treson' (V.4.29 – 31). The appearance of the Governor in a judicial role suggests that he may put things right, but even more than with similar figures in contemporary plays like Shakespeare's

Measure, for Measure (1604), the Governor is part of the problem, not the solution.

Several critics have objected to the unsatisfactoriness of the play's ending, but it seems to be deliberate. Lysander and his wife do not speak to each other, but what could they say? His despairing cry of 'What have I done?' (V.5.87) moves *The Widdowes Teares* towards tragedy, and the lasting effect of generic uneasiness is only increased by the announcement at the very end of a wedding between a girl and boy who fell in love at first sight, in a reminder of more conventional comedies. *The Widdowes Teares* is perhaps best described as an early instance of the vogue for tragi-comedy, as defined by Fletcher in the preface to *The Faithful Shepheardesse* (printed 1609), for which Chapman wrote a commendatory poem. *The Faithful Shepheardesse* is based on Guarini's *Il Pastor Fido: Tragicomedia Pastorale*, one of several Italian plays cited in the dedicatory letter to *The Widdowes Teares*. Fletcher writes: 'A tragie-comedie is not so called in respect of mirth and killing, but in respect it wants deaths, which is inough to make it no tragedie, yet brings some neere it, which is inough to make it no comedie.' *The Widdowes Teares* is similar in this respect to Chapman's earlier tragi-comedy *The Gentleman Usher* (1602–3). The lesson of *The Widdowes Teares* is one of accommodation – 'learne to live as other mortalls doe' (IV.2.177). Tharsalio is 'a Man, and not a Giant' (I.2.81–2) – whereas Bussy wants to be a giant and not a man – and he asserts: 'All natures are not capable of all gifts' (IV.1.124). *The Widdowes Teares* is a play written against the all-embracing absolutism so often driven towards by Chapman. If *Bussy D'Ambois* is England's first heroic tragedy, this is Chapman's answering anti-heroic comedy.

FURTHER READING

Ayers, P. K., 'Staging Modernity: Chapman, Jonson, and The Decline of the Golden Age', *Cahiers Elizabethains*, 47 (1995), pp. 9–28

Chapman, George, *The Widow's Tears*, ed. Ethel M. Smeak (London: Edward Arnold, 1967)

— *The Widow's Tears*, ed. Akihiro Yamada (London: Methuen, 1975)

Hopkins, Lisa, 'Marlowe, Chapman, Ford and Nero', *English Language Notes*, XXXV (1997), pp. 5–9

Juneja, Renu, 'Widowhood and Sexuality in Chapman's *The Widow's Tears*', *Philological Quarterly*, 67 (1988), pp. 157–75

Tricomi, Albert, 'The Social Disorder of Chapman's *The Widow's Tears*', *JEGP*, 72 (1973), pp. 350–59

TEXTUAL NOTES

The text is based on the copy of *The Widdowes Teares* in the Bodleian Library, Oxford (Shelfmark: Mal. 240 [7]). In the notes that follow, the first readings are from this edition and the second readings record those of the base text.

The Actors

Governour] *Thir. Gouernour*
Lycus] *Lycas*
[*Rebus . . . friends of Rebus*]] *3.*
Lords suiters to Eudora the widdow
Countesse.
Gent[lewomen] . . . Eudora] *only*
Ianthe thus described in Q

Dedicatory Epistle

5 *therefore [I]* ~ ∧
6 *disposition.*] ~,
13 *rest,*] ~.
14 *affected,*] ~.

Act I. Scene 1

81 brother,] ~?
84 bed?] ~.
87 done)] ~,
88 interred,] ~)
107 example?] ~.
120 quarters?] ~.
134 faith.] ~,
148 her, Nephew, this] ~ ∧ ~; This

Act I. Scene 2

34.3 STHENIO] *Sthenia*
45 Sir;] ~,
65 Madame?] ~:
126 Shoulders] Soulders
132–4 What . . . sight] Q *prints as prose*
136–7 Yet . . . immortall] Q *prints as prose*
148–9 If . . . him] Q *prints as prose*
157 PSORABEUS] *Lurd.*
158.1 *Exeunt*] *Exit*

Act I. Scene 3

16 erected?] ~;
82 How . . . Brother?] Q *prints as separate line*
127 Now forth] Nowforth
129 commodities] commodoties
155 SD *out.*] ~:
156 Ladie?] ~.
172 heirs] ears
173 alwaies-] ~.
174 unprovided-] ~.
182 SD *Exeunt*] *Exit*

Act II. Scene 1

10 Heavens;] ~.
34 h'as] has
34–5 All . . . know?] Q *lines:* All . . . a/ Bone . . . know?
44 manhood,] ~;

Act II. Scene 2

5–8 A shrew . . . her] Q *prints as two speeches* (A . . . comparison/ Lets . . . her) *both prefixed* 'Sthe.'
23.1 *Laodice, Argus*] Laodice, Reb, Hiar Psor. comming after, Argus
24–5 Here's . . . you] Q *prints as verse:* Here's . . . ant/ Please . . . Tennants/ Desires . . . you
50.1 ARSACE *comes forward*] Enter Arsace
83 when] When
123 SD EUDORA . . . *enter*] *Exit.*
127 SD *Exeunt*] *Exit*

Act II. Scene 3

57 probabilitie?] ~.
88 wit?] ~,
95 me.] ~:

Act II. Scene 4

8 letters] letrers
13 *Sthenio*?] ~.
92 you?] ~.
114 it were] It ∧
154–7 Or . . . bed] Q *prints as prose*
157 head?] ~.
176 businesse?] ~.

Act III. Scene 1

3 doe?] ~.
6 tast; . . . away.] ~, . . . ~,
9–12 I . . . to] Q *prints as prose*
13–19 Let . . . selfe] Q *prints as prose*
15 good;] ~,
18 observance?] ~,
25 shew;] ~,
29 night?] ~.
38 unbanded!] vn-/ banded,
44 in?] ~.
52–3 Which . . . Foe] Q *prints as prose*
54 come,] ~ ∧
70 brother-] ~.
78–82 Brother . . . nuptialls] Q *prints as prose*
84–5 atchievement?] ~.
102 stoop't . . . affection?] stoo'pt
    . . . ~;
109–15 But . . . wife?] Q *prints as prose*
113 th'] the
120 No, wife?] ~ ∧ ~.
124 *Paphos* ∧] ~;
137 Fare-well] Fare-will
141.1 *Exeunt*] *Exit*
146 heeld,] ~;
147 in-step?] ~.
159 pleasures?] ~.
183 death?] ~.
207 comfort,] ~;
212 arrivall?] ~.
219 place; . . . passe.] ~, . . . ~,

221 neare?] ~.
223 himselfe.] ~,
223–4 And . . . Sonne] Q *prints as prose*
225–6 Whom . . . speede] Q *prints as
    prose*
225 hear] here

Act III. Scene 2

22 may] my
24 within] with in
34 Revellers,] ~.
35 Nuptialls.] ~,
38–9 Can . . . well?] Q *prints as prose*
39–41 But . . . house] Q *prints as prose*
40 ill] all
55 then] than
74 *Phoenix*; there, . . . cheere:] ~,
    . . . ~ ∧ . . . ~ ∧
78 heaven,] ~.
79 Mistris;] ~,
79.1–2 SD] *in Roman except 'Musique',
    'Hymen', and 'Sylvanes'*
81 not] Not
83 bride,] ~ ∧
107.2 *places,*] ~.

Act IV. Scene 1

20 true);] ~) ∧
26 well?] ~.
45 well?] ~,
77–80 A lance . . . us] Q *prints as prose*
96–7 For . . . light] Q *lines:* For . . .
    These/ Grieves . . . light
99 wi'th'] with
111 sustenance?] ~.
134 upon't?] ~.
136–7 But . . . weake] Q *prints as prose*

Act IV. Scene 2

4 Accus'd; ... Gods] Q *lines*.
Accus'd condemn'd/ Now ...
Gods

13 quick,] ~.

14 In ... there] Q *lines*: In ...
Ho!/ Who's ... there?

14 bosome?] ~:

20 dwell?] ~.

21–2 What ... dead?] Q *prints as prose*

22–33 Good ... *Lysander*] Q *prints as
three separate groups of prose
sentences*

33 Bandittos] Bantditos

34–7 And ... mournes?] Q *prints as
prose*

46 spoile] spoil'd

78 Mistris] *omitted in* Q

79–86 Say ... thankes?] Q *prints as
prose*

90 Now ... none?] Q *lines*: Now
... husband./ No? ... none?

101 Let ... to] Q *lines*: Let ...
starve/ Fall ... to

108 A noble] Noble

110 Come, Wench,] ~ ^ ~ ^

111–12 Thou ... command] Q *lines*:
Thou ... within/ The ...
command

119 lost] lost'

124 What ... me?] Q *lines*: Will ...
enow/ What ... me

131 it?] ~.

149 an't's] ants,

152 Posterionds-] ~.

156–8 Right ... tongues] Q *prints as
prose*

Act IV. Scene 3

73 What,] ~ ^

76–8 Comfortable ... hunters] Q

prints as verse. Comfortable ...
edifie/ Me ... *Dido*/ And ...
hearke/ Me ... hunters

Act V. Scene 1

11 foode,] ~;

23 see!] ~ ^

30 Your] Our

36 me,] ~ ^

43 mindes] windes

60 jealousie,] ~.

74–6 When ... signe] Q *lines*: When
... bodies/ Stolne ... fast/ In
... signe

Act V. Scene 2

9–12 What? ... wealth?] Q *prints as
prose*

15–16 The ... opinion-] *one line in* Q

16 opinion-] ~.

58 carelessly] caresly

59–75 He ... enemies] Q *prints as prose*

Act V. Scene 3

7–8 Yet ... earth] Q *prints as prose*

10 for't.] ~,

11–13 Die? ... husband] Q *prints as
prose*

20–22 That ... Gibbet] *one line in* Q

22 Cancro!] ~.

37 truth;] ~ ^

38 thee] the

42 truant] tenant

55–6 Ha? ... love?] Q *prints as prose*

66 Devill?] ~.

68 this,] ~ ^

73 Achelous] Achelons

73 ill] all

74 enough;] ~.

76 Ida] Ilea

127 there?] ~.
139.1 *Ero . . . &c.*] Q *prints in roman as part of Tharsalio's speech*
171–9 Nay . . . Tomb] Q *prints as prose*

Act V. Scene 4

34 Mountainers;] ~,
40–41 Truth's . . . square] Q *prints as prose*
40 Truth's] Truth
45 Night,] ~ ʌ
47 herse?] ~.

Act V. Scene 5

8 true ʌ] ~;
8 thee] her
18 SD *enters.*] ~ ʌ
25 a way] away
25 resolv'd?] ~.
36 It] I
40–41 His . . . it] Q *lines:* His . . . with/ Gore? . . . it
49–50 I . . . knowne] Q *lines:* I . . . this/ Brake . . . knowne
57–8 But . . . it] Q *lines:* But . . . thee/ Swallowes . . . doubts/ Can . . . it

59–60 Neither . . . worke] Q *lines:* Neither . . . toth'/ Proofe . . . worke
64 Fore ʌ] ~,
72 soft-roed] soft-r'ode
78 most-] ~.
87–8 What . . . more] Q *prints as prose*
92 We . . . duties] Q *prints as separate line*
115 Say . . . Captaine?] Q *prints as separate line*
132 Governour.] ~,
133 LYSANDER] *speech prefix omitted in* Q
140 but] bur
140 Corps?] ~.
146 Martyrs.] Martys
173 a Foole] ʌ Foole
186 Let . . . away] Q *prints as separate line*
264 SD ARGUS stalkes] *on preceding line in* Q
268 in't!] ~?
276 from] for
288 1 SOLDIER] *Soul.*
289–91 These . . . hand,] Q *prints as prose*
291 hand,] ~.
298–9 Come . . . hand] Q *prints as prose*

COMMENTARY

The Actors

Translations are given where names are based on Greek.

Tharsalio: Boldness, confidence, also punning on the English 'tarse', an old term for the penis.

Lysander: Loose man.

Lycus: Wolf.

Argus . . . Usher: Bright, idle. In myth Argus had 100 eyes which were always open. When killed on Jove's orders, his eyes were used to deck a peacock's tail. A Gentleman

Usher – a sort of head butler – was the second most important servant in noble households, behind the Steward.

Hiarbus: Named in Book IV of Virgil's *Aeneid* as a king from Gaetulia (Morocco), unsuccessful wooer of Dido.

Psorabeus: Itchy, starving.

Eudora: Generous, richly endowed.

Sthenio: Strength.

Ianthe: Violet. Also the name of a mute maid in Chapman's comedy *The Blinde begger of Alexandria* (1596).

Ero: Hero, as in *Hero And Leander*, and Love, as in Eros.

Arsace: Joiner, one who gives relief.

Dedication

Jo. REED . . . Glocester: Mitton is actually in Worcestershire near Tewkesbury, and the manor there was sold to Giles Reed in 1571 by the poet Sir Fulke Greville, 1st Baron Brooke. Giles Reed married Katherine Greville, and John Reed was their eldest son. John succeeded his father in 1611.

4–5 *Injusti . . . fido*: Gli Ingiusti Sdegni is a five-act pastoral comedy in prose by Bernardino Pino, printed in 1553. *Nuova Favola Pastorale* (i.e. *Il Pentamento Amoroso*) is a five-act pastoral in verse by Luigi Groto, printed in 1576; *La Calisto: Favola Pastorale* is another five-act pastoral in verse by Groto, printed in 1583. The most interesting reference is to *Il Pastor Fido: Tragicomedia Pastorale*, a five-act verse play by Giambattista Guarini, written in 1589 in emulation of Tasso's pastoral play of 1573, *Aminta*. The play was printed in 1590, translated into English in 1602 as *Il Pastor Fido: Or The faithfull Shepheard*, and proved popular throughout the seventeenth century. It was the basis for John Fletcher's *The Faithfull Shepheardesse*, for which Chapman wrote a commendatory poem when it was printed in 1609.

Act I. Scene 1

SD *Tharsalio . . . Glasse*: Tharsalio alone with a mirror.

18 *how, are . . . aspect*: Compare the devil Ophioneus in Chapman's tragedy *Caesar And Pompey* (1604–5), II.i.142–3: 'Say, dost not love me? art not enamourd of my acquaintance?' Compare also Commentary on I.1.60–63 below. The attitudes struck fill out Lysander's complaint at II.1.41–9 that Tharsalio has 'Turn'd Devill'.

33 *in written Bookes I find it*: Adaptation of a stock phrase used in Italian romance poems and English ballads to assert the truth of something unlikely to be true. Written books also means tailors' account books: Tharsalio has got his new suit on credit.

60–63 *there is . . . errands*: Compare the devil Ophioneus in *Caesar And Pompey*, II.i.110–14: 'Nor skils it for degrees in a knave, or a fooles preferment; Thou shalt rise by fortune: let desert rise leisurely enough, and by degrees; fortune preferres headlong, and comes like riches to a man; huge riches being got with little paines, and little with huge paines.' Compare also *Bussy D'Ambois* (1604), I.1.134–9, where the word 'headlong' is used again, and V.3.19 where 'huge riches' recurs.

65–7 *draw you up . . . shoot at*: In Volume 2 of his edition of *The Plays of George Chapman: The Comedies* (New York and London, 1914), p. 807, T. M. Parrott notes: 'The reference is to the well-known story told of Virgil in the Middle Ages. According to this tale a lady whom the poet-magician was courting promised to draw him up to her room by night in a basket. She left him, however, suspended half-way to be mocked at in the morning by the passers-by. In revenge Virgil extinguished all the fires in Rome, and prevented their being rekindled until the lady stooped to the disgrace of appearing in her smock in the Forum and allowing torches to be kindled by contact with her body.' The allusion is picked up again at I.3.125–7.

75 *blind Goddesse*: Confidence, not Fortune. Compare Chapman's translation of *Homer's Odysses* (1614), III.308–9: 'blind Confidence/ (The God of Fooles).'

88–90 *to feede . . . Lent*: Eating meat during Lent was forbidden by law.

99–100 *adore . . . adhorne*: Compare *All Fooles* (1599), II.1.241: 'hee adores you, and adhornes me'. 'Adhorne' means to fix with the horns of the cuckold.

104 *poisoner*: In Shakespeare's tragedy *Hamlet* (1600), Hamlet's father is poisoned by Claudius, who then marries Hamlet's mother.

115 *Monopolies . . . cryed downe*: James I called in monopolies granted under Elizabeth I in a proclamation on May 17, 1603. Monopolies gave their holders the right to corner the market in certain goods. The allusion helps to fix the play's date.

122 *Italian aire*: Compare George Whetstone's elegy 'Sir Philip Sidney, his honorable life, his valiant death, and true vertues', published in 1587, for a typical expression of the period's anti-Italian sentiment: 'An English-man that is Italianate:/ Doth lightly prove a Devell incarnate.' (Tharsalio is said to have 'Turn'd Devill' at II.1.46.) Italy was a theatrical byword, particularly after John Marston's early plays, for lasciviousness and the sort of corrupt and ruthless conduct associated with the political philosopher Machiavelli.

123 *ingenuous Nature*: Compare *Bussy D'Ambois*, III.2.107: 'th'ingenuous soule of D'Ambois'.

Act I. Scene 2

14–15 *Ulysses . . . voice*: In fact Ulysses got his crew to put wax in their ears and bind him to the mast so that he could hear the Sirens safely, according to Book XII of Homer's *Odyssey*. See Introduction.

34 SD *going over the Stage*: A theatrical convention. Argus and Lycus come in from different sides of the stage, not from doors at the back, with no one noticing them until later (I.2.62).

107 *out at window*: Tharsalio is suggesting that Hiarbus is a bastard.

108 *bag-pipe*: A mocking reference to James I's Scottish followers as puffed-up. Also slang reference to getting an erection.

112–13 *Magick Characters . . . booke*: Compare Chapman's *Hero And Leander* (1598), III.97–9: 'Then laid he forth his late inriched armes,/ In whose white circle Love writ all his charmes,/ And made his characters sweet *Heros* lims, . . .' Magicians were supposed to make marks ('characters') inside a magic circle. Here the image is of a sexually diseased lord entering the body ('Magick Characters' = limbs) of a whore – 'an unlawful booke'.

115–17 *I perceive . . . dresse him*: Sexual innuendo. 'Goose' is slang for prostitute, 'proud' is used of animals on heat.

140–41 *the Elements . . . generate*: According to Book A of Aristotle's *Metaphysica*, Empedocles first suggested that the elements of fire, water, earth and air are segregated by love and aggregated by strife. Compare I.3.31–2: 'All thinges by strife engender.' Compare also ll. 39–46 of 'Hymnus in Noctem' in *The Shadow Of Night* (1594).

158 *Or begg'd . . . Viceroy*: i.e. have Tharsalio committed as a madman. Henry VIII established the right to 'beg a person', i.e. to petition the Court of Wards (suppressed under Charles II) 'for the custody of a minor, an heiress, or an infant, as feudal superior or as having interest in the matter' (*OED*).

Act I. Scene 3

100 *Conquerours . . . overcome*: An allusion to Julius Caesar's famous comment after invading Britain: *Veni, vidi, vici* – I came, I saw, I overcame. Hence 'Conquerours stile'.

125–7 *as famous . . . her nose*: See Commentary on I.1.65–7.

139–41 *the Asse . . . seise it*: Like the Trojan Horse in the Trojan Wars.

Act II. Scene 1

20–22 *wandring Aeneas . . . throat*: Aeneas is the hero of Virgil's *Aeneid*, and this is the first of several allusions by Chapman to the story of Dido and Aeneas. Dido is the Queen of Lybia, who falls in love with Aeneas after he is shipwrecked. When he leaves her to pursue his destiny, she throws herself on a pyre. 'Reversion' is a legal term for something left after death. The 'Turtle' is a common symbol of faithfulness – as for example in Shakespeare's poem 'The Phoenix and the Turtle' (1601). '*Atropos*' is one of the Three Fates entrusted with the thread of life, as in *Bussy D'Ambois*, III.2.391–5 (see 'A List of Historical, Mythological and Geographical Names'). The two clauses about the Turtle and Atropos may be imaginatively expanded from a reference to fate in Petronius' *Satyricon*, where the maid asks the Widow of Ephesus why she should breathe her last innocent breath before fate demands it. This question is posed immediately before a quotation from Virgil's *Aeneid*, IV.34: 'Believe you that ashes or the buried ghosts can know?' Petronius takes this line from a scene where the lovesick Dido is being consoled by her sister. Chapman adapts it and transfers the maid's speech to Lysander at IV.2.84–6.

27–8 *Diana . . . monckey*: The goddess Diana never changed a man into a monkey, but she did turn the young hunter Actaeon into a stag after he chanced upon her bathing naked. Actaeon was then killed by his own hounds. Compare 41.7–9 and gloss in *Ovids Banquet of Sence* (1595).

Act II. Scene 2

5–7 *Argus . . . sleepe*: Argus' mythical name is ironic. He's an idiot like Poggio in Chapman's tragi-comedy *The Gentleman Usher* (1602–3).
51 *Cypriane Goddesse*: Aphrodite/Venus. Worshipped in Cyprus, often said to land at Paphos after being born in the waves. One of the changes Chapman makes to Petronius is to shift the setting of the tale from Ephesus, a place sacred to Diana, the moon-goddess of chastity, to Cyprus, island of the love-goddess of Venus, who's referred to by name throughout the play.
122 *Contentment . . . beings*: Compare *Ovids Banquet of Sence*, 54.1–4.

Act II. Scene 3

18–19 *spun . . . concupiscence*: Alluding back to the web-spinning Penelope (see 'A List of Historical, Mythological and Geographical Names') at I.1.140 and I.2.9–15.

Act II. Scene 4

26 *lawfull adulterie*: This may have been Chapman's own opinion. The character of Bellamont in *Northward Hoe* (1605) by Thomas Dekker and John Webster is based on Chapman. Bellamont is told: 'You were wont to say venery is like usery that it may be allowed tho it be not lawfull.' (III.i.87–8)
36 *as Ptolemie . . . windes*: The Greek polymath Ptolemy does not say that the winds have a special influence on women.
45 *two fortunate Stars*: Parrott notes (*Comedies*, p. 809): 'St. Elmo's fires, the electric phenomenon sometimes seen in storms at the mast-head or on the yard-arms of ships. In ancient days this phenomenon was regarded as a manifestation of the Twin Brethren, Castor and Pollux, stellified by Zeus, who were regarded as the protectors of travellers by sea . . .'
76–7 *There stand . . . againe*: Compare the opening scene of *Hamlet*.
124 *flering*: Smiling falsely and obsequiously. Compare *Hero And Leander*, VI.19–22.
173–4 *our Countrie-man Hercules*: No classical writer thought that Hercules was born in Cyprus. Traditionally his birthplace was Thebes or Argos – never Cyprus.
174–6 *for love . . . businesse*: Hermes sold Hercules as a slave to Omphale, Queen of Lydia, who made him do women's work, such as spinning. According to some versions of the story, he fell in love with her. Compare Ovid's *Heroides*, IX.53–118, and Book One Chapter 12 of *The Countesse of Pembrokes Arcadia* (1590) by Sir Philip Sidney, where Pyrocles has disguised himself as an Amazon warrior in order to get access to the princess Philocleia, whose father does not want her to get married.

Pyrocles wears a brooch which shows Hercules holding Omphale's spinning-distaff, and carries the ambiguous motto: '*Never more valiant.*'

181 *Sparta-Velvets*: 'Velvet-wearing Spartans'. With implications of foppish softness.

186–7 *and beg . . . to me*: Compare II.1.20–22 and Commentary.

188 *Calidonian Bore*: Diana sent a boar as a curse to the kingdom of Calydon, as told in Homer's *Iliad*, IX.536ff. Compare l. 84 of 'Hymnus in Noctem'. Caledonia is also the old name for Scotland.

196 *dub'd*: Suggests that ladies slept around to get their husbands knighthoods. An attack on the creation of new knights by James I and, as in *Bussy D'Ambois*, a pointer to the play's date.

Act III. Scene 1

3–4 *strange curiositie . . . lay in*: The Roman Emperor Nero killed his mother, then inspected and commented on her dead body. It's not historically certain that he did rip open her womb.

23 *loth to depart*: The name of a popular tune.

38 *wrapt in carelesse cloake*: Compare Chapman's comedy *Monsieur D'Olive* (1605), V.ii.6, where D'Olive is spotted entering in disguise: ''Tis he by heaven, wrapt in his carelesse cloke.'

50–51 *magnis . . . ausis*: From Phaethon's epitaph in Ovid's *Metamorphoses*, II.328–9: 'yet he failed as he dared to accomplish great things'.

53 *Fortune . . . Foe*: An allusion to a popular tune, starting 'Fortune my foe, why dost thou frown on me?'

153 *shame . . . lost*: Compare *All Fooles*, III.1.62 and Commentary.

Act III. Scene 2

14 *he hangs . . . Hymens shape*: Hymen probably 'hangs' down from the ceiling over the stage by means of a pulley system before he finally '*descends*' at III.2.79 SD. It is also possible, however, that he simply appeared high up in the gallery at the back of the stage.

68–9 *ship . . . abilitie*: From Erasmus's *Adagia* (1500): 'Ne uni navi facultates' – do not load all your resources in one ship. Compare *Hero And Leander*, IV.501.

Act IV. Scene 1

1 *by this time*: About a week has passed since the end of Act III. News of Lysander's 'death' has arrived, his funeral has taken place, and Cynthia has carried on mourning in his tomb for four days – see IV.1.110.

21 *Dipolis*: 'Double city'. No such place in Cyprus, but Paphos may be intended, as it included Old and New Paphos.

26 *strange Knights*: Another allusion to James I's creation of new knights.

45 *Nuntius*: Lycus goes on to parody the style of the messenger in Greek and Roman tragedies. Compare *Bussy D'Ambois*, II.1.25 – 137 and Commentary.

107 *These . . . light*: Compare the proverbial 'Small sorrows speak, great ones are silent' and l. 607 of Seneca's play *Phaedra*: '*Curae leves loquuntur, ingentes stupent*' – 'light cares speak out, enormous ones stun'.

99 – 100 *over-doing Actor*: Compare *Hamlet*, III.ii.4 – 14, where Hamlet complains about over-acting.

127 – 8 *My sister . . . woman*: Compare Commentary on V.3.93, also *Ovids Banquet of Sence*, stanzas 2 – 11, and *Hamlet*, I.ii.149.

Act IV. Scene 2

0.2 SD *the Tombe*: The Tomb may have been either a sort of small booth, possibly set up against the façade of the tiring-house at the back of the stage, or the space behind the doorway in the middle of the façade.

57 – 8 *As did . . . winded*: Compare ll. 1 – 2 of the sixteenth sonnet in *Certain Sonnets* by Sir Philip Sidney, printed in 1598: 'A satyre once did runne away for dread,/ With sound of horne, which he him selfe did blow.' The whole sonnet is relevant to *The Widdowes Teares*. See *The Poems of Sir Philip Sidney*, ed. William A. Ringler, Jr. (Oxford: Clarendon Press, 1962), p. 145.

79 – 89 *Say that . . . for you*: Based on a speech by the Widow's maid in Petronius' *Satyricon*, and at IV.2.84 – 6 adapting Petronius' own quotation of Virgil's *Aeneid*, IV.34. See Commentary on II.1.20 – 22.

95 – 6 *Did . . . life*: Closely based on Petronius' *Satyricon*, part of the narration here being turned into a question by the maid.

136 SD *bibit Ancill[a]*: 'The maid drinks'.

145 *Verolles*: From the French verole, meaning pox.

152 – 5 *Aristotle . . . tongue*: Aristotle did write *Analytica Posteriora* ('his Posterionds'), but Ero seems to be mistaken in her source.

Act IV. Scene 3

36 *black Santus*: Sanctus is sung just before the consecration in the service of the Mass. A black Sanctus is a hymn distorted to express contempt or dislike, and formerly used as a kind of serenade to a faithless wife, as well as a monk-ridiculing hymn to St Satan.

40 – 78 *Honourable . . . hunters*: In Petronius' *Satyricon* the inducements used by the soldier to persuade the widow to eat lead on to a sexual appeal supported by the maid who quotes Virgil's *Aeneid*, IV.38: 'Would you fight even a pleasing passion?' The soldier and the Widow end up sleeping together. Things don't go so far in Chapman, but the encounter in these lines is based on Petronius, with the maid urging her mistress to 'pledge him in love too' and the Widow and soldier (Lysander) kissing at IV.3.64. Later in Book IV of the *Aeneid* Dido and Aeneas are out hunting when a storm forces them to take shelter in a cave, where they exchange vows of love. Chapman's conflation of the Widow's tomb with this cave is made explicit by Ero at the end of this scene.

49–50 *Wine . . . drinke*: Compare *Hero And Leander*, V.59–60: 'Then layd she wine on cares to make them sinke;/ *Who feares the threats of Fortune, let him drinke.*'

Act V. Scene 1

26 *drawing on*: A sarcastic play on words – Tharsalio gives Lycus the impression that Cynthia is drawing on towards death, whereas she's sexually leading on the soldier.

31–2 *She, she . . . chastitie*: An adaptation of ll. 6–7 of the seventh piece in *The Third and Last Booke of Songs or Aires* (1603) by John Dowland, about the one woman in the world with a constant mind: 'Shee shee shee and onelie she,/ she onely Queene of love and beautie.' The song is reprinted with modern spelling in *English Madrigal Verse 1588–1632*, ed. E. H. Fellowes (Oxford: 1967, third edition), pp. 481–2.

42 *What . . . was I*: Compare Rynaldo's reaction in *All Fooles*, V.2.79: 'What a dull slave was I to be thus gull'd.'

45–7 *Shee . . . conjunction*: 'Interjection' and 'conjunction' are both parts of speech. 'Interjection' here refers to Cynthia's earlier ejaculations of grief at Lysander's death, 'conjunction' to her sexual entanglement with the soldier.

Act V. Scene 3

63–4 *the shirt . . . banefull*: An allusion to the shirt of Nessus, a centaur killed by Hercules. The shirt was soaked in the centaur's poisonous blood, and when Hercules' wife sent it to him, innocently supposing it would be a charm to regain his love and put him off his mistress Iole, it poisoned him. Compare Book IX of Ovid's *Heroides*.

72–6 *Thou foolish . . . leaves*: The passage tells fools who like to soak up news of other people's secrets and misfortunes to look in their own homes, count up what they see and then choke, because there's plenty ('copie') enough troubles there: ills fill a horn that's thus the opposite of a cornucopia ('*Achelous* horne'), as many ills as there are streams flowing into the river Alizon, as many ills as there are leaves in the woods on the mountain range of Ida.

93 *why . . . incomprehensible*: Compare Hamlet talking about his mother Gertrude remarrying in *Hamlet*, I.ii.149–51: 'Like *Niobe* all teares, why she, even she/ O God, a beast that wants discourse of reason/ Would have mourn'd longer!'

Act V. Scene 5

0.1 SD *Lysander . . . yron*: Lysander alone with an iron crowbar.

158 *wooden dagger*: A wooden dagger was often carried by the Vice, the main character in some Morality plays and sixteenth-century interludes. Compare V.5.207 and *Bussy D'Ambois*, I.1.204.

216–49 *Ile turne . . . ath' Towne*: The Governor's speech is made deliberately nonsensical and contradictory. It threatens to expand the 'topsie turvy world' described by 1 Soldier at V.4.29–31. The Governor's 'new discipline' is also reminiscent of the topsy-turvy after-life described by the devil Ophioneus in *Caesar And Pompey*, II.i.152–5: 'he that sold Seacoale here, shall be a Baron there; he that was a cheating Rogue here, shall be a Justice of peace there; a knave here, a knight there'. Parrott suggested (*Comedies*, p. 798) that the satire on the Governor showed 'Chapman's personal resentment' for his imprisonment in the case of *Eastward Hoe*, so the play must have been finished late in 1605. However, Albert H. Tricomi points out Chapman's 'abjectness' in prison: see 'The Dates of the Plays of George Chapman', *English Literary Renaissance*, XII (1982), p. 250. He faced severe punishment – having his ears cropped and nose slit – and Tricomi argues that Chapman would have been far more likely to avoid antagonizing the authorities. With *Eastward Hoe* being written early in 1605, and *Monsieur D'Olive* in the middle of the year, 1604 and perhaps early 1605 seems a more plausible date for *The Widdowes Teares*.

228–9 *no . . . neede*: Compare *Bussy D'Ambois*, I.1.97, and l. 48 of Chapman's poem 'A Great Man' in *Petrarchs Seven Penitentiall Psalms, Paraphrastically Translated: With other Philosophicall Poems, and a Hymne to Christ upon the Crosse* (1612): 'Good never doing, but where is no need'. Also l. 186 of his poem *Eugenia* (1614): 'None will doe good, but where there is no neede'.

249 *Cart*: Whores in particular were carted through the streets as a punishment.

279 *Go to, be comforted*: Michael Neill comments on 'the uncomfortable cobbling up' of a destroyed marriage 'against the background of an outrageously violated family monument' on pp. 61–2 of ' "Feasts Put Down Funerals": Death and Ritual in Renaissance Comedy' in *True Rites and Maimed Rites: Ritual and Anti-Ritual in Shakespeare and His Age*, eds. Linda Woodbridge and Edward Berry (Urbana and Chicago: University of Illinois Press, 1992). Neill adds: 'It is a satiric catastrophe whose full effect is very much dependent on its scenic recollection of tragic dramas, like *Titus Andronicus*, *Romeo and Juliet* and *Anthony and Cleopatra*, where tombs and monuments are deployed as symbols of lineage and the heroic transcendence of mortality.'

294–6 *Asse . . . feard*: The story of the ass is one of Aesop's fables, also alluded to in *Bussy D'Ambois*, I.2.154–6.

NOTES TO *POEMS*

The best introductions to Chapman's poems are his own dedicatory letters in *The Shadow Of Night* (1594) and *Ovids Banquet of Sence* (1595). These books were his first publications, and their dedications are acts of self-presentation which set the stage for the rest of his career. They show Chapman's scorn for other contemporary writers who lust after 'profit' and the 'affection of great mens fancies' ('great' here meaning the opposite of good). They proclaim his belief that plainness of style leads to barbarism. Chapman prefers a sort of venerable obscurity: 'where it shroudeth it selfe in the hart of his subject, uttrd with fitnes of figure, and expressive Epethetes; with that darknes wil I still labour to be shadowed: rich Minerals are digd out of the bowels of the earth'. The subsequent talk of his 'new pen' may suggest that Chapman is venturing a new kind of art, but his arguments for obscurity go back very far indeed, as is later acknowledged in the first lines of the preamble to *A Free And Offenceles Justification, Of A Lately Publisht and most maliciously misinterpreted Poeme; Entituled Andromeda liberata* (1614): 'As *Learning*, hath delighted from her Cradle, to hide her selfe from the base and prophane *Vulgare*, her ancient Enemy; under divers vailes of *Hieroglyphickes*, Fables, and the like; So hath she pleased her selfe with no disguise more; then in misteries and allegoricall fictions of *Poesie*.' '*Hieroglyphickes*' refers to the symbols carved on Egyptian temples; Chapman consistently associates the Poet with the figure of the inspired priest revealing 'misteries' only to initiates. Hence, in the dedication to *Ovids Banquet of Sence*, his dismissal of 'ignorants' and his hatred of the 'prophane multitude'. Etymologically, 'prophane' means 'before (i.e. outside) the temple'. Chapman wants an audience which is not necessarily noble through birth; his poems often criticize the social system which puts blood and inheritance above merit (see, for e.g., *Ovids Banquet of Sence*, 90.8–91.7 and the Commentary). The new kind of 'judiciall' readers sought by Chapman are those 'whom learning hath made noble, and nobilitie sacred', qualities which the poet himself should exemplify: the best work can only be produced by the best of men. This is one reason why Chapman identifies himself with mythological heroes, particularly Hercules, in his rapt endurance of 'th'extremes incident' to 'the deepe searche of knowledge' and the 'divine discipline of Poesie'.

For Chapman, poetry is not a game for amateurs. It is sacred, religious, ceremonial. It has to be prepared for by 'invocation, fasting, watching' (l. 18 of the dedicatory letter in *The Shadow Of Night*) and it comes when the poet enters into a 'blissfull trance'. This is what Chapman prays for at the start of 'Hymnus in Noctem' in *The Shadow Of Night*, ll. 10–15:

> . . . let soft sleepe
> (Binding my sences) lose my working soule,
> That in her highest pitch, she may controule
> The court of skill, compact of misterie,
> Wanting but franchisement and memorie
> To reach all secrets: . . .

'Franchisement and memorie' is an allusion to Plato's thesis that learning is nothing but recollection. The idea depends on a belief that humans were created knowing everything already. If that's accepted, then the search for knowledge becomes a process of trying to remember what must still be inside the mind – like digging minerals 'out of the bowels of the earth' – and it follows that it should indeed be possible to 'reach all secrets' through the use of memory systems. Ted Hughes describes such systems in his essay 'Shakespeare and Occult Neoplatonism' in *Winter Pollen* (London: Faber, 1994), p. 294: 'Memory systems were already naturalized in classical and theological tradition. Basically these were mental maps, fixed in imagination, on which the whole summa of knowledge and speculation could be arranged, with each item anchored to its place on the map by a mnemonic visual image.' Hughes sees such systems as vital tools for activating the Occult Neoplatonist vision.

Occult Neoplatonism reached its height in England in the late sixteenth century. The movement began in Florence at the end of the fifteenth century. A key text was Marsilio Ficino's translation of the *Corpus Hermeticum* (*c.*1490), a collection of writings supposedly by the ancient Egyptian God Thoth, or 'Hermes Trismegistus'. The *Corpus Hermeticum* taught that 'by mystical regeneration it was possible for man to regain domination over nature which he had lost at the Fall': see Keith Thomas, *Religion and the Decline of Magic* (London: Penguin, 1973), p. 267. The two foremost proponents of the movement in England were the Italian philosopher and spy Giordano Bruno (?1548–1600) and the mathematician and astrologer John Dee (1527–1608). Both men influenced the literary and scientific grouping which included Sir Walter Ralegh and Henry Percy, the ninth Earl of Northumberland; they and their associates are discussed in detail by the historian Christopher Hill in *Intellectual Origins of the English Revolution Revisited* (Oxford: Clarendon Press, 1997). Northumberland was interested in mathematics, astronomy, anatomy, medicine, geography, and cosmography. George Peele praised him in *The Honour of the Garter* (1593) for '(Leaving our Schoolemens vulgar trodden pathes)/ And following the ancient reverend steps/ Of Trismegistus and Pythagoras'. Figures linked with Ralegh and Northumberland included the scientist and explorer Thomas Harriot, the mathematician and navigational expert Robert Hues, the mathematician Walter Warner, the poet and playwright Christopher Marlowe, and the poet and mathematician Mathew Roydon to whom Chapman dedicated *The Shadow Of Night* and *Ovids Banquet of Sence*. The activities of 'deepe searching *Northumberland*' are 'reported' to Chapman by Roydon, says the letter in *The Shadow Of Night*.

Chapman's involvement with the grouping of freethinkers around Sir Walter

Ralegh made his 'strange muse ... aspire' (ll. 31–3 of 'To *M. Harriots*', 1598). *The Shadow Of Night, Ovids Banquet of Sence*, 'De Guiana' (1596), 'To *M. Harriots*', and *Hero And Leander* (1598) are all part of a poetic venture calling to mind this pronouncement by Ezra Pound: 'Obscurities inherent in the thing occur when the author is piercing, or trying to pierce into uncharted regions; when he is trying to express things not yet current, not yet worn into phrase; when he is ahead of the emotional, or philosophic sense (as a painter might be ahead of the colour-sense) of his contemporaries': see 'Early Translators of Homer', *Literary Essays of Ezra Pound*, ed. T. S. Eliot (London: Faber, 1960), p. 268–9. Ted Hughes finds Chapman's works 'saturated with the occultists' magical outlook', and he argues that the same enquiring spirit touched 'the hard-headed sceptic Ralegh and the mathematician Hariot, whose combined enterprise opened North America to English settlement'. Hughes goes on to outline some of the features of the intellectual study of magic that may have caught Shakespeare's attention, and by implication Chapman's, including: 'The idea of meditation as a conjuring, by ritual magic, of hallucinatory figures – with whom conversations can be held, and who communicate intuitive, imaginative vision and clairvoyance' ('Shakespeare and Occult Neoplatonism', pp. 300 and 309). 'Hymnus in Noctem' is one such conjuring ('See now ascends, the glorious Bride of Brides' – l. 384) and *The Teares of Peace* (1609) is similar. Chapman is sat in 'silent meditation', when suddenly a light breaks through the shade and a goodly person appears who can see 'past, and future things' (ll. 23–37). Chapman finds himself in conversation with Homer, who grants him a vision of Peace on her way to the funeral of Love. Chapman and Peace then have a conversation about what's wrong with the world, and the poem ends with another series of visions.

Most of Chapman's poetry is in rhyming couplets. Blank verse is only used in 'De Guiana'. The reasons for this are partly nationalistic and political. Chapman belonged to a generation that wanted to rival the literary achievements of Italy, France and Spain. The Elizabethans felt that England's last great poet had been Chaucer, and by the second half of the sixteenth century, the English language had changed so much, they could barely understand him any more. Significant numbers of talented young Elizabethans felt the time had come for their country's literature to be a powerful national force. An argument is decked out in 'Hymnus in Cynthiam', ll. 86–91, in *The Shadow Of Night*:

> ... as sweet poesie
> Will not be clad in her supremacie
> With those straunge garments (Romes Hexameters)
> As she is English: but in right prefers
> Our native robes, put on with skilfull hands
> (English heroicks) to those antick garlands, ...

'Antick' here means antique and also antic, as in clownish and grotesquely dressed, and the hexameters are 'Romes' not just because they are Latin poetical metres but because Rome contains the Vatican, the capital city of the Catholic church, opposed to the Protestantism of England and the separatist religious supremacy declared by Henry VIII. This religious and political conflict is the basis of a plea to the 'Queene celestiall' not to quit her 'Ephesias state' (an allusion to the famous chastity of the Widow of Ephesus, whose story figures in Chapman's play of 1604–5, *The Widdowes Teares*), and not to spoil with foreign grace 'The purenesse of thy never-tainted life,/ Scorning the subject title of a wife' (ll. 95–9). This leads on to a further call (ll. 116–19):

> Then set thy Christall, and Imperiall throne,
> (Girt in thy chast, and never-loosing zone)
> Gainst Europs Sunne directly opposit,
> And give him darknesse, that doth threat thy light.

'Europs Sunne' draws on a tradition of imagery associating the Pope with the sun, but it may also allude to the French nobleman Alençon, the Monsieur of *Bussy D'Ambois* (1604), who sought to marry Elizabeth I, and whose personal emblem was a rising sun. The identification of Elizabeth I with the chaste moon-goddess Cynthia is one of the ways in which *The Shadow Of Night* is a poem about the current state and future prospects of England.

Chapman's poetry normally has a public purpose. It's often occasioned by specific events. *The Teares of Peace* seeks to draw lessons from the truce in the War of the Netherlands reached in the spring of 1609. Two of the long poems which follow in the next five years are written to bemoan deaths – firstly, 'the most disastrous Death' of Chapman's patron Henry Prince of Wales (*An Epicede on Henry Prince of Wales*, 1612), secondly, 'the most religiously noble' Lord William Russell (*Eugenia*, 1614). Two other poems from this period – 'A Hymne to Hymen' (1613) and *Andromeda Liberata* (1614) – are composed to celebrate important marriages. Of course these works cannot be divorced from Chapman's private situation. *Andromeda Liberata*, for example, was written when he was desperate for money. The death of Prince Henry meant he hadn't received the £300 he was promised for his translations of Homer, nor had he been paid for *The Memorable Masque of the two Honourable Houses or Innes of Court; the Middle Temple, and Lyncolnes Inne* performed in 1613. With *Andromeda Liberata* he hoped to win the patronage of the Earl of Somerset, but instead Chapman's allegory caused such displeasure that he had to explain himself with *A Free And Offenceles Justification, Of A Lately Publisht and most maliciously misinterpreted Poeme; Entituled Andromeda liberata*. The preface to the *Justification* sets out the principles underlying all of Chapman's laureate-style compositions. It argues (parenthentically) for the poet's socially curative role: '(For howsoever Phisitions alledge; that their medecins, respect *non Hominem, sed Socratem*; not every, but such a speciall body: Yet *Poets* professe the contrary, that their phisique intends *non Socratem sed Hominem*, not the individuall but the universall)' (ll. 17–21). Poets are healers and their work contains the soul of truth. It might seem insignificant, but in the words of the dedicatory letter to the Earl of Somerset in *Andromeda Liberata*, ll. 35–44:

> This little Soules Pulse, *Poesie*, panting still
> Like to a dancing pease upon a Quill,
> Made with a childes breath, up and downe to fly,
> (Is no more manly thought); And yet thereby
> Even in the corps of all the world we can
> Discover all the good and bad of man,
> Anatomise his nakednesse, and be
> To his chiefe Ornament, a Majestie:
> Erect him past his human Period
> And heighten his transition into God.

The last lines derive from Ficino's *Commentary on Plato's Symposium* (1474) and inform Chapman's vision of the poet as an acknowledged anatomiser of 'all the world', a figure so empowered because he is the epitome of learning and 'good life' ('For good life is th'effect, of learnings Act' – *The Teares of Peace*, l. 396). The power of the poet's work – centred in his own self – is also asserted in Chapman's commendatory poem about Ben Jonson's play *Sejanus* (1603): 'Thy *Muse* yet makes it the whole Sphaere, and Lawe/ To all State Lives: and bounds Ambitions strife' ('In Sejanum Ben. Jonsoni', 1605, ll. 31–2). Chapman's favourite image of perfection is the 'Sphaere' or circle, created literally in 'A Coronet for his Mistresse *Philosophie*' (1595), a sequence of ten sonnets. The second sonnet starts with the last line of the first, the third starts with the last line of the second, and so interweavingly on, until the very last line of the sequence is the same as the first. Chapman's belief in the civilizing function of 'bounds' also raises the possibility that his rhyming couplets are a series of mini-circles, acts of learning meant to control the strife of language.

Chapman's style is shaped by the poet's duty to 'anatomise' all the world. In the poems and plays, his favourite word is 'all'. In *Bussy D'Ambois*, for example, it's used 194 times. By his own profession, what drives Chapman's imagination is 'not the individuall but the universall'. His medicinal addiction to the word 'all' is like Auden's devotion in the 1930s to the definite article 'the' as a tool for reducing experience 'to classifiable elements, as a necessary preliminary to diagnosis and prescription': see Bernard Bergonzi, *Reading The Thirties* (London and Basingstoke: Macmillan, 1978), p. 48. Chapman's totalizing prescriptiveness forms part of the paradoxically imperious character of Bussy in *Bussy D'Ambois*. The same desire for a power that defies challenging can be felt in the second verse paragraph of 'Hymnus in Noctem' ('Let them breake harts . . . That all mens bosoms . . . may be lanced wide' – ll. 25–7) and Bussy's second speech in Act III. Scene 2 ('let me but Hawlke at him,/ Ile play the Vulture' – III.2.36–7). In Chapman's plays the characters have hard outsides, for defensive and aggressive purposes, and the 'bounds' of his poems are similarly like dry stone walls, built to keep in and keep out. They are mostly rough-textured, interconnected, hard to dismantle, they fit odd shapes and sizes together because

Chapman is more interested in the place of his subjects in relationships than in the subjects themselves. His imagination is gripped by the idea of the world as a system of correspondences which can be anatomized through analogy and multi-layered mythological manipulation in order to 'Discover all the good and bad of man'. Hence the sometimes bafflingly rapid moves from particular things to general statements, and the increasing tendency to announce propositions like a speaker at a public meeting ('See, All;' – *The Teares of Peace*, l. 7) instead of letting them emerge. (In the plays, Chapman's predominant fascination with the elaboration of connections helps to explain the intrigue plots in the comedies and minor characters' lack of individual definition, as well as the sudden occurrences and the outward-looking soliloquies. See also the Introduction.)

Chapman always tried to keep his work for the theatre up to date, but his poetry can seem oddly old-fashioned when read today. Part of the reason for this may be that he fell between two generations, and started writing late. He was almost certainly born in 1559, about seven years after Edmund Spenser and five years after Sir Philip Sidney, both of whom were producing important works 15 years before his first publication. Chapman was born about four years before the poets Samuel Daniel and Michael Drayton, and for most readers he's in a kind of limbo with them, before the stars of the next generation. John Donne was born in 1572, Ben Jonson in 1572–3, John Marston in about 1575. It is time to look again at Chapman's 'uncharted regions'.

FURTHER READING

Huntington, John, ' "This Ticklish Title": Chapman, *Nennio*, and the Critique of Nobility', *English Literary Renaissance*, 26 (1996), pp. 291–312

—— 'Furious Insolence: The Social Meaning of Poetic Inspiration in the 1590s', *Modern Philology*, 94 (1997), pp. 305–26

Lewis, C. S., 'Hero and Leander', *Proceedings of the British Academy*, XXVIII (1952), pp. 23–37

—— *English Literature in the Sixteenth Century, Excluding Drama* (Oxford: Oxford University Press, 1954), especially pp. 510–19

Waddington, Raymond B., 'Visual Rhetoric: Chapman and the Extended Poem', *English Literary Renaissance*, 13 (1983), pp. 36–57

Wilcox, Joel F., 'Ficino's Commentary on Plato's *Ion* and Chapman's Inspired Poet in the *Odyssey*', *Philological Quarterly*, 64 (1985), pp. 195–209

'Hymnus in Noctem'

The way Chapman presented his first publication in 1594 shows how seriously he wanted to be taken as a poet. The title page doesn't just say *The Shadow Of Night*. It says: *Skia Nuketos. The Shadow Of Night: Containing Two Poeticall Hymnes*, Devised by G. C. Gent. The first hymn is 'Hymnus in Noctem', the second 'Hymnus in Cynthiam', but those words '*Containing*' and 'Devised' suggest there's far more to this book than a couple of poems. There's also a Latin epigraph, a dedicatory letter, and forty-one glosses, with quotations in Latin and Greek from more than twenty sources. The reader is meant to be intimidated and impressed. The overall effect is rather like that of *The Waste Land* (1922) by T. S. Eliot, and indeed it has been suggested that Eliot took the idea for his notes from Chapman: see Raymond B. Waddington, 'T. S. Eliot's Reading of George Chapman: One Model for *The Waste Land*', *Yeats–Eliot Review*, 6 (1979), pp. 26–8. Waddington returns to this argument in 'Visual Rhetoric: Chapman and the Extended Poem', *English Literary Renaissance*, 13 (1983), pp. 40–41, where he quotes A. Walton Litz, '*The Waste Land* Fifty Years After', *Eliot in His Time* (Princeton: Princeton University Press, 1973), p. 9. Litz writes that Eliot's notes 'were the top-secret information needed for any successful revolution; they flaunt the fact that modern literature must be intricate and difficult, that it involves hard intellectual effort, and that for a time it must be nurtured by a coterie of those who know'. Chapman's dedicatory letter to *The Shadow Of Night* likewise speaks of '*Herculean* labour' (l. 3) and addresses members of the coterie of Sir Walter Ralegh and the Earl of Northumberland.

The Shadow Of Night may have been written by the summer of 1592. This suggestion was first made by Charles Nicholl in *A Cup Of News: The life of Thomas Nashe* (London: Routledge & Kegan Paul, 1984), p. 109. Nicholl quotes the opening quatrain of a sonnet composed in 1592 by Nashe in praise of 'Amyntas', i.e. Lord Strange, the 'most ingenious *Darbie*' of Chapman's dedicatory letter to *The Shadow Of Night*:

> Perusing yesternight, with idle eyes,
>   The Fairy Singers stately tuned verse,
> And viewing after Chap-mens wonted guise,
>   What strange contents the title did rehearse . . .

It does seem likely that 'Chap-mens' is a pun on Chapman's name, particularly given the other references to '. . . night', 'strange contents', and the trance-like 'idle eyes'. Nicholl adds: 'This glance at Chapman's poetic and philosophic stance is aptly made in the context of the *Faerie Queene*, which is shot through with occultist and neo-Platonic themes' (*A Cup Of News*, p. 109). Books I–III of Spenser's *Faerie Queene* appeared in 1590. The poem was dedicated to Elizabeth I, but Spenser also addressed an explanatory letter to Sir Walter Ralegh. A date of 1592 for *The Shadow Of Night* allows

Nicholl to set Chapman's work beside Marlowe's contemporaneous tragedy *Dr Faustus* and Nashe's *Pierce Penilesse his Supplication to the Divell* (1592):

> The three works run the gamut of reactions. At either end are Chapman and Nashe, devotee and sceptic: Chapman immersed in occult study, dedicated to 'invocation, fasting, watching'; Nashe out and about in the daily world, reacting to the idea of invocation with the spoof diabolism of Pierce's 'supplication'. And somewhere between the two, oscillating and ambiguous, is Marlowe, poetically 'ravisht' by the aspirations and ethos of 'magick', yet thumping home the orthodox line that invocation is black, unlawful and damnable' (*A Cup Of News*, p. 110).

Nicholl proposes that 'some kind of debate on the value of occultism is going on', with the figures involved including Sir Walter Ralegh and Lord Strange.

The Shadow Of Night should also be set against the contemporary vogue for erotic Ovidian poetry. Chapman regarded this as trivial:

> Presume not then ye flesh confounded soules,
> That cannot beare the full Castalian bowles,
> Which sever mounting spirits from the sences,
> To looke in this deepe fount for thy pretenses: . . .

This section of 'Hymnus in Cynthiam', ll. 162–5, probably alludes to the lines from Ovid's *Amores*, I.15.35–6, prefixed to Shakespeare's *Venus and Adonis*, which was printed in 1593: 'Let the mob admire base things; may golden Apollo serve me full cups from the Castalian spring.' Like *Ovids Banquet of Sence* (1595), *The Shadow Of Night* is meant to be 'deepe' and chaste like the moon-goddess Cynthia, identified with Elizabeth I, as in the surviving fragments of Ralegh's long poem, 'The 11th: and last booke of the Ocean to Scinthia' and 'The end of the bookes, of the Oceans love to Scinthia, and the beginninge of the 12 Boock, entreatinge of Sorrow'. Chapman's poems are not meant for 'flesh confounded soules'.

He seems to have wanted *The Shadow Of Night* to be read in the spirit of Orphic hymns. These poems addressed to Greek divinities were thought to reveal to initiates the secrets of the ancient mystery religion of Orphism, and they were attributed to Orpheus (modern scholars have been unable to prove who wrote the hymns, or when). Orpheus is quoted five times in the notes, a hymn by Callimachus is cited twice, a Homeric hymn once. Raymond B. Waddington notes that Ficino interpreted the Orphic Hymns as astrological invocations: see *The Mind's Empire: Myth and Form in George Chapman's Narrative Poems* (Baltimore and London: Johns Hopkins University Press, 1974), p. 95. Ficino practised Orphic magic. He tried to cure his melancholy by drawing down the 'virtues' of planets, and Waddington suggests *The Shadow Of Night* adapts similar invocatory procedures: '*Noctem* should be considered as providing a context for the invocation in *Cynthiam*, which expresses the character of the moon goddess. The "magic" which the poet attempts to invoke is both subjective, medically curative as it was for Ficino, and transitive, an effort to work a quasi-religious, wholly political "influence" upon his audience' (*The Mind's Empire*, p. 95). Millar Maclure also turns to Ficino in a helpful account of the relationship between the two hymns: see *George Chapman: A Critical Study* (Toronto: Toronto University Press, 1966), p. 36. 'Between them the two hymns deal with the two sorts of "temporal beatitude" according to Ficino: the contemplative (*religio*) and the active (*justitia*). The first hymn is contemplative, concerned with poetic wisdom and its enemies; the second turns to the life of action, to politics and morals. The first is concerned with art, the second with nature'. 'Hymnus in Noctem' has been chosen here to better illustrate Chapman's art.

FURTHER READING

Battenhouse, R. W., 'Chapman's *The Shadow Of Night*: An Interpretation', *Studies in Philology*, XXXVIII (1941), pp. 584–608

TEXTUAL NOTES

The base text is from the copy of *The Shadow Of Night* (1594) in the Bodleian Library, Oxford (shelfmark: Mal. 299 [6]). In the notes that follow, the first readings are those of this edition and the second record those of the base text.

95 fire ∧] ~)	381 ¹¹] *omitted in* Q
104 price.] ~:	394 Is] In
120 drudgerie:] ~.	Gloss
139 *marginal note*: Muse] Muses	no. 1 *Astronomicis]* Astronimicis
144 Fortitude.] ~,	'ΑΛλ] Α'λλ
148 exemplified;] ~.	no. 3 *discere*] *dicere*
149 *indented in* Q	no. 6 *advolaverat*] *advolverat*
190 jestes;] ~.	no. 12 *inga*] *fuga*
260 beames:] ~.	no. 13.3 *quae fert*] *quaefert*
296 ne'er] nere	no. 13.5 *decora*] ∧ ~
301 villanies:] ~.	

COMMENTARY

Dedicatory letter

Master Mathew Roydon: Chapman's next publication *Ovids Banquet of Sence* (1595) is also dedicated to Roydon, a poet, mathematician and Hermeticist. Roydon studied at the Inns of Court in London, and was part of the circle of 'University Wits' in the 1580s, writing commendatory verses for Thomas Watson's sonnet sequence *The Εκατομπα Θια or Passionate Centurie of Love* (1582). He was friendly with Christopher Marlowe, and part of Sir Walter Ralegh's circle. Roydon's 'Elegie, or Friends passion for his

Astrophill', about Sir Philip Sidney, appeared in *The Phoenix Nest* (1593). He was praised by Thomas Nashe in the preface to Robert Greene's *Menaphon* (1589): 'Neither is he [Spenser] the onely swallow of our Summer . . . there are extant about London many most able men to revive Poetry . . . as namely, for example, *Matthew Roydon*, *Thomas Achlow*, and *George Peele*; the first of whom . . . hath shewed himselfe singular in the immortall Epitaph of his beloved *Astrophell*, besides many other most absolute Comike inventions (made more publike by every mans praise, then they can be by my speech) . . .' Roydon was clearly respected by Chapman.

3–7 *from flints . . . Medusa*: The references come from Natalis Comes's *Mythologiae*, Book VIII, Chapter II, first published in 1551. The allusion to 'the eyes of *Graea*' is inaccurate: see Introduction. Frank L. Schoell first showed how Chapman quarried Comes's compendium of classical mythology in his book *Études sur l'Humanisme continental en Angleterre à la fin de la Renaissance* (Paris: Champion, 1926).

15–16 *supererogation . . . pierst*: Chapman uses the word 'supererogation' to mean something like 'overweening pretension', but its close proximity to 'pierst' calls into play a contemporary literary controversy. Only a very simplified account is given here; for many more details see *A Cup Of News: The life of Thomas Nashe* by Charles Nicholl (London: Routledge & Kegan Paul, 1984). In *Foure Letters and certaine Sonnets* (1592), the Cambridge University tutor Gabriel Harvey scathingly condemned the dying writer Robert Greene as a dissolute hack. Greene was a friend of Thomas Nashe, and Nashe replied to Harvey in *Strange Newes, of the intercepting certaine Letters and a convoy of Verses as they were going Privillie to Victuall the Low Countries* (1593). In *Strange Newes*, Nashe took the word 'supererogation' from Roman Catholic theology to make it mean 'doing more than is needed'. The *OED*'s first citation of this sense is from *Strange Newes*. Harvey responded to Nashe with *Pierces Supererogation* (1593), a reference in part to another of Nashe's works, *Pierce Penilesse his Supplication to the Divell* (1592). In *Pierces Supererogation*, Harvey explains that an unnamed friend of his has been defending Nashe as a proof of the argument that it's better for writers to experience life than read books. Frances A. Yates in *A Study of Love's Labour's Lost* (Cambridge: Cambridge University Press, 1936) shows that Harvey's friend was the writer John Eliot, and she suggests that Chapman's dedicatory letter was written partly to take issue with Harvey's long account of Eliot's remarks. For example, Harvey reports his friend as saying: 'they that will seeke out the Archmistery of the busiest Modernistes, shall find it nether more, nor lesse, than a certayne pragmaticall secret, called Villainy, the verie science of Sciences, and the familiar Spirit of Pierces Supererogation'. The words 'secret . . . science . . . familiar . . . Pierces Supererogation' all have their indignant echoes in Chapman's letter. And it certainly does seem as if Chapman is attacking Nashe ('Pierce'), a rival for the patronage of two of the noblemen referred to below. See particularly pp. 108–12, 179–80 and 201 of *A Cup Of News* for the diametric oppositions between Chapman and Nashe, and the idea that *Pierce Penilesse* contains 'elements of discrete propaganda' against Ralegh's circle. See also the Commentary on l. 19.

16–17 *that she . . . secrets*: Compare l. 74: '(Most harlot-like) her naked secrets shows'.

The 'passion-driven men' of ll. 10–11 inhabit the 'blindnesse of the minde' castigated in the poem. See also the Commentary on l. 27–8.

19 *Intonsi Catones*: From Horace's *Odes*, ii.15, 11. Means 'unshaven Catos' – a reference to the Roman Stoic philosopher Cato who may have looked unkempt but had integrity. Chapman's suggestion is that the 'passion-driven' and 'profit-ravisht' men condemned in his letter don't have any integrity, and they look scruffy. It's possible that Chapman is giving a sarcastic classical twist to Harvey's attack on Greene in *Foure Letters and certaine Sonnets*. One of Harvey's numerous taunts concerns Greene's 'fonde disguisinge of a Master of Arte with ruffianly haire, unseemely apparell, and more unseemely Company'. Nicholl suggests in *A Cup Of News* that the main target of Chapman's jibes is Nashe's *Christes Teares over Jerusalem, whereunto is annexed, a comparitive admonition to London* (1593). He thinks Chapman sees Nashe as 'a yob masquerading as a preacher' (p. 180).

27 *ingenious Darbie*: Ferdinando Stanley, Lord Strange, 5th Earl of Derby (?1559–1594), patron of the theatrical company Strange's Men. Probably called 'ingenious' because he wrote poetry and was interested in alchemy. *Darbie* was the model for Amyntas in Spenser's *Colin Clouts come home againe* (printed 1595). Thomas Nashe's *Pierce Penilesse* was also dedicated to 'Amyntas', while his entertainingly obscene poem 'The choise of valentines', about visiting a prostitute, was addressed 'To the right Honorable the lord S.', that is, Lord Strange. It is possible that Chapman's use of the word 'prostitutely' in l. 16 is barbed against Nashe.

28 *Northumberland*: Henry Percy, 9th Earl of Northumberland (1564–1632), known as the 'wizard Earl'. See Notes to Poems.

31 *heire of Hunsdon*: Sir George Carey (1547–1603), Lord Strange's brother-in-law and friend. Carey's father Henry, 1st Lord Hunsdon, was Queen Elizabeth's first cousin and Lord Chamberlain: he succeeded to the title of 2nd Lord Hunsdon in 1596. Nashe dedicated *Christes Teares over Jerusalem* to Lady Elizabeth Carey, and at Christmas 1593 Carey helped Nashe escape a legal summons brought by the Aldermen of the City of London over insinuations in that work. Nashe's *The Terrors of the Night* (printed 1594), about dreams and nightmares, was dedicated to the Careys' daughter, and can be seen as a rationalist counter-pull to Chapman's more occultist *The Shadow Of Night*. In 1597 Carey became Lord Chamberlain and patron of Shakespeare's company of actors. He helped many artists and scholars, and was also Governor of the Isle of Wight.

'Hymnus in Noctem'

1–4 and **Gloss 1** *Great . . . reliefe*: Derived from a reference in Comes's *Mythologiae*, III, 12. 'De Nocte'. The Latin quoted in the gloss is Comes's adaptation of ll. 408–10 of Aratus' Greek astronomical poem *Phaenomena* ('Aratus in *Astronomicis*'). In English: 'Night, the ancient [goddess], with her chariot enfolds this Altar all around, and she gave to sailors these most certain signs, as she felt pity for men who are exposed to dangers from every source.' Comes has added to Aratus the image of

Night enfolding the constellation of the Altar with her chariot. Probably misled by the usual image of Night going round *the earth* in her chariot, Chapman fails to recognize that the 'ara' (altar) mentioned in Comes's text is the constellation of the Altar. He thinks it applies to the earth. The last line of Comes's translation also seems to be largely based on Cicero's version of Aratus (see ll. 189–91 of *Carmina Aratea*).

> *Haec tamen aeterno invisens loca curriculo nox*
> *signa dedit nautis, cuncti quae noscere possent,*
> *Commiserans hominum metuendos undique casus.*

Thus, in quoting from Comes, Chapman is also, probably unknowingly, quoting from Cicero. Textually, a misprint in Chapman's original reference in the Gloss to '*Aratus in Astronimicis*' has been corrected to '*Astronomicis*'.

5 and **Gloss 2** *nurse of death*: Derived from Comes's Latin translation in his *Mythologiae*, III, 12, 'De Nocte', of ll. 211–13 of Hesiod's Greek *Theogony* ('*Hesiodus* in *Theogonia*'). In English: 'Night bore harsh Fate and the black Parca, and Death, and Sleep, and all the many sorts of dreams, she bore these children without being joined to any husband.' Parca was originally the Roman goddess of birth, but then owing to an etymological mix-up, the Parcae became the three Fates of Latin poetry.

10 *shipwracke*: One of Chapman's favourite images. See Introduction.

14 and **Gloss 3** *franchisement and memorie*: The Latin *discere* means 'to learn', *reminisci* means 'to remember'. Chapman's original text has *dicere*, 'to say': this misprint has been corrected. Compare Plato's *Phaedo*, 72e to 76. See Notes to Poems.

19 and **Gloss 4** *Heavens christall temples*: In Gloss 4 the reference to '*Homer & aliis*' means 'Homer and others'.

21–2 *fierce bolts . . . Artillerie*: Compare *Bussy D'Ambois* (1604), IV.2.16–17, and Chapman's *Caesar And Pompey* (1604–5), II.v.3–4: 'those dreadfull bolts,/ the *Cyclops* Ram in *Joves* Artillery, . . .'

29–49 *Sorrowes . . . pride*: This whole verse paragraph, particularly the section about the elements, is indebted to a passage in *La Semaine ou Création du monde* (1578) by Guillaume de Salluste, Sieur Du Bartas, which was translated into English as *Bartas his Devine Weekes and Workes* by Josuah Sylvester. The first fragments came out in 1592, the complete translation in 1608. Compare ll. 247–60 of the First Day of the First Week:

> That first World (yet) was a most forme-lesse *Forme*,
> A confus'd Heap, a *Chaos* most diforme,
> A Gulph of Gulphes, a Body ill compact,
> An ugly medly, where all difference lackt:
> Where th'Elements lay jumbled all together,
> Where hot and colde were jarring each with either;
> The blunt with sharpe; the danke against the drie,
> The hard with soft, the base against the high;
> Bitter with sweet: and while this brawle did laste,

> The Earth in Heav'n, the Heav'n in Earth was plaste:
>
> Earth, Aire, and Fire, were with the Water mixt,
>
> Water, Earth, Aire, within the Fire were fixt,
>
> Fire, Water, Earth, did in the Aire abide,
>
> Aire, Fire, and Water, in the Earth did hide.

Quoted from *The Divine Weeks and Works of Guillaume de Saluste Sieur du Bartas*, translated by Josuah Sylvester, ed. Susan Snyder (Oxford: Clarendon Press, 1979), p. 118.

60 *As in*: 'As they were in . . .'

63–74 *A stepdame . . . shows*: Derived from Comes's *Mythologiae*, III, 12, 'De Nocte'.

67 *then*: i.e. before then, before the arrival of the 'stepdame Night of minde'.

70 *shadow*: In the 'shadow' because of the 'hell obscuring wings' of l. 64, and the 'shadow' in the title *The Shadow Of Night*.

74 *Most . . . shows*: Compare Commentary on ll. 16–17 of the dedicatory letter.

77 *create*: i.e. 'created'.

83 *Now . . . paramores*: Refers back to 'Religious curb' in l. 81.

84 *Calydonian bores*: Sent by Diana as a curse to the kingdom of Calydon, as told in Homer's *Iliad*, IX.536ff. The reference here is possibly derived from Comes's *Mythologiae*, VII, 3, 'De Apro Calydonio'. Compare Chapman's *The Widdowes Teares* (1604–5), II.4.188.

91 *without*: i.e. 'to be without'.

95–104 *Who . . . price*: The 'tender Chevrill' is the skin from a kid-goat which is 'shruncke with fire' so the arms and legs metaphorically burn back into the body out of a selfish desire to avoid being used or having to give anything away. The phrase 'fierce rape forebeare' is difficult to paraphrase. In context it seems to mean something like: 'Leave aside the question of fierce rape, which really would be an intrusion, man even wants to shirk his duty of hospitality, because he is greedy.' The lines make more sense when those following have been read. In ll. 105–11 the image of the goat-skin leads on to the contrasting kindness of the mythical goat Amalthaea (see 'A List of Historical, Mythological and Geographical Names').

105–11 *Kinde . . . harts*: Derived from Comes's *Mythologiae*, VI, 11, 'De Capri Celesti'.

112–16 *The sencelesse . . . exclude*: Derived from Comes's *Mythologiae*, VI, 10, 'De Argonavi'. The 'Argive ship' is the vessel which carried Jason and the Argonauts to Colchos on their quest for the Golden Fleece. The 'fautor' (patron) and 'God of gratitude' is Jove, whose transformation of Amalthaea into a star 'for her love' to him has just been described.

117–22 *A thousand . . . the best*: Chapman says he could give a thousand examples of Jove creating stars, examples which would condemn ('damne') men. The description of men as 'stone-pesants' looks back to l. 108: 'Basenesse is flintie; gentrie softe as silke'. Typhon is a monster with a hundred serpentine heads who rebelled against the Gods, was crushed by a thunderbolt, and then buried under Mount Aetna: compare *Bussy D'Ambois*, III.2.136–9, where Monsieur predicts that Bussy will be struck 'under th'*AEtna* of his pride'. Men 'like Typhons' might try to be the equal of kings, but in fact they are the 'abject slaves of drudgerie'. Compare ll. 329–30, 'pale day . . . Is but a drudge'. Even worse, men are proud of their 'thraldome' and in not responding to kindness are the opposite of star-creating Jove. They hate not to be hated by 'the best'.

124–6 *And that . . . intelligence*: 'And accept that to begin with man was given a shape of God-like excellence, for the sake of his soul and the intelligence of that (female) soul.'

135 *prime*: Compare l. 61, 'extract out of the prime'. Poets are figured as the best surviving men.

139 *the sweetest*: The Latin in the marginal gloss means 'the sweetness of the song, or its modulation'.

139–58 *So when . . . hel-danting kinde*: Derived from Comes's *Mythologiae*, VII, 14, 'De Orpheo'.

159–70 *The golden . . . with will*: Derived from reference in Comes's *Mythologiae*, II, 4, 'De Junone'. The 'golden chaine' represents 'Ambition' and 'cursed avarice' (compare 'thanklesse avarice', l. 103) because the Gods try to use it to pull down Jove. The chain comes from Homer's *Iliad* where Jove tells the Gods not to side with either Troy or Greece in the Trojan War. In Chapman's translation of *The Iliads Of Homer* (1611), VIII.16–25:

> '. . . Indanger it the whiles and see let downe our golden chaine,
> And at it let all Deities their utmost strengths constraine
> To draw me to the earth from heaven: you never shall prevaile
> Though with your most contention ye dare my state assaile.
> But when my will shall be dispos'd to draw you all to me,
> Even with the earth it selfe and seas ye shall enforced be.
> Then will I to to Olympus' top our vertuous engine bind
> And by it everie thing shall hang by my command inclind.
> So much I am supreme to Gods, to men supreme as much.'
> The Gods sat silent and admir'd, his dreadfull speech was such.

Lines 163–70 are some of the most difficult (and worst) ever written by Chapman, 'Intending this' being a particular insult to the reader's patience. The 'supreme' part of Jove seems to be occupied in this allegorical 'explanation' by the 'sweetest Muses sonne' of l. 139 who could draw men 'To civill love of Art, and Fortitude' (l. 144). So 'him' in l. 169 is the Poet whose adorning the 'shape' of man 'with vertue, and his powre with will' matches the aforementioned 'Art, and Fortitude'. The role of the ambitious gods is played by the representative man 'that manlesse changes hates': that is the man who because he is 'manlesse' hates the sort of changes that the Poet would like to see made in him and his kind through seeing 'accounts' which 'Might mend their mindes' (l. 138). It's also because he is 'manlesse' and hates changes that the representative man strains against the 'powrefull chaine' and so tries to keep men from the 'true vertue' and 'pristine states' upheld by the Poet. It is thus the 'powerfull chaine' and not the man which – stretch the syntax though this does – 'is ennobled with a deathlesse love/ Of things eternall, dignified above'. The next verse paragraph continues the theme of how men should become men.

189 *Bacchanalean feasts*: Bacchus is the god of wine, 'Bacchanalean' means riotously drunken and debauched.

195 *Saturnes golden scepter*: The Golden Age. Compare *Bussy D'Ambois*, III.2.103–7.

203 and **Gloss 6** *The morning . . . stead*: Derived from Comes's Latin translation in his *Mythologiae*, VI, 2, 'De Aurora', of ll. 16–17 of Lycophron's obscure Greek poem 'Alexandra'. In English: 'Dawn was just swooping down on the high Phegion mount on the swift wings of Pegasus', i.e. Pegasus is 'the Muses stead [steed]'. Textually, a misprint in Chapman's original quotation has been corrected (on the basis of Comes) from '*advolverat*' to '*advolaverat*' because the former is grammatically impossible and makes no sense.

204 and **Gloss 7** *Vulcans golden bed*: Derived, as the Gloss acknowledges, from Comes's *Mythologiae*, V, 17, 'De Sole'.

207 *this inferiour element*: i.e. daylight.

215–17 and **Gloss 8** *Eagle-like . . . deepe*: Expanded from Comes's Latin translation in his *Mythologiae*, III, 12, 'De Nocte', of a Greek hymn then attributed to Orpheus. In English: 'You [Night] who drive the light under the ground.' Compare l. 10 of 'To Night': see *Orphei hymni*, ed. W. Quandt (Berlin: 1962, 3rd edition). This is the first of several references in *The Shadow Of Night* to Orphic hymns, ancient Greek mysteries (see also the Headnote). Chapman's elaboration of the Orphic verse in ll. 215–17 of 'Hymnus in Noctem' is an instance of ingenious invention characteristic of the Greek hymns. Other devices imitated by Chapman from the hymns are listed by Gerald Snare in *The Mystification of George Chapman* (Durham, USA, and London: Duke University Press, 1989), p. 153. Snare cites 'the passion for compounding epithets and names (especially in Orpheus) and for inventing ingenious metaphors and similes; the inclusion of numerous place names and geographical detail (especially in Callimachus); extending epic similes into mininarratives; mythological narratives meant to be emblematic of the nature of the gods and their services; topical, even historical, allusion; prayers, usually at the conclusion; a kind of high-minded exclusiveness, sometimes expressed in asking the uninitiated to leave the temple.' Snare suggests that Chapman's imitation of 'a form relatively unknown in England, . . . the classical hymn', is the 'reason for the poem having the apparatus of a gloss, a gloss which consistently points out how successful the imitation is' (*Mystification*, p. 152). 'Chapman's glosses emphasize the construction of the poems, not a construct we may wish to derive from them. The application or the moral, that last step in the typical Renaissance gloss, is not taken' (*Mystification*, p. 166). This is partly why the glosses speak of the poet in the third person: 'He calls . . .' (Gloss 1), 'Here he alludes . . .' (Gloss 9), 'This *Periphrasis* . . . he useth . . .' (Gloss 10). The notes flaunt Chapman's wish to be taken seriously as an accomplished new voice in English poetry. Snare suggests that 'Chapman's habits as a glosser argue against taking the poems as mysterious documents meant to baffle the unworthy and keep outsiders out' but, among the conflicting evidence, note in the FINIS to the Gloss Chapman's address to 'such as understand . . . for the rest, God helpe them'.

227 *Art . . . heart*: Night is black except where she glitters with stars as if from within.

230 *deface*: Means to 'cover with clouds' and 'attack'.

232–4 *All the . . . love*: The lines refer back to ll. 105–22 about Jove transforming 'kinde Amalthaea' and the 'Argive ship' into stars.

246 *chiefe . . . Garlands*: Obscure, but probably ironic. As l. 243 refers to 'Vertues obscur'd' and l. 248 to 'vertues overthroes' it seems likely that 'vertues Garlands' are not meant to be the usual straightforward symbols of distinction or victory. Quite the opposite: the 'chiefe flowrs' are flesh-imprisoning stone and steel which then help to create the shape of the following oxymoronic image of Night as the 'tender fortresse of our woes' (l. 247). Night is 'tender' because the flesh is 'spongie' (l. 244), like a 'fortresse' because of the stone and steel, and full of 'woes' because of the oppressed state of 'vertues'.

255–9 and **Gloss 9** *Fall Hercules . . . oxen*: Compare Comes's *Mythologiae*, VII, 1, 'De Hercule'. The 'beastly stable' is the Augean stable which was notorious for its size and filth; it was one of Hercules' labours to clean it in a day. The Latin in the Gloss means 'as Pherecides says in the third book of his histories'.

260 *his*: Refers to the 'Sunne'.

268 and **Gloss 10** *Rich-tapird . . . blest*: Derived from Comes's *Mythologiae*, III, 12, 'De Nocte'. Compare Commentary on ll. 1–4 and Gloss 1.

280–87 *And when . . . miseries*: Very obscure. The following interpretation is only tentative. The 'matter of our kind' and the 'materiall substance of the mind' are everyone's bodies, not just the death-seeking poet's as in l. 276: 'There will I furnish up my funerall bed'. Bodies' status as matter links them to the Earth and metaphorically they move like the Earth until they die as well ('cease their revolutions'). The end comes about because they live in the detestable time described in the rest of the poem ('in abode/ Of such impure and ugly period'). The next line – 'As the old essence, and insensive prime' – is not a further description of the current 'impure and ugly period'. Rather, it seems to mean that the current period will be concluded just as the old one was: 'So all things now (extract out of the prime)/ Are turnd to chaos, and confound the time' (ll. 61–2). The *OED* does not have an entry for 'insensive', but it seems to correspond to a rare meaning given there for 'insensible', that is, 'non-material' and 'incapable of being perceived by the bodily senses': hence the opposing stress given in ll. 280–81 to 'matter' and 'materiall substance'. The last three lines are even more obscure, but they seem to look back to the start of the poem. The 'time' just passed may be 'fourefold' because it refers to the 'fighting parents' (l. 38) of the universe – earth, air, sea and fire. The world is then turned to a 'lumpe' just as the end of the elements' combat saw 'bodies live without the soules of men,/ Lumps being digested' (ll. 48–9). At this later stage of the poem bodies are dying, but Chapman's imagination works in the same way, and, as ll. 48–9 were followed by an image of streams 'Let forth' from a 'wealthie fount', so now 'rapting Torrents rise' and 'murmure forth my miseries'. The word 'rapting' (meaning 'enrapturing') is used four years before the *OED*'s first citation. The rise of the 'rapting Torrents' reflects Chapman's wish in ll. 8–10: 'now let humor give/ Seas to mine eyes, that I may quicklie weepe/ The shipwracke of the world'.

289 *Whom . . . give*: 'In whom the same extreme situations have produced the same desires.'

295 *Whose . . . sustain*: 'Whose sisters suffer rape and bondage.'

302 *Aspire . . . quintessence*: 'Aspire th' extraction' means aspire to that. Both 'extraction' and 'quintessence' are terms used in alchemy: 'quintessence' is the 'fifth essence' of ancient and medieval philosophy, the substance of which heavenly bodies were supposed to be composed.

314 *Should . . . eyes*: 'Should' refers back to the 'triviall and remissive mones' (l. 311) and seems to mean 'which would'. The 'hearers eyes' are the mirrors ('glasses') to their souls – a popular Renaissance idea.

321–3 *Vertue . . . puts on*: Examples of the 'extreames' resulting from 'Chaos' (l. 319). 'Vertue' gives rise to 'scorne', and 'noblest honor' is a cause of shame. 'Pride' is so arrogant he likes to bath in tears: 'purple' is the imperial colour. Compare *Bussy D'Ambois*, III.2.69–70, where Bussy taunts the Guise about wearing purple: 'Heere would I make thee cast that popular purple,/ In which thy proud soule sits and braves thy soveraigne.'

340 *Iveryport*: One of the two gates of Sleep – made of ivory – is transferred to Night. Compare Homer's *Odyssey*, XIX.562, and Virgil's *Aeneid*, VI.893–6. Also referred to in Chapman's comedy *All Fooles* (1599), III.1.14. Sleep's other gate of horn is referred to in l. 352. The subjects of the dreams from the 'Iveryport' look oddly forward to *Bussy D'Ambois*, where Monsieur is a 'Prince', the friar Comolet ends up 'in habit of deceased friends', and Tamyra is a 'Lady'.

352 *port of horne*: One of the two gates of Sleep. See note above to l. 340.

361 *the second light*: i.e. Night.

362–7 *Since day . . . sorrowes wings*: These lines reflect the Protestant distrust of the visual imagination. Between 1536 and 1658, between the dissolution of the monasteries by Henry VIII and the death of Oliver Cromwell, Protestants in Britain smashed up tens of thousands of religious images. A good account of their iconoclasm is given by Andrew Graham-Dixon in Chapter One of *A History of British Art* (London: BBC Books, 1996). On p. 36 he notes: 'Defaced images often had their eyes scratched away, as though, by breaking visual contact between image and viewer, the suspect power of the image might be defused'. Chapman's assertion that 'the eyes most quicke and dangerous use,/ Enflames the heart' lies behind the narrator's warning to Ovid not to look at Corynna in stanzas 42–3 of *Ovids Banquet of Sence*. Lines 366–7 point towards *Ovids Banquet of Sence* in saying that mournings should be preferred to banquettings. An explanation for why this should be is contained in ll. 190–91 of *The Teares of Peace* (1609): 'Free sufferance for the truth, makes sorrow sing,/ And mourning farre more sweet, then banqueting'.

381–2 and **Gloss 11** *Themis . . . horse*: Derived from Comes's *Mythologiae*, IV, 16, 'De Horis'. In the Gloss, the tag '*ut Orph*.' means 'as [says] Orpheus', the Latin verse means 'The Hours born from the seed of Jupiter and Themis, etc'. See ll. 1−3 of 'To the Horai' in Quandt's edition of *Orphei hymni*.

388 *the Cyprian starre*: The planet Venus.

392−3 and **Gloss 12** *a brase . . . Hynds*: Derived from Comes's Latin translation in his *Mythologiae*, III, 18, 'De Diana', of ll. 110−12 of Callimachus' Greek hymn 'To Artemis'. In the Gloss '*ut ait*' means 'as says', the verses translate as: 'Golden, Diana, slayer of Titys, are all your weapons, and your maiden girdle, and golden are the yokes you put on the neck of the deer, when you lead them to your golden chariot'. Titys was a son of Earth. Textually, a misprint in Chapman's original quotation has been corrected (on the basis of Comes) from '*fuga*' (meaning 'flight, the action of running away') to '*iuga*' (meaning 'yokes') because '*fuga*' is grammatically impossible and makes no sense.

394−6 and **Gloss 13** *Hyperions . . . incantations*: Derived from Comes's Latin translation in his *Mythologiae*, VI, 2, 'De Aurora', of ll. 371−4 of Hesiod's *Theogony*. The Latin '*in his versibus*' means 'in these lines', the verses translate as: 'Thea gave birth to mighty Sun, and shining Moon, and Dawn, who brings life-giving light to all, to mortals and to the gods who dwell in heaven, for noble Thea conceived them from the seed of glorious Hyperion.'

A minor correction has been made to a misprint in Chapman's quotation, on the basis of Comes.

395 *disparent*: Means 'diverse, of varying appearance'. Compare Chapman's *Ovids Banquet of Sence*, 11.5, and his continuation of Marlowe's *Hero And Leander* (1598), III.123−4, where the Goddess Ceremonie wears 'A rich disparent Pentackle . . . Drawne full of circles and strange characters.'

Ovids Banquet of Sence

Ovids Banquet of Sence was published in 1595 in a volume with three other poems. 'A Coronet for his Mistresse *Philosophie*' is a sequence of ten sonnets definitely by Chapman. He may also have translated 'The amorous Zodiack' from a French poem by Gilles Durant. 'The amorous contention of *Phillis* and *Flora*' is a medieval poem probably translated from Latin by Chapman's friend Richard Stapleton. The title page of the book boasts a Latin epigraph from Persius and a cryptic emblem; inside are a dedicatory letter, five commendatory sonnets, and twenty-two marginal glosses to *Ovids Banquets of Sence*. As with *The Shadow Of Night* (1594), Chapman seems to have devised a volume designed to deter riff-raff while conveying his meanings. The epigraph reads: '*Quis leget haec? Nemo Hercule Nemo, vel duo vel nemo.*' This condenses ll. 2−3 of Persius' 'Satire I'. Persius is approached by an anonymous interlocutor who asks him: 'Who'll read that?' Persius replies: 'Not a soul by Hercules. One or two perhaps or nobody.' The lines hark back to the dedicatory letter in *The Shadow Of Night* (source of 'Hymnus in Noctem'). There Chapman claims to be content 'if but a few, if one, or if none' (l. 36) like his work. 'Satire I' is also quoted in the *Prologus* to Chapman's comedy *All Fooles* (1599), and in both cases the citation is a useful pointer. Persius' poem attacks the fashionable decadent verse of his day: Chapman's target in *Ovids Banquet of Sence* is the vogue for erotic Ovidian narratives such as Shakespeare's *Venus and Adonis* (1593), already swatted in *The Shadow Of Night*. Persius' reference to Hercules calls to mind Chapman's talk of '*Herculean* labour' in l. 3 of the dedicatory letter to Roydon in *The Shadow Of Night*, while in 'Hymnus in Noctem' Hercules is urged to shoot at the sun: 'Suffer no more his lustfull rayes to get/ The Earth with issue' (ll. 264–5). Chapman's antipathy to 'lustfull' verse (his 'Mistresse' is '*Philosophie*') means that *Ovids Banquet of Sence* must be read from a 'judiciall perspective' (l. 20), as Roydon is told in the dedicatory letter. The operation of such a perspective is illustrated by the emblem on the title page. It shows a straight stick seemingly bent when half placed in water, with the motto: *Sibi Conscia Recti* (Conscious in themselves of the right). The lesson of this optical illusion is to trust to what the mind knows is right, not judge by the evidence of the senses. Raymond B. Waddington suggests that Chapman may well have been the first poet to use a metaphoric title-page emblem 'with such sophistication, integrating it into the entire design of the book': see 'Visual Rhetoric: Chapman and the Extended Poem', *English Literary Renaissance*, 13 (1983), p. 46. The emblem – like *Ovids Banquet of Sence* itself – is another of Chapman's 'optike' pictures (see Introduction).

Ovid is meant to be seen as misguided because of the way he feasts on his senses. Chapman's summary of 'The Argument' of his poem makes clear how self-reflexive Ovid's banquet is: '*to himselfe uttered the comfort he conceived in his sence of Hearing*' (ll. 5– 6). This process of 'reverberate vigor' (49.5) continues throughout the poem and culminates in Ovid's declaration that for the sake of 'Sweete touch' (113.1) he will write 'the Art of love' (113.5). 'Ovid always ends up inspired by his own poeticization of what he senses rather than by what he senses itself ', notes Gerald Snare, 'Chapman's Ovid', *Studies in Philology*, p. 444. Snare adds: 'Chapman's assumption is that his readers should *not* be like Ovid . . . As proper readers are virtuous, they will not misinterpret and transform what is before them into some series of metaphors that will delight a heightened sensuality' ('Chapman's Ovid', p. 445). Chapman's poem is not finally a celebration of Ovid's spiritual ascent but a critique of his sensual descent. In 'The Banquet of Sense', *Shakespeare, Spenser, Donne*, pp. 84–115, Frank Kermode writes: 'The Platonic Banquet represents love, the ascent from sense to the higher powers of the soul, and ultimately the apprehension of the divine beauty. The Banquet of Sense represents a descent from sight to the senses capable of only material gratification – what Ficino calls "bestial love" ' (p. 99). Kermode's argument for 'a descent' is now largely accepted. But part of the difficulty of *Ovids Banquet of Sence* is the encouragement that Chapman seems to give to both views of his 'optike' picture: see, for example, the Commentary on 41.6–9 and gloss. This counter-attractiveness is also one of the main reasons for the work's value as a poem. Kermode calls it 'one of the most difficult poems in the language' ('The Banquet of Sense', p. 84), and at least one of Chapman's contemporaries seems to have agreed. Millar Maclure in

George Chapman: A Critical Study, p. 46, makes the persuasive suggestion that John Marston is alluding to Chapman and *Ovids Banquet of Sence* in his poem *The Scourge of Villanie* (1598), Satyre.IX.54–9:

> I am too milde, reach me my scourge againe,
>
> O yon's a pen speakes in a learned vaine.
>
> Deepe, past all sence. Lanthorne & candle light,
>
> Here's all invisible, *all mentall spright.*
>
> What hotchpotch, giberidge, doth the Poet bring?
>
> How strangely speakes? yet sweetly doth he sing . . .

FURTHER READING

Gless, Darryl J., 'Chapman's Ironic Ovid', *English Literary Renaissance*, 9 (1979), pp. 21–41

Huntington, John, 'Philosophical Seduction in Chapman, Davies, and Donne', *English Literary History*, 44 (1977), pp. 40–59

Kermode, Frank, 'The Banquet of Sense', *Shakespeare, Spenser, Donne* (London: Routledge & Kegan Paul, 1971), pp. 84–115

Myers Jr, James Phares, " 'This Curious Frame": Chapman's *Ovids Banquet of Sense*', *Studies in Philology*, 65 (1968), pp. 192–206

Ribner, Rhoda M., 'The Compasse of This Curious Frame: Chapman's *Ovids Banquet of Sence* and the Emblematic Tradition', *Studies in the Renaissance*, 17 (1970), pp. 233–58

Smarr, Janet Levarie, 'The Pyramid and the Circle: "Ovid's Banquet of Sense" ', *Philological Quarterly*, 63 (1984), pp. 369–86

Snare, Gerald, 'Chapman's Ovid', *Studies in Philology*, 75 (1978), pp. 430–50

Waddington, Raymond B., 'Chapman and Persius: The Epigraph to *Ovids Banquet of Sence*', *Review of English Studies*, 19 (1968), pp. 158–62

TEXTUAL NOTES

The base text is the copy of the first quarto in the Bodleian Library, Oxford (shelfmark: Mal. 210 [5]). In the notes that follow, the first readings are those of this edition and the second record those of the base text.

Epistle:	18.6 repayre:] ~?
9 *olentis*] *dentis*	21.9 eare,] ~.
11 ornament] ornamrnt	34.4 spices,] ~ ∧
36 others] other	37.9 merits.] ~;
	38.9 frames.] ~;
11.5 grounde] rounde	41.6 neede:] ~ ∧
12.4 divinitie.] ~,	46.7 enter;] ~,

47.7 fix,] ~ ∧
51.3 fade,] ~ ∧
53.1 is] in
   60 *marginal note*: office of her fingers]
     ~ ∧ ~~
63.3 finde] minde
65.6 told:] ~ ∧
65.7 it.] ~,
73.7 ensnare,] ~ ∧
73.8 subtlest] subtelst
83.2 unrest,] ~ ∧

86.3 breathes] breath's
90.9 childeren,] ~.
91.5 imperance,] ~ ∧
91.9 scorning.] ~,
93.4 the] thy
105.9 Globes.] ~ ∧
108.6 liken'd] likened
112.5 mindes,] ~ ∧
112.9 utterd] uttered

COMMENTARY

Dedicatory letter

Mathew Royden: See first note in Commentary on 'Hymnus in Noctem' in *The Shadow Of Night* (1594) and Note to *Poems*.

6–8 *materiall . . . utilitie*: Closely based on Xylander's Latin translation (published in 1572) of the essay 'De Homero' in Plutarch's *Moralia* (Plutarch's authorship of the piece has been questioned by modern scholars). The essay says that Homer was the first to show the use of '*Schema*'. So (whoever did write it) it's not surprising that Chapman's belief in the importance of 'varying' is also expressed in 'The Preface To The Reader' in his translation of *The Iliads Of Homer* (1611): '*Yet how much I differ, and with what authoritie, let my impartiall and judiciall reader judge – alwaies conceiving how pedanticall and absurd an affectation it is in the interpretation of any Author (much more of Homer) to turn him word for word, when (according to Horace and other best lawgivers to translators) it is the part of every knowing and judiciall interpreter not to follow the number and order of words but the materiall things themselves, and sentences to weigh diligently, and to clothe and adorne them with words and such a stile and forme of Oration as are most apt for the language into which they are converted.*' The words 'materiall' and 'Oration' here recur, along with the idea of ornamentation. Note also the need for 'judiciall' readers and the critique of '*pedanticall . . . affectation*'.

8–9 *This of . . . addito*: The Latin *olentis* is corrected from the misprinted *dentis* in the original, following a suggestion first made in a letter by George G. Loane to *The Times Literary Supplement* on 21 February 1935. Translated it means: 'When you cook a lentil soup do not add any perfume'. The remark started life as a jibe by the comic poet Strattis about ('of') the Greek tragedian Euripides' over-refinement of style. But, as Loane points out, the sense changed over time to 'Don't cast pearls before swine'. It's difficult to say where Chapman found the quotation. He may have translated it straight from Aristotle's 'De Sensu', 443b, where Strattis is quoted. Chapman's version of the adage does not correspond with other Latin translations of 'De Sensu' which could have been available to him. Strattis' jibe is translated in

Erasmus' *Adagia* (1500), which Chapman knew, but again the Latin is different. It is possible that Chapman rephrased the line from Erasmus.

13 *and give Cammels hornes*: An allusion to one of Aesop's *Fables* about a camel asking Jove for horns. Compare Chapman's tragedy *The Revenge Of Bussy D'Ambois* (1610–11), II.1.176–81:

> . . . those foolish great-spleen'd Cammels,
>
> That to their high heads, beg'd of Jove hornes higher;
>
> Whose most uncomely, and ridiculous pride
>
> When hee had satisfied, they could not use,
>
> But where they went upright before, they stoopt,
>
> And bore their heads much lower for their hornes; . . .

14–16 *That, Enargia . . . phrase*: Sir Philip Sidney writes in *A defence of poetry* (1579–80, printed 1595) of the 'forciblenesse or *Energia* (as the Greeks call it) of the writer'. It's a quality brilliantly described by Seamus Heaney, who calls it 'this sensation of clear water springing through sand', in an essay which is mostly about Marlowe's translation of *Hero And Leander*, but also touches on Chapman's 1598 continuation; see 'Extending the Alphabet: On Christopher Marlowe's "Hero and Leander" ', in *The Redress of Poetry* (London: Faber, 1995), pp. 17–37. Chapman's use of the word '*Enargia*' calls on the sense of 'forciblenesse' while wanting to make sure it's not mistaken for brute force, hence the qualifications immediately following. The overall definition needs to be read against the paragraph below about 'Obscuritie'. The call for 'unaffected phrase' accords with the assertion that 'Obscuritie in affection of words, & indigested concets, is pedanticall and childish' (ll. 26–7).

22–30 *There is . . . dust of it*: Chapman is drawing on Erasmus's *Parabolae sive similia*: 'I have not chosen what was ready to hand, nor picked up pebbles on the beach; I have brought forth precious stones from the inner treasure-house of the Muses. The barber's shop, the tawdry conversation of the market-place are no source for what is to be worth the ears and eyes of educated men. Such things must be unearthed in the innermost secrets of nature, in the inner shrine of the arts and sciences.' Translated by R. A. B. Mynors, *The Collected Works of Erasmus* (Toronto: University of Toronto Press, 1978), XXIII, p 131.

25 *which . . . patch*: A dismissive phrase reused in Chapman's poem commending John Fletcher's tragicomedy *The Faithful Shepheardesse* (printed 1609), 'To his loving friend M. *J. Fletcher* concerning his Pastorall, being both a Poeme and a play', l. 16.

28–9 *with that . . . shaddowed*: A defiant assertion which suggests that Chapman may have been mocked or criticised for the obscurity of *The Shadow Of Night* (1594).

The Argument

2 *Corynna . . . Garden*: Corynna is the name of Ovid's mistress, her garden is where the action of *Ovids Banquet of Sence* is to occur.

Glosses *Auditus . . . Tactus*: The first three senses are placed in the same order as they are in Chapman's continuation of Marlowe's *Hero And Leander* (1598), V.42−7, just before Hero makes 'a friendly feast'. The procession through 'Musick . . . odorous . . . Beautie' appeals in turn to the senses of Hearing, Smell and Sight:

> They came; sweet Musick ushered th'odorous way,
> And wanton Ayre in twentie sweet forms danst
> After her fingers; Beautie and Love advanst
> Their ensignes in the downles rosie faces
> Of youths and maids, led after by the Graces.
> For all these, Hero made a friendly feast, . . .

Neoplatonic tradition places Hearing, Smell and Sight higher up the spiritual ladder than Taste and Touch because they do not depend on bodily contact. They are more intellectual. In his influential *Commentary on Plato's Symposium* (1474), Ficino puts Sight ahead of the other four senses. No source has been found for Chapman's own ordering in *Ovids Banquet of Sence*, where Sight is given a pivotal role. See especially stanzas 42 and 43.

Narratio

1.1−2.3 *The Earth . . . desire*: Darryl J. Gless in 'Chapman's Ironic Ovid', *English Literary Renaissance*, 9 (1979), p. 29, glosses these lines by reference to *Marsilio's Ficino's Commentary on Plato's Symposium*, edited and translated by Sears R. Jayne, *University of Missouri Studies*, 19 (1944). Gless writes: 'As Ficino explains, love is the "perpetual knot and binder of the world, the immovable support of its parts and the firm foundation of the whole creation" (III.iii, p. 152), for from "common relation[s] a common love is born, and from that love a common attraction. . . . [Hence] the magnet draws iron . . . . the sun turns many flowers and leaves toward itself, the moon attracts the seas . . ." ' (VI.x, p. 200. Cf. III.i, p. 148). The bracketed references are to Ficino's *Commentary*. Compare Chapman's comedy *All Fooles* (1599), I.1.97−123 and Commentary.

3.1−9 *Stone . . . shewed*: The description of the statue is adapted from the Greek traveller and geographer Pausanius as quoted in Natalis Comes's *Mythologiae* (1551), VI, 13, 'De Niobe'. The phrase 'optike reason' is translated from Comes's *ad opticam rationem*. See Introduction for discussion of 'optike pictures'. Chapman himself has made up the story of Augustus Caesar moving the statue from Mount Sipylus (named after Niobe's son listed first in 5.1), and surrounding it with statues and pyramids.

4.1 *In Sommer . . . exstasie*: Means that the extreme suffering ('exstasie') of Niobe can only be seen during the summer. Why is unclear.

5.1–3 *Her sonnes . . . Tantalus*: Niobe's sons are also listed by Comes in *Mythologiae*, VI, 13, 'De Niobe'.

6.8 *living beauties essence*: i.e. Corynna.

8.7–8 *Venus . . . desire*: An allusion to the beauty contest judged by Paris and won by Venus, which led to the Trojan War.

9.1–10.9 *A soft . . . them*: Some of the flowers and herbs in these two stanzas are obscure; Chapman may be using forgotten local names, such as 'Twillpants'. On 'the bewildering range of local plant nomenclature' see Keith Thomas, *Man and the Natural World* (London: Penguin, 1984), pp. 81–7. The only recorded usage of 'Melanthy' in the *OED* is from *Ovids Banquet of Sence*, and it's said to mean Gith. The *OED* then defines Gith as 'A name for plants of the genus *Nigella*, esp. *N. sativa*.' It also refers to *Nigella damascena*, or Damask Gith, better known nowadays as Love-in-a-mist, which is a member of the Buttercup family, and therefore quite possibly attractive to bees. However, Gith was also a name applied in the late sixteenth century to the Corn-cockle (*Lychnis Githago*), also known as Kiss-me-quick, an attractive cornfield plant with purple flowers. Both vernacular names suggest fitting occupants of Corynna's garden, and it is impossible to be sure exactly what Chapman had in mind. Nor is it clear what 'Amareus' is in modern botanical terms, although it might be amaracus, or dittany of Crete, 'formerly famous for its alleged medicinal virtues' (*OED*). 'Pansies' are still pansies, their name a sixteenth-century derivation from the French for thoughts – *pensées* – hence probably the flowers' symbolic use at 'Nuptials'. It's grammatically possible that '*Dianas* arrow' and '*Cupids* crimson shielde' are alternative terms for the pansy, which thus make it symbolic of chaste thoughts, as Diana is the moon-goddess of chastity and hunting, and Cupid is the god of love, the beautiful son of Mercury and Venus. Or they may be separate plants, in which case their identities are obscure. 'Ope-morne' could be anything, and seems to be included to balance 'night-shade', a family of plants with several members. All wild nightshades are poisonous, although Richard Mabey in his excellent *Flora Britannica* (London: Sinclair-Stevenson, 1996), p. 300, notes the ancient practice of using extracts from deadly nightshade (*Atropa belladonna*) as stomach sedatives. The plant is also thought to be the origin of the Latin compliment 'belladonna' (as in "beautiful woman"). Mabey writes: 'Italian women used water distilled from the 'beautiful lady herb' as a cosmetic, to enlarge their pupils' (*Flora Britannica*, p. 300). This sounds the kind of practice which would appeal to Corynna. '*Venus* navill' was a name given in the sixteenth century to the Pennywort (*Umbilicus rupestris*), now better known as the Navelwort, so called because of the dimple where the flower-stalk joins the centre of the fleshy circular leaf. Geoffrey Grigson writes: 'The 5th century Latin name for the plant was *umbilicus Veneris*, "Venus's navel"; an earlier Greek name – less polite, suggesting the hairless smooth statues – was *kepos Aphrodites*, "Aphrodites' privates" (literally "garden").' See *A Dictionary of English Plant Names* (London: Allen Lane, 1974), p. 150. The early name of *kepos Aphrodites* is of obvious relevance to a garden where a woman just compared to Venus (8.7) is appearing naked. Mabey also notes the Navelwort's vernacular name of 'Coolers', probably deriving 'from the use of the sappy leaves as an ointment for burns' (*Flora Britannica*, p. 177). 'Violets' are still violets, *Calamintha* is a genus including Common-, Cushion- and Wood-Calamint. There is a genus of plants called *Nepenthes*, but function is here more important than species. What's meant is a plant capable of producing the sedative drug Nepenthe, drunk to expel sadness and melancholy ('purgative of care'). *Rumex* is a genus of plants including the Broad-leaved Dock, used most commonly as a salve against nettle stings, although Mabey includes a recollection of the plant being mixed with pig's lard to produce a treatment for piles (*Flora Britannica*, p. 111). 'Sya' is obscure (although sye is an old dialect name for chive). 'Hyacinth' is probably the aquamarine-coloured *Hyacinthus orientalis*, which was introduced to England in the mid-sixteenth century, although the name 'hyacinth' was also given to larkspur and the South-East European *Scilla bifolia*, which flowers in spring. Whichever, it's the mythological aspect that's important. The hyacinth is supposed to have sprung from the blood of the dying vegetation god Huakinthos, who was accidentally killed with a discus by Apollo. Mabey notes that Apollo is supposed to have inscribed the letters AIAI – 'alas' – on the plant's petals to express his grief (*Flora Britannica*, p. 412). 'White and red Jessamines' are jasmine (*Jasminum officinale*) introduced to England from Persia in the sixteenth century. 'Merry' is a corruption of the French for cherry – *merise* – and is probably a kind of wild black cherry which also used to be known as the honey cherry. 'Melliphill' is obscure, but is a plant again linked in some way to honey; to 'mellify' is to make honey, or sweeten with honey. 'Crowne-imperiall' (*Fritillaria imperialis*) is another plant imported to Europe from Persia in the late sixteenth century. The name describes the crown-like appearance of its flowers and leaves. It's one of the flowers that Proserpina drops from Dis's wagon in Shakespeare's *The Winters Tale* (1610–11), IV.iv.126. 'Amaranth' is 'Immortall' because its name derives from the Greek word *amaranton*, which means 'unwithering'. Chapman's 'Amaranth' is another plant whose exact botanical identity is difficult to establish. It may be a species of the genus *Amaranthus*, such as love-lies-bleeding (which would sit nicely alongside the hyacinth), or, going back to the Greeks, a golden-flowered species of the genus *Helichrysum*, possibly a kind of chrysanthemum. Whichever, it's again the mythological aspect which is more important. Grigson notes: 'As an everlasting it symbolized immortality, was represented on tombs, and was woven into chaplets' (*Dictionary*, p. 8). It's also called 'Immortal Amarant' in Milton's *Paradise Lost* (1667), III.353. The name of the 'white Aphrodill' comes from the French 'fleur d'aphrodille': it is the white daffodil (*Narcissus poeticus*), also known in the late 16th century as the White Narcissus and the Poet's Lily. The 'cup-like Twillpants' is obscure, although it's obviously a plant which reminded somebody of nether-garments fashioned in the diagonally ridged pattern of the cloth still known as twill.

11.5 *disparent*: Means 'of varying appearance' and refers back to the different flowers named in the previous two stanzas. Compare l. 395 of 'Hymnus in Noctem' and Commentary.

12.8 *Joves bird . . . dove*: Jove's bird is his Eagle, superior to all other birds, but taken ('ceaz'd') by Venus's dove, symbolizing lust.

12.18 *fate*: Compare 84.8 and gloss and Commentary.

13.3 *How mercifull . . . prove*: A joke. The historical Julia was a notorious adultress. Seneca described her banishment by 'the deified Augustus' in 'De Beneficiis', VI.32. Augustus — Julia's father — declared her to be 'shameless past the indictment of shamelessness'. He also said that 'she had been accessible to scores of paramours, that the very forum and the rostrum, from which her father had proposed a law against adultery, had been chosen by the daughter for her debaucheries, that she had daily resorted to the statue of Marsyas, and, laying aside the role of adultress, there sold her favours'. Quoted by Gless ('Chapman's Ironic Ovid', p. 34) from Seneca's *Moral Essays*, translation by John W. Basore (Cambridge, Massachusetts: The Loeb Classical Library, 1935), Vol. III, pp. 431 – 2. In Ovid's *Amores*, Corynna is also painted as a lover of sensual pleasure.

13.7–9 *Trusting . . . directed*: An astrological conceit. Ovid's 'constellation' is what today would be called his star sign, his ruling 'star' in this case being Julia's (Corynna's) beauty.

14.6 *shader*: Probably means 'shadier'. I.e. if Ovid had been in a darker place, he might not have been so blinded with 'love'.

16.5 *to smite the starrs*: Compare l. 19 of 'De Guiana' and Commentary.

16.6 *furious trance*: A reference to the idea of divine inspiration ('furor poeticus'). Compare l. 15 of 'Hymnus in Noctem' and l. 65 of *The Teares of Peace* (1609) and Notes to *Poems*.

17.4 *numberd laughter*: Laughter that's in time with her music and musical itself.

17.5 *species*: 'The emanation from the voice which constitutes the direct object of cognition for his sense of hearing': note in *The Poems of George Chapman*, ed. Phyllis Brooks Bartlett (New York: MLA, 1941), p. 431. Compare 93.8.

18.1 *guilt . . . Attick Bees*: Corynna's tunes are 'guilt' as in gilded or golden like the honey carried by the bees. The best honey in classical times is supposed to have come from the Hymettic region of Attica in central Greece, hence '*Attick Bees*'.

19.3 *daughters of the wood*: i.e. nymphs, who were meant to be fond of dancing. If Chapman has any particular nymphs in mind, they may be Hamadryades, the life-spirits of trees, supposed to die as their trees wither.

21.7 *As much . . . priz'd*: 'As much prized by heaven as by my hearing.'

23.2 *Shooke . . . braine*: Compare l. 2 of the sonnet addressed to Walsingham, and affixed to one copy of Chapman's comedy *All Fooles* (printed 1605): 'The least allow'd birth of my shaken braine.' See notes to *All Fooles*. Compare also l. 1207 of *The Teares of Peace*: 'Thus shooke I this abortive from my braine'.

24.4 *Bred*: i.e. 'having been bred'.

24.5 gloss. *The Philosopher . . . transit*: The philosopher is Aristotle (compare *De Anima*, 429b), and the saying is used elsewhere by Chapman. It means 'The intellect passes into the intelligible things themselves' or as Chapman himself translates in 24.5–6: 'Intellects themselves transite/ To eache intelligible quallitie.' Compare ll. 423–6 of *Eugenia* (1614) where the assertion is quoted as a gloss to these lines:

> . . . That as Philosophie
> Saies there is evermore proportion
> Betwixt the knowing part, and what is knowne
> So joynd, that both, are absolutely one; . . .

Compare also ll. 856–61 of *The Teares of Peace* and Chapman's note to l. 343 of Book XIV of his translation of *The Iliads Of Homer* (1611): '*And (indeed) where a man is understood, there is ever a proportion betwixt the writer's wit and the writee's (that I may speake with authority) according to my old lesson in Philosophy*: Intellectus in ipsa intelligibilia transit.'

25.3–4 *My life . . . dygested*: Compare ll. 29–49 of 'Hymnus in Noctem' and Commentary. Compare also the dedicatory letter to the Earl of Somerset in *Andromeda Liberata* (1614), ll. 129–30: 'so this small world of ours/ Is but a *Chaos* of corporeall powers'.

26.5 and **gloss** *before*: i.e. as in the process described in stanza 23.

27.4–7 *So my . . . common sence*: These lines are difficult. 'So my loves soule' refers to Corynna's soul, not to Ovid's, and it's her soul 'together smit' with her desire which 'doth lighten' – i.e. produce the design ('pretence') of the notes resembling flashes of lightning – in the same way that 'sparkes of fire' result from the clash of steel and flint in the lines immediately preceding. However, 'lighten' may also be used in its old metaphorical sense of 'give birth', which is why Chapman's own gloss to these lines refers back to the gloss to stanza 23, where '*the species of every object propagates it selfe by our spirites to our common sence*'. So it's the spirits which convey the 'notes' to the metaphorical Wardrobe of 'the common sence' as in the gloss to stanza 23.

31.3 *sensor of his savour*: i.e. his nose.

31.4–7 *the Phenix . . . Apollos eye*: The phoenix is a mythical bird, supposedly the only one of its kind. It lives for five or six hundred years in the Arabian desert, then burns itself on a nest of aromatic twigs (hence 'Arabian spicerie'), ignited by the sun ('*Apollos eye*') and fanned by its own wings. From the ashes the phoenix then rises renewed.

33.5–8 *And if . . . breath*: The '*Ganges*' is the Indian river. The men living on scent are an appropriation of Pliny's description of the Astomes: 'They live only by the aire, and smelling to sweet odours, which they draw in at their nosthrils: And yet if the scent be anything strong and stinking, they are soone therwith overcome, and dy withall' – quoted from *The Historie of the World Commonly Called the Naturall Historie of C. Plinius Secundus*, translated by Philemon Holland (1601). Chapman's use of Pliny is pointed out by Danielle Nagler in 'Towards the Smell of Mortality: Shakespeare and Ideas of Smell 1588–1625' in *The Cambridge Quarterly*, 26 (1997), pp. 42–58. Nagler comments: 'Chapman's use of this legend in his veiled attack on Renaissance imitators of Ovid's sensuous love poetry seems significant. The association of naturally generated sweet smells with the divine, forces their use within this context to suggest a love bordering on the sacrilegious, a lust that is seriously out of hand as "odors feede love, and love cleare heaven discovers".'

37.1 *Odor . . . concite*: The idea that odour springs from dryness and is stimulated by heat ('concite' means excited) is expressed by Aristotle in 'De Anima', 422a, and 'De Sensu', 443b.

41.1 *vulture . . . liver*: An allusion to the Greek myth of Prometheus, who's chained by Zeus and then has to suffer the torment of an eagle being sent to attack his liver every day. As Prometheus is immortal, his liver grows again at night (hence 'encreasing').

41.5 *Myne of knowledge*: The same phrase is used in l. 31 of 'To *M. Harriots*' (1598).

41.5–6 *enricht . . . neede*: In Platonic tradition, 'povertie' is the parent of love, while 'neede' can serve as a stimulus to higher things, hence 'enricht'.

41.7–9 and **gloss** *A sight . . . eye*: Compare Shakespeare's *Twelfe Night, Or what you will* (1601), I.i.18–22, where Orsino alludes to the same myth and is pursued by his own 'desires', just as Ovid's own thoughts ('the thought of sight') drive him through the poem. Compare also the self-reflexive reverberations afflicting Lysander in Chapman's tragi-comedy *The Widdowes Teares* (1604–5), and the allusions to Diana and Actaeon at I.3.63–7 and II.1.27–8. Another interpretation is proposed by John Huntington, 'Philosophical Seduction in Chapman, Davies, and Donne', *English Literary History*, 44 (1977), pp. 43–5, who sees the allusion as ambiguous, including the conventional view already given, then possibly a kind of unorthodox reading following Giordano Bruno's *De gli eroici furori* (1585). Bruno suggests the result of Actaeon being devoured by his dogs is 'to make him dead to the vulgar, to the multitude, free him from the snares of the perturbing senses and the fleshly prison of matter, so that he no longer sees his Diana as through a glass or a window, but having thrown down the earthly walls, he sees a complete view of the whole horizon'. Quoted by Huntington from *The Heroic Frenzies*, translated by Paul Eugene Memmo, Jr., *University of North Carolina Studies in the Romance Languages and Literatures*, 50 (1966), pp. 225–6, as part of his contention that *Ovids Banquet of Sence* is 'an extended exercise in encompassing in a single verbal structure the double possibilities of rapturous experience: its potential for transcendent insight and its potential for self-deception and debauch'.

47.1–9 *Great . . . gracing*: Derived from Comes's *Mythologiae*, II, 4, 'De Junone'.

48.2 *Aspen*: As in the tree, well known for trembling in the air. Compare 56.9.

48.7–9 *Attemps . . . graunted*: A version of the philosophy proclaimed by Tharsalio in Chapman's tragi-comedy *The Widdowes Teares*.

49.9 *riches in a little Roome*: Compare Marlowe's *The Jew of Malta* (1592): 'Infinite riches in a little roome' (I.37).

50.4–5 and **gloss** *And as . . . star*: Compare *The Teares of Peace*, ll. 1010–12 and l. 1187 and *Bussy D'Ambois*, V.3.187–9. In the Gloss, the Latin *Stellas cadentes* means 'falling stars'. The phrase is not used by Virgil, but it does occur in Servius' commentary on the *Aeneid*, V. 527.

51.1–2 *This beauties . . . witchcraft*: Compare *Ficino's Commentary*, p. 199: 'Now anyone beautiful bewitches us through our vulnerable eyes'. Also compare Commentary on 'Hymnus in Noctem', ll. 362–7.

51.4 *chapmen*: Means 'vendors', but is also a pun on Chapman's own name.

51.7–9 *Unlesse . . . alone*: These lines draw on an idea of love which derives from

Plato and is extensively discussed in Ficino's *Commentary on Plato's Symposium*. In brief, 'those who . . . are born under the same star, are so constituted, that the image of the more beautiful of the two flowing through the eyes into the soul of the other, corresponds to and agrees completely with a like image formed from its very generation both in the celestial body and in the inner part of the soul. The soul, thus struck, recognises that image meeting it as something its own' (*Ficino's Commentary*, p. 188). This self-reflexive theory helps to explain why Chapman's 'enricher' ('the more beautiful of the two') may see 'her owne . . . in another'. The process is probably compared to 'good selfe-love' because the soul is searching for its own beauty, and is not contented in and with the body.

53.1–4 *Then . . . gold*: The first line has been emended here from 'Then in the truest wisdome' to 'Then is . . .', for three reasons. Firstly, it provides a verb, without which the sentence does not make sense. Secondly, 'Then is' balances 'That nothing wisdome is . . .' in 53.4. Thirdly, stanzas 51, 52, 54 and 55 all start with a declaration using 'is' as a verb – 'This beauties fayre is . . .', 'For sacred beautie, is . . .', 'Contentment is . . .', 'But as weake colour alwayes is . . .', so emendation makes this stanza conform to the pattern of Chapman's 'digression' (56.1). 'Then is the truest wisdome' follows on from 'The summe and court of all proportion' (52.7), 'proportion' referring to one of Chapman's favourite sayings from Aristotle – see the gloss to 24.5 and Commentary. The 'all-things-nothing' of 53.4 is wisdom; the paradoxical description yokes together the philosopher's view of wisdom as 'all-things' (looking back to 'all proportion') and the view of 'publique . . . worldlings' that it's nothing, because there's no money in it ('no gold').

54.1–4 *Contentment . . . reposde*: The idea is that the metaphorical circle of 'Contentment' is seldom or never joined up, any more than the letter 'C' at the start of the word 'Contentment' is itself completely circular. The last line is difficult, but could mean something like: 'And to bring about ("conduce") contentment, because it's like a C, and because people's actions are like a compass ("all our deedes/ Bend in that circle"), everyone must always try to redraw ("repose") that circle.' Chapman elsewhere uses 'repose' to mean something like 'replace': Compare his translation of *Homer's Odysses* (1614), IX, 702–3: 'Nor thinke my hurt offends me, for my Sire/ Can soon repose in it the visuall fire'.

54.5–6 *More force . . . composde*: i.e. 'There is more force and art . . . and joys thus made up . . .'

56.5 *Where silver past the least*: Very obscure. Possibly alchemical.

57.5 *tropicke*: Probably the 'tropicke' of Cancer, which covers the start of July and so corresponds with Corynna's true name of Julia. Janet Levarie Smarr in 'The Pyramid and the Circle: "Ovid's Banquet of Sense" ', *Philological Quarterly*, 63 (1984), p. 379, comments: 'This tropic is so called because it marks the turning point of the sun, thus signaling the lengthening darkness of approaching winter. According to neoplatonic tradition, it is therefore the gate through which souls descend from the light of heaven into the darkness of an earthly body'.

58.7 *Lameate*: What this bird would be called now is not known.

59.3 *Gehon . . . Euphrates*: Four rivers that spring from one source and run through Eden in the Bible, Genesis 2, 10–14. In Renaissance England the rivers often represented the four prime virtues of prudence, temperance, fortitude and justice, flowing from God's wisdom: see A. D. S. Fowler, 'The River Guyon', *Modern Language Notes*, 75 (1960), pp. 289–92.

59.8 *tenne pure floods*: i.e. her fingers, as explained in the gloss to 60.1.

60.4 *And bound . . . section*: Obscure. The sense depends on whether 'bound' refers back to the 'fresh sorts of flowers' in 60.3 or the fingers which 'winde theyr courses . . . And raise such sounds' in 60.1–2. The latter seems more likely, with 'section' meaning finger, and 'every section' rounding off part of the body ('that booke of life'). The word 'bound' then echoes the fingers 'Bounding themselves in length' in 59.9.

61.6–7 *so excellent . . . Olympiad*: The Olympic Games, founded in 776 BC.

63.8–9 *Shee shall . . . for ever*: 'She shall live through Time, and Time which has never been so feasted shall grow forever stronger because of her fame.'

64.3 *chapter*: From the Latin 'capitulum' meaning 'little head', hence the top of the pyramid as opposed to the 'base' referred to in the next line.

65.4 *Draw his desires*: 'Lead on his desires'.

65.5 *tell it . . . conceale it*: i.e. count and hide it, like a 'Treasurer' with his 'Gold'.

65.8–9 *O Beautie . . . pine*: These paradoxical lines are very difficult to paraphrase. They play with the idea that it's more usual for the object of a seige to yield after being starved out than it is to yield and still to starve, as is said to happen here when Beauty is the besieger. The sense then depends on the idea of Beauty's simultaneous unattainability and desirability. Giving in to the desirability of Beauty means the yielder 'starves' because Beauty still can't be grasped (as earlier in the stanza 'None can peculier joy'). But Beauty also wins if it 'feedes' the object of a seige because desires build up to the point where, owing to Beauty's unattainability, those desires cannot be realized, and this causes pining. Compare 101.1–3.

66.5 *Or as it*: 'As if it . . .'

67.1–3 *Thus . . . bewraide*: Obscure. These lines seem to suggest that intentions are always discovered because '*Argus*' – a symbol of watchfulness – alerts the avenging agent of Fate.

68.4 *Troy . . . Art*: An allusion to Helen's role in the Trojan War in Homer's *Iliad*. The verb 'swum' is also used in Chapman's translation of the scene where Helen is fetched by 'Iris the raine-bow' to the 'Scaean towrs' to see her first husband and friends again:

> . . . (though she tooke a pride
> To set her thoughts at gaze and see, in her cleare beautie's flood,
> What choice of glorie swum to her yet tender womanhood) . . .   (III.148–50)

And the same word is used again shortly after when Priam 'cals Helen to informe him of the Greeke Princes' (gloss to l. 178):

Come: do not thinke I lay the warres, endur'd by us, on thee:

The gods have sent them, and the teares in which they swumme, to me.   (III.181-2)

And compare 67.8: 'O Beauty, still thy Empire swims in blood.'

69.1 *the Autumnale Starre*: Sirius.

69.5-6 *Shee lifts . . . blood*: The sun's 'Meridian' is its highest point, thus Corynna is pictured stretching her arms up as far as she can.

69.9 *scorch the Center*: Compare 7.3-5. Another allusion to the myth of Phaeton, son of the sun-god Apollo, whose attempt to drive his father's chariot caused a scar in the sky – the Milky Way – and threatened to set the world on fire. Smarr notes the Milky Way's position between Libra and Scorpio, signs covering the months September to November. Compare 57.5 and Commentary, the reference at 69.1 to 'the Autumnale Starre' and the emblem of '*the Sun going downe*' in the marginal gloss to 70.7.

70.1-5 *Thus when . . . graced*: Gless ('Chapman's Ironic Ovid', pp. 36-7) takes Corynna's efforts with her hair, her song in stanza 12 and 'her Glasse' (mirror) at 74.1 to indicate her derivation from medieval personifications of 'luxuria' or idleness, and her role as a siren. The siren who appears in Act IV Scene 2 of John Lyly's *Loves Metamorphosis* (1589-90) is directed to sing with a mirror in her hand and a comb.

70.8-9 *sable . . . obscuri*: 'Charectry' spelt thus is not in the *OED*. It seems to mean a set of letters (characters) which express a thought. The Latin means: 'As nobility declines, undistinguished people gain ground.'

71.3 *Medio caret*: 'It lacks a medium.'

71.7 *Teipsum et orbem*: 'Yourself and the world.'

72.1 *Tygris . . . Euphrates*: Three rivers. Compare 59.3.

72.6-7 *Each . . . styll*: Compare the similar expression of this Neoplatonic idea in *Bussy D'Ambois* (1604), III.1.104-5.

74.6 *the heavenly Goate*: The star Capella.

78.5-78 *honor . . . attaineth it*: Difficult to paraphrase because of Chapman's syntax. The lines mean that 'honor' should be kept in a state of purity diametrically opposed to that 'defiled' state which comes about as soon as nakedness is seen. Bartlett (*Poems*, pp. 432-3) points out that 'Chapman uses the verb compress as equivalent to "embrace"; sometimes with an implied, sometimes with a definite meaning of "to rape".' So 'incompressed' means 'unembraced, not raped'.

78.8 *Nature bides defame*: 'Nature suffers the loss of its good name . . .'

79.4 *Vulgar Opinion*: Compare l. 463 of *The Teares of Peace* and Commentary.

80.1-4 and gloss *As in . . . frame*: Translated, the gloss ascribed to Aristotle means: 'The action of discerning with the eyes must be ascribed in both man and animals to the one who sees.' In simple terms the question asked is: How can it be harmful to see something that's part of you? The question is meant to be a rhetorical one, such self-awareness being held to distinguish humans from the 'Beast' in the lines immediately following.

81.7-9 *But you . . . remedie*: 'Because you are unwronged and without dishonour no ill dares touch you, and one of your kisses can quickly remedy affliction and sorcery.'

82.1−2 *I could . . . affects*: The 'times' which Ovid says he was unable to respect, because his desires ('affects') are not 'cold', are the 'private times' referred to by Corynna at 77.2.

84.5 and **gloss** *Where rules the Prince of sence*: Compare Chapman's comedy *The Blinde beggar of Alexandria* (1596, printed 1598), Scene vi.68: 'my braine . . . my prince of sence'. The gloss means: 'The seat of sensorial perception is in the brain, and it is from here that the nerves, which are the means of voluntary motion, originate.'

84.8 and **gloss** *Nature (my fate)*: Compare 12.19. The gloss means: 'Nature is the Fate of every person, as Theophrastus [says].'

86.6 *Brats of dearth*: i.e. the 'vapours' of 86.1 which are blown away by the wind.

87 and **gloss** *If now . . . sence*: The Latin gloss means: 'To perceive by the senses is equal to experiencing a change [of state]' or, as Chapman puts it in 87.6, 'To suffer change'. The 'three sences' in 87.2 are hearing, smell, and sight, already experienced by Ovid ('put in act'). He now wants his 'other sences' of taste and touch put 'into fact', 'fact' being opposed to the 'fantasie' of 87.1 because these two senses depend on the material gratification of bodily contact. The phrase 'now changde that offence' is very difficult to understand because Chapman is asking his compressed words to do too much. The following interpretation is only tentative. The clause seems to mean that if Corynna doesn't grant Ovid's wishes, then what has so far been 'put in act' and what he wants to be made 'fact', will wrongly (in the light of the philosophical argument expressed in 87.6−9) be 'changde' into an 'offence' by *him* − 'that offence' thus connecting with a second sense of the word 'fact'. In the sixteenth century it meant 'a crime'. This is why, earlier in the stanza, Ovid asks for 'justice'. However, in 87.5 the repetition of the word 'now' also suggests that if Corynna does now refuse Ovid's wishes, then *her* action too is 'changde' into an 'offence' in relation to the previous situation when Ovid's senses were activated. The aim of Ovid's rhetoric is to make it impossible for Corynna to 'grant not'. If she refuses to act, that in itself will constitute a 'changde . . . offence' against the philosophical argument of the rest of the stanza that 'every sence, must serve societie' (87.9). Far better therefore 'To suffer change' willingly and give Ovid what he wants. Corynna's reward will be that change consolidates sensual perfection ('doth perfect sence compact').

88.6 gloss *He . . . sensuum*: i.e. 'He intends the common sence which is *centrum sensibus et speciebus* [what the senses and the outward forms centre around], & cals it last because it dooth, *sapere in effectione sensuum* [is responsible for producing the senses].' Compare the 'common sence' referred to in the gloss to 23.3 and 27.7.

90.6 *perills soveraignties*: Obscure. May mean something like 'supreme dangers'.

90.8−91.7 *Tis for . . . inheritance*: Compare ll. 326−30 of *The Teares of Peace* and Commentary, and ll. 27−30 of 'To M. Harriots' and Commentary. In 1595 − the year that *Ovids Banquet of Sence* was published − Chapman wrote a commendatory sonnet for a translation by William Jones of *Nennio, Or a Treatise of Nobility: Wherein is discoursed what true Nobilitie is, with such qualities as are required in a perfect Gentleman*. Chapman's sonnet and *Nennio* are discussed by John Huntington in ' "This Ticklish Title":

Chapman, *Nennio*, and the Critique of Nobility', *English Literary Renaissance*, 26 (1996), pp. 291–312. Chapman's 'critique of nobility' is here voiced by Ovid.

93.8 *species*: Compare 17.5 and Commentary.

94.1 *that giv'st . . . event*: 'That makes speech possible . . .'

95.8 *Long . . . detection*: 'Long courtships never make a bad choice ("detection") good'.

96.7 *Force . . . skyll*: Compare the attitude of Tharsalio in Chapman's tragi-comedy *The Widdowes Teares*, e.g. I.1.139–42.

98.1 *The motion of the Heavens*: Ptolemy proposed that the universe consisted of spheres which made music when they were in harmony.

100.1–6 and **gloss** *But . . . fled*: An explanation of echoes. The Latin gloss means: 'This is the principle by which echo occurs.' Bartlett (*Poems*, p. 433) compares the first four lines with Aristotle's 'De Anima', 419 b.

101.1–3 *And thus . . . store*: Compare 65.8–9 and Commentary.

102.5 *my sences . . . Feeling*: The idea that Feeling is the main sense is expressed in Aristotle's 'De Anima'. Compare 103.5 and also Chapman's *The Tragedie Of Chabot Admirall Of France* (1611–13), IV.i.189–93:

> . . . this same sence of feeling
> (Being ground to all the sences) hath one key
> More than the rest to let in through them all
> The mindes true apprehension, that thence takes
> Her first convey'd intelligence.

103.4 *ist*: 'Is it . . .'

104.1 *The mind then cleere*: The mind is said to be 'cleere' because of the assertion at the end of the previous stanza that it's not tainted by 'bodies touch or tyre' (103.8).

104.3–4 *As by . . . Golde*: An alchemical image. The 'great elixer' is the (mythical) substance supposedly capable of turning an element like copper into gold. Compare l. 404 of 'Hymnus in Cynthiam' in *The Shadow Of Night*: 'O then thou great Elixer of all treasures'. Chapman's own gloss to this line is: 'The Philosophers stone, or *Philosophica Medicina* is cald the great Elixer to which he here alludes.'

104.5 *Such as trans-forme*: 'Such people as do transform . . .'

107.1–9 *And thus . . . guise*: Ovid is apostrophizing his hand. In l. 6 'Proportions odnes' is partly a reference to the hand's five fingers, five being an odd number, but two hands make the number 10, an 'even' number. In l. 9 the hand represents God's world-making power, as it also does most famously in Michaelangelo's painting on the ceiling of the Sistine Chapel in Rome.

109.8–9 *Ever . . . bestowing*: Compare the image of the 'perpetual-motion-making kisse' at 99.5. A 'fruitfull Iland' in 'Hymnus in Cynthiam' in *The Shadow Of Night*, ll. 368–9, is also described as 'Ever with child of curious Architect,/ Yet still deliverd: . . .' and the idea is used again in l. 12 of the 'Dialogus' of *A Free And Offenceles Justification Of Andromeda liberata* (1614).

110.1–6 *This sayd . . . retire*: Possibly derived from Comes's *Mythologiae*, III.4, 'De Junone'. *Saturnia* is Juno, *Alcydes* is Hercules.

111.8–9 *enemie . . . pleade*: The 'enemie' is the body – Ovid must 'pleade' with the 'fleshlie engine' (111.5) of the tongue.

113.5 *For . . . love*: 'For thy sake' refers back to 'Sweete touch' in 113.1. The 'Art of love' is Ovid's *Ars Amatoria*, a mock didactic treatise.

114.7 *Mummers mask*: Mummers' plays are a kind of English folk-play. There are numerous local variations but the main characters are a St George figure, a Turkish Knight and a Doctor.

116.5–9 *And as . . . rue*: Possibly taken from Plutarch's essay 'On tranquility of mind' in the *Moralia*.

117.8 *knew . . . intended*: Huntington ('Philosophical Seduction', p. 58) compares Ovid's *Amores*, I.v.25.

117.10–11 *Intentio . . . convivium*: 'It is an activity proper to the mind to make efforts. End of the banquet.'

'De Guiana, Carmen Epicum'

'De Guiana, Carmen Epicum' is a plea for support for the colonialist ambitions of Sir Walter Ralegh, who led an expedition to Guiana in 1595. Ralegh's voyage was made partly to try to win back the favour of Elizabeth I. This had been lost when Ralegh secretly married one of the Queen's Maids of Honour, who were meant to be virgins, in 1592. He and his wife were punished by two months' imprisonment in the Tower of London, and on his release Ralegh was forbidden to attend the royal court. He retired to Sherborne Castle in West Dorset, where such heretical and free-thinking conversations were rumoured to be held with his entourage – including friends of Chapman – that in 1594 allegations of atheism were formally investigated by the authorities. Stephen Greenblatt characterizes Ralegh's mood during these years as one of 'restless discontent': see *Sir Walter Ralegh: The Renaissance Man and his Roles* (New Haven, Connecticut: Yale University Press, 1973), p. 99. The voyage to Guiana was carefully planned as a 'theatrical gesture calculated to dazzle the Queen' (Greenblatt, p. 104). In this respect it failed. She still refused to see Ralegh, and her 'wry skepticism' (Greenblatt, p. 104) about his reports was shared by potential backers of future voyages and the public. In an effort to vindicate himself and stimulate enthusiasm, Ralegh wrote *The Discoverie of the Large, Rich, and Bewtiful Empyre of Guiana, with a relation of the great and Golden Citie of Manoa (which the Spanyards call El Dorado) And of the Provinces of Emeria, Arromaia, Amapaia, and other Countries, with their rivers, adjoyning*, which was published in 1596. Chapman's poem 'De Guiana' was probably commissioned as part of the same propagandist process, either by Ralegh himself, or perhaps by Thomas Harriot, who was the expedition's scientific expert. 'De Guiana' was written after Ralegh returned from South America in September 1595, and before a second voyage to Guiana was made by Lawrence Keymis, who had sailed with Ralegh on the first expedition. Keymis set out on 25 January 1596. 'De

Guiana' was prefixed to Keymis' account of his voyage, published in 1596 as *A Relation of the second voyage to Guiana. Perfourmed and written in the yeare 1596*. Keymis, a former fellow of Balliol College, Oxford, a geographer and mathematician, killed himself during a third trip to Guiana in 1618.

Ralegh's first voyage has been described by the historian Simon Schama in *Landscape & Memory* as 'the prototype of all imperial upstream epics' (London: Harper Collins, 1995), p. 312. It's passed down through time into the imaginations of such figures as Joseph Conrad (*Heart of Darkness*), John Huston (*The African Queen*) and Francis Ford Coppola (*Apocalypse Now*). Chapman's poem contributes to one of the main features of the poetic myth identified by Schama, that of the search for Eldorado, 'A golden worlde in this our yron age' ('De Guiana', l. 32). Charles Nicholl in *The Creature in the Map* (London: Jonathan Cape, 1995), p. 323, has also described Ralegh's voyage as 'a kind of alchemical field-trip, if not a full-blown, purgatorial, *opus*-like quest', undertaken partly under the guidance of the magus Dr John Dee. Nicholl suggests that 'the motifs that emerge from the *Discoverie* and Chapman's *De Guiana* – the idea of the 'golden world', the idea of 'chaste' colonizing, the idea of "virgin" territory as related to the Virgin Queen cult – spring in general from Dee's occultist musings on the new British Empire (as he was the first to call it)' (*The Creature in the Map*, pp. 311–12).

Across Europe throughout the sixteenth century explorers set off in search of riches and glory. Their efforts were widely written up. In Chapter Four of Richard Helgerson's *Forms of Nationhood: The Elizabethan Writing of England* (Chicago and London: University of Chicago Press, 1992), 'De Guiana' is compared to other expeditionary verses by the Hungarian Stephen Parmenius ('De Navigatione', about a voyage to Newfoundland made by Ralegh's half-brother Sir Humphrey Gilbert) and by the Portuguese writer Luis de Camões (*The Lusiads*, 1572). Each poem, notes Helgerson, is 'marked by the same stylistic as well as social elevation, the same proclamation of inspiration, the same prophetic vision of empire, the same rarified evocation of boundless wealth, the same neglect of commerce, the same nationalist emphasis, and the same identification of the monarch and the arms-bearing nobility' (*Forms of Nationhood*, p. 173). *The Memorable Masque of the two Honourable Houses or Innes of Court; the Middle Temple and Lyncolnes Inne*, written by Chapman for the marriage of Princess Elizabeth in 1613, also recapitulates themes from 'De Guiana'.

TEXTUAL NOTES

The base text is the copy of the quarto in the Bodleian Library, Oxford (shelfmark: 4° L 80. Art.). In the notes that follow, the first readings are those of this edition and the second record those of the base text.

> 68 death,] ~.
> 77 ought,] ~;
> 94 confident;] ~.
> 166 them,] ~)

COMMENTARY

De Guiana, Carmen Epicum means 'Epic song about Guiana'.

1–6 *What worke ... my mind*: The 'worke of honour' is the possible conquest of Guiana that the rest of the poem will promote. Chapman's 'furie' is not anger but divine inspiration ('furor poeticus'). From 'and gives' to 'my mind' Chapman is attempting to describe a state of being that's difficult to paraphrase. The 'armed handes' point towards the 'sworde' of l. 9, and suggest that Chapman has been inspired by Ralegh to try to achieve what in his 'heartes peace' his body and thoughts would otherwise turn to in 'rapt' fascination anyway. 'Thirsted' means both that such enterprise is longed for, and that the mind's own workings have become dry in the absence of 'action'. 'Thirsted' also looks towards the 'aged throte' of l. 11. Lastly it's a joke about Ralegh's name – Queen Elizabeth I called him 'water'.

9 *his Eliza-consecrated*: 'His' refers to Sir Walter Ralegh, '*Eliza*' is Elizabeth I.

11 *her aged throte*: 'Her' refers to England. What's proposed is the country's rejuvenation.

17 *Joves Eagle*: Jove's eagle bore thunder beneath its wings. Compare the marginal gloss to Chapman's *Eugenia* (1614) ll. 742–5: 'The soule, Mythologisd is the Eagle which is said to beare the thunder under her wings ...' Also compare *Bussy D'Ambois* (1604), III.2.4–5.

19 *forehead ... Starres*: Compare Chapman's continuation of Marlowe's *Hero And Leander* (1598), VI.197–8: 'And up he [Neptune] rose, for haste his forehead hit/ Gainst heavens hard Christall'.

21 *kissing her hand*: Compare the willing submission of the Virginian Princes in Chapman's *The Memorable Masque of the two Honourable Houses or Innes of Court; the Middle Temple and Lyncolnes Inne* (1613), when they are summoned to convert their devotions 'To this our Britan *Phoebus*' (l. 330), i.e. King James I.

24 *sacred Maide*: The unmarried Elizabeth I.

38 *him*: Sir Walter Ralegh.

41 *squint-eyd Envies*: An image possibly derived from Plutarch's essay 'On envy and hate' in the *Moralia* where envy is compared to an evil or diseased eye, offended by everything bright. Compare Chapman's address 'To the Reader' in his translation of

The Iliads Of Homer (1611), l. 77, and the dedicatory poem to *Andromeda Liberata* (1614), ll. 174–6.

56 *as a river*. One of Chapman's favourite images.

64 *Iberian Neptune*. Spain.

65 *triple worlde*. Earth, seas and hell. Compare 'Hymnus in Cynthiam' in *The Shadow Of Night* (1594), ll. 1–3: 'Natures bright eye-sight, and the Nights faire soule/ That with thy triple forehead dost controule/ Earth, seas, and hell . . .'

92 *And let*. 'If you let . . .'

117–29 *But how . . . her powers*. The 'heroike Author' is Sir Walter Ralegh, whose comparison to the 'wrong'd soule of *Nature*' means the second part of this passage (ll. 123–9) serves as Chapman's own explanation of the first (ll. 117–23). Thus the answer to 'How in excesse of Sence is Sence bereft her?' (l. 119) is that she is 'much like a bodie numb'd with surfets' (l. 127). But the first part is still difficult. It seeks an explanation for the lack of support for Ralegh, and possibly because this is a politically sensitive question, it's not phrased in easily understandable terms. It's suggested that England's disregard is so baffling that Nature herself must somehow be 'corrupted'. As in 'Hymnus in Noctem' ('Suffer no more his lustfull rayes to get/ The Earth with issue' – ll. 264–5) the degradation of the present state of things is expressed in sexual terms ('lightening-like effectes of lust'). The effects are 'lightening-like' as in *Bussy D'Ambois*, IV.2.165–6, 'A politician, must like lightening melt/ The very marrow, and not Print the skin . . .' This is why the flesh is 'unwounded' and the 'soule' is wounded through the flesh. The 'soule' is thus 'that part she hurtes', identified over the next few lines with Sir Walter Ralegh who 'sustainst/ Paine, charge, and perill for thy countreys good . . .'

161 *Guianian Orenoque*. The Orinoco river.

167–79 *A world . . . Avarice*. Guiana is imagined as a pre-lapsarian Golden Age, free of the need to strive for wealth because treasures present themselves. Compare the description of the Golden Age in Ovid's *Metamorphoses*, as translated by Arthur Golding in 1567: 'The fertile earth as yet was free, untoucht of spade or plough,/ And yet it yeelded of it selfe every things inough.' See also Ralegh's own summing-up in *The Discoverie of the Large, Rich, and Bewtiful Empyre of Guiana, with a relation of the great and Golden Citie of Manoa (which the Spanyards call El Dorado) And of the Provinces of Emeria, Arromaia, Amapaia, and other Countries, with their rivers, adjoyning* (1596): 'To conclude, *Guiana* is a Contrey that hath yet her Maydenhead, never sackt, turned, nor wrought, the face of the earth hath not beene torne, nor the vertue and salt of the soyle spent by manurance, the graves have not beene opened for gold, the mines not broken with sledges, nor their Images puld down out of their temples.'

170 *Estridge-like*. 'Estridge' means ostrich. Compare John Lyly's *Euphues* (1578): 'the *Estrich* disgesteth harde iron to preserve his healthe'.

172 *Gallique*. French.

'*To M. Harriots*'

'To My Admired and Soule-Loved Friend Mayster of all essentiall and true knowledge, *M. Harriots*' was first printed in 1598. It appeared at the end of *Achilles Shield*, Chapman's translation of Book XVIII of Homer's *Iliad*. The '*M. Harriots*' of the title is the mathematician and astronomer Thomas Harriot (1560–1621), one of the greatest scientists of his time, whose many other interests included navigation, optics, alchemy and phonetics. Chapman's poem is an academic love-letter; he seems to have admired his friend more than anyone except Homer (in the title 'Soule-Loved' also puns on 'Sole-Loved'). In fact, Chapman's expressions of desire for Harriot's 'instructive light' are so strong it's difficult to be sure exactly where the shadows of influence fall. For example, Harriot was the first Englishman to make a telescope: hence Chapman's reference to his 'perfect eye' (l. 41). But it's not so clear how much Harriot's scientific investigations informed Chapman's own enquiring spirit. Jean Jacquot notes that Harriot's explorations of the skies with his telescope (paralleling Galileo's) 'questioned the validity of the traditional world-order, based on the opposition between the Heavens and the Earth, their natures, and their motions. The Copernican theory had challenged the world-order by making the Earth move with the other planets': see 'Harriot, Hill, Warner And The New Philosophy', in *Thomas Harriot: Renaissance Scientist*, ed. John W. Shirley (Oxford: Clarendon Press, 1974), p. 107. 'Now is it true, earth mooves, and heaven stands still': this line from Chapman's tragedy *Bussy D'Ambois* (1604), V.1.153, certainly reflects Copernican theory, but does it also owe something to Harriot? All that can generally be said with confidence is that Chapman sought to move in Harriot's orbit.

The two men may have met at Oxford University, if Chapman did indeed go there. Mutual friends included Mathew Roydon, to whom Chapman dedicated *The Shadow Of Night* (1594) and *Ovids Banquet of Sence* (1595), and the navigational expert and geographer Robert Hues. Anthony Wood reports in *Athenae Oxonienses* (1691–2) that Hues was 'noted for a good Grecian'. In the preface to *The Whole Works Of Homer, Prince Of Poetts* (1616) Chapman declares that he has conferred about his translation with two people: '*Only some one or two places I have shewed to my worthy and most learned friend, M. Harriots, for his censure how much mine owne weighed: whose judgement and knowledge in all kinds, I know to be incomparable and bottomlesse – yea, to be admired as much as his most blameles life and the right sacred expence of his time is to be honoured and reverenced . . . Another right learned, honest and entirely loved friend of mine, M. Robert Hews, I must needs put into my confest conference touching Homer, though very little more than that I had with M. Harriots. Which two, I protest, are all, and preferred to all . . .*' This repeats the praise of 'To *M. Harriots*'. John W. Shirley notes that Harriot too was considered to be 'a good Grecian': see *Thomas Harriot: A Biography* (Oxford: Clarendon Press, 1983), p. 65.

By about 1582 Harriot had entered the household of Sir Walter Ralegh as a mathematical tutor. He was close to Ralegh during the next 'jubilant years of his rise to wealth and prominence': see John W. Shirley, 'Sir Walter Ralegh and Thomas Harriot', *Thomas Harriot: Renaissance Scientist*, p. 18. In 1583, for example, Ralegh was selected as escort to the visiting Duke of Alençon, the Monsieur of *Bussy D'Ambois*. In 1585 Harriot went on Ralegh's expedition to Virginia, and stayed a year. His job at sea was to help with navigation, on land to study the inhabitants and survey their territories. '*A briefe and true report of the new found land of Virginia: of the commodities there found and to be raysed, as well marchantable, as others for victuall, building and other necessarie uses for those that are and shalbe the planters there; and of the nature and manners of the naturall inhabitants: . . .*' – to give just part of the full title – was published in 1588. It was the only work of Harriot to be published during his lifetime: hence Chapman's reference to 'when thy writings . . . breake forth' (ll. 89–90).

When the authorities investigated the alleged atheism of Christopher Marlowe and Ralegh in 1593–4, Harriot was implicated several times. The spy Richard Baines testified that Marlowe 'affirmeth that Moyses [Moses] was but a Jugler, & that one Heriots being Sir W. Raleghs man can do more than he'; and the playwright Thomas Kyd wrote that Marlowe had atheistic conversations with Harriot, Roydon, and the mathematician Walter Warner: see *Thomas Harriot: A Biography*, pp. 67–8. Chapman moved in dangerous circles: atheism was punishable by death. Harriot was probably questioned, but no evidence has survived and he does seem to have been a blameless Christian. As Ralegh's fortunes waned, Harriot sought the patronage of the 9th Earl of Northumberland, who is referred to by Chapman in the dedicatory letter to *The Shadow Of Night*. Harriot, Warner and Hues were to become known as the Earl's 'Three Magi'.

TEXTUAL NOTES

The base text is from the copy of *Achilles Shield* (1598) in the British Library (shelfmark: C.39.d., 54). In the notes that follow, the first readings are those of this edition and the second record those of the base text.

46 earth;] ~.	97 cleare ∧] ~,
48 learne.] ~ ∧	98 appeare:] ~.
49 kisse:] ~.	141 impudence,] ~.
50 is;] ~:	142 excellence.] ~ ∧
80 reverence, . . . emperie ∧] ~ ∧ . . .	153 ames:] ~ ∧
~,	155 show,] ~ ∧
88 you.] ~ ∧	164 tombes.] ~,
96 sitte,] ~.	

COMMENTARY

1–2 *To . . . weight*: The way that Harriot's 'depth of soule' can measure the dimensions of 'all workes of weight' is an illustration of one of Chapman's favourite maxims from Aristotle, that 'there is evermore proportion/ Betwixt the knowing part, and what is knowne' (*Eugenia*, 1614), ll. 424–5. See also Commentary on *Ovids Banquet of Sence* (1595), 24.5 gloss.

7–8 *this shield . . . bookes*: This poem was originally printed at the end of the 1598 volume *Achilles Shield*, Chapman's translation of Book XVIII of Homer's *Iliad*. The other 'bookes' are the *Seaven Bookes Of The Iliades Of Homere, Prince of Poets* (1598), a translation of Books I, II, VII–XI.

13–15 *and take . . . mind*: Compare 'A Coronet for his Mistresse *Philosophie*' (1595), 4.13–14, where referring to '*Philosophie*' Chapman writes: 'Vertue is both the merrit and reward/ Of her remov'd, and soule-infusde regard'. Compare also *Bussy D'Ambois* (1604), I.2.132–40, where Monsieur compares Bussy to the sea that will never be settled 'Till he be croun'd with his owne quiet fome', for another expression of the idea that the soul's satisfactions are good in themselves.

26 *Or . . . spirits*: The syntax is unclear, but the simple sense seems to be that without food and drink bodies 'sterve' and thirst ('quench'). The word 'fierie' may be sarcastically set against the 'Sphere of fire' in l. 34.

27–30 *Thus as . . . Parasites*: John Huntington, ' "This Ticklish Title": Chapman, *Nennio*, and the Critique of Nobility', *English Literary Renaissance*, 26 (1996), p. 299, quotes these lines as an explicit complaint 'about the injustice and humiliation of the patronage situation'. He adds: 'By championing virtue and learning as good in themselves, Chapman lays claim to a cultural capital that is usually the prerogative of the aristocracy, but he also calls into question the common values of the social system.' Chapman's stance – 'a poor man of modest social standing assuming an aristocratic culture and yet condemning the shortcomings of the aristocracy' – is seen by Huntington as evidence that Chapman 'is working in a newly opened social space'. Compare *Bussy D'Ambois*, where Bussy makes 'friends/ Of the unrighteous *Mammon*' in the shape of Monsieur, at the same time as he declares his ambition to 'bring up a new fashion,/ And rise in Court with vertue' (I.1.125–6). Bussy certainly 'calls into question the common values of the social system'. Huntington also discusses Chapman's conception of virtue in 'Furious Insolence: The Social Meaning of Poetic Inspiration in the 1590s', *Modern Philology*, 94 (1997), pp. 305–26. He doesn't refer to Chapman's plays, but his argument suggests Bussy's hinterland in the poems: ' "virtue", so insisted on by Chapman in his early work, is easily understood as an ascetic moralism, while it is also intimately coupled with inspiration, both as a moral prerequisite to inspiration and, in a socially inflected sense, as *virtus*, an ideal of integrity explicitly opposed to the privileges of "blood" ' ('Furious Insolence', p. 308).

31–40 *Rich . . . remembers*: See Introduction.

31 *mine of knowledge*: Compare *Ovids Banquet of Sence*, 41.5.

41 *perfect eye*: i.e. Harriot's telescope.

43 *Gloweworme*: Compare *The Teares of Peace* (1609), l. 502.

46 *fowle panther earth*: 'Chapman likens earth to the panther because that animal was supposed to attract by its sweet breath and then destroy': note by Phyllis Brooks Bartlett in her edition of *The Poems of George Chapman* (New York: MLA, 1941), p. 479. Chapman may also be referring back to a long, complicated and mysterious allegory in 'Hymnus in Cynthiam' in *The Shadow Of Night* (1594). In ll. 210–19, quoted in the Commentary on *The Teares of Peace* (1609), the Goddess Cynthia creates a nymph given the sacred name of Euthimya 'Since she the cares and toyles of earth must tame'. Euthimya can 'turne her selfe to everie shape' (l. 226) just as 'Wisedome conformes her selfe to all earths guises' (l. 229). Euthimya first changes herself into a panther. Cynthia also makes a pack of hounds and a group of huntsmen; and the hounds with 'licorous [i.e. lecherous] hast' (l. 268) chase the metamorphosed panther to a vast and thorny thicket. The hounds cannot get to the panther inside, but the Huntsmen then arrive 'Mounted on Lyons, Unicorns, and Bores' (l. 285). Because these are 'the Princeliest, and hardiest beasts' (l. 295) they are able to open up the thicket. Inside are the 'soules of such as liv'd implausible' (l. 272), some of them eaten by Cynthia's dogs (compare the myth of Actaeon) after 'she had transformd them into beasts' (l. 279). A moral is suggested in ll. 320–21: 'Eyes should guide bodies, and our soules our eyes,/ But now the world consistes on contraries' (compare Commentary on ll. 362–7 of 'Hymnus in Noctem'). Such 'contraries' upset the world of 'To *M. Harriots*', where the soul's 'genuine formes . . . struggle for birth,/ Under the clawes of this fowle Panther earth' (ll. 45–6) partly because of the hidden guises of 'Wisdome'/Euthimya. Chapman's soul is held down by the baseness and desires of the body.

65–7 *Not . . . conceites*: Compare the warning against 'faulty apprehensions' given by Bussy in *Bussy D'Ambois*, III.1.22.

70 *shiver . . . Hercules*: The syntax makes this ambiguous, but the presentation of Hercules elsewhere in Chapman's work suggests that he is less likely to be one of the 'ignorants', than the figure needed to make them 'shiver'.

77–80 *merite . . . dignitie*: Another example of Chapman's belief that 'merite' should determine people's place in society. Compare *Ovids Banquet of Sence*, 90.8–91.7 and Commentary, and ll. 326–31 of *The Teares of Peace* and Commentary.

78 *Timpanies of state*: Compare *Bussy D'Ambois*, I.1.10: 'Tympanouse statists'.

83–5 *and much . . . ignorance*: Obscure, but seems to mean that the 'Tympanouse statists' of l. 78ff also ('much more') regard Harriot's learning as but a 'chink' compared to the 'great Sunne'. They 'adore' the sun 'In staring ignorance' because they're imagined to be looking straight at it, so it blinds them. Their adoration also suggests idolatry.

111 *judiciall*: See Introduction, note 4.

113 *inverted world*: The idea of the world turned upside-down and moving is also used in 'A Coronet for his Mistresse *Philosophie*' (1595), 5.5–6: 'Th'inversed world that goes upon her head/ And with her wanton heeles doth kyck the sky'.

118 *And make . . . exempt*: Compare the first two lines of Chapman's commendatory sonnet on William Jones's translation of *Nennio, Or a Treatise of Nobility: Wherein is discoursed what true Nobilitie is, with such qualities as are required in a perfect Gentleman* (1595): 'Accept thrice Noble *Nennio* at his hand/ That cannot bid himselfe welcome at home' ('G. Chapman to the Author', ll. 1–2). The sonnet expresses the same sense of alienated homelessness.

145 *Courtly question now:* The question is whether the Earl of Essex, to whom Chapman dedicated his versions of the *Seaven Bookes Of The Iliades Of Homere, Prince of Poets* and *Achilles Shield*, will now sponsor a complete translation, or help Chapman to find other sources of patronage at court.

The Teares of Peace

Euthymiae Raptus; Or The Teares of Peace was published in 1609. It was Chapman's first long poem since *Hero And Leander* (1598) and is a celebration of two events. Firstly, the truce called in the war between Spain and the Netherlands, which came about in the spring of 1609 partly through the mediations of King James I of England and King Henry IV of France. Also in 1609, Chapman published *Homer Prince of Poets: Translated according to the Greeke in twelve Bookes of his Iliads.* This volume added Books III–VI and XII to the eight books published in 1598 (I, II, VII–XI, XVIII). It was dedicated to Prince Henry, who then commanded Chapman to translate the remaining books. The second cause for celebration in *The Teares of Peace* is this 'Command,/ To end his *Iliades*' (ll. 1210–11). Chapman seeks to excuse his 'delaie' (l. 1208) in finishing by saying that Homer himself had a hand in *The Teares of Peace.* Homer's spirit appears to Chapman in a vision, and tells him that being Henry's subject is an honour prized 'Past all his honours helde in other Lands' (l. 1223).

The Teares of Peace is dedicated to Prince Henry. Chapman was appointed sewer-in-ordinary (head-waiter/food-taster) to Prince Henry in 1604. The young prince – he was eighteen when he died in November 1612 – had a martial spirit and Protestant zeal. British opponents of the Catholic country of Spain in particular hoped he would adopt more belligerent policies than his father. David Norbook notes that Henry seems to have had 'considerable influence' in the production of masques for the marriage of Princess Elizabeth early in 1613: see *Poetry and Politics in the English Renaissance* (London: RKP, 1984), p. 204. One of the entertainments was Chapman's *Memorable Masque of the two Honourable Houses or Innes of Court; the Middle Temple, and Lyncolnes Inne* which 'glorified projects of colonisation in the New World, a topic which aroused Henry's enthusiasm, particularly as it was a means of resisting Spanish power in the part of the world from which they drew their chief financial strength' (*Poetry and Politics*, p. 204). But Chapman also seems to have wanted to steer Henry away from outward warlike thoughts. *The Teares of Peace* tells him that 'a Princes maine state stands/ In his owne knowledge, and his powre within' (ll. 1224–5) and this accords with the dedicatory epistle to the *twelve Bookes*, designed 'To furnish your youths groundworke, and first State' (l. 17). The first lines of the epistle assert that 'perfect happinesse . . . makes him blest/ That governes inward' and

> . . . in his minde
> Holds such a scepter, as can keepe confinde
> His whole lifes actions in the royall bounds
> Of Vertue and Religion; . . .   (ll. 1–12)

Homer and Chapman 'create/ All sorts of worthiest men' (ll. 19–20 of the epistle) to serve as examples for the Prince.

Several sources have been suggested for *The Teares of Peace*. The French critic Jean Jacquot first proposed that the apparition of Homer is based upon that of Pimander ('Divine Intelligence') to Hermes Trismegistus in 'Book I of The Pimander' (i.e. the *Corpus Hermeticum*), which was translated by Ficino in about 1490 (see Notes to *Poems*). Jacquot also argued that Book X of *The Pimander* helps to explain the attributes given to Homer – the light which 'Brake through the shade' (l. 34), the 'sacred bosome . . . full of fire' (l. 39), and the kindly advice given to the poet that he may look at the apparition without fear, because all men have the power within themselves to become like him: see *George Chapman (1559–1634), sa vie, sa poesie, son théâtre, sa pensée* (Paris, 1951), pp. 74–5. Another likely source is Petrarch's *Secretum* (*c.*1342), which Chapman adapted in Act III. Scene 1 of *Monsieur D'Olive* (1605). Millar Maclure in *George Chapman: A Critical Study* (Toronto: Toronto University Press, 1966), p. 70, first compared the *Secretum* with *The Teares of Peace*: 'like this poem, it is an *apologia pro vita sua*, in which St Augustine is introduced to Petrarch by Truth, and the opinions of the crowd are abjured in favour of self-reverence, self-knowledge, self-control – as in Chapman'. The importance of self-knowledge in *The Teares of Peace* also prompted Maren-Sofie Rostvig to point to the possible influence of sections 13 and 14 of Pico della Mirandola's *Oration on the Dignity of Man* (1492): see *The Hidden Sense, Norwegian Studies in English*, 9 (Oslo, 1963), p. 78n. 'Thus Pico makes the point that only moral philosophy is capable of checking "the leonine passions of wrath and violence" and in this connection he recalls Homer's definition of wrath as strife. And if nature is strife, then only the study of moral philosophy can induce in a man "a true quiet and unshaken peace".' Finally Raymond B. Waddington traces the form of the poem back to Boethius via Chaucer and Spenser: see *The Mind's Empire: Myth and Form in George Chapman's Narrative Poems* (Baltimore and London: Johns Hopkins University Press, 1974), p. 182. 'The entire formal concept of vision projecting the narrator into a consolation-debate with a personification who represents a didactically superior position, originated with Boethius. Here, although Chapman probably knew Boethius, the use of conventions Englished from the *Roman de la Rose* and the entire medieval flavor suggest that Chapman is emulating both Chaucer and the vision of medievalism which Spenser projects in his poetry'. Waddington points to the stress laid on temperance, and ll. 457–9 and ll. 1130–67, as particularly Spenserian.

FURTHER READING

Waddington, R. B., 'The Iconography of Silence and Chapman's Hercules', *Journal of the Warburg and Courtauld Institutes*, 33 (1970), pp. 248–63. An article about the figure of 'Herculean silence' in l. 1108 of *The Teares of Peace*: its findings are summarized in Waddington's book *The Mind's Empire: Myth and Form in George Chapman's Narrative Poems* (Baltimore and London: Johns Hopkins University Press, 1974).

TEXTUAL NOTES

The Teares of Peace

The base text is the copy of *Euthymiae Raptus; Or The Teares of Peace* (1609) in the British Library (shelfmark: c.30.e.3). In the notes that follow, the first readings are those of this edition and the second record those of the base text.

79	acclamations] exclamations (*a seventeenth-century hand has made this alteration in three of the five surviving copies of the book*)	670	seated)] ~,
		805	Penne ∧] ~.
		853	ignorant,] ~.
		941	me] we
262	Spleene;] ~.	983	∧ As] (~
325	warre.] ~;	1002	these,] ~)
326	rude?] ~,	1086	unworldly] unwordly
327	multitude.] ~?	1134	erre,] ~.
345	wrackt.] ~,	1137	Nightingall.] ~;
351	Diadem.] ~,		

COMMENTARY

Euthymiae: In 'Hymnus in Cynthiam' in *The Shadow Of Night* (1594), ll. 210–19, the Goddess Cynthia creates a precursor of Peace:

> She frames of matter intimate before,
> (To wit, a bright, and daseling meteor)
> A goodlie Nimph, whose bewtie, bewtie staines
> Heav'ns with her jewells; gives all the raines
> Of wished pleasance; frames her golden wings,
> But them she bindes up close with purple strings,
> Because she now will have her run alone,
> And bid the base, to all affection.
> And Euthimya is her sacred name,
> Since she the cares and toyles of earth must tame: . . .

'Euthimya' is a name invented by Chapman from the Greek for cheerfulness. In 'Hymnus in Cynthiam' she represents spiritual Joy or Contentment of the mind.

Teares: Compare Ulysses' response to the minstrel Demodocus in ll. 720–23 of Book VIII of Chapman's translation of *Homer's Odysses* (1614):

> In teares his feeling braine swet: for in things
> That move past utterance, teares ope all their springs.
> Nor are there in the Powres that all life beares
> More true interpreters of all than teares.

Inductio: i.e. Introduction

1–6 *Now . . . Mars*: Britain's 'Soveraign' James I is acclaimed for helping to negotiate the Truce of Antwerp, halting twelve years of war between Spain and the Netherlands. In ll. 2–3 'her' refers back to 'Peace', in l. 3 'his' refers to Hercules. The Pillars of Hercules are the rocks on either side of the Strait of Gibraltar, supposed in classical times to have been set up by Hercules to support the western boundary of the world. Hence the allusion brings in Spain geographically, but it also means that James I has exceeded the limits of Hercules' achievements. *'Mars'* is the god of war and lover of Venus. Vulcan used a net to catch them committing adultery. Compare *All Fooles* (1599), III.1.270–71, and *Bussy D'Ambois* (1604), V.1.62.

16 *shipwrackt*: One of Chapman's favourite images. See Introduction.

17 *Religion . . . One*: Compare the devil Ophioneus in Chapman's tragedy *Caesar And Pompey* (1604–5), II.i.38–41: 'The world's out of frame, a thousand Rulers wresting it this way, and that, with as many Religions; when, as heavens upper Sphere is mov'd onely by one, so should the Sphere of earth be, and Ile have it so.'

36–7 *blind . . . sawe*: The apparition is Homer, and the paradoxical suggestion is that he can see 'inward; past and future things' precisely because he is blind, just as in 'Hymnus in Noctem' in *The Shadow Of Night* the darkness of Night is superior to 'day, or light, in anie qualitie' (l. 362). Compare also ll. 72–3 and ll. 1005–6 of *The Teares of Peace*.

61–2 *Remember . . . well*: This sounds like it should be a quotation from another poem by Chapman, but it's not in his surviving work.

65 *trance*: Compare 'Hymnus in Noctem', l. 15, and Notes to *Poems*.

75 *Elysian*: From Elysium, described by Chapman in a gloss to *Ovids Banquet of Sence* (1595), 57.1, as 'the blisfull state of soules, as Virgill faines'.

76–85 *That . . . english me*: Chapman was born near Hitchin in Hertfordshire, probably in 1559. These lines suggest that the spirit of Homer has visited him once before, when he was meditating on a hill near Hitchin, and that Chapman temporarily ('for the time then') inherited Homer's 'spirit' and so understood the 'true sense' of his works. This encouraged him to start translating Homer's poetry ('english me'). As Chapman's first translation appeared in 1598, some invisible colloquy must have occurred before then. It's not clear whether anywhere in particular is meant by 'fayre

Greenes'. (Perhaps it's a reference to the lawns of colleges at Oxford or Cambridge, where Chapman might have gone as a student or to consult libraries?)

87–90 *It was . . . delight*: The Prince is James I's son Henry, and 'the grace' he did Chapman was to agree to sponsor his translation of Homer's works, hence 'my Princes *Homer*'. The spirit's face suggests to Chapman that Homer is delighted with this move.

92 *stay*: The main meaning here seems to be 'support', but it could also mean 'staying power' (bolstering that 'search I still intend' in l. 98) and further be used in its old sense of 'being a calming influence' on the journey 'through Earths peace-pretending strife' (l. 97).

94 *Advancing Colours*: A figurative reference to military 'Colours' such as flags and ensigns. Compare ll. 843–5 of *The Teares of Peace* and Shakespeare's *The Merry Wives of Windsor* (1597), III.iv.85: 'I must advance the colours of my love'.

120 *The ayrie Nation*: i.e. birds that fly in the air.

151–4 *the Sunne . . . from her*: Compare the gloss to *Ovids Banquet of Sence*, 70.7: '*At the Sun going downe, shadowes grow longest, whereupon this Embleme is devised*'.

184–5 *Homer . . . no share*: In her edition of *The Poems of George Chapman* (New York: MLA, 1941), p. 442, Phyllis Brooks Bartlett says that a Dr Rutledge suggested to her that Chapman might have been thinking here of a passage in Book XXIII of Homer's *Iliad*, about the mourning for Patroclus, part of which is quoted in the gloss to l. 853 of *Eugenia* (1614). In Chapman's translation of *The Iliads Of Homer* (1611), XXIII.7–8: 'When with our friend's kind woe our hearts have felt delight to do/ A virtuous soule right, . . .'. Compare l. 195 of *The Teares of Peace*: 'Griefe, that dischargeth Conscience, is delight'.

191 *And mourning . . . banqueting*: Compare 'Hymnus in Noctem', l. 366: 'Since mournings are preferd to banquettings'.

215–16 *Heaven moves . . . moving Heaven*: The reason 'men say it stands' is the discovery of Copernicus that it was in fact the earth which moved and not the heavens. Compare *Bussy D'Ambois*, V.1.153.

224–5 *And in . . . throwne*: Compare ll. 29–49 of 'Hymnus in Noctem' and Commentary.

228 *O ye . . . Quiristers*: 'Quiristers' means choristers, 'three-times-thrice' means there are nine of them, hence they are the Muses – Calliope, Clio, Euterpe, Terpsichore, Erato, Melpomene, Thalia, Polyhymnia, and Urania.

238–40 *our Thames . . . falls*: The scene is now the banks of the River Thames, the wave-lending 'her' of l. 239. In l. 240 'yours' are the Muses, the Thames is their holy Sister, and 'falls' refers to the Muses' fountain of inspiration on Mount Helicon, and to the Thames's own descent to the sea.

242 *great Prince of men*: i.e. Prince Henry.

246 *Heavens deare Lamb*: The Lamb of Christ.

248 *thrice great Britaine*: Called 'thrice great' because it combines the kingdoms of England, Wales and Scotland.

259 *tragique daughters bosome*: i.e. Religion – see ll. 205–7.

317 *polisht*: Compare 'Hymnus in Noctem', ll. 223–4: 'We basely make retrait, and are no lesse/ Then huge impolisht heapes of filthinesse.'

324 *long Robe*: As worn by lawyers.

328–31 *For regular . . . Lord alike*: The phrase 'chiefe stroke strike' means that 'regular Learning' should be the mightiest factor in distinguishing 'all mens worths'. But it isn't. The point is made elsewhere in Chapman's works, for example in ll. 80–85 of the dedicatory letter to his translation of *Seaven Bookes Of The Iliades*, addressed in 1598 to the Earl of Essex: 'If the crowne of humanitie be the soule, and the soule an intellectual beam of God, the essence of her substance being intellection and intellection or understanding the strength and eminence of her faculties, the differencing of men in excellencie must be directed onelie by their proportions of true knowledge.' The language used here reflects Chapman's favourite saying from Aristotle (compare 24.5–6 and gloss of *Ovids Banquet of Sence* and Commentary, and ll. 856–61 of *The Teares of Peace*) and it echoes throughout the poem 'To *M. Harriots*' suffixed to *Achilles Shield* (1598). What's proposed is a different social structure. See Notes to *Poems*.

362–5 *But . . . the Cote*: Called 'their terms' because they are heraldic and reflect noblemen's obsession with birth-right instead of Learning. In heraldic terms, the 'Roote' is the family tree entitling a man to a 'Cote' of Arms. The 'Crest' is a figure or device borne above the shield and helmet in the 'Cote' and the 'Field' is the surface of the shield. In Peace's adaptation of these terms, 'Life' itself is the top ('Crest') and bottom ('Roote') of 'all mans' potential nobility – a state which can be attained through 'learning'. It's learning which distinguishes ('differences' is used as a verb) between people.

408 *Those Giants . . . heaven*: A reference to the mythological Giants who fought against the Gods but were defeated and buried under various Greek and Italian volcanoes.

435–6 *like Kites . . . garbidge*: Kites are birds of prey. Compare *Bussy D'Ambois*, II.1.5–8, where Envy is compared to a Kite feeding on 'outcast entrailes'. Chapman's use of the word 'bangle' – meaning to beat about – predates the *OED*'s first hawk-related citation by six years.

444 *manlesse*: Compare 'Hymnus in Noctem', l. 93.

462 *Opinion*: Associated with the multitude by Plato in Book VI of *The Republic*, and a word always used pejoratively by Chapman to mean the opposite of Knowledge, Judgement and Truth. Compare ll. 213–14 of 'A Hymne to our Saviour on the Crosse' in *Petrarchs Seven Penitentiall Psalms, Paraphrastically Translated: With other Philosophicall Poems, and a Hymne to Christ upon the Crosse* (1612): 'we are tost out of our humane Throne/ By pied and protean Opinion'. Peter Ure notes that Chapman's use of the word is bound up with a 'Stoic and Calvinist emphasis on inward discipline and virtue, to which Opinion is an exterior ill': see p. 336 of 'A Note on "Opinion" in Daniel, Greville and Chapman', *Modern Languages Review*, 46 (1951), pp. 331–8. On p. 334 Ure also points out Greville's view – relevant to *The Teares of Peace* – that 'Opinion is one of the natural allies of outward destructive powers (kings and wars in *Alaham* and *A Treatie of Warres*)'.

503 *like gould-worms*: i.e. like glow-worms, although glow-worms do not make a noise. Compare 'To *M. Harriots*', ll. 43–4.

552 *the Blaze*: Compare the fiery brightness of this image with the obscure glow-worms representing true learning in l. 503.

596–604 *And as . . . Muse*: The image is derived from Plutarch's essay 'On being a busybody,' in the *Moralia*. It's used again in *Andromeda Liberata* (1614), ll. 203–10:

> . . . as in certaine Cities were
> Some ports through which all rites piaculare [means 'sinful'],
> All Executed men, all filth were brought,
> Of all things chast, or pure, or sacred, nought
> Entring or issuing there: so curious men,
> Nought manly, elegant, or not uncleane,
> Embrace, or bray out: Acts of staine are still
> Their Syrens, and their Muses . . .

For the 'Syrens', see Introduction.

610–13 *To bee . . . adorne her*: 'Justice is to be wondered at. For Proportion and Ornament none of the Graces is as excellent as her. She's so excellent that vile things (which would be vile on any other figure) actually adorn her.'

613–30 *me thought . . . composed there*: In l. 614 'giving lawe' means 'giving order'. Raymond B. Waddington argues in *The Mind's Empire: Myth and Form in George Chapman's Narrative Poems* (Baltimore and London: Johns Hopkins University Press, 1974), p. 187, that 'the globe of empire, Astraea's book of law, and her position by the seashore serve to suggest that the earthly embodiment Chapman once saw was Elizabeth, as Astraea and as Cynthia, queen of the ocean': as in 'Hymnus in Cynthiam'. For Queen Elizabeth I's role as Astraea – the goddess of Justice in the Golden Age – see Frances A. Yates, *Astraea: The Imperial Theme in the Sixteenth Century* (London: Routledge & Kegan Paul, 1975). Waddington also points out that emblems of Doctrina depict her with a book in her lap, while the 'goulden bridles' belong to Temperance.

634 *The large . . . wrote*: It's not clear which of his works Chapman is referring to here. But 'large' and 'long since' suggest it could be *The Shadow Of Night, Ovids Banquet of Sence*, or his continuation of Marlowe's *Hero And Leander* (1598).

675–6 *Spirits . . . Circle*: The magician's magic circle was supposed to protect him from any devils ('Spirits') he raised. Compare *Bussy D'Ambois*, III.2.288, where Bussy is compared by Monsieur to 'a spirit rais'd without a circle'.

677–84 *And then . . . their eares*: Compare the choric speech delivered by Epernon in *The Tragedie Of Charles Duke of Byron* (1607–8), V.iii.193–8:

> We have not any strength but weakens us,
> No greatnes but doth crush us into ayre.
> Our knowledges, do light us but to erre,

> Our Ornaments are Burthens: Our delights
> Are our tormentors; fiendes that (raisd in feares)
> At parting shake our Roofes about our eares.

See the Notes to *Bussy D'Ambois*.

685 *Th'imprison'd thirst*: i.e. 'The imprisoned thirst for . . .'

695-9 *beheaded Hydra's . . . conquers*: The Hydra was a mythical many-headed monster which lived in the stinking Lernean Fen. Every time one of its heads was cut off, two more would appear ('ever double rise'). The monster was eventually destroyed by Hercules as one of his Labours, hence 'Herculean Learning conquers'.

743-4 *wright . . . Savadges*: An image suggesting the mythical musician Orpheus, whose lyre-playing could 'charme' animate and inanimate objects.

753 *creating Fire*: An allusion to Promotheus' theft of fire from the gods. Compare the gloss to l. 131 of 'Hymnus in Noctem'. See Introduction.

856-61 *As in Rules . . . skill*: An exposition of one Chapman's favourite sayings from the Greek philosopher Aristotle. Compare ll. 327-31 of *The Teares of Peace*, also 23.5-6 and gloss of *Ovids Banquet of Sence* and Commentary.

874-81 *But . . . sincere*: Expanded from the last five lines of a speech in Chapman's tragedy *Caesar And Pompey*, where the Soothsayer tells Caesar how he sacrificed an ox for him (III.ii.4-26). The last five lines describe the beast's limbs burning on the altar:

> Not like the Elementall fire that burnes
> In household uses, lamely struggling up,
> This way and that way winding as it rises,
> But (right and upright) reacht his proper sphere
> Where burnes the fire eternall and sincere.

The Soothsayer's speech in its turn is based on a scene between Tiresias and his daughter Manto in Seneca's *Oedipus* (ll. 299ff.).

912 *Rubarb . . . Thessalie*: Rhubarb imported from China and Tibet via Russia and the Levant was used in the Renaissance as a purgative drug. Thessalie – part of northern Greece – was famed among the ancients as a breeding ground for dangerous narcotics. The sour taste of such substances is meant to be contrasted with the 'sweet' of l. 911.

913-17 *O trie . . . beneath*: Obscure, but 'contradiction' and 'lode' seem to refer back to the 'deare yoke' of l. 903.

942 *calme Shore . . . Sonne*: The phrase 'calme Shore' is repeated from l. 99. 'Sonne' means Christ, 'him' is God.

944 *in my haven, wracke*: One of Chapman's favourite images, which may derive from Quintilian's *De Institutione Oratoria* via Erasmus's *Adagia* (1500). See Introduction.

1003 *balls . . . Race*: An allusion to the myth of the huntress Atalanta, who refused to marry anyone who could not beat her in a race. So Hippomenes borrowed three golden apples (here 'balls') from Aphrodite, threw them under Atalanta's feet, and won. Compare *Hero And Leander*, V.449, which refers to 'bals of Discord'.

1005–6 *the gaudie . . . Night*: Compare the theme of 'Hymnus in Noctem'.

1010–12 *And how . . . Starres*: Compare 50.4–9 and gloss in *Ovids Banquet of Sence* and Commentary.

1016–22 *To which . . . till death*: A passage reworked from *The Tragedie Of Charles Duke of Byron*, V.iv.31–8, where Byron is preparing to be executed for treason and feels his soul rousing and threatening Death:

> At whom I joyfully will cast her off:
> I know this bodie but a sinck of folly,
> The ground-work, and rais'd frame of woe and frailtie:
> The bond, and bundle of corruption;
> A quick corse, onely sensible of griefe,
> A walking sepulcher, or household thiefe:
> A glasse of ayre, broken with lesse then breath,
> A slave bound face to face to death, til death: . . .

Compare also Tamyra's pleading with her husband Montsurry in *Bussy D'Ambois*, V.1.108–11.

1023 *consecrate*: Compare 'Hymnus in Noctem', l. 372.

1053 *gratious Princes*: i.e. Prince Henry.

1108–11 *Peacefull . . . ayre*: The image of 'Herculean silence' is very complex and has best been elucidated by R. B. Waddington in 'The Iconography of Silence and Chapman's Hercules', *Journal of the Warburg and Courtauld Institutes*, 33 (1970), pp. 248–63. Waddington's argument is summarized on pp. 190–92 of his book *The Mind's Empire*. The following explanation is simplified from Waddington. The image of 'Herculean silence' has its roots in Egyptian iconography, where Isis' son Horus is usually pictured as a chubby infant childishly holding his finger to his mouth. The Greeks called this figure Harpocrates (Horus the child); they mistook his childishness for silence, and so, when a cult of silence as a high form of eloquence was developed by mystery religions, Pythagoreans and Platonists, Harpocrates became the god of silence, an idea which continued into the Renaissance. Hence Chapman's reference to 'his forefingers charme'. Silence is 'Herculean' because Chapman associates Hercules with learning, e.g. in ll. 1–3 of the dedicatory letter to *The Shadow Of Night* and l. 699 of *The Teares of Peace*. Waddington also refers to 'the tradition, which Spenser used in Book 5 of *The Faerie Queene*, of Hercules as god of justice; and the tradition of the "Gallic Hercules", which celebrated the hero for his eloquence rather than for physical strength' (*The Mind's Empire*, p. 191).

1135–7 *the bird . . . Nightingall*: i.e. the robin.

1161 *Both sorts of Ignorance*: i.e. the learned sort castigated at l. 528 and the traditional unlearned sort.

1189–90 *The Phoenix . . . renew*: The phoenix is a mythical bird supposed to rise renewed from its own ashes. See also 31.4–7 of *Ovids Banquet of Sence* and Commentary.

Corollarium ad *Principem:*
'*A crowning appendix dedicated to the Prince.*'

1207 *Thus . . . braine:* Compare 23.2 of *Ovids Banquet of Sence* and Commentary and the first line of the sonnet quoted in the 'Note on the Text' of *All Fooles.*
1211 *Great Prince:* Prince Henry.

'*A good woman*'

'A good woman' was published in 1612 in *Petrarchs Seven Penitentiall Psalms, Paraphrastically Translated: With other Philosophicall Poems, and a Hymne to Christ upon the Crosse.* It was placed after the translations of Petrarch, the *Hymne to Christ,* and three other philosophical poems – 'Virgils Epigram of a good man', 'A great Man' ('great' being opposed to 'good'), and 'A sleight man' (between 'great' and 'good'). 'A good woman' was then followed by three more of Virgil's epigrams, 'A Fragment of the Teares of peace', twenty more philosophical poems with titles like 'Of Ambition', 'Of Friendship', and five similar 'Fragments'. A list of the contents suggests some thematic ordering as Chapman continues to preach the Christian-Stoic philosophy developed through *The Teares of Peace* (1609) and *The Revenge Of Bussy D'Ambois* (1610–11). Many of the poems reiterate points familiar from his earlier work. 'A good woman' stands out as a new pronouncement on the ideal nature of relations between the sexes. At a time when women had little formal education, Chapman's obsession with 'learning' prompts him to go against the 'foolish' and 'false opinion,/ That learning fits not women' (ll. 16–17). The volume also shows Chapman emptying out his commonplace book. Like John Webster he copied out sentences and passages from many other men's works, then used these borrowings in his plays and poems to make strange mosaics of his own. Several of the poems in the 1612 volume are versified from the work of the Stoic Epictetus. The last fifty-four lines of 'A good woman' are heavily indebted to Plutarch's 'Conjugalia praecepta' ('Advice to bride and groom') in the *Moralia,* which is also adapted with very different emphasis in *The Revenge Of Bussy D'Ambois.* From the plundering of Natalis Comes's *Mythologiae* (1551) for *The Shadow Of Night* (1594), throughout his career Chapman had a magpie mind. Hence the often rugged texture of his poetry and drama; he bulked in material like an explorer equipping himself for uncharted regions.

TEXTUAL NOTES

The base text of 'A good woman' is from the copy of *Petrarchs Seven Penitentiall Psalms, Paraphrastically Translated: With other Philosophicall Poems* (1612) in the Bodleian Library, Oxford (shelfmark: 8° G. 67. Th.).

COMMENTARY

29–82 *She is . . . doubles more*: Closely based on Plutarch's essay 'Advice to bride and groom'.

36 *Yet . . . shame*: Quoted by Plutarch from Herodotus. Compare Chapman's tragedy *The Revenge Of Bussy D'Ambois* (1610–11), III.ii.162–5, where Charlotte – wife of the spy Baligny – is urging Clermont to revenge Bussy's death:

> . . . I would once
> Strip off my shame with my attire, and trie
> If a poore woman, votist of revenge
> Would not performe it . . .

47–54 and Gloss *And as . . . powres applies*: The gloss means: 'students of Geometry affirm that lines and surfaces do not move of their own accord, but accompany the movement of bodies.' Compare *The Revenge Of Bussy D'Ambois*, I.ii.53–61, where Tamyra is speaking to her husband Montsurry:

> But as Geometricians (you still say)
> Teach that no lines, nor superfices,
> Doe move themselves, but still accompanie
> The motions of their bodies: so poore wives
> Must not pursue, nor have their owne affections,
> But to their husbands earnests, and their jests,
> To their austerities of lookes, and laughters,
> (Though ne'er so foolish and injurious)
> Like Parasites and slaves, fit their disposures.

The differing emphases of poem and play show Chapman's methods of working with material stored in his commonplace book being adapted for the job at hand.

59 *And as . . . Hippocrates*: An image not taken from Plutarch, but used elsewhere by Chapman. Compare his tragicomedy *The Gentleman Usher* (1602–3), IV.iii.17, and *The Memorable Masque of the two Honourable Houses or Innes of Court; the Middle Temple, and Lyncolnes Inne* (1613), ll. 320–27. In *The Poems of George Chapman* (New York: MLA, 1941), p. 448, Bartlett suggests that Chapman may have found the image in Robert Cawdray's *Treasurie of Similes* (1600), p. 851. She notes that Hippocrates was supposed to have pronounced a pair of brothers twins because they sickened at the same time, and the course of their disease was the same.

65–7 *And as . . . scarlet*: Compare *The Conspiracie Of Charles Duke of Byron* (1607–8), II.ii.39–40, where King Henry IV is discussing how to govern and correct Byron:

> To Buls, we must not shew our selves in red,
> Nor to the warlick Elephant in white; . . .

GLOSSARY

able warrant

abodement foreboding, omen

aboding portending

absolute perfect

acceptive suitable for acceptance (coined by Chapman in 1598)

accomplements things which adorn or perfect

Additions honorific titles

adhorne endow with cuckold's horns (Chapman's coinage)

after-times time after death

ameld enamelled

amities friendship

Ancetors ancestors

Antique invariably rustic, often grotesque, sometimes obscene

apposde put in juxtaposition to

Argosea large trading ship

arrive bring to, bestow on

assay put to the test

attended waited for

Attorney deputy, backer

Autumnal Starre Sirius

baffeld disgraced, duped

balls obstacles

bangle flap about, not bothering to swoop on prey

Barks coverings, clothing

Barly-breake a game; one couple in a central area called 'hell' try to catch other couples

Basilisks fabulous serpents whose looks or breath could kill

Bayly bailiff

beare state hold office

becks callings, invocations

beholding beholden

Bents stalks

Bever lower face-guard of a helmet

bewrayes reveals

Bisogno beggarly person (especially of inexperienced soldiers)

blandation illusion (*OED*'s only example of this sense)

blaze blazon; proclaim in a formal manner

blister'd slanderous

bloud a) family, descent b) sexual desire c) sexually rampant male

blowse a tart

boote reward, booty

bracke a flaw, usually in cloth

Brake literally, a vise; thus, a fixed position

braving boasting

breathing life-giving

Broker dealer in the second-hand

brookes tolerates

bruits spreads rumours

brunt assault

Buckler sword

bugge bugbear

bullets thunderbolts

buske points ties which secure a whalebone corset, i.e. bosom

Buzz rumour

by slip minor fault

Callenders signs; indications suggested in almanacs

Cancro Italian oath: cancer take you!

Capricions caprices

capricious lecherous

case a) disguise   b) female sexual organs

cast throw of a dice

Cates exotic foods

Center of the universe

chaffe husks of corn which burn out rapidly

chapmen vendors

checke pursue (hunting term)

Chevrill kid leather, which was most pliable

Christmast provided with Christmas cheer (Chapman's coinage)

Cockatrice a serpent, identified with the basilisk

chop bandy words

clapdish alms-dish, the lid of which announced a beggar's approach

cloth tapestry

Colestafe pole for carrying burdens

collections indications

compasse reach

Complexion temperament

conceipted imagined

concretion connection with material substance

Confidence a) assurance
   b) over-boldness

Conge bow, invariably sycophantic

Coniskins rabbit skins

conscience consciousness

conseave plant the conception in, i.e. deceive

consite excited

contentation satisfaction

contents plural of 'content', i.e. kinds of satisfaction

Copesmates antagonists; but cope (= grapple) also often has a bawdy sense

cornetting playing the cornet or horn

Cornutos cuckolds

correspondent responsible

Covert wooded growth providing shelter

crackt damaged, decrepit

crankes labyrinths

creaming forming scum or froth on the surface of

cries Clinke chimes

crosse-capers from dancing; unexpected move which confounds another person (antedates *OED*'s earliest usage)

crowned cup brimming glass

crownes five-shilling coins

cuckooes note cuckolds' song

cullion rascal, but with play on the original sense, 'testicle'

cullour pretext

curious elaborate

currant genuine

curtoll curtail, bring to an end

Cycatrice scar of a healed wound

Cyprian of Venus; licentious

danting vanquishing

dating claiming to be

deare dire, dangerous

debate contention (more acrimonious than current usage)

decent appropriate

defalcation diminution, cutting down

defesances legal acts rendering former contracts null and void

determinate final

devise elaborate workmanship

Diall compass

digestion shape, structure

disparag'd technical term: dishonoured by marriage to an inferior

disparent diverse, of varying appearance (Chapman's coinage; antedates *OED*'s earliest usage)

dispence evade the law

displow reverse the beneficial effects of

the plough (Chapman's coinage)

disposure disposition (antedates *OED*'s only example of this sense)

distemper afflict

divines spiritual elements, mind and soul

draught outline drawing

drudgerie sexual satisfaction

dwell endure

earnest a) advance payment b) seriousness

effection formation, production

elixer quintessence (from alchemy)

eloigne remove to a distance

embrewd stained (often with blood)

Empale encircle

emploiments implements

Empresse impress, motto

enchase exhibit

engine scheme, project

ennamild beautified with a variety of colours

enseame bring together, introduce (with sexual implications)

entertaine a) take into service b) while away (time)

equall equitable, balanced

errant a) arrant b) erring

erre wander

Estridge ostrich

everted overturned, upset

exhales draws up

Exiturus going

Exordion introduction, proem

expansure expansion (Chapman's coinage)

exploded driven off (from Latin 'explosus'; antedates *OED*'s earliest usage)

expresse represent emblematically

expugn'd vanquished

exquire find the identity of

extensure state of being extended, protracted

extrude thrust out

facts actions

fancie imagination

fat fatten

fautor a) patron b) adherent, partisan

fending defensive remarks

fin'd purified

fine for pay to secure exemption

fircke whip, beat (often with a pun on 'fuck')

fivers fibres (of life)

flering smiling falsely and obsequiously

Flotes waves

foile defeat; a failure (from hunting)

fond foolish

forced enforced, violated

forehead assurance

franchisement liberty, release from restraint

frantique crazy

French mesells venereal disease

frivall frivolous

froes Bacchantes; wild female revellers

front a) defy b) take precedence over, replace

frontlesse shameless

frubber burnisher, polisher (Chapman's coinage)

gainst in preparation for the time when

geniale generative

Gentrie rank of gentleman

glorious boastful

Gnomons rods which cast the shadows on sun-dials

gob large mouthful of food, especially meat

gorget armour for the throat

gratulate appease

grissells gristle, of which the ear was thought to consist

Guaicum drug made from the resin of the guaiacum tree

Gudgion small fish used as bait, i.e. a false tale

Guiserd a) a partisan of the Guise   b) fantastically dressed masquerader

habituate habitual

Hackster whore's thug (*OED*'s first usage)

Haies elaborate and/or meandering country dances

Haling hauling, dragging

hangbyes hangers-on

hant (haunt) subject under discussion

hartlesse lacking in courage

Harpye mythical rapacious monster, with female body but birdlike wings and talons

haughtie high-minded, aspiring

Hebrew any unintelligible language

height elevated rank

Hermean rodde peacemaker; Hermes used the caduceus to resolve quarrels

Heronshawe young heron

high Naps luxurious clothing

hight called

hinde servant

horned bony

hoysed hoist, raised

huge great in rank

humor personal temperament

ignorant unknown

Illustrious manifest, obvious

Immanitie capacity for cruelty

impe graft on to, mend

impeach check, rebuke

imperance commanding quality (Chapman's coinage)

implide employed

impostume abscess

imprecations curses

impulsion external influence on the mind

incompressed free from sexual violation (unique usage; not in *OED*)

indepressed not dejected (Chapman's coinage; not in *OED*, but antedates earliest usage of 'undepressed')

indew'd endowed

indigest shapeless, formless

inennerable indescribable

ingenuous generous, noble

in graine indeed; genuine

in print in perfect order

in sadnesse in all seriousness, in truth

insensive non-material (unique usage; not in *OED*)

inspired animated

integuments outer coverings

Intellective possessed of understanding

intend deem, believe

irrevitable nonce version of 'irrenitible', not to be withstood

Iveryport the ivory door to the realm of sleep

jade worthless horse

jogges nudges

kennell gutter

kilbuck fierce-looking man (Chapman's coinage)

kinde natural state

lamps eyes

lard fat

lasts measures of weight (1 last of gunpowder equalled 24 barrels)

lay wager

leeful just, allowed

legerdeheele nonce version of legerdemain; thus a conflation of 'trickery' and the bawdy innuendo of 'kicking up the heels'

let hinder, prevent

levels aims

Linstock forked stick holding the flame by which a cannon was fired

low a short distance

lucerns lynxes, famed as courageous hunters

lycorous obsessed with exotic food (with pun on lecherous)

lymbo a) place near hell where the just who lived before Christ dwelt   b) any confinement

lymn illuminate

lyripoope literally, a hood worn by a scholar i.e. wits, understanding

making personal appearance

malipert insolent

Manlesly unmanfully, inhumanly (*OED*'s first usage)

marginall glossing, commenting upon

maritorious nonce word: absurdly fond of their husbands

mate a) rival   b) checkmate

maynd maimed

mazer head

meane steady route

Medlar rotten fruit

Meere a) absolute   b) nothing other than

meritorious earning cash through sex (*meretrix* in Latin = whore)

Mewd hidden, locked away

miching skulking

misprision misunderstanding

monster a prodigy or freak, displayed at fairs

Moon-calves children of the moon; fickle, unstable persons (*OED*'s first usage)

mountaners outlaws from mountainous regions

muckinders handkerchiefs

muske-Cats musk was used for strong perfumes; hence, fops

Mutton loose woman

myddins dunghills

Mylor French designation for an English lord

nasty disgusting, foul (far stronger than current usage)

nice precise, fussy

nicke device which makes a clock strike

not-headed a) close-cropped   b) free of cuckold's horns

noyse band of musicians

Nuntius messenger in ancient tragedy

objection objective, end

observing paying court to

officious dutiful

Opinion 'a light, vain, crude, imperfect thing . . . never arriving at the understanding' (Ben Jonson)

opportunities importunities

Ordinaries the lowest grade of drinking house

ostents portents

ouches sores (*OED*'s only example of this sense)

outlandish foreign, fantastic

outraying going beyond the bounds of moderation

outweare cast aside

oversee overlook

over-weene confound with self-regard

owght owed

paise balance

panch't stabbed in the belly

Pantable pantofle; slipper, shoe

paring rind

partles impartial (Chapman's coinage)

part'st departs, comes away

passport any document granting permission

peculier (as verb) privately own (unique usage; not in *OED*)

Pegmas originally stages bearing descriptive inscriptions; hence contents of an entertainment

Pelopian ivory (see List of Historical, Mythological and Geographical Names, 'Pelops')

perboile sweat in a tub to cure the pox

perdu's profligates

Period conclusion

perviall transparently obvious (Chapman's coinage)

phanes fanes, i.e. temples, but with a possible play on vanes (= weathercocks)

picked punctilious

platts plots

pole-deedes deed poll

politicke scheming

Pompists ostentatiously wealthy persons (Chapman's coinage)

Posie inscription on jewellery

post-issue children of a second marriage

potable flowing; intoxicated (unique usage)

Poultron poltroon

preace the crush of conflict

pregredience a going before (Chapman's coinage)

presentments entertainments

pressing crowding

presumed presumptuous

prevent anticipate

prickesong singing from musical notation (with sexual pun)

privitie private knowledge

proface obsolete greeting at a meal: you're welcome to it!

project thrusting, impudent

proper handsome

prorected directed straight at (unique usage; not in *OED*)

proud eager, confident (sexually)

prove a) sustain   b) test

Puttock bird of prey, a kite

Pyes magpies

Pyramis pyramid

qualified appeased

Quatorzanies Quatorzains; true sonnets of fourteen lines

queimishlie unique variant of 'squeamishly', i.e. coldly, distantly

quite requite

rackt strained

radicall essential

rapting ravishing (antedates *OED*'s earliest use)

Rate scold

reaches maximum spread of canvas (of sails)

receit reception

recognizance legally binding obligation, usually financial

redition the action of returning (*OED*'s first usage)

reflection turning back

Regiment authority

regreete return of a greeting

Rejoinders replies of a defendant to a plaintiff

remainenances nonce word, implying 'remnants'

reminiscion remembrance (Chapman's coinage)

remissive careless

replications plaintiff's replies to a defendant

Residence residents, inhabitants

respective respectful

responsive corresponding with

retrive from hunting: to flush out game for a second shoot

reversion legal term for something (a job, estate, or widow) left after death

Revive restore from depression

Revolts rebels against

Rip[p]ier fish-seller, notorious for gossiping

rocke distaff

Rushes floor coverings

Ruth sorrow, lamentation

sacietie feeling of disgust caused by over-indulgence

sadly seriously

say assay, make trial of

scute scudo; coin of varying but small value

Sdruciolla triple or dactylic rhymes

seeled with eyes stitched shut (of pigeons used for hunting)

sees flares up

seld seldom

set elaborately constructed

sett bet with

Sfoote God's foot

shack-rags low-born rascals (unique usage)

shift device

side accompany

simples remedies

skal'd removed the scabs from

skathe dangerously harmful emotion

skittish a) coy   b) frivolous

sleight adroitness, cunning

slight (as exclamation) God's light

smockage nonce word conflating 'smock' (= whore) and 'socage' (= tenure of land in return for money or services)

smocke-faces effeminate faces (Chapman's coinage)

soft-roed like the sperm of a male fish

Soldado soldier (Spanish)

Sollar loft, attic

sophisticate adulterated

sorted assorted

sorts accords

sound swoon

sounds has a suggestion of

spaded spayed, have ovaries removed

sparke woman of outstanding beauty or wit

Speeder a successful executor of a suit

speeding vulnerable, prone to fatal wound

spenders those of spendthrifts

sperst dispersed

spinners spiders

spurrie radiating light (Chapman's coinage)

stand a) job   b) place of observation

standing fixed, settled

standish portable writing desk

Stewes brothels

stild distilled

still a) ever, perpetually   b) distill

Stilladoe stiletto (?), unique usage

stocke tree stump

stoope Gallant humble themselves

strangenesse aloofness

strappl'd strapped, protected (of legs – *OED*'s only example of this sense)

string a) cord for tying a purse   b) ribbon of a knight's order

Stroddle variant of 'straddle' (*OED*'s first usage)

stupid generated by stupor

sublimate mercuric chloride, a strong poison

superficies outer crust

supererogation performance of more than is necessary

surfets lightning bolts

tall tough, forceful

Theorbo large double-necked lute

thirsted longed for

threshals thresholds

tickle sensitive

Timbrels musical instruments, like tambourines

tire from falconry: to tear with the beak

Topt literally, to put a top-sail on a ship

tracts traces, tracks

traduction translation

transite pass across

tread a) walk   b) copulate

trenches wrinkles

trow (in question) do you suppose?

trull common prostitute

Trumps trumpets

trusse seize

tumult mob

Tympanouse tympany is a swelling, thus, arrogant

Tynsell thin cloth incorporating gold or silver

Under a) disguised as   b) for any less

unparagond without equal (Chapman's coinage)

unshuting unfitting (Chapman's coinage; not in *OED*, but antedates earliest usage of 'unsuiting')

unusering giving no return (Chapman's coinage; antedates *OED*'s sole usage)

utmost outermost

valure valour

vant best/foremost part

vaulting houses brothels

Venerean addicted to sexual pleasure (*OED*'s first usage)

Venery a) hunting   b) sexual activity

venie a bout

waft guard (maritime)

warning peece signal-gun

weather storm

weed garment

Wethers male sheep

Wezand throat

Wifler one who prepared the way in processions; proverbially thick

widgine notoriously stupid kind of duck

wilde gathering of wild beasts

wires ornamental supports of either hair or a ruff

withall at the same time

wittals fools

wonted lacked, missing

worthlesse not commensurate with one's true worth

wot know

wrap't crazy

wreake avenge

yron shackle with irons

Zoones By God's wounds (euphemistic abbreviation)

LIST OF HISTORICAL, MYTHOLOGICAL AND GEOGRAPHICAL NAMES

ACCIUS NOEVIUS A Roman augur in the time of Tarquin; according to Livy he cut a whetstone with a razor at that king's command.

ACHELOUS The river god who assumed the form of a bull during combat against HERCULES. One of his horns was torn away and duly replaced with the cornucopia.

ACHILLES Legendary Greek warrior who, having been immersed in the River Styx by his mother, had almost attained immortality. After killing the Trojan hero Hector in vengeance for the death of his companion Patroclus, he was then slain by PARIS, who exploited ACHILLES' only weakness by shooting an arrow through his heel.

ACTEON The hunter who was torn to pieces by his own hounds after being turned into a stag by DIANA, the wood goddess, when he espied her bathing naked in the forest.

ADONIS Archetype of male beauty with whom the goddess VENUS was obsessed.

AENEAS Hero of Virgil's *Aeneid*, founder of Rome and short-lived lover of DIDO, queen of Carthage.

AJAX Greek warrior who, when not awarded the weapons of ACHILLES, ran mad and slaughtered a flock of sheep he believed to be the Greek army.

ALCIDES *see* HERCULES.

ALIZON Homer mentions a people of this name from Asia Minor, but no River Alizon exists.

AMALTHAEA She-goat nurse of ZEUS/JUPITER, transformed by him into a star with horns filled with nectar and ambrosia, one of which was the cornucopia, the 'horn of plenty'.

APHRODITE *see* VENUS.

APOLLO *see* PHOEBUS.

ARGOLIAN From the Argo, the ship that carried Jason on his quest for the Golden Fleece.

ARGUS A creature with a hundred eyes and thus a symbol of watchfulness.

ATLAS The giant who was compelled to hold up the sky as punishment for his part in the rebellion of the TITANS.

ATROPOS Of the three Fates to whose custody the thread of life was entrusted, Atropos was the one famed for her eagerness to sever it.

ATHENIAN PRINCE Hippolytus, falsely accused of incest by and with his step-mother Phaedra, was torn to pieces, but returned to life by the intervention of Artemis and the healing of Aesculapius.

AUGEAN STABLES Notorious both for size and filth; it was one of HERCULES' labours to clean them in one day.

AURIGA A constellation, also known as the Waggoner.

BOÖTES A northern constellation, known also as the Waggoner, resembling a hunter with a club and two dogs.

CALYDONIAN BOAR Fearful beast let loose by DIANA as a punishment for the king of Calydon's neglect of her religious rites; eventually killed by the king's son, the Argonaut Meleager.

CAMILLUS Recalled from exile to repel a Gallic invasion in 387 BC, he was thereafter known as the second founder of Rome.

CANDIA Capital of Crete, famous for its wines.

CENTAUR[E]S A Thessalian race of creatures, half-man and half-horse.

CEPHALUS By accident, Cephalus killed his loving but jealous wife Procris, while they were out hunting, with his infallible javelin.

CERBERUS Many-headed dog that guarded the entrance to the Underworld.

CHARIBDIS Monstrous whirlpool in the Straits of Messina that stood opposite SCYLLA, who was invariably characterized as a voracious female.

CHLORIS Goddess of flowers and wife of Zephyrus, god of the winds.

CHYMAERA Monstrous amalgam of a lion, a goat and a dragon; eventually killed by Bellerophon, who had been sent to fight the monster as a punishment for an adultery he didn't commit.

CLIO A daughter of ZEUS and the Muse of History; she particularly recorded the heroic and the virtuous and was often depicted bearing a book and a trumpet.

CLOTHO The Fate responsible for spinning the thread of life on her distaff.

CORYNNA Ovid's poetic name for his mistress; in reality she was probably Julia, the Emperor Augustus' daughter.

CRATINUS (?484 BC – ?419 BC) Ranked with Aristophanes and EUPOLIS as one of the greatest writers of Greek 'Old Comedy'.

CUPID God of love, the beautiful son of MERCURY and VENUS, usually represented either as a warrior or as being blind, with a bow and arrows.

CYCLOPS One-eyed giants who forged JOVE's thunderbolts.

CYNTHIA *see* DIANA.

CYPRIS *see* VENUS.

CYTHAERON Mountain in Boeotia, and scene of Dionysiac orgies.

DANAË The daughter of Acrisius, the king of Argos, who was imprisoned in a bronze tower when an oracle predicted that her son would murder Acrisius. While she was incarcerated, JOVE visited her in a shower of gold and she later bore his son PERSEUS.

DELPHIC ORACLE The supreme oracle of ancient Greece, presided over by APOLLO. Situated on the slope of Mount Parnassus, and supposed to be the centre of the earth, marked by the sacred navel-stone known as the omphalos.

DEUCALION The son of Prometheus who, like Noah of the Old Testament, survived a great flood by building a boat. When the flood receded, he and his wife Pyrrha threw stones overboard which were transformed into the new people.

DIANA Goddess of the moon, chastity, woodland and hunting. She is often known by the alternative designations Artemis, Phoebe and Cynthia.

DIDO Queen of Carthage; she fell in love with the Trojan AENEAS who deserted her in order to fulfil his destiny as the founder of Rome, and she killed herself in despair.

DIPOLIS Probably an error; a minor Syrian town mentioned in Pliny, but certainly not in Cyprus.

EPAMINONDAS Fourth-century BC Theban statesman, celebrated as the military strategist whose skill defeated the Spartans.

EPIMETHEUS Curiosity prompted him to open Pandora's Box, from which issued all the evils which have afflicted humanity ever since.

EUMENIDES, or FURIES The avenging spirits who punished wrongs. They were typically depicted as three female figures with snakes in their hair, brandishing whips, firebrands and scorpions.

EUPOLIS Ranked with Aristophanes and CRATINUS as one of the greatest writers of Greek 'Old Comedy'. Flourished 430 BC – 410 BC.

EURIPIDES Fifth-century Greek dramatist, noted – and often ridiculed – for being innovative, sophisticated and over-refined.

EURIPUS Narrow strait in Boeotia, famed for the frequency and violence of its tides.

EURUS The east wind, brother of Zephyrus, usually portrayed as an impetuous young man.

EURYDICE Wife of ORPHEUS who went to reclaim her from the Underworld but broke PLUTO's stipulation that he should not look back at her and thus lost her.

EUXINE The Black Sea.

EVIPPE Wife of King PIERUS; their nine daughters, the Pierides, challenged the Muses to a song contest and were turned into magpies for their presumption.

FLORA see CHLORIS.

GANIMED Beautiful son of Tros, King of Troy, who was carried away by ZEUS to become his cup-bearer; he is usually regarded as an icon of homoerotic love.

GORDIAN Legendary knot which Alexander the Great cut with his sword when he couldn't untie it.

GORGON MEDUSA A monster whose hideous head turned anyone who looked at it into stone.

GRAEA The Graeae were three sisters who were born ancient and who shared one tooth and one eye between them; they lent the latter to PERSEUS for his battle with their sister, the GORGON MEDUSA.

HAEDY A small double star in the band of AURIGA.

HARPIES Monsters with the faces of women but the bodies of vultures.

HEBE Goddess of youth, daughter of JUPITER and JUNO, cup-bearer to the gods and archetype of female beauty.

HECCATE Goddess of night, the Underworld and sorcery.

HELICON Highest mountain in Boeotia, seat of the Muses before their transfer to OLYMPUS and Parnassus; at its foot was Aganippe, the fountain of inspiration.

HERCULES Also Heracles and Alcides. The son of JUPITER and Alcmene and the greatest mythological hero who became renowned for his strength and endurance, having successfully completed twelve heroic labours.

HESIODUS Hesiod, Greek poet and mythologist of the eighth century BC.

HIPPOCRATES Greek physician of the fifth and fourth centuries BC; alleged to have pronounced two brothers twins because they grew sick simultaneously.

HITCHIN Hertfordshire town which was Chapman's birthplace.

HYDRA Many-headed monster, each of whose heads, if cut off, would be replaced by two more.

HYMEN Greek god of marriage, conventionally portrayed as a veiled young man, bearing a flaming torch.

HYPERION Sun-god and TITAN. Husband of Thea, father of the Sun, Moon and Dawn.

IDA Phrygian mountain range, famed for its wooded slopes.

IRIS Messenger to JUNO.

ISIS In Egyptian mythology, the wife of Osiris and mother of Horus. Identified by the Greeks and Romans with many other goddesses.

JOVE *see* JUPITER.

JUNO Wife to the promiscuous JUPITER who fastidiously defended the sanctity of marriage by seeking the destruction of those who were implicated in his adultery.

JUPITER King of the gods who expressed an insatiable sexual appetite and was best known for administering divine judgements through the use of thunderbolts. Commonly referred to as JOVE as well as being designated ZEUS in Greek mythology.

JUPITER HAMMON [H]Ammon was a Libyan ram-god often conflated with JUPITER; the much-consulted oracle at his temple was discredited after pronouncing Alexander the Great to be the son of JUPITER.

LACHESIS The Fate responsible for drawing out the thread of life and thus determining its length.

LAPITHES A people from Thessaly who successfully repelled an attack by drunken CENTAURS and whose leaders included NESTOR and Theseus.

LATONA Beloved of ZEUS, mother of both Artemis and APOLLO, more usually known by the Greek form of her name, Leto.

LEDA A Spartan queen, loved by ZEUS.

LERNEAN FENNE A stinking swamp, home to the monstrous HYDRA which was eventually destroyed by HERCULES.

LYCURGUS   Possibly apocryphal founder of the Spartan constitution, whose legislative measures were supposedly inspired by the Delphic oracle.

MACEDON   Alexander the Great.

MARS   God of war and lover of VENUS.

MEDUSA   The GORGON who was slain by PERSEUS; her hair was comprised of snakes and anyone who directly looked at her would turn to stone.

MENELAUS   *see* PARIS.

MERCURIE, MERCURY   Messenger of the gods, as well as patron of travellers, thieves and lawyers.

MINERVA   *see* PALLAS ATHENA.

MORPHEUS   God of sleep.

NAVARRE   Kingdom which used to include part of south-west France; now part of Spain. Henry of Navarre fought against King Henry III of France in the War of the Three Henries (1585–8); the other chief combatant was Henry of Guise. Navarre became King Henry IV after Henry III was assassinated in 1589.

NEPTUNE   God of all waters, including the sea; he shared the dominion of the world with JUPITER and PLUTO, and was usually depicted bearing a trident.

NESTOR   The oldest and wisest of the Greeks who besieged Troy. According to Juvenal (see *Satires* VI.326), he was rendered impotent by a hernia. His story is most famously recounted in Homer's *The Iliad*.

NIOBE   She was punished for her presumption and pride in her many children by having all but one killed; she metamorphosed into an incessantly weeping statue.

NISUS   King of Corinth, possessed of a lofty tower upon which APOLLO was said to have laid his lyre; the same tower also witnessed the murder of his treacherous daughter SCYLLA by her disenchanted lover Minos.

OCTAVIUS AUGUSTUS CAESAR   Roman Emperor from 27 BC until his death in AD 14; patron of Virgil and Horace but banisher of Ovid.

ODYSSEUS   *see* ULISSES.

OEDIPUS   Legendary king of Thebes, who was disgraced for his incestuous relationship with his mother Jocasta. This legend was famously dramatized by Sophocles and later adapted by SENECA. He was also known for solving the riddle of the Sphinx.

OLYMPUS   The highest mountain in Greece, which was reputedly the habitation of the twelve gods, as well as being recognized as the birthplace of the Muses.

OMPHALE   Queen of Lydia, bought HERCULES as a slave, and made him do ·omen's work, such as spinning.

ORPHEL   Mythical musician whose lyre-playing could transform or control animate or inanimate objects; offended by his frigidity, the Bacchantes (female followers of Dionysus) tore him to pieces, but his severed head continued to sing.

OSSA   A high peak in the same range in Thessaly as PELION.

PALLAS ATHENA Also Minerva. She sprang, motherless, from the head of ZEUS/ JUPITER to become the goddess of war, wisdom, justice and the liberal arts, carrying a reflective shield to which was fixed the snaky head of the GORGON MEDUSA.

PAPHOS Town in Cyprus where stood the famous temple of APHRODITE/VENUS, goddess of love.

PARIS The son of Priam and Hecuba, who became a symbol of male seductiveness when he took flight with Helen, wife of Menelaus, the king of Sparta, who had hospitably entertained him. This incident later became the pretext for the Trojan War.

PELEUS Thessalian king, falsely accused of adultery and left to perish on Mount Pelion before being rescued by VULCAN and JUPITER.

PELION Mountain in Thessaly, famed as the haunt of wild (and lecherous) beasts, including the CENTAURS.

PELOPS After being killed and served to the gods by Tantalus, Pelops was restored to life and his missing shoulder, which had been eaten by Ceres, was replaced by an ivory one with restorative properties.

PENELOPE Wife to ULISSES/ODYSSEUS and archetype of marital fidelity who frustrated her many suitors by insisting that she would not remarry until she had completed a woven shroud. During the ten-year period of her husband's return voyage, she would spend each night unravelling the shroud, thus ensuring that it would never be finished.

PERSEUS The son of JUPITER and DANAË who, with the help of PALLAS ATHENA, a magic helmet and an adamantine sword, undertook a number of daring feats, notably, the decapitation of the GORGON MEDUSA; the rescue of Andromeda, who was chained to a rock; and the saving of his mother from the tyrant Polydectes.

PHAETON The son of APOLLO, the sun god, who ignored warnings not to ride his father's chariot. When he lost control, he inflicted a scar in the sky (the Milky Way) and plummeted to Earth; JUPITER destroyed him with a thunderbolt during his descent, and thus prevented the destruction of the Earth.

PHOEBE see DIANA.

PHOEBUS PHOEBUS APOLLO, the sun god.

PIEREAN From Mount Perus in Thessaly, home to the nine daughters of King Pierus who challenged the Muses to a song contest and were turned into magpies for their presumption.

PINDUS Mountain range in northern Greece.

PLUTO King of the Underworld.

PROTEUS Omniscient sea god who could change shape.

PYRRHO Third-century BC Greek philosopher who founded the brand of Sceptic philosophy that advocated indifference as the proper response to matters of life and death.

PYTHAGORAS Greek philosopher, ascetic and mathematician (c.6 BC) who originated the doctrine of metempsychosis and the transmigration of the soul.

SABAEAN Arabic, thus, exotic.

SAMOS An island and town in the Aegean, reputed to be the site of both the birth and marriage of JUNO.

SATURNE God of Time and leader of the TITANS who presided over the Golden Age until he was overthrown by JUPITER.

SATURNIA *see* JUNO.

SCYLLA A nymph who was punished for her frigidity by having her lower parts turned into a knot of voracious dogs; later she became a dangerous rock in the Straits of Messina and a symbol of indiscriminate lust.

SENECA Lucius Annaeus Seneca, first-century AD Roman philosopher, founder of Stoicism and tutor to Nero, who forced him to commit a painful and public suicide.

SICILIAN GURMANDIST Gnatho, Plutarch's archetypal glutton.

SOLON Sixth-century BC Athenian statesman, celebrated for his legislative and constitutional innovations.

SOMNUS God of sleep.

SYBILLA Female prophet, known as the Cumaean Sybyl, whose cave AENEAS visited before his descent to the Underworld.

THAMYSIS The River Thames.

THEMISTOCLES Fifth-century BC Athenian statesman, whose expansion of the Greek navy helped thwart an invasion by XERXES at Salamis in 480 BC.

THESPIADS The Muses, so called after the town of Thespia, which was situated on a slope of Mount HELICON in Boeotia.

THESPIAN From Thespia, near Mount HELICON, the seat of the Muses.

THESSALIE Part of northern Greece, famed among the ancients as a breeding ground for sorcery and dangerous narcotics.

TITAN (probably) the sun god HYPERION; the Titans were a family of gods who ruled the world until their overthrow by ZEUS.

TYPHON A monster with a hundred serpentine heads who rebelled against the gods in retaliation for the suppression of the revolt of his brothers, the Giants; he was crushed by JUPITER's thunderbolt and thereafter confined beneath Mount Aetna.

ULISSES Also ODYSSEUS, the king of Ithaca, whose legendary journey was the subject of Homer's epic poem, *The Odyssey*. This tale famously recounts the many incidents that hampered the return voyage of Ulysses and his crew, such as the alluring song of the sirens and the difficult passage through SCYLLA and CHARIBDIS, the encounter with the lotus-eaters and the transformation of his men into swine by the goddess Circe.

VENUS Goddess of erotic love and beauty who won the Golden Apple in the Judgement of PARIS – an event that eventually precipitated the Trojan War.

VESPERS Of the planet Venus, when visible in the West after sunset; thus, a simile for evening.

VULCAN Roman god of fire who embarrassed both his adulterous wife, VENUS, and her lover, MARS, by casting a net over them while they were in bed together.

XERXES King of Persia; led punitive and ultimately unsuccessful expedition against the Greeks in 480 BC.

ZEUS *see* JUPITER.

READ MORE IN PENGUIN

RENAISSANCE DRAMATISTS

The *Renaissance Dramatists* series provides scrupulously prepared texts with original spelling and punctuation, edited by leading scholars with extensive explanatory notes. The General Editor is John Pitcher.

Published or forthcoming:

The Spanish Tragedie by Thomas Kyd, ed. Emma Smith
includes the anonymous *The First Part of Jeronimo*

Plays and Poems by George Chapman, ed. Jonathan Hudston
includes *All Fooles*, *Bussy D'Ambois*, *The Widdowes Teares* and a selection of poems

Three Tragedies by Renaissance Women, ed. Diane Purkiss
includes *The Tragedie of Iphigeneia*, by Jane, Lady Lumley; *The Tragedie of Antonie*, by Mary, Countess of Pembroke; and *The Tragedie of Mariam*, by Elizabeth Cary

Volpone and Other Plays by Ben Jonson, ed. Lorna Hutson
includes *Every Man in his Humour*; *Sejanus, His Fall*; *Volpone, or the Foxe*; and *Epicoene, or the Silent Woman*

The Malcontent and Other Plays by John Marston, ed. David Pascoe
includes *The History of Antonio and Mellida*; *Antonios Revenge*; *The Malcontent*; *The Dutch Courtezan*; and *Parasitaster, or the Fawne*

A New Way to Pay Old Debts and Other Plays by Philip Massinger, ed. Richard Rowland
includes *The Roman Actor*, *Believe as you List*, *The Maid of Honour* and *A New Way to Pay Old Debts*

The Complete Plays by Christopher Marlowe, ed. Frank Romany

READ MORE IN PENGUIN

In every corner of the world, on every subject under the sun, Penguin represents quality and variety – the very best in publishing today.

For complete information about books available from Penguin – including Puffins, Penguin Classics and Arkana – and how to order them, write to us at the appropriate address below. Please note that for copyright reasons the selection of books varies from country to country.

In the United Kingdom: Please write to *Dept. EP, Penguin Books Ltd, Bath Road, Harmondsworth, West Drayton, Middlesex UB7 ODA*

In the United States: Please write to *Consumer Sales, Penguin Putnam Inc., P.O. Box 999, Dept. 17109, Bergenfield, New Jersey 07621-0120.* VISA and MasterCard holders call 1-800-253-6476 to order Penguin titles

In Canada: Please write to *Penguin Books Canada Ltd, 10 Alcorn Avenue, Suite 300, Toronto, Ontario M4V 3B2*

In Australia: Please write to *Penguin Books Australia Ltd, P.O. Box 257, Ringwood, Victoria 3134*

In New Zealand: Please write to *Penguin Books (NZ) Ltd, Private Bag 102902, North Shore Mail Centre, Auckland 10*

In India: Please write to *Penguin Books India Pvt Ltd, 210 Chiranjiv Tower, 43 Nehru Place, New Delhi 110 019*

In the Netherlands: Please write to *Penguin Books Netherlands bv, Postbus 3507, NL-1001 AH Amsterdam*

In Germany: Please write to *Penguin Books Deutschland GmbH, Metzlerstrasse 26, 60594 Frankfurt am Main*

In Spain: Please write to *Penguin Books S. A., Bravo Murillo 19, 1° B, 28015 Madrid*

In Italy: Please write to *Penguin Italia s.r.l., Via Benedetto Croce 2, 20094 Corsico, Milano*

In France: Please write to *Penguin France, Le Carré Wilson, 62 rue Benjamin Baillaud, 31500 Toulouse*

In Japan: Please write to *Penguin Books Japan Ltd, Kaneko Building, 2-3-25 Koraku, Bunkyo-Ku, Tokyo 112*

In South Africa: Please write to *Penguin Books South Africa (Pty) Ltd, Private Bag X14, Parkview, 2122 Johannesburg*

READ MORE IN PENGUIN

A CHOICE OF CLASSICS

Francis Bacon	**The Essays**
Aphra Behn	**Love-Letters between a Nobleman and His Sister**
	Oroonoko, The Rover and Other Works
George Berkeley	**Principles of Human Knowledge/Three Dialogues between Hylas and Philonous**
James Boswell	**The Life of Samuel Johnson**
Sir Thomas Browne	**The Major Works**
John Bunyan	**The Pilgrim's Progress**
Edmund Burke	**Reflections on the Revolution in France**
Frances Burney	**Evelina**
Margaret Cavendish	**The Blazing World and Other Writings**
William Cobbett	**Rural Rides**
William Congreve	**Comedies**
Thomas de Quincey	**Confessions of an English Opium Eater**
	Recollections of the Lakes and the Lake Poets
Daniel Defoe	**A Journal of the Plague Year**
	Moll Flanders
	Robinson Crusoe
	Roxana
	A Tour Through the Whole Island of Great Britain
Henry Fielding	**Amelia**
	Jonathan Wild
	Joseph Andrews
	The Journal of a Voyage to Lisbon
	Tom Jones
John Gay	**The Beggar's Opera**
Oliver Goldsmith	**The Vicar of Wakefield**
Lady Gregory	**Selected Writings**

READ MORE IN PENGUIN

A CHOICE OF CLASSICS

William Hazlitt	**Selected Writings**
George Herbert	**The Complete English Poems**
Thomas Hobbes	**Leviathan**
Samuel Johnson/ James Boswell	**A Journey to the Western Islands of Scotland** and **The Journal of a Tour of the Hebrides**
Charles Lamb	**Selected Prose**
George Meredith	**The Egoist**
Thomas Middleton	**Five Plays**
John Milton	**Paradise Lost**
Samuel Richardson	**Clarissa**
	Pamela
Earl of Rochester	**Complete Works**
Richard Brinsley Sheridan	**The School for Scandal and Other Plays**
Sir Philip Sidney	**Selected Poems**
Christopher Smart	**Selected Poems**
Adam Smith	**The Wealth of Nations** (Books I–III)
Tobias Smollett	**The Adventures of Ferdinand Count Fathom**
	Humphrey Clinker
	Roderick Random
Laurence Sterne	**The Life and Opinions of Tristram Shandy**
	A Sentimental Journey Through France and Italy
Jonathan Swift	**Gulliver's Travels**
	Selected Poems
Thomas Traherne	**Selected Poems and Prose**
Henry Vaughan	**Complete Poems**

READ MORE IN PENGUIN

A CHOICE OF CLASSICS

Leopoldo Alas	**La Regenta**
Leon B. Alberti	**On Painting**
Ludovico Ariosto	**Orlando Furioso** (in 2 volumes)
Giovanni Boccaccio	**The Decameron**
Baldassar Castiglione	**The Book of the Courtier**
Benvenuto Cellini	**Autobiography**
Miguel de Cervantes	**Don Quixote**
	Exemplary Stories
Dante	**The Divine Comedy** (in 3 volumes)
	La Vita Nuova
Machado de Assis	**Dom Casmurro**
Bernal Díaz	**The Conquest of New Spain**
Carlo Goldoni	**Four Comedies (The Venetian Twins/The Artful Widow/Mirandolina/The Superior Residence)**
Niccolò Machiavelli	**The Discourses**
	The Prince
Alessandro Manzoni	**The Betrothed**
Emilia Pardo Bazán	**The House of Ulloa**
Benito Pérez Galdós	**Fortunata and Jacinta**
Giorgio Vasari	**Lives of the Artists** (in 2 volumes)

and

Five Italian Renaissance Comedies
   (Machiavelli/**The Mandragola**; Ariosto/**Lena**; Aretino/**The Stablemaster**; Gl'Intronati/**The Deceived**; Guarini/**The Faithful Shepherd**)
The Poem of the Cid
Two Spanish Picaresque Novels
   (Anon/**Lazarillo de Tormes**; de Quevedo/**The Swindler**)